Dictionary of Literary Biography

Dictionary of Literary Biography Documentary Series

Dictionary of Literary Biography Yearbooks

Concise Series

Concise Dictionary of American Literary Biography, 7 volumes (1988-1999): *The New Consciousness, 1941-1968; Colonization to the American Renaissance, 1640-1865; Realism, Naturalism, and Local Color, 1865-1917; The Twenties, 1917-1929; The Age of Maturity, 1929-1941; Broadening Views, 1968-1988; Supplement: Modern Writers, 1900-1998.*

Concise Dictionary of British Literary Biography, 8 volumes (1991-1992): *Writers of the Middle Ages and Renaissance Before 1660; Writers of the Restoration and Eighteenth Century, 1660-1789; Writers of the Romantic Period, 1789-1832; Victorian Writers, 1832-1890; Late-Victorian and Edwardian Writers, 1890-1914; Modern Writers, 1914-1945; Writers After World War II, 1945-1960; Contemporary Writers, 1960 to Present.*

Concise Dictionary of World Literary Biography, 10 volumes projected (1999-   ): *Ancient Greek and Roman Writers; German Writers; African, Caribbean, and Latin American Writers; South Slavic and Eastern European Writers.*

Dictionary of Literary Biography® • Volume Two Hundred Forty-Four

American Short-Story Writers Since World War II
Fourth Series

Dictionary of Literary Biography® • Volume Two Hundred Forty-Four

American Short-Story Writers Since World War II
Fourth Series

Edited by
Patrick Meanor
State University of New York College at Oneonta

and

Joseph McNicholas
State University of New York College at Oneonta

A Bruccoli Clark Layman Book
The Gale Group
Detroit • San Francisco • London • Boston • Woodbridge, Conn.

Printed in the United States of America

The paper used in this publication meets the minimum requirements
of American National Standard for Information Sciences–Permanence
Paper for Printed Library Materials, ANSI Z39.48-1984. ∞™

Library of Congress Cataloging-in-Publication Data

American short-story writers since World War II. Fourth series / edited by Patrick Meanor and
Joseph McNicholas.
    p. cm.–(Dictionary of literary biography: v. 244)
"A Bruccoli Clark Layman book."
Includes bibliographical references and index.
ISBN 0-7876-4661-X (alk. paper)
1. Short stories, American–Dictionaries. 2. American fiction–20th century–Bio-bibliography–
Dictionaries. 3. Authors, American–20th century–Biography–Dictionaries. 4. Short stories, American–
Bio-bibliography–Dictionaries. 5. American fiction–20th century–Dictionaries. I. Meanor, Patrick.
II. McNicholas, Joseph. III. Series.

PS374.S5 A3966 2001
813.0109054–dc21   2001033596
[B]

10 9 8 7 6 5 4 3 2 1

In honor of poet and short-story writer Dr. Robert Kelly, with undiminished
admiration and affection for all that he has given me,
with gratitude to Richard Burnside and Edward Morehead
for enriching my life in Oneonta immeasurably,
and in loving memory of Lucy Meanor (1987–2001)
–P. M.

With thanks to Dr. Luz Elena Ramirez
for her support and her insight
–J.M.

Contents

Plan of the Series

. . . Almost the most prodigious asset of a country, and perhaps its most precious possession, is its native literary product—when that product is fine and noble and enduring.

Mark Twain*

The advisory board, the editors, and the publisher of the *Dictionary of Literary Biography* are joined in endorsing Mark Twain's declaration. The literature of a nation provides an inexhaustible resource of permanent worth. Our purpose is to make literature and its creators better understood and more accessible to students and the reading public, while satisfying the needs of teachers and researchers.

To meet these requirements, *literary biography* has been construed in terms of the author's achievement. The most important thing about a writer is his writing. Accordingly, the entries in *DLB* are career biographies, tracing the development of the author's canon and the evolution of his reputation.

The purpose of *DLB* is not only to provide reliable information in a usable format but also to place the figures in the larger perspective of literary history and to offer appraisals of their accomplishments by qualified scholars.

The publication plan for *DLB* resulted from two years of preparation. The project was proposed to Bruccoli Clark by Frederick G. Ruffner, president of the Gale Research Company, in November 1975. After specimen entries were prepared and typeset, an advisory board was formed to refine the entry format and develop the series rationale. In meetings held during 1976, the publisher, series editors, and advisory board approved the scheme for a comprehensive biographical dictionary of persons who contributed to literature. Editorial work on the first volume began in January 1977, and it was published in 1978. In order to make *DLB* more than a dictionary and to compile volumes that individually have claim to status as literary history, it was decided to organize volumes by topic, period, or

From an unpublished section of Mark Twain's autobiography, copyright by the Mark Twain Company

genre. Each of these freestanding volumes provides a biographical-bibliographical guide and overview for a particular area of literature. We are convinced that this organization—as opposed to a single alphabet method—constitutes a valuable innovation in the presentation of reference material. The volume plan necessarily requires many decisions for the placement and treatment of authors. Certain figures will be included in separate volumes, but with different entries emphasizing the aspect of his career appropriate to each volume. Ernest Hemingway, for example, is represented in *American Writers in Paris, 1920–1939* by an entry focusing on his expatriate apprenticeship; he is also in *American Novelists, 1910–1945* with an entry surveying his entire career, as well as in *American Short-Story Writers, 1910–1945, Second Series* with an entry concentrating on his short fiction. Each volume includes a cumulative index of the subject authors and articles.

Since 1981 the series has been further augmented by the *DLB Yearbooks*, which update published entries, add new entries to keep the *DLB* current with contemporary activity, and provide articles on literary history. There have also been nineteen *DLB Documentary Series* volumes which provide illustrations, facsimiles, and biographical and critical source materials for figures, works, or groups judged to have particular interest for students. In 1999 the *Documentary Series* was incorporated into the *DLB* volume numbering system beginning with *DLB 210, Ernest Hemingway.*

We define literature as the *intellectual commerce of a nation:* not merely as belles lettres but as that ample and complex process by which ideas are generated, shaped, and transmitted. *DLB* entries are not limited to "creative writers" but extend to other figures who in their time and in their way influenced the mind of a people. Thus the series encompasses historians, journalists, publishers, book collectors, and screenwriters. By this means readers of *DLB* may be aided to perceive literature not as cult scripture in the keeping of intellectual high priests but firmly positioned at the center of a nation's life.

DLB includes the major writers appropriate to each volume and those standing in the ranks behind them. Scholarly and critical counsel has been sought in deciding which minor figures to include and how full their entries should be. Wherever possible, useful references are made to figures who do not warrant separate entries.

Each *DLB* volume has an expert volume editor responsible for planning the volume, selecting the figures for inclusion, and assigning the entries. Volume editors are also responsible for preparing, where appropriate, appendices surveying the major periodicals and literary and intellectual movements for their volumes, as well as lists of further readings. Work on the series as a whole is coordinated at the Bruccoli Clark Layman editorial center in Columbia, South Carolina, where the editorial staff is responsible for accuracy and utility of the published volumes.

One feature that distinguishes *DLB* is the illustration policy–its concern with the iconography of literature. Just as an author is influenced by his surroundings, so is the reader's understanding of the author enhanced by a knowledge of his environment. Therefore *DLB* volumes include not only drawings, paintings, and photographs of authors, often depicting them at various stages in their careers, but also illustrations of their families and places where they lived. Title pages are regularly reproduced in facsimile along with dust jackets for modern authors. The dust jackets are a special feature of *DLB* because they often document better than anything else the way in which an author's work was perceived in its own time. Specimens of the writers' manuscripts and letters are included when feasible.

Samuel Johnson rightly decreed that "The chief glory of every people arises from its authors." The purpose of the *Dictionary of Literary Biography* is to compile literary history in the surest way available to us–by accurate and comprehensive treatment of the lives and work of those who contributed to it.

The *DLB* Advisory Board

Introduction

These essays continue the plan set out in *Dictionary of Literary Biography 130: American Short-Story Writers Since World War II* (First Series) and developed in the Second Series (*DLB 218*) and the Third Series (*DLB 234*). The editors of the Fourth Series are pleased to offer through their contributors a sustained critical engagement with American short-story writers since World War II; many of the entries in *DLB 244* fill in a lacuna on the subject. In previous series the editors have established a few important concepts for approaching short fiction. In particular, the *American Short-Story Writers Since World War II* series has focused on the nature of a changing literary marketplace; it has tracked the rise of academic havens for short-fiction writers; and it has examined the ways in which varied and sometimes competing schools of writing exert influence over short-story writers.

Editors and contributors have also pointed out the role of the short story in understanding society. In taking this approach, the editors have, with some reservation, agreed with critic Gary Krist, who asserted in *The New York Times Book Review* (18 April 1999) that "those interested in what it means to be alive in late twentieth-century America need to concern themselves not with the totalizing vision of the novel, but with the fragmentary mosaic tiles which are short stories." However, while Krist polarizes the short story and the novel, many contributors to the Fourth Series have observed that the two genres overlap. The question of definition, among other debates, surfaces repeatedly in attempts to provide a clear, organized, academic account of literary production. Notwithstanding the distinctions between the short story and the novel, it can be safely argued that short fiction expresses dynamic postmodernity, thereby garnering support from many quarters and eliciting argument from many others.

The experimental literary techniques of such avant-garde writers as Samuel Beckett, André Breton, and Franz Kafka sometimes replaced the earlier traditional models of Ernest Hemingway and F. Scott Fitzgerald, whose stories were more eagerly received by a wide readership. Literature since World War II is marked by a kind of innovation and invention not typically seen in previous periods. Not surprisingly, short fiction has been caught up in this zeitgeist. In a survey of American literature since the 1940s, it is clear that Thomas Pynchon, Donald Barthelme, Djuna Barnes, and many others refused to write "traditional" novels. Such writers as R. H. W. Dillard opt to blend the novel and the short story, producing amalgams that juxtapose thematically and symbolically related short works. Since it is such a protean form, one area of contention concerning the short story has been whether authors should emphasize the experimental element of short fiction or craftsmanship.

The University of Iowa Writers' Workshop formalized creative writing as a discipline in the 1930s, stressing originality of method rather than content. This program signals a major departure from the old view of short fiction as "nutshelling," as the practice of telling a good story. The Iowa school encouraged experimentation that had already begun to appear in the work of younger experimental authors such as Donald Barthelme, Barth, and Pynchon—writers additionally influenced by the labyrinthine prose of Jorge Luis Borges and the magical realism of Gabriel García Márquez, as well as by the practices of American literary outlaws Charles Bukowski and William Seward Burroughs. Whatever long-term effects that creative-writing programs may have had on fiction writing since 1945, they play an important role in this *DLB* volume because almost all of the writers included have graduated from, have worked in, or are presently involved with creative-writing programs as teachers.

Along with the increased institutional support for creative writing during this period, a boom of "little magazines" supported the outpouring of creative short fiction. These publications often sought no direct connections with either the commercialized New York literary scene or the academic world. Just as the writing programs became new "centers," so, too, did the little magazines create their own independent communities, where they were free to develop their own aesthetics. Many of the editors of and contributors to these magazines strongly objected to the homogenized eclecticism coming out of the more conservative writing programs and academic journals such as the *Kenyon Review, Sewanee Review,* and *Southern Review,* or a more trendy liberal journal such as the *Partisan Review*. The more open-minded founders of magazines such as *Big Table, Kulchur,* the *Black Mountain Review, Io, Lillabulero, Caterpillar,* the *Evergreen Review,* the *Chelsea Review,* and scores of other maverick publications positioned themselves strategically in the debate of craft versus experimentation. Some claimed that the M.F.A. workshops' emphasis on craft and technique had inadvertently replaced viable aesthetic and cultural traditions that had previously activated innovative fiction writing.

Among the most important of such radical journals was the *Black Mountain Review* (1950–1956), which published work by students and teachers at Black Mountain College in North Carolina. The journal emerged from a tradition that revered Ezra Pound, William Carlos Williams, and other objectivist writers such as Charles Olson and Louis Zukofsky, along with the additional influences of Europeans and modernists such as Henri Gaudier-Brzeska, Paul Klee, and Pablo Picasso, as well as Jackson Pollock and Franz Kline. Craft, as such, was discussed only in relation to a specific tradition and never became the major focus that it assumed in the workshop approach at Iowa and other creative-writing departments. As critic Michael Anania explains in his comprehensive history of little magazines: "In the almost totally decentralized literature of the late Sixties and early Seventies, these associations are measures of what was once called influence" (*TriQuarterly,* Fall 1978).

Other important forms of support that both contribute to the complex world of the contemporary American short story and substantially promote a writer's career are the prizes that various organizations award each year and, in most cases, the influential anthologies in which these prizewinning stories appear. The anthology *Best American Short Stories,* edited by Shannon Ravenel and (after 1990) Katrina Kenison and published by Houghton Mifflin, has accelerated the careers of many short-story writers over the past twenty years. Kenison sifts through between 1,500 and 2,000 short stories yearly and sends 100 to a co-editor for the final awarding of the prizes. Her co-editors have included the most respected short-story writers in America, such as John Updike, John Cheever, and Gina Berriault. Not only do prizewinners earn national recognition and a monetary award but also their stories appear in an annual collection along with other winners. Besides *Best American Short Stories,* the major awards honoring short-story writers are the O. Henry Prize, the Iowa Short-Fiction Award, the PEN/Hemingway Award, the Pushcart Prize series, and the John Simmons Short Fiction Award. Most of the writers in this volume have been recipients of one or more of these awards, an achievement that advances their careers.

Publishers often look to the award winners first when scouting for fresh talent. A common pattern with prizewinning writers is that such an award leads to more public recognition that, in turn, leads to offers of academic positions that allow them to support a family and have the time to devote to new work.

The university presses have also played a key role in awarding prizes and publishing series of annual short-story collections. The University of Pittsburgh Press, for example, awards $5,000 annually to an outstanding young short-fiction writer and publishes his or her first collection. The University of Missouri Press, under editor Clair Wilcox, also initiated a short-fiction series of publications known as "The University of Missouri Press Breakthrough Series." The University of Georgia Press sponsors the Flannery O'Connor Award for Short Fiction, while the University of Iowa extends to its winners the Iowa Short Fiction Prize. Similarly, the University of Illinois Press has published more than sixty volumes in its "Illinois Short Fiction Series," while literary journals such as *TriQuarterly* award prizes for short fiction. Journals devoted primarily to short fiction now include *Short Story,* under editor Mary Rohrberger; the *Journal of the Short Story in English; Story,* edited by Lois Rosenthal; Francis Ford Coppola's *Zoetrope: All Story;* and *Studies in Short Fiction,* edited by Michael O'Shea at Newberry College in Newberry, South Carolina.

As suggested earlier, debates about short fiction involve the definition of the genre itself. In his 1975 study *Form and Meaning in Fiction,* short-story theorist Norman Friedman calls for a critical consensus on rigorously, logically articulated criteria for distinguishing the short story from other kinds of writing. Rohrberger, one of the leading American short-story scholars, presents a different approach in her studies of the genre, suggesting that literary developments do not lend themselves to the kind of logical rigor Friedman is looking for. In the decades following World War II, the short stories produced by American writers have defied generalization. In the introduction to her *Collected Stories* (1975) Hortense Calisher has offered readers one of the more useful metaphorical definitions of the short story as it has evolved since World War II: the short story today, she writes, "is an apocalypse, served in a very small cup." A survey of the writers considered in this volume reveals a field of individualistic writers, many passionately involved in expanding the boundaries of their art.

Paradoxically, even while critics worry about the stifling effects of the academic writing programs where increasing numbers of younger writers sojourn, the works these younger authors produce are invariably fresh and inventive. The short story has flourished since World War II, continually redefining the paradigms employed to interpret it and serving as a richly varied chronicle of a tumultuous age. Today's writers are using new tools to explore new territory–an historical and intellectual landscape of technology, immigration, civil rights, and corporatization, shadowed with profound philosophical and religious doubts.

The short-story form has a rich and varied history as well. There are many competing claims for the honor of having produced the first short story; some scholars point to the Bible as a primary source. As Charles E. May observes in *The Short Story: The Reality of Artifice* (1995), "The wellsprings of the form are as old as the primitive realm of myth . . . a myth not only expresses the inner meaning of things . . . but it does so specifically by telling a story." The short-story form is identifiable in narratives as ancient as *The Satyricon* by Petronius (first century A.D.) or the tales of Scheherazade. In the Western literary tradition, the honor of producing the first collection of short stories belongs to Giovanni Boccaccio. However, Boccaccio's *Decameron,* as with *The Thousand and One Nights,* is essentially a compilation of traditional tales that does not pretend to be original work, and both present a frame narrative: a central story that wraps around various other tales told. In the case of *The Thousand and One Nights,* first "published" in about 1450, Scheherazade holds her execution at bay by entertaining a sultan with tales told every day, but with the climaxes of those tales deferred until the next night. This strategy enables her to do what all good writers (with a degree of traditional skill) do: she informatively teases, yet defers gratification so as to hold the audience's attention. Boccaccio's Italian aristocrats are seeking to escape one of the waves of plague that swelled throughout the fourteenth century, and they seek to pass the time away from reality, secluded in their convent in the country, by telling tales grouped around various thematic treatments. Boccaccio's aristocrats, and the characters in the tales themselves, are not recognizable, but rather functional; they have little of the characterization or psychological depth associated with the growth in modern consciousness. Nevertheless, in *The Decameron* readers are treated to stories of the local, the particular, and to tales of lives lived in the interstices of history. So entertaining was Boccaccio's creation that Geoffrey Chaucer adopted several of his stories and the overall design to produce the masterful *Canterbury Tales*–the frame narrative of which also includes a "holiday" from the mundane.

As Miguel Cervantes, who did more than re-present traditional tales in his *Exemplary Novels* in the seventeenth century, or as Wilhelm Kleist, E.T.A. Hoffmann, and others continued the narrative tradition in the eighteenth and nineteenth centuries, one sees clock-

work automatons and tales of the fabulous connected purely to the local and not the universal. By the time that Edgar Allan Poe began writing short stories in the early nineteenth century, the dominant literary form was the novel. Poe's famous statements about the "requirements" of short fiction–that each story should be digestible in one sitting and that a singularity of effect should mark the composition–established him as one of the first theorists of the genre. Other genre theorists such as Ian Watt and Michael McKeon link the development of the recognizably modern world–industrialized, urban, goal-oriented, individualistic, and capitalistic–to the growth of the novel. The short-story form continued to develop well into the twentieth century in contradistinction to the novel by telling stories that might otherwise be overlooked in the sweeping scope of the novel.

After World War II, however, such distinctions began to break down again as the world became both a much bigger place and, as David Harvey illustrates in *The Condition of Postmodernity: An Enquiry into the Origins of Cultural Change* (1989), a much smaller one. And the innovations within fiction, as within society, have continued to outpace one's ability to control them. When this *DLB* series began in 1993, the Internet was in its infancy. Already it has spawned new forums of literacy and literature. The short story is the natural genre for adaptation to this medium. Many of the traditional journalist powerhouses such as *The New Yorker, The Atlantic Monthly,* and *Harper's,* now have a presence online either for marketing their print journals or for presenting fiction via the World Wide Web. Journals appearing in hard copy have also moved online, such as Coppola's *Zoetrope: All Story.* Likewise, the National Endowment of the Arts has a "Writer's Corner" with full-text short stories available online.

As a counterpart to online fiction are new journals that exist only in cyberspace, such as *The Blue Moon Review.* In addition, literary communities are developing electronically in the realms of *Salon* and *The Electronic Book Review,* websites devoted to critical reception of new and traditional print format works of fiction. The web also facilitates short-story publishing for niche audiences whose interests might not otherwise make it into print. This category includes sites devoted to fiction about animated cartoon characters, fishing, and Generation Xers. But it also includes truly innovative work that refashions narrative and language by taking seriously the hypertextual, typographical, and multimedia potential of computer-mediated literature. *The Electronic Poetry Center* hosted by the State University of New York at Buffalo, for example, provides an excellent introduction to literature that has literally moved off the page (and onto the screen). Though this body of work is not the subject of this volume, it represents the important next chapter for the history of the short story.

There are many differences among the authors discussed in this series, but there is also a great deal of common ground. As in previous series, certain unifying strands may be detected as the writers try to balance the aesthetic and stylistic realms with the social and political realms. Much of the work of these writers displays a fascination with culture undergoing profound change. Such metamorphoses often result in complications surrounding social roles and norms and elide distinctions between the local and the universal. Many writers in this volume explore the tensions between society and the individual (which has always been popular in American literature), especially as those tensions result in alienation, nonconformity, or violence that exposes the darker side of the American dream.

As cultures change, the maps by which writers make sense of reality begin to fade. In her essay on Allegra Goodman, Ann V. Simon observes that "most contemporary souls juggle multiple, overlapping, and sometimes contradictory allegiances." Goodman's characters seem to lose their way while trying to balance orthodox religious values with their desire for self-advancement. In trying to strike that balance, they experience the personal confusion brought about by cultural change, as exemplified by the "orthodox Jewish communities in Hawaii, where Passover seders are held outdoors among mango trees and thirteen-year-old girls don muumuus to celebrate their bat-mitzvahs." Similarly, Ha Jin's work often deals with a culture in transition and the human costs such change can exact. Paula E. Geyh claims that the "characters in Jin's stories find themselves caught in heart-breaking conflicts between political dogma and private devotion," as seen when a character from a village commune is forced to choose between obeying his mother's dying wish to be buried (tradition) or observing the party mandate to cremate the deceased (law). Often, the choices to be made in a changing culture are not as black and white as in Jin's story. Dennis Held captures the sense of ambiguity well while describing one of David Long's stories, which "illustrates the difficulty of finding connection . . . in a world where the old order no longer works, and whatever will replace it has yet to arrive."

Sometimes cultural tensions and ambiguity generate an eclecticism that includes different cultural elements. Tess Gallagher, for example, "draws on the literature and culture of places as distant as Ireland, Eastern Europe, and Japan." William L. Stull and Maureen P. Carroll suggest that "the unifying pattern of Gallagher's life and art has been the harmony of opposites." Such efforts at accommodating radically different worlds characterize American culture after World War

II, and the theme of trying to do justice to the multiple and contradictory realities of life runs throughout the work of many of the short-story writers represented here. Mary Beth Long, in her entry on John Rolfe Gardiner, points out that in addition to his affiliation with local Southern culture, Gardiner has been recognized as having a gift for "searching out the quirky, the unusual person or turn of events and weaving it into a perfectly logical if bizarre tale." Such logical but bizarre tales can be taken as a sign of the acceptance of norms and the recognition of their mutability.

Not surprisingly, social roles and expectations are disrupted as cultures transform. In his entry on Frederick Barthelme, John Hughes argues that the author's characters "struggle to find moral footing on the slippery slope of contemporary life, where conventional values such as marriage, monogamy, fidelity, and even heterosexuality have been exhausted." Because the exhaustion of traditional values has been a common experience in society since World War II, the social roles assigned by gender, race, and class have changed. Pam Houston's *Cowboys Are My Weakness* (1992) illustrates such changes. Kathryn West suggests that Houston's "stories of adventurous women rafting through white water rapids, guiding Dall sheep hunters in Alaska, and attempting to establish relationships with men of the American West tapped a little-explored but ripe territory in contemporary consciousness."

Many women writers in this volume register the fact that the rules for self-identity have shifted. The work of Mary Gaitskill, who left home in her teens and worked at "a variety of jobs: street vendor, clerk, stripper, and apparently at least once as a prostitute," exemplifies the loss of norms. As Joseph J. Wydeven points out: "Gaitskill is adept at probing the consequences of female adolescent drift and disrupture, which precludes normal family life and complicates sexual development." Indeed, contemporary existence complicates sexuality in general. For example, Cynthia A. Davidson points out a "recurrent theme" in Alyson Hagy's work: "the exploration of gender identity and sex-role transgression and the expression of sexual differences." In exploring the fragmentary and the individual, short stories provide a good means of imaginatively coming to grips with cultural and psychological disruptions.

The skilled story writer unearths broad human experiences even while focusing on particular groups. As a genre, short stories allow an author to sketch the character of a people as a means to access deeper human truths. Herman Beavers perceives in the fiction of James Alan McPherson just such an effort to move through the specifics of, in his case, race, to a more expansive vision of humanity. Beavers writes of McPherson that he "fell under the influence of Ralph

Ellison and adopted the older man's sense that embracing his American citizenship, despite the contradictions of the racial divide in America, would lead him closer to the core of human values he wanted to depict in his fiction." Similarly, John Breitmeyer praises the perception of Louis Auchincloss in both bringing to life a specific class of people and for seeing through their specificity: "For quantity and quality of observation of changing times and mores of the upper classes on the American East Coast and especially Manhattan, Auchincloss has had few equals in the last two-thirds of this century. This region, seen through the lens of Auchincloss's short fiction, has become a microcosm of America, or perhaps more accurately, of the human condition." Josephine Jacobsen's work, which consistently evokes compelling characters, also takes up through specifics the more general themes such as "the effects of sorrow, the conflicts within love and marriage, and the ethical/moral dimensions of human conduct."

Another favorite theme is the tension between the civilized and the barbarous that dwells beneath any character's surface. Carol Frost finds George P. Elliott particularly illuminative in his depictions of "how people behave with each other in various contexts: nakedly, in their guises, as families, with the loved and unloved, and in ordinary social interactions" while nevertheless disturbing readers with "the mongrel and baser motivations of human behavior." Michael Brodsky's protagonists also suffer from an advanced sense of alienation. John C. Hawley describes how "The rat race not only of personal relations but also of the business world pushes Brodsky's characters into an internal paralysis (and fugue-like repetitive thoughts) often masked by external freneticism."

Ron Carlson's fiction typifies the "soft alienation" of the post–World War II era, in which society is less an individual's enemy, as it is for Kafka, than a source of generalized discomfort. As Jay Boyer observes, Carlson grew up in Salt Lake City but was not a Mormon; and while he "was not ostracized . . . he learned that full assimilation into this particular community could not be won." David Pink asserts that much of the work of Josip Novakovich–who, as a Croatian Baptist, always felt like an outsider to American culture–"is about characters examining, developing, or defending their individuality, much as Novakovich has done himself." Other writers were moving so far in this direction that they began to wonder what there was to "fit into." Hilary Masters, for example, explores the awkward relationship between the individual and society. He describes his own work as sounding "themes of abandonment–all kinds of abandonment, physical, spiritual and moral–while it represents men and women caught in the socio-political fabric of America." Richard L.

Blevins points out that for Douglas Woolf, a major theme was "the alienation of the individual in the postmodern New World." Often this alienation is because of psychological pressure exerted by or upon the family, and the theme of familial constraints was particularly strong during the 1950s and 1960s as the nuclear family gained dominance in American iconography.

Of course, one of the ways to stand out in a crowd is to develop a signature style. Among the more aesthetically minded authors represented in this volume, Russell Edson has been described by Robert Miltner as holding a distinctive position among both poets and fiction writers, since Edson "helped develop the rising status of the contemporary prose poem and was a forerunner of the movement in prose toward microfiction, flash fiction, short-shorts, and other categories of brief fiction and prose writing." Employing a personal style characterized by "close attention to language and nuance, torqued syntax, density, sound quality, imagery, and metaphor," Edson reflects the radical reconfiguring of genre appropriate to a society dispensing with broad categories, whether they be social or literary. Perhaps the most well-respected stylist represented in this collection is the Russian-born Vladimir Nabokov. Alexandra Smith observes that "some critics have accused Nabokov of being indifferent to social and political issues of his time, comparing his stories and novels to elegantly constructed, labyrinth-like narratives and riddles." Rather than poring over his work for a better understanding of social problems, Nabokov's reader pieces together a puzzle and luxuriates in beautiful designs.

If American society has grown more violent since World War II, it has become less concerned with the physical struggle for existence. One might wonder what, then, is at stake in American anger? Brad Vice's entry on Pinckney Benedict provides a way of understanding the themes of anger and frustration that must concern any fictional treatment of American life. In Benedict's story "The Sutton Pie Safe," Vice points out, "What in the beginning appears to be nothing more than the depiction of a paltry domestic row becomes a poignant exploration of the ways that class and poverty conspire to injure dignity." This ability to elevate social issues characterizes a good deal of short fiction. John William Corrington is another writer represented in this series whose work transforms violence into significance. Geoffrey H. Goodwin contends that "his stories use metaphors of war, justice, and the human capacity for evil to illuminate vital responses to the moral dilemmas that concerned him." Sometimes, however, the violence is not universal, but directly related to cultural change. Kelli Wondra indicates that Melanie Rae Thon's short stories depict tension between African-

American and white characters: "In her small-town settings, where resources are scarce and personal stakes often high, Thon finds that a 'pervasive aspect of that culture is violence.'"

But violence occurs in more abstract ways as well, in little betrayals within families and between lovers, in the attacks on character that undermine self-esteem. The short-story writer also captures these moments of psychological pain. Jay Boyer says that Alan Cheuse "has asked readers consistently to consider the monstrous harm people inflict on one another, all in the name of love." Sarah R. Gleeson-White also discusses this submerged violence in Antonya Nelson's work under the category of "'family terrorism'–games of power and manipulation, the little techniques perfected over the years to get under the skin of kinsfolk and close friends." Such little techniques are the perfect subject for short stories, in which one can read a whole lifetime of struggle through the unfolding of a single episode. These oscillations between pain and love, between base behavior and sublime significance, are the raw material for many authors. While confronted with the primal nature of power of anger and violence, writers such as Lester Goran also look for redemption. Patrick Meanor suggests that "Hope and the promise of a better life constitute the major quests throughout many of Goran's stories."

Such a range of stylistic and content choices foregrounds authorial voice and purpose. The reader of the short story should consider the decision making involved in such brief pieces, investigate the authors' choices, and use this invitation to expose the authors' hands, be they motivated by ideological or aesthetic considerations. For in the writers' choices, readers gain access to a creative world that informs and is informed by the second half of the twentieth century.

–*Patrick Meanor and Joseph McNicholas*

Acknowledgments

This book was produced by Bruccoli Clark Layman, Inc. Karen L. Rood is senior editor. Tracy Simmons Bitonti and Nikki La Rocque were the in-house editors.

Production manager is Philip B. Dematteis.

Administrative support was provided by Ann M. Cheschi, Amber L. Coker, and Angi Pleasant.

Accountant is Ann-Marie Holland.

Copyediting supervisor is Sally R. Evans. The copyediting staff includes Phyllis A. Avant, Brenda Carol Blanton, Melissa D. Hinton, William Tobias Mathes, Rebecca Mayo, Nancy E. Smith, and Elizabeth Jo Ann Sumner.

Editorial associates are Andrew Choate and Michael S. Martin.

Database manager is José A. Juarez.

Layout and graphics supervisor is Janet E. Hill. The graphics staff includes Karla Corley Brown and Zoe R. Cook.

Office manager is Kathy Lawler Merlette.

Photography supervisor is Paul Talbot. Photography editor is Scott Nemzek.

Digital photographic copy work was performed by Joseph M. Bruccoli.

The SGML staff includes Frank Graham, Linda Dalton Mullinax, Jason Paddock, and Alex Snead.

Systems manager is Marie L. Parker.

Typesetting supervisor is Kathleen M. Flanagan. The typesetting staff includes Jaime All, Patricia Marie Flanagan, Mark J. McEwan, and Pamela D. Norton. Freelance typesetters are Wanda Adams and Vicki Grivetti.

Walter W. Ross did library research. He was assisted by Steven Gross and the following librarians at the Thomas Cooper Library of the University of South Carolina: circulation department head Tucker Taylor; reference department head Virginia W. Weathers; Brette Barclay, Marilee Birchfield, Paul Cammarata, Gary Geer, Michael Macan, Tom Marcil, Rose Marshall, and Sharon Verba; interlibrary loan department head John Brunswick; and interlibrary loan staff Robert Arndt, Hayden Battle, Barry Bull, Jo Cottingham, Marna Hostetler, Marieum McClary, Erika Peake, and Nelson Rivera.

American Short-Story Writers Since World War II
Fourth Series

Dictionary of Literary Biography

Louis Auchincloss

(27 September 1917 –   )

John Breitmeyer
University of South Carolina

See also the Auchincloss entries in *DLB 2: American Novelists Since World War II* and *DLB Yearbook: 1980.*

BOOKS: *The Indifferent Children,* as Andrew Lee (New York: Prentice-Hall, 1947);

The Injustice Collectors (Boston: Houghton Mifflin, 1950; London: Gollancz, 1951);

Sybil (Boston: Houghton Mifflin, 1952 [i.e., 1951]; London: Gollancz, 1952);

A Law for the Lion (Boston: Houghton Mifflin, 1953; London: Gollancz, 1953);

The Romantic Egoists (Boston: Houghton Mifflin, 1954; London: Gollancz, 1954);

The Great World and Timothy Colt (Boston: Houghton Mifflin, 1956; London: Gollancz, 1956 [i.e., 1957]);

Venus in Sparta (Boston: Houghton Mifflin, 1958; London: Gollancz, 1958);

Pursuit of the Prodigal (Boston: Houghton Mifflin, 1959; London: Gollancz, 1960);

The House of Five Talents (Boston: Houghton Mifflin, 1960; London: Gollancz, 1961);

Reflections of a Jacobite (Boston: Houghton Mifflin, 1961; London: Gollancz, 1962);

Edith Wharton (Minneapolis: University of Minnesota Press, 1961);

Portrait in Brownstone (Boston: Houghton Mifflin, 1962; London: Gollancz, 1962);

Powers of Attorney (Boston: Houghton Mifflin, 1963; London: Gollancz, 1963);

The Rector of Justin (Boston: Houghton Mifflin, 1964; London: Gollancz, 1965);

Ellen Glasgow (Minneapolis: University of Minnesota Press, 1964);

Louis Auchincloss (courtesy of the author)

Pioneers & Caretakers: A Study of 9 American Women Novelists (Minneapolis: University of Minnesota Press, 1965; London: Oxford University Press, 1966);

The Embezzler (Boston: Houghton Mifflin, 1966; London: Gollancz, 1966);

Tales of Manhattan (Boston: Houghton Mifflin, 1967; London: Gollancz, 1967);

A World of Profit (Boston: Houghton Mifflin, 1968; London: Gollancz, 1969);

Motiveless Malignity (Boston: Houghton Mifflin, 1969; London: Gollancz, 1970);

Second Chance: Tales of Two Generations (Boston: Houghton Mifflin, 1970; London: Gollancz, 1971);

Edith Wharton: A Woman in Her Time (New York: Viking, 1971; London: Joseph, 1972);

Henry Adams (Minneapolis: University of Minnesota Press, 1971);

I Come as a Thief (Boston: Houghton Mifflin, 1972; London: Weidenfeld & Nicolson, 1973);

Richelieu (New York: Viking, 1972; London: Joseph, 1973);

The Partners (Boston: Houghton Mifflin, 1974; London: Weidenfeld & Nicolson, 1974);

A Writer's Capital (Minneapolis: University of Minnesota Press, 1974);

Reading Henry James (Minneapolis: University of Minnesota Press, 1975);

The Winthrop Covenant (Franklin Center, Pa.: Franklin Library, 1976; Boston: Houghton Mifflin, 1976; London: Weidenfeld & Nicolson, 1976);

The Dark Lady (Boston: Houghton Mifflin, 1977; London: Weidenfeld & Nicolson, 1977);

The Country Cousin (Boston: Houghton Mifflin, 1978; London: Weidenfeld & Nicolson, 1978);

Persons of Consequence: Queen Victoria and Her Circle (New York: Random House, 1979; London: Weidenfeld & Nicolson, 1979);

Life, Law, and Letters: Essays and Sketches (Boston: Houghton Mifflin, 1979; London: Weidenfeld & Nicolson, 1980);

The House of the Prophet (Boston: Houghton Mifflin, 1980; London: Weidenfeld & Nicolson, 1980);

The Cat and the King (Boston: Houghton Mifflin, 1981; London: Weidenfeld & Nicolson, 1981);

Three "Perfect" Novels and What They Have in Common (Bloomfield Hills, Mich.: Bruccoli Clark, 1981);

Watchfires (Boston: Houghton Mifflin, 1982; London: Weidenfeld & Nicolson, 1982);

Narcissa, and Other Fables (Boston: Houghton Mifflin, 1983);

Exit Lady Masham (Franklin Center, Pa.: Franklin Library, 1983; Boston: Houghton Mifflin, 1983; London: Weidenfeld & Nicolson, 1984);

The Book Class (Boston: Houghton Mifflin, 1984; London: Weidenfeld & Nicolson, 1984);

False Dawn: Women in the Age of the Sun King (Garden City, N.Y.: Anchor, 1984);

Honorable Men (Boston: Houghton Mifflin, 1985; London: Weidenfeld & Nicolson, 1986);

Diary of a Yuppie (Franklin Center, Pa.: Franklin Library, 1986; Boston: Houghton Mifflin, 1986; London: Weidenfeld & Nicolson, 1987);

Skinny Island: More Tales of Manhattan (Boston: Houghton Mifflin, 1987; London: Weidenfeld & Nicolson, 1988);

The Golden Calves (Boston: Houghton Mifflin, 1988; London: Weidenfeld & Nicolson, 1989);

The Vanderbilt Era: Profiles of a Gilded Age (New York: Scribners, 1989);

Fellow Passengers: A Novel in Portraits (Boston: Houghton Mifflin, 1989; London: Constable, 1990);

J. P. Morgan: The Financier as Collector (New York: H. N. Abrams, 1990);

The Lady of Situations (Boston: Houghton Mifflin, 1990; London: Constable, 1991);

Love Without Wings: Some Friendships in Literature and Politics (Boston: Houghton Mifflin, 1991);

False Gods (Boston: Houghton Mifflin, 1992; London: Constable, 1993);

Three Lives (Boston: Houghton Mifflin, 1993; London: Constable, 1994);

The Style's the Man: Reflections on Proust, Fitzgerald, Wharton, Vidal, and Others (New York: Scribners, 1994);

Tales of Yesteryear (Boston: Houghton Mifflin, 1994; London: Constable, 1995);

The Collected Stories of Louis Auchincloss (Boston: Houghton Mifflin, 1994);

The Education of Oscar Fairfax (Boston: Houghton Mifflin, 1995; London: Duckworth, 1996);

La Gloire: The Roman Empire of Corneille and Racine (Columbia: University of South Carolina Press, 1996);

The Man Behind the Book: Literary Profiles (Boston: Houghton Mifflin, 1996);

The Atonement and Other Stories (Boston: Houghton Mifflin, 1997);

The Anniversary and Other Stories (Boston: Houghton Mifflin, 1999);

Woodrow Wilson (New York: Viking, 2000);

Her Infinite Variety (Boston: Houghton Mifflin, 2000).

PLAY PRODUCTION: *The Club Bedroom*, New York, Theatre de Lys, 1967.

OTHER: *The Edith Wharton Reader,* edited by Auchincloss (New York: Scribners, 1965);

Anthony Trollope, *The Warden, and Barchester Towers,* edited by Auchincloss (Boston: Houghton Mifflin, 1966);

Fables of Wit and Elegance, edited by Auchincloss (New York: Scribners, 1972);

Deborah Turbeville, *Unseen Versailles,* introduction by Auchincloss (Garden City, N.Y.: Doubleday, 1981);

Quotations from Henry James, selected by Auchincloss (Charlottesville: Published for the Associates of the University of Virginia Library by the University Press of Virginia, 1984);

The Hone & Strong Diaries of Manhattan, edited by Auchincloss (New York: Abbeville Press, 1989);
Deborah Turbeville's Newport Remembered: A Photographic Portrait of a Gilded Past, text by Auchincloss (New York: H. N. Abrams, 1994).

Louis Auchincloss's clear and accessible style, dry wit, compelling plots, psychological acuity, and strong moral sense characterize his short fiction as it surveys the troubled lives of its generally "privileged" characters. During the second half of the twentieth century Auchincloss observed the changing times and mores of the upper classes on the American East Coast and especially Manhattan. This region, as seen through the lens of Auchincloss's short fiction, has become a microcosm of America and of the human condition.

Since the publication of his first novel in 1947, Auchincloss has become one of the most prolific and respected postwar American authors, and he has also been a working lawyer on Wall Street for most of that time. Known primarily as a novelist, with twenty-seven novels to date, he has nevertheless produced some dozen short-story collections and fifteen nonfiction books ranging from history to biography to collections of critical essays. In 1965 he was elected to the National Institute of Arts and Letters (and then to the National Academy of Arts and Letters in 1991); and in 1967 he became president of the Museum of the City of New York, a position he held until the mid 1990s. In 1997 he was elected to a three-year term as president of the reconstituted American Academy of Arts and Letters. Though his peak of public recognition was the 1960s, he has continued to write and to garner favorable reviews. Auchincloss has become a fixture in American letters as well as a significant cultural critic, historian, and arbiter of taste.

Auchincloss belongs to a select minority of writers, such as Wallace Stevens, who have managed to combine a practical and demanding bourgeois nonliterary career with significant artistic achievement. Though the subject of his dual careers is "boring" to Auchincloss, his success as a lawyer and his production of a large and varied body of material, not to mention his presidency of the museum and the maintenance of a rich family and social life, make him something of a Renaissance man for the twentieth century.

A discussion of Auchincloss's writings necessarily partakes of a larger conversation about class, money, and the observation of both in American fiction; it is the starting point of most discussions of Auchincloss, and he focuses on this subject himself when he discusses his own work. As such, his fiction adheres to the conventions of the "novel of manners," with its focus on the customs, manners, conventions, and mores of a

Auchincloss in 1921 (courtesy of Louis Auchincloss)

specific social group. Even Auchincloss's most casual readers know that he most often takes for his settings the places and times of his own experience: the New York country clubs, drawing rooms, auction houses, and law offices of the modestly well-off to the extremely rich. The stories have moved outside of New York occasionally, to Massachusetts boarding schools, Maine or Massachusetts resorts, Virginia plantations, European cities, or navy ships, but Manhattan is his touchstone. In this world he has succeeded in portraying a complex and varied cast of characters whose thoughts and experiences can—many of his supporters insist—speak to and for people of all social and economic circumstances, despite the apparent narrowness of their society and location. His detractors (such as the critic Granville

Hicks, who has been a kind of cordial opponent of Auchincloss over the years) see Auchincloss as inhabiting too small a social and geographic space, writing coolly detached character studies of his affluent associates and neighbors, which limits the relevance of his otherwise sharply observed fiction.

Auchincloss writes in a strain of "mannered" and socially attuned American realism that includes William Dean Howells, Henry James, and Edith Wharton, and also to some extent F. Scott Fitzgerald, Sinclair Lewis, John O'Hara, and John P. Marquand. Comparisons to these authors, particularly James and Wharton, have become distressing to Auchincloss over time, not because they are inaccurate or because he dislikes the comparison (he has, in fact, written extensively and positively about both James and Wharton, and somewhat more critically of O'Hara and Marquand), but rather because the use of these comparisons in advertising and book-jacket copy has sometimes had the effect of casting Auchincloss as an anachronistic "society" writer in the eyes of the book-buying public, whose associations with this tradition are often negative despite the fact that these authors are all excellent in varying degrees. Allusions to several of these writers in his stories, along with frequent references to various painters, French theater and architecture, Richard Wagner, William Shakespeare, and other elements of high culture give the impression of characters, and an author, existing in a rather rarefied literary and artistic world, which some readers can find alienating. Time, however, has freed many writers such as James and Wharton from contemporaneous prejudice and will likely do so for Auchincloss as well.

Louis Stanton Auchincloss was born into an affluent family. His parents, Joseph Howland (known as Howland) and Priscilla (née Stanton) Auchincloss, were from affluent and prominent families and were part of a wide-ranging clan of New Englanders who belonged to that group of Americans most typically referred to as WASPs (white Anglo-Saxon Protestants). The unusual family name is Scottish. The family kept several servants, had two vacation homes, and as able to send Louis and his three siblings (John, Howland, and Priscilla) to private schools during the Great Depression.

Howland Auchincloss was a Wall Street lawyer who, along with Louis's mother, expected Louis to follow in his footsteps, an expectation the son eventually did fulfill, though this vocation was balanced by the authorial career his parents never envisioned. The "gray" world of drudgery and responsibility young Louis saw his father as inhabiting was at odds with the gayer social and literary world represented by his mother, a world Auchincloss vastly preferred. Priscilla

Auchincloss was a caring and perhaps too-attentive mother of her four children; she was an extremely intelligent woman, with discriminating literary and aesthetic tastes. Auchincloss has described her as "brilliant," but also consumed by fears and inhibitions that hampered her potential as an individual: fears for her children's safety and futures, and exaggerated concern with appearances and propriety. Auchincloss's mother has clearly inspired several of the various matriarchal figures in Auchincloss's short stories that alternately conform to aspects of the interesting split in her nature: a sharp mind and strong personality combined with a circumscribed and limited ambition, and perhaps even spirit.

Young Louis had the irrepressible writerly habits of observation and inquiry—stories of who had money and how they got it, for example, were fascinating to him, sometimes to his parents' embarrassment—and so Auchincloss developed into an observer of his family and its social set. Auchincloss's early experiences shaped and inspired much of his short fiction. He attended prep schools as a child, first Bovee (a now-defunct Manhattan elementary prep school), then Groton, the most exclusive boys' school in the country at the time. Groton was a particularly formative experience; versions of it frequently appear in his stories.

While at Groton, Auchincloss began as a poor student. He felt alienated from his peers and too timid to assert himself academically or socially. By the end of his second form, however, he settled on grades as a way to assert his presence and eventually became one of the top students in the school. He also began to write while at Groton and published twelve items in the *Third Form Weekly* and *The Grotonian*, the school literary magazines. The essays he wrote were apparently quite good (the stories, however, he and his biographers agree would only be of interest to an Auchincloss collector). Auchincloss graduated third in his class, having gained more confidence during his last years there through his involvement in literature and drama.

He was admitted to Yale University, his father's alma mater, in 1935. While at Yale, Auchincloss came further out of his shell and allowed himself more time away from his studies than he had at Groton. He attended parties and went to movies; took literature, French, and history courses; and generally had a good time. He met and befriended a brilliant but troubled young man named Jack Woods, who became an occasional presence in his short stories. Woods committed suicide in 1941, and his death figures as a motif in the stories more often than his living presence is asserted. As he had at Groton, Auchincloss became involved in the school literary scene and trod the boards for the drama club. The eight stories he published in the Yale literary magazine were, like those printed at Groton, indicative of a bright mind but as yet no significant or original literary skill.

At Yale, Auchincloss first attempted to write seriously—that is, for outside publication—but upon the completion of what he admits was an unpublishable novel titled "A World of Profit" (a title Auchincloss resuscitated in 1968 for a different novel), Auchincloss saw his literary career as a bust and thought he should get on with what he considered his "duty," which was to become a lawyer. He left Yale and enrolled in the University of Virginia Law School in 1938. To his surprise, Auchincloss found he actually liked the law; he found some outlet for his literary energy in the editorship of the school's law review and in the mastering of that legal genre, the brief. After three years, Auchincloss graduated at the top of his class. He received his law degree in 1941 and worked briefly as a lawyer in the firm of Sullivan and Cromwell prior to his enlistment in the navy that same year. He served in the navy from 1941 to 1945, and reentered Sullivan and Cromwell after the war, where he stayed until he temporarily retired from law to write full-time from 1952 to 1954. Auchincloss returned to the law in 1954 to work for Hawkins, Delafield and Wood in trusts and estates, married Adèle Lawrence in 1957, and remained at the same firm until his retirement in 1986, writing all the while.

Auchincloss's experience in the navy was a long struggle to be of some concrete use in the war effort. He seemed destined never to see combat. Though he initially applied for work in naval intelligence, he soon attempted to change the status of his application to active sea duty. Before this transfer could be accomplished, he received his first post, in Panama, which turned out to be an experience of navy bureaucracy and ineffectiveness he found galling. He worked constantly to be transferred to ship duty, and finally succeeded after almost a year in Panama. While in Panama, Auchincloss read books, did some defense work in courts martial, played tennis, and generally tried to stave off tedium as best he could. Auchincloss undertook training and continued his petitioning to be moved to an active theater of the war. He was stationed next in the Caribbean and did not see real combat (and not much of that) until 1943, when he received second-in-command posts on landing ship tanks in the Atlantic theater and then the Pacific, prior to the end of the war and his return home.

Even in wartime, Auchincloss led a remarkably literary existence; he read dozens of books (novels in Panama, drama in the Atlantic) and wrote hundreds of pages of letters home. The general tedium of navy service did not abate entirely after Panama, and the

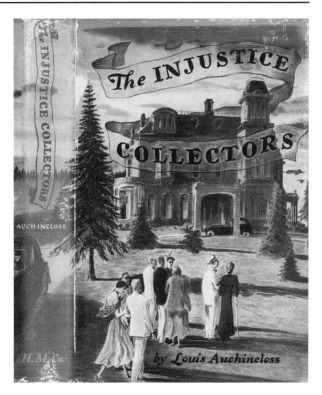

Dust jacket for Auchincloss's first collection of short stories (1950), which earned the praise of Evelyn Waugh and is considered one of Auchincloss's best books

uneventful nature of Auchincloss's World War II experience accounts for its rare appearance in his short stories. World War II has been the setting for perhaps four short stories by Auchincloss.

Upon returning to New York, Auchincloss resumed his law career and began writing almost immediately. Although his first publication was a novel, the circumstances of its publication are worth mentioning because his personal difficulties with it reveal something of his ambivalence, in those early years, toward the idea of being an author. The publication of Auchincloss's first novel, *The Indifferent Children* (1947), caused something of a scandal in his family. His parents (with whom he was living) objected to it, as they had years earlier to the doomed "A World of Profit," on the basis that it might hurt his fledgling law career by calling his dedication to that career into question. Auchincloss's mother specifically objected because she felt that he could do better and that there was no room for "second-rate" literature in the world. Auchincloss himself tended toward this view; as he later put it in his autobiography, *A Writer's Capital* (1974), his and his mother's "neuroses were complementary." He put off his personal doubts, however, and held fast to the idea of publishing. As a compromise with his parents, he decided to publish under a pseudonym, Andrew Lee (the name of an abstemious ancestor). The novel came out to mixed reviews, but the most positive of them, a review by William McFee in the 27 May 1947 edition of the *New York Sun,* compared Auchincloss favorably with Henry James. As Auchincloss puts it, that portion of McFee's review "pleased me as no line of print had before or has since." From that point, Auchincloss decided to be a writer.

The publisher for *The Indifferent Children* was Prentice-Hall. Auchincloss had submitted the novel to a friend, James Oliver Brown, the New York editor for the firm. Following publication of the novel, Brown started his own literary agency and helped Auchincloss establish the relationship with Houghton Mifflin that Auchincloss has maintained throughout his career (with Brown as his agent until 1984). Houghton Mifflin was the publisher of *The Injustice Collectors* (1950) and has been the publisher for every one of Auchincloss's subsequent short-story collections.

Autobiographical elements in Auchincloss's short stories are so profuse that one is tempted to call even the stories that are not directly autobiographical a kind of speculative autobiography. Auchincloss has said "all a novelist's characters are himself," and although not every author would agree, it certainly seems true in Auchincloss's case. Many of Auchincloss's characters and plots correspond not directly to himself or his life, but rather to impressions of Auchincloss that others have had, or to possibilities of what he could have become. For example, the enigmatic object of narrative scrutiny in "The Gemlike Flame," Clarence McClintock (from *The Romantic Egoists,* 1954), is a reclusive, asexual young man whose lifestyle is the studied opposite of his mother's. He is perceived as homosexual by others, including his mother and the narrator of the story. It is no great leap to connect this character to Auchincloss who, though neither homosexual nor asexual, was undoubtedly perceived by many in his social circles to be one or the other as he remained an unmarried man of refined tastes (and an infrequent dater) into his middle thirties. Another example of such a character is Reggie Turner in "Polyhymnia, Muse of Sacred Song" from *False Gods* (1992). Reggie reflects upon himself, "I suppose, by the new Freudian rules, I should have turned out a homosexual. Was that not the common fate of the coddled darlings of dominating mothers and abdicating fathers? But such was not to be my fate." Auchincloss's father, while busy, was not quite "abdicating," but still, one senses the general autobiographical pattern in this character's confession. Repressed homosexuality is a recurring theme in Auchincloss's stories, but it is possible to make too much of this fact; other recurring themes include insider trading, adultery, and reckless dissipation (besides autobiography, it is important to remember that one of Auchincloss's major sources is society gossip). Auchincloss's short stories are written in an inclusive realism, and he would be remiss to avoid any phenomena common to his society. Characters such as Clarence McClintock or Reggie Turner abound in Auchincloss's stories: characters that are exaggerations, or misperceptions, or even incarnations of himself that Auchincloss may at one time have feared were possible.

Auchincloss generally appears in his own stories in one of two distinct ways: either a major character, perhaps the character whose voice narrates the story, is like him in some respect, or another, secondary character will correspond to Auchincloss in some telling way. The first kind of inclusion occurs clearly enough in "Portrait of the Artist by Another," from *Skinny Island: More Tales of Manhattan* (1987). The first-person narrator, Jamie Abercrombie, is a conservative boy at boarding school who befriends an older, liberal teacher, Eric Stair, who becomes his art instructor; but Jamie is rejected by his teacher's new wife. In retaliation he opportunistically sees her at her bedroom window and sketches her in the nude, then allows the sketch to be found by school administrators. The Stairs leave the school, and Jamie is quietly guilt-ridden until years later, when he meets with his former teacher and confesses. Stair forgives him, and they both go off to war. Stair is killed in battle, and Jamie reflects that he is saved by that final confession, though a ghost of his former regret remains. The themes and methods are typical for Auchincloss: conflict with, or over, a male mentor or busybody matriarch (here, the former); the power or value of art; and the death of a loved character (often, as here, in the war) spurring regret and self-realization. This last is a recurring Auchincloss conclusion, a kind of combination of the Jack Woods theme and tragedies arising from war; although Auchincloss's specific World War II experience is an infrequent subject of his stories, the more generalized theme of war as a conscience-pricking or destructive force is a specter that haunts many more.

The effect of Auchincloss's second approach to self-inclusion, through a peripheral character, can seem at times almost casually metafictional, like L. Frank Baum's Wizard of Oz appearing from behind his curtain, or Alfred Hitchcock becoming fleetingly visible in a cameo in one of his own movies. For example, in "Hermes, God of the Self-Made Man," from *False Gods,* a secondary character, Horace Aspinwall, became exactly what another character predicted: "a respected partner in his firm, in charge of a minor department." For anyone familiar with the events of Auchincloss's life, moments such as these create almost a little in-joke between Auchincloss and his readers. Through devices

Louis and Adèle Auchincloss with their sons, Andrew, Blake, and John, during the 1960s (courtesy of Louis Auchincloss)

such as these, Auchincloss makes clear that he is toying with elements of his own life in his short stories, combining and recombining them in endless permutations that constantly illuminate new areas of the world he inhabits.

There is less division between Auchincloss's short stories and novels than exists for many authors who write both. Several of his short stories have subsequently developed into novels, such as "The Great World and Timothy Colt" (1954), which became a novel of the same title in 1956; and several of his book-length works, such as *The Partners* (1974), *The Winthrop Covenant* (1976), and *The Book Class* (1984), exist as something between "novel" and "short-story collection," because they include longish, separated but thematically bound narratives that can be alternately defined as stories in a short-story cycle, chapters of a novel, or related novellas. Christopher Dahl, in his critical biography *Louis Auchincloss* (1986), attributes this phenomenon to what he describes as Auchincloss's "quest for unity" in theme and content in his short-story collections and in his work in general. David B. Parsell, in his 1988 critical overview of Auchincloss's work, believes this "pressure against the boundaries that appear to separate the short story from

the novel" is Auchincloss's "major contribution" to the short-story form. A large percentage of Auchincloss's stories are written exclusively for inclusion in collections, supporting the theory that his intention is to create works with a great deal of coherence.

Just as he has been labeled a novelist of manners, Auchincloss can also be described as a short-story writer of manners. His characteristic settings and characters are found in both his novels and short stories, and his concerns with propriety, social place, and disgrace and its avoidance are pronounced in both fictional forms.

Auchincloss's first collection of short stories, *The Injustice Collectors* (1950), came out to generally favorable reviews, including kudos by Walter Lippman and Evelyn Waugh, and is still frequently regarded as being among his best works. Negative critical responses circled around the same themes: "coldness" or emotional detachment, indebtedness to Wharton, and unsympathetic characters. Most reviews, however, were overwhelmingly positive, and more than one reviewer noted the emergence of a major talent. Perhaps because of Auchincloss's relatively late start, even these first stories are polished, disciplined, and mature, and include many themes and character types that appear in his later collections: fortunes gained and lost, old maids, public humiliation, asexual fops, and meddling parents. "Maud," the first short story Auchincloss published (in *The Atlantic Monthly,* December–January 1949–1950), is a tale of an old maid in the making. Like Clarence McClintock in "The Gemlike Flame," a story Auchincloss wrote three years later, Maud Spreddon is emotionally reserved to the point of misanthropy. Unlike the austere choice of Clarence, however, one senses a kind of impediment in Maud, a sort of emotional autism that is highly reminiscent of John Marcher's in Henry James's "Beast in the Jungle" (1903). Maud eventually loses her chance at emotional redemption when her potential love interest dies (as in the James story), and she must face the future with a determined stoicism.

The remaining six stories in *The Injustice Collectors* introduce other themes and plots that reappear in Auchincloss's later collections. In "The Miracle" a worried father successfully heads off what he sees as a bad union between his son and the daughter of uncultured, grasping neighbors. In "The Fall of a Sparrow" the narrator, a navy seaman, observes a former high-school classmate, newly made captain of a ship, botch a shipside mooring and retire in humiliation. In "Finish, Good Lady" a middle-aged assistant to an elderly matriarch, Mrs. Lorne, discovers and reveals, to terrible effect, the financial straits Mrs. Lorne's daughter is hiding from her mother to preserve her mother's sense of luxury and importance. In "The Ambassadress" (predictably, from its title, a Jamesian tale of Americans abroad), an expatriate artist and dandy approaching middle age contemplates marriage with a languid divorceé but, immaturely, requires something he cannot define from his older sister before making a decision. In "The Edification of Marianne" the protagonist is a kind of benign Maud; Marianne is a perfect little girl who grows up to be the spirit of charity and a perfect wife and mother, but her perfection is a kind of spiritual hollowness that contains no passion or love for individuals, and she ends up driving away her husband and a potential suitor even as her fame as a philanthropist grows. In "Greg's Peg" the narrator, for mysterious reasons, encourages Greg, a simple and pathetic man approaching middle age, to assert himself in life. Greg follows this counsel by turning himself into an embarrassing spectacle at the Maine resort where he and his mother spend their summers.

Auchincloss's stories tend to turn on three primary axes—moral, material, and aesthetic. Any character can be placed on a sliding scale along one or more of these axes, and the most significant character's movement—or failure to move—constitutes the primary drama of the story. Narrators are implicated in this pro-

cess more often than not; Auchincloss tends to favor first-person narration in his short stories, and usually the narrator is an active character in the fiction, often the protagonist. Auchincloss's authorial stance is, of course, sometimes detectable as something distinct from his narrators', especially in those stories where the narrators are less than entirely sympathetic (such as the manipulative narrator of "Greg's Peg" from *The Injustice Collectors*). However, Auchincloss generally eschews an evenhanded, omniscient narratorial stance in favor of one that is more involved, more down in the muck and murk of his characters' ostensibly elegant lives.

The eight stories in *The Romantic Egoists* (1954), Auchincloss's second short-story collection, were written between 1952 and 1954, and they continue in much the same vein as those in *The Injustice Collectors.* Unlike that collection, however, *The Romantic Egoists* has a single narrator, Peter Westcott, and includes two short stories derived from Auchincloss's wartime navy experience ("Wally" and "Loyalty Up and Loyalty Down"). The stories of *The Romantic Egoists* show Auchincloss settling into what became his enduring style; his stories had become a bit looser, displaying fewer attempts at Jamesian perfection of form and more scene-by-scene plausibility and depth of character. Plot events and incisive, categorical descriptions of characters are handled with dispatch until the reader arrives at one of Auchincloss's trademark clipped, compact dialogues between often powerful, almost always sophisticated characters in which the ambitions and doubts of one or both are laid bare.

Like James, Auchincloss has a certain difficulty creating character voices that are easily distinguishable; all his characters, even the pathetic ones (and there are many of those), tend to sound educated, genteel, and literate, sometimes despite narrative descriptions to the contrary. Biographer Carol Gelderman shows that Auchincloss is aware of this problem in James and has recognized it in his own writing. However, Auchincloss's command of dialogue in *The Romantic Egoists* (and in subsequent collections) had much improved from that of *The Injustice Collectors;* the characters' exchanges are remarkable for their believability, consciousness, and brevity. Terse, aware, ironic, and understated, his characters' words present a standard of wry sophistication that is both entertaining and informative of their society, and matches in observational shrewdness the pitiless social typologies given for the characters in narration.

Critical response to *The Romantic Egoists* was also positive. There were the usual comparisons to James, Wharton, and Marquand, but on the whole, Auchincloss's growing presence as a distinctive voice was beginning to be acknowledged. His rarefied sensibility earned him at least one epithet: Angus Wilson, writing for *The Spectator* (1 October 1954), called Auchincloss an "arrogant neo-aristocrat"; but even Wilson's review concludes favorably. The critics had begun to read Auchincloss on his own terms, most acknowledging and praising the thematic unity imposed on the stories of this collection by a single narrator observing a series of troubled, nonconformist characters, alternately pitiable and admirable.

During these years away from the law, while writing the stories of *The Romantic Egoists,* Auchincloss entered psychoanalysis. The effect of this therapy upon his short stories, in this collection and thereafter, is occasionally detectable in their content (such as in "Oberon and Titania" in *The Partners* [1974], which recaps some of Auchincloss's psychiatric experiences through its female protagonist), but is more generally manifested in Auchincloss's increased output; with the help of Freudian analysis, Auchincloss was able to reconcile his dual careers as writer and lawyer. He returned to the law in 1954 and settled into a highly productive routine of writing in his spare time, frequently at his law desk.

Also during this period Auchincloss made his first (and only) sustained attempt to become part of a literary "scene." He kept up his habit of fraternization with old, established New Yorkers, frequently older ladies, picking their brains for gossip, history, and mores of past eras, but he also found time to attend parties put together by John Aldridge and Vance Bourjaily, editors of *Discovery,* a serialized paperback put out by Pocket Books featuring Auchincloss's stories along with those of writers such as Norman Mailer, George Plimpton, and Herman Wouk. Auchincloss failed to integrate himself fully into this social scene, but he did stay long enough to garner a compliment from Mailer about "The Gemlike Flame"–that, as Auchincloss quotes him, Mailer "wouldn't have minded having written it himself." He also, through these gatherings, had the opportunity to renew an acquaintance with Gore Vidal, a once-stepcousin by marriage, with whom he has remained friends.

During the nine years following publication of *The Romantic Egoists,* Auchincloss turned his attention to his career, his love life, and novel writing. In this highly active period he established himself at his firm, wooed and married Adèle Lawrence and fathered their three sons (John, Blake, and Andrew), published five novels, edited a volume of Wharton's works, and published a collection of essays (*Reflections of a Jacobite,* 1961). He and Adèle moved into an apartment on Park Avenue in 1959 after the birth of their second child, and they bought a renovated farmhouse in Bedford, New York, for weekends in the country. Auchincloss wrote short stories only occasionally until 1962, when a sudden

Dust jacket for Auchincloss's 1970 collection of short stories, all of which examine changes in American manners and mores during the 1960s

flurry of story publishing culminated in the collection *Powers of Attorney* (1963).

Powers of Attorney is Auchincloss's first work to be set exclusively in the world of law and lawyers. The setting for all the stories is the Wall Street law firm of Tower, Tilney, and Webb, and the recurring central character is the founding partner, Clitus Tilney. These stories produce new variations on consistent Auchinclossian themes ennobling the past, such as the changing of the guard as partners retire and successors vie for power, and also a more general sense of better days gone by in the profession–a kind of dry-eyed nostalgia for days more ethical, or at least more concerned with ethics, if no better–days less bureaucratic and less mechanized. Auchincloss, as a lawyer, was well known for his own high standard of ethics as well as a marked preference for the spirit and theory of the law over routine application of statutes. He was not primarily a litigator–he tried only one case in his entire career (which he won)–thus, his law stories are not courtroom dramas but tales of the inner workings of partnerships and the politics, crises, and ethical dilemmas and temptations that lawyers can face in seemingly staid law firms. The specialized subject matter of the volume perhaps increased its feeling of distance or limitation for reviewers, who were positive but less effusive in their praise for this collection than for the previous two. Given Auchincloss's firsthand knowledge of the subject and setting, the lack of drama or intensity in the stories that some readers noted may be simple realism concerning the mood and manner of a Wall Street law firm.

Auchincloss was hitting his stride as a successful writer at this point in his career. His contributions to magazines, most of them popular journals such as *McCall's, The New Yorker,* and *Cosmopolitan,* were voluminous. He had pieces of novels (serialized and individual) and short stories appearing in more than a dozen magazines, and his literary income was exceeding his income from the law. He was courted and feted by society, the public, and the intelligentsia of New York. His success was not total, however; nominated for both a National Book Award and a Pulitzer Prize for the best-selling *The Rector of Justin* in 1964, he won neither, and was not nominated for a Pulitzer again (he received one more National Book Award nomination in 1966 for *The Embezzler*). Still, the 1960s were a triumph for Auchincloss, marked more by conspicuous success in novels than short stories, but general acclaim was the rule until the close of the decade.

The thirteen stories in *Tales of Manhattan* (1967), his fourth collection, unfold in three groupings—"Memories of an Auctioneer," "Arnold & Degener, One Chase Manhattan Plaza," and "The Matrons." The "auctioneer" of the first group is Roger Jordan, an art auctioneer through whom Auchincloss explores what was becoming a favorite theme—the possession and valuation of art objects and what they reflect about their owners. Auchincloss shares this theme of art and its effects with both James and Wharton. The second group of stories is a small legal collection in which the law firm of Arnold & Degener is depicted indirectly through its partners' writings about the others in the firm. "The Matrons" is, exactly as its title implies, a collection of portraits of old society ladies of New York, and an exploration of how they keep up (or not) with changing times. Reaction to the volume was, once again, mostly positive; but some critics were beginning to accuse Auchincloss of having a superficial or antiquated sensibility. One can surmise that in the rapidly changing world of 1960s America, readers were beginning to prefer more blood and guts in their fiction than Auchincloss customarily offered.

Auchincloss won back some of his critics with *Second Chance: Tales of Two Generations* (1970). The collection has a binding theme of generational difference, realized more concretely than the usual Auchinclossian sense of the past haunting the present. Most of the twelve stories in the collection depict some kind of a generational shift, such as between father and son ("Black Shylock"), or mentor and successor ("The Prince and the Pauper"), or deceased husband and new suitor ("Suttee"). Dahl has called *Second Chance* Auchincloss's most topical collection; the theme of a generation gap, as well as some of the politics in the stories, is well within the zeitgeist of this period of American history. Auchincloss generally achieves a balance between present and past in this collection.

One exception to the quotidian topicality of *Second Chance*, however, is "The Prison Window," an exception both to the theme of current events and generational division and to Auchincloss's usual adherence to realistic and mundane subject matter. "The Prison Window" is a kind of muted tale of the supernatural, reminiscent of Edgar Allan Poe's or Wharton's ghost stories. In it, a museum curator is faced with first the ethical and then the (ectoplasmically) spiritual ramifications of displaying an eighteenth-century prison window as an objet d'art. The mood of otherworldly menace is conveyed effectively in this story, and as with certain other departures in setting and subject matter (for example, *The Winthrop Covenant*), Auchincloss demonstrates his capability to occasionally step outside of his favorite settings and subjects—real-world family dramas in late-nineteenth- and twentieth-century New York. Not until the next collection, however, were changes in America reflected in a dramatic shift in Auchincloss's style.

The Partners (1974), Auchincloss's sixth collection, is the second collection of "legal" stories, and though it shares the major structural features of *Powers of Attorney*—a recurring central figure (Beekman "Beeky" Ehninger) operating a law firm (Shepard, Putney, and Cox), to which all the characters have a connection—the tenor of the stories is somewhat different. *The Partners* is in several ways Auchincloss's least polite or mannered collection, and that may have something to do with the passing away of his mother in the previous year. (His father had passed away in 1968.) Priscilla Auchincloss had been a faithful reader of her son's work, often before the manuscripts were submitted for publication. Given their close relation, her naturally modest sensibilities, and Auchincloss's high regard for her opinion, her death may have had a freeing effect on the content of his stories. Auchincloss was also writing his autobiography, *A Writer's Capital,* during the same period he wrote the stories of *The Partners,* so perhaps it is natural that a certain confessional straightforwardness spills over from that writing into this collection. Although the perennial Auchincloss themes are all represented, the tone of the stories is more brash, sexy, and angry; the characters have frequently ceased to understate or imply, and often simply state what they feel in what is, for Auchincloss, brutally frank language. Irony and satire, so frequently but subtly present in his stories, are at their most naked in *The Partners.*

Auchincloss is clearly trying to keep up with the times in this collection, and to a large degree he succeeds. Critical reception was mixed; Auchincloss's shift in tone and sensibility is something only a few reviewers picked up on at the time of publication, most being content to keep him in the category of "novelist of manners" and to judge the content on that basis. The collection was originally marketed as a novel, most likely because of its unity of setting and theme, and also possibly because of Auchincloss's greater notoriety as a novelist than a short-story writer at this point in his career. Reviewers had become more partisan by this time; critical preferences for more-visceral, experimental, or minority-centered fiction—preferences that had begun to shift as early as *Tales of Manhattan*—were now quite pronounced in many cases. Some readers were siding with Auchincloss for conservative reasons, while others used adjectives such as "bloodless" to condemn not only this collection but also Auchincloss himself, his preferred genre, and perhaps even his society.

"The Marriage Contract," the best story in the volume, tells the tale of Marcus and Felicia Currier, a working couple whose conflicts arise from their separate legal careers. In the battle of wills over whether the husband should accede to his wife's wishes or she to his, the story teeters on the brink of an Ibsenesque conclusion wherein the wife will simply storm out of the marriage. She does not, and by her remaining, the story ends on an unresolved question of what she has lost. Felicia's acidic reflections on her husband's firm, its members, and its stifling priorities are by turns hilarious and unsettling; and frequently her sensibility clearly controls the narrative. This loosening and extending of third-person character perspective was unheard of in the days of Auchincloss's first collection. *The Partners* was a relative commercial success, and Auchincloss was proving himself an artist of flexibility as well as mature talent. For his seventh collection, however, he took his readers in an entirely new direction.

The Winthrop Covenant moves out of the present century into the history of "the rise and fall of the Puritan ethic in New York and New England," as explained in the foreword. Primarily, it is the story of the Winthrop family and its increasingly tenuous connection to its Puritan heritage. Critical biographer Vincent Piket, in his *Louis Auchincloss: The Growth of a Novelist* (1991), marks the publication of this collection as a "break" in Auchincloss's work. Piket sees this collection as the

Dust jacket for Auchincloss's 1997 collection of short stories, including the satiric "Realist in Babylon," about the rise of an amoral newspaper magnate

point at which Auchincloss ceased trying to remain "current" and turned more actively to the past as a source of inspiration. There is certainly validity to this thesis; no short fiction Auchincloss has written since then matches the startling (for Auchincloss) contemporary sensibility of *The Partners;* and later stories (such as "The Atonement," from *The Atonement and Other Stories,* 1997) do tend to have older characters and more frequently use digressive flashbacks to provide back stories for the characters.

The Winthrop Covenant marks the longest sustained attempt Auchincloss makes in his short fiction to alter his customary subject matter and setting of present-day New York. Given his interest in history, it was natural for him to occasionally cast his sights back from the time of writing, but he had done so usually by having a narrator about his parents' age and clearly used the material gleaned from all those late-night conversations with society dowagers. *The Winthrop Covenant* generally remains in or near New York, but its historical scope goes back to the seventeenth century. The nine stories move chronologically forward, tracing the mishaps of the branches of the Winthrops as they go. "In the Beauty of the Lilies, Christ Was Born Across the Sea" is its most frequently reprinted story, possibly because it provided direct inspiration for the novel *Watchfires* (1982) six years later. Auchincloss has cited *The Winthrop Covenant* as a personal favorite. Its historical ambition, while perhaps not fully realized, certainly distinguishes it from the rest of Auchincloss's short-story output.

In a return to a more traditional collection format, Auchincloss published the twelve stories of *Narcissa, and Other Fables* in 1983. The title story uses a familiar Auchinclossian character and theme: the amoral artist. Elise Marcy, a successful artist, poses nude for a fellow artist whom she supports, a man less successful but of greater talent. Her posing nude is to satisfy a narcissistic desire, but reality asserts itself when the artist tries to blackmail her for further support. In an epiphanic moment, Elise realizes her love of his art is greater than her desire to defend herself from him, and she accedes to his demands. Though Auchincloss has returned to a more traditional approach in this collection, these stories, and those written hereafter, retain some of the bluntness that characterizes those of *The Partners;* the dialogue more often includes profanity, and sex remains less taboo a subject than it was for Auchincloss through the 1950s and 1960s. The collection ends with a sequence of twelve almost-stories under the title "Sketches of the Seventies," which are written in an unusual format: they are a series of one-paragraph to one-page descriptions, vignettes, and prose snapshots of characters and situations that are pure Auchincloss in their observation (somehow without being completely judgmental) of hypocrisy, shallowness, and social climbing. Though together these sketches do not comprise a larger narrative, their fragmentary nature is intriguing, perhaps a rare nod to postmodern sensibility. Also, they are valuable in offering a reader new to Auchincloss an instant immersion in typical Auchincloss moods and observations.

Auchincloss retired from the law in 1986. His coworkers during thirty-two years at Hawkins, Delafield and Wood had appreciated Auchincloss's gentlemanly manner, his objectiveness, and his responsible, ethical commitment to the business of lawyering and to the committees on which he sat. An associate and friend at the firm, Paul Golinski (quoted in Gelderman's *Louis Auchincloss: A Writer's Life*), attests to these qualities, adding that Auchincloss's "belief in the importance of English to the lawyer almost amounted to a religion."

Skinny Island, Auchincloss's ninth collection, was published the year after his retirement and is reminiscent of the previous collection in its loose associations between stories. Although it is a strong collection over-

all, its weakest story of the twelve, "Marcus: A Gothic Tale," shows by exception how entrenched Auchincloss's habits have become. The story is indeed Gothic, a condensed narrative of a romantic, hypersensitive young literature teacher at a Groton-ish private school (a distant variation on the Malcolm Strachan type) who spends his life denying his homosexuality and comes to a shattering self-awareness at the conclusion of the story as a result of an offhand remark by the headmaster. Though its narration and dialogue are overwrought and purplish (as Auchincloss intended), it succeeds as neither parody nor example of any Gothic genre. It is, however, a testament to Auchincloss's reflexive talent as a storyteller that even this tale is speedy and entertaining.

Auchincloss's wife, Adèle, passed away in 1991, a victim of cancer at fifty-nine. While Auchincloss had written his books and worked downtown, she had raised their three children and become heavily involved with the New York City park system and nationwide ecology and preservation concerns. An artist, Adèle illustrated her own book of natural wonders from the Alaskan countryside (*Tongass Tides,* 1984) as well as the book jackets for three of her husband's novels—*The Embezzler, The Rector of Justin,* and *Tales of Manhattan.* She and Auchincloss had a house built in 1988 outside of Liberty, New York, to replace the Bedford house they had by that time sold. Following her death, the house outside Liberty went to their three sons. Auchincloss returned to his beloved New York City, where he has kept on writing.

False Gods (1992) is a lively but uneven collection of six longish stories that are bound by the theme of characters' false ideas of themselves or empty ideals, epitomized in the titles associating the stories with specific Greek gods. "Polyhymnia, Muse of Sacred Song" is a rather rambling, digressive tale that uses a structuring device to hold it together. In this story a Protestant, Reggie Turner, desires to be a writer but feels he does not have the requisite gifts and becomes a Catholic priest instead. He grows to question his vocation after several trials of his faith, the greatest of which is when his marriage advice sends a young couple off to die in a plane crash en route to be married. He eventually leaves the church. Auchincloss frames the story as an explanation to the archbishop. Though Auchincloss has used story-framing, epistolary formats (such as in "The Penultimate Puritan" from *The Winthrop Covenant*), and other such structural devices occasionally, he generally prefers straightforward narration. Such overt structuring in this story is a substitute for a more integral cohesion.

"Hephaestus, God of Newfangled Things" is a much more successful story. In it, Humphrey Gilbert, an architect, must give up his passionate but platonic (later turned fully adulterous) relationship with his uncle's much younger wife in order to marry a woman whom both he and his dictatorial mother can see is "right" for him. This story explores, in greater depth than in "Polyhymnia, Muse of Sacred Song," aesthetic questions of the value of art to an artist: How much sacrifice is required to excel in one's field? To what extent should the public's taste dictate the direction of an artist's career? Humphrey is persuaded by his wife-to-be to pursue modern architecture instead of the older French architecture he loves. The story cleverly, and poignantly, parallels Humphrey's abandoning his impractical dreams with both the love affair he must leave behind and his mother's abandoned stage career.

"The Man of Good Will," the best of the eight stories in Auchincloss's tenth collection, *Tales of Yesteryear* (1994), brings Auchincloss back to the themes of generational split and disillusionment of the young. The "man" in question is Seth Middleton, grandfather to a suicidal young man, Mark Storey, who opposes the Vietnam War. Seth's visits to Mark at college, in place of Mark's estranged parents, are futile, and the suicide (reminiscent of Jack Woods's) eventually takes place. The old man's despairing questions at the end–"Why should he worry about being fatuous now? Why should he worry about anything?"–are a telling reminder of the emotional intensity that sometimes exists in Auchincloss's stories, and a clear counterexample to those who have accused Auchincloss of being passionless, or more concerned with decorum than spirit.

Such charges could be leveled perhaps a bit more justifiably at "The Lotos Eaters," another story from *Tales of Yesteryear*. "The Lotos Eaters" is a farcically light treatment of a recently married, beginning-to-be elderly couple, Joyce and Dick Emmons. It is a second marriage for both of them, and the central conflict of the story occurs when Joyce leaves her–now their–summer beach resort to get involved in fundraising, following a discussion in which Dick admits he considers their vacation home "heaven." He confesses he misses her, and they agree to reunite. Stories such as this one exhibit the characteristics some people have grown to dislike in Auchincloss's work: the dialogue of these aging sophisticates sounds brittle and forced, especially when the characters are discussing religious matters–glibness supersedes wit. Try as he might, Auchincloss cannot quite achieve the profound whimsicality of a Noël Coward or an Oscar Wilde when handling such inconsequential characters or situations. Past stories such as "The Ambassadress" dealt with similarly light characters,

but the subject matter was complicated by suggestions of depth in characters and their relations that is not to be found in "The Lotos Eaters." Nevertheless, this story is at worst amusing and quickly forgotten, an appetizer for more-satisfying fare.

The Atonement and Other Stories (1997) shows his powers, while not quite at the peaks of polish or ambition represented in *The Injustice Collectors* or *The Winthrop Covenant*, essentially undiminished. "The Hidden Muse," a brief story of Auchinclossian nostalgia, is basically pure autobiography with a few details rearranged. "Realist in Babylon," perhaps the best story in the collection, is a concise and evocative tale of the rise of an amoral newspaper magnate, Hugh Orrick, as seen through the eyes of a boyhood friend. Readers watch with the narrator in cynical amusement as Hugh, in the role of philanthropist and ethical exemplar, delivers a speech to the seventy-fifth class of his former high school. Auchincloss, in his preferred milieu of the wealthy and powerful, is continuing to make astute observations concerning the ethical complexities, compromises, and realities of everyday life.

The Anniversary and Other Stories (1999) exhibits similar qualities. Some stories show Auchincloss reverting a bit to the Jamesian wordiness characterizing his earliest work, and some of the dialogue has that narrativelike quality Auchincloss has never been entirely able to shake, but the exploration of ambition, social standing, and moral dilemmas and the examination of motivation in these stories are still sharp. Some stories, such as "Decicco v. Schweizer" (not a legal story, despite its title), suffer from abrupt endings or too-hastily summarized narrative events, but in general, the pacing of these stories is just right. The continuing fruitful use of autobiographical material continues unabated: "The Devil and Guy Lansing" is a Groton tale; "Man of the Renaissance," successfully combining themes from stories such as "The Man of Goodwill" and "The Novelist of Manners," is a tale of an artist facing the devils of mediocrity, and is also a story of a paternal figure facing the role he played in the death of his son. These and other stories exhibit Auchincloss's limitless use of limited subject matter, a secret known to all prolific authors who do not rely primarily on research for inspiration, but rather mine the human heart and the smaller world of particular situations.

Dignified and unsentimental, restrained yet compassionate, Louis Auchincloss's corpus of short fiction provides a lasting overview of a culture and society more central in American history and heritage than its comparative neglect by other authors would have it seem. Readers are indebted to Auchin-

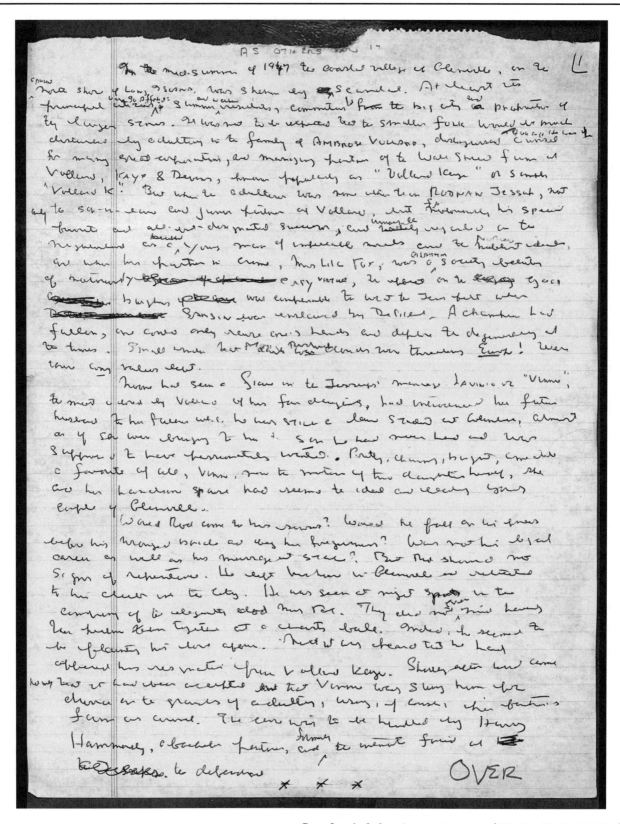

Pages from drafts for a short story in progress (Collection of Louis Auchincloss)

In the mid-summer of 1947 the coastal village of Glenville on the opulent north shore of Long Island was shaken by scandal. At least its principal citizens were so affected: summer and weekend residents, commuters to the big city and proprietors of the larger stores. It was not to be expected that the smaller folk would be much affected by adultery in the family of Ambrose Vollard, distinguished counsel though he was to many great corporations and managing partner of the Wall Street law firm of Vollard, Kaye & Devens, known popularly as "Vollard Kaye" or simply "Vollard K". But when the adulterer was none other than Rodman Jessup, not only the son-in-law and junior partner of Vollard but his special favorite and all but designated successor, a young man universally admired in the neighborhood for his impeccable morals and high ideals, and when his partner in crime, Mrs. Lila Fisk, was a middle-aged Manhattan society woman of fading charms and loose behavior, the effect on the good burghers of Glenville was comparable to that of the Hebrews when Delilah cut off Sampson's curly locks. A champion had inexplicably fallen; they could only raise their hands and deplore the degeneracy of the times. Small wonder that the planet was menaced again with world war!

Noone has seen a flaw in the Jessups' marriage. Lavinia, or "Vinnie", the most adored by Vollard of his four daughters, had introduced her future husband to her father when he was a law student at Columbia, almost as though she were bringing him the son he had never had and that he was supposed to have passionately wanted. Pretty, bright, charming and amiable, now the mother of

1

closs for chronicling a moneyed and cultured society that has more in common with the rest of America than one might have otherwise thought. In many ways, of course, his world is different from that of the less privileged, but this difference may actually make his role as observer of that world even more valuable.

Interviews:

Lewis Nichols, "Talk with Mr. Auchincloss," *New York Times Book Review,* 27 September 1953, p. 28;

Nichols, "Talk with Mr. Auchincloss," *New York Times,* 21 October 1956, p. 6;

Roy Newquist, "Louis Auchincloss," in *Counterpoint,* edited by Newquist (Chicago: Rand McNally, 1965), pp. 31–38;

Dinitia Smith, "The Old Master and the Yuppie," *New York,* 18 August 1986, pp. 30–34;

Patricia Lindin, "The Museum that Saved the City," *Town and Country* (September 1987): 230–233;

Vincent Piket, "An Interview with Louis Auchincloss," *Dutch Quarterly Review of Anglo-American Letters,* 18 (1988): 20–37;

Jean Ross, "Auchincloss, An Interview," in *Contemporary Authors,* New Revision Series, 29 (Detroit: Gale Research, 1990): 26–31;

George Plimpton, "Louis Auchincloss: The Art of Fiction CXXXVIII," *Paris Review,* 132 (Fall 1994): 73–94.

Bibliography:

Jackson Bryer, *Louis Auchincloss and His Critics: A Bibliographical Record* (Boston: G. K. Hall, 1977).

Biography:

Carol Gelderman, *Louis Auchincloss: A Writer's Life* (New York: Crown, 1993).

References:

C. D. B. Bryan, "Under the Auchincloss Shell," *New York Times Magazine,* 11 February 1979, pp. 35, 37, 61, 66;

Christopher Dahl, *Louis Auchincloss* (New York: Ungar, 1986);

John Leonard, "What Have American Writers Got Against Businessmen?" *Forbes,* 15 May 1977, p. 121;

David B. Parsell, *Louis Auchincloss* (Boston: Twayne, 1988);

Vincent Piket, *Louis Auchincloss: The Growth of a Novelist* (New York: St. Martin's Press, 1991);

Scott Rosenberg, "A Double Life in Perfect Balance," *American Lawyer* (February 1983): 42–44;

James Tuttleton, "The Image of Lost Elegance and Virtue," *American Literature,* 43 (1972): 616–632.

Papers:

A collection of Louis Auchincloss's papers is housed at the University of Virginia, in Charlottesville.

Frederick Barthelme

(10 October 1943 –   )

John Hughes
Valencia Community College

See also the Barthelme entry in *DLB Yearbook: 1985.*

BOOKS: *Rangoon* (New York: Winter House, 1970);
War and War (Garden City, N.Y.: Doubleday, 1971);
Moon Deluxe (New York: Simon & Schuster, 1983; Harmondsworth, U.K.: Penguin, 1984);
Second Marriage (New York: Simon & Schuster, 1984; London: Dent, 1985);
Tracer (New York: Simon & Schuster, 1985; London: Dent, 1986);
Chroma (New York: Simon & Schuster, 1987; Harmondsworth, U.K.: Penguin, 1988);
Two Against One (New York: Weidenfeld & Nicolson, 1988);
Natural Selection (New York: Viking, 1990);
The Brothers (New York: Viking, 1993);
Painted Desert (New York: Viking, 1995);
Bob the Gambler (New York: Houghton Mifflin, 1997);
Double Down: Reflections on Gambling and Loss, by Barthelme and Steven Barthelme (New York: Houghton Mifflin, 1999);
The Law of Averages: New & Selected Stories (Washington, D.C.: Counterpoint, 2000).

SELECTED PERIODICAL PUBLICATION–
UNCOLLECTED: "On Being Wrong: Convicted Minimalist Spills Bean," *New York Times Book Review,* 3 April 1988, p. 1.

Frederick Barthelme (courtesy of the author)

Though he published two books in the 1970s, Frederick Barthelme began to draw serious attention only with the publication of his short-story collection, *Moon Deluxe,* in 1983. In the seventeen stories of that book Barthelme traces the lives of men and women through the shopping malls, fast-food restaurants, and apartment complexes of postmodern America. He works with characters stunned by consumer overload and shaken by radical shifts in gender roles following the cultural revolutions in sexuality and gender relations of the late 1960s and 1970s. Throughout his subsequent novels and short stories, Barthelme's characters are searching for a new way to live that allows for meaningful relationships in an era of changed notions of masculinity and femininity. Essentially a moralist, though not of the traditional kind, Barthelme treats characters struggling to find moral footing on the slippery slope of contemporary life, where conventional values such as marriage, monogamy, fidelity, and heterosexuality have been exhausted. Barthelme's characters are on a search, not for a code that might work for an entire nation, but for a set of principles by which to guide their own individual choices.

Frederick Barthelme was born in Houston, Texas, on 10 October 1943 to Donald Barthelme, an architect and professor, and Helen (née Bechtold) Barthelme, an English teacher. He is one of five children, four of whom grew up to be fiction writers. His brother Donald was a world-famous metafictionalist before he died of cancer in 1989; Peter writes mystery novels, including *Push, Meet Shove* (1987) and *Tart, with Silken Finish* (1988); and Steven, who teaches creative writing at the University of Southern Mississippi, has published a book of short stories, *And He Tells the Little Horse the Whole Story* (1987). His sister, Joan, is retired from a career in public relations. Frederick Barthelme attended Tulane University from 1961 to 1962 and the University of Houston from 1962 through 1965. He took his undergraduate degree at the Museum of Fine Art in Houston, Texas, in 1966.

After graduation Barthelme began pursuing a career as a visual artist. From 1966 to 1974 he exhibited in shows around the country, in Canada, and in Buenos Aires, Argentina. He said in a 1988 interview in *Contemporary Authors* that he was interested in replacing the idea of "creating" art with one of "buying" art, of taping work gloves and PVC pipes to gallery walls. He says his first two books, *Rangoon* (1970) and *War and War* (1971), were the literary equivalents of those plastic art experiments. The first two books either received poor notices or were ignored.

Rangoon, a collection of stories, drawings, and photographs, and *War and War,* billed as a novel, were both metafictions, literary artifacts, experiments similar to the works of John Barth, Robert Coover, and Frederick's brother Donald Barthelme. As Frederick Barthelme stated in his essay "On Being Wrong: Convicted Minimalist Spills Bean," which appeared in *The New York Times Book Review* in 1988, he abandoned metafiction because he sensed it had been done as well as it could be by its most famous practitioners.

In 1976 he began studying with Barth at Johns Hopkins, where he won the university's Eliot Coleman Award for Prose and received his M.A. in 1977. That same year he began teaching at the University of Southern Mississippi and became the director of the university's Center for Writers in 1978. Since 1977 he has also edited *Mississippi Review,* an influential literary magazine that has published such writers as Barth, John Hawkes, and Martin Amis.

In the late 1970s Barthelme began publishing short stories. He began the search for a new voice, a search that resulted in his adoption of a minimalist, or neorealist, style that helped to short-list him among the top story writers of the 1980s and provoked Bret Easton Ellis to describe him as "one of the most distinctive prose stylists since Hemingway." Throughout the 1980s he published in magazines such as *Chicago Review, North American Review, Esquire, New Orleans Review, Kansas Review,* and most notably, *The New Yorker*. In 1983 thirteen of his stories from *The New Yorker* and one from *Esquire* appeared in his first collection, *Moon Deluxe*. In this collection Barthelme's male protagonists negotiate the minefield of contemporary sexual relations, with varying degrees of understanding and success.

In many ways *Moon Deluxe* is a primer for postmodern minimalism. The collection firmly establishes in terms of plot and point of view what is possible in fiction after the extravagances of the metafiction of the 1960s and early 1970s, such as Barth's *Giles Goat-Boy* (1966), which is narrated by a computer, and Thomas Pynchon's *Gravity's Rainbow* (1973), a sprawling book with no discernible plot and a protagonist whose orgasms can predict V-2 rocket strikes in World War II London. Barthelme's fictions are especially informed by definitive metafictional work, such as the work of his brother Donald, Barth, Hawkes, and William Gass, the writers Barthelme calls the "four big guys" who were able to write metafiction and write it well. If metafiction suggested, through its playful approach to form, genre, and point of view, that stories and novels should never, and could never, be mistaken for reality, that realism in literature was just an impossible writing trick, then for Barthelme and other neorealists their fiction had to acknowledge this hard-won understanding. Barthelme's stories in *Moon Deluxe* do not participate in the traditional form of the epiphany story. In such standard epiphany stories as John Updike's "A&P" and Frank O'Connor's "Guests of the Nation," the protagonists usually find themselves moving through the events of the plot toward a moment of sudden insight or realization, a moment that changes the protagonist's life in some small or large way. That does not happen in a typical Barthelme story, for that is precisely the kind of "trick" of realistic writing that metafiction had gone about skewering to such good effect. Barthelme (and other postmetafictional writers) could hardly go back to such plot devices now that they had been so fully parodied. Barthelme is less interested in plot and story than in character and description, and this occupation with character and description is generally true of the stories in *Moon Deluxe* and *Chroma* (1987).

Barthelme's short stories offer only three points of view: first person, third-person limited omniscience, and second person. Barthelme never uses the fully omniscient point of view, which mimics a God-like perspective on the characters and events. His decision seems appropriate for writing in a period in which belief in God has declined. If there is no God, then there ought to be no God-like perspective from which to see human beings and their actions. There are only human perspectives with their necessary limitations. First-person and third-person limited points of view probably more accurately reflect life as it is lived, with the inherent limitations on knowledge that they imply and impart. The use of second-person point of view is an uncommon convention; using that point of view as a tool to emphasize his narrators' extreme self-consciousness allows Barthelme to experiment with literary technique.

The first of the seventeen stories in *Moon Deluxe* is "Box Step." In this story the first-person narrator, Henry Pfeister, a prototypical Barthelme protagonist, finds himself attracted to his secretary, Ann. He invites her to his house for a drink, and she then invites others: coworkers, Henry's sister and brother-in-law, and some friends, which in turn raises the question of whether Ann is avoiding being alone with Henry. She asks, "I play hostess? Are we sure about this?" Uncertainty pervades this piece and seems to point to the notion that nothing is sure. The language is often slippery; what is said among the characters is rarely completely clear. At the party Henry shows everyone a plastic toy dinosaur he bought. When he says he bought it at the T. G. & Y., one of the characters becomes angry and storms out of the party, slamming the door. The next day at work, Henry learns that the woman who had stormed out has a daughter working at the T. G. & Y. and living with the store's manager. That same day Henry happens to be near that store and goes in again. He tells the girl, Connie, he has talked to her parents. She says she is not sure how to deal with her parents. He tells her to do what she wants and have a good time because she can change it all later if she wants.

Henry's final statement to Connie summarizes the ethos of Barthelme's fictional world: no decision is final, no marriage permanent, no error unfixable. This world is not a bleak existential one where every choice carries with it the responsibility of determining one's identity. It is a postmodern ethos, a happier and more optimistic one that suggests that there are always more options. The story concludes with a trip to Biloxi, a tourist town on the Mississippi Gulf Coast, and a lyrical description of the gaudy colors and outrageous come-ons of the tourist traps. "Box Step" is a summary study of the themes that Barthelme habitually examines in his stories: postmodernism, social comment, women in control, and the social construction of reality.

Four of the stories in *Moon Deluxe*—"Shopgirls," the title story "Moon Deluxe," "Pool Lights," and "Safeway"— use the second-person point of view. While fairly common in poetry, its use in narrative fiction is rare, though there are certainly prominent examples such as in Italo Calvino's *Se una notte d'inverno un viaggiatore* (1979; translated as *If on a winter's night a traveler,* 1981) and Jay McInerney's *Bright Lights, Big City* (1984). Reviewing *Moon Deluxe* for *Harper's* in 1986, Madison Smartt Bell called Barthelme "a pioneer of what is becoming a very irritating mannerism of contemporary fiction: second person narration." Bell quotes a paragraph from the story "Shopgirls" in which the protagonist plays self-consciously with the food on his plate, and then Bell writes "*The hell I do,*" indicating that he believes

Dust jacket for Barthelme's 1983 book, seventeen stories in which men and women attempt to cope with the sexual revolution of the 1960s and 1970s

Barthelme is telling him that he, Bell, is the character playing with his food. That is to say, Bell believes that Barthelme intends the reader to understand that the reader and the protagonist of the story are the same person. While this identification between reader and character in a story is what some writers using second-person point of view intend the reader to experience, Bell has misunderstood Barthelme's use of the technique. Drawing the reader into complicity in the story is not what Barthelme is doing in the second-person stories of *Moon Deluxe*. Instead, the use of the "you" as both a narrative technique and character in a Barthelme story embodies the extreme self-consciousness of the Barthelme protagonist. Barthelme's narrators in these four stories are, in fact, first-person narrators who are talking to themselves, calling themselves "you," thereby emphasizing and reinforcing the distance those protagonists feel from the world around them, especially from the women in their lives.

One of the most important recurring themes in Barthelme's stories is the question of what a man's role is in the postfeminist-revolution world. How do men relate to these radically free women? Barthelme's protagonists are stunned and nearly paralyzed into inaction by the powerful "new woman." In Barthelme's stories, especially in these second-person stories, the women are in charge of every situation. For example, in "Shopgirls" the second-person narrator likes to admire the beautiful women who work in the shops in the mall. The women are disarmingly self-confident; they know they are beautiful and know that is why they have been hired to work in the upscale shops. The unnamed protagonist, who lies to the women and the reader about his name, is something of a voyeur. The shopgirls have noticed him watching them, pretending to shop, and they invite him to lunch; then they talk about him right to his face, as if he were a child or not there at all. They discuss how he has followed them around through the stores. The women speculate upon which one he likes the best. They comment that he is handsome. One of them rises from the table, comes around to his chair, and "opens her blouse slightly. 'See, Robert? Isn't it pretty? Tell the girls I'm the one you really like.' 'You're the one I really like,' you say." One of the women, Andrea, takes him to her apartment that night, and there, in a sexually charged situation, talks to him about her father, an ineffectual man who botched his own suicide. The story ends when Andrea goes to bed around midnight: "you make no move to follow her into the bedroom, and she makes no special invitation. You sleep on the sofa, fully dressed, without even a sheet to cover you." He imagines that tomorrow he will go back to the mall and buy some useless object from another beautiful woman. This character is an extreme example of the Barthelme protagonist, one so unsure of his relationship to women that he becomes paralyzed by his fear of them and, at the same time, his desperate need for them. The familiar interplay between men and women is displaced: instead of sleeping with her, he sleeps fully clothed on the couch; instead of buying something for a woman, he will buy something from one.

"Moon Deluxe" opens with a quasi-surrealist image of a man stuck in traffic who sees a beautiful woman in another car. She makes a tantalizing gesture toward him and is then borne away by the traffic, seemingly out of his life. Later he is set up with another woman, Lily, at a dinner party and goes home with her. There he meets the woman from the traffic jam, a six-foot blonde with the masculine nickname of Tony. The relationship between the women seems to the narrator to be sexual. Yet, he is there, invited by Lily. What is his role? What is expected of him? Is he the interloper, or the third party in a ménage à trois? Tony is confused and upset, though whether because of the narrator's presence or because of something else is not clear. She says, "'Edward's not a threat, is he? You're

not a threat, are you, Edward?' 'I don't guess so. To my dismay.'" Thoroughly frustrated, he decides to leave. The women do not attempt to stop him. He wishes he would be invited to spend the night, even if only to sleep on the couch. They both kiss him good-bye, with their lips innocently shut, and go back into the apartment hand in hand. The story ends with him standing outside, looking at the moon and feeling pool water in his shoes. The title "Moon Deluxe" indicates the feminine principle of the moon, but of the "deluxe" variety, which is to say that there is, for this protagonist, the possibility of two women, of a ménage à trois, complicated by the fact that if the two women are together, they do not really need him. Here again Barthelme creates conflict but excludes resolution, a traditional plot structure he has largely abandoned. He creates his fictions to reflect life as it is truly lived, with conflict, confusion, and retreat.

Some readers may believe that Barthelme's viewpoint of the breakdown of the traditional roles between men and women is symptomatic of a decline in American values and culture. Barthelme's tone, however, in the stories of *Moon Deluxe* does not offer out-and-out condemnation but rather displays dispassionate neutrality. He dramatizes the new relationships between the sexes but does not comment upon them satirically or ironically. There is, in fact, a decided lack of irony in all of Barthelme's work. Kim Herzinger, in an article on minimalism, comments that minimalists are "hesitant about irony as a mode of presentation, and profoundly uneasy with irony as a mode of evaluation." Barthelme is not judging his strong women and his weakened men. He sometimes invites the reader to laugh at the situation his characters find themselves in, but he rarely asks the reader to laugh at the characters themselves. He presents the unvarnished world as it is.

"Pool Lights" is the third of the second-person stories in *Moon Deluxe*. In this story the image of J. Alfred Prufrock pervades. Prufrock is the narrator of T. S. Eliot's poem "The Lovesong of J. Alfred Prufrock" (1915), a man paralyzed into inaction by an extreme self-consciousness and by the emergence of a new kind of woman. The unnamed protagonist in "Pool Lights" is extremely self-conscious (he watches himself undress in a mirror), and he confesses to Dolores, a woman who lives in the same apartment complex and who is pursuing him, that he does not like to sit by the pool because he worries other tenants are watching him through their windows. Dolores suggests that it is hard not to look at the sunbathers, and he thinks she suspects him of that same voyeurism. Again much like Prufrock, this protagonist imagines he knows what women think of him, projecting his own self-image onto them. In fact, watching the tenants around the pool through his window is exactly what the narrator is doing.

The opening sentence of "Pool Lights" reveals Barthelme's postmodern obsession with the slippery nature of language and the potentially devastating implications for interpersonal communication and for literature: "There are things that cannot be understood—things said at school, at the supermarket, or in this case by the pool of the Santa Rosa Apartments on a hazy afternoon in midsummer." Dolores says he has a "pretty face," and the narrator ponders that particular word choice. A curious reversal of sex roles ensues, wherein Dolores plays the pursuer and the narrator takes on more traditionally feminine traits and behaviors, a favorite technique Barthelme uses to deconstruct the familiar and comment on contemporary gender roles. Later in the story the narrator watches a pool party through his window and sees Dolores look up and beckon him to come down. He is certain she cannot see him, but, of course, he cannot be sure. He retreats, closes the curtains, goes back to bed, and mindlessly flips through magazines. Later she stands him up when their date is inconvenient for her but expects him to come running when she calls. This situation parodies the traditional suburban romance and puts the narrator in a comic bind: the fact that she takes the lead in getting things started between them takes the possibility of rejection off him but simultaneously robs him of the male role in the relationship.

The final of the second-person stories is "Safeway." In this story Barthelme continues to examine the leading, initiating woman. In the Safeway grocery store, the second-person narrator meets a beautiful, well-dressed woman who makes sexual overtures to him. A dreamlike quality pervades the events in the grocery store, from the two raucously sexual plumbers in the checkout line with their non sequitur humor to the scene in which a soda bottle mysteriously explodes:

> Your aisle is stared at like a traffic accident. Then you are surrounded by boys mopping and being solicitous, and everyone is laughing. The woman is laughing. The manager, who appears from nowhere, is laughing and trying to blot her blouse dry with a yellow sponge. The checker is laughing and at the same time apologizing. The boys are laughing as they fall to their knees in order to clean up the mess. Someone goes after another bottle of Tab, and while the lane is still crowded with people, while everyone is still laughing, the checker shoves your purchases to the foot of her counter, where yet another tall, thickset, smiling teenager stuffs the goods into a brown sack.

Following this surreal slapstick, she invites him for coffee, then offers to come to his apartment, telling him her husband is out of town. Though he has already fantasized about submitting sexually to her—"touching her

hair, and her shoulders, and her skin in response to stern commands"—he gives her a phony address so that she cannot find him. The scene at the checkout stand has predicted for him the pitfalls of becoming involved with her. Involvement means chaos and conflict, a clumsy, sticky mess where everyone is laughing except him. In "Safeway" the narrator has taken the "safe way" in navigating this encounter: he simply avoids it.

One of the most common narrative strategies in *Moon Deluxe* is to have events, people, and situations unexpectedly emerge into the protagonist's life, angling in on the protagonist seemingly out of the corner of his eye, casting a surreal spell over him and putting him into disturbingly strange conjunctions of people and circumstances, all of which seem to control him more than he controls them. In "Violet," the protagonist, Philip, who lives in another of the existentially empty apartment complexes that dot Barthelme's Southern landscape, is heating a frozen dinner and watching on television a CNN newswoman with whom he is somewhat obsessed, speaking her name to the television, commenting on her makeup, and mentally cataloguing her wardrobe. When a teenage girl, Violet, knocks on his door and asks to use the phone, he cannot say no. Eventually she insists that he take her out for dinner, and afterward, they go to a bar. When they go out to his car, they find a seven-foot-tall man examining Philip's car. Vaguely threatening, maybe drunk, he asks to drive the car. Violet decides that they should take the man, Sidney, for a ride, which they do, eventually stopping to let Sidney take over the wheel and drive. They end up back in the parking lot of the bar, where Violet reveals she knows Philip from Pie Country, where she works and he frequents. The story ends with the waitress emerging from the bar to ask if Sidney really drove the car.

"Violet" is an unconventional story because the events are unconnected and bizarre. From Violet arriving uninvited at his door to Sidney driving his car, the things that happen to Philip are strange and menacing, events that might, in the hands of a suspense writer, portend dangerous outcomes, serious consequences, and bodily harm. In this story, however, the events unfold and end benignly. The notion that unforeseen, uncontrollable events can generally turn out all right is a recurring theme in Barthelme's work. As Philip floats along in "Violet," like a leaf on a current of events seemingly beyond his control, finally coming home safely again, he is Barthelme's parody of the mythic hero on his journey-quest, a quest that in contemporary times no longer has a grail or purpose but is just a circle bringing the hero home again, with nothing to show but the thrill of the journey.

The threat of radical lesbianism, one of Barthelme's early thematic concerns and one he has dealt with earlier in the story "Moon Deluxe," returns in "Monster Deal."

Dust jacket for Barthelme's 2000 book, twenty-nine stories in which Barthelme identifies a common thread of "polite anarchy"

In this story a six-foot-two-inch woman named Tina (paralleling the six-foot Tony in "Moon Deluxe") shows up at Jerry's house and announces she is spending the night. Though Jerry has never seen her before, she says she is a friend of his landlord. She is attractive and forceful, moving him around and taking charge. When she says "Tell you what, you check me out. Meanwhile, I'll catch some sleep. . . . Which bedroom do you want me in?" she sounds vaguely sexual, but neither the reader nor Jerry knows for sure. Tina is a mover and a shaker. Currently she is planning to deliver three hundred chickens to a church bazaar, though she has not decided whether to lease a refrigerated truck or haul them in her Cadillac. Compared to her vivacity and drive, the retiring Jerry practically disappears into the background. Jerry previously had made a date with Karen, the woman who delivers his paper. Before he knows it, Tina has left with Karen, and they are gone all night, the night he was supposed to take Karen out. When they get back to his house, they stagger around giggling at jokes he does not get, then "arm in arm, and after a lot of maneuvering and laughing, get into the bedroom and shut the door." The next morning Tina emerges and watches him cook breakfast. In a nearly perfect male-female role reversal, he cooks and cleans, and she watches and eats, making messes he has to clean up. Finally Tina leaves to make her chicken deal, and he is left alone in the kitchen looking at the newspaper. Jerry does not want to read; he just looks at the headlines. This evasion of particulars suggests that he likes broad outlines but does not want to engage with specifics, which are scary. Karen has not yet come out of the bedroom.

After *Moon Deluxe* was published, Barthelme wrote the novels *Second Marriage* (1984) and *Tracer* (1985). Both are tentative explorations of the novel form. *Second Marriage* is an expanded version of a story from *Moon Deluxe,* "The Browns." At just 126 pages, *Tracer,* in length and complexity, is more akin to a long short story than to a novel. In *Second Marriage* and *Tracer* Barthelme examines one of his ongoing themes: that marriage, the traditional relationship between men and women, formerly a sacred institution, must now be recognized in postmodern times to be a purely secular one, socially constructed rather than divinely ordained. Inasmuch as it is a socially constructed institution, people may partake of it or not. If they choose not to do so, they may redefine or reconstruct it in any fashion that suits them: marry in a church or courthouse, or live together without benefit of clergy or government sanction, raise children or live child-free, practice monogamy or not, divorce and remarry as many times as desired. There is even the possibility that one man might have two women as his mates. But, by the same token, if two women can be brought together into a relationship, maybe they will not need the man at all—which is the great fear of many of the men in Barthelme's stories and novels.

In 1987 Barthelme published his second collection of short stories, *Chroma*. The pieces therein address similar questions of secular matrimony, and the protagonists move from the Prufrock-like lone male of the *Moon Deluxe* variety to married people. In his *Chroma* stories and in the novels that follow, Barthelme shows that postmodern marriage will be different from traditional marriage and that it will be the partners who define the parameters of their marriages—not the church, the state, or public opinion. *Chroma* also continues his examination of characters struggling with life in the frenetic consumer culture in which traditional values and roles have been jettisoned, but no new signposts have been erected.

The first of the fifteen stories in *Chroma* is "Driver." The unnamed protagonist is a man whose life has settled into a routine. His wife goes to bed without him and leaves him to watch late-night television. One night he is moved to tears by a show about Los Angeles low-riders. As the owners of the cars put them through their paces, using their custom shock absorbers to make the vehicles hop up and down, the protagonist imagines himself a part of that subculture. The next day he buys just such a customized car, and it enlivens him. In turn, it enlivens his wife, Rita. As he rides around at the end of the story, he is struck for the first time by the unexpected beauty of the world in which he lives, even the cars and factories and apartment complexes. This story suggests that marriages can bog down and must be shaken up by something unexpected, as in the protagonist's purchase of a car completely out of step with his life.

In "Perfect Things" another couple, Jerry and Ellen, have come to a point in their marriage where they are bored, tired of the same old thing every day. Speaking of their life together, Ellen says, "It's all under control, right? I hate it. I hate the lawn, Jerry, know what I mean?" He does. He does not like the lawn either, but he is not happy with how Ellen is dealing with their routine lives. She has taken a lover, a younger man named Toby. As Jerry and Ellen sit at breakfast and argue over Toby and their lives, Jerry comes to realize just how much he loves Ellen. When she tells him he would like Toby, he denies it, saying he hates Toby. But he thinks that is not true; he does not feel hate for Toby: "What he did feel was much in love with Ellen, more in love than he had been in a long time." He then recites a litany of the things he loves about her. This story leaves the issue of Toby unresolved and implies that somehow Jerry and Ellen will

find a way to stay married, even if it means he has to accept her relationship with Toby.

In the title story, "Chroma," the unnamed first-person narrator also has a wife who is openly having an affair. He is not sure how he feels about the situation. He should be angry, upset, and jealous because his wife, Alicia, spends every other weekend and the occasional weeknight with her boyfriend, George. The narrator says that at first he thought he might go crazy, but eventually he begins to enjoy the time alone, the quiet, and the clean house. The idea is that women are messy, or rather that relationships are messy, and that it is simply cleaner and quieter without anyone around. "Chroma" ends with Alicia getting cleaned up in the bathtub as the narrator sits on the floor by the tub talking with her about their situation. Like Jerry from "Perfect Things," this protagonist is also struck with how beautiful his wife is, how much he loves her despite the unusual marital situation they live in. He is willing to try to find a new way to negotiate marriage, a way that stretches the boundaries of what marriage is by jettisoning possessiveness, jealousy, and monogamy.

Not every story in *Chroma* details the new conception of marriage. "Trick Scenery" is a story that uses a second-person narrator talking to himself, addressing himself as "you." There are no other characters in the story. Barthelme tries to imagine the consequences of a narrator so self-conscious, so paralyzed by his fear of women, that he recedes into a world of pure fantasy. The narrator imagines himself driving on a highway, and as he drives, he tries to imagine the scenery going by, but all he can picture is trick scenery, "as if painted on a movie flat," he says. His imagination is limited. He is no better at imagining the woman he wants. At one moment he imagines a woman who would wear cheap dresses from a department store; a moment later he believes his own suit, about which he cannot make up his mind—black with pinstripes or black with chalkstripes—"would be perfect for a man with a blond woman, a tall woman." This story oscillates between the sensual and the horrible. He is at times strongly attracted to the imaginary woman, sometimes repelled by her. In one scene he describes running his fingers over her bare arms and admiring her breasts. In another he sees her mouth during her nap as "an ugly hole laced at its edges with blown hair." This story plays on, in an unusual way for Barthelme, a recurring theme in most of his fiction: men who simultaneously want and do not want women. His male characters often desire beauty and sexuality but also want to avoid the awkward entanglements, the emotion, the conflict, the mess.

Another story from *Chroma* is "Restraint," which also takes place in the mind of the narrator. This story is quite short, just over three pages, and consists of only one paragraph, an internal monologue by a man who, in the hall at work, passes the most striking and beautiful woman he has ever seen. It is nothing less than a paean to all that is best in the sensual appreciation of women by men. Finally the story is about the small amount of restraint it takes for him to pass her by, without speaking, without leering, without grabbing her. He returns to his office and counts his blessings; he accepts what is given. Again, for the Barthelme protagonist, it is easier, neater, cleaner, and simpler to be alone than to engage in a relationship with another person.

Chroma ends with a story titled "Reset." Though a few of the details have changed, it is a continuation of "Box Step," the opening story of *Moon Deluxe,* and brings the two collections full circle. The first-person narrator of "Reset," though not named, has a woman named Ann working for him, as does the protagonist in "Box Step." They are close enough that everyone in their office assumes they are having an affair, just as everyone did in "Box Step." In this final story of *Chroma,* Ann is leaving, quitting her job to move to Texas. The narrator does not want her to leave. Again, as in all of Barthelme's stories about men and women, the woman has the power. He cannot make her stay; indeed, everything he says comes out wrong and pushes her away. He is ineffectual to such a degree that at one point she finally says, "Wouldn't it be nice if you could make me stop. I mean, wouldn't that be something?" That scenario is not to be. She is the decision maker of the relationship, and they both are aware of her power. One of Barthelme's continuing themes is that the roles men and women occupy in the contemporary world have changed irrevocably. New ways of relating have to be found, even if the search is painful and awkward, even if no resolution is found.

The narrator invites Ann on one last business trip with him to Tennessee to scout a location for one of their company's clients. The issue of her leaving and his barely spoken love for her hangs in the air as they ride around the small town with one of the local politicians—who, the narrator is sure, is interested in Ann. The ending of the story is typically unresolved: the narrator is staring out a window of his bungalow at Ann, who is sitting on the front porch of her bungalow. His window seems to frame a scene, as if a tableaux or opening from an Alfred Hitchcock movie; the story ends with the line "I tried to see the future." Of course, like the reader, the narrator cannot see the future. The future in the story, as the future in life, is open, not fixed, not determined. The traditional epiphany story has been thwarted again.

Following his second collection of short stories, Barthelme published three novels in the late 1980s and early 1990s that deal with the question of the nature of marriage. In *Two Against One* (1988), *Natural Selection* (1990), and *The Brothers* (1993) Barthelme examines the issue of marriage: what constitutes marriage now that it is a purely secular institution, a (revokable) license issued by the (his-

torically transient) state rather than an indissoluble union forged by an eternal God? If marriage is a socially constructed institution, how will people construct their marriages in the postmodern world? The stories in *Chroma* were a movement toward some of the questions that Barthelme addresses in these novels. Often the marital issues at stake in the three novels are that of the ménage à trois and the power of women over men, continuing themes from *Moon Deluxe.*

The idea that monogamy may have to be discarded if some marriages are going to last is worked out in minute detail in *Two Against One.* The protagonist's estranged wife returns after a six-month separation to ask if there is some way they can be together again while she keeps her new lover. The novel ends on an unresolved note: the protagonist is lying in bed with his lover, who is trying to convince him that his wife does in fact love him, regardless of whatever other issues may be in the way. He has a lover, and she has a lover, and yet they want to find a way to be together regardless. *Two Against One* is also concerned with the issue of cleanliness, of order, or lack thereof, in relationships and how it affects the characters.

In the 1997 novel *Bob the Gambler* Barthelme more fully develops his idea that postmodern marriage may need disorder, shaking up, to survive in a meaningful way. A stagnating married couple decide on a whim to try the casinos on the Mississippi Gulf Coast. They begin a downward spiral into obsession and debt but also find a revitalized sense of their love of and commitment to each other.

Frederick Barthelme figured in the shaping of literary minimalism. Raymond Carver may have been the progenitor of the movement, but Barthelme most fully exemplifies and stays true to the principles of minimalist writing. Barthelme used minimalism to chronicle in an unblinking fashion the aftermath of the sex wars that changed the way men and women relate to each other. His writing acknowledges and records the way men and women began to fumble toward rapprochement. Barthelme shows the contemporary world—the fast-food restaurants, the crummy motels, the glittering malls, the Dickensian microcosms of apartment complexes—without irony, without disdain, celebrating the world for what it is, not what it used to be.

References:

Madison Smartt Bell, "Less is Less," *Harper's,* 272 (April 1986): 64–69;

Kim Herzinger, "Minimalism as Postmodernism: Some Introductory Notes," *New Orleans Review,* 16, no. 3 (1989): 73–81;

John Hughes, "Sex Wars in *Moon Deluxe:* Frederick Barthelme and the Postmodern Prufrock," *Studies in Short Fiction,* 33 (1996): 401–410.

Pinckney Benedict

(12 April 1964 –   )

Brad Vice
Arkansas Tech University

BOOKS: *Town Smokes* (Princeton / New York: Ontario
    Review, 1987);
The Wrecking Yard: Stories (New York: Doubleday, 1992);
Dogs of God (New York: Doubleday, 1994).

PRODUCED SCRIPT: *Four Days,* based on John
    Buell's novel, motion picture, Amerique Films,
    1999.

SELECTED PERIODICAL PUBLICATIONS–
UNCOLLECTED: "Micracle Boy," *Esquire,* 130
    (December 1998): 112–117;
"The Gleaners," *Story,* 47 (Autumn 1999): 29–39;
"Zog-19: A Scientific Romance," *Zoetrope: All-Story,* 4
    (Spring 2000): 28–35;
"Pony Car," *Ontario Review,* no. 54 (Spring–Summer
    2001).

"Beware of the wise who are young and gifted,"
wrote novelist Russell Banks in a cover blurb for Pinckney Benedict's first short-story collection, *Town Smokes*
(1987); "They quickly become irreplaceable." *Town
Smokes* had just been published to rave reviews, and
many, like Banks, thought of the then-twenty-three-
year-old Benedict as a short-fiction prodigy. By struggling to diversify his skills as a storywriter, Benedict has
made a contribution to almost every significant prose-
publishing niche. To date Benedict has published
another book of short stories, *The Wrecking Yard* (1992);
a novel titled *Dogs of God* (1994); and many interviews,
book reviews, and nonfiction articles with magazines
such as *Bomb* and *Esquire.* With the 1999 release of the
feature movie *Four Days* Benedict made a foray into
screenwriting as well. Benedict is primarily known as a
writer of short fiction; nine stories appear in *Town
Smokes,* and ten more stories appear in *The Wrecking Yard.*

The son of Cleveland Keith and Ann Farrar
Arthur Benedict, Arthur Pinckney Benedict was born
on 12 April 1964 in southern West Virginia and grew
up on his parents' dairy farm near the town of Lewisburg. Benedict's father was a military pilot turned politi-

*Pinckney Benedict (photograph © C. C. F. Gachet; from
the dust jacket for* The Wrecking Yard, *1992)*

cian who enjoyed taking his family flying in his
single-engine bush plane on weekends. As a teenager
Benedict attended The Hill School, a preparatory
school outside Philadelphia, and graduated in 1982.

At an early age Benedict discovered he had a gift
for making up things when he found he could stave off
playground bullies by telling them entertaining jokes
and stories. Always fond of reading, Benedict fueled his
imagination with the sophisticated sea-adventure novels
of Herman Melville and Joseph Conrad as well as the

novels of popular horror and science-fiction writers such as Stephen King, Phillip K. Dick, and H. P. Lovecraft. The writer credited with having the most influence on Benedict's own fiction is fellow West Virginian Breece D'J Pancake, who populated his own short stories with Appalachia's working-class, rough-and-tumble hill people, fond of hunting, fishing, and fighting.

The Stories of Breece D'J Pancake (1983), a slim volume of Pancake's collected fiction, was published posthumously after the author's suicide at the age of twenty-seven. This collection struck a chord with Benedict, who also wanted to write simply and sparingly about the natives of his home state. In fact, it is easy to think of Benedict's early stories in *Town Smokes* as elegies for Pancake. Benedict adopted Pancake's style, marked by its cool, laconic prose and its careful attention to local dialect, making a powerful vehicle for its subject matter, the colorful, often frightening underclass of West Virginia. Soon after the publication of *Town Smokes* in 1987, the author was heralded as the most promising hybrid that gritty minimalism and Southern regionalism had to offer. Even the grande dame of Southern literature, Eudora Welty, came out in favor of the book, writing, "With the appearance of *Town Smokes* we are beyond question in the presence of a strong talent. It is one assured and also venturesome; we have been introduced to an original."

Most of *Town Smokes* was composed during the young author's time as an undergraduate at Princeton University, where Benedict greatly benefited from the tutelage of the novelist Joyce Carol Oates. She encouraged her student to submit what is now the most famous story in the collection, "The Sutton Pie Safe," to the Nelson Algren Short Story Contest, sponsored by *The Chicago Tribune,* and in 1986 Benedict became the youngest recipient of one of the most coveted prizes in American literature.

Like many of the stories in *Town Smokes,* "The Sutton Pie Safe" is narrated through the eyes of a young boy whose family has fallen on hard times. The protagonist, Cates, finds himself torn between his father's pride and his mother's pragmatism when a wealthy antique hunter, Mrs. Hanson, offers to purchase a family heirloom—Cates's grandfather's bread box, or "pie safe," as Mrs. Hanson calls it. The pie safe is the product of a West Virginia original, Samuel Sutton, a turn-of-the-twentieth-century furniture maker famous for his fine workmanship. Cates's family is unaware that the old beat-up bread box has anything other than sentimental value until Mrs. Hanson offers to buy it.

The story begins with Cates's father about to show his son how to make a belt out of a blacksnake, a trick handed down from Cates's grandfather. The tanning lesson is interrupted by the attractive Mrs. Han-

son's arrival. Cates and his father quit work to greet their guest, but the visit turns tense when Mrs. Hanson announces that she absolutely must have the pie safe as a gift for her husband, Judge Hanson. Mrs. Hanson's presumption offends Cates's father, but Cates's mother reluctantly argues in favor of the sale, knowing that Mrs. Hanson's money will enable them to repair their decrepit barn and keep the farm running for another year. Cates quietly watches the argument until his father loses his temper with their presumptuous houseguest. "'We aren't merchants,' he said. 'And this isn't a furniture shop.'" Cates's father storms out of the house in a huff, dragging his son back to the dead blacksnake outside. Cates watches as his father begins the ritual of skinning the snake, but the boy's attention wavers as Mrs. Hanson leaves, carrying the Sutton pie safe off in her Cadillac. Cates loses the real treasure, the blacksnake belt, when the boy returns his attention to his father, who is now holding a partially digested mouse plucked from the snake's intestines. The sight of the dead mouse sickens Cates, and this weakness further angers his frustrated father. He spitefully destroys the blacksnake with his knife, telling his son "you think about that the next time you decide to want something."

Like most of Benedict's fiction, "The Sutton Pie Safe" is deceptively simple. What in the beginning appears to be nothing more than the depiction of a paltry domestic row becomes a poignant exploration of the ways that class and poverty conspire to injure dignity. Nowhere is this theme more clearly rendered than in the title story, "Town Smokes," which is narrated by a boy even poorer than Cates, a boy so poor he does not even have a family. Again the notion of inheritance plays an important role in the story. When the nameless protagonist of "Town Smokes" loses his father in a logging accident, he decides to leave his mountain home and his only living relative, the alcoholic Uncle Hunter, in order to see what the world below the mountain is like. He tells only his uncle that he is going to town to get store-bought cigarettes, but both the uncle and the boy know that he will not return from his trip. During the journey the boy is robbed by two older boys, poor "ridgerunners" like himself, who not only strip him of his father's pistol and money but also take the boy's shoes. In a final act of pettiness, the two robbers break an arrowhead the boy had collected while digging his father's grave. The robbers leave the boy with a warning, telling him that the people in town do not like ridgerunners and that he would be better off to turn back up the mountain and go home. Broke and barefoot, the nameless protagonist wanders into town anyway, where he is befriended by the owner of a drugstore, who shares a pack of Camels with him. Though the narrator is now absolutely destitute, he has found a momentary reprieve from the isolation of the mountain.

Other stories, such as "Booze" and "All the Dead," are similarly painful coming-of-age stories. The story "Booze" is a West Virginian version of *Moby-Dick* (1851) in miniature. The adventure begins when Benedict's protagonist, Eli, and his friend Kenny catch a glimpse of the legendary Booze, a fearsome, wild pig that weighs more than six hundred pounds and is colored mostly white. After the death of his owner, Booze broke out of his pen, driven by hunger to flee into the woods and turn feral and carnivorous. In this state Booze becomes a danger to the whole county. As sheep and calves begin to disappear, Eli's neighbors even begin to fear for their small children, and Eli's father, also a farmer, promises the boys $50 if they can kill the wild boar. Armed with pistols and shotguns, they stalk the woods surrounding Eli's father's farm but never find Booze. Calves continue to disappear. On two different occasions Eli's father wounds the boar but is unable to kill it.

Years pass, yet, Eli, whose favorite dog has been killed by the boar, cannot let go of his obsession with Booze. Kenny has his doubts about the hog's ability to survive the wounds Eli's father inflicted and dismisses any rumors that the creature is still alive. "It's like Bigfoot," Kenny explains to Eli. "People aren't sure what they see, so they call it Bigfoot. You call it Booze." Kenny is proven wrong when he is attacked by the mythic Booze. The ending is dramatic, almost cinematic, as Kenny splits the crazed hog's snout and drives the sling blade into his skull, a one-in-a-million shot that saves Kenny from having his legs broken. Still the charging boar's momentum knocks over Kenny, and he is momentarily penned under the corpse's dead weight. The story ends with Eli helping his friend out from under the six hundred pounds of white flesh. While Benedict brings an epic sense of drama into "Booze" through Eli and Kenny's wondrous adventures, he does so only to reinforce the grim vision of bloody rural existence where survival is a struggle and must be fought for.

Sometimes Benedict's fatalism is mixed with a little more irony. Benedict allows his wry sense of humor to take over in stories such as "Dog," in which two goofy trailer-park residents borrow a gun with which to do away with a rabid German shepherd that has decided to die under their double-wide. Broom and Eldridge visit a motorcycle repairman, Fat Ed, to borrow a pistol in order to kill the pitiful, yet savage, creature under their home. The humor in the story derives from the stoogelike arguments that characterize Broom and Eldridge's relationship. They bicker and spat through the entire narrative and fight about who is

Cover for Benedict's first book, a collection of short stories published in 1987, the year before he graduated from Princeton University

going to go under the house with the pistol. Eldridge finally wins out because Fat Ed does not like Broom and has warned Eldridge that if Broom ever touches his gun he will never loan them anything again.

The tone of the story shifts dramatically when Eldridge crawls into the darkness under the trailer alone. Here he meets a vision of death when the weakened dog manages to stand and bare his teeth. "A loop of saliva hung from its long snout. It presented its chest like it wasn't afraid, like it wanted the bullet. Most animals could smell guns, Eldridge knew." Eldridge reluctantly shoots the pathetic creature. Before he can drag the corpse out from under the trailer, digger beetles crawl up from under the soil, drawn to the surface by the dog's blood. Benedict concludes the story with Eldridge sitting quietly under the trailer with the dead dog and the beetles as Broom calls to him over and over again. It now seems the friends live in two separate worlds, Broom in the comic world of daylight and Eldridge in the ineffably sad underworld. The moment is filled with pathos. Benedict is adept at channeling the emotion most people feel for pets into powerful fiction. Dogs hold a special place in the author's work, and ultimately he uses them as mirrors for the humans they come into contact with.

The author also frequently uses blood sport–dogfights, bare-knuckle boxing–as the subject of his fiction. "Pit" begins at a dogfight in which Brunty, a nervous gambler, mistakenly stabs Paxco, a local good-old-boy crime boss, after the gambler misinterprets the criminal's wave as a threatening gesture. The rest of the story unfolds like a mini action-adventure movie filled with gangsters, bikers, and prostitutes. In one *Macbeth*-like moment, Paxco's taunting ghost even returns to poke fun at the hounded Brunty. Like a dog in a pit, Brunty is doomed. No matter how many times he evades death, he will inevitably be thrown back in the pit to do battle with the sinister forces determined to do him in. Paxco's underlings will pursue him to the ends of the earth to get revenge. Even after Brunty's friend Sister Sue sells him out to "Paxco's boys," and the twitchy gambler is dispatched with a shotgun blast, Benedict hints that this cycle of violence is just beginning again. "The big one was in charge now. He figured that maybe Paxco had got what was coming to him. He figured that with him running things they all stood to do a lot better. He was grateful to the corpse in the trunk of the Dodge, in a strange way." The rapid transitions and goofy characters in this story foreshadow the kind of writing Benedict perfects in his later work; but for the most part *Town Smokes* is a deeply sad and serious book populated with lonely, desperate people.

No matter what the tone of the stories in *Town Smokes,* it is clear that the collection draws its power from a dual sense of place and misplacement. Or as Benedict said in his first interview with *The New York Times Book Review* (12 July 1987), *Town Smokes* is a book of "border" fiction full of "independent people" with "strong personalities." The state of West Virginia is sometimes called a border state because Northerners think of it as a Southern state, and Southerners hold the opposite opinion. "Neither region wants us," Benedict told *U.S. News & World Report* in a later interview (16 May 1994). "So it does feel like we're sort of a doorway. And that's fine. Because that's the area I like to explore in my work–these places where there's no mainstream to be outside of."

After Benedict's graduation from Princeton, the author enrolled in the University of Iowa Writers' Workshop to earn his M.F.A. These two years marked a period of doubt and uncertainty for the young author, compounded by an ill-fated stint as a writer for the award-winning television producer David Milch (*Hill Street Blues, NYPD Blue*). None of Benedict's scripts was ever produced. Soon after graduation in 1988 Benedict

found himself back on his feet again. After his marriage to Laura Philpot in 1990, the author published another collection of short fiction, *The Wrecking Yard* in 1992. In 1996 he became a professor of creative writing at Hope College in Michigan.

The Wrecking Yard marks a further maturing of Benedict's style. His stories became more compact, and his sense of humor became more sophisticated, but the "border fiction" subject matter remained the same. In this collection Benedict seems to have learned that violent confrontation is the key to heightening tension in his stories. In "Getting Over Arnette" a fight between a jealous boyfriend and a crazed Vietnam veteran interrupts the nightly festivities at a local bowling alley. Two good old boys, Loftus and Bone, go out for a night on the town in hopes of helping Loftus get over Arnette, an insatiable redhead that Loftus hopes to marry. Arnette, however, had "run off with some 'college puke' a couple of days before and had broken Loftus's heart and shattered his life." Bone convinces Loftus to go to the bowling alley where it is ladies' night, hoping that a night out will take Arnette off his friend's mind. Before long Loftus and Bone make a nuisance of themselves and are thrown out of the Bowl-a-Drome with their bowling shoes still on. Outside the doors of the bowling alley Loftus and Bone run into Leonard Meadows, a Vietnam veteran fond of telling old war stories. When Meadows mentions that he too is in love with the luscious Arnette, Loftus goes mad and attacks the former soldier. Even with Bone's help, Loftus is no match for the large Meadows. The next day Loftus has a concussion and Bone is missing teeth; they wake just in time to greet Arnette, who is returning from her last fling with the "college puke." Benedict concludes the story by implying that Arnette will now remain faithful to Loftus because of his heroism. She touches his wounds gently, and Loftus takes this tenderness as a sign that "for his suffering she would never leave him for another man again."

In "Getting Over Arnette" the author shows a romantic lightheartedness missing in his previous work. Much of the isolation and loneliness that thematically dominated *Town Smokes* is renovated into a sort of comic aggression in *The Wrecking Yard*. Benedict's prose is more polished than in his previous border fiction.

In the title story Benedict populates a haunted junkyard with a wide cast of comic mechanics. Mr. Papaduke's wrecker service eventually becomes the home of all cars involved in accidents in Dywer County, West Virginia, and the yard becomes the setting for one of Benedict's more-eerie stories. Rather than constructing "The Wrecking Yard" around a single plot with a single conflict and resolution, as in "Getting Over Arnette," Benedict allows Papaduke's scrap heap to become the communal site for several stories, each of which ends in death and destruction. Within the walls of "The Wrecking Yard" the reader stumbles across several vehicles: a twisted cattle trailer responsible for the death of almost a hundred steers, a sports car that is responsible for a mangled teenage girl, and even a perfectly good Impala used as the instrument of death in a depressed young man's suicide.

While the stories that occupy the middle section of *The Wrecking Yard* have more-exotic settings than those at the beginning of the book, they, like "Getting Over Arnette," rely heavily on violent confrontation for their power. For instance, a girl from a carnival electrocutes her lovers in "The Electrical Girl," and an Old West posse hunts down an accused murderer in "Washman." These stories are departures from Benedict's usual form both stylistically and in setting. "Washman" is set in the Old West at the turn of the twentieth century, and "The Electrical Girl" is written as a radio play, totally narrated in dialogue.

Many critics took issue with these stories, calling them simple fictive experiments, too absurd or violent to take seriously; but in retrospect it seems that these more experimental stories should be read as evidence of Benedict's growing interest in less traditional narratives. This move away from realism proved important for Benedict's development as a writer of novels and screenplays. However, the two most significant stories in the collection are written in Benedict's trademark border realism.

The most memorable confrontation story in the collection, "Bounty," is also the most subtle and haunting. This time the conflict takes place between Candles, an eccentric sheep farmer from the mountains, and the local sheriff, Gallantin. The story begins with Candles's visit to the courthouse carrying a dead dog on his back. He announces his presence by laying the dog's carcass across the desk of the receptionist. When the irate Sheriff Gallantin begins to question him, Candles replies that the dead dog is a "coydog," a cross between a coyote and a dog, and he has come to claim the five-dollar bounty the state offers for coyotes. In fact, Candles possesses a whole truck full of dead coydogs that is parked outside the courthouse, and he wants $5.00 a head for them. When Gallantin exits the courthouse to count the number of dead coydogs in Candles's truck, he finds not a pack of feral sheep killers but a load of German shepherds and even a beagle–in short, a massacre of pets. Of course, Gallantin refuses to pay the bounty, but he is also hesitant to push the eccentric Candles too far. The story ends with Gallantin telling Candles, "I'm not sure exactly what went on here . . . and I don't believe I care to know." Then Gallantin sends the farmer back up the mountain, leaving the confrontation unresolved.

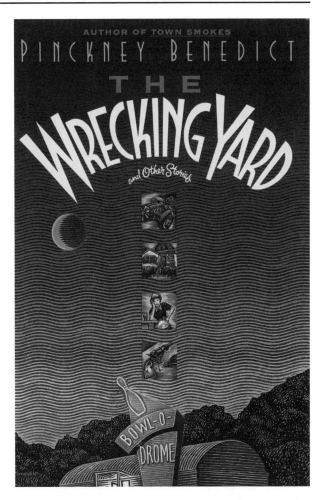

Dust jacket for Benedict's 1992 book, stories that have been favorably compared to the short fiction of Flannery O'Connor and Eudora Welty

While this ending seems disappointing, the unresolved tension actually makes "Bounty" the most intriguing story in the collection. The reader is unable to stop pondering the mysterious circumstances behind the dead dogs. In *Town Smokes* Benedict's characters live in an isolated, violent, chaotic world, but in *The Wrecking Yard* this sense of violence is pushed beyond regionalism to its absurd limits. No longer does Benedict write tender coming-of-age stories about boys hoping to find peace and acceptance in the world at the foot of the mountain. Now that Benedict's characters are fully adult, the point of view is more distant, more equally weighted, and not a little mocking. In short, Benedict's fiction has developed beyond the early influence of Pancake to a form more closely resembling the Gothic stories of Flannery O'Connor or Welty.

Understanding this perfection of style becomes important when reading the last story in *The Wrecking Yard,* "Odom," which revisits the familiar isolated mountain territory of *Town Smokes.* "Odom" can be read as a sort of reversal of the title story of Benedict's first collection. Like "Town Smokes" and the "Sutton Pie Safe," "Odom" is a father-son story, but this time the story is told from the mature perspective of the father. The story opens with Enier Odom and his seventeen-year-old son clearing trees off their property with dynamite. Odom secretly believes that if he builds a new house for his son, it will prevent him from moving to town and leaving his father alone on top of the mountain. The black-market dynamite they use to uproot the stumps is old and unstable, and Odom's hearing is damaged when one of the sticks of dynamite goes off too early. Later that night Odom's son takes his father's truck into town and does not return the next day.

After a few days pass Odom discovers that his son has been thrown in jail for being drunk and disorderly. "I dealt with enough of you crazy backward ridge-running mountain rats in my lifetime," the inhospitable sheriff tells Odom. "You want my advice, I'd keep him closer to home." Even though the sheriff promises to release Odom's boy, he still does not return, and Odom becomes positively sick with worry. Ten days later when Odom's prodigal son finally returns to the homestead, he finds his father has turned into a shriveled old man, rail thin, hands bleeding, face blistered by another dynamite accident, and almost completely deaf from the first one. The son takes over the heavy work while Odom holds the bit. The two are reunited by their labor, but it is a bittersweet reunion, for Odom realizes that his son is now a man and will soon have little need for him.

Like *Town Smokes, The Wrecking Yard* was well received by readers and critics alike. Louise Kennedy of *The Boston Globe* (10 January 1992) focused her review of *The Wrecking Yard* on its authentic voice: "Pinckney Benedict lives in West Virginia, where he grew up. The jacket of his second collection of stories, *The Wrecking Yard,* tells us this, but it doesn't have to: the best of these stories have so sharp and clear a sense of the state, and of its people, that they could only come from a native writer. . . . The place, the people and the tough scrappy battle between them are subtly drawn and utterly real. Like the blue vistas at the top of a nasty mountain, they're worth getting to."

Even though Benedict laid the foundation of his literary reputation with short fiction, the author proved himself to be equally adept at novel writing. In 1994 Benedict published his first novel, *Dogs of God.* The book is set in West Virginia and is written in Benedict's trademark lucid, laconic prose, but Benedict's mastery over realistic narrative actually creates a strangely postmodern novel. *Dogs of God* was awarded Britain's John Steinbeck Award in 1995 and was favorably compared to literary masters such as William Faulkner and Cormac McCarthy.

The novel centers on Tannhauser, a mad, twelve-fingered drug lord, who grows marijuana utilizing the labor of enslaved Mexicans. His sprawling, though decaying, compound (Tannhauser has dubbed it "El Dorado") is located atop Little Hogback Mountain. Little does Tannhauser know that DEA agents are planning to raid El Dorado and that the corrupt local sheriff is helping them as a means of covering up his own misdeeds. The protagonist of the novel, Goody, a down-and-out bare-knuckle boxer, gets caught up in the middle of the assault on the mountain when he agrees to take part in a fight arranged for the amusement of visiting gangsters sent to report on Tannhauser's drug production. Added to this cinematic plot, there are underground secret passages, ghosts, and even a spaceship, as well as an apocalyptic ending that might have been dreamed up in Hollywood.

Many critics lavished praise on the novel for its over-the-top pyrotechnics. In the *Los Angeles Times* (27 March 1994) reviewer Chris Goodrich coined the word "Benedictland" to describe the setting of the novel, which "brims with odd characters and creatures driven by primal, irrefutable urges. These desires regularly fail to make sense to the reader, but part of the novel's magnetic attraction is a logic both alien and commonplace, a logic that doesn't so much defy analysis as render it irrelevant." Goodrich called *Dogs of God* "about as fine a first novel as one could want," and many other reviews, such as in *The Chicago Tribune* and *The Times Literary Supplement,* agreed with Goodrich's assessment. In an interview with *U.S. News and World Report* (16 May 1994) Benedict's former teacher Oates reported that upon reading the manuscript of the novel she told her former student: "Pinckney, you're going to set the tourist industry in West Virginia back one hundred years." Benedict replied, "I may have some vested interest in keeping tourists out."

Since the publication of *Dogs of God,* Benedict has dedicated much of his time and effort to writing screenplays. His talent for writing taut, action-packed prose attracted the attention of Amerique Films, a small Toronto motion-picture company interested in adapting Canadian novelist John Buell's psychological crime thriller *Four Days* (1962) to the big screen. The movie, released in the fall of 1999, tells the story of a young boy whose father coerces him into participating in a bank robbery. When the boy's father is killed by an armed guard, the orphan flees with the heist money. Soon he finds himself pursued not only by the police but also by his father's manic partner in a four-day chase that leads him through most of Ontario. The movie *Four Days* echoes many of the themes familiar in

Benedict's early work in *Town Smokes*. The figure of the isolated youngster caught up in a hard world of greed and violence is particularly reminiscent of Benedict's first published stories.

Also in 1999 Benedict moved closer to his home in West Virginia when he became a professor of creative writing at Hollins University, where he teaches writing for the screen as well as fiction workshops. The author has been working on another novel and a motion-picture adaptation of *Dogs of God*. He and his wife, Laura, have two children, Nora and Cleveland.

Since the 1992 publication of *The Wrecking Yard*, Benedict has yet to produce another book of short fiction. He has not abandoned the form, however. On the contrary, Benedict has published several stories in prestigious periodicals such as *Story, Zoetrope: All-Story* and *Esquire*. Many of these stories have been anthologized in prizewinning collections such as *The Pushcart Prizes: Best of the Small Press (1998), New Stories From the South (1999),* and *Prize Stories 1999: The O. Henry Awards* (1999). His best-known short story, "The Sutton Pie Safe," has been anthologized in *The Oxford Book of American Short Stories* (1992) and is frequently touted as one of the best stories of the last two decades. For his outstanding contribution to American literature the author was recently awarded an NEA grant, with which he hopes to complete his second novel.

From his early stories in *Town Smokes* to his most-recent appearances in *Esquire*, Pinckney Benedict's particular brand of border fiction has revitalized the Southern Gothic short story, a form that many critics thought was doomed to hollow self-parody. Like short-story masters before him such as O'Connor, Welty, and even his boyhood hero, Pancake, Benedict is capable of writing prose that is at once simple and spare but also philosophically complicated. There are no easy answers for the poverty-stricken farmers and ridgerunners that populate his stories. Endurance seems to be Benedict's most consistent theme; it is the only virtue in a world where the powers of chance and fate conspire to extinguish both the ignominious and the noble alike.

Interviews:

Bruce Weber, "Making It Strange," *New York Times Book Review,* 12 July 1987, p. 14;

Thomas E. Douglass, "Pinckney Benedict," *Appalachian Journal,* 20 (Fall 1992): 68–74;

Viva Hardigg, "A Vision from the Border," *U.S. News & World Report,* 116 (16 May 1994): 63;

Brad Vice, "Pinckney Benedict: Transforming Fiction for Film," *Novel and Short Story Writers' Market* (1 January 2000): 35–38.

References:

Angela B. Freeman, "The Origins and Fortunes of Negativity: The West Virginia Worlds of Kromer, Pancake, and Benedict," *Appalachian Journal,* 25 (Spring 1998): 244–269;

Jim Wayne Miller, "New Generation of Savages Sighted in West Virginia," *Appalachian Heritage,* 16 (Fall 1988): 28–33;

Bob Snyder, "Pancake and Benedict," *Appalachian Journal,* 15 (Spring 1988): 276–283;

John Alexander Williams, "Unpacking Pinckney in Poland," *Appalachian Journal,* 20 (Winter 1993): 162–175.

Michael Brodsky

(2 August 1948 –   )

John C. Hawley
Santa Clara University

BOOKS: *Detour: A Novel* (New York: Urizen, 1977; London: Calder, 1979; expanded edition, Houston: Scrivenery Press, forthcoming 2001);

Wedding Feast, & Two Novellas (New York: Urizen, 1981);

Project and Other Short Pieces (Tivoli, N.Y.: Guignol, 1982), revised and republished as *Project: Stories and Plays* (Annandale-on-Hudson, N.Y.: Begos & Rosenberg, 1991);

The Envelope of the Given (*Der Tatbestand und Seine Hulle*) (Berlin: Suhrkamp Verlag, 1982);

Circuits (Rhinebeck, N.Y.: Guignol, 1985);

Xman (New York: Four Walls Eight Windows, 1987);

X in Paris (New York: Four Walls Eight Windows, 1988);

Dyad (New York: Four Walls Eight Windows, 1989);

Three Goat Songs (New York: Four Walls Eight Windows, 1991);

*** (New York: Four Walls Eight Windows, 1994);

Southernmost and Other Stories (New York: Four Walls Eight Windows, 1996);

We Can Report Them (New York: Four Walls Eight Windows, 1999).

PLAY PRODUCTIONS: *Terrible Sunlight,* New York, South Street Theater, 2 April 1980;

Dose Center, New York, Theater for the New City, 15 February 1990;

Night of the Chair, New York, Theater Club Funambules, 13 December 1990;

Six Scenes, New York, Ontological-St. Mark's by Target Margin Theater, 26 May 1994;

The Anti-Muse, reading, New York, Ontological-St. Mark's by Target Margin Theater, March 1996; performance, New York, Theatorium, 26 January 2000.

TRANSLATION: Samuel Beckett, *Eleuthéria* (New York: Foxrock, 1995).

SELECTED PERIODICAL PUBLICATION–
UNCOLLECTED: "Svevo: The Artist as Analyzand," *Review of Existential Psychology and Psychiatry,* 15, nos. 2–3 (1977): 112–133.

Michael Brodsky (courtesy of the author)

"My relation to words is a sullied one," writes the narrator of Michael Brodsky's story "Postal Clerk" (in *Wedding Feast, & Two Novellas,* 1981), and the same might be said of the author. Brodsky has been praised as a gifted literary technician whose writing consistently challenges readers to reimagine the purposes of fiction. He has gained a reputation as an author whose principal concerns are not necessarily related to the advancement of a story line: "I feel enormous resistances to straightforwardly telling a story," he said in a 4 February 2000 personal letter, "–to *just* telling a story–providing the required story-entertainment drug that everybody craves all the more so as the powers that be at the present moment virulently, regressively, demand a story and nothing but a story." Brodsky has received the Ernest Hemingway Citation from PEN and is increasingly compared to Thomas Pynchon, Donald Barthelme, Henry James, and Franz Kafka as a serious short-story writer.

Michael Mark Brodsky was born in New York City on 2 August 1948 to Martin and Marian Brodsky. His father was a businessman and his mother a clerical worker before marriage. Brodsky received his bachelor's degree from Columbia University in 1969, and then attended the School of Medicine at Case Western Reserve University from 1970 to 1972. He has taught mathematics and science in New York (1969–1970) and French and English in Cleveland (1972–1975). Since 1975 he has worked as an editor for various companies and organizations. On 28 November 1976 he married Laurence Lacoste; the couple have two sons and live in New York.

Brodsky's protagonists are distinctly uncomfortable with the world around them: alienated and alienating, they have a difficult time getting through the day. On the stylistic and technical level, one might speak of Brodsky's sentences as microcosmic versions of the same existential struggle. The narrator of the story "Southernmost" (in *Southernmost and Other Stories,* 1996) describes the process: "At every turn I will be trying to catch myself in a spasm of recoiling detachment from each and every poetic effect so as to be able to analyze it, catch it in the act of having its effect, discover through it what constitutes acceptable mass-thrillable poetic license, tellable meaning." Thus, the process of storytelling is made cerebral, part of the subject matter. Brodsky's introduction to his translation of Samuel Beckett's *Eleuthéria* (1995) expresses his admiration for Beckett's "fascination with shardlike colloquializings," and Brodsky's own complex and impressive grammar dazzles the reader. In fact, the precision of diction and syntax might be one means of combating an environment thick with paranoia, distraction, and exhaustion. Brodsky's is a world in which a great deal is in flux, with characters in transit between jobs and relationships. In one story after another, the significance of external action pales before the focus on interior psychic malaise.

After Brodsky's first novel, *Detour* (1977), met with mixed reviews—a critic for the *Virginia Quarterly Review* (Spring 1979) called it a "brilliant but grotesque first effort"—the author established his unsettling style. Four years later, with his first story collection, *Wedding Feast, & Two Novellas,* he again offered a menagerie of fascinating individuals in detailed (and often objectively humorous) crises. The rat race not only of personal relations but also of the business world pushes Brodsky's characters into an internal paralysis (and fuguelike repetitive thoughts) often masked by external freneticism. In "Wedding Feast" the central character, Sam, a failed writer, gets a job as a waiter. This situation provides something like a plot, but the real "happenings" in the story center around the characters' obsessions with

the manipulation of words and of thought processes. Thus, a character "began to weep as if aware she could never create sentences like the last." Absurdism plays a large role in Brodsky's work, as signaled on the first page of this story when the soon-to-be-waiter cannot shift his focus away from the tortured phrase "void erect."

Sam finds life difficult, yet he enjoys occasionally being ruffled; he had, after all, been finding it fatiguing to be a "bystander at the hypertrophy of one's vigilance." The solace of finding a position—suitable employment, on the one hand, but also placement in a world of assigned meaning—comes as both an occasional comfort and a persistent threat in most of Brodsky's stories. Sam recoils from or engages with words passing through his head in a far more committed way than he can with any person at his place of employment. Thus, he finds that "you needed to oppose to the sentences of others your own sentence."

In this first collection of stories a character refers to Wittgenstein's artichoke, something like the conundrum of stripping away the layers of an onion to find its core. In the world of these stories, "denudation" of self in encounters with others is treated similarly as "the mock epic of a penetration to my essence." Sent as a waiter for a wedding feast during which a murder may or may not be committed, Sam "secretly craved the cleavage of bride and groom." Whether he means the joining, or the splitting apart, is unclear. In either case, his wishes seem granted by Brodsky, who offers his character a bizarre droit du seigneur when the groom can no longer accept the role of husband, his apparent placement by society. Brodsky leads the reader to surmise that Sam may, in fact, have been the groom all along, in a twist reminiscent of Ambrose Bierce's "An Occurrence at Owl Creek Bridge" (1890).

The other major story in this collection, "Postal Clerk," deals with a title character who does everything he can to avoid delivering the mail. He sometimes reads the letters; he often just throws them all away. Sometimes he delivers garbage instead of letters. In this story reminiscent of Herman Melville's "Bartleby, The Scrivener" (1853) Brodsky seems to be taunting his readers through this not-so-civil employee, who remarks:

> after a few sentences their faces took on a blank look not so much of resistance as of immersion in an unknown element, my voice. . . . They felt my sentences were not so much statements as flecks of coercion. . . . But I wanted to come to the end of all sentences, make the sentence that would transfix both me and my listeners. . . . And all the time I was less speaking than plowing toward the annihilation of speech.

Late in the story he points out that "unlike Bartleby I did not limit my vocabulary to five words." For one who has almost given up on the delivery of "letters," this postal clerk is nonetheless quite fluent in his obsession with them. A fellow worker falls in love with him, but the relationship goes nowhere. Finally he is fired; left embittered, he takes a job at a mental institution. There, phrases take on more reality in the narrator's life than people, who slip into abstraction: "For to hear D speaking of 4," he assures himself, "and C of 8 and to say to myself D4 and C8, demonstrated that I did make contact." He meets a woman, apparently marries her, and has children. But these mundane plot details barely ripple the surface of Brodsky's story. "I was left alone," the postal clerk writes, "with the words, over and over, the woman and children beside me, repercussions in, repercussions of, the old bones." All the material that would lay the groundwork for a traditional short story seem as irrelevant to readers as they do to Brodsky's starkly isolated hero.

Such lyricism put to the service of remarkably meager expectations from life typifies many of Brodsky's stories. In the title story from *Project and Other Short Pieces* (1982) the protagonist is again obsessed with the avoidance of being situated by those around him. He does not want to be "localized," so he avoids watching the news or coming into contact with anyone who will prompt him to take a position on any issues. He wishes to maintain a sense of his own decision making, his own spontaneity, and therefore he cannot tolerate being fully understood by others. His immediate problem is recommitting himself at work to the latest project to which his group has been assigned. "How does one attach oneself and go on sustaining belief in the attachment," he asks; "How do I manage to sustain this fever pitch of credulity in the face of an essential. . . . arbitrariness. Why this particular project?" He does not respect his coworkers, O'Grady, Morgan, and Chichpop; he tries to take some comfort in a woman, Hedda Kumquat. The nights in anonymous towns and the repetitive meals in overlit diners wear down his enthusiasm for various projects, and he marvels at his previous dedication ("Naming words," he notes, "are accessible only to those vociferating novices who must convince themselves through overuse that they are at last in the project's domain"). This attitude changes when a coworker is run over by a truck; shaken free from his last vestiges of individuality, the protagonist is ready to recommit to the project. "Rejoice," he is told, "that you participate in the being of what will always outlive every effort to localize."

In one of the few stories with a female protagonist, "The Envelope of the Given," a young European woman comes to New York City to begin a new life as a writer. She envisions her job at a boutique as a temporary distraction. The real focus for her life is her relationship

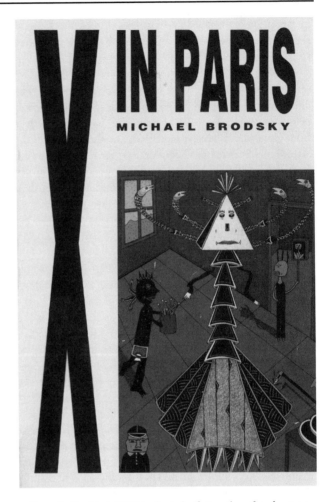

Cover for Brodsky's 1988 book, stories that continue the adventures of the unnamed protagonist he introduced in his 1987 novel, Xman

with two men: her agent and an artist. She struggles with the agent's attempts to categorize her work and thereby make it marketable, and with the artist's demand that she resist telling stories. "Light is never supposed to break through the words," he advises; "But light can of course seem to be about to break through the words." She herself loves a story, loves piecing it together into a meaningful narrative; in fact, she longs to have someone take her in hand and show her how it all fits. But details keep disrupting the flow. This story is a cautionary tale that Brodsky is telling himself, his recounting of the great temptation of giving in to readers' expectations. "A story," his narrator writes, "is the sum of impossible connections between impossibly compatible details." As a recovering storyteller she recognizes that she is "prey to irrelevant associations," but in them she finds her ironic salvation. She chooses to "deform" her stories with irrelevancies and arbitrary phrases. She finally learns that she "needed details for becoming these details she was no longer reducible to the given."

At the same time, "The Envelope of the Given" is about the anxiety of influence, as Brodsky's narrator gains the confidence to discard the masters. When asked who inspires his writing, Brodsky responded in the 4 February 2000 letter: "I'd like to think I'm beyond being influenced or inspired (not said self-congratulatorily, just stolidly)," but he then went on to mention Marcel Proust, Fyodor Dostoevsky, and Melville. He likes detective writers (Agatha Christie, Raymond Chandler) for their effort to "fight one's way out of a closed system," and thriller writers (Celia Fremlin, Patricia Highsmith) "most of all for their redemption of the everyday." On the other hand, Brodsky concludes "The Envelope of the Given" with the caution that the artist "awaited breathlessly any attention to himself and his work but when it came it was always inadequate, defective." Like many authors (and many of his characters), Brodsky resists having his work summed up, judged, or fixed—but he does not want it ignored.

He next published two novels: *Circuits* (1985) and *Xman* (1987). Referring to the former ("a monologue in which the speaker flees and then submits to imprisonment and judgment by vaguely defined authorities") and to *Wedding Feast, & Two Novellas,* Lois Gordon noted in *The New York Times Book Review* (14 September 1986) that "Mr. Brodsky mines veins of epistemology and ontology that were once the domain of philosophy but have more recently become that of linguistic deconstruction." *Xman* is the tale of a man whose job is to convince the sick that they are well. The notice for this novel in *Publishers Weekly* (11 September 1987) exemplifies the mixed reviews that often meet Brodsky's work: "The result is a 500-page tirade of rhapsodic complaint that honors its sources in Beckett's novels and Wallace Stevens's poetry. Although most readers' eyes are likely to glaze over early on, those devoted to serious writing will find many rewards."

The next collection of short fiction, *X in Paris* (1988), continues the adventures of this underdetermined everyman. As in *Project and Other Short Pieces,* the exact vocation he undertakes is left unnamed, and therefore appears totally arbitrary—"we will call it X." Having been trained in science, and working on "a long story uniting all my torments and an interest in metamathematics (Gödel, Cantor, infinity, with a big nod to Pythagoras)," Brodsky tends toward abstraction. In the 4 February 2000 letter he noted that "the thoughts that have been abstracted from heterogeneous collisions with the world don't exist until they're part of the very story they seem to curse as an obstruction of their own coming to eternal rest therein." In a similar vein the narrator in *X in Paris* warns readers that "specification will only obstruct the elaboration of a network of relations, connections, to which X lends itself easily enough when unencumbered by, depopulated of, specific features,

ubiquitous nuances." X, which could be many things, becomes a pretext for thoughts. In a swipe at René Descartes's first principle, he concludes, "I acquire thoughts, therefore I am." As in "The Envelope of the Given," the narrator is plagued by, saved by, and tortured by details. And in his arbitrary, tentative engagements with others, Xman continues to render even the infrequent unselfconscious moment distressingly conscious, obsessively observed and recorded.

Like a Henry James character, Xman concludes that "anticipation of participation is always delicious." Xman finds himself spending more and more time in the parking lot, like the postal clerk who stopped delivering letters, like Beckett's Estragon and Vladimir waiting for Godot in an agnostic challenge to teleology. Until he can be "placed" by his colleagues, Xman is an irritant in their workaday lives, one of the "details" that refuses to fit into the story they rehearse each day in the office. When characters actually accept their lives, their "story" comes to an end because it no longer has "story elements" in the traditional sense: "this does not mean however that they are not constantly growing, transforming themselves, enhancing vitality and commitment to each other and to their life together. That life simply resonates at a frequency which is inaccessible to story and its elements." This statement seems more a commentary on the telling of stories than on the meaningfulness of such lives, however. In "Origin," a brief exploration of parental ties reminiscent of Franz Kafka's *Die Verwandlung* (1915; translated as "Metamorphosis," 1936–1938), Brodsky adds a heavy dollop of Freudian determinism, quickly limning a son who is "fixed, localized beyond appeal."

In "Breadwinner's Ethic" Brodsky combines the ineptitude at finding comfort in simple human ties with the vacuity of the business world. The protagonist, Loophole, dreads celebrating New Year's Eve in New York; he fears committing the sin of "conspicuousness"; he avoids his boss, Flatulong, and is alienated from his work. In later stories he is alienated from nature, as well ("There was nothing in the configuration of the new dawn that seemed to offer an apology for its essential sameness"). And in the concluding piece in the volume ("A Plight"), almost computer-generated in its random splattering of meaningless phrases amid advertising copy and a mock attempt at detective narration, Brodsky pushes his techniques to their limits and offers the reader an experience of complete alienation from "story." In the 4 February 2000 letter the novelist concedes that "the story comes into being best when the writer appears to be preoccupied with something else entirely, to wit, disembarrassing himself of his thoughts, the accumulated booty of his collisions with the horrible and beautiful world within and without—getting rid of them by simultaneously offering them habitation in the coffin of the story."

John Byrum of the *Columbus Dispatch* (1989) concluded that *X in Paris* was "a tour de force. It is a multi-leveled, complex interrogation of the text, context, and experience of being human." Most reviewers remarked on the impossibility of summarizing or, for that matter, "placing" these stories. That result is precisely what Brodsky wanted. The novel *Dyad* (1989) confirms this attempt at mutual discomfiture. Though this novel purports to be a detective investigation of a life, presented in fugal form, reviewer Robert Nye in *The Guardian* (15 March 1990) noted that the book is in fact "about the mind that makes it, and the mind that reads it."

Three Goat Songs (1991) is an experiment in postmodern formalism, three variations on a theme, in which a man sits on a rock contemplating the sea and herds of goats. Like Brodsky, the man is married, with two children, and he is "terrified of living up to the demands of any rubric." These three novellas continue to vary the story elements discussed in *X in Paris* and other works. As in various other stories, the apparent object of observation—in this volume, the goats—is arbitrary, ephemeral. The title of this book is taken from the literal translation of the Greek term for tragedy, suggesting on another level that readers are observing a rubric for storytelling, like the three-part Greek tragedies. But as a reviewer for *Publishers Weekly* (22 March 1991) noted, Brodsky "writes not of the individual's desire for order, the theme of tragedy, but of the individual's desire for order in a unified narrative of the self." Such a narrative is not forthcoming.

Writing for *The New York Times Book Review* (26 January 1992), Albert Mobilio demonstrated that the model for *Three Goat Songs* is Beckett's minimalist *Nouvelles et textes pour rien* (1955; translated as *Stories and Texts for Nothing,* 1967) and suggested that the three novellas "explore our systems of perception, speculating on how what we see becomes what we think and ultimately the story we tell." Early in the first novella the narrator notes that "all this made sense only within walking distance of a confessor," and he later says it is ironic that a goat "should see fit to install itself in the copiously dreaded and eagerly invoked too long vacant role of confessor for the excess of unspeakables." This goat could as easily be analyst, lover, or reader, as the narrator seeks "auditors, confessors, interlocutors, bystanders, coadjutors, mufti, dragomen," but is unclear whether he should offer up "the story of my connection to the rocks—one with beginning, middle, and end," or "the slaver of incidents," or "sheer amorphousness." As with *X in Paris,* this thrice-told tale ends with a seeming paean to the end of telling, where "at last somebody was scratching the surface of the unchanging underlying, the underlying unchanging, that eventless

Dust jacket for Brodsky's 1996 book, in which the title story describes a fictional meeting between poets Wallace Stevens and Hart Crane in Key West

substratum of substrata immune to a telling. At any moment, therefore, the telling must give way."

With his next novel, one with the unpronounceable title *** (1994), Brodsky rehearses some familiar themes and techniques. The novel is a convoluted detective story about Stu Potts, who works in an asterisk factory (thus, the actual product is unimportant; only the process is of interest). Intermittent chapters are used to comment upon and subvert narrative chapters. Those who liked Brodsky before, liked this experiment; reflecting the ambivalence that others displayed, a critic for *Kirkus Reviews* (1 April 1994) wrote that "from its title of three asterisks one can tell that the master of the oblique is out to make life miserable for those who dare to try to make sense of his purposefully impenetrable novel." Brodsky followed this novel with his translation of Beckett's play *Eleuthéria.* In his "Translator's Introduction" Brodsky writes that "it became clear that Beckett's struggle with/resistance to creating the work was to be transmogrified into the very thew and sinew—the living fiber—of that work's unfolding over stage time."

In some sense that idea might be seen as a theme running through Brodsky's next collection, *Southernmost and Other Stories*. The title story presents an imagined meeting between Wallace Stevens and Hart Crane in Key West, before the latter's suicide. The Key is used metaphorically as an extreme jumping-off point into the unknown, a fit meeting place between two representatives of varying approaches to the imagination. Whether or not Brodsky "accurately" imagines the two writers, he presents them as advocates for competing aesthetics: as Thomas Lecky noted in the *Review of Contemporary Fiction* (Spring 1997), "For Brodsky, Stevens and Crane reflect two poles: Stevens the corporate man, whose willingness to dive into fictions Brodsky's narrator often sees as a tendency for rationalization, and Crane the recalcitrant bohemian, whose intractable imagination destined him to his final plunge." The narrator, again something of a detective, is hunting down the "truth" about Crane and, as in earlier stories, soon concludes that "there was only a story once it began to be untellable." He wishes to become one with his subject, to achieve anonymity, and recognizes that in Key West "the terror and delight of anonymity were exacerbated to breaking point."

In "The Son, He Must Not Know" another Kafkaesque metaphor plays itself out as a man repeatedly reinforces his placement as a father, almost as if to stave off the anonymity so desired in the earlier story. By embracing the role of father and being seen to play the part, he actually submerges himself all the more deeply into the common anonymity that the son must not be allowed to acknowledge until he, too, slips into fatherhood. Where this accommodation to normalcy can lead shapes "A Fifty-Thousand-Dollar-A-Year Man," another of Brodsky's takes on the organization man. Brodsky shows in later pieces that the everyman story as he imagines it is just too specific to have the same voice, moving from the mildly hysterical mathematics of some narrators to the cerebral detachment of "Bagatelle" and "Bill Brandtford, Stage Designer."

Early in his career Brodsky wrote an article on the novelist Italo Svevo, comparing him to Proust and Kafka, distinguishing him for his interest in "rehabilitation as a way of life," and noting that "there is a curious self-acceptance behind all his ironical self-revelations." He concludes by praising Svevo, Proust, and Kafka for remaining ever "alert to the possibilities for creative expression afforded by the relentless ambiguity of the phenomena around and inside them." A similar preoccupation with ambiguity and rehabilitation informs Brodsky's fight against giving in to any comforting stories that suggest a beginning, middle, and end, that settle one into a fixed position and transparent meaning in one's ongoing and ever-unfolding life. His narrators stop several times in midsentence because the achievement of closure, so common in typically plotted stories, has already been done before—and in ways no longer salvageable. Brodsky is in agreement with Virginia Woolf's condemnation of modern fiction as materialistic, preoccupied with surfaces, and thereby redundant.

The narrator of "Southernmost" clearly speaks for his author when he admits that

> unlike all other beloved, best-loved storytellers I cannot refrain from scalding my public—punishing them for failing to reprobate the massive deformation resident in any faithful rendering . . . . For once within the true storyteller has but one aim: to thrash his way clear of story, to undo the undoing of him that is story. But why is story an undoing? Not only because in embodying life, but with all the boring parts excised (Hitchcock), it maladapts him for the preordained return to life's pitiless duration. Story also exalts closure, ending, as an allegorizing of humus-pretty death.

As Nye noted in *The Guardian,* Brodsky's "reputation, as they say, is subterranean, a bit special, limited to those who can appreciate the peculiar flavour of Proustian cunning that pervades his work." And Paul West concluded in *The New York Times Book Review* (24 December 1989) that Brodsky "has learned the lesson the minimalists never will: it doesn't matter how little the thing you write about is, if your prose style can conquer the vacancy. His does." But the only "little" things that Brodsky turns his attention to are in fact the details of common life. Finally, he lets the narrator of "Southernmost" expresses what many writers have felt:

> I rob my commentators, should there be any, of what they arrogantly—erroneously—take to be their missionary (position) birthright. My work is no longer so much raw material—on the uncultivated level of soil and wind and arable wheat—awaiting the definitive transmutation into selfhood attainable only through the calisthenics peculiar to their superior art, that of definitive interpretation. The work embodies its own commentary, doesn't need the intercession of these bogland buzzards. Let them, as buzzards must, feed on boglands' rush-fringed tonsures of cloudless sky.

Reference:

Gerry Dukes, "The Second Englishing of *Eleutheria*," *Samuel Beckett Today* (Amsterdam), 7 (1998): 75–80.

Ron Carlson

(15 September 1947 –   )

Jay Boyer
Arizona State University

BOOKS: *Betrayed By F. Scott Fitzgerald* (New York: Norton, 1977);

Truants (New York: Norton, 1981; London: Murray, 1982);

The News of the World (New York: Norton, 1987);

Plan B for the Middle Class (New York: Norton, 1992);

The Hotel Eden (New York: Norton, 1997).

Born and raised in the post–World War II American West, Ron Carlson is a short-story writer known for his self-styled regionalism that allows for characters to suffer through comic, tender, and hard moments of self-examination and realization. Though he has lived on the East Coast, Carlson identifies himself as a Westerner and wishes to be known as such. "The light and space here sustain me," he explained in an unpublished interview: "I couldn't go to New York and type. I wouldn't want to go back to Connecticut. It's beautiful: rolling green hills. But I found it ultimately oppressive and enclosed." Currently a professor at Arizona State University, Carlson has said that the secret to his sympathetic portrayals of human quirks and foibles is his "practice to pay hard, hard attention."

Ronald Frank Carlson was born on 15 September 1947 in Logan, Utah, to Edwin Carlson, an engineer and welder, and Verna Mertz Carlson, a homemaker and writer, who were living at Utah State University on the G.I. Bill. The Carlsons moved to the west side of Salt Lake City in 1949, where Ron Carlson's two brothers were born, Robert in 1950 and Reagan in 1953. Salt Lake City in the 1950s was a Mormon town. Living among a close religious group of which they were not a part drew the family together. Carlson was not ostracized in the Mormon community, but like many characters who appear in his later stories, he learned that full assimilation into this particular community could not be won.

His parents, both members of large farming families from South Dakota, were storytellers, and Carlson himself began to write sketches when he was in elementary school, particularly after he saw a fifth-grade classmate's spiral notebook full of writing and pictures. Marvin Wharton, Carlson recalled in an unpublished interview, "was writing a book, with illustrations and everything! It took the top of my head off. I remember it vividly. I thought to myself, that's right, you can write your stories. I guess I'm writing to try to catch up to Marvin, wherever he is."

Growing up in Salt Lake, a town between the Rocky Mountains and the great American desert, shaped the kind of writer Carlson became. He sets many of his stories in Utah, using the landscape as background to his baseball, fishing, hunting, and hiking adventures. These boyhood passions, learned from his father, have all filtered into Carlson's work to become part of his fictional landscape.

Carlson graduated from West High in 1965 at age seventeen. That fall his family moved to Houston, where he entered the University of Houston. Because he was removed from friends and in a strange city, his education took on new dimensions: lectures, poetry readings, and road trips to Galveston to surf cast at night. He avoided majoring in English, trying biology, geology, and history instead. His work in English classes, however, was easier for him than his other studies, and his professors encouraged his poetry and storytelling. Some would accept creative work in lieu of formal literary analysis. A member of the honors program, Carlson transferred to the University of Utah in 1966 and graduated in 1970 with a B.A. in English.

He married his high-school and college sweetheart, Georgia Elaine Craig, on 14 June 1969 and worked for a year as an art supply salesman before entering the graduate program in English at the University of Utah, where he was awarded his master's degree in 1972. His thesis was a collection of short fiction, "The Larry Stories," sections of which were seedbeds for his first novel and other subsequent fiction. One story, "The Big Two Hearted Film Review," about a monster movie and a rent-raising party, was woven into his first novel, *Betrayed by F. Scott Fitzgerald* (1977).

Ron Carlson (courtesy of the author)

After earning his M.A., Carlson accepted a job on the English faculty at the Hotchkiss School, an elite boarding school in Lakeville, Connecticut. The Carlsons remained there until 1981. Carlson taught English and coached the hockey team, while his wife tutored. Both served as dorm advisers.

Carlson became increasingly involved in writing at Hotchkiss, serving as adviser to the literary review and as editor of the *Hotchkiss Alumni Magazine,* for which he wrote a series of features about campus life. In Utah he had started a novel that was difficult to complete because of coaching, dormitory life, and teaching, which included Saturday classes. The intense schedule was overwhelming. Carlson recalled in an unpublished interview that it was like "swimming under water the length of a pool" for nine months straight, coming up in June to "wonder where you've been." The Carlsons were considering leaving when his chairman, Blair Torrey, relieved Carlson of his dorm duties and gave him leave to take the following spring off to write the book.

In March 1974 Carlson and his wife drove to Cholla Bay in Mexico, where Carlson expected to finish his novel. Once there, however, he realized he had less of a novel than he had anticipated. Working

with what he did have–the voice of Larry Boosinger, "a kind of tender, smart aleck voice"–Carlson took the scenes he had completed and strung them together with Larry as the speaker. When the Carlsons returned to the East Coast in fall 1974, he had two-thirds of the novel completed, which then sat in a box for nearly a year. In 1976 Carlson began researching publishers and sent the volume off to Norton blind. Carol Smith bought it, and Carlson finished the book in the summer of 1976.

Betrayed by F. Scott Fitzgerald is a rites-of-passage novel. Larry Boosinger believes that nothing real will claim him so long as he remains a graduate student at the University of Utah. Armed primarily with what he knows of life from movies, books in general, and the novels of F. Scott Fitzgerald in particular, Larry begins an odyssey that will take him from Utah to Mexico and back again, only to discover that–literally and metaphorically–he is where he started. Now living on the fringes of the city, Larry is falsely implicated in a crime, indicted, then imprisoned. He breaks out of jail in order to confront the lowlifes who have framed him and to clear his own name.

Larry aspires to the same kind of romantic heights that filled the hearts and blurred the visions of Fitzgerald's characters, but he ultimately realizes that Fitzgerald had nothing to teach him about the world as it actually is. Fitzgerald's vison had been an innocent one, as was Larry's. To be armed with books is to be armed only with air. In the end, Larry suspects that he has forever turned some corner in his life. Perhaps he is through with being a boy. He senses his fate rests not in grand dreams but in the simpler pleasures of routine, home, friends, and a garden.

Because of the locales, some may suspect *Betrayed by F. Scott Fitzgerald* to be autobiographical. Carlson conceded that "This one though was more autobiographical than I probably intended it to be. It was my first time out. . . . My impulse to write it was not unlike writing a love letter to the life I'd known at twenty." *Betrayed by F. Scott Fitzgerald* was glowingly reviewed in *The New York Times,* but the review "appeared" in July of 1977 on the day of the second New York City blackout, and the paper never hit the streets. In what is now a collector's edition of the paper, reviewer Richard Lingeman praised this Sturm und Drang rites-of-passage novel as being a tender and comic version of a graduate student's quest for self-discovery, perhaps smarter than it was serious.

Carlson began writing his second novel during the spring of 1977 while teaching and coaching at Hotchkiss; then he and his wife returned for the summer to Salt Lake to begin his sabbatical. He finished *Truants* late in the fall of 1977. He recalled in an unpublished interview, "I wanted to evoke the West through characters I was going to put on the road, the openness, the rough edges." Carlson said he wrote the novel "at a distance," allowing the characters to shape the flow of the story. He sent the manuscript to Smith at Norton in the spring. Without knowing its fate, Carlson and his wife flew to London. When they returned that July there was a letter of acceptance, and Carlson "went to work on the ending. I wrote it fifteen different ways, at least, opting finally for the open-ended situation in which Collin finds himself now." Barry Yourgrau, writing for *The New York Times Book Review* (15 February 1981), praised *Truants* for the author's decent heart and tart tongue, praising Carlson's capacity to capture a passing moment of daily life with a vivid, tender touch.

With the publication of *Truants* in 1981, Carlson faced a difficult decision about his teaching career. His intense teaching schedule simply did not allow Carlson to write full-time; however, neither *Truants* nor *Betrayed By F. Scott Fitzgerald* had brought in the kind of money that would support a family without some other form of income. Carlson was a writer with promise but without the ability to make a living solely through writing.

Carlson decided to resign from Hotchkiss and returned to Salt Lake City late in 1981. Taking a job as a technical editor for Sperry Corporation, Elaine Carlson became the primary breadwinner while her husband wrote and brought in money in various ways: selling Christmas trees and pumpkins, modeling, and parking cars. He taught in the Continuing Education Program at the University of Utah beginning in 1982; he went into the schools of Idaho as a member of the Idaho Commission on the Arts Artist in Residency Program beginning in 1983, and with success at this project, went on to two-week residencies in Utah and Alaska.

Carlson spent most of his days writing. He wrote a series of short stories based on his boyhood on the west side of town, and he worked on a novel about marriage. Some of this work found homes in literary magazines such as *Western Humanities Review, Carolina Quarterly,* and *Tri-Quarterly,* and his stories were cited as "among the year's best" in the *Best American Short Stories* for 1984, 1985, and 1986.

The mid 1980s was a period of change for the Carlson household. Their sons, Nicholas and Colin, were born in 1984 and 1985, the same year that Carlson was awarded a Fellowship from the National Endowment for the Arts (NEA). There was other encouragement in 1984–1986: an Alan Collins fellowship to the Breadloaf Writers' Conference and a PEN Syndicated Fiction Prize. Carlson was also taken on by an agent, Gail Hochman at the Brandt and Brandt Agency.

Along with the NEA grant in 1985 came a Wang word processor. Carlson sold his electric typewriter, put aside his novel, and began gathering new stories, many of them with children as characters, for his first collection. He was at home with two infants, and his wife was thriving in her editing career. In 1986 he sold the manuscript that became *The News of the World,* and he accepted a position at Arizona State University as writer in residence. Carlson quickly made a place for himself in the budding creative writing program. In 1987 he was asked by the Department of English to stay on and became an assistant professor. In 1988 *Esquire* honored him with its Green Thumb Award for his skills as a mentor to promising young writers. One point he makes repeatedly to his students is that writing is a form of labor, work that must be practiced daily. "When I'm in a project, I work a lot," Carlson said; "I march through the whole draft. The only thing in my life that's interesting is surviving the draft—not making it good, not making it bright, light, dark, but surviving."

Dust jacket for Carlson's 1987 book, stories in which he says his "imagination, when it had its options, took the sunny turn"

The News of the World was published in 1987 just as Carlson was beginning his professorship, and it was a defining moment in his career. In this work, characters leading modest lives are buoyed against all the things that go wrong in their worlds by small, familial pleasures. "There's something wishful about *The News of the World*," Carlson said: "I think, in that collection, the imagination, when it had its option, took the sunny turn." His friend, writer Bob Shacochis, later called Carlson "the crown prince of domesticity," and in a collection with such stories as "The H Street Sledding Record" and "Blood and its Relationship to Water," one can understand why. These are charming, heartfelt tales of the young, in love, and newly married who are putting their toes into the waters of parenthood and finding those waters magical.

The midsection of the collection is devoted to a half dozen short, highly comic pieces. Their subject matter is generally a wrenching experience recounted by someone who has survived and is attempting to make peace with the event. Several of the stories in *The News of the World* have been performed on stage as

monologues. While he has gone on to write some material specifically for the theater, much of Carlson's work that has been staged–at the Sundance Playwright's Institute, the Philadelphia Festival Theater, the Manhattan Punch Line, and the Salt Lake Acting Company– has appeared first in print.

The most well known of these, and perhaps the comic monologue with which Carlson is most identified, is "Bigfoot Stole My Wife." Rick's wife has left him after years of neglect, taking the dog and the Toyota. First performed on stage in Philadelphia in 1986, "Bigfoot" begins:

> The problem is credibility. The problem, as I'm finding over the last few weeks, is basic credibility. A lot of people look at me and say, sure Rick, Bigfoot stole your wife. It makes me sad to see it, the look of disbelief in each person's eye. Trudy's disappearance makes me sad, too, and I'm sick in my heart about where she may be and how he's treating her, what they do all day, if she's getting enough to eat.

Such monologues reveal how the speakers adapt to what they have been through; they look to what they know best, whether it applies in this case or not; they spare themselves as much as they can. Carlson is never more serious than when he uses humor in his stories. This concern surfaces as well in several of the more-somber stories in this collection such as "Halflife," "Milk," and "The Status Quo." In these stories too, old ways of coping no longer work.

Carlson recalls that the work in *The News of the World* came out of a particularly "sunny, lucky" time in his life. "*The News of the World* is a kind of sweet book." His next collection of short stories, *Plan B for the Middle Class,* came out in 1992. Carlson called this volume "tougher stuff." He began trying a manner of writing he refers to as "going to ground," a literary style that allows for more honesty about life choices and their consequences. This development resulted in the stories in *Plan B for the Middle Class* being "much less wishful, more substantial than some of the stuff in *News*."

In *Plan B for the Middle Class,* the protagonist is often introduced just as a dark cloud seems to be creeping into an otherwise crystalline sky. In "Sunny Billy Day" a failed-big-leaguer-turned-sports-columnist recounts the season in which Billy Day threatened the integrity of baseball itself, then salvaged it in a stroke. Billy is one of those fellows who leads a charmed life, getting all the breaks everyone else longs for. Billy charms umpires into reversing their calls against him. This manipulation goes on for a season until, in a big game played before thousands of people, Billy insists, at his own expense, that an umpire make the call properly: "The ballpark was back, everyone standing now, watching. . . . Oh god, the cheer. The cheer went up my spine like a chiropractor. There was joy in Ohio and it went out in waves around the world. . . . Not joy at the out; joy at order restored. It was the greatest noise I've ever heard."

Order is not so easily restored in all the stories found in this second collection, however. In several of the stories the pleasures of domesticity have immediately definable limits. The perils of the world cannot be kept at bay. In "DeRay" the protagonist is hard at work one summer fencing his desert backyard, turning it into a grassy playground for his infant daughter, Allie. He is caught up in the pleasures of mindless physical labor: "It would be a little world, safe, enclosed, where my daughter, when she got around to walking, would tumble in the thick green grass." The title character, DeRay, his next-door neighbor, several years his senior, is a longhaired, tattooed, Harley-riding engineer, married to his third wife. The narrator's wife recognizes the threat DeRay poses. She senses a change in her husband since he has been having nightly beers with their neighbor and staying out late.

DeRay represents a kind of freedom and abandon that the narrator has forfeited in the name of domestic-

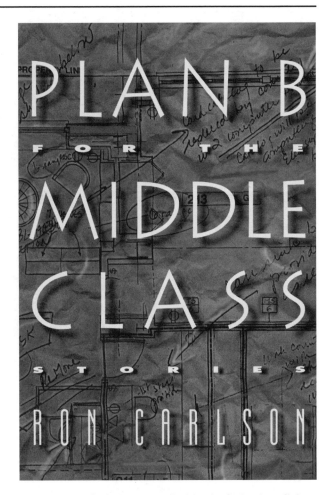

Dust jacket for Carlson's 1992 book, stories Carlson has called "less wistful" and "more substantial" than those in his previous collection

ity. The narrator's wife sees why her husband seems distant, different: a fence meant to keep evil at a distance also has become a fence that hems him in. The most important lesson DeRay has to offer is something more simple, however. The tight-lipped DeRay articulates what the narrator has known all along but refused to admit: "You're a nice kid, but that fence around your place won't stop a thing."

The need to stake out one's own plot of ground, the need to build a fence of one kind or a wall of another—and the futility of all these desires—became a recurring concern in Carlson's later stories. The narrator in "DeRay" says, "When you have a baby, you have to put in a lawn. You're suppose to build a fence. There's no surprise in that. I am like every other man in that." Anxiety creeps into the lives of Carlson's protagonists at precisely the moment they are old enough to realize this fencing is more for their peace of mind than it is for the protection of their loved ones. Like the daily routines in which his characters find pleasures, or the rules with which they guide their futures, the walls

The Speed of Light   ~~Butch and Penn Stories~~ (26)

"Oh, you're crazy," Butch stands and walks over to the new hole in his basement. The desk lamp still shines on the empty bureau top. He returns. "You couldn't see that cat. He's fully recovered. His appetite has come back."

We pick ~~glass~~ debris off our sleeping bags for a while and then get in them and then the li~~ght~~   and the neighborhood grows

"We come from fi

"Seventy-eight."

got the record." Butc

sky. "Stars," he says.

"Where?" Fenn say

"The speed of ligl

"How are the scien

"Bug off, Parley."

"No, how is play

Look at the river." He

fourteen.

"Bug off. Scared w

"Sleep out forever

games. Big deal."

"What is it, Parley?" Butch says. "What's going on?"

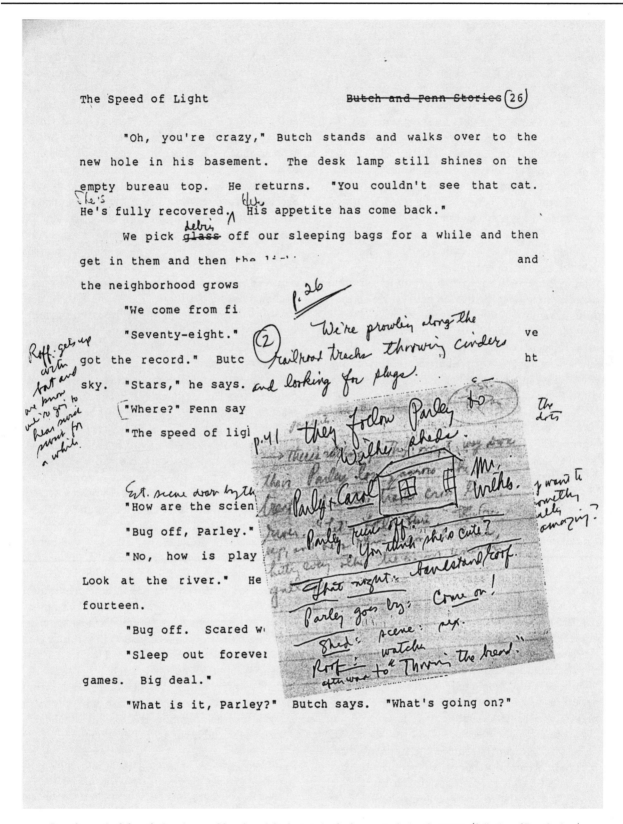

Page from a draft for a forthcoming novel based on eight short stories Carlson wrote during the 1980s (Collection of Ron Carlson)

and fences they build are fragile structures, flimsy measures, virtually helpless before the tremors of the earth, the full forces of life.

In the title story, "Plan B for the Middle Class," the narrator, Zoo Lewis, has just lost his job as a nature columnist for a newspaper syndicate. For years he has made his living answering questions submitted by his readers about animals and wildlife, but now he is not sure of what the questions should be, much less the proper response. When he is told it is probably time to go to plan B, he answers that this work is already plan B: he had wanted to become a veterinarian, not a writer, and now he is not even that.

Zoo cannot quite bring himself to break news of his unemployment to his wife, Katie, for he realizes that the loss of his income may wreak havoc on the life they have built for their two young sons. To delay having to tell her, he goes to plan C. He accepts a writing assignment that will take him to Hawaii and provide himself and Katie some time away from the boys. He believes that if he can just make love to his wife as her lover, rather than the mother of his sons, he can somehow turn back time, make things right, and begin again. But his plan does not unfold. Still wide awake after his wife is asleep, he leaves their hotel room and goes out onto Waikiki Beach, bathing himself in the surf, braced at last for whatever life was remaining: "I was already on Plan B—or was it C? What a deal. How could I not smile? What would stop me there, half in the ocean, from smiling? Plan B. A person could go right through the alphabet. With a little gumption and love, a person could go through every single letter of the alphabet."

In an unpublished interview, Carlson stated that he considers "Plan B for the Middle Class" and another story, "Blazo," to be "the central axis of this book. . . . The title story feels today a little like a younger version of me musing about his own life. There was too much happening in our lives, the new job, directing the MFA program, making a place for myself at school, making a life for ourselves in Phoenix. The book simply gathered." Carlson considered this period in his career as a time "when the range of my material was as wide as it will ever be."

Carlson's third collection of short fiction, *The Hotel Eden* (1997) explores some of the ways in which life not only demands change as people age but demands as well that people continue to learn. The title story, the first in the collection, follows Mark and Allison, a young American couple fresh from their studies, living in London on a lark. They feel as if they are perched on the threshold of the real world and are eager to partake. Their guide is an expatriate named Porter. A magnetic personality, he is a raconteur who has been everyplace one might want to go and has all the requisite, charming stories. He befriends them both, showing them his city and its pubs. Mark, the narrator, says of Porter, "He was a character, and I realize now that we'd never met one. I'd known some guys in the dorms who would do crazy things drunk on the weekend, but I'd never met anybody in my life who had done so much and seen so much. He was out in the world, and it called to me."

Porter stages a trip for himself and Mark to Scotland, purportedly to give Mark a glimpse of the Gulf Stream in its full measure; but actually Porter has his eye on Allison. Creating a ruse, Porter returns to London before his traveling companion. Coming back on his own, Mark realizes Porter has betrayed him with the woman he loves. He goes back to their favorite haunt, the bar of the Hotel Eden: "It would be three hours before Allison and Porter came in from wherever they were, and then I would tell them all about my trip to Scotland. It would be my first story."

These are stories about rites of passage, if one defines that phrase loosely. Rites of passage take place in adolescence ("Keith"), but they take place as well in young adulthood ("Oxygen," "Santa Monica," "A Note on the Type," "Down the Green River") and into one's middle years ("The House Goes Up," "Nightcap," "Prisoner of the Bluestone"). At various stages in their lives Carlson's characters must reinvent themselves and begin anew.

"Oxygen," the longest story in the collection, and one of the longest that Carlson has ever published, won a 1997 Pushcart Prize. A university student comes home to Phoenix in 1967 and works a summer job in the stifling desert heat delivering oxygen cylinders to home-care patients. Bringing the breath of life to the dying might seem to have special rewards, its own satisfactions. Yet, it brings out the worst in the protagonist, David. He takes a sadistic pleasure in bedding the daughter of one of the patients within earshot of her failing father, and in the final episode, he abandons an aged emphysemic, Gil Benson, leaving him to bake in the heat. The story ends with David's train of thought:

> Outside, the cooked air filled my lungs and the bright dish of Phoenix glittered to the west. I drove toward it carefully. Nothing had cooled down. In every direction the desert was being torn up, and I let the raw night rip through the open car window. At home my suitcases were packed. Some big thing was closing down in me; I'd spent the summer as someone else, someone I didn't care for and I would be glad when he left town. We would see each other from time to time, but I also

knew he was no friend of mine. I eased along the empty roadways trying simply to gather what was left, to think, but it was like trying to fold a big blanket alone. I kept having to start over.

In an unpublished interview, Carlson revealed something of the origins of "Oxygen": "With the narrative distance of thirty years, I mined my own experience to get this story. I did deliver oxygen in Phoenix during the summer of 1967, and it was a great and tough job." Carlson said he was interested in the "shadow of the story" and "didn't want the kid to have an easy passage." For David, Carlson wrote a complicated "passage" that ends with David's acknowledgment of his other, darker self. Carlson also explained how the writing of this particular collection worked: "It was a period when I'd write a draft and move on, leaving it unfinished for months. When you write on sabbatical, you don't finish, polish, re-edit. You cut new ground leaving all the roads unpaved. You tell yourself there's going to be time enough for paving once you get back to teaching."

More recently, Carlson has worked on "The Speed of Light," a young adult novel drawn from eight stories that he first wrote and published individually between 1982 and 1987 in such periodicals as *Sports Illustrated, Carolina Quarterly,* and *Epoch.* In the fall of 1999, while on sabbatical, Carlson revised these stories into a rites-of-passage novel set in 1959. The novel is scheduled for publication in 2002. "The Speed of Light" follows three twelve-year-old boys trying to invent the world in their last summer as friends. The coming-of-age story, and the fact that humans repeat that learning process in variations as they age, has been the center of gravity for Carlson as a writer for nearly a quarter of a century. "Perhaps the biggest lie we're told as we enter the inferno of adolescence is that it will pass," Carlson said; "The people who say this, obviously, don't know they're lying; they love us and are desperate to say something that might offer us a kernel of hope as we enter that violent region from whose bourne no traveler returns."

Carlson's writing has met with wide approval. His readers have embraced his range, his sense of humor, and his compelling emotional honesty. They see in the body of work he has produced a consistent vision exercised in a variety of ways. Reviewing *The Hotel Eden* for *The Los Angeles Times* (6 July 1977), Ilene Cooper wrote:

> Ron Carlson's *The Hotel Eden* is a strange eclectic mixture of some of the funniest and saddest stories ever to cozy up together in one volume. Some stories are brilliant and deeply moving; others are wild and surreal. Taken together they represent the idiosyncratic vision of an original writer who does what only good writers can do: make us see and feel what his characters see and feel and draw us into their world as if we had been born there.

In an unpublished interview Carlson reflected, "I am just a mid-career guy writing books and teaching. . . . I have been able to write what I want as fiercely as possible without thinking about the market, and my stories have, fortunately, found homes and an audience."

Alan Cheuse

(23 January 1940 –   )

Jay Boyer
Arizona State University

BOOKS: *Candace & Other Stories* (Cambridge, Mass.: Apple-wood, 1980);

The Bohemians: John Reed and His Friends Who Shook the World (Cambridge, Mass.: Apple-wood, 1982);

The Grandmothers' Club (Salt Lake City: Peregrine Smith, 1986);

Fall Out of Heaven: An Autobiographical Journey (Salt Lake City: G. M. Smith, 1987);

The Light Possessed (Salt Lake City: Peregrine Smith, 1990);

The Tennessee Waltz and Other Stories (Salt Lake City: Peregrine Smith, 1990);

Lost and Old Rivers (Dallas: Southern Methodist University Press, 1998);

Listening to the Page: Adventures in Reading and Writing (New York: Columbia University Press, 2001).

OTHER: *The Rarer Action: Essays in Honor of Francis Ferguson,* edited by Cheuse and Richard M. Koffler (New Brunswick, N.J.: Rutgers University Press, 1970);

The Sound of Writing, edited by Cheuse and Caroline Marshall (New York: Anchor, 1991);

Listening to Ourselves, edited by Cheuse and Marshall (New York: Anchor, 1994);

Talking Horse: Bernard Malamud on Life and Art, edited by Cheuse and Nicholas Delbanco (New York: Columbia University Press, 1996).

Alan Cheuse (courtesy of the author)

Alan Cheuse is probably best known to American book lovers through his work on National Public Radio, both as book commentator on *All Things Considered* and as host of its short-story magazine, *The Sounds of Writing.* He is also a writer of fiction, having published three collections of short stories, three novels, and a memoir. His articles, reviews, and short stories have been published in periodicals such as *The New Yorker, Black Warrior Review, The Nation, The New York Times Book Review, The Los Angeles Times Book Review, The Saturday Review, The Chicago Tribune, Ms., The Dallas Morning News,* and *The Antioch Review.* The nature of commitment and the sundry ways in which people betray one another has been a concern of Cheuse's fiction for more than twenty years. Cheuse appreciates the beat of the human heart, even as he wonders at its cry for love despite all the wounds people suffer, so it is not at all surprising that so much of his work deals with relationships under strain. He has asked readers consistently to consider the monstrous harm people inflict on one another, all in the name of love.

Alan Stuart Cheuse was born on 23 January 1940 to Philip Kaplan and Henrietta Diamond Cheuse in

Perth Amboy, New Jersey. He attended Lafayette College from 1957 to 1958 and then graduated from Rutgers University with a B.A. in 1961. He was variously employed in the following years as a New Jersey Turnpike Authority toll taker (1961), a reporter for Fairchild Publications (1962–1963), and a staff member for *Kirkus Reviews* (1963–1964). On 7 October 1964 he married Mary Agan, with whom he has a son, Joshua. In 1965 the couple moved to Guadalajara, Jalisco, Mexico, where Cheuse worked as a history and English teacher at the Butler Institute. In 1966 he left and became a case worker for the New York City Department of Welfare (1966–1967). Cheuse obtained his Ph.D. from Rutgers in 1974, the same year he and his wife divorced. He married Marjorie Lee Pryse on 22 June 1975; they have two daughters, Emma and Sonya.

Cheuse has spent much of his life as a teacher as well as a writer. He was a member of the division of literature and languages at Bennington College in Vermont from 1970 to 1978. After leaving Bennington, he moved to Knoxville, Tennessee, where he supported himself as a journalist while finishing his first book.

Cheuse published his first work, *Candace & Other Stories,* a collection of four short stories and the novella of the title, in 1980. One of these stories, "Fishing for Coyotes," is Cheuse at his best. April, her husband, William, and their infant daughter, Marina, come to Corpus Christi for the Christmas holiday. It is April's first visit since going off to college in the North. Trying to put as much distance as possible between herself and her roots, after graduation she had moved to New York City, where she met William, an artist, moved into his loft in Lower Manhattan, married him, and had a child. Since Marina's birth, they have moved to Guadalajara, Mexico, where April has taken a teaching position, an arrangement that allows William to oversee the care of their daughter while also beginning a career of his own as a painter.

April had set off into the world meaning to create a life entirely different from what she knew as a child, but in the forty-eight hours she is at home she sees her alcoholic mother in herself and realizes she has married a man who is sure to become like her father. The marriage she has made for herself is merely a variation of her parents'. The final scene takes place when April and her family drive to Padre Island to celebrate Christmas Day with a cookout. Standing on the beach, April notices three men, her husband among them, casting their rods toward a range of dunes, rather than the Gulf of Mexico. They have baited their hooks for coyotes, not fish. Coyotes run wild in the sand dunes, scavenging food, and April recalls a moment from her childhood on a Christmas much like this one when she had seen an angler reeling in a yowling, wounded animal, a

hook visible through its jowl. She feels similarly snared. She is part of a bloodline, and instinctively she responds to its call: "A high-pitched shriek, but whether of beast or bird or woman or baby she cannot immediately determine, rises suddenly on the wind. Something catches in her throat, and she races along the shifting sand to answer a cry of distress."

In "The Call," a journalist has come to Mexico on assignment in search of an interview with a famous figure. The man's aged and unstable wife answers the phone when the journalist calls their villa from his hotel room. It turns out that the celebrity he has come to interview is leaving his wife after forty-five years of marriage and going off with another woman. Cheuse's journalist is about to get a glimpse of who the man is aside from his worldly achievements and what he and his wife have done to one another in their many years together. Her husband picks up the phone in another room, however, and shoos him away summarily. The story ends as the journalist looks out his window:

> Doves congregated on the rooftops, flapping their wings in protest against the metal-heavy air. From dozens of tubs and basins, boisterous water gushed, like sound through wires, setting the walls to trembling with its passage. Surprising me where I lay brooding in my solitude, the maid used her master key to enter my room. She apologized for intruding, bowing her head as she backed out the door. Later the piercing shriek of rending steel, wailing sirens, voices shrilling in pain and dismay summoned as many of us as could hurry downstairs as witnesses to an accident other than our own.

The air only seems "metal-heavy" when one has just had a glimpse of a stranger's broken heart. In a 1990 interview with Neila Seshachari, Cheuse spoke about the effect he means to achieve:

> I think in images, which shape themselves into a fluid scene, very much as the twenty-four frames per second of film give the illusion of action on the screen. What we call memory is all of the images we have stored in our brains as we recollect them in the present. Thus the past is never past, it is always the present, as Faulkner says. If life is a series of present moments, then narrative fiction seems to be connected to lyric poetry in a much more intimate way than the theorists of narrative would have it. Fiction, like poetry, works at its best when it brings together emotion as well as idea, passion as well as characters in the illusory unfolding we call time—when it works close to the timing of the human heart, to the flow of our blood, to the beat of our heart.

In a Cheuse story, the past is never wholly gone, and the heart alone is instructive. Since the feeling of the moment is what he means to evoke, the endings

Cheuse at his great-grandmother's house in Perth Amboy, New Jersey, 1956 (courtesy of Alan Cheuse)

Cheuse prefers merely resound with that feeling, rather than move to resolve the dramatic conflict.

About as near as Cheuse comes to bringing events to a plot resolution is in "The Quest for Ambrose Bierce." Even in that story the final passage is as much a poem to be savored as it is a full-fledged dramatic finale. A journalist from Columbus, Ohio, Tommy Alman has come to Mexico on the trail of the self-exiled writer Ambrose Bierce, an assignment that takes him deeper into Mexico than he anticipated and ultimately deeper into himself. He has found his wife in the arms of another man and accepted any assignment that might take him away. He is fleeing from what awaits him at home as much as he is seeking a story.

Aboard a Mexican bus he befriends an American girl, a refugee from the Woodstock era, a flower child nursing a baby. She tells Tommy she has come to Mexico from New York City with her Puerto Rican boyfriend. The boyfriend is in jail on a drug charge. The girl is headed north. Tommy wonders as he listens to her whether she is capable of commitment to anyone, including her child or the child's father. The only thing of which he is absolutely certain is that he is no less lost than she is, no more uncentered, and he feels his fate being tied to her own once he gives up on the story he

has been sent to cover, allowing the bus routes to take him to wherever she is headed.

The girl disappears once they get through customs and are safely in America, leaving Tommy alone with the infant at the bus depot. Tommy is hardly equipped to take care of himself, much less a child, but he is desperate for anything that might serve as a center of gravity to his life, any sort of commitment at all. In the final passage of the story he makes one:

> Later, as they departed for Las Cruces, with the morning sun behind them, Alman, hands trembling, heart beating wildly despite the calm and certitude of the humming American bus, patted the wailing infant on its bottom until its noisy fears subsided. In Tucson, amidst the ammoniac fumes of the men's room, he changed the infant yet one more time. In Phoenix, after picking a cigarette butt from the drain, he sat the naked creature in the sink, bathed it with a paper towel and rubbed it with ointment he found in the knapsack. Dabbing water on its brow, he took a deep breath and gave the child an old-fashioned masculine name.

In 1982 Cheuse made his debut as a novelist with *The Bohemians: John Reed and His Friends Who Shook the World*, a faux autobiography of John Reed, one of the most famous American romantics. The focus of the book is commitment and betrayal. Cheuse explores Reed's commitment to revolutionary politics at a watershed moment in American history, but *The Bohemians* is equally interested in human relationships, particularly Reed's love of Louise Bryant and her bittersweet affair with playwright Eugene O'Neill.

Cheuse briefly worked as a writer in residence at the University of the South in Sewanee, Tennessee, in 1984. He was also divorced from Pryse that year and began a two-year stint as the writer in residence at the University of Michigan at Ann Arbor. In 1986 Cheuse published *The Grandmothers' Club,* a novel relating the experiences of the Jewish immigrant in the United States. From 1986 to 1987 Cheuse was acting director of writing workshops at Bennington College. In 1987 he became a professor on the writing faculty of George Mason University in Fairfax, Virginia. That same year he published his memoir, *Fall Out of Heaven: An Autobiographical Journey.*

In 1990 Cheuse published his second collection of short fiction, *The Tennessee Waltz and Other Stories.* It includes fourteen stories, most of which seem rawer than the stories in the first collection. Cheuse was older at their creation, a more seasoned and established writer. These pieces often seem less calculated to impress a reader with his capacity for carefully tuned prose or the lyrical moment. Many of these stories are set in or around Tennessee, and Cheuse makes the most of his appreciation for regional speech and how many languages are spoken in America. He reminds readers that in matters of the heart they share a common tongue.

In the first story, "Slides," a mudslide near Santa Cruz, California, has caused several deaths and obliterated many homes. As the storm raged, the speaker's parents called, and she now means to reassure them through audio and visual proof that she and their grandchildren are among the survivors. After putting together an audio cassette and a box of slides, the speaker describes the photos of the aftereffects of the mudslide. Deserted by her husband, left to raise her children on her own, she knows something of the emotional effects of having the earth symbolically fall out from beneath oneself. The story is less concerned with detailing the natural disaster than it is in affirming her spirit. She counts herself among the lucky and means to stay where she is, to make the best of what she has: "I've got a job beginning next week at a big drugstore in Santa Cruz–they've been busy because of the way people lost a lot of things in the storm up here and need to replace them, and because, I guess, people just keep struggling during both sickness and in health, storms and sunny days."

"Sources of Country Music" presents a newlywed who is taking the Music Tour of Nashville by herself while her groom, Billy, sleeps off a hangover. Bit by bit the reader learns she has married Billy in search of a family she has never had, and Cheuse makes it clear that she should have kept searching, for Billy is already flirting with other girls by the time she gets back to their motel. Brenda has discovered a painting on the walls of the Country Music Hall of Fame that she wants him to share, Thomas Hart Benton's *The Sources of Country Music.* What has touched her heart is its depiction of simple people in perfect step with one another as they dance to the tune of several country musicians. The story ends as she stands Billy before it: "Well doesn't that just get you?" she says. But Billy is indifferent: "It'll take a lot more than that to get me."

"The Pac-Man Murders" follows a father as he accompanies his two children to a penny arcade in Knoxville to play Pac-Man, doing his best to entertain them in the absence of his wife. Although as far as their children are concerned she is spending the time at her "drama group," Arlene, Martin's wife, has taken to spending this night each week dancing provocatively at the Pussy Cat Village. Martin is a Tennessee physicist who moonlights writing murder mysteries. In Martin's creative world, nothing is random; he plans out every detail of his mystery books; there is always a pattern to everything. If not, how could detectives solve crimes? Why Arlene should choose to betray him in this particular way, however, defies all of his skills of equation.

Martin appears once again in "The Tennessee Waltz," this time with Sue Beth Reals, a woman he has been seeing on the side since his wife began stepping out. Normally they spend the evening dancing at a country music bar, then repair to a nearby motel. They have managed this activity on the sly because Sue Beth's spouse, Andy Goins, works nights at the telephone company. This particular evening he comes to the bar in search of her. Cheuse offers the reader the evening from all three perspectives: Martin's, Andy's, and Sue Beth's. A reader is reminded of how the lyrics to the song "The Tennessee Waltz" speak sweetly of betrayal; there is nothing sweet about it off the dance floor, however, and the story ends with this disturbing recognition. Sue Beth says, "Sometimes it seems like our lives was made of trying to be music, but nobody was singing now."

"Seals," the final story of the collection, is set in the Santa Cruz area of California. Burr's wife, Buffy, has packed her bags and gone off to Europe, leaving him without explanation. Buffy's sister, Sally, and her teenage daughter, Tish, arrive from Houston for a visit. Having women in his home after living so long without them awakens in Burr long-forgotten desires, particu-

separates me from the rawness of it. I'm going to see my children. I'm bound away, for love of

them.

14. Milk Bath

In the center of the room--a high ceilinged kitchen at the back of the old house--stands a

table where the white-haired woman prepares the vegetables for meals, peeling, breaking off

stems, slicing. Meat she works on at the large sink, a separate place for meat. Here on this table

she set the tin tub that she filled with the warm milk. Calling to the front of the house she waits

for her daughter to bring the child.

Her daughter! Nearly a child herself, to give birth at this young age. Dark-haired,

big-boned, she had the hips for it. But what did she know about life? She needed her mother on

occasions like this. When her daughter came in the woman took the infant from her, holding the

child up to her face, cooing at it, making small noises with her lips to match the noises of the

babe.

This February child--she needed soothing, she needed protection against the elements

outside. The wind howling. The snow falling. The frozen Raritan ~~down the street.~~ leaps. The early dark.

All these things conspire against a healthy season. Keep the child warm, keep the child in fluids,

that's all you can do. Unwrapping her tiny granddaughter the white-haired woman whose

wide-cheeked face showed many wrinkles gently lowered the infant into the warm liquid,

keeping her broad hand beneath the girl's silky bottom. With the other hand she began to lave the

"On the Millstone River"
55

Page from the corrected typescript for a story collected in Cheuse's 1998 book, Lost and Old Rivers *(Collection of Alan Cheuse)*

larly when he sees their bodies intertwined in sleep. It has not been simply sex that has been missing from his life. It has been romance, magic, the wonders of the heart that only the presence of women can call out in a man, and his first evening with them under his roof seems charged with some special cosmic force.

The longer he is with the mother and daughter, however, the sharper the tensions between them become. Tish is seriously ill, though from what disease Burr does not know. They travel to Stanford in hope of accessing experimental treatment, apparently a last-ditch effort to keep her alive. Tish's dying is complicated by her mother's pregnancy. Sally is in danger of losing one child at the same time she gives birth to another. Burr has been watching the two women struggle to find a way to part from one another, to distance themselves as they prepare for final separation. On the last day of their visit Burr takes them along the coastal highway to a vantage point from which they can enjoy the sea lions below in the ocean. Sally and Burr remain on the edge of a cliff, while Tish climbs down toward the surf. In the last lines of the story, Cheuse carefully balances the human need for love and human savagery in seeking that love. Sally asks if Burr wants to know about how his wife betrayed him before she left:

> "I can wait," he said, spying Tish walking out from behind a clump of reed and sea grass to point, with a clean motion of her finger and hand, at two young elephant seal bulls splashing about in the surf, playing or fighting—it couldn't be said clearly which, at least not by an ignorant observer. Towering grey-black creatures with glistening hides and teeth like fence pickets sticking from their hideous elongated snouts, they shrieked and lunged and butted and slashed each other under a morning sun that lit the scene with the odd intensity of a fire in space.

Many of the concerns seen in Cheuse's earlier work are addressed as well in his 1998 collection, *Lost and Old Rivers*—the loneliness of what it means to be human, broken bonds, loyalties divided, promises made and too easily forgotten, the grip of the past on a character's life. The title is drawn from the story "An Afternoon of Harp Music in Lake Charles, Louisiana," in which Louise, a Minneapolis businesswoman, travels from a business meeting in Texas to visit her twin sister, Lindy, in Lake Charles. The two have not seen one another for five years. During that time Lindy has married, settled down, and settled in.

As they were growing up, Louise had always seen her own life and her own experience of the world in her sister. They are, to her, one person. Through Lindy, Louise sees how her life might have turned out if she had married Alex, a man from whom she is estranged,

and settled down. She feels lost, confused, empty by half. What would her domestic life have been? Is that what is missing? Or is it Lindy herself who is missing? On the way to Lake Charles, Louise passes a sign promising "Lost and Old Rivers," and she is taken by the thought. What if the waters of all the old rivers they had known when they were growing up together came rushing back to her, came rushing back to them both?

Lindy and her husband, Harry, have prepared a duet in honor of Louise's arrival. Harry plays his harp and Lindy her flute, and for moments at a time Louise feels at peace with herself, though this sensation is fleeting: "It used to be that having Lindy in her life made things seem balanced and comprehensible. But seeing her this time after so long an absence was having the opposite effect from what she had anticipated—not order, but fear bordering on chaos, unless it was true, as she had felt more and more, that fear ordered things as much as hope."

Cheuse's interest in what he has called "the creative process of memory and the retrieval of history" is the central thematic thread running throughout *Lost and Old Rivers*. One of the longest and most beautiful stories in the collection is based on the life of an actual historical figure, "Hernando Alonso," the first Jew to settle on Mexican soil. The story begins in 1528, then takes the reader back through the seven years that separate his arrival in the country from his eventual martyrdom. In some of his most polished prose, Cheuse details the role Hernando has played in settling the area, how he began his family, and the place he has found for himself among his neighbors. Hernán Cortés has been his protector for much of this time, and when Cortés goes to Spain in 1528, Alonso becomes a visible and vulnerable figure. Dominican friars are sent to the area to establish their monasteries during Cortés's absence. Alonso is persecuted and finally martyred, burned at the stake.

"The Mexican Maid" is set in Washington, D.C. Its protagonist, Birnhaus, has recently separated from his wife, Sara, and he is salving his wounds. He spends his day crunching numbers for his firm, something he thinks is ironic since Sara was sure he could not figure out anything. He entered therapy shortly after she left, but any hope he has held that therapy would put him in touch with himself and his past have diminished by the time the story begins. He now spends his nights carousing trendy bars such as Paolo's with his friend, Chuck Johnson, chasing anything in skirts, while his apartment becomes septic with filth. Birnhaus is not the sort of man who cleans up a mess, literally or otherwise.

One day in his psychologist's office he meets a cleaning woman, Señora Claro, whom he puts on his payroll. The story takes the reader through the months Señora Claro tends his apartment. After Señora Claro

Lost
and
Old
Rivers

STORIES BY ALAN CHEUSE

Dust jacket for Cheuse's 1998 book, in which the central theme of the stories is what he calls "the creative process of memory and the retrieval of history"

misses a weekly visit, he learns that she has developed a heart problem and is a patient at the Washington Hospital Center. Long before she should, she goes back to work. One night he returns to his apartment to find her dead on his floor. He does his best to resuscitate her, putting his mouth on hers, until all the bile within him after all of his troubles with women will not stay down any longer:

> There came a pounding at the door, and as if that were the signal he was waiting for, Birnhaus collapsed onto the woman even as his gorge rose and he spewed forth his own late supper and all the beer and—it seemed all of the drinks he had drunk at Paolo's, all of the meals he had taken there and at other exotic restaurants, and all of the smokes and the hors d'oeuvres and the snacks and desserts, and candy and medicine and syrups and toppings and the saliva of a thousand kisses, from his mother's to those on the lips of every woman he had ever tasted, this wretched acid gush of

waste that flowed down over his shirt and poured onto the prone body of the Mexican maid, sloshed over her chest and neck, and left an indelible stain on the rug beneath her.

Like Birnhaus, the protagonist of "Man in a Barrel" is a bilious character, at odds with women and marriage and what family life demands. The story is set in Niagara Falls, where a divorced father is taking his three young sons. He has picked them up in Albany from his former wife, Nancy. The speaker now lives in Detroit, where he works on the assembly lines building cars. Nancy delights in making it as difficult as possible for him to see his boys. He is going ahead with this trip despite the fact that he could have gone to Cancun, Mexico, with friends for a sunny weekend of cold beers and sex. Cheuse recounts the torturous car trip from Albany into Canada to delightful comic effect. It is every single father's nightmare.

The speaker is much more ambivalent about fathering his unruly children than he cares to admit. The trip is made worse when the Canadian customs guard demands a notarized letter from Nancy that the children are allowed across the border. Returning in a rage to the American side of the falls, he does his best to raise their spirits and salvage the trip with a bit of sightseeing.

While he is showing them wonders of the cascading waters before them, a nearby turbaned Pakistani throws his infant over the rail, to the horror of the man's wife. The Pakistani flees and the speaker pursues him, finally knocking him to the ground and holding him in place until the police arrive to take him into custody. As he is being taken away, the Pakistani looks into the eyes of the speaker: "I looked over at the Indian guy an he looked up at me and it was so crazy because just then he nodded at me, nodded, like he was saying, Don't worry, it's okay, or, Right, we did what we had to do, or, We did a good job together, right?" The Pakistani has seen in the speaker a man just like himself, no more born to care for a child than he, no more eager to face the sacrifices that having children demands. The reader understands this moment of communion better than the speaker seems to care to.

The story ends once the speaker gets his boys to bed in their motel room. Leaving them alone, he goes to a nearby bar and drinks beer, haunted by the Pakistani's face as it seems to float up before his eyes. Returning to his room, he sits before the phone, nodding off from the alcohol, then brings himself awake long enough to look at himself in the mirror and try to gauge who he really is. In the last lines he phones a girl for a date.

The final story in the collection is "On the Millstone River." In an unpublished letter, Cheuse admitted:

The Millstone River story is so straightforwardly autobiographical, you might wonder why I didn't write it as autobiography. I wondered, too, as I was writing it. But what I saw evolving was something much more shaped and transformed than autobiography. I mix the real with the invented, the imagined with the actual, and I allowed myself to make things up, to lie! in a way I would have felt was dishonest had I been writing autobiography.

"On the Millstone River" takes water as its central conceit. The story is comprised of fourteen vignettes of various lengths, each in its own way lyrical. Collectively, they take the reader from Cheuse's beginnings as a writer in Greenwich Village, through his various wives, the birthing of children, and the deaths of loved ones, through his travels, teaching, and writing career, toward who he is today. In the thirteenth section Cheuse writes, "Yes, there is something visible behind me when I look over my shoulder, certain forms looming out of the fog of memory—the travels, the loves, the marriages. And I'm moving away from all that, I hope, with as much speed as this train putting downstate stations behind it. Onward from now on."

Cheuse's sense of place sets him apart stylistically from other writers of his generation. Where others briefly locate a reader in space and time and then move along, Cheuse makes his landscapes fully charged energy fields in which to explore his characters and develop the plot. This characteristic is particularly evident in his third novel, *The Light Possessed,* published in 1990, before his marriage to Kristin M. O'Shee on 17 August 1991. Reminiscent of the work of photographer Alfred Stieglitz and artist Georgia O'Keefe, the book deals with Ava Boldin, who comes to the city from the Midwest and begins an affair with a New York photographer old enough to be her father, eventually making her home in the desert apart from him, where light and life seem truest. Cheuse's sense of a landscape and its effect on the soul reminds the reader that the harmonies found by the pair in their work only served to counterpoint the differences that held them apart. His use of light in this regard is particularly stunning:

Of late I have spent much time alone with clouds. And I have discovered that when I am out under the sky and notice these configurations that only he could truly capture with his camera, I think of Stig, and all the desert land around me, and the sky itself seems to contract in an instant into an ice-cold pain no smaller, I say, than my first—all of it exquisitely there, compressed and pressing into my stomach. But I can shrug off the pain.

And then I sigh, and I wish with that sigh that he were walking along the trail northwest to the top of the mesa, so that we might take home with us the sight of those clouds on his photographic plates.

He and I certainly had no quarrel about light.

Cheuse often employs this technique in shorter work, as in his short story "Accident" (in *The Tennessee Waltz and Other Stories*), Joe is recently widowed. A member of a dam-inspecting team working for the Tennessee Valley Authority, he drops his young son off at what is clearly a troubled day-care center and proceeds on to work. A reader learns of his edgy emotional state by sharing his view through the windshield:

He could see clouds as he drove; he could see the ghostly shapes of the mountains rising out of the hazy east. There were huge constructions out there he had been hired to maintain. Water rose, locks clicked, fields of transformers hummed and buzzed beneath towering shields of concrete and steel. His life on the other hand was a mournful mess, shards of metal on a highway, blood, bone, an empty place at the table, a narrow bed.

Cheuse prefers to leave the well-wrought plot and the meticulous development of character to the novels he undertakes. He offers a sequence of events in the life of a solitary character in transit, someone far from home in several possible ways. He favors the third-person subjective point of view, rendered most often in the immediate past tense. This point of view allows the reader retrospectively to experience events from the character's perspective. Cheuse traces for his readers a pattern to events that his characters missed while living through them. While this technique lends authority and value to the idea of "the big picture," it leaves little dramatic tension in the short fiction. Cheuse's stories more often end with a deeply resonant image than a finely honed conclusion. Explaining in an unpublished letter his difference in writing style between the short story and novel forms, Cheuse said:

I try to do short stories in water colors, not a good medium for the novel. The novel needs oils, or at least acrylics. When I write stories, I discover that I'm usually focusing on the feeling soul—essence?—of the character, and the emotive aspect of the setting. The link between the character's interior life and the landscape through which the character moves always fascinates me, and I concentrate first on getting that right . . . I know at the same time that I keep a certain distance from the material, I try to keep the language sharp, evocative, incisive, pared close to the bone. Though I try to illuminate the beautiful instance—or glimpses—in nature when they come along or when characters spy them out.

Cheuse has been reviewed more widely (and warmly) as a novelist than as a short-story writer. Those who admire Cheuse's short fiction tend to embrace the way his stories shun conventional development in favor of some final, epiphanic flourish. For instance, Grace Anne Candido of *Booklist* wrote in a 1 December 1998 review of *Lost and Old Rivers,* "Wounded, unfinished men—and a few wounded women—stride through these stories with the bulk and aroma of life about them." Candido praised how "Each story is a fully realized universe, with a tale that tends to move languorously toward a pinpoint conclusion," and she was particularly taken with "On the Millstone River": "The last piece . . . is a sinewy musing on two marriages, three children, Europe and its effect on the young, and other things, saved from terminal mushiness by Cheuse's control and edge. His gorgeous delineation of the night of his daughter's birth in a raging snowstorm—unsentimental, diamond bright—is worth the price of admission."

Those critical of Cheuse often resist his depiction of America's disenfranchised. They tire of characters who are more self-concerned than self-aware. In a 15 October 1998 assessment *Kirkus Reviews* called *Lost and Old Rivers* "Heavy-handed academic fiction" by a gifted critic "whose insights into other writers and literary styles doesn't seem to have rubbed off on his own. . . . Pompous, dull, and provincial, Cheuse's characters never seem to realize that it's the narrowness of their own world rather than the strangeness of anyone else's that's the source of their dilemma."

Despite these criticisms, Cheuse has joined the ranks of short-story writers such as Richard Ford, Raymond Carver, and Mark Richard as a commentator on the broken hearts of those who are often not given a voice in literature. What sets Cheuse apart from many of his contemporaries is that he is less concerned with pinpointing fault, guilt, and obligation than in detailing how his characters will find the strength to survive.

Interviews:

Neila Seshachari, "The Light on Alan Cheuse: A Dialogue," *Weber Studies,* 72 (Fall 1990): 1–21;

Andrew Wingfield, "Voices: A Conversation with Alan Cheuse," *Pleaides: A Journal of New Writing,* 20 (1999): 145–163.

John William Corrington

(28 October 1932 – 24 November 1988)

Geoffrey H. Goodwin
Naropa University

See also the John William Corrington entry in *DLB 6: American Novelists Since World War II, Second Series.*

BOOKS: *Where We Are* (Washington, D.C.: Charioteers, 1962);

The Anatomy of Love and Other Poems (Fort Lauderdale: Roman Books, 1964);

Mr. Clean and Other Poems (San Francisco: Amber House Press, 1964);

And Wait For The Night (New York: Putnam, 1964; London: Blond, 1964);

Lines to the South and Other Poems (Baton Rouge: Louisiana State University Press, 1965);

The Upper Hand (New York: Putnam, 1967; London: Blond, 1968);

The Lonesome Traveler and Other Stories (New York: Putnam, 1968);

The Bombardier (New York: Putnam, 1970);

The Actes and Monuments (Urbana & London: University of Illinois Press, 1978);

The Southern Reporter (Baton Rouge: Louisiana State University Press, 1981);

Shad Sentell (New York: Congdon & Weed, 1984); republished as *Shad* (London: Macmillan, 1984);

So Small a Carnival, by John William Corrington and Joyce H. Corrington (New York: Viking/Penguin, 1986);

A Project Named Desire, by John William Corrington and Joyce H. Corrington (New York: Viking/Penguin, 1987);

A Civil Death, by John William Corrington and Joyce H. Corrington (New York: Viking/Penguin, 1987);

All My Trials (Fayetteville: University of Arkansas Press, 1987);

The White Zone, by John William Corrington and Joyce H. Corrington (New York: Viking, 1990);

The Collected Stories of John William Corrington, edited by Joyce H. Corrington (Columbia: University of Missouri Press, 1990).

John William Corrington (photograph from the dust jacket for William Mills, ed., John William Corrington: Southern Man of Letters, *1994)*

PRODUCED SCRIPTS: *Von Richthofen and Brown,* script by John William Corrington and Joyce H. Corrington, motion picture, United Artists, 1970; retitled *The Red Baron,* 1971;

The Omega Man, script by John William Corrington and Joyce H. Corrington, motion picture, Warner Bros., 1971;

Box Car Bertha, script by John William Corrington and Joyce H. Corrington, motion picture, American International Production, 1972;

The Battle for the Planet of the Apes, script by John William Corrington and Joyce H. Corrington, motion picture, Twentieth Century-Fox, 1973;

Search for Tomorrow, episodes 6949–7426 by John William Corrington and Joyce H. Corrington, television, CBS, 1978–1980;

Another World, episodes 4058–4081 by John William Corrington and Joyce H. Corrington, television, NBC, 1980;

Texas, episodes 1–147 by John William Corrington and Joyce H. Corrington, television, CBS, 1980–1981;

General Hospital, episodes 52–106 by John William Corrington and Joyce H. Corrington, television, ABC, 1982;

Capitol, episodes 104–271 by John William Corrington and Joyce H. Corrington, television, CBS, 1982–1983;

One Life to Live, episodes 4122–4219 by John William Corrington and Joyce H. Corrington, television, ABC, 1984;

Superior Court, episodes 1001–1170 and 2001–2170 by John William Corrington and Joyce H. Corrington, television, Ralph Edwards/Stu Billet Productions, 1986–1989.

OTHER: *Southern Writing in the Sixties: Fiction,* edited by Corrington and Miller Williams (Baton Rouge: Louisiana State University Press, 1966);

Southern Writing in the Sixties: Poetry, edited by Corrington and Williams (Baton Rouge: Louisiana State University Press, 1967);

Eric Voegelin, *The Nature of the Law and Related Legal Writings,* edited by Corrington, Robert Anthony Pascal, and James Lee Babin (Baton Rouge: Louisiana State University Press, 1991).

John William Corrington's contribution to American literature is generally underappreciated. In James Dickey's assessment—quoted on the cover of *The Collected Stories of John William Corrington* (1990)—"A more forthright, bold, adventurous writer than John William Corrington would be very hard to find." Such praise was well earned. Corrington looked at the depths of human experience, examining the interplay between the human extremes of the grotesque and the spiritual and offering insights into how the two opposing natures co-exist. Though Corrington produced quality work in several genres, his reputation rests most securely on his short stories.

In the nineteen stories published in his three collections of short fiction, Corrington examined a changing—at times frightening—society, demonstrated by his characters' questionable adherence to the manners and customs of time and place. His stories use metaphors of war, justice, and the human capacity for evil to illuminate vital responses to the moral dilemmas that concerned him.

The son of John Wesley Corrington, an insurance adjuster, and Viva (Shelley) Corrington, John William Corrington was born on 28 October 1932 in Memphis, Tennessee. He was raised in Shreveport, Louisiana, which figures prominently as a setting in much of his work. Corrington earned a B.A. in English from Centenary College of Louisiana in 1956. After two years as a correspondent in Europe for the *Houston Post,* he entered graduate school at Rice University. He married Joyce Elaine Hooper, a chemistry professor, on 6 February 1960. The couple subsequently had four children, and Joyce Corrington worked with her husband on several projects, including mystery novels, television scripts, and screenplays.

Also in 1960, Corrington earned his M.A. from Rice and took a job in the English Department of Louisiana State University, where he remained until 1966. Having passed the required oral examinations and written a dissertation on James Joyce, he earned a D.Phil. from the University of Sussex in 1964. Throughout his career as a writer, Corrington remained a devoted scholar with a voracious appetite for learning. After serving as a professor (and chairman for some of his tenure) at Loyola University of the South from 1966 to 1973, Corrington left teaching and earned a J.D. from the Tulane University Law School (1975). He then practiced civil law in New Orleans.

In his poetry, novels, short stories, television scripts, screenplays, and literary criticism, Corrington interwove themes derived from his studies. The history of the Civil War, music, philosophy, science, and religion helped to deepen his treatment of such subjects as war, justice, human nature, and the manners and customs of American culture. His characters speak from experience as they encounter troubling events. His flawless dialogue allows his work to flow smoothly, giving the reader a genuine sense of other voices. Calling this easy rhythm of speech "the Faulkner tradition," Corrington explained another important link: "I invented the definitions of the traditions. There's the Shakespeare tradition and the Dante tradition. In the Shakespeare tradition, the artist vanishes in his work." Corrington frequently vanishes in his work, embracing the characters of each story fully, and giving them distinctive speech characteristics. He avoids using an omniscient authorial persona and lets his characters speak for themselves. In an essay collected in *John William Corrington: Southern Man of Letters* (1994), Thomas Preston described these facets of Corrington's work, noting "its density of wit, humor, language, its laughter, character, narrative poetics, grotesqueness, and, finally, its reach for transcendence." Corrington's humor is often called dark, ironic, and localized. His technique of focusing on sudden and ironic twists of fate heightens his ability to show the grimness of reality.

Corrington's first collection of short stories, *The Lonesome Traveler and Other Stories,* appeared in 1968, after the publication of four collections of his poetry and his novels *And Wait For The Night* (1964) and *The Upper Hand* (1967). The first novel is set during the Civil War, as are six of the nine stories in *The Lonesome Traveler.*

The opening story, "If Time Were Not / A Moving Thing," takes place in 1868 and 1968. Two alternating narrators—a former nun, Marie Ducote, and a railroad brakeman, Mr. Posey—tell separate but similar stories of lost children, describing events that occurred in two different centuries. The dueling tragedies seem to echo across time, with each distinctive voice left hanging at a moment when each narrator struggles to define his or her emotions about personal loss. Marie Ducote finds God once again, even though her twin sons have died in a plague. Mr. Posey finds a connection to a fate he has dreamed of while watching the nightly news. Through a misguided desire to allay a stranger's fears for her missing child, he confuses the searchers and accidentally contributes to the boy's death. The possibility that death can awaken an individual's moral code is introduced in this first story and continues to be a theme throughout Corrington's work.

In *Publishers Weekly* (28 September 1990) Sybil Steinberg referred to the "quirky turns" in Corrington's stories. This technique of unpredictable plot twists allows the unexpected to provoke reader responses, in much the same way that the shock of death can help Corrington's grieving characters to reevaluate life.

First published in the Spring 1965 issue of *The Georgia Review,* the second story in *The Lonesome Traveler,* "First Blood," begins with a scene in which Confederate soldiers are pinned down by Federal artillery. Old Milburn helps injured Southern troops who are trapped in his barn. Later, his son, fresh from thirteen weeks in battle, comes home and kills a wounded Yankee, whom his father shot in self-defense but has since been helping to recuperate. Appalled by the heartlessness of his son's act, an enraged Milburn kills his own son. In his essay for *John William Corrington: Southern Man of Letters,* Robert B. Heilman called Corrington "the equal of any writer in recreating the brutal realities of war." "First Blood" illustrates the mixture of loyalty, compassion, and brutality that occurs in war.

In Corrington's fictive framework, history does not collapse into useless, romanticized fabrication. The story displays Corrington's ability to use an unexpected plot turn—in this case, a father's killing his son—to provoke the reader into examining the value of life.

The remaining stories of *The Lonesome Traveler* move forward through time, further bridging the gap between past and present and revealing the constants in human nature. Corrington referred to Faulkner's saying that "The past isn't dead, it isn't even the past." As he noted in his introduction to *Southern Writing in the Sixties: Fiction* (1966): "We are told that the Southerner lives in the past. He does not. The past lives in him, and there is a difference." Corrington believed that old truths live throughout time, and actions of the past carry much weight in his stories.

Corrington illustrated his concern for the continuance of history and tradition throughout *The Lonesome Traveler.* In "Reunion," first published in *The Southwest Review* (Summer 1963), a grandfather brings his two grandsons to Gettysburg fifty years after the historic battle there. In revisiting the scene, he feels once again the reality of the Confederate loss and quietly says, "We should have gone on.... We never should have stopped." Though fifty years have passed since the battle, emotional wounds reopen easily. Corrington often used older males, frequently fathers or grandfathers, to teach the lessons of the past—which often become poignant or bittersweet because the younger generation refuses, at least initially, to hear their elders' words of wisdom.

In "A Time to Embrace," first published in *The Denver Quarterly* (Winter 1968), a father tells a story about the kindly Mr. Sentell to show "a grown man's knowledge" of how to "handle that burden the way a man handles whatever comes his way, whether he has sought it or not." Corrington's powerful prose reveals the elderly man's ambiguous parentage. Two men loved Sentell's mother and helped to raise him. The unanswered question of which man is Sentell's biological father contributes to rivalry between the two men. Finally, at her grave the men come to terms with one another and become friends, recognizing their mutual love for her as a bond. Transcendence of difficulties, as a metaphysical lesson to "handle whatever comes," becomes an increasingly important theme in Corrington's three short-story collections.

First published in *The Arlington Quarterly* (Spring 1968), "The Retrievers" is perhaps Corrington's most whimsical work, as he looks at the powerful effect of the past on human nature in a more tangible way. Two impoverished children, Malissa and Nathan, find a map that locates a hidden fortune under their kitchen and secretly begin to dig through the floor in the mid-

Started 14 May 1976
Completed 1 December 1976   Version II

'<u>E</u>very <u>Act</u> <u>Whatever</u> ~~of~~ <u>Man</u>
I

1st draft
John W. Corrington
1976

It was his habit to come to the courthouse ~~early~~
when he had ~~business~~ there. He would nod to
the janitor as the large ancient doors opened,
& then, the rising sun behind him, he would
walk "up &" down the silent, shadowed corridor, a dog-run
with offices, chambers, & courtrooms off to either
side.

When he had a trial, he would do the last-minute acts
of mental construction at this time, search out the
questions to be asked that he had not discovered yet.
On those days, he would pace rapidly through the
shadows, hardly noticing the dark obscure portraits
of long-dead judges that adorned the walls along
the corridor, or ^even^ noticing later the growing number
of lawyers & functionaries as they came in to begin
their day. Not until his opponent, or the clerk of
the court where he was to try, came up to him
would he cease his pacing & look up. distracted,
to see that the sun was high & it was time
to work.

Other times, when there was no trial, he would go to
five o'clock mass in the tiny church of the ~~Blessed~~ Holy
^Redeemer^ ~~Sacrament~~, & then, christ upon him, would pace

Page from a draft for a story collected in Corrington's 1978 book, The Actes and Monuments
(Corrington Collection, Magale Library, Centenary College of Louisiana)

dle of the night. The hidden riches they discover serve as a metaphor for the wealth of history that can be unearthed. Corrington avoids celebrating their material gain and instead emphasizes the symbolic pleasure that can be found in retrieving history. The last lines also reveal his humor: "'After all, we weren't what you'd call new rich,' Malissa said. 'Our money had been in Caddo Parish for almost eighty years.'"

First published in the Winter 1968 issue of *The Arlington Quarterly*, the title story in *The Lonesome Traveler* focuses on a budding journalist from the North, Robert Pleasance, who travels to a small Southern town to write about a lynching that is expected to take place. As he watches the local sheriff trying to ensure that his black prisoner will receive a fair trial, Pleasance attains "the sudden total and immitigable knowledge of what spiritual pain, bereavement really mean," finding a deeper sense of personal truth. When the mob corners the sheriff and the black man, the sheriff shoots his prisoner rather than let the angry mob hang him—creating one of Corrington's typical plot twists. A mysterious, ghostlike Bible salesman leads Pleasance away from the mob, so that he can race back to his editor with the story, only to discover—in another twist of plot—that comedian and pundit Will Rogers has died in a plane crash, and there is no room in the paper for Pleasance's story. Much of Corrington's fiction includes such multiple and layered "quirky turns." By the end of the story it is obvious that Pleasance's travails have been for his own growth: the "immitigable knowledge" he has learned helps him develop a sense of his place in life.

Set in 1946, "The Dark Corner," about a brother bringing home a dead soldier's body from Europe, suggests that present actions can undo mistakes made in the past. Even though the soldier asked not to be returned to his native Shreveport if he died in combat, his brother decides to bring him home, saying: "He knows better now. If he doesn't know better the whole thing is absurd." The brother thinks that war must have changed his sibling's mind; war, with its connection to death, must have clarified and thus enhanced the soldier's sense of the value of life and community connections.

Set in 1958, "The Arrangement" depicts the breakdown of a marriage, chronicling Sarah's tormented life through the eyes of a male acquaintance. Corrington shows how her husband's philandering causes Sarah's emotional collapse. Even as she tries to turn the tables by engaging in her own affair, their modern "open" marriage—the "arrangement" of the title—shatters her spirit.

The narrator of "The Night School," first published in *The Massachusetts Review* (Summer 1968), sees that "To move a finger is to risk moving the axis of the earth"—repeating the lesson Mr. Posey learned in "If Time Were Not / A Moving Thing" when he altered the course of events and prevented a young boy from being rescued. Yet, the narrator of "The Night School" realizes that action at the right moment is necessary: destiny must be seized when the "ripeness" arrives. The art of "Being happy is not being unhappy," he says, displaying a rugged power of faith in self and tradition.

Corrington's second short-story collection, *The Actes and Monuments* (1978), was published ten years after *The Lonesome Traveler*. Corrington spent the intervening decade studying the thought of historian-philosopher Eric Voegelin, earning his law degree, and writing screenplays and a World War II novel, *The Bombardier* (1970). His experiences in law school and as an attorney obviously influenced his choice of subjects for the five stories collected in *The Actes and Monuments*.

In *The Actes and Monuments* Corrington's already well-honed skill at creating narration and dialogue seems even keener and more accomplished and his character development seems more refined than in his first collection. This increased subtlety allows a deeper examination of the complex nuances of meaning lying between right and wrong. At the same time his graphic, increasingly ironic depictions of violence are always used to heighten the importance of key points in the stories, never just for shock value.

The Actes and Monuments begins with the title story (first published in *The Sewanee Review*, Winter 1975), in which Harry Cohen, a thirty-eight-year-old Jewish lawyer, begins to question the value of his life after suffering a nearly fatal heart attack. The title is a reference to John Fox's *Actes and Monuments of These Latter Perilous Days* (1563), better known as his *Book of Martyrs*. This allusion reveals how Corrington, like other Southern Christian writers such as Flannery O'Connor or Walker Percy, see his stories as a means of bearing witness to the powers of grace and transcedence in human life. He decides to leave a job that offers power and prestige and to move to Vicksburg, Mississippi, to help rural African Americans. Cohen's response to his heart attack is to define his fears—particularly those to which one is simultaneously attracted—and to face them:

> I wondered afterward, when I came to understand at least the meaning of my own choice, if we do not usually fail ourselves of happiness—of satisfaction, anyhow—by ignoring the possibilities of perversity. Not perversion. Those we invariably attempt in some form. No, perversity: How few of us step into a situation which both terrifies and attracts us. If we fear water, we avoid it rather than forcing ourselves to swim. If we

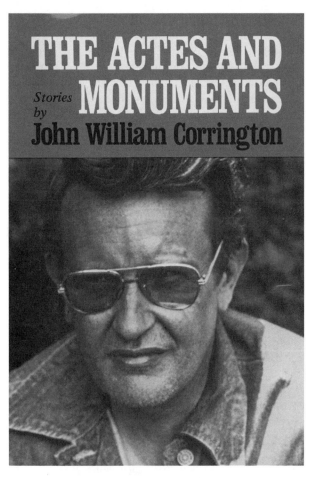

Dust jacket for Corrington's second collection of short fiction, for which he drew on his experiences while studying and practicing law

fear heights, we refuse to make that single skydive which might simultaneously free and captivate us. If we cannot abide cats, we push them away, settling for a world of dogs.

Through his simple metaphors, Cohen demonstrates how he made his life-altering choice.

In Mississippi, Cohen meets W. C. Grierson, an old and philosophical lawyer whose rooms piled with thousands of old and rare books suggest how deeply he treasures the lessons of history. One of Corrington's father figures, Grierson re-evaluates the arguments used in old cases that have been decided and put to rest long ago, considering the principles behind these decisions to help himself learn from the mistakes of the past. Drinking corn whiskey with Grierson, Cohen discovers the true meaning behind the man's love of books and history: the legal system values precedent and interpretation; the art (of life and of the story) is developing consistent moral and ethical codes.

First published in *The Sewanee Review* (Winter 1972), "Old Men Dream Dreams, Young Men See Visions" is perhaps the only one of Corrington's published short stories that seems autobiographical. In his essay for *John William Corrington: Southern Man of Letters,* Lloyd Halliburton claims that this story is based on a date Corrington had when he was a teenager. While kissing and talking about their dreams, the fifteen-year-old narrator, Bill, and a young girl named Helena lose track of time on a date and stay out many hours beyond the time Bill has agreed to have her home. Bill could leave Helena outside her house and drive off, but to salvage his somewhat tarnished reputation, he walks Helena to the door to face her father. There he has a disorienting encounter with the angry man, who has become so anxious about his daughter while waiting that he breaks down in tears. Courage seems to come naturally to Corrington's characters once they see the ramifications of their actions.

"Pleadings," first published in *The Southern Review* (Winter 1976), depicts a lawyer worn down by his practice and developing a personal attachment to a client. Howard Bedlow tells his lawyer that, as the result of an adulterous affair, his wife has become pregnant and given birth to a deformed child. In fact, however, the boy is Bedlow's own son. The story ends when the Bedlows' home catches fire, and Bedlow rushes into the burning structure to save his son. All three die, fused into one by the fire. The "pleadings" of the title are court proceedings, but they are also a metaphor for Bedlow's desire to hide from the truth. Even with repeated assurances of his wife's fidelity, he refuses to accept fact and take responsibility for his child until a sudden emergency forces instant reconciliation.

In "Keep Them Cards and Letters Comin' In," first published in *The Sewanee Review* (Winter 1970), a man with a poverty-stricken and emotionally barren past toured as a musician until he ran out of songs of his own and took a job as a country-music DJ in California, not a place where he particularly wants to be. When a musician friend visits him at work, it becomes clear that neither man will permanently settle down; they have become too rootless and restless. The musician leaves to smoke his "funny cigarettes," and the DJ talks to his fans while drinking from a bottle of liquor hidden under his desk. "Keep Them Cards and Letters Comin' In" shows how time can gradually grind people down.

First published in *The Southern Review* (Summer 1978), "Every Act Whatever of Man" is one of Corrington's strongest stories. After fifty years of serving his community, eighty-year-old Father O'Malley is comatose, and his doctors are certain the speech centers of his brain have been destroyed. Suddenly, however, while a lawyer, a judge, and a representative of the church are arguing over whether to discontinue life support, Father O'Malley begins loudly proclaiming remembered confessions. Through this recitation of the tawdry details of his parishioners' lives, the past enters into the affairs of the present in a more immediate way than in earlier Corrington stories. Appalled that the priest is repeating parishioners' secrets, even involuntarily, the representative of the church reverses his position and wants to end Father O'Malley's life. The lawyer is the only one of the three who wants to keep the priest on life support.

Finally, as the representative from the archdiocese is performing the last rites, Father O'Malley appears to awaken and look around the room, causing the judge to admit to the lawyer that the legal system has failed in this case. This moment reveals Corrington's respect for tradition, valor, and honesty, as well as his belief that admitting one's mistakes allows one to develop integrity.

Corrington continued to employ surprising plot twists, "quirky turns," and darkly humorous settings in *The Actes and Monuments,* but in these later stories the shifting complexities of his narrators' descriptions, his regional center in the Deep South of Shreveport, and his often graphic imagery have challenged critics to probe his stories more deeply. As Heilman has explained, "The better the story, the more it is like an iceberg: the visible part is vast enough, but one knows how much more still lurks below the surface." Corrington's early work reveals his ability to tell a story well, but the later work is more subtle in its use of details to suggest the uncertainty of life. His skill in employing nuance and gesture grew progressively more powerful, becoming one of the great strengths of his last collection.

Intentionally complex plots, which draw on Corrington's fund of knowledge from his studies of literature and the law, make interpretation of his short stories challenging. Further complicating Corrington's stories is his obsession with the darker aspects of human nature and his examination of topics such as violence, abortion, euthanasia, suicide, lynchings, Satanism, and war. These topics evoked the strongest responses from Corrington as he grew older. Yet, he proposed that respect for tradition and place could help ameliorate some of his characters' pain.

The contribution of the past in shaping the present is a theme in nearly every story Corrington wrote. History became increasingly important in his final collection, *The Southern Reporter* (1981).

In the first of the five stories, "The Man Who Slept with Women," Uncle Shad Sentell is described as a womanizing curmudgeon. Unlike the idolized father figures in "Reunion" and "A Time to Embrace," Shad is demythologized, seducing a nurse while visiting the nephew he has injured.

First published in *The Southern Review* (Winter 1980), "Nothing Succeeds" is about extremism. Corrington describes the childhood room of Lancelot Boudreaux in language similar to that with which he presented the lawyer's library in "Pleadings." Boudreaux's cluttered and disheveled room represents the mind of a man who has studied widely, but his lack of discipline has driven him to madness. A cult leader in California, Boudreaux, with degrees in everything from physics to medicine, is an evil, counterculture deity figure. Surrounded by his shallow believers, he lacks authenticity. Landry and Fourier, two lawyers who travel to Boudreaux's decadent, urban realm to inform him of the immense fortune he has inherited from his grandfather, are daunted by the dark twists of the city. The story displays the blurry lines of moral ambiguity. When Landry tracks down Boudreaux, the two men reminisce and drink brandy like Southern gentlemen. Landry's sense of tradition helps Boudreaux reconnect with the Southern culture he left behind.

In "A Day in Thy Court" the life of a successful lawyer is shattered by the death of his wife. Corrington juxtaposes memories of life and love in disturbing, almost surreal images: the man's thoughts of his wife are linked to simple things he notices while fishing. Now dying of cancer, he imagines his oat-cell carcinoma as a living organism hunting him. Staring at the shore and the water, he reflects on his accomplishments and mourns his wife. As her image floats back into his mind, he commits suicide by leaping into the river. The concluding sentence takes him to eternity with a simple image: "A court adjourned, another opening." This sense of completion is new to Corrington's work, developed through maturation.

Showing different aspects of his mature vision, "The Great Pumpkin" portrays deeply disturbing sexual violence. When punks in Halloween costumes invade the home of a peacefully retired couple, the Twittys, Mr. Twitty picks up a sawed-off shotgun and shoots the hooligans while they are assaulting his wife. In a perverse plot twist the authorities, misguided by the impression that the punks are harmless local boys, put Mr. Twitty in jail instead. Twitty's wife dies from her injuries, and Mr. Twitty is beaten to death in his cell. With a moral ambiguity that is common in Corrington's late stories, "The Great Pumpkin" mixes dark humor with compassion. Society, the story implies, is unaware of the depths of its depravity, and in its ignorance it is capable of swal-

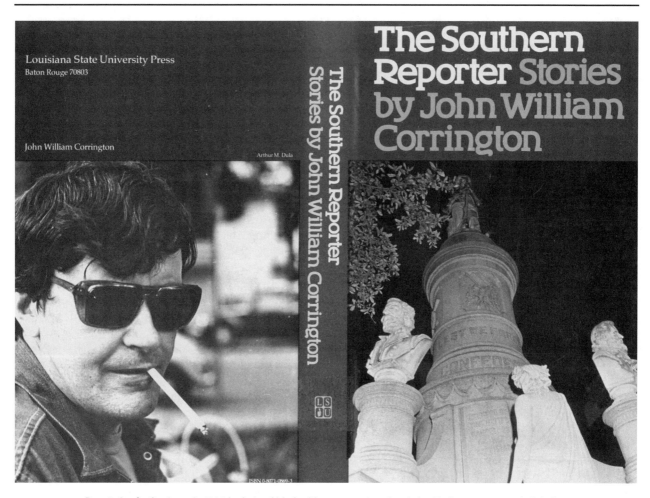

Dust jacket for Corrington's 1981 book, in which the title story examines the relationship between revenge and the law

lowing the story of the boys' innocence and Twitty's guilt. Yet, Corrington shows his readers Twitty's core values and his willingness to stand up for them.

The title story, "The Southern Reporter," one of Corrington's longest, is a study of the relationship between revenge and the law, a major theme of Corrington's later work. He was deeply concerned with how justice manifests itself as an organized belief system. The reporter, Dewey Domingue, feels a moral obligation to avenge a violent rape because the courts failed to accomplish the task. Like many of the killers in Corrington's fiction, Domingue has only one means of escape after his act, to turn the gun on himself. Protecting the voiceless becomes a cause worth dying for.

A previously uncollected story, "Heroic Measures / Vital Signs," was published in the Fall 1986 issue of *The Southern Review* before it was included in *The Collected Stories of John William Corrington* (1990). As Harry Rawls's daughter, Doreen, lies in a coma after a car accident, his former wife and her spiritual guru want to declare her brain-dead, but some

believe she can recover. As the confused Rawls is drinking in a bar, he remembers that Doreen once told him he had to do more than "watch and listen" if he wanted to have a life. Gradually he realizes that Doreen's life has become a symbol of commitment. This realization, however, does not help Harry accept that his daughter will not recover. His anger boils over, and, in an act of violent panic he shoots the man his former wife has brought to the hospital.

Heilman has referred to Corrington's "ambiguity" and "inconclusiveness" as a "tincture of mystery." Corrington's increasing sense of the ambiguous nature of morality is also apparent in the four New Orleans mystery novels that he wrote with his wife, Joyce. Certainty rarely plays a role in his short stories, and as his sensibilities developed over time the line between good and evil became less and less apparent.

In his fiction Corrington artfully balanced a world of evil with a less obvious world of good. War, justice, and revenge are balanced by family, tradition, and hope. Corrington's well-constructed plot twists mix with his subtle, dark humor to create a world of honest characters somehow managing to survive. Corrington's "quirky turns" and his stylistic integrity enabled him to re-create traditional Southern themes in new, credible ways and to make the often violent aspects of human affairs somehow familiar and oddly redeemable but never glamorized. Over and over Corrington's stories teach the reader that honoring the lessons of the past and respecting history can prevent repeating its mistakes.

Corrington's short stories were included in *The Best American Short Stories* volumes for 1972, 1976, and 1977 and the 1976 O. Henry Awards collection. Other than *John William Corrington: The Southern Man of Letters* (1994), a collection of essays written by friends and associates, little attention has been paid to his work. John William Corrington died from a heart attack on 24 November 1988 at the age of fifty-six.

Interview:

Interview conducted 4 September 1981, *Contemporary Authors Online* <www.galenet.com>.

Bibliography:

Joyce H. Corrington, "A Complete Bibliography of the Works of John William Corrington," in *John William Corrington: Southern Man of Letters,* edited by William Mills (Conway, Ark.: UCA Press, 1994), pp. 202–228.

References:

Joseph M. Flora and Robert Bain, eds., *Contemporary Fiction Writers of the South* (Westport, Conn.: Greenwood Press, 1993), pp. 83–90;

William Mills, ed., *John William Corrington: Southern Man of Letters* (Conway, Ark.: UCA Press, 1994);

Lewis P. Simpson, "Southern Fiction," in *The Harvard Guide to Contemporary American Writers,* edited by Daniel Hoffman (Cambridge, Mass.: Harvard University Press, 1979), pp. 179–184.

Papers:

John William Corrington's journals are at the Samuel P. Peters Research Center of Centenary College in Shreveport, Louisiana.

R. H. W. Dillard

(11 October 1937 –   )

Joseph McNicholas
State University of New York at Oneonta

See also the Dillard entry in *DLB 5: American Poets Since World War II, First Series.*

BOOKS: *The Day I Stopped Dreaming about Barbara Steele, and Other Poems* (Chapel Hill: University of North Carolina Press, 1966);

News of the Nile: A Book of Poems (Chapel Hill: University of North Carolina Press, 1971);

After Borges: A Sequence of New Poems (Baton Rouge: Louisiana State University Press, 1972);

The Book of Changes: A Novel (Garden City, N.Y.: Doubleday, 1974);

Horror Films (New York: Monarch Press, 1976);

The Greeting: New & Selected Poems (Salt Lake City: University of Utah Press, 1981);

The First Man on the Sun: A Novel (Baton Rouge: Louisiana State University Press, 1983);

Understanding George Garrett (Columbia: University of South Carolina Press, 1988);

Just Here, Just Now: Poems (Baton Rouge: Louisiana State University Press, 1994);

Omniphobia: Stories (Baton Rouge: Louisiana State University Press, 1995);

Sallies: Poems (Baton Rouge: Louisiana State University Press, 2001).

OTHER: Oliver Goldsmith, *The Vicar of Wakefield,* introduction by Dillard (New York: Harper, 1965);

"The Little Man with the Long Red Hair," in *The Girl in the Black Raincoat,* edited by George Garrett (New York: Duell, Sloan & Pearce, 1966), pp. 317–338;

"Even a Man Who Is Pure at Heart: Poetry and Danger in the Horror Film," in *Man and the Movies,* edited by W. R. Robinson (Baton Rouge: Louisiana State University Press, 1967), pp. 60–96;

The Experience of America: A Book of Readings, edited by Dillard and Louis D. Rubin Jr. (New York: Macmillan, 1969);

R. H. W. Dillard, 1977

The Sounder Few: Essays from "The Hollins Critic," edited by Dillard, Garrett, and John Rees Moore (Athens: University of Georgia Press, 1971);

"Their Wedding Journey," in *The Wedding Cake in the Middle of the Road: 23 Variations on a Theme,* edited by Garrett and Susan Stamberg (New York: Norton, 1992), pp. 189–198;

Robert Louis Stevenson, *Treasure Island,* introduction by Dillard (New York: Signet, 1998);

"Nabokov's Christmas Stories," in *Torpid Smoke: The Stories of Vladimir Nabakov,* edited by Steven G. Kellerman and Irving Malin (Amsterdam & Atlanta: Rodopi, 2000), pp. 35–52;

James Branch Cabell, *Let Me Lie*, introduction by Dillard (Charlottesville & London: University Press of Virginia, 2001).

SELECTED PERIODICAL PUBLICATIONS–
UNCOLLECTED: "Projection C," *Roanoke Review*, 2 (Spring 1969): 13–21;
"The Loneliness of Mr. Tolliver," *Virginia Southwest*, 2 (December 1992): 55–57;
"The Saintliness of Rufus Griswold," *Southern Review*, 33 (Spring 1997): 335–343;
"Forgetting the End of the World," *Virginia Quarterly Review*, 75 (Autumn 1999): 649–655.

Respected as a poet, storyteller, critic, and influential English professor at Hollins University in Virginia, R. H. W. Dillard has enjoyed a substantial and varied writing career. Author of a growing body of work that includes short and long fiction, literary scholarship, poetry, and screenplays, Dillard has been hailed by fellow writer George Garrett as a master of "new Southern Fiction." For his influence on generations of students, Garrett Epps of *The New York Times* (7 August 1988) categorizes him as "one of the most remarkable teachers in America."

Born in Roanoke, Virginia, on 11 October 1937, Richard Henry Wilde Dillard was named after his great grandfather. The Dillard family had arrived in the New World in the 1650s and had distinguished themselves as doctors, lawyers, and military officers throughout the nineteenth and twentieth centuries. His father, Benton Dillard, was an attorney and elected mayor (Democrat) of Roanoke, Virginia. He describes his mother, Mattie Dillard (née Mullins) as a housewife who imparted her love of reading on her only child. Though as a child he was not always enamored of school, he fell in love with writing and saw an academic life as a way of fulfilling his dream of being a writer. He completed a B.A. at Roanoke College in three years, graduating in 1958, and went on to a graduate school at the University of Virginia on a Woodrow Wilson Fellowship, earning an M.A. in 1959. He completed his coursework for the Ph.D. in August 1964, the same year he took a position at Hollins College (now Hollins University). The following year he was awarded his doctorate and married Annie Doak (who became the well-known memoirist and novelist Annie Dillard) on 5 June. A year later he accepted a position as assistant professor at Hollins, where he continues to teach creative writing. His work bears the marks of extended learning. As Kelly Cherry points out, his "vocabularies of reference are astonishingly varied and knowledgeably detailed, encompassing among others, science, cinema, literature, art and linguistics."

In his primary volumes of fiction–*The Book of Changes* (1974), *The First Man on the Sun* (1983), and *Omniphobia* (1995)–and in his short stories published independently of these works, Dillard synthesizes literary conventions, moods, settings, and characters. Language, with its potential to operate according to a logic different than the material world, is what directs his amusing eclecticism. Thus, his narratives take on qualities of the absurd, sometimes verging on surrealism.

Dillard's prose is rooted in intertextuality. He weaves allusions to other writers into his narratives while revisiting and reinventing his own themes, linguistic quirks, and imagery. His academic orientations led critic Brian Kenney to say that his fictional tapestry "will be best appreciated by fellow academics and students of writing" (*Library Journal*, 15 March 1995). In spite of formal experimentalism, however, his themes appear fairly conventional for twentieth-century authors, as he addresses male and female sexuality (both fear of and overindulgence in), consumption (both gastronomic and commercial), death (of the body and mind), and a hyperextended self-awareness. Dillard introduces these subjects with ironic humor and irreverent playfulness.

Although several artists and thinkers influence Dillard (whose writing often begins with and plays upon quotation), Russian-American Vladimir Nabokov and Argentine Jorge Luis Borges figure prominently in both his fiction and criticism. For example, in *The Sounder Few: Essays from "The Hollins Critic"* (1971) Dillard explains that the author of *Lolita* (1955) and *Pale Fire* (1962) "plays God and Fate to his characters, and gives us in that game a share of the divine." Similarly, Dillard imbues his stories with a sense of authorial divinity, even whimsy. While Dillard's characters express their individuality in quirky ways, their overall behavior seems ruled by forces outside themselves. The reader feels sympathy for them, trapped as they are within a perverse universe ruled by a sadistic, albeit comic, intelligence.

Traces of Borges's labyrinthine plots can be seen in many of Dillard's short stories, in which the challenge to the characters is to figure out just what kind of world they inhabit. Dillard seems to view this struggle with the highest regard: "to be able to see the perplexed artistry of the pattern in which one lives and sees is to be able to take real pleasure in the moment and to live truly." He often foregrounds a character's ability or inability to perceive that pattern. Dillard also tips his hand to the reader, who observes the interplay between reality and fiction, as in "Projection C" (1969). Finally, he invents stories that promise revelation but simultaneously confound it through nontraditional uses of time and place.

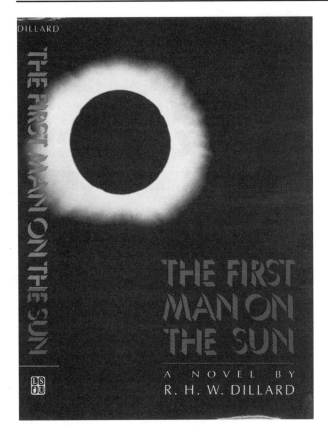

Dust jacket for Dillard's 1983 book, a novel made from essays, poems, and one short story

In 1966 Dillard published his first short story, "The Adventures of Butterfat Boy," in John William Corrington and Miller Williams's *Southern Writing in the Sixties: Fiction.* Later collected in *Omniphobia* (1995), the story parallels experiments in his first collection of poetry, *The Day I Stopped Dreaming about Barbara Steele, and Other Poems,* also published that year. Complex use of imagery and perspective energize both kinds of writing. "The Adventures of Butterfat Boy" also establishes two of Dillard's signature prose approaches. First, he creates a narrative that refers to its own structure and emphasizes discontinuity rather than coherence. Comprised of three separate vignettes, the story begins with a framing fragment depicting a nameless individual in an abject state of sickness on a bathroom floor, waiting for "the Butterfat Boy." The second fragment depicts a character one assumes might be the Butterfat Boy riding a motorcycle, pursued by women in a menacing car—women who (as in a James Bond movie) want to inject the motorcyclist with a hypodermic needle. The sexual liaison between an enormous woman and a midget occupies the third fragment, again a disturbing situation, a postmodern puzzle.

Dillard's second signature approach resides with the resolution, almost by narrative fiat, of these scenes.

The motorcyclist finally dismounts, crosses the room where the fat woman and the midget are entwined, and enters a bathroom, where he collapses—with the narrative suggestion that he, too, will begin waiting for the Butterfat Boy. Thus the work becomes an M. C. Escher drawing or David Lynch subplot, a textual adventure, which uses circular narration to force vignettes that otherwise do not make sense.

"Projection C" revisits and revises the elements of sex, motorcycles, and the power of fantasy. In this story a boy dressed in motorcycle garb goes to a brothel and is paired with a woman who, as in the atom-defying science fiction of *Star Trek,* shape-shifts from thin to plump, from muscular to full-figured. Indeed, as with the psychological rhetoric in Gene Roddenberry's work, Dillard's bent toward surrealism allows this woman to fulfill the protagonist's mercurial fantasies, by appearing as a little girl, a cheerleader, a maid, a prostitute, and a mother. The fantasies themselves resemble a lesson in modern American psychology concerning man's desire to return to his youth, to be the captain of the football team, to be the bourgeois master, to be part of the underground, and to return to the womb. Not surprisingly, then, fragmentary memories of an earlier encounter with the boy's cousin become part of the narrative, and so perhaps a premature guilt feeds the fantasy. Ultimately, the boy seems to understand the intermingling of reality and desire as he sees a woman pass by on a motorcycle:

His legs began to bow out as he stretched his hands before him onto airy handlebars.
"Brroom," he said softly, "brroom."

Boyhood innocence returns in his wonder and admiration, but the possibilities of his future have already unfolded, and that awareness confuses the reader's sympathies.

Another coming-of-age story, "The Little Man with the Long Red Hair" (1966), features boy-men who embark on sexual escapades, ending on an awkward but relatively tender note. Rather than operating in one setting, the boy-men move from urban to rural and to indeterminate spaces—a room filled with cigar smoke, a train plowing through a field of grass, and a tiled bathroom where the title character sits in a tub. As in his other early fiction, Dillard blurs the lines between the imaginary and the real world, for the narrative centers on the infatuation of some fraternity boys with what seems to be a mysterious red-haired transvestite. The boys fixate upon this sexually ambivalent character, who, as they bathe her, rises in a dreamlike state, her hair falling no longer in red streams, but in blonde. The unifying idea in an otherwise incoherent arrangement of scenarios is the impossibility of fulfilling one's fantasy because desire changes it into something new and different. Dillard's transvestite figure maintains an obscure relationship to its environment, becoming an object of interest and repulsion that readers will recognize from Franz Kafka's *Die Verwandlung* (1915; translated as "Metamorphosis," 1936–1938), another literary influence.

Following this early, experimental work, which actively disorients linear reading and deliberately blurs the line between fiction and reality, Dillard became director of the creative writing program at Hollins College in 1971. During this period he wrote two collections of poetry, *News of the Nile* (1971) and *After Borges* (1972). His next work, *The Book of Changes,* presents a cycle of interrelated short fiction whose classification merits some explanation. While it lacks unity in plot, character, and setting, it is labeled a novel; the actual content reveals that its four untitled narratives coexist uneasily. Each becomes a discrete short story or novella punctured occasionally by surprising intrusions of the other stories and by allusions to other works of literature. Stephen Hall, in *The Washington Post Book World,* (3 November 1974), noted that what unites the different tales are "objects—a coin, a talisman, a scrapbook, a mask, a purloined diamond—objects that retain their integrity and tangibility in the blur of lifetimes that revolve around them." Four protagonists—Sir Hugh Fitz-Hyffen, Pudd, Albert Longinus, and Gridley Quayle—occupy each story. These postmodern creations correspond roughly with, respectively, Sir Arthur Conan Doyle's Sherlock Holmes, Mark Twain's Pudd'nhead Wilson, the historical Greek rhetorician Longinus, and Nabokov's Clare Quilty.

The Book of Changes raises intertextuality to a principle of composition, thus making each story a distinctive and often unrelated contribution to the whole. The framing story begins with Sir Hugh Fitz-Hyffen, who maintains several roles as detective, international agent, and museum thief. Unlike the hyperobservant Sherlock Holmes, Fitz-Hyffen is blissfully ignorant of obvious clues in a murder as he wanders through new, ever-changing settings. As a guest in an Eastern European castle in a region plagued by werewolves, Fitz-Hyffen casually searches for suspects while ignoring the blood-caked jowls of the butler. Playing on the convention that "the butler did it," Dillard convolutes the gothic impulse to get to the bottom of things. Blind to the cliché, Fitz-Hyffen displays a dark, mysterious side less interested in solving the crime than in plotting his next, seemingly purposeless, move. The scenario ends with a comic resolution, as the octogenarian sleuth drives off with a young beauty, abandoning his Watson.

An undercurrent of violence infuses the next story about Pudd, a sex-crazed executioner who is fired from his job for a gruesome scene in which he fails to fully decapitate his victim on the first stroke of his sword. Dillard's choice of weapon creates a nineteenth-century atmosphere in conflict with Pudd's municipal bus ride home. Less a character than a point in a constellation of characters, Pudd betrays little emotion.

Also within this constellation is Albert Longinus, who has an analytical mind and drives a laundry truck in Newark, New Jersey—a city known not merely for its airport but for its vast receptacles of human and industrial waste. In the spirit of his namesake, the Greek rhetorician and presumed author of *On The Sublime* (circa first century A.D.), Longinus labors to discover the source and meaning of epigrammatic notes that he finds attached to his laundry bags. This plot device allows Dillard to engage in extensive wordplay, generating nonsensical notes of foreboding and Nabokovian lists that rearrange book titles and authors' names, as in *The Deer Mailer* by Norman Park or *The Book of Dillards* by R. H. W. Change.

Gridley Quayle's dubious claims of patrimony parallel the denouement of *Lolita,* when Humbert Humbert claims to be Lo's father. In these passages Dillard revels in creating mirrored and anagrammatic appellations such as Otto N. Otto (listed as ONO/ono on typed missives) to express his fascination with the "enormously allusive texture" of Nabokov. Through allusion, Dillard seeks not to place his work on any one literary level or within any one genre, but rather to perceive literature as language that can be reorganized and reconceived. In this case, Dillard's fiction reminds the reader of the innovations of contemporary language poets.

Divorced from Annie Dillard in 1975, Dillard was already working on *The First Man on the Sun* (1983). In 1978 Mary MacArthur's *Carry Me Back: An Anthology of Virginia Fiction* included "The Death Eater," later collected in *Omniphobia.* This story focuses on an alienated and self-aware short-order cook who dishes food out to the pedestrian tastes of a local clientele. Through detailed description—which replaces the dreamlike, shifting settings of his experimental fiction—the cook allows entry into the greasy world of the diner and the spectacle of consumption: "I watch them chew and swallow, talk to each other with their mouths stuffed with half-chewed food—pasty bread and grainy burger, split pickle and oozing ketchup, a swirl of mustard, crinkles of lettuce in the mushy mix." Obsessed with the human need to "eat dead things faster than we die," the cook plots the murder of the "Fat Family," obese regulars who shovel food into their mouths hand over fist. Death comes to this corpulent group silently, in the form of botulistic chili prepared especially for them.

After cleaning up any evidence of his culinary crime, the narrator retreats home to digest his own "fat feast" of death itself.

Following his marriage to writer Cathy Hankla on 24 March 1979, Dillard satirized the unhealthy effects of academic isolation on sexuality in "The Bog," first published in *The Iowa Review* (Fall 1980) and subsequently collected in *Omniphobia*. The philosopher-narrator, Cotswaldo, contemplates his life after years of languishing at a small liberal arts college. Dillard makes fun of overspecialized academic work with Cotswaldo's early paper: "Moral Implications of Overcrowding as Exemplified by Desmond Morris' Homosexualization of Ten Spined Stickleback." Cotswaldo has produced a longer work, *Darwin's Bassoon,* which has propelled him to some fame and professional recognition. Notwithstanding this success, Cotswaldo's background exposes the ups and downs of an academic career. Following the success of his book, Cotswaldo is invited to the Institute of Theoretical Studies (ITS) to work on ESP and non-language-based methods of communication. But this institute fails to change the course of Cotswaldo's career in the way such associations are supposed to.

Written in diary form, "The Bog" chronicles Cotswaldo's summer at ITS, a woodsy, remote setting worthy of the protagonist's pastoral name (the Cotswalds are a summer vacation spot in England). Dillard returns to the English canon for literary ideas, particularly in the opening of the story and the characterization of its narrator. The story begins with a quotation by G. E. C. Challenger, the fictional craniologist of Doyle's *The Lost World* (1912). Thus, the reader expects Dillard to engage with nineteenth- and early-twentieth-century discourses of science.

Readers are not disappointed, but again Dillard's treatment of science takes it out of the heroic realm of Doyle and into his familiar terrain of paranoia and absurdity. Cotswaldo and his colleagues work in silent isolation as if, as an institute, they have already moved beyond the need for interpersonal connection. Cotswaldo describes one geologist as having "pressed the mind deeper into the inanimate than almost anyone before him." In Frankensteinian fashion, his own project involves endowing "mindless" matter with intelligence and, inversely, restoring "mind to matter." Keith Mano of *The New York Times* (16 April 1995) aptly describes "The Bog" as a satire of the naturalist genre (with which Annie Dillard had become well associated).

Surrounded by murderous nature and outside of normal social intercourse, the researchers regress to an adolescent obsession with sex. The introduction of a female researcher, Sara Band, intensifies feelings and dispositions of a primal nature. Dillard plays on the trope of civilized man's entry into the wild and his sub-

sequent return to his barbaric origins. Kenney views Band as Dillard's "classically misogynist creation," because although she is a colleague, she is passed around to men who enjoy orgiastic copulation with her. Meanwhile, Cotswaldo suffers a deeper sense of alienation and self-revulsion about the whole state of affairs. He begins to realize that his own goal of domination over nature has been ill-conceived, and he learns to succumb to nature's own form of consciousness, to bring his awareness into it rather than try to reign over it. Nevertheless, his dream of fusing the mind with the material world is ultimately realized when Cotswaldo and Band finally engage in sex. At this moment, Cotswaldo imagines her turning into a praying mantis; to escape the image, he runs into the woods, accidentally plunging into the bog. There, alone, he slowly sinks in a wet, dark pit, vacantly acknowledging the material consequences of this impromptu liaison.

The Greeting: New and Selected Poems appeared in 1981 and was followed in 1983 with *The First Man on the Sun*. Like Dillard's previous volume of fiction, *The First Man on the Sun* is billed as a novel, but its format includes essays, a short story, and a book of poems spliced together. The work exhibits Dillard's genre-bending frame of mind and represents an identifiable stylistic shift. The prose is more contemplative, and the rhythm is slower.

Pursuing Dillard's interest in the mind/matter divide, *The First Man on the Sun* meditates on the historical, physical, and philosophical properties of the central body in the solar system. Through its characters, who are fictional figures and doubles of real people (among them Xhavid, Seamus Heaney, and Sean Siobhan), Dillard reflects on man's place in the universe, human mortality, natural frailty, and the moods associated with changing seasons. The work fuses the worlds of literature, popular culture, and science. In the essays, the unnamed narrator, who is rather transparently the author, wishes to say good-bye to the late Nabokov in one chapter and lists his favorite writers, such as Edgar Allan Poe, Herman Melville, Henry Miller, and Jorge Luis Borges, in another. These authors obviously constitute Dillard's inspirations, as suggested in *After Borges,* the repeated references to Nabokov's *Lolita* in *The Book of Changes,* and, in later work, the quotation of Poe, who affirms that "To originate, is carefully, patiently, and understandingly to combine." This method has, of course, become Dillard's.

In *The First Man on the Sun* Dillard combines the peculiarities of ethnic groups, the Cold War race between the Russians and Americans to use spaceships for discovery and conquest, and the penchant for writers to overly self-examine. To that end, the narrative is written in future tense as a nod both to Irish habits of speech ("What will you be having") and to the futuristic subject of the tale. Set in Dublin, Virginia, near Hollins College, the plot involves international spies, love intrigues, and personal rivalries. Dublin has become an international hub of groups from "small abused lands" such as the "Welsh, Kurds, Eritreans, Basques and Khmers" among others. A bizarre and imaginative story bordering on science fiction, "The First Man on the Sun" takes its cue from a clichéd joke in which an Irishman, not wanting to be outdone by the accomplishments of a Russian and American, boasts that Ireland will land the first astronaut on the solar surface. In response to his interlocutors' objections, the Irishman replies, "Do you think we're stupid? . . . We're sending him, you know, at night."

The patent absurdity provides a counterpoint to the pathos of the reflections in the essays on man's place in the universe and among his rivals. The joke reappears in various contexts, as does the theme of creating jokes at the expense of others. According to Dillard's solarnaut Seamus Heanus, there are those who say "Ouch, help" and those who say "Ha, ha, there's one on you." That categorization structures events as characters struggle to have the last laugh over others, often to find that they have made a mistake. For example, Xhavid has lost his honor in Albania and tries to reclaim it by killing his rival, the Russian Piotr Prostranstvo. The Albanian's last laugh is ruined, however, when Prostranstvo survives the attack. Therefore, acting within a new cast of international figures (as in the Interzone of William S. Burrough's work), Xhavid joins the solarnauts to be the first man on the sun, which he is. However, because of profound interpersonal fusing on the sun, so too are his Irish companions. He is not to be the new Yuri Gagarin or Neil Armstrong; instead he is left in an ambiguous position, perhaps not a shameful one, but not an heroic one either.

Published at a high point during the Ronald Reagan era of the Cold War, the book manages to escape facile geopolitical binaries, while it jumps beyond the standard narrative boundaries as well. One of the solarnauts, Sean Siobhan, writes a book of poems, *Confessions of an Irish Solarnaut,* which ambiguously communicates his love to his intended while reflecting on the difficulty of communication generally.

Throughout the work, Dillard plays with the formal means of presenting a story. Poems break off into depictions of semaphore. Drawings of objects appear in the text to supplement descriptions. In a self-conscious effort to organize a tumult of emotion, Siobhan devises a list of discrete elements and numbers his paragraphs. One of the chapters, "Pegeen in Love," is further subdivided into chapters. Dillard's efforts reduce the text to absurdity at points because the abbreviations and other

Dust jacket for Dillard's 1995 book, which includes stories written from the mid 1960s through the early 1990s

tricks render the language largely incomprehensible. Impossible dialogues take place between Sean and Seamus in which each is identified only by "S." Lists of people and writers appear, only to be supplemented and corrected by other lists. Cats walk across the typewriter: "fgma X Z   X," disturbing the surface of the text; the cats' typing is then recycled as a message in a secret spy code known only to a political faction within Dublin. Throughout *The First Man on the Sun* Dillard fuses his broad knowledge of genres and plots, his fascination with language, and the ontological concerns that pervade even his earliest pieces.

Collected in *Omniphobia,* "The Road" (*Quarterly West,* Spring-Summer 1985), winner of *The Quarterly West* novella competition, continues Dillard's move toward a more contemplative style, one that draws upon the strength of history and philosophy for meaning. In a departure from his earliest stories, Dillard encourages identification with the protagonist, maintains narrative unity, and elaborates a linear plot. Announced as "A Modest Final Chapter for the Southern Literary Renaissance," and clearly a satire on that tradition, the story recounts the difficulty and pain involved for the protagonist, Abel Boyd, in revisiting the South of his childhood. In the recent past, Boyd's grandfather wielded political and racial privilege over the largely black community. More specifically, he lobbied for a main artery in the county to veer from its likely course to serve his own ends. That decision leaves the black town isolated, creates a conduit for bootleggers, and actually helps bring an end to his own plantation.

Returning to his home county to better understand his roots, Boyd encounters a community that continues to be deeply divided by race and scarred by the frequent highway collisions caused by the poor design of the road. As in "Projection C," the search for self involves a bizarre encounter with a prostitute, in this case a virgin and devotee of Alfred Tennyson who is collecting material for her graduate work. Boyd discovers her pure state unexpectedly during foreplay and "is struck still, caught rigid and unhinged." Dillard then connects the woman's body with the ravaged landscape, for "in the bush was but a hard and tight-lipped line, the pursed and stern feature of a New England maiden aunt on a chill February's morning." D. Keith Mano, who reviewed *Omniphobia* for *The New York Times* (16 April 1995), interprets "The Road" as set in just such a geography, "some sort of mountainous pudendum." In this case, the "hard and tight-lipped line" is recognizable as Clytter's Ridge, which divides the "long oval" of Slote Valley into the white section and the black section. At the northern limit of the valley, the fateful twist in the road creates death after death. The prostitute's mission, to bring love and healing to the South, paradoxically drives the narrator to suicide on that same curve. Therefore, although Dillard relies on traditional techniques, his plots continue to frustrate ordinary beliefs in right and wrong, and redemption continues to be evasive.

The desperate, the suicidal, and the hopeless inspire Dillard's next major short fiction, "Omniphobia" (*New Virginia Review*, 1988). In conveying the fear of everything, Dillard returns to his hallmark fragmentary vision. The compositional technique is closely related to that used in *The Book of Changes;* Dillard creates a mood of disjunction and narrative interruption by interspersing four unrelated scenarios. The scenarios do not present themselves in discrete sections; rather, recalling *The First Man on the Sun,* the paragraphs appear in numbered sequence with the integer indicating the scenario and the decimal indicating the paragraph number for that scenario. Thus, 1.01 is the first paragraph of the omniphobe's visceral account of fear; 1.02 continues in that vein; 2.01 introduces a voice further from the pain of dementia describing the symptoms of mental illness; and 3.01 begins a narrative describing the escape of an inmate from an institution (perhaps a prison or a psychiatric hospital). The most fully developed tale, 4.x, recounts the self-destructive passions of a punk-rock singer. The story, then, is really an amalgam of fragments producing a mood through thematic preoccupation, an abstract expression more than a coherent, plot-driven tale.

Divorced from Cathy Hankla in 1991, Dillard wrote "Their Wedding Journey," which appeared in Susan Stanberg and George Garrett's *The Wedding Cake in the Middle of the Road* (1992), and was later collected in *Omniphobia.* The story recalls Dillard's earlier, experimental style. Dillard resolves this tale of the failure of love through the deus ex machina of a postmodern insistence on the fictionality of the fiction itself. The characters seem realistic enough, however, and the setting is lifelike. Syd and Lorna are en route to a friend's wedding, their children finally settled down in the backseat. The landscape is powdered with snow, and the mood is drowsy and dreamlike. The romance and sexuality have gone from their marriage, and Syd reflects back upon their own wedding night, arousing himself in the process. The straightforward style draws the reader into their personal conundrums and evinces compassion.

Their drama, however, perhaps too real for Dillard, resists resolution. Opting neither for a syrupy solution to this couple's alienation nor for a cold intensification of their distance, Dillard turns toward the surrealistic. As they drive through the snowscape, the scene shifts to the surface of a wedding cake, recalling Dillard's unreal, obscene geography in "The Road." A plastic bride and groom appear dimly monumental in the distance like Mount Rushmore. The sky opens with the flash of a knife as another bride and groom participate in the cake-cutting ritual. The scene changes again to Syd and Lorna's ceremony, presenting a taste of the saccharine promise of marriage. Lorna looks through the "singular moment in time to where the future stretches out before them like a smooth white road curving indefinitely into unending days of delight." Those days, of course, are not to be, as the surreal apocalypse draws to an end their "unending" days without delight.

The star-crossed lovers of another story in *Omniphobia,* "That's What I Like (About the South)" also encounter the perverse fate of arbitrary, writerly patterns. First published in George Garrett and Paul Ruffin's *That's What I Like (About the South)* (1992), the story charts the clash between Roy's desire to find a husband as her biological clock ticks on and the noncommittal manner of her boyfriend, Shirley. Sympathetically sketched, Roy looks for the operations of fate in her life and superstitiously tries to influence it. As Shirley says, "All Roy's choices . . . seem to be made before she makes them." However, Roy overlooks the most telling sign that Shirley is not "the one": his book collection. While he is not a voracious reader, he is an eclectic one, expressing his interest (and Dillard's) "in doubles, in things that repeat." Thus, he possesses the Ed McBain series with detective Meyer Meyer, Joseph Heller's *Catch-22* (1961) with Major Major, Edward Lytton Bulwer-Lytton's work, the philosophy of James McTaggart Ellis McTaggart, and a book titled *Poe Poe Poe Poe Poe Poe Poe* (1972). He even orders mahimahi at restaurants. Thus, when Shirley meets a woman named Shirley, Roy's fate is sealed.

Like "Their Wedding Journey" and "The Adventures of Butterfat Boy," "That's What I Like (About the South)" resolves itself less through the logic of human activity or philosophical ruminations than through play with formal elements of repetition, of transposing one level of reality, in this case fascination with double names, onto another level of reality, such as the choice of romantic partner. At the same time, Dillard's tale parodies formulaic prescriptions for Southern literature by organizing itself around seven qualities of the genre outlined by editor Shannon Ravenel, including deep involvement in place, family bonds, and the celebration of eccentricity. In satirizing such categorizations, Dillard points out the shortcomings of critical work and hints at the stultifying effects of attempts to organize reality.

In that sense, "The Loneliness of Mr. Tolliver" (1992) continues Dillard's vexed tone of sympathy with human characters. A brief character sketch, a slice-of-life poem about a retired widower who lives with a cat and dog, the story introduces dreams as simple wish fulfillment. Mr. Tolliver spends another Christmas alone; he has forsaken the Christmas rituals and retires early to bed. He dreams of his wife and wakes to his cat and dog in the cold darkness before falling into a dreamless sleep. It is tempting to read the nostalgic tale as another turning point for Dillard as he explores the traumas of advancing age.

Following on the publication of the poetry collection *Just Here, Just Now* in 1994, Dillard's first self-announced collection of stories, *Omniphobia,* was published through Louisiana State University Press in 1995. The book is divided into three parts around the themes of love, the South, and death. Influenced strongly by his academic career and frame of reference, *Omniphobia,* was not a collection for popular tastes, but it was recognized among fans of Southern literature for its craftsmanship. Stephanie Merritt, writing for *The Times,* (22 February 1996), observed that Dillard is "above all

a craftsman of language" and that his "rich, highly-wrought prose draws the reader into a grotesque caricature of modern society."

Combining Dillard's efforts in scholarship and fiction writing, "The Saintliness of Rufus Griswold" (1997) is a fictionalized essay on Poe's literary executor; it claims that only the forgotten dead are free of their concerns in this world. In the piece, the narrator argues that by misrepresenting Poe in his biography, Griswold spared Poe from the pain of being remembered, liberating him to enjoy paradise. Therefore, concludes the narrator, "despite my absence from that list of canonized names, I had done myself a favor, perhaps the greatest favor of all, by giving my life to poetry." The essay continues the melancholic tone of "The Loneliness of Mr. Tolliver," and the preoccupation with the record of literary merit may reflect Dillard's own misgivings over his thirty-year career in writing, despite praise from contemporaries such as Garrett.

In 1999 Dillard published "Forgetting the End of the World" in *The Virginia Quarterly Review.* Another fictionalized essay, this work recounts a moment of epiphany born of the same themes as "The Loneliness of Mr. Tolliver" and "The Saintliness of Rufus Griswold": aging and forgetting. In this piece, the narrator's treasured memory of a fleeting moment of pure love is destroyed at a college reunion. His lost love recalls the episode differently and points out that the song he recalls hearing in the background had not yet been released. The narrator imagines his individual failure to share a common recollection as a social apocalypse wherein the world loses the possibility of communication, purpose, and lawfulness as it descends into greater levels of forgetfulness.

As a formal experimenter with a sensitivity to the sadness and distress of so much of human life, Dillard has created an opus rich in contradiction. Garrett cites Dillard's contribution to fiction as formative of a new type: "Southern writers of the past fit into two camps, the straight types and the off-the-wall types. The new writers fit a third category of eclectic sophistication, and their best representative is R. H. W. Dillard."

References:

Kelly Cherry, "The Two Cultures at the End of the Twentieth Century: An Essay on Poetry and Science," *Midwest Quarterly,* 35 (Winter 1994): 121–136;

George Garrett, "Soil of Hope: New and Other Voices in Southern Fiction for the Nineties," *American Notes & Queries,* 5 (October 1992): 193–195;

R. S. Gwynn, "Stars Bright, Stars Light," *Sewanee Review,* 57 (Spring 1999): 296–306.

Susan M. Dodd

(22 May 1946 –   )

Leslie Haynsworth
Columbia College

BOOKS: *Old Wives' Tales* (Iowa City: University of
  Iowa Press, 1984);
No Earthly Notion (New York: Viking, 1986);
Mamaw (New York: Viking, 1988);
Hell-Bent Men and Their Cities (New York: Viking, 1990);
The Mourner's Bench (New York: Morrow, 1998);
O Careless Love (New York: Morrow, 1999);
The Silent Woman (New York: Morrow, forthcoming
  2001).

A native Midwesterner who spent much of her
adult life in the Northeast and now lives in the South,
Susan M. Dodd writes fiction that reflects this diversity
of habitats and the variety of perspectives that such a
peripatetic life affords. While many of her stories are
imbued with a strong sense of place, Dodd herself
hardly could be characterized as a regionalist author,
for there is no one particular place that she is wedded to
as a writer. As she explained in a 26 July 1999 interview
with *Publishers Weekly,* "I used to see it as a deficiency in
me that I didn't come from deep roots in a place that
had this endless well of history like Faulkner or O'Connor did. The place where I grew up could have been
anywhere. It had no individual character." She discovered, however, that this lack of connection to a specific
place was an asset to a writer seeking to capture a range
of different experiences in her fiction. "I can go places
and soak everything up," she said, "I'm always asking
what it's like to be this person in this place."

Dodd's work is also notable for the diversity of its
characters. Delving into a collection of her stories, readers might find themselves at one moment seeing the
world through the eyes of a forty-year-old man experiencing a midlife crisis in suburban Virginia, at another
moment sharing the perspective of an elderly woman in
New England, a homeless couple in Florida, or a widower in California. Yet, despite their different backgrounds and experiences, Dodd's characters tend to
share certain traits and tendencies. Speaking of the kind
of reading she prefers, Dodd has remarked that, "My
soul tends to jump up and claim books belonging to a

Susan M. Dodd (photograph by Ed Bailey; from the dust jacket for
The Mourner's Bench, *1998)*

certain kind of character–half-cracked, whole-hearted,
pained, brave, lost, innocents who simply refuse, no
matter what, to loosen their grip on such faith and hope
and love as they possess." These "innocents," reso-
lutely individualistic and yet steadfastly searching for or
seeking to preserve the kinds of sustaining connections
with others through which "faith and hope and love"
are maintained, people Dodd's own fiction as well. Persistently concerned with exploring the complexities of
the needs and desires that draw people together and the
frictions that push them apart, Dodd's stories uncover
and illuminate the subtle interplay between the heart
and the mind, between her characters' needs to maintain a distinct sense of self and their quest to understand
themselves in relation to others.

Dodd was born Susan Mooney on 22 May 1946 in Chicago, the oldest child of Mark M. Mooney, an attorney, and Geri Mazy Mooney, an artist. After earning a B.S. in Foreign Service from Georgetown University (where she challenged classmate Bill Clinton for sophomore-class president) in 1968, she worked as a speechwriter for Senator Thomas J. Dodd of Connecticut. On 8 August 1970 she married the senator's son, Christopher J. Dodd, and moved to Louisville, Kentucky, where she served as assistant director of Project Upward Bound and pursued an M.S. in community development at the University of Louisville, which she received in 1972. Relocating to her husband's native Connecticut, where he eventually took over his father's seat in the Senate, she was employed from 1974 to 1978 as assistant director of United Community Services in Norwich. In 1981 she enrolled in the M.F.A. program in creative writing at Vermont College, from which she graduated in 1983. She and her husband were divorced in 1982; they have no children.

In 1983 Dodd began her career as a creative writing instructor, teaching first at Vermont College (1983–1984). She has also taught writing at the University of Iowa (1985–1986), Harvard University (1988–1993), and Bennington College (1994–2000). Dodd is a strong proponent of creative writing programs, primarily because she feels most fledgling writers need a great deal of feedback and support. As she explained in the 1999 interview, "When you're just starting, being able to gauge your own strengths, and to keep going with no feedback is very difficult." Moreover:

> While every writer starts with natural strengths, she has to learn to foster other talents. I was born with an ear for voice, but I had to work on my eye. My teachers told me my early stories were like disembodied voices—they could have been taking place inside a ping-pong ball. So I had to work really hard on the visual component of my fiction. But, finally, one day it was just there—it had come naturally. And that's a story I love to tell my students, that with perseverence and helpful feedback, you can and will grow as a writer.

Dodd also reveals a philosophy that is central to her own practice as a writer when she reminds her students that "at some point in her existence, every artist has to make a choice about how they're going to fail—by not going far enough or by going too far. I heartily endorse going too far, opening up your heart and the heart of the story."

That process of opening up, of learning to overcome reticence and fear, particularly on an emotional level, is central to the evolution of many of Dodd's characters as well. In her first collection of stories, *Old Wives' Tales* (1984), Dodd develops the central themes

that inform her corpus of short fiction and novels—the fragility of human connections, the power of emotional bonds as a sustaining force in characters' lives, and the difficulty of negotiating between one's needs and desires as an individual and as a participant in relationships with others. Winner of the prestigious Iowa Short Fiction Award for 1984, *Old Wives' Tales* also garnered praise for Dodd from *The New York Times Book Review,* which hailed her as "a natural storyteller" who "creates characters, quite a variety of them, who sit well on the page and afterward in the mind." Dodd herself spoke of the collection as an outgrowth of her belief that the short story is a "kind of miracle where beauty, bravery, and delicacy exist" and that the genre is "made to illuminate those moments when humanity burns through its layers of sorrow with astonishing light."

Sorrows, both small and large, often beset Dodd's characters, but the stories in *Old Wives' Tales* typically take these characters through a process of gradually increasing awareness and insight, often culminating in a subtle but life-altering epiphany, which gives them newfound strength to cope with a painful or difficult situation or offers hope for a brighter, more self-determined future. In this sense these stories might broadly be described as having a therapeutic rhythm. Frequently starting with moments of emotional loss, despair, or impasse, they chart the process through which their characters gain both clearer self-perceptions and greater attunement to the needs and feelings of those with whom they are in relationships. Both of these forms of emotional maturation are necessary if the characters are to successfully navigate their way through times of emotional stress or crisis.

In "Snowbird," for example, a retired widower who has migrated from his native New Hampshire to California frets over his daughter back east, whose husband has left her and whose voice seems "to get damaged in transit" over transcontinental phone wires. Though recognizing that their relationship has become strained as a result of the physical distance between them, he nevertheless cannot stop trying to provide direction for her life. In the California desert he remains deliberately estranged from his immediate neighbors, dreaming incessantly of his New England past, refusing to participate in communal activities and rejecting all overtures toward friendship: "Exclusion suited the old man. Having foraged among the leavings of his life to piece together a kind of contentment, he was not about to brook interference." His solitary contentment is invaded, however, by the widow living next door, who, in return for the weekly privilege of borrowing his car, persists in bringing him homemade food: "The old man wished she would simply take his car keys and leave him be. Wished she would keep her soups and puddings to herself. He ate them, of course, but only to get rid of them." While he cannot refuse her culinary offerings, he nevertheless remains stiffly aloof from her, until one evening, she breaks down in front of him, after having just received news of a family tragedy. Confronted with her emotional outburst, he finds himself confounded by "the way some people permitted disorder to take over their lives."

Infuriated by the way she has allowed "her grief to seep through their common wall, staining his private enclave," he is startled into empathy when he catches a glimpse of the old woman's feet and realizes she is wearing the same kind of bedroom slippers his daughter has always worn. This small and arbitrary token of connection between the two women drives him to reach out to his neighbor, however awkwardly and tentatively, to try to comfort her, just as he has always sought to comfort and protect his daughter. Utterly distraught, the widow hardly responds to his clumsy ministrations. Yet, in the act of committing them, the old man discovers that his emotional life is not in fact all behind him, in the past in New England, that the present too demands his careful attention. That night, in a conversation with his daughter, he becomes newly attuned to her emotional needs and is stunned to realize that he has failed her. Determining to bridge the literal space between them by visiting her, he finds that by the simple act of making this decision he has begun to bridge their emotional distance as well.

Emotional barriers thrown into sharper relief by a character's concern with physical barriers also constitute a central theme of the story "Walls." A young woman does not want to marry her live-in boyfriend and is forced to confront the reasons for her reticence after repeatedly listening to her next-door neighbor crying over the death of her child. "It's strange, and sort of terrible," she muses, "how you can practically live with somebody, nothing but a flimsy piece of beaver-board and some pipe and wire between you, and not have the slightest idea what's going on with them." Yet, she comes to realize, the same failure to understand another person is also taking place within the walls of her own apartment. As her boyfriend pushes her to get married, their relationship begins to deteriorate. "Getting married seems like rope to me," she says, "if it doesn't strangle you, you trip on it. Why take the chance? We'd talk and talk and get no place fast. Finally we'd go to bed feeling all used up and empty." Already divorced after an earlier, disastrous marriage to her high-school boyfriend, she finds herself unwilling to let her emotional barriers dissolve completely. As they both sit listening to their neighbor wailing over her dead son, over the loss of a child loved without reservation, the narrator's boyfriend tells her, "That's what you're afraid of"—a truth she cannot deny but is unwilling to change: "I tried to think of something to say, but sometimes there just isn't any use talking. I knew what Ray was thinking: he was wishing that wall wasn't there. But I was glad it was. The difference between us . . . I guess that's what it comes down to." She ultimately discovers walls and concealments are perhaps an inevitable part of any relationship, and while confronting them may cause moments of emotional strain or insecurity, they need not destroy otherwise healthy bonds.

When her boyfriend decides to visit family in Seattle, she learns that he too has hidden fundamental aspects of his life from her; not until they are driving to the airport does he tell her one of the people he is going to see is his daughter—a daughter whose existence he had never so much as mentioned before:

> So when Ray told me the whole story, it really threw me. A kid—I mean, how could he keep something like that from me all this time? He tried to pass it off like it wasn't all that important. I could tell he was afraid I'd blow up or something. But I didn't. . . . With him leaving, I didn't want to get into saying anything I'd only want to take back later. I didn't want him to, either. Still, I felt like bawling. Not that it would have changed anything.

The connection between them is clearly fragile and attenuated at this point. Both of them recognize this fragility and tread carefully so as not to further distress each other—which suggests that each is beginning to learn, not so much how to dismantle walls as to work around them.

In "Rue," the story that opens the volume, the barrier between Miss Rainey Roth and her husband appears insurmountable—after less than one year of marriage, he abandoned her, never to be heard from again. Now a sixty-one-year-old, self-sufficient businesswoman who has reclaimed her maiden name, has "no time for hazy notions," and firmly believes "nothing was apt to help a person who wouldn't help herself," Miss Rainey is nevertheless haunted by the inexplicable motives for her husband's departure: "It was this, the mysteriousness of John Amos Dudley's spirit, that most tormented Rainey. . . . She could not abide knowing her life had been shaped and confined by something whose nature she failed so totally to grasp." Thus, when she wins $10,000 in the state lottery ("not through luck, but through carelessness; someone had dropped the ticket on the path to her small herb and spice shop"), she hires a private detective to locate her husband, intending to make him look her in the eye, explain himself, and then divorce her.

Perplexed by her need to find a man missing from her life for more than three decades and by her refusal to simply initiate divorce proceedings herself, the detective is reluctant to take her money until she explains: "He left me, so he should divorce me. . . . people must take responsibility for what they do." Her quixotic quest is destined for failure; the result of the detective's investigation is the discovery that her husband has been dead for almost fifteen years. "Seems he drank himself to death," the detective tells her. "Put in a state institution in '65, died within a year. . . . No living relatives, he told 'em." Feeling that nothing has been resolved, Miss Rainey "tried to summon up satisfaction over the loose ends snipped from her life, and she kept about her work." Although she "looked well enough . . . her step seemed slightly less determined, her shoulders less straight. . . . The lines in her face were deeper, yet softer too, as if sorrow had won a victory over disapproval."

Finally, since her husband will never confront her, she travels to his grave and confronts him. She stands patiently "studying the two lines of letters and numbers meant to memorialize him, and trying to recall his face." Even now, his essence eludes her:

> The face of the young Lieutenant Commander was darkly tarnished and dim, and the forty-nine-year-old drunkard buried here was unimaginable to her. . . . Miss Rainey waited. Behind the brutal wind, she thought she detected a waltz. But even as she listened, she knew she was making it up . . . as deftly as she had made up the contentment of her life.

With this insight, she at least finds peace and the capacity for forgiveness, which she expresses as she scatters dried herbs over her estranged husband's grave: rosemary, thyme, and, most important, "rue, the herb of grace."

Another older woman is the central figure in the most whimsical—and yet perhaps most profoundly meditative—story in the volume. In "One Hundred Years of Solicitude" Dodd wryly revisits the world of Gabriel García Márquez's 1970 novel *Cien años de soledad* (translated as *One Hundred Years of Solitude,* 1970) from the perspective of Ursula, the aged matriarch who, in her declining years, becomes a kind of plaything for the children of the family ("They dress me like a doll. A baby doll") but whose mind has only grown sharper after a century of life. "I sometimes think I wasn't cut out to be a matriarch," she muses, hoping that, at best, those who remember her will conclude that "she tried." Nevertheless, she has "a million stories—average compensation, no more, for the time I've put in;" and she has her own ideas about the value of such stories: while, "Naturally, everyone wants to hear about my son the hero, the favorite among those inclined to worship or ridicule. . . . I find the stories of the women in my family more fascinating than the men's." Perhaps, she

concludes, this preference is because "the stories the women tell tend to be cautionary, and lend themselves more readily to my manner of telling. With women's stories, I have an edge of insight, a center of empathy." So while the men in the family create the kinds of bold, epic narratives of which history is woven, Ursula is content to "keep my stories where they do the least harm: in my head." What the narratives that she values most have taught her is that "history is folly. Thank God that is something we don't understand for the first hundred years."

The other stories collected in *Old Wives' Tales* display a similar diversity of characters—from a young woman in Minnesota struggling to come to terms with the way her parents' influence has shaped her adult life in "Coelostat," to a political wife struggling to preserve her own identity in her charismatic husband's shadow in "Public Appearances," to a young father whose memories of a troubled boyhood friend irrevocably color his feelings about his own small daughters in "Berkie." All explore similar themes of individuals confronting the implications of significant relationships with others, and, however subtly, all are illuminated and enriched by this particular process of self-discovery.

Dodd's second collection of stories, *Hell-Bent Men and Their Cities* (1990), again addresses both the challenges and the rewards of relationships, but in this collection she explores two particular recurring themes: the difficulty of understanding what others are really thinking and feeling (and the concomitant temptation to "invent" others' identities based on one's own, possibly flawed impressions of them) and relationships between parents and their adult children.

These two themes are conjoined with particular clarity in the story "Third World," wherein a man and his estranged wife are forced to confront their inability to interpret each other when they visit their daughter, Melissa, dying of anorexia, in the hospital. Narrated by the husband, Stephen, who wonders if perhaps his daughter sees her deliberate self-starvation as "the surest means of cutting us loose from each other, her mother and me," the story explores the feelings of helpless guilt and frustration both parents experience as they watch their child slip away from them. "I am the culprit here," the husband concludes, while his wife wonders, "Have we done this to her?" As they agonize over their daughter's stubborn refusal to live, it becomes clear that, indeed, they, and especially he, have been responsible for her fate by stubbornly ignoring the warning signs as they appeared, believing instead that whatever was wrong with their relationship, they had at least produced a bright and well-adjusted child. When Melissa's weight began to drop, her parents "colluded and conspired, refusing to

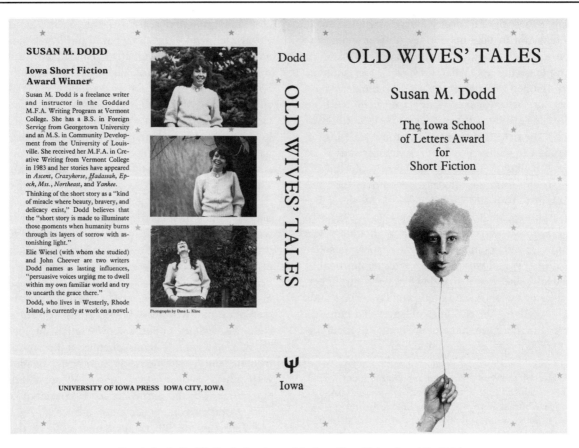

SUSAN M. DODD

**Iowa Short Fiction
Award Winner**

Susan M. Dodd is a freelance writer and instructor in the Goddard M.F.A. Writing Program at Vermont College. She has a B.S. in Foreign Service from Georgetown University and an M.S. in Community Development from the University of Louisville. She received her M.F.A. in Creative Writing from Vermont College in 1983 and her stories have appeared in *Ascent, Crazyhorse, Hadassah, Epoch, Mss., Northeast,* and *Yankee.*

Thinking of the short story as a "kind of miracle where beauty, bravery, and delicacy exist," Dodd believes that the "short story is made to illuminate those moments when humanity burns through its layers of sorrow with astonishing light."

Elie Wiesel (with whom she studied) and John Cheever are two writers Dodd names as lasting influences, "persuasive voices urging me to dwell within my own familiar world and try to unearth the grace there."

Dodd, who lives in Westerly, Rhode Island, is currently at work on a novel.

Photographs by Dana L. Kline

UNIVERSITY OF IOWA PRESS IOWA CITY, IOWA

Dodd

OLD WIVES' TALES

Ψ
Iowa

OLD WIVES' TALES

Susan M. Dodd

The Iowa School
of Letters Award
for
Short Fiction

Dust jacket for Dodd's first book, winner of the Iowa Short Fiction Award for 1984

acknowledge anything awry with our succès d'estime, our perfect child." More than that, however, her mother began to diet with her, and Stephen, who used to call his wife "my baby girl," is so "entranced" by her "revived girlishness" that he "scarcely noticed Melissa at all . . . except insofar as she resembled her mother." In this respect, Stephen's fascination with this new version of his former wife, this vision of her as the childlike bride he had always imagined her to be, understanding her thus in order to imagine himself as being more powerful and in control, causes Melissa, too, to elude his grasp. He realizes when he sees her that "In a sense, then, I've given Melissa an alibi for her disappearance." Moreover, he now recognizes it was his very besottedness with his own unrealistic but self-empowering view of his wife that brought about the demise of their relationship in the first place: "My wife let me get away with a number of things, diminutives and endearments and such. I should have kept account of her allowances. And I might have, had I understood I'd eventually foot an astronomical bill for them. But I was smitten beyond calculation."

As a consequence, he now faces irreparable loss. Melissa, who, lying in her hospital bed, "seems to be watching us, her mother and father, from a vast distance," has internalized the dynamic of her parents' relationship and is now reenacting its death throes through her own relationship with her dwindling body, refusing to give her parents any hope. "Her wishes are modest, even selfless, yes," Stephen acknowledges. "But she makes them known with an authority that is sublime." An appreciation for irony, he realizes, is one of the few things he and his wife have ever had in common: "Not much to build on; but our daughter claims it like a prized heirloom. Keeps it in high polish." Now Melissa has become a literal embodiment of the fragile ties that once seemed to bind her family together but ultimately tore it apart: "How brave she always seemed," Stephen muses, "even as a small child, irony holding martyrdom at bay. Or so I once thought. Now I wonder if martyrs are not the supreme ironists of our species."

Dodd revisits the theme of a relationship held together only by each parent's bond with their child in "I'm Right Over There," in which an elderly widower finds himself drawn to his new neighbor, Vera Cudahy, with whom he feels a kind of kinship even as he recognizes that this feeling may be illusory: "Most of what's written on Vera's face I wouldn't dream of mentioning. But I like to think I read her, understood her, right from the start." Vera has moved to this remote community from Boston with her husband, Paul, who is rumored to have fled the consequences of some shady business dealings, and their teenage son, Liam. As the old man observes them, he sees that "there was tension between Vera and Paul. They didn't bicker, but they were so careful with one another that it made me uneasy." Things are different when Liam is present, though. "The way he transformed his parents was really something to see. Paul Cudahy's face eased and Vera's brightened. I stayed longer than I meant to, just for the pleasure of watching them dote on that boy."

When Liam is killed in a car accident, however, the tie between his parents is severed; Paul disappears on increasingly long business trips, and the widower, normally a reticent man, finds himself compelled to reach out to Vera. When you have lived long enough, he observes, you see a lot of tragedy, and "mostly you discover how little you've got to offer by way of consolation, and you try to live with that." Nevertheless, he visits Vera, who receives him warmly, and over the course of the next few months they form a restful and mutually comforting friendship. As their relationship develops, the old man realizes that he loves Vera, but in a different way from that in which he loved his wife:

> I've always been drawn to quiet women with a look of sorrow about them. Maybe they remind me of my mother, who seemed a little lost, wandering around the edges of my father's life. A lot of women wore that look fifty years ago; not so many any more. I married a girl who was funny, outspoken, sometimes even tough. I loved Fran for her sharp edges. Still, soft, sad ladies can put the squeeze on my heart. I read Vera Cudahy's face and longed to take care of her.

What he discovers, though, is that love can take various forms and result in different kinds of relationships, that one can be in love with more than one person without violating the truth of one's feelings for either of them. Recalling his abiding affection for his wife, he concludes, "But you can love other women. You should, too. You should love anyone you've got it in you to love, as I see it." "I'm Right Over Here" becomes a meditation on the sustaining power of love that comes from unexpected sources because marriage, the relationship into which people are conditioned to channel all their emotional energy, may not always provide the sustenance that it is imagined to hold. Those who have and exercise the capacity to recognize the existence of other, less conventional kinds of love will find their lives infinitely enriched by it.

Love can, however, also be a destructive force in Dodd's fiction, as it is in the sly and playful but sharply observed "The Great Man Writes a Love Story," in which a young woman who serves as secretary to a celebrated writer reflects on the treacherous permeability of the boundary between art and life. Caustically self-aware and defiantly self-conscious as a narrator—"I may get us lost" she warns the reader from the start. "Would you mind? Are you coming? What if there is, finally, no end? Would that be too awful for you?"—she describes the process by which she enters into a love affair with her employer despite knowing that neither he nor such a relationship is particularly good for her. "Those deprived of the company of Great Men," she remarks, "presume that consorting with greatness is like edging close to a fire. . . . In short, greatness is perceived as wildfire, wondrous and contagious. But in fact a kind of opposite is true. The stature of a Great Man scales down his intimates to miniatures. The vitality of Great Men is sucked from the marrow of slight bones."

The affair begins when his wife suggests that he write a love story, a project about which he seeks his secretary's advice. Rather than writing one, however, he enacts one, seducing his secretary with a crude pass to which she responds with a kind of passive submission: "the Great Man had concluded I could enlarge and enliven his knowledge of love. . . . It cost me little to yield to him. Or so I thought at the time." As the affair continues, she recognizes that it is depleting them both, robbing her of autonomy and self-determination and him of the creative power it purportedly was supposed to inspire. Thus she determines to leave him, only to find herself incapable of doing so when he mocks her plans to go abroad, for even in his mockery she recognizes sorrow and supplication. "The pathos of Great Men," she concludes, "is, I think, that they have so little hand in their own greatness. And so they are pursued to the heights by a sense of irretrievable loss." Admitting that she is frustrated by the very lack of a clear sense of resolution or closure that she feared from the start of her story, and concerned that as a result of her entanglement with the Great Man, "I have fallen out of love with my own mind," the narrator nevertheless continues—albeit with obviously mixed feelings—to pursue "the exhausting work of reinventing love."

Love, and the shifts in perspective it can bring about, is also the central theme of the title story of the volume. "Hell-Bent Men and Their Cities" chronicles the genesis of a relationship between two people who ostensibly have little in common: a woman who lives quietly in the country, where she is habituated to living "life on a reduced scale," and a man who lives on an extravagantly wealthy scale in New York City. When they meet at the home of mutual friends in the suburbs—a literal middle ground between their respective worlds—she is drawn to him but, because their lives are so different, she doubts the validity of her impressions of him: "She had tried to read things into his ruined shoes, like a gypsy woman short on cash grasping at the dregs of a tourist's teacup. Yes, the whole of him, filling her mind, was pieced together from circumstantial evidence. Unsubstantiated. Something she had made up as she went along." Even when he invites her to visit him in the city and clearly indicates that her feelings for him are reciprocated, she continues to approach the relationship with trepidation. "Here, now, in the city with a lover," she realizes, "she was at a loss, sure everything she did and felt was wrong." Painfully self-conscious, she wants to go home, where she is sure of who she is and where she can put her flirtations with "the fatal charm of cities for hell-bent men" behind her.

He, however, seems to recognize instinctively that she has a "long history of escape attempts" and that her fear of this unfamiliar environment is at its heart a fear of intimacy; he refuses to be put off by her attempts to keep a distance between them. The meal he prepares for her becomes a metaphor for their relationship itself. At first, despite the richness and bounty of the food, she cannot eat, but as he holds her captive with his eyes, she realizes that "He disapproved of caution, of thrift. Perhaps that was what lovers were meant to do." Newly awakened to the possibility that she can be incautious with her feelings without losing control of her identity altogether, she finds that her appetite has returned with a vengeance. "I'm awfully hungry," she tells him, suddenly confident for the first time that, once she has expressed such a need, he will fulfill it.

Dodd's critically acclaimed novel, *The Mourner's Bench*, published in 1998, brought her national recognition as a writer of great talent and promise. Praised by *The New York Times Book Review* for "the strength of its characters—their complexity and courage; the subtlety of their reactions; the humor, irony and plain old *interest* they manage to find in the trouble that invades their lives," *The Mourner's Bench* mines familiar terrain for Dodd, exploring the lingering effects of a blighted love affair between two reticent and emotionally fragile people with the author's typical subtlety and understatement.

Because *The Mourner's Bench* was such a critical success, Morrow republished Dodd's second novel, *Mamaw*, in 1999. Dodd's father's favorite of all her books, *Mamaw* tells the story of Zerelda James (1865–1911), the mother of Frank and Jesse James, a woman whose fortitude was surpassed only by her love for her family. Spanning nearly a century of turbulent American history, the novel covers her sons' rise to ignominious celebrity, but it focuses mainly on the remarkable

events of Zerelda James's own life. After rescuing her husband from a suicide attempt, she was jailed on suspicion of being a Confederate spy and later had her house bombed by Pinkerton agents. Based on historical figures and historical fact, this story becomes in Dodd's hands a testimony to the sustaining power of a mother's love even in times of trial and upheaval.

The importance of love as a sustaining force in times of difficulty is also a recurring theme in *O Careless Love* (1999), Dodd's third collection of stories. In many of these stories moments of quiet but profound human connection both illuminate and change her characters' lives. Speaking in 1999 about the title of the volume, Dodd remarked, "My characters are not careless, but love is. I think of love as being a capricious and often not benevolent force that undoes people, and lets them down. It forces hearts to open and then plays tricks on them. But the heart that can open itself to love despite a painful history is a real triumph of the spirit."

Perhaps nowhere is that triumph more clearly illustrated than in the longest piece in the volume, a novella called "Ethiopia," in which Nola, a shy and unassuming novelist, meets and develops a literary friendship with Marcus, a prizewinning writer of considerable renown. When Marcus abruptly disappears, Nola summons up the courage to track him down and finds him in a mental hospital where, catatonically depressed, he seems impervious to help. Nola refuses to leave him in such a state. "I know you're tired, pal," she says, "and very sad. So I'm trying not to get too noisy about it. But I am hurling myself against you . . . against what's wrong with you. I'm not going to *let* you be this way." By the end of the story Marcus has begun to heal and Nola has, with his help, become more attuned to the recklessly "profligate" side of her nature, which gives her the heretofore unrecognized strength to hurl herself "against everything she knew she could not remit or revise, could never emend, could only begin to imagine."

Far more lighthearted in both theme and tone—if no less concerned with the difficulties of sustaining emotional bonds—is the story "I Married a Space Alien," which is also a somewhat autobiographical piece that recounts some of the more bizarre challenges of being a political wife. Grace is a divorcée whose life in a small town is quiet and serene until the day when a tabloid newspaper announces that her former husband, Bryan, a United States senator, is actually a space alien. Suddenly finding herself at the center of a great deal of sly gossip and teasing on the part of her neighbors, Grace is also overcome by memories of the time when she and Bryan were married, and she begins to almost obsessively pick apart the reasons why she left him. "That we're entirely different species is something we both figured out a long time ago," she remarks. While he, who fed off being surrounded by adoring crowds, was content to overlook their differences, she, who "craved peace and quiet and anonymity," found that after twelve years of marriage she was more lonely than she had ever been. She needed to leave "to find out what, if anything, was left of me." Still, she thinks now with poignant regret of the early days of their relationship, when they both believed they could be happy together despite their different needs and perspectives. Ultimately, despite its whimsical subject matter, "I Married a Space Alien" reaches conclusions–rare for Dodd–about what love cannot overcome, suggesting that an individual whose sense of self is undermined by the ties that bind her to another person is better off alone. For all that Grace rues the demise of her relationship, she does not regret her decision to leave it. For her the ridiculous tabloid headline contains a kernel of truth–she and Bryan truly are from, and belong in, different worlds.

"Lady Chatterly's Root Canal" is another story that couches serious subject matter in a lighthearted tone. "This is a story about imagination, really," announces Margaret Chatterly, whose "friends call me Lady, of course":

> If I hadn't imagined all those heartaches and dreams to fill in the blank spaces in Baily Randall's clueless blue eyes, I wouldn't have gotten my heart broken again. And if that hadn't happened, who knows what the old man–Dr. Scheetz–might have sniffed out in me when I dropped like a pile of cruddy laundry into his cruddy little waiting room on the morning after my hallucinatory heart had been smashed to smithereens for the fifth and final time.

The "old man" is a dentist whom Margaret visits after discovering that her boyfriend is cheating on her with her landlady–a scenario that is at once so painful and so absurd, "the first thing I wanted to do was laugh." Determining that "A root canal seemed as good a way as any to celebrate," Margaret puts herself in the hands of "a wiry old guy in a bloodstained white smock with a drill in his hand"–hardly a figure likely to inspire confidence that the next few hours will be pleasant ones. Yet, despite the fact that "his office was the color of Band-Aids and had–I swear I'm not making this up–one picture on the wall, the one where a bunch of dogs are smoking cigars and playing poker," Margaret finds that she and the crotchety old dentist share the same wry and stoical outlook on life, and that, after feeling battered and reduced by her discovery of her boyfriend's infidelity, the time she spends in Dr. Scheetz's company helps her recover her native sensibility. Moreover, to her surprise, the dentist confesses that he has

Dust jacket for Dodd's 1999 book, stories in which Dodd depicts love as what she calls "a capricious and often not benevolent force"

seen her around the neighborhood, that, in fact, he has kept an eye on her. "You are really something," he tells her, and this knowledge that, unbeknownst to her, she has been the object of interest and speculation for a cynical old man restores her confidence and sense of self to the point where she leaves his office feeling invigorated, "Like a kid with nothing to lose, like a woman with someplace to go."

Another character who draws sustenance from what is originally an insignificant connection is Junie in "What I Remember Now." A freelance artist who lives alone in a tiny Vermont town because "Solitude suits me. . . . Some people do best on their own," Junie feels at home in a community where people have a habit of "not going out on any limbs" to be sociable. Her relationship with Barter Cunningham is typical: after seeing each other around town for a while, they fall into the habit of saying "Hey," to each other–but never anything more. When Junie goes so far as to append a "How you doing?" to this greeting, he responds wordlessly. "I never knew before," she remarks, "that a person could nod using just one side of their head." Paltry as they seem, such interactions please Junie: "With him I got to be kind of like a kid with an imaginary friend, having him talk to me in my mind. He kept me company at a distance."

This distance dissolves, however, when she runs into him in a Montpelier bookstore one day, and they strike up an actual conversation, which leads to a meal together, which in turn is the start of a tentative relationship. Intimacy is not easy for either of them, though, and despite the fact that both find comfort in their physical closeness, she comes to realize that they do not really know one another at all. Eventually drifting apart, they resume their previous habit of casual greetings when they pass by one another in town, and Junie finds that perhaps this is the best kind of relationship to have after all. "Things I might have asked him come back to me sometimes," she reflects, "things like where his money comes from and how often he cries in bookstores and whether he believes in God." Still, "Distant sightings, a weekly *hey* . . . not a lot to get by on. But knowing he was around, or might be, made me happy in a funny way."

One character who learns, with the help of a new lover, to break through the self-protective barriers she has erected between herself and others is Glory in "Adult Education." Remarking that "I was, as a youngster, forever falling in love—not with boys, I mean, but with old folks, little children, bus drivers and librarians and clerks in the five-and-dime. Anybody who'd bother to show me any kindness." Glory recalls how her mother tried to caution her against such reckless emotional attachments. "I tried for the longest time to disbelieve the truth she meant to acquaint me with. But life makes no bones about teaching the hard way what your mama would try to soften." Now middle-aged and twice-divorced, Glory deliberately keeps to herself until the evening when, stranded on a broken-down city bus, she strikes up a conversation with her seatmate, Gabriel, a mailman with a kind and open face. Despite the fact that it "seems like we did everything backward, Gabriel and me"—for they wind up in bed together that first night and only thereafter begin to get to know one another—his kindness and refusal to be put off by her emotional reticence encourage in her a similar willingness to trust that their relationship can be a nurturing, as opposed to a destructive, force in her life. Habituated to being let down by love, "I lay in that big bed now, the jungle animals all gone tame and Gabriel wrapping every bit of himself around me, and I can't help believing God's come into it somewhere. How else are you going to explain . . . the light in Gabriel's eyes that, when the light goes off, seems enough to see by? Or me, all of a sudden singing?"

Peopled by divorcées, orphans, and deliberate loners, Dodd's stories locate readers in a world where it can seem difficult to establish meaningful and sustaining human connections. Yet, these stories generally suggest that even the most lost souls deserve and benefit from love. Dodd also persistently reminds readers that emotional sustenance can come from unexpected sources: a widowed neighbor, a stranger on a bus, even a crotchety dentist.

Citing literary influences ranging from Eudora Welty to John Cheever, Anton Chekhov, and Willa Cather, Dodd has clearly established a voice and a terrain that are distinctively her own. If her stories are not revolutionary in terms of their use of form or language, they nevertheless resonate with a deep, if quiet, perceptiveness about human needs and human nature. Regarding her writing philosophy, Dodd said, "I'm not one of those writers who spends a lot of time thinking about what is and isn't true. That's just not how my mind works. But I am in search of emotional truth. I'm not trying to create new literary forms, I'm just trying to tell people's stories." Her novel *The Silent Woman* is scheduled for publication in November 2001.

Interview:

Leslie Haynsworth, "Susan Dodd: An Open Heart," *Publishers Weekly* (26 July 1999): 56–57.

Russell Edson

(9 April 1935 –   )

Robert Miltner
Kent State University, Stark Campus

BOOKS: *Ceremonies in Bachelor Space* (Asheville, N.C.: Grapnel Press, 1951);

A Stone is Nobody's: Fables and Drawings (Stamford, Conn.: Thing Press, 1961);

Appearances: Fables and Drawings (Stamford, Conn.: Thing Press, 1961);

The Boundry: Prose Poems with Wood Engravings (Stamford, Conn.: Thing Press, 1964);

The Very Thing That Happens: Fables and Drawings (New York: New Directions, 1964);

The Brain Kitchen: Writings and Woodcuts (Stamford, Conn.: Thing Press, 1965);

What a Man Can See: Fables (Penland, N.C.: Jargon Society, 1969);

The Clam Theater (Middletown, Conn.: Wesleyan University Press, 1973);

The Childhood of an Equestrian (New York: Harper & Row, 1973);

A Roof with Some Clouds Behind It (Hartford, Conn.: Bartholomew's Cobble, 1975);

The Falling Sickness: A Book of Plays (New York: New Directions, 1975);

The Intuitive Journey and Other Works (New York: Harper & Row, 1976);

The Reason Why the Closet-Man Is Never Sad (Middletown, Conn.: Wesleyan University Press, 1977);

Edson's Mentality (Chicago: OINK! Press, 1977);

The Wounded Breakfast: Ten Poems (New York: Red Ozier Press, 1978); expanded as *The Wounded Breakfast* (Middletown, Penn.: Wesleyan University Press, 1985);

With Sincerest Regrets (Providence, R.I.: Burning Deck, 1980);

Wuck Wuck Wuck! (New York: Red Ozier Press, 1984);

Gulping's Recital (Rhinebeck, N.Y.: Guignol Books, 1984);

Tick Tock: Short Stories and Woodcut (Minneapolis, Minn.: Demitasse/Coffee House Press, 1992);

The Song of Percival Peacock: A Novel (Minneapolis, Minn.: Coffee House Press, 1992);

Submarine Bells (Minneapolis, Minn.: Red Egypt Press, 1994);

The Tunnel: Selected Poems (Oberlin, Ohio: Oberlin College Press, 1994);

The Tormented Mirror (Pittsburgh: University of Pittsburgh Press, 2001).

RECORDING: *A Performance at Hog Theatre* (Washington, D.C.: Watershed Intermedia, 1979).

OTHER: *Occurance,* special Edson issue, no. 5 (1976);

"Portrait of the Writer as a Fat Man," in *A Field Guide to Contemporary Poetry and Poetics,* edited by Stuart Friebert and David Young (New York: Longman, 1980), pp. 293–302.

SELECTED PERIODICAL PUBLICATION–UNCOLLECTED: "Dick and Jane and the Mayonnaise Factor: An Apprenticeship," *Ohio Review,* 5 (Winter 1990): 100–102.

Russell Edson emerged during the late twentieth century as one of the most significant practitioners of the prose poem in America. Because his writings, which have been called prose poems, fables, and parables, often resist easy categorization, it has been difficult for critics to locate Edson's work comfortably within the mainstream of American literature. Edson told Peter Johnson in an interview for *The Writer's Chronicle* (May/Summer 1999):

> What name one gives or doesn't give to his or her writing is far less important than the work itself. I called my first published books fables, looking, with the help of this label, for a way to describe the pieces I had been writing since sexual awareness. But fables are message stories, and I don't like messages. Fairy tales say in their openings, we're not real, but we're fun. My purpose has always been reality, and it still is.

Edson's works appear as prose on the page, comprising narratives, characters, dialogue, scenes, or epipha-

Russell Edson (photograph by David Edson; from the dust jacket for The Childhood of an Equestrian, *1973)*

nies; yet, they also include elements often associated with poetry, such as close attention to language and nuance, torqued syntax, density, sound quality, imagery, and metaphor. It is unlike the kind of prose that is typically called fiction and that is primarily narrative, offering instead prose that can use any of the devices of poetry except the line break. Edson has helped develop the rising status of the contemporary prose poem and was a forerunner of the movement in prose toward microfiction, flash fiction, short-shorts, and other categories of brief fiction and prose writing. Edson creates inventive, surreal, dizzying miniatures that illuminate language in an original way.

While several of his early books were self-published, several others have been published by reputable small-press publishers such as Burning Deck and Coffee House, often in limited-edition runs of between two hundred and five hundred copies, or in a run as small as twenty, as he did with *Submarine Bells* (1994), an artist's book with original etchings by David Rathman. Other books by Edson have been published with important commercial presses such as New Directions and Harper and Row, as well as distinguished university presses such as Wesleyan University Press and Oberlin College Press.

Offering a critique of culture, society, family, and identity, each of which expresses and limits itself through language, Edson's work, which is basically anti-autobiographical, tends toward the metaphoric, symbolic, and surrealistic. According to Lee Upton in her 1998 book *The Muse of Abandonment: Origin, Identity, Mastery in Five American Poets,* Edson's surrealism can be seen in his "disruptions of time and space" and in his "willingness to engage in extreme images, to conflate reference areas, and to shift speech registers." Because he has worked in a specialized subgenre, Edson has built a reputation among writers who admire his skill and innovations, though the critical establishment has lagged behind in recognition of his achievements, and he has remained relatively unrewarded by grants and fellowships. If anything, his international reputation exceeds his national reputation as a prose poet, short-story writer, novelist, playwright, printer, and artist.

An intensely private individual, Russell Edson admits to being born in Connecticut on 9 April 1935; beyond the facts that his wife is named Frances and that he lives in Stamford, Connecticut, little is publicly stated about Edson, who, like fellow writers J. D. Salinger and Thomas Pynchon, eschews publicity. He told *Contemporary Authors* in 1978, "I make it a point not to be a celebrity . . . if I have any public value, it is in my published works, not in my secret dreams." Edson's early aspirations were apparently for a career in art. When he was sixteen, he won the Kimon Nicolaides competitive scholarship at the Art Students League in New York City. Evidence of this early avocation is seen in the wood engravings, woodcuts, and drawings that accompanied his early books of poems, which he himself typeset and printed. Woodcuts and wood engravings yield images that are small, iconographic, and not always representational. Once used as the primary means of illustrating books, wood engravings helped William Blake express his visions and later were revived by Edvard Munch for his nightmarish distortions. Like woodcuts, Edson's short fictions and prose poems are designed to fit on a single page, and they range from hard-edged to blurred, from visionary to nightmarish.

Edson is the son of Gus Edson, a former sports cartoonist and writer of the *Streaky* Sunday comic who was selected in a national competition to replace Sidney Smith, creator of the "Andy Gump" newspaper comic character, upon Smith's death. Gus Edson held the position for nearly a quarter century, from 1935 until the demise of *The Gumps* in 1959. Michel Delville, in *The American Prose Poem: Poetic Form and the Boundaries of Genre* (1998), compares Edson's pieces to newspaper cartoons and sees several recurring similar features, including "an interest in burlesque situations and grotesques" as well as "an apparent economy of effort, and the use of the short narrative format." Considering the format for a comic strip—especially the Sunday comics editions, which use ten to twelve frames—it would seem as though a typical Edson prose work emulates the style. Delville notes how "almost all of Edson's prose poems . . . consist of a series of short paragraphs, most of which are only one sentence. . . . The different phases of the narrative, which testify to the author's fascination with the eccentric and the bizarre, reflect his predilection for short 'scenes' with a strictly limited narrative scope and with plotlines built upon a particular detail or a succession of details." Thus, Edson's short "scenes" emulate the small frames of the comics narratives, and his brief dialogues are similar to the "balloons" in which the short lines spoken by the characters in the comics appear.

Edson turned to writing at Black Mountain College near Asheville, North Carolina, where he studied briefly with Charles Olson. Black Mountain College, which operated from 1933 to 1957, was an experiment in interdisciplinary self-directed arts education. The faculty included, in addition to Olson, writers

Robert Creeley and Robert Duncan, as well as painter Josef Albers, fiber artist Anni Albers, choreographer Merce Cunningham, architect R. Buckminster Fuller, and composer John Cage. Black Mountain students included artist Robert Rauschenberg, as well as writers Fielding Dawson, Edward Dorn, and Jonathan Williams. Edson's poems appeared in the 1951 inaugural issue of *Black Mountain Review* at the time when it was a venture of students and faculty only. His first separate volume, *Ceremonies in Bachelor Space* (1951), was published by fellow student Tommy Jackson as part of the student press movement at the college. Whether it was through his father's work with the newspapers, or because Black Mountain College had its own printing press, Edson had an interest in typesetting. When Edson established his own Thing Press in the early 1960s, he handset the pages, printed his own woodcuts and wood engravings to illustrate the books, and hand-bound the volumes himself. As he told Johnson, "I like the idea of one's own shop. The idea of the home-made and simple."

Edson's first books include *A Stone is Nobody's: Fables and Drawings* (1961), *Appearances: Fables and Drawings* (1961), and *The Boundry: Prose Poems and Wood Engravings* (1964). Denise Levertov, another poet associated with Black Mountain College, drew selections from these volumes for Edson's first full-length book from a major press, *The Very Thing That Happens: Fables and Drawings,* published by New Directions Press in 1964. In her introduction Levertov, who identifies Edson's themes as suffering and solitude, immobilization by failure to communicate, and interaction without interrelation, sees the book as a sequence of poems that "begins with marriage as a story of mutual destruction and leads through the deformation of offspring to the wan hope for the possible escape of the survivors." Regardless of themes that "sound grim," Levertov praises Edson for stories that are "wildly funny. It's as if *King Lear* had been written and illustrated by Edward Lear."

Part of what lends humor to Edson's pieces is the sense of surrealism that infuses his work, allowing him to liberate pictorial ideas from their traditional associations and to explore the juxtaposition of unexpected objects within a fantasy atmosphere. In "The Plaything," for example, Edson offers such metamorphosis as a man's left leg turning into a wheel, one of his arms turning into a canoe paddle, and his head turning into "a child's fort with lead soldiers along its ramparts." The man, however, is not distraught or diminished, but rather amusedly transformed: he considers the wheel to be "quite ingenious of God; the plaything from that distance must be amusing." As for the canoe-paddle hand, Edson has the man consider the inevitability of change: "And why not? he murmurs, if it happens it is surely possible, and if it is possible why should it not have happened?"

Edson, an admitted "neo-surrealist," considers his work a kind of "dreaming awake." As he told Johnson, dream thinking is important to the development of what occurs within the poems: "Dreams create their own art works at night in a language of signs, images, gestures, and metaphor, all in a dumb show. The subconscious does not know how to speak in the conscious language. Trying to put a dream into words is like trying to translate a painting into words." The dream images thus supplant the reality of objects, as legs become wheels, with uncertain metaphor remaining the bridge between the real and the surreal. In "A Man Who Writes" Edson further explores the difficulty of using language to convey meaning. A man labels things on his body—*head* on his forehead, *hand* on his hand—then continues by writing *father* on his father and *dinner* on his dinner. Recognizing the literal, denotative emphasis of his son's actions, the father asks if the son will write *belch* (an abstract) on his belch, only to have the son write *God bless everyone* on God. This leap to the hierarchical, to the connotative, not to mention the campy reference to Charles Dickens's Tiny Tim, emphasizes one characteristic of Edson's work: the quick, snap-shut ending with its faux epiphany and pseudo punch line.

What a Man Can See: Fables (1969) expands upon Edson's connections with Black Mountain College. Jonathan Williams, who operated the Jargon Society Press, was a former Black Mountain student who published poems by Creeley and early editions of Olson's *Maximus Poems* (1953, 1956); further, *What a Man Can See* was illustrated not by Edson but by former Black Mountain student Ray Johnson. One important motif consistent in Edson's work that is evident in *What a Man Can See* is the use of inside-outside substitution, in which the interior of the house is described in the language of the outdoors, or in which humans transform through metamorphosis into objects from the outdoors. In "The Fall," for example, a man who "found two leaves and came indoors holding them" tells his parents that he is a tree, only to be told to go back outdoors so that his roots do not ruin the carpet. There is a sense of loss in the man's being denied the opportunity to grow, to be nurtured within the family unit. When the man drops his leaves, his outdoor prop, however, and announces he is not a tree but a man again, his parents turn around and accept the very thing they previously rejected: they take him to be a tree, commenting as he drops his leaves, "look it is fall." The piece is an example of

what Delville sees as Edson's way of writing in a method reminiscent of Franz Kafka's parable: turning points gone wrong in the narrative in which the protagonist is propelled "into a logic-of-the-absurd sequence, the stages of which are depicted, one after the other, with painstaking, almost hallucinatory precision," leading toward "the most unlikely and uncanny metamorphoses."

The Clam Theater (1973) was praised by Gerrit Henry in *Poetry* (August 1974) for offering "a happy marriage of French Surrealist techniques with a Marx Brothers-like insouciance and haplessness." One piece, "The Kingdom," offers an image reminiscent of Salvador Dali, as the narrator, who states that he is "living in his mind," observes that "my watch is melting on my wrist." Henry further commented upon the humor in these pieces, observing how these short prose poems "abound with puns, literary 'sight gags,' metaphors taken to their wildly illogical conclusions." One such example is the brief piece "The Broken Daughter," in which a man takes his broken daughter to a mechanic for repair, hoping to have her backside pumped up and her hair rewired, but the mechanic tells him,

> This girl needs a whole new set of valves, and look at all those collision marks around her face, said the mechanic.
> I just want her fixed-up enough to use around the house; for longer trips I have my wife.

The representation of the daughter and the wife as cars offers a troubling metaphor concerning the limitations of women in a patriarchal society; as cars, they are objects to be owned and used. Edson explores forbidden content, especially including societal limitations and cultural ideologies concerning women. By presenting the women as cars, as objects, he parodies the kind of definition by diminishment that exists in society, evidence of the dark and cruel side of human nature. Such an epiphany may be evident to the reader, but not to the narrator, offering "failed epiphanies" that Upton says "unreel horizontally, as narrative is swiftly impelled along an irreversible track in which language conventions are brought to an inevitable conclusion in violence." The violence—"all those collision marks around her face"—suggests more than mere language, for the interchangeable nature of lives reduced to mere objects implies the kind of thinking that lies at the core of incest, suggested by the narrator's concern with surface cover-up, and regular use for "longer trips" of his wife after the "broken" daughter eventually moves out.

As Upton notes, families in Edson's work generate cruelty: "Parents destroy children by demands for a ludicrous conformity; their attachment to a symbolic idea or expectation compels them to render their offspring into manipulable objects." As is often the case in Edson's pieces, parents turn their children into extensions of themselves, warped doubles. Equally as often the wife is made into a child who can be manipulated and controlled by her husband, who represents patriarchal authority. To emphasize the ubiquitous nature of such social activity, Edson uses universal tags, "the generic names of Father and Mother," continues Upton, "as if they were symbolic of ritualistic functions in families that are addicted to arbitrary displays of cultural authority," though often these functions are cruel, dysfunctional, and debilitating.

The figures of the old man and the old woman, and of the father and the mother, reoccur frequently in *The Childhood of an Equestrian* (1973). In "The Pattern" a woman who gives birth to an old man, in an inversion of the natural pattern, "wonders if she is the only mother with a baby old enough to be her father." In "A Journey Through the Moonlight," the figure of an old man sleeping melts like wax, drips from the bed, and moves out under the back door "into the silver meadow, like a pool of sperm, frosty under the moon, as if in its first nature, boneless and absurd." Each is an example of Edson's vision of the world as presented in "Antimatter": "On the other side of a mirror there's an inverse world, where the insane go sane; where bones climb out of the earth and recede to the first slime of love." This inverse world is where many of Edson's prose pieces are set, leading alternately to comic and tragic tales. The man in "The Father of Toads," for example, who comically "just delivered a toad from his wife's armpit," encounters a conflict when the mother, who has already named her first child (also a toad baby) George Jr., seeks to name the second toad baby George Sr. The father acquiesces by offering to hide in the attic so that both toad babies can be named George. The shift in mood from strangeness to sadness, from playfulness to pathos, occurs when the father says, "Yes, if no one talks to me, then what need have I for a name?" indicating how public identity defines personal identity. Ultimately, societal functions transcend personal identity as well, as suggested in the wife's reply that, "No, no one will talk to you for the rest of your life. And when we bury you we shall put *Father of Toads* on your tombstone."

As Upton comments, Edson's works are "profoundly political, questioning forms of power summoned in language. . . . like rather remarkable mirrors, they reflect the psychic consequences of

The Intuitive Journey
and Other Works

Russell Edson

Dust jacket for Edson's 1976 book, which includes the stories in The Childhood of an Equestrian *(1973), as well as previously uncollected works*

social and cultural behaviors." On the one hand, Edson is making use of the universal figure, of "everyman" and "everywoman." Yet, on the other hand, limiting a person merely to a social role, stripped of personal identity, keeps that person a stock figure, unable to change self or situation, a kind of paralysis in which problems perpetuate without resolution. Identification of characters as types only—mother, father, old man, old woman, husband, wife, daughter, son, fat man, fat woman—reduces the human condition to one of severely limited possibility and perpetual social and familial dysfunction.

The Intuitive Journey and Other Works (1976) includes *Childhood of an Equestrian* and a newer work, *The Intuitive Journey.* "The Gentlemen in the Meadow" offers a typical Edson transformation, yet this one is two-fold: first, the gentlemen are seen "floating in the meadow over the yellow grass," hovering by the "wonderful blue little flowers," drifting in any way the wind blows them. In the second transformation, the reader is told that "Butterflies flutter through" the gentlemen. Another metamorphosis takes place in "The Feet of the Fat Man," as the fat man literally melts into a pool, his face where his ankle should be on one foot, the hair from his head on the other foot. The fat man is typical of Edson's universal characters; Henry wrote in the *Virginia Quarterly Review* (Spring 1977) that Edson's "concerns, while idiosyncratic as ever, have increasingly become everyone's." But the fat man is more, as expressed in Edson's essay "Portrait of the Writer as a Fat Man," published in *A Field Guide to Contemporary Poetry and Poetics* (1980). For Edson, the fat man is a symbol of the artist, the outsider who must draw from his "own hidden life," and he must work toward "bits and pieces formed from memory," that is, he can craft prose poems instead of large novels and still produce worthy prose. Ultimately, the fat man is "only capable of symbolic work," for, in a paraphrase of Charles Baudelaire, inventor of the prose poem, the fat man discovers "A poetry freed from the definition of poetry, and a prose free of the necessities of fiction; a personal form disciplined not by other literature, but by unhappiness; thus a way to be happy. Writing is the joy when all other joys have failed."

The motif of inside-outside reversal appears again in "The Canoeing," in which a narrator is paddling a canoe up the stairs to the second floor of the house, his paddles catching on the banisters, until he arrives in "the quiet waters of the upstairs hall." The reconfiguring of the interior of the house challenges the reader to consider standard perceptions, and to recognize that any change in perspective generates additional metaphors. Interestingly, the narrator sees "salmon passing us, flipping step by step" which he describes as being "like the slippered feet of someone falling down the stairs, played backward as in a movie," establishing the forward-reverse motif that operates in later Edson pieces. The inside-outside reversal motif reoccurs in "Grass" as a living room is overgrown with grass that stretches through the dining room and kitchen, extending "for miles and miles into the walls." Edson offers variation by adding an upside-down motif, as "In a cellar under the grass an old man sits in a rocking chair," and an age-reversal motif, as this old man "holds an infant, the infant body of himself."

Of Edson's books, *The Reason Why the Closet-Man is Never Sad* (1977) is his most socially charged, taking up many of the issues associated with the rise of the women's movement and its social ramifications. As Edson told Johnson, "I always write what needs to be written at the time of its writing." Delville has stated that Edson's most significant contribution to the history of the narrative prose poem is "the neo-Surrealist, absurdist 'fable.'" In his narratives Edson examines a principle of human behavior, often one of brutality or absurd action or reaction, only he ends by offering the reader an epiphany, an insight, in lieu of the stock moral of a fable; in many cases, the absurdity is the only "moral." Additionally, Edson appropriates the classic beast fable, stories in which personified animals speak and act as humans; further, he replaces the beasts with objects, at times through metamorphosis, inventing the "object fable," that is, stories in which personified objects speak and act as humans.

In "The Double Bed" a woman turns into a double bed: "The time was coming when she could no longer be able to leave the house, when she would have to remain in one of the bedrooms." Edson's transformation of the woman into a double bed is a case of metonymy: the sexual connotation of the double bed reduces the woman to a sexual object, as is evident when the father says, "perhaps if she had gotten married there would have been a man in her double bed, and she wouldn't have to become a double bed all by herself." Yet, there is a hint of rebellion on the part of both the mother and the woman, the mother murmuring that "it's such a lovely thing for a woman to become a double bed all by herself," and the woman thinking, "it's a lot more comfortable, even in a double bed, to be alone." Expressing sentiments associated with the women's movement that was growing in the 1970s, these women claim their right to their own independence, a double bed of their own, instead of succumbing to patriarchal and societal dictates concerning their own bodies.

The "zero population" movement toward childless families during the 1970s is considered in "The Parental Decision," a piece concerning a couple who have decided not to have any children:

> A man splits into two who are an old woman and an old man.
> They must be his parents. But where is the man? Perhaps he gave his life for them.

A man marries and divides his life with his spouse, like their respective parents—only in Edson's world, they are old the moment they commit to being childless. The query "where is the man?" pertains both to the child who never was, and thus will never achieve manhood, and to the man who, procreation deferred, cannot be defined by his biological role.

"Erasing Amyloo" addresses another societal change of the 1970s, the issue of abortion:

A father with a huge eraser erases his daughter. When he finishes there's only a red smudge on the wall.

His wife says, where is Amyloo?

She's a mistake, I erased her.

The patriarchal figure of the father controls the fate of the daughter, while the woman is not allowed to control her own body or choices concerning it; the father is the one who deems Amyloo a mistake and acts alone to erase her. The simplicity of erasure works as a metaphor to explain the action of abortion, a quick fix of a mistake, or unwanted pregnancy. The incident is pushed further by the father dictating his wife's response as he erases Amyloo from his wife's memory with the same eraser, in essence making the wife jettison, like the husband, any sense of conscience. When the wife asks her husband "Are you my Amyloo, whom I don't remember anymore?" he replies with the question "Do I look like a girl?" With the wife's confused final line, "I don't know, I don't know what anything looks like anymore," Edson shows the societal and biological disruptions to the psyche that occur when women have abortions, making clear what Upton identifies as "the cultural vulnerability of women" who are "in one way or another, expunged—by political will, by the patriarchal family, and by metaphorical construction."

This issue continues in "The Pregnant Ones" as a pregnant woman's husband and two doctors become pregnant themselves, so that, rather than the act of her giving birth being the central event of the narrative, she is abandoned as the "three men argue about names for their own unborn children, which they fully expect will be sons." Upton notes how this reaction demonstrates men's "anxieties about women and reproduction," as they "take on the pregnant woman's experience as their own and further suppress difference by presuming that their offspring will be male, that is, gender duplicates of themselves."

Black humor pervades these pieces; as Donald Hall commented in *The Atlantic Monthly* (October 1977), Edson's work is "fanciful, it's even funny—but this humor carries discomfort with it, like all serious humor." Concerning his use of humor, Edson told Johnson that "there's nothing wrong with a sad prose poem as long as it's funny. The sense of the funny is the true sense of the tragic. That's what *funny* is all about." One piece in *The Reason Why the Closet-Man is Never Sad* that offers counterbalancing humor, or verbal and visual sleight of hand, is "The Taxi." This surrealist romp utilizes the forward-reverse motif, with some carryover of the indoor-outdoor motif: in the first paragraph a taxi crashes through the wall of a third-floor apartment, amazing both narrator and reader when it is revealed that "the yellow driver is really a cluster of canaries arranged in the shape of a driver, who flutters apart, streaming from the windows of the taxi in yellow fountains." In the second paragraph the narrator, realizing that he is "in the midst of something splendid," reverses the action by canceling the taxi, an act that causes the canaries to reassemble themselves into the shape of a man, though in the third paragraph, the narrator calls again for the taxi, and the action begins again. This cinematographic effect, much like playing with forward and reverse on the old-fashioned film projectors or on a VCR, is certainly entertaining. Reducing life experiences to replicable acts, however, is also a limitation, a denial of the endless open possibilities of human experience.

Edson suggests the human tendency toward denial in the title piece, "The Reason Why the Closet-Man is Never Sad," in which the house is used as a metaphor for those who live within; it is also, according to Upton, "a symbol of unchallenged forms of relationship" that not only confine body space but also "restrict the occupants' range of emotions and their ability to initiate any possible redemptive actions." Thus, the closet-man chooses to live in a house that has "no rooms, just hallways and closets," and closets are comforting, predictable, for "you take things out of closets, you put things in closets, and nothing happens." The fear of experience is eliminated by eliminating rooms, for "*Things happen in rooms*," and the closet-man "does not like things to happen." The endless movement and backward-forward action, the coming or going of the closet-man, the limiting of experience to hallways and closets only, leads away from sadness to, if not artificial happiness, at least lack of sadness. As Upton suggests, "if a closet-house makes for no feeling, perhaps (to reverse the figure) no feeling makes for strange houses, indeed, for closet houses." Edson shows that denial of experience, the things that happen, is sadly characteristic of the American life: denial and lack of feeling lead to acceptance of the kinds of cruelty and emptiness that result from personal, familial, societal, and cultural limitations.

In a 1989 review of the 1985 collection *The Wounded Breakfast* (1985) in *Parnassus: Poetry in Review*, Sven Birkerts compares Edson's prose to "the more mordant moments of Monty Python—unruffled equanimity chirping in the face of some unfolding piece of ghastliness." One motif that Edson has used since early in his career, and often with "ghastly" results, is the motif of having a house take on the metonymous role of the humans who live within it. In fact, Upton observes that among the images of constricting forms used by Edson, "perhaps none is more dominant than that of the house." Edson compares the house to "cultural patterns that enable practices of oppressive violence, particularly within the contemporary family as a site of violence, neglect, and abandonment of children and the aged. In particular, the image of the house discloses calcified forms of human relationships as these are channeled by language." At times, the house is presented in fractured images, as in "How Things Will Be," in which the kitchen "will always be hungry"; the cupboard, parodying Old Mother Hubbard, "won't even find a bone"; and the bedrooms "lie awake at night, blank-eyed against the whispery shuffle of hallways wandering back and forth." In "The Unforgiven" the house functions as a single unit while a man guilty of indiscretions and of acting out something other than his "true self" in a social arena comes home seeking—presumably from his wife—forgiveness:

> But when he got to the threshold of his house his house said, go away, I am not at home.
> Not at home? A house is always at home; where else can it be? said the man.
> I am not at home to you, said his house.

The seeming indeterminacy and interchangeability of *house* and *home,* the denotative physical dwelling and the connotative emotional projection, could just as easily be read as a hurt woman replying that she is not a wife if her husband does not treat her as such. A boundary has been breached, emotionally and linguistically, and this disruption offers the man a failed epiphany, for the piece ends with him "stumbling away into another series of indiscretions" and with the destructive pattern repeating itself. Part of the "ghastly" destructive nature of such narratives lies in their being rooted in the limitations of language and the limitations of cultural ideology.

In "Feeding the Dog" a woman melts her husband and pours him into "little husband molds," a reducing and diminishing act; it is also a controlling act, for the woman still needs the husband to perform his sexual function within the marriage, as evidenced by her "diddling" the little naked husband into producing erections, and her throwing one damaged mold—its genitals did not set correctly—to the family dog. The act of diminishing her husband empowers the woman, who in the end "might melt her husband again. She likes melting him. She might pour him into an even smaller series of husband molds." Domestic violence, another destructive societal force, is explored in "The Philosophers," as a

mother and son seek to define themselves in contradictory ways: "I think, therefore I am, said a man whose mother quickly hit him on the head, saying, I hit my son on the head, therefore I am." The two dichotomous philosophies—violent and intellectual—are not only incompatible, but as Edson suggests, the violent means of self-definition is more powerful than the intellectual means, as the actions speak louder than the words. As the mother states, "I hit, therefore we both are, the hitter and the one who gets hit"; language again makes the final distinction, one that in this case transcends both gender and family roles.

Irving Malin, reviewing *Tick Tock* (1992) in the *Review of Contemporary Fiction* (Fall 1992), noted how Edson's short fictions work against the traditions of linear narratives, pointing out how Edson's texts "disrupt rational expectations. They represent a curious world which has its own sense of time, characterization, faith; they include transformations of men into machines (and vice versa), logic into non-logic. They are surrealists' *transgressions*." Edson's writing, which appears in a faux-simplistic style, reads in a manner reminiscent of fairy tales, fables, children's books, or early readers. Discussing his style, Edson told Johnson, "I've never seen anything wrong with Dick and Jane." In "Dick and Jane and the Mayonnaise Factor: An Apprenticeship" (*Ohio Review,* Winter 1990) Edson discusses his use of a primerlike writing style:

> The first book I mastered was the primer. And it was here that I first met Dick and Jane, and a dog named Spot. Little did I know that this book would become the spiritual matrix for all that I would ever do.
> Simple paragraphs of Dick and Jane living in their nouns and verbs.
> The Dick and Jane stories are flat, distracted by grammar and spelling, and never achieve a true fiction of developed description and story. If the Dick and Jane stories are not great literature, they still provide a holding place where one's own substitutions and inventions can find root. A matrix, as it were, of possibility.

Malin sees this style as a device to evoke a transgressed world: "Edson writes in an apparently plain, childlike manner so that he seduces us to read—to see—the inner workings of his tick-tocks, his universe." The simplicity of a text hides the truth in obvious places, free of adornment and calling no attention to itself. Edson writes in "Portrait of the Writer as a Fat Man" that on the surface, the prose poem "should look like a page from a child's primer, indented paragraph beginnings, justified margins," which of course echoes the typeset pages of Edson's early self-published books. Tension is produced in

Edson's stories by the juxtaposition of competing levels of language, as evident in the story "Breakfast Conversation," in which an old woman "Suddenly" squeezes toothpaste into her husband's oatmeal. Despite the seeming connections between the actions, readers want to know, as Malin asks, "the reasons for her 'sudden' action." In Edson's work, the what is usually evident in the text, at least on its minimalist narrative level; the why, however, is at best hinted at through metaphor or surrealist juxtapositioning.

With the publication of *The Tunnel: Selected Poems* (1994), Edson brought together the best works from seven of his books from major presses published over a twenty-year period. Malin observed in the *Review of Contemporary Fiction* (Spring 1995) that while Edson "has been acclaimed in Europe . . . he has never received much recognition in this country," and suggested that with the publication of *The Tunnel* this oversight might begin to change. He sees Edson as one who offers readers a Lewis Carroll kind of through-the-looking-glass world "of antimatter, a world in which mysterious, strange beauty can flourish." *The Tunnel* solidifies Edson's position as one of the most important prose poets writing at the end of the twentieth century and the beginning of the twenty-first. He is, as Hall noted, a writer whose "imagination is revolutionary. He explores a small

territory, but it is unmapped land." Yet, the personal, familial, social, and cultural landscapes Edson traverses are often confusing terrains, in need of exploration and explication. As Edson told Johnson, "My pieces, when they work, though full of odd happenings, win the argument against disorder through the logic of language and a compositional wholeness." Because Russell Edson's prose style is so Dick-and-Jane simple, yet suffused with the connotative and metaphorical dimension of poetry, his work is accessible, offering readers the ability to laugh equally at the darkest side of human nature and at the workings of the mind at play.

Interview:

Peter Johnson, "An Interview with Russell Edson," *Writer's Chronicle,* 31 (May/Summer 1999): 30–36.

References:

Michel Delville, *The American Prose Poem: Poetic Form and the Boundaries of Genre* (Gainesville: University Press of Florida, 1998);

Lee Upton, "Cruel Figures: The 'Anti-Forms' of Russell Edson," in her *The Muse of Abandonment: Origin, Identity, Mastery in Five American Poets* (Lewisburg, Pa.: Bucknell University Press, 1998), pp. 54–74.

Deborah Eisenberg
(20 November 1945 –   )

Robin A. Werner
Tulane University

BOOKS: *Pastorale* (New York & London: French, 1983);

Transactions in a Foreign Currency (New York: Knopf, 1986; London: Faber & Faber, 1986);

Under the 82nd Airborne (New York: Farrar, Straus & Giroux, 1992; London: Faber & Faber, 1992);

Air, 24 Hours: Jennifer Bartlett (New York: H. N. Abrams, 1994);

The Stories (So Far) of Deborah Eisenberg (New York: Noonday, 1997)—comprises *Transactions in a Foreign Currency* and *Under the 82nd Airborne;*

All Around Atlantis (New York: Farrar, Straus & Giroux, 1997; London: Granto, 1997).

PLAY PRODUCTION: *Pastorale,* New York, Second Stage Theatre, 1981.

The characters in Deborah Eisenberg's stories are often lost. Whether they travel through a foreign country or their own equally alien, familiar worlds, they are on quests of discovery. Throughout her three volumes of short fiction, this theme is consistently honed and refined. Employing vivid descriptions and poignant symbols, Eisenberg takes her readers along into a world that is strangely familiar. Her witty prose and dramatic delineation of character deepen the sensations of confusion and loss that pervade her fiction.

Deborah Eisenberg was born on 20 November 1945 to George and Ruth Eisenberg in Chicago, Illinois. Her father was a pediatrician, her mother a housewife. Eisenberg has described her childhood in the Chicago suburb of Winnetka as a "hermetically sealed" middle-class existence. In the early 1960s Eisenberg left suburban Illinois for Vermont, where she attended boarding school and later studied Latin and Greek at Marlboro College. Then, in the mid 1960s, Eisenberg moved to New York City, where she earned her B.A. in 1968 from the New School for Social Research in the New School College. For the next seven years she remained in New York, holding a variety of secretarial

Deborah Eisenberg (photograph by Diana Michener; from the dust jacket for All Around Atlantis, *1997)*

and waitressing jobs, until in 1975 she "stopped smoking and started writing."

In 1981 her play, *Pastorale,* was produced by the Second Stage Theatre in New York and was published in 1983. The switch from writing for the stage to writing short fiction seems to have been a movement centered on Eisenberg finding her voice. Explaining why she likes the short-story form best, Eisenberg said in a

1992 interview: "I like the bristling, sparky, kinetic effect you can get from condensing something down to the point where it almost squeaks."

During the mid 1980s Eisenberg traveled sporadically throughout Latin America. These travels have had a tremendous impact on her writing. She claims to have visited every Central American country with the exceptions of Costa Rica and Belize. In the 1992 interview Eisenberg explained why she loves travel: "even though there are always horrible experiences . . . the thing that guides you in the ordinary round of your day is not there–the stability that carries you from one moment to the next is gone." In 1986 Eisenberg published her first collection of short stories, *Transactions in a Foreign Currency,* and received the first of three O. Henry Awards (the others followed in 1995 and 1997).

Eisenberg's writing is dreamlike; it projects a great variety of moods different from the narrow focus of many short-story writers. The seven stories that comprise *Transactions in a Foreign Currency* deal with protagonists who, in some way, are alienated from their surroundings. Travel, a major theme throughout Eisenberg's writing, surfaces here both in actual movement into new surroundings and in the inward journeys of her troubled heroines. The narratives reveal the dysfunctional world, and the epiphanies the characters achieve generally center on self-awareness.

"Flotsam," the first story in this collection, depicts a woman's struggle to define herself rather than constantly viewing her identity in relation to others' perceptions. The story opens in a flashback; the narrator displays herself in a relationship that has grown sour. Her academic boyfriend begins to grow more and more fastidious, ultimately lashing out with a phrase typical of Eisenberg's occasionally florid prose: "You're like the Blob. You remember that movie *The Blob?* You're sentient protoplasm, but you're as undifferentiated as sentient protoplasm can get. You're devoid of even taxonomic attributes." In this early volume such passages seem to break up the narrative flow; however, Eisenberg's wit and her vivid characters make such moments humorous rather than distracting. The narrator of "Flotsam," Charlotte, then travels to New York City to live with a stranger, dramatically altering her surroundings and associates. New York is described vividly through a stranger's eyes as the problems of Eisenberg's heroine are brought out in this alien environment. The subway itself becomes mystical: "How gaudy and festive it was, like a huge Chinese dragon, clanking and huffing through its glimmering cavern." Despite the vast differences in the people and places that now surround her, Charlotte continues to define herself through her former boyfriend's dismissive

assessment, living under a smiling picture of him that she has hung prominently in the apartment.

The narrator's new roommate, the stunning, scintillating, and drug-addicted Cinder, leads Charlotte into a new realm. Through her encounters with two men Charlotte begins to break her identification with her former boyfriend and her dependence on Cinder. After-work drinks with her married employer and an impromptu date with Cinder's castoff boyfriend begin to guide Charlotte to a new view of her life. Finally Cinder bursts out in anger at Charlotte, and Charlotte realizes the extent to which her life has been molded by her perceptions. As she prepares to leave Cinder's apartment she notices the picture of her former boyfriend:

> And, Lord–I'd almost forgotten my photograph of Robert. What was it doing up there anyway–as if he were the president of some company? I yanked it from the wall with both hands, and it tore in half . . . to my surprise, I didn't care. Robert had never looked like that picture anyhow. That was how I'd wanted him to look, but he hadn't looked like that.

"A Lesson in Traveling Light" is also about a female protagonist's growing awareness of herself and those around her, but this narrative is framed in a seemingly endless cross-country journey by van. Through this story of a relationship on the verge of self-destruction Eisenberg illuminates the ways in which people understand their intimates through their interactions with others. Despite having lived with Lee for several years, the narrator knows little about him. Through his interactions with old friends, whom they stay with at various intervals in their random journey, the narrator sees her lover and their relationship in a new way. The first moment of this insight is presented almost supernaturally: "Lee and I had always drunk wine out of the same glasses we drank everything else out of, and it was not the kind of wine you'd have anything to say about, so Lee with his graceful raised glass was an odd sight. So odd a sight, in fact, that it seemed to lift the table slightly, causing it to hover in the vibrating dimness."

The story becomes one of watching and waiting. As they travel, rootless, the narrator philosophizes: "'It's incredible,' I said, 'how fast every place you go gets to be home,'" and Lee replies, "That's why it's good to travel . . . It reminds you what life really is." Travel in Eisenberg's stories brings the human relationships into sharp relief, and nowhere is this more apparent in *Transactions in a Foreign Currency* than in this story. "A Lesson in Traveling Light" ends, as do many of Eisenberg's narratives, on an ambiguous down note as the narrator stands alone in a parking lot realizing that one day soon she will be there boarding a bus, her rela-

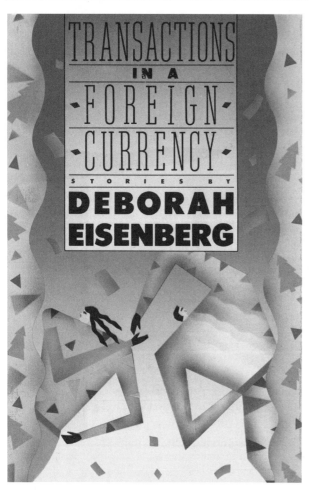

Dust jacket for Eisenberg's 1986 book, seven stories about travelers who experience alienation in strange surroundings

tionship with Lee finally finished. Despite the loneliness of her final musing there is a sense of greater strength and self-knowledge in the final moments:

> I watched the van glide out onto the road, and I saw it accelerate up along the curve of the days ahead. Soon, I saw, Lee would pull up in front of Kathryn's house; soon he would step through the door and she would turn; and soon—not that afternoon, of course, but soon enough—I would be standing again in this parking lot, ticket in hand, waiting to board the bus that would appear so startlingly in front of me, as if from nowhere.

In the end the relationship itself is what must be shed in order to truly travel light.

The title story, "Transactions in a Foreign Currency," appears near the end of the collection. This story, like "A Lesson in Traveling Light" and so much of Eisenberg's work, examines relationships and the effect of travel on a woman's ability to see herself. "Transactions in a Foreign Currency" presents the reader with a heroine enmeshed in a destructive

on-again-off-again nine-year-old relationship. As the story opens, the narrator's lover, Ivan, calls to ask her to come visit him in Montreal:

> I turned with the receiver to the wall as I absorbed the fact of Ivan's voice, and when I glanced back at the man on my sofa, he seemed like a scrap of paper, or the handle from a broken cup, or a single rubber band—a thing that has become dislodged from its rightful place and intrudes on one's consciousness two or three or many times before one understands that it is just a thing best thrown away.

Eisenberg's vivid description immediately sets the tone of this relationship. The unnamed narrator puts her own life on hold while she flies to Ivan. When her relationship with Ivan began, the narrator had hoped for marriage. Despite Ivan's claim that she has "just as much power as I do" in the relationship, it appears to have been rather one-sided for some time. The narrator describes being with Ivan as feeling "as if I were standing in the sun, and it never occurred to me to hesitate or to ask any questions." This story is not so much about a relationship, however, as about a woman finding her own power.

Soon after the narrator's arrival in Montreal, Ivan decides to fly home to spend Christmas with his son and former wife. Left alone in Ivan's world, the narrator confronts her own loneliness and questionable self-sufficiency: "I felt I had been equipped by a mysterious agency: I knew without asking how to transport myself into a foreign city, my pockets were filled with its money, and in my hand I had a set of keys to an apartment there." This feeling is only the beginning of her quest for self-identification. The narrator descends first into sleep, unconsciously fasting, and then goes on a grocery-shopping spree in the clothes that some other woman has left in Ivan's closet. When she returns to Ivan's apartment she finds it inhabited by a waiflike man who claims that Ivan owes him money. This man, Eugene, offers her drugs, but what makes an impression on the narrator is Eugene's beauty: "He was beautiful, I saw. He was beautiful. He sparkled with beauty; it streamed from him in glistening sheets, as if he were emerging from a lake of it." They sleep together, and the narrator uses the remainder of her foreign currency to pay off Ivan's debts.

By the time Ivan returns, the city has become, somehow, no longer foreign, and the story ends with a sense that the narrator is beginning to claim her power in their relationship. She realizes her relationship with Ivan is hollow: "How I wished I could contain the golden wounding hope of him. But it had begun to diverge from me—oh, who knew how long before—and I could feel myself already reforming: empty, light." As she and Ivan walk along the street, the same way she had walked on her quest for groceries, the city ceases to be foreign:

> How familiar it was, as if I'd entered and explored it over years. Well, it had been a short time, really, but it would certainly be part of me, this city, long after I'd forgotten the names of the streets and the colors of the light, long after I'd forgotten the feel of Ivan's shirt against my cheek, and the darkening sight separated from me now by a sheet of glass I could almost reach out to shatter.

These final words, with Eisenberg's enigmatic symbolism, flow into the title of the final story, "Broken Glass," and recall the major thematic connections between the stories of this collection: how the foreign becomes familiar and the ways in which people see themselves through relationships with others.

Transactions in a Foreign Currency was greeted with a generally positive critical reception. Michiko Kakutani of *The New York Times* (5 March 1986) wrote that in Eisenberg's first collection of short fiction "she delineates her characters' lives with a full palette of colors, using not just the earth tones of fashionable alienation, but also the pastel brights of comedy and the darker, more luminous shades of an artist blessed with emotional wisdom." Kakutani's criticism is couched in flattery: "at times, Miss Eisenberg's ease in capturing the way we speak today combined with her sure sense of craft, can result in 'slice of life' studies that suffer from a certain patness."

Bob Shaccochis's review in *The New York Times Book Review* (9 March 1986) focuses on the element of travel, both literal and figurative, in these narratives. Characters are "made to travel outside the native land of their inner selves into a world that appears astonishingly regulated, where ostensibly enlightened men collect women the way superpowers assert spheres of influence." Many of her characters seem lost, a fact pointed out in Richard Panek's more critical article for *The Chicago Tribune* (13 July 1986). Panek complained that the "balance between introspection and overstatement is delicate, especially in first-person fiction, and sometimes Eisenberg slips." Lynne Sharon Schwartz's review for *The Washington Post* (11 May 1986) began by praising Eisenberg as "a writer of considerable talent—she has wit, deftness and grace, and she can cut through her characters' trivial and overlong conversations with an arresting, illuminating metaphor." Schwartz goes on to complain, however, that Eisenberg's gifts "do not, for the most part, relieve the spell of monotony cast by the voice of enervated sophistication."

Virtually all of the criticism focuses on Eisenberg's language, relating it to her early success as a playwright. Kakutani began by saying that Eisenberg "writes with a playwright's quick, bristling ear for dialogue and a painter's affection for nuance and image." Most of the critics, even those who pointed out flaws, praised *Transactions in a Foreign Currency* for Eisenberg's use of dialogue, her wit, and her character depiction.

From the mid 1980s through the early 1990s Eisenberg held a series of academic appointments. In 1987 she was awarded the PEN Hemingway citation, the Mrs. Giles Writing Foundation Award, a Guggenheim Fellowship (1987–1988), and the Whiting Foundation Award (1987–1988). She served the first of her two terms as the visiting Hurst professor at Washington University in St. Louis in 1989. In 1991 she served as the Shirley Sutton Thomas visiting writer and was awarded the Deutscher Akademischer Austauschdienst Stipendium. She participated in the Iowa Writers' Workshop at the University of Iowa in the fall semesters of 1990, 1992, and 1993.

Her second collection of short stories, *Under the 82nd Airborne,* was published in 1992. One of the most striking of the seven pieces in the volume is the title story, which appears second. "Under the 82nd Airborne," like much of Eisenberg's work, is set in Latin America, and Eisenberg's travels in the area obviously contribute to the vivid descriptions. The heroine of this story, Caitlin, is older than many of Eisenberg's protagonists and works as an actress. She has traveled to the small town of Tegucigalpa, in Honduras, in order to spend time with her daughter, Holly, who is accompanying her fiancé on a business trip. Caitlin's need to connect with her daughter is motivated by her dissatisfaction with her normal round of auditions and casting calls in New York City. Caitlin is searching for understanding, trying to know her daughter who is now, almost miraculously, "as old as Caitlin and Todd had been" when Holly was born. Caitlin has just broken up with her live-in boyfriend, and her life has suddenly taken a downturn. Thus, this story is also about her attempt to reconnect with herself. Caitlin's age becomes a significant factor as she tries to assess the woman she has become:

> Her gray-blue eyes were still clear and wide, her pale-brown hair still gave off light. From a distance she could have been a girl, but tonight her face was disfigured by the meaningless history of a stranger. Surely her intended self was locked away somewhere, embryonic and protected. She searched the mirror, but the impostor on duty there stared bafflingly back.

As her trip progresses, the story moves back and forth between the present and Caitlin's reflections on her past: how she became pregnant with Holly, the dissolu-

Dust jacket for Eisenberg's 1992 book, in which the protagonist of the title story visits a bar in Honduras,
where American journalists are "waiting to watch the 82nd Airborne Division fall out of the sky"

tion of her marriage, and how her husband managed to limit her contact with their daughter after the divorce.

Instead of connecting, however, Caitlin and her daughter just fight: "Jesus, Caitlin thought. How idiotic. Holly would be sorry later–she always was. But in the meantime . . . Oh, well. Out for adventures." As she travels out into the foreign world around her, she realizes there are troops and many Americans present. A "burly, red-faced boy who was drinking a beer as he walked" bumps into her and says "Gramma's looking good."

As in "Transactions in a Foreign Currency," this woman's fevered walk through the city becomes a significant turning point. She meets up with a businessman (who may actually be a CIA agent) whom she had encountered on the plane. Over drinks they discuss the city. As they talk, it becomes clear that the country is on the brink of war, a strategic point that the Americans and the communist countries are about to fight over. The tensions in the country contrast sharply with the world of the Americans in the bar as it fills with journal-

ists, "All waiting to watch the 82nd Airborne Division fall out of the sky." The bitterness of the men and the emptiness of the journalists there to document the aerial attack lead Caitlin's thoughts back to Holly and what has brought her here. Eisenberg offers no concrete resolution in this story. It ends with reflections: the memory of the day she left Holly and her husband and the sight of a fish "darting and circling in the flickering light, bumping against the glass as though at any moment its cloudy little bowl could be a great fresh pond, strewn with leaves and flowers." The reader is left to contemplate whether in fact Caitlin has moved through the tale like the fish in its bowl.

"The Custodian" is the most acclaimed story in *Under the 82nd Airborne* and was chosen for the *The Best American Short Stories of 1991*, edited by Alice Adams and Katrina Kenison. In this story Eisenberg repeats her focus on the confrontation of past and present by opening the story with two women who meet again in the small town in which they grew up. The narrator, Lynnie, confronts her memories of Isobel all around her, but when the two actually meet, their discussion is stiff and awkward. After the opening the story moves fluidly back into the past to narrate the events that led to Isobel being sent away—her seduction by a married professor for whom the girls baby-sat.

Lynnie and Isobel were friends more from a lack of anything better to do than from any real affinity for one another. Lynnie idolized the beautiful, wealthy, and slightly older Isobel. During summer bike rides they often visited a wonderful house that becomes central to the rest of the story:

> The house is stone, and stands empty on a hill. Clouds float by it, making great black shadows swing over the sloping meadows below with their cows and barns and wildflowers. Inside, in the spreading coolness, the light flows as variously clear and shaded as water. Trees seem to crowd in the dim recesses. The house is just there, enclosing part of the world. . . . The girls walk carefully when they visit, fearful of churning up the delicate maze of silence.

One day this silence is broken by the arrival of a family. Through Ross, Claire, and their children, the family who come to inhabit this house, Lynnie and Isobel obtain a glimpse into an intellectual and artistic world quite different from their small-town existence. The idyllic life they are allowed brief glimpses of, however, is ultimately threatened. Lynnie witnesses Ross visiting Isobel at night when her parents are not home:

> It is the following week that Isobel leaves. Lynnie watches from her window as Isobel and her mother and father load up her father's car and get into it. They are taking a trip, Lynnie thinks; they are just taking a trip, but still she runs down the stairs as fast as she can, and then, as the car pulls out into the street, Isobel twists around in the back seat. Her face is waxy with an unhealthy glow, and her hair ripples out around her. Lynnie raises her hand, perhaps imperceptibly, but in any case Isobel only looks.

It is never made clear who is responsible for the anonymous letter that informed Isobel's parents of her improper relationship with Ross.

After Isobel's departure, life changes for Lynnie. Isobel's mother barely contains her distaste when she passes Lynnie on the street, and suddenly, Lynnie sees herself as the woman must see her:

> an impassive, solid, limp-haired child, an inconveniently frequent visitor, breathing noisily, hungry for a smile—a negligible girl, utterly unlike her own daughter. And then Lynnie sees Isobel, vanishing brightly all over again as she looks back from her father's car, pressing into Lynnie's safekeeping everything that should have vanished along with her.

Only in this final line does the significance of the title become clear.

"The Custodian" is followed by another story set in Central America: "Holy Week." The style of this story is unusual for Eisenberg. It begins under the heading "Sunday" with a breathless list: "Everything as promised: Costumes, clouds of incense—processions already begun; town tingly with anticipation." This style continues for the first three paragraphs and then resolves itself into the notes that Dennis, the narrator, is taking for his travel article. This note-taking is interrupted by Sarah, the girl he has brought with him on this trip. The rest of the story progresses with the narrative periodically interrupted by another heading and more notes. Generally this stylistic device is interesting, but it does become strained at points as Dennis takes notes on his crumbling relationship. The inclusion of the travel-article notes, however, shows the difference between how the reality of foreign cities differs from the fantasy fed to tourists. The notes waver between descriptions obviously intended for the article and Dennis's own reflections:

> Indians impenetrable as they watch Jesus pass by, ribs showing through white plaster skin, trickling red plaster blood; they watch so intently, holding their babies up to look. Unnerving, the way they watch, way they walk, gliding along in those fantastical clothes of theirs. Silent emissaries from a vanished world, stranded in ours.

Once again, as in "A Lesson in Traveling Light," Eisenberg uses the foreign setting to throw the relationships between her characters into relief. Dennis muses on the advantages and disadvantages of his relationship with the much younger Sarah: "On the one hand, the intensity, the clarity (generally) of Sarah's reactions. On the other, her impatience, stubbornness, unwillingness to see the other point of view. Fundamentally youth's refusal to acknowledge the subtlety, complexity of a situation; at worst, adds up to a sort of insensitivity." The more time he spends in this foreign town, the more lovely it seems. Once more, Eisenberg's description evokes powerful emotions:

> Gets more beautiful as the eye adjusts. So high, so pale, so strange. Flowers astonishing—graceful rococo shapes, sinuous, pendant, like ornamentations on the churches. Every hour of the day, in every changing tint of air, new details coming forward. The ancient stillness. All the different ancientnesses—Spain, Rome, themselves so new compared to the Indians. All converging right here in the square. Concentrated in the processions, in every dark eye.

As in the title story of this collection, the military forces its presence into the heady existence of the tourists. This time it is the local militia: "The soldiers—the hard-eyed, ravenous-looking boys." They rule over the parade, seemingly unnoticed by the locals.

By "Friday" Dennis's notes begin to reveal a portrait of himself as a self-deluded, rapidly aging man, and he comes to the realization that his time with Sarah will soon be over. Dennis pictures her at a future cocktail party discussing "her first involvement with a mature man," comforting himself that he will not have meant nothing to her. As their trip comes to a close, the combination of evidence of a secret guerilla war and Dennis's brooding over the foreseeable demise of their relationship spoils their enjoyment of the elegant restaurants and hotels. Sarah, with her youthful enthusiasm, cannot forget what she has seen or understand why it has not appeared in newspapers. Dennis, however, puts the conflict between the rich and the poor out of his mind and begins to return to his normal life. After all, he thinks:

> would it improve, the world, if Sarah and I stay in and subsist on a diet of microwaved potatoes? Because I really don't think so . . . I suppose—that by the standards of any sane person it could be considered a crime to go to a restaurant. To go someplace nice. After all. Our little comforts—The velvet murmur, the dimming of the street as the door closes, the enfolding calm of the other diners . . . that incredible moment when the waiter steps up, smiling, to put your plate before you.

At this enigmatic point Eisenberg leaves the reader, pondering the distinctions between places so close and yet so distant.

Criticism of *Under the 82nd Airborne* focused on the occasional lack of warmth evinced by these technically brilliant stories. In his laudatory review for *The New York Times* (9 February 1992) Gary Krist claims that this second collection is "darker, more complex and more thematically opulent than their predecessors, suggesting a conscious attempt on the author's part to thicken the psychological texture of her fictional world." If this "conscious attempt" to write a more psychologically complex work occasionally leads to descriptions that are "abstract, cold, even unapproachable," he concludes, this detraction is less important than the evidence that Eisenberg "is a writer who is not afraid to extend her range."

In a review for *The Chicago Tribune* (31 March 1992) Bill Mahin wrote that Eisenberg "creates vibrant, vivid characters that linger in memory long after reading." Mahin's review is unabashedly glowing, but other reviews critiqued this second collection as lacking in some of the virtues of her first. According to Richard Eder in his 13 February 1992 review for *The Los Angeles Times,* Eisenberg's first collection had a "fierceness in the insult and an energy in the sensibility." In *Under the 82nd Airborne,* however, "that urgency, that insistent wind pressure, has died down . . . In some of the stories, the characteristic voicing remains, but it is underpowered, and as a result is a sporadically successful ornamentation." Yet, even Eder must admit, at times these stories display the fact that "Eisenberg has her own authentic sharpness, and the narration is perfectly done." Overall, the response to this second collection was laudatory, and in 1993 Eisenberg received three awards: the Friends of American Writers Award, the Ingram-Merrill Foundation Grant, and the Award for Literature from the American Academy of Arts and Sciences.

After *Under the 82nd Airborne,* Eisenberg devoted herself to a variety of projects while working on her third short-story collection. She served as a visiting professor at the City College of New York in the spring of 1993 and 1994. In 1994 Eisenberg published *Air, 24 Hours: Jennifer Bartlett,* a 167-page monograph on a series of paintings. In the summer of 1995 she participated in the Prague Summer Writers' Workshop. She served as an adjunct professor at New York University in the spring of 1995 and 1996. In 1997 Eisenberg's first two collections were published together as *The Stories (So Far) of Deborah Eisenberg.* Her third volume of short stories, *All Around Atlantis,* was published in 1997.

The story that opens *All Around Atlantis,* "The Girl Who Left Her Sock on the Floor," vividly illustrates how far beyond her two earlier collections this volume has moved. It is a witty, moving depiction of a girl's search that begins with the death of her mother and ends on the verge of meeting the father she thought had died before she was born. The central character, Francie, immediately engages the reader. In some ways, Francie, like most of Eisenberg's protagonists, is lost, but her situation is deeper and more complex, more of a comment on the current state of the world. The opening pages range back and forth between beautiful descriptions of the snowy world outside her boarding-school dorm window and humorous commentary to her roommate: "'You know,' Francie said, 'there are people in the world—not many, but a few—to whom the most important thing is not whether there happens to be a sock on the floor. There are people in the world who are not afraid to face reality.'" This passage provides not only a rapid-fire character study but also hints at the deeper themes evoked in this tale. Left alone in the world by her mother's death, Francie must travel home musing on the ephemeral nature of life:

If you were to break, for example, your hip, there would be the pain, the proof, telling you all the time it was true: *that's then and this is now*. But this thing–each second it had to be true all over again; she was getting hurled against each second. *Now*. And *now again– thwack!* Maybe one of these seconds she'd smash right through and find herself in the clear place where her mother was alive, scowling, criticizing.

Francie does not grieve and hurt because her relationship with her mother was idyllic. In fact, it seems to have been rather strained, but it was her only link, her only connection. As she travels to the hospital, Francie believes that she is orphaned.

The mortician, to whom her mother's body has been sent for cremation, reveals that Francie's father is alive and living in New York City. Francie furthers her odyssey, almost out of money and carrying her mother's ashes, desperate to find this man who may not even know she exists. In the end Eisenberg holds back from this confrontation. Instead of her father, Francie finds a man named Alex who invites her in to wait for her father's return. Sitting on the sofa, clutching the box of ashes, Francie does not dare reveal the reason for her visit. She imagines her father, walking down the street: "He fished in his pocket for change, and then glanced up sharply. Holding her breath, Francie drew herself back into the darkness. *It's your imagination,* she promised; he was going to have to deal with her soon enough–no sense making him see her until he actually had to."

"Rosie Gets a Soul" is in some ways a continuation of the themes in "The Girl Who Left Her Sock on the Floor." It also examines the precarious place of humanity in the world and the fragility of identities. In this story Rosie's quest begins by quitting the heroin that has kept her in a dreamlike existence and leaving her boyfriend and drug dealer, Ian. Depending on the mercies of a high-school friend, Jamie, Rosie finds herself caught up in his world. Jamie is an artist who supports himself by painting and stenciling on the walls of the extremely rich, and as the story opens, Rosie has been hired as his assistant: "almost thirty years old, Rosie thinks, and this is where she finds herself–on someone's bedroom ceiling." Throughout this story the conflict between the dull business world of the rich and the colorful yet far less privileged world of artists presents a vivid social commentary. Rosie's motivation to get off the drugs is prompted by just such a comparison: "Those people had treated their lives so well, tending them and worshipping then and *using* them (however moronically), and she had just tossed hers into the freezer, like some old chunk of something you didn't exactly know what to do with."

Dust jacket for Eisenberg's 1997 book, in which the title story focuses on the relationship between a Holocaust survivor and her daughter

As the story progresses and Rosie gains a sense of herself, she begins to fixate on the couple whose apartment she is painting. After meeting Elizabeth, the wife, Rosie is tempted by a silk slip that has been hanging tantalizingly in the bathroom for some time: "when Rosie gives the slip just the gentlest tug, it tumbles down, twinkling, into her hands. The slip pours tremblingly around her body, transforming it into a thrilling landscape, all gleams and shadows." This one item, casually left by the owners, is a clear symbol for the world of privilege. After meeting the husband, however, Rosie is drawn into their lives. One evening they exchange a serious flirtation and a passionate kiss; but then his failure to call, or even acknowledge their connection, prompts Rosie to assert herself and enact a small form of revenge: "The slip glimmers as though it's been waiting for her; it tumbles into her arms as she touches it. A rescue? Oh, no, not at all." She muses that the owners will be forced to think about her, to think about what she has done, in stealing the slip but she will just shove it on a back shelf and never think of them again—in this way she will get her revenge.

Three of the stories in this collection continue Eisenberg's focus on Latin America: "Across the Lake," "Someone to Talk To," and "Tlaloc's Paradise." All three continue the thematic thread begun in the earlier collections by stories such as "Broken Glass," "Under the 82nd Airborne," and "Holy Week." They examine the conflict between the worlds of the pampered tourist and the impoverished locals, adding in politics and war as grim reminders of the world outside the individual's search for understanding. The title story of the collection also examines these themes, but from a different perspective: that of the daughter of Holocaust survivors who is trying to come to terms with her own past and her relationship with her troubled mother.

All Around Atlantis is Eisenberg's most polished collection of short fiction. Eisenberg herself has said that her stories need to be read slowly—carefully—because each includes far too much meaning for a casual or cursory reading. R. Z. Shepard commented on this depth in his 15 September 1997 review for *Time:* "Powerful currents of the subconscious run beneath Eisenberg's winsome surfaces."

In her review of *All Around Atlantis* titled "City of the Drowned," Wendy Brandmark commented in *The London Times Literary Supplement* (13 March 1998):

> Deborah Eisenberg writes with the lucidity of a wise child who pushes aside the excuses of adults and yet understands their ambivalence and hypocrisy. We may not identify with her characters, but we are pulled into the stories by their emotional accuracy and the ease and economy with which she reveals people and their relationships.

This statement is telling, particularly since some of the most impressive stories in this collection, such as "The Girl Who Left Her Sock on the Floor," "Mermaids," and "All Around Atlantis" focus on children and adolescents.

Jim Shepard commented on this fact in his review for *The New York Times* (21 September 1997). Shepard compares Eisenberg's treatment of children and teenagers to that of Henry James, whom he quotes: "Eisenberg uses children to make seemingly ignoble people worthy of our attention . . . by the play of their good faith, these children make their parents 'concrete, immense and awful.'" This review is not entirely favorable; Shepard pointed out that "not all the strategies that recur in Eisenberg's stories are endlessly pleasing. Occasionally, the noticed detail is too flatfootedly an object correlative . . . and there's a fondness for pointedly illuminating chance encounters with eccentrics, who through their ramblings focus the stories' themes while bringing the usually somewhat baffled protagonists up to speed." Overall, however, the critics seem to have deemed *All Around Atlantis* the best collection that Eisenberg has yet produced. As Shepard said in his concluding sentence: "these stories are spirited and masterly road maps through sad and forbidding and desolate terrain."

Eisenberg continues to be read by a growing audience: her fiction has been translated into six languages. She has held a variety of collegiate positions and served as contributing editor for *Bomb Magazine*. Eisenberg currently splits her time between Manhattan and Virginia, teaching fiction writing every fall at the University of Virginia. Her short stories continue to appear in such periodicals as *The New Yorker, The Yale Review,* and *The Voice Literary Supplement*. In the fall of 1999 Eisenberg began to pursue a new interest—acting—rehearsing the role of Judy in Wallace Shawn's *The Designated Mourner* under the direction of André Gregory.

In the worlds Eisenberg creates, humanity is viewed through interrelationships, and the characters' surroundings, no matter how exotic, all include a certain familiar pang. Throughout her three volumes of short fiction, Eisenberg presents witty and urbane characters on voyages of self-discovery. As her style has matured, Eisenberg's prose has become increasingly sharp and symbolic. Eisenberg's vivid and intense reflections on characters juxtaposed against their surroundings have gained her a place among the most accomplished short-story writers of the late twentieth century.

Interview:

Nancy Sharkey, "Courting Disaster," *New York Times Book Review,* 9 February 1992, p. 11.

George P. Elliott

(16 June 1918 – 3 May 1980)

Carol Frost
Hartwick College

BOOKS: *Poems* (N.p.: Porpoise Books, 1954);

Parktilden Village (Boston: Beacon, 1958);

Among the Dangs: Ten Short Stories (New York: Holt, Rinehart & Winston, 1961; London: Secker & Warburg, 1962);

Fever & Chills (Iowa City: Stone Wall Press, 1961);

David Knudsen (New York: Random House, 1962);

A Piece of Lettuce: Personal Essays on Books, Beliefs, American Places, and Growing Up in a Strange Country (New York: Random House, 1964);

14 Poems (Lanham, Md.: Goosetree Press, 1964);

In the World: A Novel (New York: Viking, 1965);

An Hour of Last Things, and Other Stories (New York: Harper & Row, 1968; London: Gollancz, 1969);

From the Berkeley Hills (New York: Harper & Row, 1969);

Conversions: Literature and the Modernist Deviation (New York: Dutton, 1971);

Muriel: A Novel (New York: Dutton, 1972);

Reaching: Poems (Northridge, Cal.: Santa Susana Press, California State University, Northridge Libraries, 1979);

A George P. Elliott Reader: Selected Poetry and Prose, edited by Robert Pack and Jay Parini (Middlebury, Vt.: Middlebury College Press / Hanover, N. H.: University Press of New England, 1992).

OTHER: *Fifteen Modern American Poets,* edited by Elliott (New York: Holt, Rinehart & Winston, 1956);

Types of Prose Fiction, edited by Elliott (New York: Random House, 1964);

Dorothea Lange, introduction by Elliott (New York: Museum of Modern Art, 1966);

Themes in World Literature, edited by Elliott (Boston: Houghton Mifflin, 1975).

A modern master of the short story, George P. Elliott published two highly regarded collections: *Among the Dangs: Ten Short Stories* (1961) and *An Hour of Last Things, and Other Stories* (1968). He has also written novels and poems, and in all genres he infuses a moral imperative. Of the older virtues associated with art—

George P. Eliott (photograph by Tappy Phillips; from the dust jacket for Conversations, *1971)*

goodness, truth, love, and beauty—beauty holds the most sway for him. His characters are often saved from their worst selves by a nearly inadvertent brush with beauty, but Elliott refuses to soothe a reader with such proximity. His stories reveal more ugliness than beauty in the human enterprise, yet without cynicism. His work considers how people behave with each other in various contexts: nakedly, in their guises, as families, with the loved and unloved, and in ordinary social interactions. If Elliott's intention is to disturb readers with the mongrel and baser motivations of human behavior, then the disturbance is all the more lasting because the writer is so clearly good-humored in his depictions of his characters' "perfect weakness."

George Paul Elliott was born on 16 June 1918 to Paul R. and Nita (Gregory) Elliott in Knightstown, Indiana. He grew up on a plantation in the Southern California desert near Riverside. He earned an A.B. at the University of California, Berkeley, in 1939 and an M.A. in 1941. That same year he married Mary Emma Jeffress, who later became an editor for *The Hudson Review;* they had a daughter, Nora. Elliott was employed in various capacities: as a shipfitter, translating blueprints into directions for shipbuilders; as a junior analyst for the war labor board during World War II; as a reporter with the American Federation of Labor *News* for the San Francisco Bay area; as a business agent for the Technical Engineers, Architects and Draftsmen labor union; and, for six months, as a real estate broker in Berkeley. In 1947 he began teaching at St. Mary's College of California, Moraga. He stayed at St. Mary's through 1955, leaving to teach at Cornell University, and later taught at Barnard College in New York City, at the University of Iowa, at Berkeley, and again at St. Mary's before going to Syracuse University. He spent seventeen years there, serving as coordinator of the graduate writing program from 1978 until his death on 3 May 1980.

Elliott's career as a teacher and a man of letters included participation in writers' conferences at such places as Bread Loaf, the University of Utah, Northwestern University, the University of Colorado, the University of Florida, the University of Santa Clara, Green Mountains, the University of Rochester, and Olivet College. He taught classes and conducted writing workshops around the country and abroad; between 1962 and 1977 he gave 118 lectures and readings. Many of his lectures were printed as essays, ranging in subject from Anton Pavlovich Chekhov (published in the *Cornell Review*) to the nature of beauty ("Snarls of Beauty," which appeared in 1978 in the *Virginia Quarterly Review*). He taught graduate and undergraduate writing workshops and literature courses (Henry James, William Shakespeare, Dante), directed doctoral dissertations and master's theses in fiction and poetry, and served on these committees in other disciplines–art, fine arts, religion, philosophy, and visual communications. His awards and honors included two Guggenheim Fellowships (1961–1962 and 1970–1971) and a National Institute of Arts and Letters Award in 1969.

Among the Dangs was Elliott's first published collection of short stories and was nominated for a 1962 National Book Award, after one revision and many reprints. The ten stories in the collection reflect Elliott's lifelong interest in forms of knowing. The flights of his fancy (in the stories "Among the Dangs," "Faq," and "The NRACP") are balanced by the disci-plines of his art, and the strangeness in some of the fiction is attributable to the author's trying to get to a truth he may not yet know. In an unpublished interview the poet Philip Booth told how during a discussion about the draft of a story Elliott had asked him to comment on, Booth noted that part of it seemed less specific than it might be, and Elliott said that was his intention. "You don't have to *see* to be a writer," he said. "But do you let *me* see?" Booth asked. "Can you see in your own mind how many windows there are in the front of your house?" Getting no reply, he asked, "Can you see it?" Elliott laughed and said he could not.

Elliott is sometimes shrewdly abstract. The withholding of visual detail makes sense when one notices Elliott's other methods and effects. In his essay "Getting Away from the Chickens," for instance, his refusal to explain how a hen once laid an egg in his mouth increases the value of the event as symbol. In earlier parts of the essay the chickens' habits, often stupid, are made easily imaginable for the reader, but when Elliott warns readers not to overinterpret the extraordinary laying, they wonder how it happened all the more.

Elliott writes with his visual imagination, and the other senses, as part of his interest in the whole of the mind as it reflects, remembers, and dreams. A writer does not add "sprigs of reality" to his fiction, but by dreaming about reality, accepting the mystery of "a great big clean egg, dyed or undyed signifying egg," Elliott notes. The germination for the title story in his first collection, "Among the Dangs," was an image from a dream, and the movement of the story is from the palpable world, with its order, to one he had dreamed, with a significance he had yet to find. His search for a durable insight in "Among the Dangs" is intellectual before it is sensual, and the positive effect on the reader could not have been so great unless the likeness it created, visual but hallucinatory, found the form of a moral dream.

For Elliott the "usable ideal" and sensory experience were two sides of a continuing dialogue. He saw the things of the world, and he listened with an inward ear to the gestating truths there, to mystery, the word he frequently used as praise for literature. In "Among the Dangs" the hero is disturbed by the possibility that when he is in a drug-induced trance (part of a ritual of a primitive tribe he visits for his research), his own prophesies are Christian, though he is not a believer. He is also disturbed by the notion that against his wishes and better sense, against probability of any sort, he feels an emotion he cannot call love, but which is nevertheless pure and strong, for Redadu, his Dang wife, a woman he married for the sake of expediency. She dies, and he is unsure of his emotions: "I can't say what sort they were, but they were fierce."

The protagonist in Elliott's satiric fable "Faq," a geographer, finds what appears to be pure reason. The impartial narrator describes a place where the men of a tribe count all day in the dark and quiet of their huts—to falter in the count, or to cheat, is punishable by death. Gradually the geographer, whose curiosity about a lost people has led him to the valley in the Atlas Mountains where "the exercise of pure reason, the counting" is practiced, joins in the activity and finds beauty and happiness in the "world of reason and sense and trance," unafflicted by "the pain of this world of ours." The chief and all the Arabic people are "hopelessly honest," but the geographer eventually comes to feel that ordered perfection is wrong—this perfection existing in the telling of "the rosary of reason's mystery." He gives up the life of pure reason and the constancy of fulfilled pleasures—lying in the sun and making love to young women—to return to the imperfections of the world. Suffering, he says, is bad; but "the lack of suffering is much worse."

"A Family Matter" and "Children of Ruth" are realistic fiction, wryly humorous. The stories concern the manners and morals of two families. The situation in "A Family Matter" is reminiscent of *King Lear:* a powerful father looks for expressions of fealty from his three children. Gordon Mott's motives are similar to the king's—to prove his power. He is aware, already, of his effect on his sons, and he toys with their affections and their pride. He is easily able to make them aware of their own shortcomings, their cruelties, their self-deceptions, and the weaknesses in their ties with their wives and children. The sense of generational obligation, of struggles with ties of love, and marked defeat also inform "The Children of Ruth." When Ruth's youngest son, Oliver, discovers that his mother has promised his half brother Gene $500 to attend a chess tournament in Europe, he maneuvers to receive some of the family inheritance due to come to him in one year when he reaches twenty-one. The narrator notes, "With all her heart she wanted to say 'yes, here it is,' so that he would love her then and forgive her for having had him out of wedlock, but she cannot go behind her decision to keep him from his destructive passion for fast cars and motorcycles." Ruth says no, and Oliver leaves home. All the sons love their mother, but the ties are too complex, and their mother is too good. They have no such generosity themselves, and they are made to feel inadequate by her disapproval, some of it quite real and some of it imagined. The result is an awful dissembling, lies, and cruel remarks. At the end of the story Gene listens with consternation to his mother's walking up and

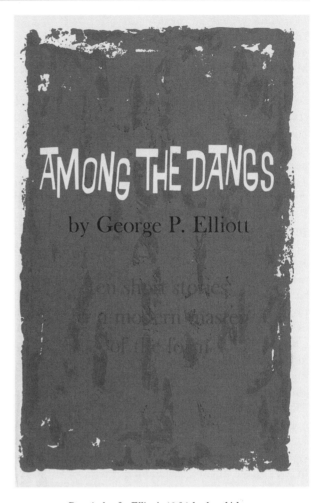

Dust jacket for Elliott's 1961 book, which was nominated for a National Book Award

down the house. "What is wrong? What is wrong?" she keeps saying. "What should I have done?" The air is unsettled by the questions.

"Hymn of Angels" is also realistic, describing Sydney Goldfarb's attempt to negotiate a record contract with Brother Dennis and the monastery where he trains young brothers in the art of pre-Gregorian chant. Goldfarb is used to dealing and is full of schemes, but he is clearly moved by the intensity and strangeness of the hymns he hears Brother Jerome and four other monks sing. Taken out of his realm, touched by "rapture" in the voices, he is at a loss for words. The effect of the beauty turns him from his business sense, and he thinks fondly of his old girl-friend, whom he phones. Her voice, however, has the familiar tones of vague suspicion, "its bold fac-simile of affection," and Sydney is restored to his more familiar emotional context. "Bye now, baby. Keep in touch," he says.

The effects of beauty are longer lasting in "Brother Quintillian and Dick the Chemist." The priest has lost his faith and the chemist, his wife. Mortality pursues them both. Yet, when Brother Quintillian visits the grieving husband and plays a recording of pre-Baroque music, the two men are restored to their separate forms of yearning and knowledge–the priest to his wonder of God's mysterious ways, and the scientist to an "unattainable and perhaps illusory quest for understanding and an explanation of the limit of things." Elliott does not choose for his readers between mathematics and faith; he only allows for what is referred to as a "high and private quest" for truth.

"The NRACP" is written in epistolary style and is allegorical. The main character, Andy, who works in public relations for the National Relocation Authority, reveals in letters to Herb his slow-dawning discovery that a "relocation center" in the Nevada desert for blacks is actually an extermination camp. The story, which is set in the 1950s, seems unrelated in plot and in style to others in the volume, but the thematic connections are similar. Andrew is reasonably fair-minded and wants to live a comfortable life. The fair-mindedness leads him finally to discover the horrible truth of the government plan, but his wish for comfort keeps him ignorant far too long. Even at the end his impulse is to try to balance the awful moral error against something good. The story shows a side of Elliott that is depressingly dismal–no one escapes from his own delusions. No one is redeemed.

Another allegory, this one tempered by Elliott's customary compassion for his characters, concerns faith. "The Beatification of BobbySu Wilson" satirizes unearned or unexamined faith and the church. Father Polycarp arrives in town to cast doubt on a miracle–a dead teenager's stigmata. In an unexpected turn of events, Father Polycarp has a vision of Bobbysu in a lovely blue robe, and Stanmer, the protagonist, is changed from doubt to faith. He plans to build a shrine with a statue of the girl–"not the acne and such but the spirit." The story is deeply ambivalent, and could likely stand as an expression of faith for the faithful, while for others the finishing impression is of having one's leg pulled. Father Polycarp has arranged his own conversion a little too neatly. The story is an example of satiric Elliott at his cleverest; his truths are contingent, his method, colloquial.

In "Love Among the Old People" Elliott's method is once again realistic and impartial. Readers overhear the conversations of people who feel their mortality, but are nevertheless ensconced in the ordinary routines of life. The characters parley and nego-tiate for loyalty, affection, and power, jockeying over a room vacated by the recently deceased Hattie, making remarks either cruel or tender, and commenting on the cost of the rent.

"Hymn of the Angels" and "Among the Dangs" summarize the collection. The situation in both stories is simply that people who have no faith are malcontented, the "real" world providing little more than the usual accoutrements: marriage, money, and the opportunity to prove oneself better than others. The result is a cool distrust. A journey to a monastery in the penultimate story and the physical and spiritual journeying into Dang country in "Among the Dangs" provide the sympathetic main characters with an altered sense of value. Both the realism in "Hymn of the Angels" and the experiment with fable in "Among the Dangs" are successful in conveying and universalizing the modern dilemma. Is what matters knowable? Elliott affirms that it is.

Fantasy and realism blend in the next collection of stories, *An Hour of Last Things*. The writing is more assured, the experimentation somehow more polished. The protagonist in "Into the Cone of Cold" shares with other Elliott characters a curiosity about what seems to hide just out of reach. Stuart, a poet, is looking for revelation, and when Brother Joseph of St. Anselm offers him a chance to participate in an experiment in cryogenics, where he will be sent to the other side of absolute zero, to the "anti-world," he agrees. The idea is that Stuart will write a poem about the experience. The experiment has been engineered from a series of equations laid out on a hunch by Carl Paulson, who has since left St. Anselm. In the laboratory the first time, Stuart attempts to find out everything he can about the physics of the experiment, but he is thwarted by his inability to ask the right questions; his not knowing becomes central to the thematic concerns of the story. Stuart returns from the antiworld with his internal organs reversed (his heart is on the right side) and his sentiments no longer benign. His former restraint has turned into an ugly sort of spontaneity. He tells his children a cruel bedtime story. He fights with his wife, Marguerite. He starts a bar brawl. Where once he felt the possibility of having a soul, he feels only a void.

A second trip into the "cone of cold" causes Stuart to feel restored at first, and filled with a sense of brotherly communion. What has really happened is that he has come to know the unknown, which is absolute nothing. The totality that he craves as a result of his new knowledge is unavailable to him. He wants too much from art, and he stops writing poems. His unbearable need for a complete spiritual "intercourse" makes him ignore his family. All he wants to do is teach, to prove that the world does mean something. He says to his increasingly estranged wife, "Immortality doesn't mean anything to me any more, just living while we can; communion; poetry's all right but you have to wait so long to see if anybody gets it and you're not even there when it happens. I like teaching better." And when he says he needs her, she replies that he has waited too long.

After his family leaves, Stuart falls into a depression. Only Brother Nicholas's apology for introducing Stuart to the absolute nothing of the machine revives him. Brother Nicholas also intervenes with Marguerite, and she and Stuart are reunited. The story ends in characteristic Elliott fashion, with the protagonist musing about what has occurred to him. In Stuart's case these last thoughts reflect a sense that some consolation can be found. An image of a black whale, an opposite of Moby-Dick, fills his mind. He feels certain the black whale can be made to communicate—by whistling or chanting. He likely will write again.

That words matter as a way to parse the truth and deliver some sense of beauty is evident in the realistic story "Words, Words, Words." Mark Birch returns to New York City from an ocean voyage with plans to propose to his lover, Jane. Having no religion, he plans a ceremony that will give significance to the sentence he plans to utter to complete the marriage proposal: "Our marriage will be a contract of equals freely joined." The plans go awry from the start, and when Jane turns him down, he doubts his own sincerity—that somehow his planning had spoiled the moment, or that there was no moment. What is left to them is several days of wonderful sex, during which he cheerlessly notes to himself that the whispers during sexual repose are in the same tone as when they were in a restaurant in the Village.

Mark's meeting with another woman in the upstate town where his minister father lives gives him back his sense of the value of language. The words Rosannah says to him seem both charmingly spontaneous and ceremonial. The two are standing at the spot where they had met once before, and he realizes that his assent to her words proves their power. Elliott's subtle partiality in the description of Mark's reasoning at the conclusion of the story—the gentle satire—is indicative of the author's stance in nearly all his fiction. While he does not meddle, he feels and thinks strongly about human frailties.

The last story in the collection, "In a Hole," is a first-person allegory about the power of language and the necessity of social complaint. A man trapped in a hole after an earthquake in a mythical city moves boulders from the stone chimney where he is imprisoned. The stones fall to the floor and he rolls them into a pile, so that he may reach high enough into the chimney to climb out. The task is dangerous; boulders fall unexpectedly. No one can hear him, but he must speak to save his own life, and the words must matter, or else the stones will not dislodge.

The characters in the other stories in *The Hour of Last Things* are often isolated and have difficulty resolving the differences between what they want (or think they want) and what they can have. In the title story Betty's husband, Winton, dies, and while she has the means and the imagination to create a new life for herself, she is overwhelmed with the freedom this loss has given her to want things. Some of these things she can buy, such as a stereo system and hundreds of records, jazz and classical. Some she can obtain by simply taking public conveyances or having a house party: companionship with ordinary people. But the affair she desires with a young black female singer is more elusive. Gradually she comes to see her past marriage as having protected her from worries about not having what she thinks she wants. When she goes to a Jehovah's Witness rally to see the object of her affection, Julia, she comes to realize that a fear of death is the motivation for all acts of desire. Mortality makes people inconsolable; they desire all they can have while in this world, then in earth's ruin, an earthly paradise.

In "Sandra" a man purchases a female slave to do his bidding. He comes to think her indispensable and frees her, then marries her. When she begins exercising her own free will, he is forced by his own sense of what he wants to enslave her again, which produces an equilibrium for the two badly isolated people for a while. But the period of freedom has, in a sense, ruined Sandra. She wavers between free will (and bad behavior) and submissiveness. The two are caught in the appearance of union. Elliott's irony prevents the fantasy from being cartoonish. The situation is exaggerated but not untrue and carries with aplomb its bitterness about human behavior. Expediency is the subject of "Is He Dead?" and betrayal in love is the concern of "Better to Burn" and "Rilla." The narrator changes in each of the stories, but to varying degrees always asks what suffices in a world of disappointment.

William Peden, in a review of *Among the Dangs* for *The New York Times Book Review* (8 January 1961), called Elliott "a writer of impeccable artistry and admirably disciplined" and extolled his "good sense, dignity, and high awareness." The strength of the stories, and a considerable amount of their tension, comes from the disproportion between what readers can easily surmise of the pessimism with which

Elliott views the characters and events, and the coolness with which he reveals human failure.

Elliott's interest in and confusion about the whole of human knowing—theology, physics, philosophy, political theory, psychology, and particularly art—are reflected in the novels, fables, stories, poems, and the especially estimable collections of essays he published subsequently. When he died, however, his work was quickly forgotten despite earlier praise from critics such as Herbert Gold in *The New Republic* (16 January 1961). *Among the Dangs,* Gold said, benefited from the "density of feeling and character, and complexity of event, that only a generous mind dares to employ in story form." Elliott's questing imagination led him to write in many genres, including the fable—stories that for J. Mitchell Morse (*The Hudson Review,* Autumn 1968) delved too deeply "into space or future times or hitherto unknown states of being." Fable had become the province of the magical realists, and American realism seems through the 1970s to have been meant to serve particular truths. Elliott's fiction was not written to soothe readers with the truth but rather to disturb and to leave enough residual tension in the reader's thoughts to have the reader continue thinking about the human predicament.

The publication in 1992 of *A George P. Elliott Reader: Selected Poetry and Prose* proved again the quality of his mind and imagination: "In an America which increasingly devalues intellectual independence, George P. Elliott's writings remain singularly important," wrote Booth in a blurb for the dust jacket. That statement could be a caution to the reader who too easily follows the current trend in fiction, whatever that trend may be. There is permanence in beauty and truth, and Elliott looked for that permanence in his fiction, which he said moved "from the recognizable order of our civilization to an imaginary world ordered barbarously." His ideals are neither simple nor set. Though the esteem in which he has been held is not widespread today, readers have only to turn to *Among the Dangs* and *An Hour of Last Things,* where the author's generosity, wit, idealism, narrative skill, and yearning prevail.

Reference:

Blanche H. Gelfant, "Beyond Nihilism: The Fiction of George P. Elliott," *Hollins Critic,* 5 (1968): 1–12.

Papers:

A collection of George P. Elliott's papers is housed at the Washington University Library in St. Louis.

Bruce Jay Friedman
(26 April 1930 –)

Brandy Brown Walker
Georgia Institute of Technology

See also the Friedman entries in *DLB 2: American Novelists Since WWII* and *DLB 28: Twentieth-Century American-Jewish Fiction Writers.*

BOOKS: *Stern* (New York: Simon & Schuster, 1962; London: Deutsch, 1963);

Far From the City of Class, and Other Stories (New York: Frommer-Pasmantier, 1963);

A Mother's Kisses (New York: Simon & Schuster, 1964; London: Cape, 1965);

Black Angels (New York: Simon & Schuster, 1966; London: Cape, 1967);

Scuba Duba: A Tense Comedy (New York: Simon & Schuster, 1968);

The Dick (New York: Knopf, 1970; London: Cape, 1971);

Steambath (New York: Knopf, 1971);

About Harry Towns (New York: Knopf, 1974; London: Cape, 1975);

The Lonely Guy's Book of Life (New York: McGraw-Hill, 1978);

Let's Hear It for a Beautiful Guy, and Other Works of Short Fiction (New York: Fine, 1984);

Tokyo Woes (New York: Fine, 1985; London: Abacus, 1986);

The Current Climate (New York: Atlantic Monthly Press, 1989);

The Slightly Older Guy (New York: Simon & Schuster, 1995);

The Collected Short Fiction of Bruce Jay Friedman (New York: Fine, 1995);

A Father's Kisses (New York: Fine, 1996);

Even the Rhinos Were Nymphos: Best Nonfiction (Chicago: University of Chicago Press, 2000).

PLAY PRODUCTIONS: *23 Pat O'Brien Movies* (one-act), produced on a triple bill with *The Floor,* by May Swenson, and *Miss Pete,* by Andrew Glaze, New York, American Place Theatre, 11 May 1966;

Bruce Jay Friedman (photograph by Benno Friedman; from the dust jacket for The Current Climate, *1989)*

Scuba Duba: A Tense Comedy, New York, New Theatre, 10 October 1967;

A Mother's Kisses, New Haven, Shubert Theatre, 21 September 1968;

Steambath, New York, Truck and Warehouse Theatre, 30 June 1970;

First Offenders, by Friedman and Jacques Levy, Detroit, Fisher Theatre, 7 August 1973;

A Foot in the Door, New York, American Place Theatre, 23 February 1979;

Have You Spoken to Any Jews Lately? New York, American Jewish Theatre, 23 January 1995.

PRODUCED SCRIPTS: *Stir Crazy,* motion picture, Columbia, 1980;

Doctor Detroit, by Friedman, Carl Gottlieb, and Robert Borris, motion picture, Universal, 1983;

The Lonely Guy, motion picture, Universal, 1984;

Splash!, by Friedman, Lowell Ganz, and Babaloo Mandel, motion picture, Buena Vista, 1984.

OTHER: *Black Humor,* edited and introduced by Friedman (New York: Bantam, 1965);

"Foreword," *No, But I Saw the Movie: The Best Short Stories Ever Made into Film,* edited by David Wheeler (New York: Penguin, 1989).

SELECTED PERIODICAL PUBLICATIONS—UNCOLLECTED: "Pebble in his Shoe," *Esquire,* 126 (July 1996): 90–93;

"Fit as a Fiddle," *TriQuarterly,* 103 (Fall 1998): 120–124.

Bruce Jay Friedman opened his *Collected Short Fiction* (1995) with an anecdotal reference to his mother's confession of dropping the young author on his head when he was two years old, thereby accounting for his trademark "tilted" quality of work. In a confession of his own in this introduction Friedman revealed that "most of these stories were written to puzzle things out for myself." For example, one of his earliest short stories, titled "The Subversive," was written to relieve him of a troubling experience he had in the U.S. Air Force concerning his shattered image of a fellow serviceman. After writing this somewhat autobiographical piece, altered by what he called "lies and other adornments," Friedman said, "I wasn't quite as troubled." Friedman's fiction often leaves the reader with the same puzzled or troubled feeling that inspired the author to tell the story. The discomfiture is passed on to the reader. The infectious nature of his often uncomfortable brand of comedy forces the reader to seriously reassess his own relationship to the society around him. In a 1988 article in *Thalia: Studies in Literary Humor,* David Seed described how Friedman's work "brilliantly evokes the anxieties of contemporary urban and suburban settings by unsettling his characters, suspending them between appalling possibilities or placing them in the midst of bizarre events which swirl round them exerting a stronger and stronger threat to their very identity."

Friedman's writing career has included working with various forms of fiction and nonfiction including novels, plays, criticism, movie scripts, and journalism. The short story, however, is arguably the focal point of his career, as so much of his other writing has developed from his work in this genre. Many of his novels expand upon themes and characters first created in short stories, and many of his stories have been successfully adapted to stage and screen. Friedman first gained recognition in the 1960s as a seriocomic writer who focused on the transient, impersonal, and extremely materialistic American culture, establishing themes of strained or nonexistent relationships between children and parents, and marriages or relationships marred by infidelity, either real or imagined. The "lonesome guy," who is only monstrous in his inability to make sense of his place in society, is a familiar character in Friedman's writing, and the neurotic and unfulfilled fantasy is a consistent theme throughout his fiction. Although all groups of people become targets of his wicked humor and caricatures, Friedman has a strong preference for shakily assimilated Jewish-American protagonists. His characters, held up for scrutiny and ridicule, are in the end always found to be wanting. Seed describes the recurring figures in Friedman's fiction as "fall-guys, schlemiels, casualties of life who either struggle in astonishment at their adversity or try to convert it into a self-mocking comedy." The most prominent themes in his fiction are the anxieties of Jewish-American identity, sexual and racial anxieties, and disjointedness from success, all delivered in the style of black humor Friedman helped to create in the 1960s.

Almost all of Friedman's stories employ a shock ending, a technique that Max F. Schulz, in his 1974 study, has identified in Friedman's style as an underlying "structural conception of the *non sequitur.*" Such endings either baffle by being completely incongruous to what the reader expects or open the reader's eyes by offering Friedman's idea of truth that lays bare the absurdity of the struggle of everyday life. As Christopher Buckley explained in a *New York Times Book Review* assessment (5 November 1995), Friedman's stories, "with their whammo endings, tend to divide into two kinds: the first leave you whispering, 'Wow'; the second go whistling over your head like an artillery round and leave you muttering, 'Huh?'"

Bruce Jay Friedman was born on 26 April 1930 in New York City, the son of middle-class parents, Irving and Molly (Liebowitz) Friedman, and he was raised in the Bronx. He showed his first interest in writing at DeWitt Clinton High School, where he wrote a column for the school paper called "AnyBuddy's Business," the title of which came from a play on his nickname. According to the jacket of his first novel, *Stern,* in high school he was voted second-funniest guy in the senior class, thus signaling both his capacity to turn his humor on himself as well as the recurring theme of inadequacy that his characters so often suffer from. He graduated from high school in 1947 and attended the University of Missouri in Columbia, where he earned his B.A. in journalism in 1951. Although his training at the University of Missouri was in journalism, he found his career in other forms of writing; Friedman has said that his move away from journalism was more of a push since, he claimed, he could not get a job with a newspaper. Instead, after graduating from college he served as an officer in the United States Air Force from 1951 to 1953, putting his journalism skills to work as a correspondent, feature writer, and photographer for the air force magazine *Air Training*. During this time he wrote several stories classified as comic fables for the periodical, with titles such as "Pvt. So-and-So and His Fairy Sergeant," but the magazine was ordered to stop printing them because they were deemed too antiestablishment.

"Wonderful Golden Rule Days," Friedman's first published short story outside of air force periodicals, was written during his time in the service and appeared in *The New Yorker* in October 1953. This story introduces the recurring character of the loser and the theme of failed hopes, combining comedy and pathos in a tale of self-inflicted humiliation. "Wonderful Golden Rule Days" tells the story of an underdog's day of glory as hard work and determination finally pay off in a vocational woodworking class. The protagonists, however, yearning for success in this antiheroic venue, thwart their own pathetic triumph by accidentally breaking their project, thus ending their brief moment in the spotlight in failure and humiliation.

In 1954, the year after this story was published, Friedman married Ginger Howard, an actress and model. That same year he started working for Magazine Management Company, publishers of men's adventure magazines. He stayed with this company for more than ten years, serving as executive editor in charge of the magazines *Men*, *Male*, and *Men's World*. Friedman and Howard, who divorced in 1978, have three sons: Josh Alan, Drew Samuel, and Kipp Adam.

The 1960s were a prolific time for Friedman as he made fiction and nonfiction contributions to popular and mainstream magazines such as *Esquire*, *Playboy*, *The New Yorker*, and *The Saturday Evening Post*. His fiction was collected with authors Saul Bellow, Joseph Heller, and Thomas Pynchon in *Nelson Algren's Book of Lonesome Monsters* (1964) and anthologized in the *Playboy Book of Science Fiction and Fantasy* (1966). Friedman used journalistic practices to imbue his writing with what he saw as the manic preoccupations of society, claiming in an interview with Jean W. Ross, "For a really direct confrontation with whatever's on your mind, there is probably nothing better than the magazine piece."

In 1962 Friedman enjoyed critical success with his first novel, *Stern*, which chronicles the racial and cultural anxieties of an emotionally spiraling thirty-something neurotic and ambivalent Jewish-American man struggling with anti-Semitism in suburbia. *Stern* began as an unpublished short story based around what became the key incident of humiliation in the novel: the protagonist's neighbor calls Stern's child and wife "kikes," then pushes her to the ground, where, legs splayed, she exposes herself. The novel focuses on Stern's shame at this event, which is compounded by the fact that his wife was not wearing any underwear at the time. Stern's response to this embarrassment is an almost complete physical and emotional collapse. He develops an ulcer and has a nervous breakdown completely disproportionate to the insult he and his family received. Stern is one of Friedman's most brilliantly realized characters, a darkly humorous victim of society's follies whose efforts to be a man and protect his wife and child are antiheroic. Friedman contrasts Stern's hesitant yearning for human contact with his spineless and self-centered obsessions, which make him wholly ineffectual yet hauntingly human for readers who also recognize the contradictions of the world around them. Overall, the novel deals with the larger issue of a man whose public image is at odds with his private feelings.

The following year Friedman published his first collection of short stories, *Far From the City of Class, and Other Stories*, comprising sixteen stories, seven of which originally appeared in periodicals ranging from *Mademoiselle* to *Playboy*. In this collection many of the formative Friedman themes such as the inability to reconcile outside appearances with inner feelings, shattered expectations, and thwarted attempts at even the most limited success are marked by some of Friedman's most bizarre and absurd plot structures. Both the title story and "The Subversive" are variations of the same situation: an Easterner visits the home of a Midwesterner and comes face to face with shattered stereotypes and the perversity at the heart of the American image. In the title story Friedman contrasts the big-city boys with the small-town yokels. The narrator of "Far From the City of Class" generally suffers from a sense of outsiderness because of his uneasiness with and inability to reconcile his Jewishness with mainstream images of Americana. Schulz wrote that in such stories, "Friedman uncovers to our eyes the hideous lie, the emptiness, in our nostalgic faith in corn-fed, small-town America."

"The Subversive" sets the Easterner-Midwesterner relationship in a military setting, ending with the horrible

Opening pages of The Saturday Evening Post *publication (7 March 1964) of a story collected in Friedman's 1966 book,* Black Angels
(illustration by M. Bodecker; reprinted with permission of The Saturday Evening Post © *1964 [Renewed] BFL&MS, Inc.)*

disclosure that the "most All-American person" the protagonist knows has at the heart of him a deeply "subversive" thing–the shame of a living skeleton in his closet, his crippled mother. The exaggerated shame he feels at having what he considers a defective and therefore perverse parent, and the violent reaction he has to having her be seen by his guest, completely subverts the ideal image the narrator has of his all-American pal.

"The Man They Threw Out of Jets" was written by Friedman during his air force years, when he was twenty-three. This story is one of his earliest attempts at forcing the reader to accept the bizarre and quixotic as normal, ending on an empty note that leaves the reader wondering what the point of the story was. The narrator, a queasy army photographer, is, like Friedman's other protagonists, uneasy and relatively useless. This photographer finds himself in a plane with a half-mad former jet pilot racing against the jets and the mountain range that seem to represent insurmountable obstacles of his past. As the story progresses, it has the potential to offer either a moral or a sense of sanity, but instead it ends with a random bit of inaction that negates the importance of the revelation that the man of the title

may be the sane one. The narrator has had an experience with the seemingly mad jet pilot that suggests that he was not mad after all but, rather, a sane hero in comparison to those who thought him mad. The narrator decides, however, not to tell anyone about his experience, ending the tale with an anti-explanation: "There were no impressive reasons for it. I just thought it over and decided I wasn't going to say anything." This ending, with its noncommentary in place of any justification for the protagonist's behavior, is typical of Friedman's style, which rejects the easy path of logic and resists that final piece that would give his characters, and his readers, the closure normally expected in fiction.

The dramatic situation and clever dialogue of another story in this volume, "23 Pat O'Brien Movies," made it adaptable for the stage, and it enjoyed a brief success as a one-act play produced in 1966 for an off-Broadway audience. The setting of this story is the well-worn scene of a man who is about to jump from a building and is confronted by the good-natured cop trying to talk him down off the ledge and in to safety. In this story, however, the cop does not get to do much talking. The jumper, recognizing the stereotypical nature of the scene he is a part of, anticipates every line of argument in the standard drill for stopping a suicide. Determined to resist the rehearsed speeches designed to get him down, the "jumper" sarcastically responds to the brief bits of dialogue the police officer utters, until finally the cop calmly rolls up his sleeves and executes "a perfect swan dive" into the pavement below. The reader and protagonist have no preparation for this twist in what seemed to be a predictable plot. Having never seen that bit before, the flabbergasted protagonist ends the story by asking the question, "What the hell do I do now?"

"Mr. Prinzo's Breakthrough" is one of Friedman's earliest potshots at psychoanalysis, in which the title character works toward his "breakthrough" in analysis by testing his analyst's claim that the analyst is there to help him in any way and that their compact is "pure and sacred." Prinzo, in Friedmanesque style, pushes that claim of loyalty beyond the limit by killing his doctor's wife, then demanding that the doctor not only help him get rid of the body but also help him escape the country. The patient, achieving a breakthrough in his treatment with this act, turns the analyst's words back on him, echoing the analyst by claiming, "I'm your patient and the only thing in the world that counts is how I feel." The doctor, feeling like a helpless victim of the extreme and perverse interpretation of the foundations of his practice, grudgingly complies. Any moral struggle between doctor and patient is shattered when the doctor suddenly realizes, as he waves goodbye to his patient, that since Mr. Prinzo has had his breakthrough, the murderer of his wife is not really his patient anymore.

Even more perverse than the logic in "Mr. Prinzo's Breakthrough" is the trajectory of another story, "When You're Excused You're Excused." This piece takes a common expression and pushes it to its illogical extreme, thereby providing a further example of the randomness of human behavior. The protagonist of "When You're Excused You're Excused," one of Friedman's anxiously assimilated Jewish-American characters, attempts to "excuse" himself from Yom Kippur, the holiest of Jewish holidays, with increasingly bizarre justifications, borne of guilt, for escalating unorthodox and even illegal behavior. Excusing himself from Yom Kippur somehow directly results in the protagonist's involvement in illegal drug use, infidelity, and murder, all in one day. This piece combines the anxiety of assimilation with materialism and the guilt of not knowing what one really believes in and stands for. In the end the protagonist can excuse the fact that he "hid a dead cop and smoked marijuana and went to a crazy party and got kissed by a Negro homosexual ballet

dancer," but he cannot excuse himself from letting someone get away with not knowing who a 1940s Jewish baseball player was, because somehow that is where he draws the line for disrespectful behavior on the holy day. This story exposes and graphically draws absurd and arbitrary lines for behavior that individuals, struggling with societal expectations, frequently try to excuse.

Friedman explores issues of chance, disillusionment, violence, and the products of a viciously consumeristic society in which death is predicted by gambling, and judgments from heaven are tied to the politics of prime-time viewing. Such is the premise of "For Your Viewing Entertainment," a satire on the amoral power television exerts over society. Similarly, "Yes, We Have No Ritchard" satirizes Hollywood's "pie-in-the-sky" plots, which overshadow reality. Both of these stories question the power of the world of make-believe, another version of a superficial surface, which prevents people from seeing the real problems and connecting with others.

Another story in the collection dealing with similar issues of misplaced loyalties and a confused sense of reality is "Foot in the Door," a laconic look at the absurd values in insurance-regulated society. In this Faustian revision of soul-selling, the body (usually someone else's, such as that of a family member) is sacrificed for financial gain. The devil is replaced by an insurance company. The insurance salesman of the story is the beneficiary of certain perks of his own, as long as his client adheres to the terms of agreement with his policy. Those terms include adultery, since the perk that the salesman earns is the client's wife. The salesman explains to the client, "my foot is in your door . . . I took asthma, a bleeding ulcer and let a Long Island train wreck have six of my grandchildren for your wife," all "under a special incentive plan" that the company provides for employees. Aside from the main gimmick and the shock ending, the underlying theme here, as in many Friedman plots, is a wife's infidelity, which is often depicted as the fault of the husband.

Many of Friedman's story lines dealing with husbands' guilt for their wives' potential misbehavior can be traced to the relationship depicted in his second novel, *A Mother's Kisses*, published in 1964. The prototype of Friedman's most memorable mother figure, the centerpiece of *A Mother's Kisses*, was created in the short story "The Trip," published in *Far From the City of Class, and Other Stories*. The novel is a developed and mature treatment of the mother and son's trip to college. *A Mother's Kisses* was well received and recognized in later criticism as prefiguring Philip Roth's *Portnoy's Complaint* (1969). *A Mother's Kisses* introduces and elaborates on a

*Dust jacket for Friedman's collection of stories exemplifying his belief
that black-humor fiction should stress "the fading line between
fantasy and reality"*

prevalent theme in Friedman's subsequent fiction, namely the history of problematic mother-son relationships that mar normal sexual development. Critic Haskel Frankel noted in a 16 August 1964 review for *The New York Times Book Review* that both Friedman's first novel, *Stern,* and *A Mother's Kisses* "suggest a world ordained by Freud but populated by the Keystone Kops." Because of the commercial success of *A Mother's Kisses,* Friedman was able to quit his executive editor job in the spring of 1966 to dedicate his time to his writing.

In the interview with Ross, Friedman described his idea of good comedy as "looking at events and people unblinkingly . . . commenting on the uncommentable, saying the unsayable, observing the uncomfortable." Such a method characterizes Friedman's style of black humor, a label he helped to create for himself and other writers in a 1965 collection titled *Black Humor,* for which he wrote the introduction. In this introduction he defined black humor by stressing "the fading line between fantasy and reality" and "a nervousness, a

tempo, a near-hysterical new beat in the air, a punishing isolation and loneliness of a strange, frenzied new kind." He further speculates whether or not "this" generation, circa 1965, might be called "the surprise-proof generation." Classed among this generation are John Barth, Joseph Heller, Vladimir Nabokov, Thomas Pynchon, and Ronald Sukenick, who all have stories in the volume. Friedman's contribution, "Black Angels," also became the title piece for his next collection, published the following year.

Consisting of sixteen stories, the collection *Black Angels* exemplifies Friedman's trademark style of black humor, including themes of frustrated human communication and shock endings that twist reader expectations and thwart any resolution for characters within the story. The title story explores the simultaneous guilt and glee that the main character, Stefano, experiences after hiring a ridiculously cut-rate team of African American gardeners to do all manner of yard work and home maintenance. Stefano is suffering from the suburban epidemic of what-will-the-neighbors-think syndrome after his wife runs away with an assistant director of daytime television. On top of that, she takes their ten-year-old son with her, leaving him abandoned with the "strain" and expense of keeping the yard and home looking respectable, for the sake of appearances and to preserve his status in the neighborhood. That status consists only of maintaining the exterior of a tidy home with no concern for the disintegration of the family that once lived in the house. Lonely and unsuccessful in his attempts to woo young girls (another prevalent Friedman theme), Stefano turns to the "Head Negro" of the Please Try Us yard service for company and counseling. The burly foreman of the work crew listens quietly to Stefano's problems and surprises him now and again with ambiguous but well-placed noncommittal questions that seem to provoke responses from Stefano and lead him, as a professional therapist would, to relief through talking. The kicker is the final scene in which the worker reveals to Stefano the outrageous fee he is charging merely to listen to him. This fee is completely incongruous with the steal-of-a-deal rate that he is charging Stefano for his official work on the yard and house. But the real work, Friedman seems to imply, is that which needs to be done not on the house but on Stefano. This bizarre ending, a parody of therapists charging exorbitant fees for monosyllabic prompts, is a reflection of the absurdities of the analysis industry feeding off suburban ills of psychological malaise and malcontent. It is also a comment on the rare value placed on one human actually listening to another.

"Brazzaville Teen-Ager" is another *Black Angels* story of failed communication. In this piece Friedman depicts a boy's struggle to find meaning through random and increasingly pointless, as well as dangerous, situations with his boss, all under the guise of attempts to save his father's life. His real goal seems to be to do something outrageous enough that will break down the barrier between him and his father so that they can make a connection. The boy thinks that if he can get his boss, whom he is terrified of, to perform wild promotional stunts, including singing backup for a doo-wop band, he can bridge some unspeakable gap and become closer to his dying father. The illogic of this reasoning is typical of Friedman's non-sequitur stories. The ending of "Brazzaville Teen-Ager" is not a triumphant celebration of how irrational behavior that risks sacrificial self-destruction can result in happiness and fulfillment, but rather anticlimactic and as pointless as the stunts themselves. These stunts ultimately leave father and son as far apart as when the story began, with an ending that promises no hope for future bonding.

Many of Friedman's stories in *Black Angels* depict man's uncertain responses to physical, emotional, and spiritual conflict in a materialistic world that the author alternatively asks the reader to mock or fear. "The Death Table" combines themes of materialism, human anxiety over death, infidelity, and a man's inability to fully know his fate. The protagonist of this story finds out through a roulette game how he will die. He procures his death card, with his fated ending on it, in exchange for not punching a man who has made advances to his wife at the casino. The protagonist wonders in the back of his mind if his wife was complicit in this potential infidelity. The conflict, as in *Stern,* is not so much between the two men as it is within the protagonist himself; he is uncertain not of his wife or of the man's motives but of his own ability to maintain and defend his manly honor. Obtaining the death card and thus overcoming the uncertainty of his future, however, feels like a certain success for the protagonist. The card explains how certain numbers on the wheel indicate specific ways of dying, from mundane heart problems to the more-exotic ways of going, such as oven explosions. The protagonist "gets lucky" and pulls a "heart" number, which is meant to be reassuring but ultimately reinforces that his uneventful life is going to end in an uneventful way. The story does not end with that bleak notion but provides a typical Friedman twist as the man broods over how the results of his death card might be wrong, thus negating any success he may have felt in winning it over defending his wife's, and by extension his own, honor.

"The Mission" is another example of a Friedman story that follows a pattern of seemingly predictable events only to leave the reader, and sometimes the protagonist, lost in the unforseeable randomness of the outcome. A masterful example of dual-track storytelling, "The Mission" is a twisted story of success, an uncommon theme in Friedman's pieces but in keeping with them because the success actually involves death. The protagonist succeeds not in having wonderful adventures but in procuring the final arrangements leading up to a death-row execution. This story seems to be a parody of what Schulz calls "the screenland superman, of the tight-lipped, little-man miracle worker, popularized by Alan Ladd," but ends up in the context of a search for the items in a death-row inmate's last meal request. What looks like an adventurous journey across exotic lands is revealed to be just an overblown shopping trip. This story takes the idea of fulfilling a last-meal request to extremes while keeping the central plot point a mystery until the end. The plot twist is successful in thwarting not only reader expectations but also the desires of every condemned man to prolong his final breath by requesting the impossible for his last meal. Typical of Friedman's style, the story ends not on a thought-provoking note, but trivializes the efforts of the adventurer-protagonist and the seriousness of death-row protocol by having the last line an articulation of the hope "that the next joker is a steak-and-apple-pie man."

The story titled "The Humiliation" revisits the themes of a failed family man reminiscent of *Stern* and the traumas of service days from many of the *Far From the City of Class, and Other Stories* pieces. This piece juxtaposes the current situation of a family man against his memories of his time in the service, exposing both parts of his life to be unfulfilled. While desperately trying to enjoy a European vacation with his family that he can neither afford nor appreciate, he sees a man from his military past who gave him the "humiliation" of the title during his early days in service. This humiliation was the result of being the butt of a senior officer's joke, not directed specifically at him for personal reasons but just because he happened to be in the wrong place at the time that the opportunity for the joke presented itself. The initial incident, a harmless prank involving answering a phone, has grown and festered in the protagonist's incredibly insecure mind to such proportions that it cannot be repaid in kind. This humiliation has shaped his uncertain and insecure life. On seeing the man responsible, in his mind, for his failed life, the protagonist both confronts and tries to repay him by repeating the prank. Out of context, however, the act of making the man from his past answer a phone call that is not for him is far too ludicrous to exact revenge. Although the act is similar, the power dynamic is completely different, and the pathetic antihero not only fails to attain closure, but relives his own humiliation. In typical Friedman style, the main character's punch line is that this chance encounter has ruined his whole European vacation, when in fact the reader sees that the humiliation of his past has left a far more permanent mark on his entire life.

In addition to novels and short stories, Friedman enjoyed commercial and financial success as a playwright. His first full-length play, *Scuba Duba: A Tense Comedy,* ran from 10 October 1967 to 8 June 1969 off-Broadway in the New Theatre. This play deals with the common Friedman themes of racial and sexual anxieties. He followed this success in 1970 with the play *Steambath,* which is set in Purgatory and deals with the protagonist's struggle to save his soul. This comedy, in Friedman's black-humor style, ends with the main character realizing that he is unworthy of being saved.

In 1970 Friedman also published his third novel, *The Dick,* which was cited by a *Washington Post* critic as one of Friedman's most ambitious works. The protagonist of this novel, Kenneth Sussman, changes his name to LePeters and, although no real reason is given, this erasure of the Jewish surname marks him as one of Friedman's typically anxious and ambiguously shameful Jewish-American characters. Consistent with Friedman's classic lead man, LePeters is just shy of any real success or accomplishment. He is not even a real "dick" on the force, but a "demi-dick," a public relations officer. This novel is heavy with symbolism and metaphor, from the title to LePeters's facial disfigurement and his psychosomatic groin injury. In this story Friedman almost lets his urban Jewish Everyman break free of the inevitable failure that his characters always achieve.

"A Change of Plan," which first appeared in *Esquire* magazine in 1966, was one of Friedman's earliest pieces to be adapted for the screen. This short story was released as a 1972 motion picture under the title *The Heartbreak Kid.* Directed by Elaine May, with a screenplay adapted by Neil Simon, this motion picture, compared to the works of Albert Brooks or Woody Allen, has been referred to as "the cinematic definition of *chutzpah.*" Charles Grodin plays the lead character in the movie, which closely follows the original story of marital infidelity and the temptations that the mainstream-society definition of WASP beauty pose to the main character, a stereotypically insecure Jewish-American man. The protagonist, a newlywed honeymooning in Florida, dumps his frumpy Jewish wife in the hopes of winning over a young Midwestern blonde whom he meets at the hotel swimming pool. Of course, there is no hope for a happy ending. The short-story title captures the mundane way in which this doomed groom goes about changing the course of his newly plotted life with his bride simply because of a chance meeting with a complete stranger. The title of the movie version captures Friedman's creation of characters prone to self-flagellating bravado, since the "heartbreak kid" is the one who always ends up heartbroken, lonely, and alienated from himself. The next year Friedman collaborated with Jacques Levy on the production *First Offenders* in New York City.

"A Change of Plan" is also included in a 1989 collection edited by David Wheeler titled *No, But I Saw the Movie: The Best Short Stories Ever Made into Film.* In the foreword he wrote for this collection Friedman explained the natural fit of a short story for motion-picture adaptation: "The traditional short story requires economy, ruthless attention to plot and narrative, particularization of character and tone and offers little opportunity for its author to stop and admire the scenery." He concludes that the genre thus has the potential to be "the perfect road map for the moviemaker."

In 1974 Friedman introduced his most enduring character in *About Harry Towns.* This book, less a novel and more of a collection of loosely connected episodic short stories involving the title character, was hailed as

A Gift From Willa Cather

As ~~it~~ is (*the case*) with most men, Harry wanted to be taken seriously and
resented the suggestion that he was not a serious man. Yet there may have
been some truth to the charge. Becuase if he were to be ruthless in
examining his life--which is not soemthing he did every ~~two~~ *twenty* minutes--
he would have to admit that he had spent most of it chasing women.
Or maybe not exactly chasing them, but pursuing them. Something along
those lines. Which is not to suggest that he had a sterling record of
catching them--or even knew what to do with them when he did--but he
certainly did pursue them. What bothered Harry is that he ~~did~~ *was doing this*
had done so much of this ~~so much of this~~ when he should have been reading Herodotus. He was
reading Herodotus <u>now</u>, but if he had been reading Herodotus when he
was chasing--or pursuing--women, he could have been <u>finished</u> with
Herodotus and moved on to someone like Tacitus. Or Willa Cather.
He could have been finished with Willa Cather, too, instead of
just starting to read her.

Harry had once sat on the deck of a film producer's house
in Malibu, exchanging war stories about the carefree Sixties and
Seventies. With a casual wave, the producer said that he had slept with
hundreds of women. Then, *turning grim, he* ~~he turned grim.~~ *said:*

"And I took no prisoners."

Harry was not in that league. He had taken plenty of prisoners.
That's all he did was take prisoners.
And he did not want to get into a numbers game with the
producer; he knew for a fact ~~that the man~~ *that the men* had slept with entire platoons
of film stars. <u>And if</u> *maybe or it. And if* he didn't know it for a <u>fact</u> *(but)* he was fairly
convinced of it. (The producer had a kind of sleazy charm and he could
see him sleazing film stars into bed.) And Harry was painfully aware
that in all his years of traveling <u>back and forth</u> to the Coast, he had

Page from the revised typescript for a story published in Playboy *(January 1988) as "Three Balconies" (Collection of Bruce Jay Friedman)*

a brilliant portrait of the emotional and moral quagmire of the 1960s lifestyle. Harry Towns has been described as Friedman's Promethean self-indulgent alter ego of the 1970s. *Washington Post Book World* critic Toby Thompson said in his 16 June 1974 review, "Each of Friedman's Harry Towns stories stands on its own . . . and each complements the other brilliantly. The book is novel, it is short fiction, it is essay. It is a goddamn heart-breaking delight and you are a fool if you miss it." *About Harry Towns* follows the title character, a mildly successful screenwriter in his forties, through separation from his family and midlife-crisis behavior as Harry desperately tries to fulfill his image of the swinging bachelor in Los Angeles. All of the Towns stories deal with Harry's various ways of coming to terms with a fairly unflattering picture of himself. "Back to Back" explores a common Friedman technique of exploiting a cliché to justify his character's unreasonable behavior. In this piece Harry, only mildly successful in his career and utterly failed in his personal life, is suffering from increasing despair fueled by unsuccessful attempts to spice up his life with drugs and women. He uses the excuse of having just lost his parents "back to back" as justification for behavior that is spiraling out of control. After sinking deeper into the self-destructive mode of drug abuse and apathy, he resolves to make positive, yet superficial changes that are never enacted. The piece ends with the randomness of fate and basic paranoia that characterizes Harry Towns and other Friedman characters. The narrative voice in this story sums up not only Harry but many of Friedman's creations: "The awful part is that he never seemed to get any huge lessons out of the things that happened to him." That is both the humor and the pathos of Friedman's writing.

In 1978 Friedman brought his brand of the comedy of the pathetic to *The Lonely Guy's Book of Life,* a collection of self-deprecating essays originally written as advice pieces for the not-so-young divorced male and published in periodicals such as *Esquire, Signature,* and *New York Magazine.* This collection, which began as "The Lonely Guy's Cookbook," was inspired by what Friedman described as his own pathetic cooking. Expanding on the theme of supermarket paperback personal guides, *The Lonely Guy's Book of Life* includes slices of the "Lonely Guy" lifestyle with titles such as "The Lonely Guy's Apartment," "Eating Alone in Restaurants," and "How to Take a Successful Nap." This collection became the basis of the 1984 movie and cult hit *The Lonely Guy.* The 1980s were a time when Friedman worked on several Hollywood projects, writing the screenplay for *Stir Crazy* in 1980, an original adaptation of Bill Manhof's novel *The Owl and the Pussycat* (1965), and collaborating with Lowell Ganz and Babaloo Mandel on the screenplay for the 1984 movie *Splash!* On 3

July 1983 he married Patricia J. O'Donohue, with whom he has a daughter, Molly.

Friedman's third short-story collection, *Let's Hear It For a Beautiful Guy, and Other Works of Short Fiction* (1984), has been referred to as part of his "manic" phase. The majority of the stories in this collection share the sadness of miscommunication and crossed signals that lead the protagonists to make outrageous or simply pathetic decisions. These tales include the familiar Friedman characters: semisuccessful screenwriters and playwrights, mostly Jewish and all anxious about race, sex, and the inevitability of failure. D. G. Myers wrote in *The New York Times Book Review* (18 November 1984), "Reading these tales consecutively is like listening to a man boasting without pause—one is left feeling pity and exhaustion." One piece in this collection that inspires pity is the selection titled "The Scientist." This story is about a man who appears to have been successful but has not succeeded in his attempt to gradually overcome his inward, uncertain identity. He seems to have become the man he always projected to the outside world, until the final scene where he is reduced to an outward display of the quivering insecurity he has been battling internally all his life. The expectations that the title "The Scientist" suggests, that of a respected, successful, highly esteemed professional, are thwarted as the protagonist, who appears to be in complete control as he takes the stage to accept a presumably deserved prestigious award, is deflated and reduced to crying out for "mommy."

"Our Lady of the Lockers" explores the outsider position of a New York City detective, who is not a part of the "tight coppish brotherhood" that LePeters (formerly Sussman) both aspired to be a part of and disdained in *The Dick.* The story is filled with hard-boiled detective bravado typified by lines such as "It was enough to make a fellow go for his weapon." The short story, however, unlike the novel, shows more affinities with metafictional writing of the time, including monologues filled with mocking asides to the reader. The protagonist even takes time off from his investigation to go to the public library and read an anthology of Jewish-American literature that includes a story by Friedman.

The title piece, "Let's Hear It for a Beautiful Guy," is the most popular of this collection and perhaps the funniest. In this story Friedman is engaged in what Anatole Broyard claimed in a *New York Times* review (29 August 1984) the author does best: "exploiting the pretensions and incongruities of a culture that takes itself too seriously." The story begins with the narrator comparing himself to Sammy Davis Jr., who, according to recent gossip reports, "is trying to get a few months off for a complete rest." The narrator, imagining some kind of camaraderie between himself and the famous star, develops a plan of rest for the two of them. In his mind they have become close enough to share a borrowed cabin in Vermont and talk about "the mystery of existence," a topic he knows Davis to be interested in from his appearances on talk shows, but begins to fear he himself knows nothing about. The tone of the story shifts as the narrator begins to doubt his ability to be a good companion to Davis. Finally, the narrator talks himself out of thinking that he is worthy of helping, but that someone certainly should.

In another story from this collection, "The Mourner," Friedman again takes a shot at superficial intimacy as the narrator, a Manhattan businessman, crashes the funeral of a complete stranger on a whim and then appears to be the only one in the room who really knew the deceased. For no apparent reason he interrupts the service to exclaim what seem to be personal comments about the individuality of the man he knows nothing about. The universality of his comments sparks responses from those who actually knew the deceased and were a part of his life, seemingly resulting in a positive expression of human relationships. Friedman's protagonist, however, in keeping with the author's style, pulls the rug out from under the mourners by admitting in the end that he has no idea who this man is, explaining his motive with the remark, "I just didn't think enough of a fuss was being made."

"Detroit Abe," written in the early 1980s as the first part of a novel Friedman never finished, was also published in *Let's Hear It for a Beautiful Guy, and Other Works of Short Fiction* after it was adapted for the movie *Doctor Detroit* (1983). In Friedman's short story, Irwin Abrahamowitz, who teaches irony at a "heavily ethnic" city university, finds himself propositioned by a pimp named Smooth to run his "business" while Smooth serves a short jail term. The struggle Abrahamowitz endures regarding his decision is less significant in the story than the definition of irony that he gives Mr. Smooth and the readers: "A way to spot irony," he says, "is when you can't quite make out the intentions of the author and when the hero ends up in puzzled defeat." This statement seems less a definition of irony and more a definition of Friedman's narrative strategy. The story ends with the protagonist having made the decision not to take up the offer, only to place a phone call to Smooth in which he identifies himself as "Detroit Abe," seemingly going back on his decision and taking on the role of pimp. The movie, which did not maintain the same level of struggle and angst with the protagonist as the original story did, was not as successful as a black-humor piece. Friedman told Ross that the movie was "so dramatically at variance with my initial work that I really didn't pay much attention to it." Having been both one who has adapted a work for the stage or screen and one who has had his work adapted by others, Friedman admits that

writing screenplays is a skill "which lies somewhere between prose and calculus" and is "the most rigorous and maddening of enterprises."

In his fourth novel, *Tokyo Woes* (1985), Friedman offers a caricature of Japan as he sends another version of his lonely guy, antihero Mike Halsey, off for foreign encounters to resolve a pending identity crisis. According to *New York Times* critic Michiko Kakutani (27 April 1985), this novel "lacks the depth of compassion and seriousness" and "lacks both the anger and tenderness" that characterized Friedman's earlier work. In another example of trying to live up to the past, Friedman's *The Current Climate* (1989) is a collection of episodic stories and a follow-up to the *About Harry Towns* series. This volume is considered by many critics as a stale attempt to recapture Harry's legendary 1960s struggle to fit in. In the 1970s the critics called Harry haunting and completely memorable. When he reappears in *The Current Climate,* however, Harry is pushing sixty and has achieved the status of a second-rate screenwriter who is "Pitched Out"—according to the title of the first story in this collection, originally published in *Esquire,* in which the only ideas Harry has left are for dog shows. Harry still likes to slip away from his comfortable yet ill-fitting suburban family for a night of anonymous city debauchery, drugs, porno flicks, and women. He is always working on a play and almost, but never, achieving something. The highlight of his life is meeting Muhammad Ali at a urinal.

In the 1990s Friedman continued to revisit earlier work. *The Slightly Older Guy* (1995) consists of essays in the vein of *The Lonely Guy's Book of Life* with titles such as "Sex and the Slightly Older Guy," "A Diet for the Slightly Older Guy," and "The Slightly Older Wife." In 1995 *The Collected Short Fiction of Bruce Jay Friedman* came out with what the author considered his best pieces throughout his career. In the foreword to this collection Friedman admitted to writing for the following reasons: "self therapy, . . . just to show off a little, to put brackets around an experience or an intriguing persona, to put in boldface what I thought of as something ridiculous or unfair in the culture." This collection spans four and a half decades of Friedman's career, featuring forty-seven stories published between 1952 and 1995. He included the most pivotal pieces that spawned several of his other projects, from the novels to stage and screen adaptations. The arrangement of stories in this collection indicates to some extent the trajectory of Friedman's career as he sees it in retrospect. He ordered the stories not chronologically but according to themes that chart some kind of progression through his career, as he recognizes his development into that slightly older guy that he lampoons at every turn. The sections progress from the first, "By Way of Introduction," to "Crazed Youth," "Halcyon Days (Family Life and the Service)," "Mother," "Sex," and "Death," and end with "The

Family Man." The stories collected under each section are tied to their thematic heading in a way that furthers the Friedmanesque style of truth through discomforting comedy.

Also in 1995 his play *Have You Spoken to Any Jews Lately?* was produced in New York City at the American Jewish Theatre, receiving mixed reviews. Some critics lauded the play as "dark, but often wildly funny vaudeville entertainment," while others felt that although "there were plenty of outrageous laughs," it was ultimately not successful as an overall comedy. The play centers around two characters who become convinced that a new Holocaust is at hand, and the major action consists of these men acting out their own bizarre panic as they are confronted with memories and fantasies of past and present.

The following year Friedman published *A Father's Kisses,* his answer thirty years later to *A Mother's Kisses.* This novel deals not with a son's neurotic relationship and hang-ups with his mother but rather with a father's innocent and somewhat overprotective love for his prepubescent daughter. Friedman introduces the character of William Binny, a fifty-something retired poultry distributor who would do anything for his daughter, even kill. In the character of Binny, Friedman creates a naive widower and small-town bore who becomes embroiled in the silliest and most suggestively dangerous situations involving bizarre characters from Miami to Tokyo to New York. Binny is somehow thrust into the role of inept assassin while still remaining a really nice guy. This novel leaves behind the dark and sometimes bitter black humor of Friedman's earlier years and replaces it with an almost sentimental comedy that still retains the wacky situations and twists that mark Friedman's work.

In 2000 the comic style and sharp wit of Friedman's nonfiction writing were assembled in *Even the Rhinos Were Nymphos: Collected Nonfiction.* The title comes from Friedman's days of writing men's pulp fiction in the 1950s, and the collection consists of essays written for various magazines from the 1950s through the 1990s. Although Friedman has had success in many genres over the past five decades, the short story is the form that best captures his fast-paced style of biting, undercutting, and ultimately touching humor.

Interview:

Jean W. Ross, "Bruce J. Friedman: CA Interview," in *Contemporary Authors,* New Revision Series, volume 25 (Detroit: Gale, 1989), pp. 148–151.

References:

Marcus Klein, "Further Notes on the Dereliction of Culture: Edward Lewis Wallant and Bruce Jay Friedman," in Irving Malin's *Contemporary American-Jewish Literature* (Bloomington: Indiana University Press, 1973), pp. 229–247;

Stuart A. Lewis, "Rootlessness and Alienation in the Novels of Bruce Jay Friedman," *College Language Association Journal,* 18 (1975): 422–433;

Max F. Schulz, *Black Humor Fiction of the Sixties: A Pluralistic Definition of Man and His World* (Athens: Ohio University Press, 1973);

Schulz, *Bruce Jay Friedman* (New York: Twayne, 1974);

David Seed, "Bruce Jay Friedman's Fiction: Black Humor and After," *Thalia: Studies in Literary Humor,* 10 (Spring–Summer 1988): 14–22.

Mary Gaitskill

(11 November 1954 –   )

Joseph J. Wydeven
Bellevue University

BOOKS: *Bad Behavior* (New York: Poseidon Press,
   1988; London: Hodder & Stoughton, 1989);
Two Girls, Fat and Thin (New York: Simon & Schuster,
   1991; London: Chatto & Windus, 1991);
Because They Wanted To (New York: Simon & Schuster,
   1997; London: Picador, 1997).

OTHER: "Revelation," in *Anchor Essay Annual: The Best
   of 1997,* edited by Phillip Lopate (New York: Doubleday / Anchor, 1997), pp. 68–74;
"The Wolf in the Tall Grass," in *Why I Write: Thoughts on
   the Craft of Fiction,* edited by Will Blythe (Boston:
   Little, Brown, 1998), pp. 155–163;
"Walt and Beth: A Love Story," sequential art, with
   Peter Trachtenberg, *Word.com* (21 June 2000)
   <http://www.word.com/features99/walt_and_beth/>.

SELECTED PERIODICAL PUBLICATIONS–
UNCOLLECTED: "The Woman Who Knew Judo,"
   Michigan Quarterly Review, 21 (Winter 1982): 170–
   181;
"The Crazy Person," *Open City,* no. 1 (1990): 49–61;
"Unearthing Dracula," *Vogue,* 182 (November 1992):
   298–303;
"On Not Being a Victim," *Harper's,* 288 (March 1994):
   35–43;
"My Inspiration: Vladimir Nabokov: Sorcerer of Cru-
   elty," *Salon.com* (12 November 1995) <http://
   www.salon.com/12nov1995/feature/nabokov.html>;
"Personal Best: Review of *The Hunchback of Notre Dame* by
   Victor Hugo," *Salon.com* (30 September 1996)
   <http://www.salon.com/weekly/hugo960930.html>;
"A Flash of Fear," review of *The Gift of Fear: Survival
   Skills that Protect Us From Violence* by Gavin De
   Becker, *Elle,* 12 (1 June 1997): 80;
"Satan Goes to Harvard," review of *Halfway Heaven:
   Diary of a Harvard Murder* by Melanie Thernstrom,
   Salon.com (13 October 1997) <http://www.salon.com/
   books/feature/1997/10/13gaitskill.html>;
"Bitch's Brew," review of *Bitch* by Elizabeth Wurtzel,
   Village Voice, April–May 1998, S16;

*Mary Gaitskill (photograph by Marion Ettlinger; from the dust jacket
for* Because They Wanted To, *1997)*

"Vein Glorious," review of *Blood: An Epic History of Medicine and Commerce* by Douglas Starr, *Village Voice* (15
   September 1998): 122;
"The Two Sides of Ethan Canin," review of *For Kings
   and Planets* by Ethan Canin, *Harper's Bazaar* (September 1998): 432;
"A Dream of Men," *New Yorker,* 74 (23 November
   1998): 88–94;
"The Rubbed Away Girl," *Open City,* no. 7 (Winter
   1999): 137–148;

"French Kisses," review of *Lila Says* by Chimo, *Village Voice,* 19 January 1999, pp. 148–149;

"Alice Adams," *Salon.com* (9 June 1999) <http://www.salon.com/people/obit/1999/06/09/adams/index.html>;

"Kubrick: A Little Kid Lost in the Sexual Darkness," review of *Eyes Wide Shut, Salon.com* (23 July 1999) <http://www.salon.com/ent/feature/1999/07/23/marcus/index.html>;

"Men at Extremes," *Salon.com* (15 November 1999) <http://www.salon.com/books/bag/1999/11/15/gaitskill2/index.html>;

"Dye Hard," review of *Blonde,* by Joyce Carol Oates, *Bookforum,* 7 (Spring 2000): 22;

"Knockout: An Interview with Joyce Carol Oates," *Bookforum,* 7 (Spring 2000): 30–31;

"A Horrible Sensation of Love," *Word.com* (21 June 2000) <http://word.com/features98/gaitskill2/text1.html>;

"See Me, Feel Me," *Villiage Voice,* 27 December 2000 – 2 January 2001, pp. 95–96.

Mary Gaitskill's range is limited, but her work is nevertheless important, as she deals with subjects that are frequently ignored in serious American fiction. Her fundamental theme is relational connection and maneuvering between "bohemian" single women and men whereby they seek, if sometimes narcissistically, to locate that mysterious moment when sex and love so infrequently come together. Although Gaitskill's women are often as inept and confused as men in her work, men often define the terms of relationships—because of power, broader insensitivities, and less interest in lasting relationships. Gaitskill's work is important largely because she confronts urban realities with a sharp-eyed and sometimes satirical empathy for the complexity of her characters, some of whom are victims of their pasts and consequent foolish decisions based on inexperience.

Mary Gaitskill was born in Lexington, Kentucky, on 11 November 1954 to Lawrence Russell and Dorothy Jane Mayer Gaitskill. She grew up in Detroit suburbs with two sisters, in an apparently troubled family. Sometime during her teen years she was briefly committed to a psychiatric hospital. At fifteen or sixteen she ran away from home and fled to Toronto, where she lived from hand to mouth and survived through a variety of jobs: street vendor, clerk, stripper, and, apparently at least once, prostitution. At sixteen she wrote in "On Not Being a Victim," she experienced an acquaintance rape, and two years later, she "was raped for real." At twenty-one she met some "Jesus freaks" and became a born-again Christian for six months.

She returned to Michigan, completed a GED, and attended a community college, then went to the University of Michigan, where she majored in journalism and wrote fiction. Her short-story collection—including "The Woman Who Knew Judo"—won the Avery Hopwood writing award. She graduated in 1981 and moved to New York. She has lived in many urban settings and has taught at Berkeley, Houston, New York University, and the New School.

Gaitskill's work appears in several formats, including in on-line magazines such as *Salon.com,* which publishes her reviews, short stories, and sequential art. Gaitskill is adept at probing the consequences of female adolescent drift and disrupture, which precludes normal family life and complicates sexual development. "When I grew up," she said in a 1994 interview with Alexander Lawrence, "I didn't have experiences of adolescent femaleness because I left and didn't do the normal thing with dating and all that." This lack of normal experience is often carried into her characters' lives. Gaitskill's interest is in the complexities of intimate relationships, as well as the character flaws and foibles that make for comically skewed communications. Although family life is crucial in the formation of her characters' lives, her characters show little interest in marriage, or in children of their own.

Principal values in Gaitskill are the unified self and meaningful connections to others, but those values exist in a cold, hard environment, where they are coupled with determining factors from childhood and adolescence: failed family life, child molestation, drugs, the false consolations of narcissism. Her work often focuses on the personal insecurities—sometimes approaching schizophrenia—of her characters, who sometimes fall into a victimhood that Gaitskill satirizes because she despises it. She uses two frequent images in her work: characters described as small, vulnerable animals and incidents in which characters describe or fear various forms of self-division, suggesting tensions in their psyches. A common method for Gaitskill is the interplay of past and present, within which old friends meet again after many years, leading to questions of causation or attempted renewals of relationships that failed in the past.

Gaitskill treats sexuality in a deliberate and complex manner. If in consumer society sexuality is exploited for its romantic qualities, Gaitskill insists on sex as a driving biological and social force. She decries Stanley Kubrick's view of sex in his motion picture *Eyes Wide Shut* (1999) as only "a dark, chaotic, destructive force," arguing that the quality of sex as "destructive and violent" is also what "makes it creative and intensely loving." Unrealistic societal understanding of the forces of sexuality is culturally damaging—especially to adolescent girls, who must make their way as "simultaneously adored and despised" sexual objects.

An important key to Gaitskill's approach in her work is her level of empathy for her characters. Her rereading of the Book of Revelation as an adult worked to increase her compassion: as she wrote in "Revelation" (1997), "Paradoxically, . . . the more you accept the pain and fear inherent in human experience, the greater your compassion can become." She sometimes writes about characters she would dislike in real life, but in processing them as fictional beings, she comes to understand their motives. This understanding encourages compassion, allowing her to deal with difficult characters and situations that more-cautious writers might avoid, for fear of being misunderstood.

Gaitskill's themes are apparent early, beginning with "The Woman Who Knew Judo," the lead story for her undergraduate collection. The story involves a young woman named Becky and her gradual comprehension of the strife between men and women derived from degrees of physical strength. The issue of self-defense is paralleled by Becky's observations of the civil rights struggle: when her mother's friend argues that blacks should defend themselves if the law will not protect them, Becky's father protests. Becky intuits a parallel between civil rights and power predicated on the physical strength of the male: her father's denial of "vigilante justice" for blacks, Becky understands, is supported by a self-interested defense of male physical superiority. With this new knowledge Becky decides not to pursue judo. She has seen that something in her father requires obeisance to authority based on physical strength, and she refuses to bend to this crude male prerogative. The exploration of gender relationships, made complex by desires for love and connection, became an important theme in Gaitskill's work.

Gaitskill's first book was *Bad Behavior* (1988), a collection of nine short stories, most of them set in New York and concerned with the angst accompanying intimate relationships in urban settings. The stories explore alienation and failed communication, sometimes in comic ways. She has said that the book explores how people "create survival systems and psychologically 'safe' places for themselves in unorthodox and sometimes apparently self-defeating ways." This view is enforced by her epigraph, from W. H. Auden, which emphasizes the ways people keep the truth from themselves in order to live—and in doing so render themselves even more vulnerable.

Gaitskill's stance regarding her characters mixes satirical insight with compassion. She is both impatient with their shallowness—their diets of drugs and jelly beans, their adolescent reliance on cartoons, psychics, and wind-up toys—and sympathetic to their circumstances. Aware of their foibles and weaknesses, she desires to redeem them in spite of themselves. In many

Dust jacket for Gaitskill's first book (1988), stories that explore how people "create survival systems and psychologically 'safe' places for themselves in unorthodox and sometimes apparently self-defeating ways"

of these relationships, the characters seem self-entrapped in static, near-claustrophobic situations: in order to grow as human beings worthy of love, they must overcome the habits that give them comfort and identity. This circumstance makes for rich comedy but little character growth.

The first story in *Bad Behavior,* "Daisy's Valentine," traces the development of a "relationship" between Daisy and Joey, two Manhattan misfits who share a bookstore workplace and a hazy dissatisfaction with their lives. Their conversations are puerile, and they seem vaguely to connect their victimization as children to their present circumstances. Joey, void of emotional intelligence, derives identity from his fantasies, in which he stars as the savior of victimized people. Daisy, on the other hand, admits she likes people who hurt her but is unable to respond to those who like her too much. They drift into an ineffectual relationship, seeing each other on the sly, so as not to disturb relations with their present sexual partners. Eventually Joey's girlfriend throws him out, and at the end Joey and Daisy find themselves on an apartment staircase feeling anxious. They achieve no insight, other than that figured in Daisy's tears at the reproach thrown at them by a well-dressed couple who identify them as vagrants.

Gaitskill's interest in these characters focuses on the irony that some relationships are founded on dysfunctional premises. This idea of relationships based in dysfunction is even more evident in the second story, "A Romantic Weekend," in which Beth, a self-proclaimed masochist, spends a miserable weekend with a new sadistic male acquaintance. Beth dislikes physical pain, though in her romantic fantasies she desires it as a means to romantic love. She wants to be mastered by some handsome, brooding man, but the boy she finds herself with is devoid of romantic imagination. When the boy takes her fantasies at face value and asserts his ego in vicious physical acts, he is repelled by her lack of "appropriate" response. Beth, on the other hand, would gladly submit under the right conditions, but while she wants to be loved, he wants someone "emptied out" of will. The weekend is a comic failure.

The title of another story, "Something Nice," indicates the desire felt by Fred (a veterinarian) when he visits Lisette, a prostitute in a brothel. The "something nice" is what his wife is unwilling to give him: she gets "docile and patient" when he suggests kinky sex. Lisette, new to the business, fires Fred's fantasies of having a "relationship" with her—despite her insistence that he would not like her in reality. By his fifth visit, on consecutive nights, he thinks of her as his "own little girl." Lisette leaves, and Fred does not see her for more than a year. Quite accidentally, Fred runs into her in a restaurant, where Lisette is in conversation with a young man. Overhearing her talk about her lesbian acquaintances, Fred finds the experience "unpleasant," and he flees the restaurant, leaving behind the gifts he had purchased for his wife and niece.

In "An Affair, Edited" Joel encounters Sara, a young woman with whom he had had an affair at the University of Michigan that "had ended badly." Although they recognize each other, Joel refuses to acknowledge her, and he is pleased to note that he is better dressed, suggesting he is the more "successful." Nevertheless, when he sees Sara a second time, he mentally reviews his relationship with her and remembers other qualities he once valued. He recalls two incidents: first, the moment when she had told him insistently that she truly loved him, and second, the time he was repulsed when she cried on the phone. He had brutally dismissed her then, but now, at the end of the story, he subconsciously wants her back.

"Connection" is another story about a friendship that ended badly, the title referring to the compulsion to study the mystery of successful friendships: "Connection was a vague word when applied to humans. What did it mean?" Revisiting Manhattan, thirty-five-year-old Susan thinks she sees an old friend, Leisha, and she remembers their troubled relationship: how after she first despised Leisha, then came to admire her, they had shared the intimate details of their lives. After Leisha had a bad affair and attempted suicide, the "connection" between them was broken. Now in New York, remembering the best parts of their relationship, Susan tries unsuccessfully to trace Leisha through old friends. At the end she determines to try again tomorrow, wanting to restore this nearly primordial connection. This story treats major themes Gaitskill is concerned with— conflicted characters looking back, comparing present "success" to the vitalities of the remembered past, and rethinking values.

"Trying to Be," like "Something Nice," involves life in a brothel, this time from the point of view of a young woman, Stephanie, who re-examines her life. The conflict is worked out through her relationship with a client, Bernard, with whom she is able to discuss "intellectual" things. Gradually she is led to examine her feelings of growing disharmony. When she begins to date Bernard outside the brothel, he insists on giving her money, and Stephanie realizes that prostitution could become her "real life." The last time she and Bernard meet, there is a cautious distance between them, and when they part this time, he does not leave money. After her initial distress she experiences a foretaste of freedom, and she contentedly buys and eats an apple.

"Secretary," set near Detroit, is a character study of a volitionless and reclusive young woman who lives at home with her parents and sister. The story appears to trace her dissolution into schizophrenia. A few weeks after she takes a job as a lawyer's secretary, her boss starts to abuse her—first verbally through insults about her work, then sexually. She allows herself to be thus victimized, perhaps because she feels she deserves abuse. At home her relations with her family deteriorate, and she begins to have sexual dreams about the lawyer. When she finally quits the job, the lawyer sends her a check for two hundred dollars more than he owes her, with a letter requesting her discretion. Some time later, when the lawyer runs for political office, she receives a call from a newspaper asking her to tell what she knows, but she refuses. The story ends with her enjoying the thought of being able to watch herself "from another place."

"Other Factors" studies Connie, another character who suffers disconnections from old friends, the "other factors" being the attenuating circumstances that keep Connie from commitments and loyalties. The core of the story is a severed relationship with an old friend,

Alice. Connie has conflicting memories of the friendship and resents the way she felt Alice had mistreated her. She begins to imagine her life as divided into fragmented "burdens," lacking cohesion. Meeting Alice, as expected, at a party, Connie feels mixed emotions, both recognizing her old friend's vulnerability and resenting her wealth. Connie resists Alice's offer to leave the party with her, and she walks home alone, with Alice's business card in her pocket. At one point she decides to throw the card into a trash can, but desists—because "One day she might come upon this card and decide it would be good to talk to somebody she hadn't spoken to in years." This ending suggests that Connie's relationships will always be tenuous and insecure.

The concluding story, "Heaven," is quite different from the others in the volume—because it is set outside the city, but more important because it deals directly with the frailties of family life. The focus is on Virginia, the mother of four children, and her relations with them, with her husband, and with a niece who stays with the family for a time. The story is told in fragments, all bearing on the difficulties of raising children (drugs, sex, headstrong independence, misunderstandings), of the silences that compound failures, and of the sadness wrought particularly by ruptures between women and their female charges. The story can be read in several ways, but at the end, when Virginia's husband declares that their family barbecue is "like heaven," the reader suspects that Virginia wistfully accepts his view as her own. In this story Gaitskill reveals a profound appreciation for the mysteries of family life and the burdens of familial love. Her ability to delineate a wide social scene and to empathize with a wider range of characters marked her as a writer of promise.

In 1991 Gaitskill published a novel, *Two Girls, Fat and Thin,* a take-off on Ayn Rand's objectivism; Rand appears in this work as Anna Granite. The novel traces the developing relationship between Dorothy Never (fat), an avid follower of Granite, and Justine Shade (thin), a journalist who seeks to expose Granite as a cultist. The novel moves between past and present, but the method is complicated by alternating chapters of Justine's third-person narration and Dorothy's more intimate first-person account. Although the title suggests contrast, the two women have much in common, not least that they were victims of child abuse. Critics generally praised the book, but some reviewers complained it was badly written—a fault others suggested was purposeful because they understood Gaitskill as deliberately imitating the weak structures of Rand's novels. Melissa Jane Hardie even views Gaitskill's "study of female masochism" as an act of "homage to Rand's own practice."

Gaitskill's second collection of short stories, *Because They Wanted To,* was published nearly a decade after *Bad Behavior,* in 1997. It was nominated for the PEN/Faulkner Award. It includes nine stories, the last of which is in four parts. The large rusty bolt and nut pictured on the dust jacket of the first edition suggest the confrontational and edgy sexual content of the collection. The title suggests the power of desires or appetites to move (and entrap) human beings, but also an inability to make firm and final decisions or to make moral judgments that might affect the lives of others. Echoes of the title are found occasionally throughout the collection, as in "Orchid," when a character has relations with two women "Because they wanted to, mostly," and in "Stuff," when a character says he had married four times, but only because the women had "wanted it so badly."

The collection varies in quality, as does Gaitskill's skill with language: sometimes the language is poetic and powerful, at other times it appears almost deliberately awkward, as if Gaitskill from paragraph to paragraph is straining to satisfy the interests of both intellectual and unsophisticated audiences. Elizabeth Young's comment that Gaitskill's "feet may be in SoHo but her heart is with the *New Yorker*" seems appropriate to this book.

Whereas in *Bad Behavior* the characters had the excuse of youth and the author the privilege of being a young writer, in *Because They Wanted To* there is a quality of weariness, of characters who have not succeeded in maturing emotionally in their twenties and now find themselves close to midlife still experimenting, all the more desperately as they get older. Gaitskill is usually willing to explore her characters' stories, but even she appears at times to be weary of their inabilities to get their lives together. Although sometimes her characters are the too-easy subjects of satire, at her best Gaitskill shows generous empathy for them and an ability to assess their frailties and failures realistically. Occasionally even the most subjective reader may yearn for some assertion of moral authority or an insistence on the exercise of adult social responsibilities.

Some of Gaitskill's characters seem frantic as they approach midlife and are still muddled about the directions of their lives. "The Wrong Thing," the concluding story, is an example of this confusion about identity. This long, four-part story features street-savvy, world-weary Susan, a poet who, on the verge of turning forty, is re-examining her life. "I have deep longings that will never be satisfied," she admits, and the story proceeds to examine how her deep longings for meaning and connection *might* be satisfied. Ultimately, however, they are not, and Susan ends up in a new-age

Dust jacket for Gaitskill's 1997 book, in which the title story depicts a teenage runaway eking out a living on the streets of Vancouver

garden releasing ladybugs. The four parts, although unified by Susan's first-person narration, do not cohere.

In the first part, "Turgor," she meets Frederick, who is only twenty-six, and she once again has to deal with the uncertainty of beginning relationships—this time with a man more than a decade younger than herself. She finds herself watching carefully, detecting an "absence" in him, and she does not encourage him. Nevertheless, in the second part, "Respect," she calls him, and at dinner he confuses her with talk of "respecting" her, which she reads almost as a weapon turned on her. When she leaves him this time, she feels physically ill but cannot "discharge the bad feeling."

In the third part, "Processing," still thinking of Frederick, Susan meets a young woman, Erin, and begins a sexual relationship with her—but one that does not "feel right," and so she ends it. The idea of "processing" personal feelings is continued in the final part, "Stuff," in which she meets and dates Kenneth, a sociologist who collects flea-market bargains—items that come

to symbolize in their abundance and variety the range and welter of her confused emotions. In the end, accompanied by a quotation from T. S. Eliot in which the characters are encouraged to "Wait without thought, for you are not ready for thought," Susan finds herself in a "healing garden" with Erin and her friends. Although she feels a terrifying loneliness there, she concludes that the ingredients for happiness are present, "abundant, breathing, and calm." The problem, however, is that this hopeful ending seems almost desperate, and the lack of resolution after all this processing is disturbing.

Another story, "The Blanket," deals with a relationship between a thirty-six-year-old woman, Valerie, and a twenty-four-year-old man, Michael. Valerie is taken with him, but given the discrepancy in their ages and the intensity of their feelings for each other, she believes the relationship cannot last. Their sexuality is acted out through mutual role-playing fantasies, but complications set in when she tells him the story of how she had once been raped. When Michael uses the rape as a springboard to another fantasy, Valerie is indignant, even though she realizes she may have inadvertently encouraged him. When they quarrel, they are astonished to find themselves exchanging admissions of love. Gaitskill's success in this story is partially because of her manipulation of point of view, as in "Romantic Weekend," allowing her to move easily among the mental anxieties of both participants, exposing both in a comic manner.

"The Girl on the Plane," selected for *The Best American Short Stories 1993,* probes the issue of acquaintance rape. It is a serious study of a difficult subject, and Gaitskill tells it through a married man, John Morton, who meets Lorraine, an attractive woman who reminds him of a girl from his youth. During his conversations with her he recollects his experiences with "poor Patty" LaForge, and in doing so comes to understand that a group orgy incident in which he had been involved during late adolescence had in fact been rape. The pivotal issue of definition is the woman's consent, which he admits to himself was never clear. Worse, he had known the girl was attracted to him, and he was unable to reciprocate except in this violent way. He feels free to admit it to this stranger on the plane because she had been forthright to him about her alcoholism—but perhaps, more important, because he wants her forgiveness. When he confesses to her, however, she freezes up, and he is left with his newly discovered remorse.

Other stories deal with contemporary therapeutic strategies; the best example is the opening story, "Tiny, Smiling Daddy." It is told from the point of view of a father who discovers that his daughter, Kitty, has published a piece about their father-daughter relationship in *Self* magazine. He feels vulnerable, and while he rushes off to get a copy of the magazine, he remembers his daughter's life with him and his wife. Although not particularly revealing, the article seems invasive. The gist is Kitty's own need to find appropriate language to help herself come to terms with her life; in polite but "ghastly talk-show language" she discusses their problems of communication and anger. She also discusses his rejection of her lesbianism—and he remembers the brutal insensitivity of his rejection, when he had responded that she meant "nothing" to him. Now, in dealing once again with his guilt, he remembers an instance of his own father's cruelty to him. At the end, he concludes, "Some kinds of loss are absolute. And no amount of self-realization or self-expression will change that." This conclusion is an acknowledgment that what he had said to her cannot be unsaid, and it serves as his acceptance of guilt with little hope for forgiveness. Whereas Kitty at least has the solace of pop psychology to help her deal with her pain, he cannot ease his guilt, ever.

In a lighter vein, "The Dentist" is concerned with Jill, who obviously needs therapy but does not understand the depth of her problem. The story begins with a huge billboard advertising Obsession perfume, which Jill thinks of as "a totem of sexualized pathology, . . . a picture made for people who can't bear to feel and yet still need to feel . . . by people sophisticated enough to fetishize their disability publicly"—an apt observation that might cover her own case (as well as those of many other Gaitskill characters). The story concerns Jill's obsession for her dentist, George, a topic she discusses ad nauseum with her friends and acquaintances, including her therapist. At every point the dentist appears to resist Jill's advances, including some crude sexual ones; he appears finally to give in to her mostly because she is so provocatively insistent. Still, his motives are not absolutely clear, leading Jill to believe that he might really be interested. Her desires are frustrated, however, despite her forwardness, and the last time they meet, it is clear that her aggression actually frightens him. Of course Jill tells this story to several "sophisticated" people who seem oblivious to sexual privacy. She wonders what they might think if she admitted to them that what first attracted her to the dentist was that "he was kind."

"Kiss and Tell" is a slight comic revenge story involving Lesly, who writes unsuccessful screenplays and obsesses over Nicki Piastrini, with whom he had carried on a brief but memorable fling. Nicki has gone on to fame and fortune as a movie actress, although she still remains friendly with him. Lesly, however, is bitterly envious: what better way, he thinks, to get back at her for her success than to write a screenplay based on Nicki's infidelities and career-minded ruthlessness. The problem is that his unknowing, excited agent sends the script to the actress who seems a perfect fit for the part—Nicki Piastrini. The movie is not made, and Nicki never speaks to Lesly again.

Another story about bad feelings between former lovers is "Orchid," involving two characters who had first known each other in college and now accidentally meet in Seattle. Margot, a social worker, feels the old attraction for the handsome psychopharmacologist, Patrick. After canceling several dates, Patrick shows her a CD-ROM he has produced that advocates the use of pharmaceutical drugs to overcome depression. Margot protests this solution, arguing that the clients she sees on a regular basis have problems for which drugs offer no cure. Margot wonders, "How had her light, heartless, lovely bête noire become this silly man?" In her review of their lives in the past, however, she discovers that Patrick had always been unable to live a meaningful, responsible life. Margot knows that his mother, who called him her "Orchid," had spoiled him, and that as a result he has hang-ups that keep him from fulfilling himself or maintaining loyalties.

Perhaps the two best pieces in the collection are "Comfort" and the title story. "Comfort," which appeared in *O. Henry Prize Stories 1997,* explores how comfort, though highly desired, seems unattainable. Daniel is called home from San Francisco to Iowa because his mother has been involved in a serious car accident. In Iowa he must confront memories of his childhood, but when he first sees his mother in the hospital he is overwhelmed with anxiety and rushes from the room. Later he has dinner with his father, a man he admires "as a suave, sneering gambler who might win at any time," even though he is presented as an insensitive and widely disliked bully. What seem to be emphasized in this story are degrees of discomfort, as when Daniel remembers the "overwhelming discomfort" between his mother and father. This feeling, the story suggests, is responsible for his anger, and perhaps for the distance between him and his brother. Possibly, too, discomfort is responsible for the difficulties he has in communicating emotions to his girlfriend, Jacquie, whom Daniel upbraids for not being comforting enough in her relationships with him and his family. Daniel's futile search for comfort is suggested with subtlety and detail.

The title story, "Because They Wanted To," however, may surpass "Comfort" in quality. It features sixteen-year-old Elise, who has run away to Vancouver, where she panhandles and does odd jobs in order to survive. She takes on a baby-sitting job in a slum tenement, although her employer says she cannot pay her for a week or two. Elise is left with two little boys and an infant in diapers. The events of her day of baby-sitting are filtered through memories of her own childhood. She remembers a history of conflict between her parents; her incestuous explorations with her brother Rick; Rick's physical abuse of their little brother, Robbie; visits to "cheap state psychiatrists"; family separations; the addition of step-parents and a new "sister"; and then running away and encountering abusive sexuality.

Despite her past, her bad habits, and her naiveté, Elise has a native goodness, and she is surprisingly intact, as shown when she persists in managing the difficult children long hours after their mother's suggested time of return. When the mother fails to return by midnight, Elise finally leaves, but not without appropriate concern for her charges: her sense of decency tells her to inform the neighbors of the situation before she departs. She knows she must not simply imitate the mother by abandoning the children, but she rightly refuses "parental" responsibility. This story is rife with menace, for as it proceeds through details of Elise's childhood, readers are led to expect a less worthy protagonist than Elise proves herself to be. That she refuses victimhood is part of Gaitskill's larger point. Unlike many others in this collection of stories, Elise is admirable in learning not to do things simply because she wants to.

Several of Gaitskill's stories remain uncollected, originally appearing in both paper and on-line periodicals. These works include "A Horrible Sensation of Love," which is archived at *Word.com,* and the chapter purportedly from a novel in progress, "Veronica," which was once found at *Thebody.com.* Two other stories, "The Crazy Person" and "The Rubbed Away Girl," have been published in the New York magazine *Open City.* Finally, with the short story "A Dream of Men," Gaitskill was published in *The New Yorker* on 23 November 1998. She was guest fiction editor of *Bookforum* for the Spring 2000 issue.

Beyond reviews of Gaitskill's books, there has been little published commentary on her work; essential foundational critical work remains to be done. She is often said to be transgressive and edgy. Young placed Gaitskill in an attenuated postfeminist "Bad Girl" tradition, along with Tama Janowitz and Catherine Texier, but it should be argued that Gaitskill's purposes are ultimately far more serious. Young states that, despite publishers' attempts to sensationalize Gaitskill, "there is far more innocence than wickedness in her work."

At this point Mary Gaitskill seems a writer still in the process of developing her ultimate voice. She has clearly retained her edge and may, in fact, be even more willing than in the past to present and argue difficult positions. Her views on sexuality may at times disturb, but her knowledge of sex and sexual identity as complex and mysterious is more accurate than the manner in which sexual politics is treated in consumer society and popular culture. Her concern for the mystery and fragility of human relationships is central to her work.

Taken as a whole, Gaitskill's fiction shows considerable repetition and a nearly obsessive thinness of content. Compared to writers such as Alice Munro, Lorrie Moore, or Ellen Gilchrist, Gaitskill is narrow and perhaps too patient with characters who sometimes have little depth or promise. Still, for some readers Gaitskill fills a gap by dealing with difficult situations faced by inexperienced and adolescent characters. Her ultimate importance may be that she earnestly addresses concerns often ignored by others and, in doing so, offers some readers glimpses into their lives and the lives of others.

Interviews:

Alexander Laurence, "Interview with Mary Gaitskill," *The Write Stuff* (1994) <http://www.altx.com/interviews/mary.gaitskill.html>;

Previewport Interview, *Previewport.com* <http://previewport.com/Home/gaitskill2-i.html>;

Charles Bock, "Interview with Mary Gaitskill," *Mississippi Review,* 27 (1999): 129–150.

References:

Mary Gaitskill Home Page, *Previewport.com* <http://previewport.com/Home/gaitskill2.html>;

Melissa Jane Hardie, "Fluff and Granite: Rereading Rand's Camp Feminist Aesthetics," in *Feminist Interpretations of Ayn Rand,* edited by Mimi Reisel Gladstein and Chris Matthew Sciabarra (University Park: Pennsylvania State University Press, 1999), pp. 363–389;

Elizabeth Young, "Library of the Ultravixens: Tama Janowitz; Mary Gaitskill; Catherine Texier," in *Shopping in Space: Essays on America's Blank Generation Fiction,* edited by Young and Graham Caveney (New York: Atlantic Monthly, 1992), pp. 165–181.

Tess Gallagher

(21 July 1943 –   )

William L. Stull
University of Hartford

and

Maureen P. Carroll
University of Hartford

See also the Gallagher entries in *DLB 120: American Poets Since World War II, Third Series,* and *DLB 212: Twentieth-Century American Western Writers, Second Series.*

BOOKS: *Stepping Outside* (Lisbon, Iowa: Penumbra, 1974);

Instructions to the Double (Port Townsend, Wash.: Graywolf, 1976);

On Your Own (Port Townsend, Wash.: Graywolf, 1978);

Portable Kisses (Seattle: Sea Pen Press & Paper Mill, 1978; expanded edition, Santa Barbara: Capra, 1992; 1994; expanded again, Newcastle upon Tyne, U.K.: Bloodaxe, 1996);

Under Stars (Port Townsend, Wash.: Graywolf, 1978);

Willingly (Port Townsend, Wash.: Graywolf, 1984);

Dostoevsky: A Screenplay, by Gallagher and Raymond Carver, published with *King Dog: A Screenplay,* by Ursula K. Le Guin (Santa Barbara: Capra, 1985);

A Concert of Tenses: Essays on Poetry, Poets on Poetry Series (Ann Arbor: University of Michigan Press, 1986);

The Lover of Horses and Other Stories (New York: Harper & Row, 1986; London: Hamilton, 1989);

Amplitude: New and Selected Poems (St. Paul, Minn.: Graywolf, 1987);

Moon Crossing Bridge (St. Paul, Minn.: Graywolf, 1992);

The Valentine Elegies (Fairfax, Cal.: Jungle Garden, 1993);

Owl-Spirit Dwelling: A Poem (Portland, Ore.: Trask House, 1995);

My Black Horse: New and Selected Poems (Newcastle upon Tyne, U.K.: Bloodaxe, 1995);

At the Owl Woman Saloon (New York: Scribner, 1997);

Soul Barnacles: Ten More Years with Ray (Ann Arbor: University of Michigan Press, 2000).

Tess Gallagher (photograph © Tim Crosby)

RECORDINGS: *Black Box 12* (Washington, D.C.: Watershed Foundation, 1977);

Some with Wings, Some with Manes (Washington, D.C.: Watershed Tapes, 1982);

Tess Gallagher: Prose and Poetry (Columbia, Mo.: American Audio Prose Library, 1994).

OTHER: Jeffrey Skinner, *A Guide to Forgetting: Poems,* selected by Gallagher (St. Paul, Minn.: Graywolf, 1988);

Raymond Carver, *A New Path to the Waterfall,* introduction by Gallagher (Boston: Atlantic Monthly, 1989; London: Collins-Harvill, 1989);

The Pushcart Prize, 1989–1990: Best of the Small Presses, introduction by Gallagher (Wainscott, N.Y.: Pushcart, 1989);

Carver, *Carver Country: The World of Raymond Carver,* photographs by Bob Adelman, introduction by Gallagher (New York: Scribners / Toronto: Collier Macmillan Canada, 1990; London: Pan, 1992);

Carver, *No Heroics, Please: Uncollected Writings,* edited by William L. Stull, foreword by Gallagher (London: Harvill, 1991; New York: Vintage, 1992);

"'3 A.M. Kitchen: My Father Talking'–Writing in Another Voice," in *Poets' Perspectives: Reading, Writing, and Teaching Poetry,* edited by Charles R. Duke and Sally A. Jacobsen (Portsmouth, N.H.: Boynton/Cook, 1992), pp. 31–36;

"Viva la Vida," in *Viva la Vida: Paintings by Alfredo Arreguin* (Tacoma, Wash.: Tacoma Art Museum, 1992), n. pag.;

"The Ghosts of Dreams," in *Remembering Ray: A Composite Biography of Raymond Carver,* edited by Stull and Maureen P. Carroll (Santa Barbara: Capra, 1993), pp. 103–107;

Robert Altman and Frank Barhydt, *Short Cuts: The Screenplay,* introduction by Gallagher (Santa Barbara: Capra, 1993);

Carver, *All of Us: The Collected Poems,* edited by Stull, introduction by Gallagher (London: Harvill, 1996; New York: Knopf, 1998);

Liliana Ursu, *The Sky behind the Forest: Selected Poems,* translated by Ursu, Adam J. Sorokin, and Gallagher (Newcastle upon Tyne, U.K.: Bloodaxe, 1997; Chester Springs, Pa.: Dufour, 1997);

"Séan McSweeney's Wild Gardening," in *Séan McSweeney: Bogland & Shoreline Sligo* (Dublin: Taylor Galleries, 1998), pp. 11–22;

"The Pure Place," in *Sleeping with One Eye Open: Women Writers and the Art of Survival,* edited by Marilyn Kallet (Athens: University of Georgia Press, 1999), pp. 167–183;

Carver, *Call If You Need Me: The Uncollected Fiction and Other Prose,* edited by Stull, foreword by Gallagher (London: Harvill, 2000; New York: Vintage, 2001);

"Soul-Making," in *Sorrow's Company: Writers on Loss and Grief,* edited by DeWitt Henry (Boston: Beacon Press, 2001), pp. 45–54;

"Two Mentors: From Orphanhood to Spirit-Companion," in *Passing the Word: Writers on Their Mentors,* edited by Lee Martin and Jeffrey Skinner (Louisville: Sarabande, 2001), pp. 39–41.

SELECTED PERIODICAL PUBLICATIONS–UNCOLLECTED:

DRAMA

Can I Get You Anything? and *The Favor,* by Gallagher and Raymond Carver, *Philosophy and Literature,* 22 (October 1998): 417–437.

NONFICTION

"Captives of the Common Good," review of *Short Stories* by Carol Bly, *New York Times Book Review,* 27 January 1985, p. 19;

"Delicate Balances," review of *A Stay by the River* by Susan Engberg, *New York Times Book Review,* 3 November 1985, p. 20;

"Privileged Peaks," *Vogue,* 178 (July 1988): 122, 125, 127;

"Island-Hopping in the Pacific Northwest," *Vogue,* 180 (June 1990): 174, 176, 178;

"Patterns of Devotion: A Collaborative Friendship of Painters and Writers," *Americas Review,* 23 (Fall–Winter 1995): 193–203;

"Staying on Earth (On Writing 'I Stop Writing the Poem')," *Poetry East,* 43 (Fall 1996): 13–15;

"What You Were Not Looking For," Baccalaureate address, Whitman College, 25 May 1997, *Whitman Magazine,* 19 (Summer 1997): 2–11;

"Angel Foot: A Double Portrait," *Evansville Review,* 8 (1998): 150–154;

"Not Translation, but Translatability: Carver to Altman/Story to Film," *Q/W/E/R/T/Y,* 9 (October 1999): 177–180.

Like the versatile denizen of Hummingbird Mountain in her story "Venison Pie," Tess Gallagher is a contemporary hybrid. Deeply rooted in her native Washington State, Gallagher draws on the literature and culture of places as distant as Ireland, Eastern Europe, and Japan. Though instinctively self-reliant, she has joined in collaborative projects with moviemakers and visual artists as well as other writers. Early recognized for her poetry, she has won acclaim for work in several genres: the essay, the screenplay, and the short story. Invoking the title of Gallagher's poetry collection *Amplitude* (1987), Emily Leider of *The San Francisco Chronicle Review* (10 January 1988) observed that her "inclusiveness allows qualities usually seen as antithetical to meet in reconciliation, or at least peaceful coexistence." In the fluid landscape of Gallagher's poems and stories, horses transform houses, saloons become salons, and "nettles could be feathers."

As these ambiguities suggest, the unifying pattern of Gallagher's life and art has been the harmony of opposites. This principle of *discordia concors* aligns her work with pre-Socratic philosophy, metaphysical poetry, and Zen koans. "I like to have these contradictions in view," she wrote in *A Concert of Tenses: Essays on Poetry* (1986), "not for one to cancel out the other, but so that the whole picture is before me." In keeping with this non-Aristotelian outlook, Gallagher has termed her favored mode of expression "lyric-narrative," a hybrid of song and story whose antecedents include broadside ballads and heroic epics. The result, whether her medium is poetry or prose, is a haunting blend of precision and suggestiveness, tenderness and toughness, that has made her, as the short-story writer Pam Houston wrote in the *Washington Post* (14 September 1997), "the female voice of the Pacific Northwest."

Tess Gallagher was born Theresa Jeanette Bond in Port Angeles, Washington, on 21 July 1943. She was the first child of migrants to the north coast of the Olympic Peninsula, the area between the Strait of Juan de Fuca and the Olympic Mountains. The strait is both barrier and gateway, separating the United States from Canada and opening the harbors of Seattle's Puget Sound to the shipping lanes of the Pacific.

Gallagher's father, Leslie Bond, was born in Oklahoma. He came from a family of itinerant farmers, laborers, gamblers, and horse traders scattered across the American Southwest. Like so many restless young men of the Dust Bowl generation, he rode the rails during the Great Depression, seeking work and opportunity. After stays in Iowa, Texas, and New Mexico, he eventually reached the Pacific Northwest. Throughout the 1930s, as related in Gallagher's memoir "My Father's Love Letters," this normally laconic man maintained a correspondence with a woman from an outwardly contrasting background. Unlike the rootless Bonds, Georgia Morris came from a family of "land rich" cattle ranchers in the Ozark Mountains of Missouri. As the ten-year courtship indicates, it took effort to persuade Morris to begin a new life in unknown territory; yet she did, arriving in Port Angeles by bus and marrying Leslie Bond in 1941.

During much of Theresa Bond's childhood, her parents toiled as "gypo loggers" in the Olympic forest. Her father rigged the cable high line from tree to tree while her mother performed the risky job of lashing the steel choker to the fallen timber. "It has always inspired me with a pride in my sex," Gallagher later said of her mother's logging. The writer credits her storytelling ability and her fascination with "the feminine heroic"—

Tess and Leslie Bond on his mother's porch in Port Angeles, Washington, in 1944 (courtesy of Tess Gallagher)

strong-willed women from Teresa of Avila to Calamity Jane—to her own mother's example.

From her father Bond learned the bitter facts of working-class life. The poems that first brought her critical acclaim, most notably "Black Money" and "3 A.M. Kitchen: My Father Talking," depict a man in violent conflict with his family and himself. Her father's alcohol-induced rages "terrorized" the writer's childhood, yet her father sometimes confessed his inmost doubts to his firstborn daughter. Called on to reconcile opposing forces—mother and father, saloon and salon, love and anger—Bond developed "ambassadorial skills" that enabled her to speak for two sides of any story. This harmonizing ability held her family together, and it became a hallmark of her art.

With three younger brothers and a baby sister, Bond was early cast in the traditional female roles of housekeeper and caretaker. Offsetting this domesticity was the wild Olympic forest, where she and her siblings played among the giant trees. Her only luxury at home was classical piano lessons. She continued her musical training into her teens, well after her parents had left the woods for jobs in town, her father as a pulp-mill worker and longshoreman, her mother as manager of the crowded household.

As Gallagher later recounted in her essay "Angel Foot: A Double Portrait," the delight of her adolescent years was a dark filly given to her by her beloved uncle Porter Morris and ridden during summers on her grandfather's farm in Missouri. She counted Angel Foot her "spirit sign" and double. "We were two beings waiting to expend ourselves in motion across space," she wrote; "She is melded onto my will, my sense of what it is to slip humanness and inhabit myself as a keen yet boundless going forth." Richly symbolic horses abound in Gallagher's writings. Although reluctant to demystify her totem animal, she has said that the horsewoman embodies "the union of animal and human spirit," a harmony of intellect and instinct, gentleness and strength.

Bond graduated from high school in June 1961. That summer she worked as a reporter and photographer for the *Port Angeles Evening News,* where she found a mentor in its outspoken publisher, Esther Webster. In the fall Bond entered the University of Washington in Seattle. She held three jobs to pay her tuition but found journalism classes dull compared to actual newspaper work. At the university she befriended a young Mexican artist named Alfredo Arreguin. The friendship has endured, and Arreguin's artworks, like those of his wife, the painter Susan Lytle, have often been paired with Gallagher's writings. This collaboration of visual and verbal artists is celebrated in her essays "Viva la Vida" (1992) and "Patterns of Devotion" (1995).

In spring 1963, seeking a more stimulating curriculum, Bond applied for admission into a creative writing course taught by the Pulitzer Prize–winning poet Theodore Roethke. She was accepted into what proved to be Roethke's final class before his death that summer. "It was the first time I had ever been *chosen* to do anything I considered of consequence," she later wrote in *A Concert of Tenses.* At once rigorous and liberating, the class gave her a sense of "awe and privilege." It was the advent of her calling as a writer.

Pursuit of that calling was delayed, however, by a series of upheavals during the 1960s. Roethke's death was followed by a tragedy in her own family when Bond's fifteen-year-old brother, Denzel, was killed in an auto accident. Also during this period Bond met an engineering student named Lawrence Gallagher, and in 1964 they married. Intent on a career in aviation, he joined the U.S. Marine Corps, a decision that took the newlyweds first to the racially polarized South, then into the nationally divisive Vietnam War.

Eventually Lawrence Gallagher was called away to fly jet planes in Southeast Asia. Tess Gallagher worked stateside in hospitals and libraries. Studying part-time, she earned her B.A. degree from the University of Washington in 1967. She felt wrenched by the personal and political tensions of the war. In what became a pattern of withdrawal and renewal, she sought perspective from afar. After traveling in Europe, she reached a place that became a refuge for her, the locality of Ballindoon in County Sligo in northwest Ireland. Both Gallaghers returned to the United States the next year, and they divorced in 1969. In retrospect, she called the marriage "a casualty of the war."

The inspiration Gallagher had drawn from Roethke's class led her back to the University of Washington in 1970–and back to writing. "I began to make a formula," Gallagher wrote in *A Concert of Tenses,* "which translates roughly: words = more than physical power = freedom from enslavement to job-life = power to direct and make meaning in your own life." Seeking verbal empowerment, Gallagher studied under the future American poet laureate Mark Strand and completed her M.A. degree in 1971. The next year she did advanced work in poetry, cinema theory, and moviemaking as a teaching fellow at the Iowa Writers' Workshop.

On 2 June 1972 her uncle Porter Morris died under suspicious circumstances on his Missouri farm. Eventually three men, accomplices in a scheme of robbery, arson, and revenge, were charged with murder. Their trial for this brutal crime resulted in short sentences for two men and release of the third, an outcome that haunted Gallagher for years. "I began, in a steady way, to move toward accepting my own death," she wrote in *A Concert of Tenses;* "In the poems I've written that please me most, I seem able to see the experience with dead-living eyes, with a dead-living heart."

At the Iowa Writers' Workshop she met the poet Michael Burkard, and the two students married in 1973. Gallagher's first book, the poetry chapbook *Stepping Outside,* was published in 1974, the same year she received her M.F.A. degree from the University of Iowa. Gallagher and Burkard shared teaching posts during the mid 1970s until marital tensions prompted her to go again to Ireland. Sheltering in a "caravan" (house trailer) near the Ballindoon graveyard, Gallagher wrote poems in which she sought to reconcile conflicting forces in her life and art: loyalty and independence, domesticity and restlessness, narrative lucidity and lyric intensity. She was welcomed by a group of writers in the divided city of Belfast, among them Ciaran Carson, Medbh McGuckian, and Michael Longley. In

1977, with her perspective once more clarified by distance, she flew home. She and Burkard were divorced that summer.

Gallagher's first commercially published books of poetry, *Instructions to the Double* (1976) and *Under Stars* (1978), chart her travels and travails. The central subject of both books is selfhood, a female writer's quest for personal and artistic autonomy. To achieve it she must cast off the stereotypical "doubles"–siren, servant, victim–foisted on her by a patriarchal culture. At the same time, she must liberate her subversive shadow double as a poet. "It's a dangerous mission," she instructs herself in the title poem of the first book. "You / could die out there. You / could live forever." In *Under Stars* a two-part arrangement, "The Ireland Poems" and "Start Again Somewhere," confirms the paradox that to come home she must leave home. Most important, by the end of her odyssey, as she writes in "On Your Own," she has found the antidote to insecurity in self-reliance: "It's like this on your own: the charms / unlikely, the employment / solitary, the best love always / the benefit of a strenuous doubt." Gallagher makes these self-discoveries in her first two books. In later poems and stories she expands them on a societal canvas.

In November 1977 Gallagher met Raymond Carver, the short-story writer and poet who became her lover, critic, and "companion soul" through the next decade. Like her, Carver was the child of Depression-era migrants to the Pacific Northwest. Born in the Columbia River hamlet of Clatskanie, Oregon, in 1938, he had grown up in the central Washington farming town of Yakima. During the years that Gallagher's father toiled in pulp mills, Carver's father worked in sawmills. Both writers were firstborn children of alcoholic men whose drinking had destabilized their families. Unlike Gallagher, Carver had inherited the disease, and when he met her he was just emerging from a near-fatal ten-year bout with alcoholism.

In spite of mutual attraction, she was wary. Carver was in the throes of ending a twenty-year marriage and starting a new life. During the next year, as he regained his sobriety and rebuilt his reputation, he and Gallagher communicated daily. They began living together in El Paso, Texas, on New Year's Day 1979. It was the start of what in her poem "Elegy with a Blue Pony" Gallagher called an "imperishable collaboration." The two writers helped reshape each other's art during the next ten years. *Instructions to the Double* and *Under Stars* had won Gallagher recognition as a promising young poet. Carver held roughly equal stature in short fiction, thanks to his debut collection *Will You Please Be Quiet, Please?* (1976). During the 1980s, even as

Dust jacket for Gallagher's first collection of short stories (1986), which prompted reviewers to compare aspects of her fiction to the works of Flannery O'Connor, Grace Paley, and Muriel Spark

each writer gained stature in his and her primary genre, a creative turnabout took place.

For Carver the first fruits of the union were two contrasting books of stories. In 1981 he published his so-called minimalist masterpiece *What We Talk about When We Talk about Love,* a book in which the astringent voice and vision reflect the bleakness of his alcoholic years. He followed this slim volume with the richer, fuller, "more generous" stories of *Cathedral* (1983). Carver credited his growth to Gallagher. "My life began to open up," he said in an interview included in *Conversations with Raymond Carver* (1990); "There is more of a fullness as a result of Tess's good eye and encouragement."

Gallagher's life and writing opened up as well, although the growth involved bereavement. Her next book of poems, *Willingly* (1984), is dedicated to Carver, but its subject is her father's death. Smoke from paper mills and cigarettes had seared the lungs of Leslie Bond for decades, and on 6 October 1982 he died of cancer. In *Willingly* Gallagher imaginatively time traveled through his life and hers, backward to her childhood and forward past the moment of his death, into a future where her father's spirit flows into hers. "And what are dreams," she wrote in "Candle, Lamp & Firefly," "when the eyes open on similar worlds / and you are dead in my living?"

A prose version of this revelation ends the title story of her first book of fiction, *The Lover of Horses and Other Stories* (1986). Gallagher had written short stories as early as 1969, but during the 1970s she concentrated on poems. Living with Carver reawakened her love of storytelling. "I had already begun writing narrative poems," she noted in a 1986 interview with Lori Miller, citing "Boat Ride" and "Woodcutting on Lost Mountain" in *Willingly*. Soon enough her partner's stories prompted her to write her own. "We edit real hard for each other," she told interviewer Paul Andrews in 1986, "and encourage each other to try new things."

The Lover of Horses includes twelve stories on themes well established in Gallagher's poems: the unruly interplay of self and family, individual and community, male and female, word and deed. The setting is the American West, and the characters are mainly working-class women from small towns. Gallagher draws inspiration from a master of the modern short story, Anton Chekhov. In her stories, as in Chekhov's, plot is subordinate to character, with emphasis less on action than on understanding. Painful insights are assuaged with wry humor and faith in human growth.

"As a poet," Michiko Kakutani wrote in her 6 September 1986 *New York Times* review of *The Lover of Horses,* "Tess Gallagher has written movingly of damaged relationships, misplaced selves, and the losses incurred by time and death." These vicissitudes pervade *The Lover of Horses,* and they converge in several stories focused on a woman's struggle to grow up. In the title story "the difficult and complex relationship between men and horses" evokes long-standing conflicts in the first-person narrator's family and soul. For years she has dutifully shuttled between mother and father, horse and house, saloon and salon, refusing to commit herself to either side. At the moment of her father's death, "in a raw pulsing of language" that signals her emergence as a writer, she claims her birthright as an outlaw: "But from that night forward I vowed to be filled with the first unsavory desire that would have me," she declares, "To plunge myself into the heart of my life and be ruthlessly lost forever." Paradoxically, from this plunge she rises a free woman.

Other stories present less dramatic efforts to rescue "misplaced selves" or gain autonomy. In the Chekhovian sketch "A Pair of Glasses" a precocious girl plays grownup by donning needless eyewear, only to be thrust back into childhood by skeptical adults. "Desperate Measures" recounts a female reporter's coming of age under the tutelage of a charming outlaw who bets his life on the toss of a coin. The story "Turpentine," although less lyrical than "The Lover of Horses," likewise depicts emerging selfhood. In this realistic yet symbolic tale, an encounter with a cosmetics saleswoman prompts Ginny Skoyles to drop the mask of impassivity she has long shown to her husband and the world.

Other stories in *The Lover of Horses* depict damaged relationships, the injuries ranging from wounded pride in "The Wimp" to emotional adultery in "At Mercy" to total war between the sexes in "Recourse." A discrepancy between her husband's words and deeds prompts the central character in "Beneficiaries" to speak up for herself. "Bad Company" is a study of belated understanding. During the course of several visits to the cemetery a widow comes to see that the "bad company" in her unfulfilling marriage included both her husband and herself. It is a humbling insight, and it prompts her to accept a grave beside the man she could not bring herself to love in life.

Matters of love, death, and loyalty are highlighted in the three remaining stories. "The Woman Who Saved Jesse James" takes its keynote from the Missouri outlaw ballad "Jesse James." Sorting through a pile of unanswered mail, Lorna Parker fears that like "that dirty little coward that shot Mister Howard" (the traitor Robert Ford, who killed Jesse under his law-abiding alias, Thomas Howard) she has betrayed her friends, both the living and the dead. The fact that loyalty has its limits proves liberating, however, when she accepts an open future. "I would just have to hope somebody, even a stranger, would give me help and comfort," she reflects; "But for now, I was ready to take up my life and do the next thing I could."

In "King Death," as in the title poem of *Willingly,* a first-person narrator is roused from sleep by the activity of a housepainter working just outside her bedroom. The awakening is spiritual and physical, as is the feeling of renewal evoked by a fresh exterior. The theme of the story is made explicit in the poem: "This is ownership, you think, arriving / in the heady afterlife of paint smell. / A deep opening goes on in you." To open to the afterlife, however, one must face down death. In the story the confrontation takes two forms. First, the narrator must overcome her antipathy to "King Death," a sodden vagrant who is the shadow double of her husband, a recovering alcoholic. Second, she must stand up to "the Mad Hatter," a raging neighbor who trains his pistol on King Death and her. When the hothead shoots his gun into the sky, she undergoes a resurrec-

Gallagher and Raymond Carver (photograph by Marion Elllinger)

tion. "I felt like I'd died and come to life," she says, her spirit renewed by her brush with violent death.

Joy Williams, a writer whose stories often focus on the young, noted in a blurb for *The Lover of Horses* that Gallagher "writes with great grace about aging people whose vision of irremediable loss is as sharp as the last daybreak." That vision is nowhere sharper than in "Girls," the closing story in *The Lover of Horses*. In this touching reprise on selfhood and mortality the title characters have become old women. After years apart Ada Gilman visits her friend Esther Cox, only to find Esther's memories of their girlhood have been erased by a stroke. The lack of recognition is daunting evidence of the ravages of time—and a blow to Ada's pride. Ada's words fail to restore the bond between the women, but Esther in her frailty knows a deeper language. She rubs Ada's feet, pats her cheek, and lies beside her through a fearful night. In the morning, as Ada primps before a mirror, she feels the years dissolve. "They could be two young women readying themselves to go out," she thinks; "Somehow the kindness and inti-

macy they'd shared as girls had lived on in them." This life-affirming insight ends the story, and the book, on a note of love and self-acceptance.

Critics found much to praise in *The Lover of Horses*. "Gallagher writes complex stories about real people," wrote Valerie Miner in a 9 November 1986 review for *Newsday*. "She refines her tales through a sophisticated intelligence and a deep empathy." Gallagher's arresting epiphanies were likened to Flannery O'Connor's. Her homespun wisdom was compared to Grace Paley's. Her offbeat humor recalled Muriel Spark's. She was praised for revealing the miraculous in the mundane. For reviewer Emily Leider, writing for the *San Jose Mercury News* (28 December 1986), the outstanding feature of the book was a paradox. "Gallagher brings together two qualities usually considered to be at odds," she wrote: "down-home naturalness . . . and the kind of spirituality that gives highest values to those qualities that are hardest to see, define, or fully comprehend."

The 1980s were richly productive years for Gallagher. From 1983 to 1987 she shared two houses in

Port Angeles with Carver. One was a weathered Victorian, the other a contemporary "Sky House" perched above the strait. Typically they worked apart by day, then spent the night together. "Only another writer can understand a writer's need for solitude," Gallagher told interviewer Tom Jenks in 1986, a point Carver seconded. Even as they wrote their separate works, they collaborated on others, including the screenplay *Dostoevsky* (1985). Together they made reading tours of England, Ireland, continental Europe, and South America. Toward the end of the decade each produced a milestone book. Hers was *Amplitude: New and Selected Poems* (1987). His was *Where I'm Calling From: New and Selected Stories* (1988).

Their collaboration, however, was cut short. Like Gallagher's father, Carver was a heavy smoker. In the fall of 1987 he was diagnosed with lung cancer. Over the next year he underwent surgery and treatment, and on 17 June 1988 the writers celebrated their eleven-year union by getting married. The cancer returned, and Gallagher bolstered Carver's spirits by urging him to write. The result was *A New Path to the Waterfall* (1989), a book of last poems that bears Carver's name but is clearly a joint work. It was completed shortly before he died, at the age of fifty, on 2 August 1988.

In the poem "Summer Fog" Carver tries to imagine the "stupendous grief" Gallagher will face after his death. "I'm in mourning and celebration for the artist and the man," she said at his memorial service in New York City, "and also for that special entity which was our relationship, which allowed such a beautiful alchemy in our lives, a kind of luminous reciprocity." Mourning and memorializing dominated her life for several years. She saw to it that Carver's remaining works were published, that his books were translated into other languages, that documentaries about him were filmed, and that friends committed their memories of him to paper.

Two books of poetry depict the process of her mourning. The first, *Moon Crossing Bridge* (1992), is an extended elegy. As in *Willingly*, Gallagher accompanies the spirit of a loved one into death and then returns to life. Like the moon in the opening poem, "Yes," she simultaneously gleams and mourns. From Kyoto's famed Togetsu bridge she watches time and eternity flow into an all-embracing sea of "dead-aliveness." In the closing poems she finds that, far from reducing her capacity to love, her husband's death has enlarged it to include the living and the dead.

Gallagher's death-defying quest in *Moon Crossing Bridge* is both heroic and erotic. Having found love constant beyond death, she celebrates love's earthly pleasures in a companion volume, an expansion of the 1978 chapbook *Portable Kisses* (1992, 1994). In this work her alter ego is the Kiss, a sassy, sexy "fishwife of the heart's raw daring." Randy and rebellious, the Kiss joins the CIA, luxuriates in her bath, and buys a fancy hat. "As a character," Gallagher observed in an interview published in *Soul Barnacles: Ten More Years with Ray* (2000), "the Kiss is a kind of double for me. She's out beyond the boundaries. And she's full of vinegar and iodine." In short, the Kiss is female flesh and blood.

A third collection, *My Black Horse: New and Selected Poems* (1995), presents the poet in midcareer. New poems reassess long-standing topics—doubles, loved ones, and the morality of art. They also point in new directions, most notably toward Eastern Europe. (In 1997 Gallagher and Adam J. Sorokin collaborated with Romanian writer Liliana Ursu on an English translation of Ursu's poetry collection *The Sky behind the Forest*. In addition, like the densely figurative work in *Moon Crossing Bridge* and *Portable Kisses,* the new poems confirm a change in Gallagher's style since Carver's death. "I think with Ray I got more and more narrative and linear," she reflected in *Soul Barnacles;* "When he was gone I moved back into this more complex psyche in the arena of my poetry, while I've tried to keep the clarity in daily life."

The emergence of new "spirit signs" in Gallagher's writings of the 1990s underscores this shift in sensibility. The earthbound horses so prominent in *Willingly* and *The Lover of Horses* are increasingly accompanied by creatures of the air. Butterflies and hummingbirds, Old and New World emblems of the active soul, figure prominently in Gallagher's poems of love and mourning. A darker, more ambiguous bird, however, becomes her totem in the poetry chapbook *Owl-Spirit Dwelling* (1995) and the fiction collection *At the Owl Woman Saloon* (1997).

Collaboration with Carver had prompted Gallagher to write short stories in the 1980s. Transformation of his stories into a movie led her back to fiction in the 1990s. Shortly after Carver's death, the director Robert Altman, acclaimed for innovative multilevel movies such as *M*A*S*H* (1970) and *Nashville* (1975), took an option on Carver's work. The result was *Short Cuts* (1993), a freewheeling adaptation of nine stories and a poem into a prizewinning movie. Gallagher consulted on the script, joined the actors on location, and stoutly defended Altman's right to reimagine Carver's work. She has since contributed an essay, "Not Translation but Translatability," to a special issue of the journal *Q/W/E/R/T/Y* (1999) devoted to *Short Cuts,* and the making of the movie figures prominently in *Soul Barnacles.*

The movie took Gallagher back to Carver's fiction, and once again his stories were a catalyst for hers. "Ray had given me confidence and a lot of his time, his faith in my fiction writing," she recalled in *Soul Barnacles;* "I had come to love the short story form. . . . And I had missed it." Initially she took the theme of her second book of fiction from a proverb about anger: "If you contemplate revenge, dig two graves." As stories accumulated, however, the title "Dig Two Graves" proved confining. "The book wouldn't adhere to that," she said in an interview in *Rustic Rub;* "It became larger and ultimately moved to include some very tender and compassionate elements."

Foremost among those elements is healing, the mysterious process of physical and spiritual renewal. This overarching theme is signaled by the title *At the Owl Woman Saloon.* None of the sixteen stories in the book bears that name, but the spirit of Owl Woman, the great Papago healer Juana Maxwell, hovers over nearly every tale. Like her ancient counterparts Lilith and Athena, whose avian emblem she shares, Owl Woman is a shadowy figure. She is associated with opposing forces—wisdom and witchcraft, light and darkness, love and death. In her healing songs she connects these powers, serving as a conduit between the living and the dead.

The setting of the stories is once again the rainy towns and forests of the author's native Northwest. At a deeper level, however, many of the tales take place in the realm of transformation. Gallagher calls attention to this ambiguity by prefacing the book with dictionary definitions of the overlapping words *saloon* and *salon.* Each denotes a traditionally gendered American space, the masculine barroom and the feminine sitting room or beauty parlor. In practice, however, the spaces and the genders tend to merge, as the stories amply demonstrate.

The convergence of opposites is happily confirmed in the first tale, "The Red Ensign," when two men invade the beauty shop where the narrator, a divorcée, is being coifed. "Are these guys illiterate or what?" she initially fumes. "'*Owl Woman Salon,*' the sign says. Did they think it said 'Owl Woman SALOON'? I am thinking: saloon or salon—you walk in one way and come out another." Just such a transformation occurs when the narrator overhears one of the men's colorful tales and her resentment turns to passionate attraction. "The Red Ensign" shows that what unites saloon and salon at a level deeper than etymology is the transformative power of stories. "This book is a storytelling saloon," Gallagher told the *Spokesman-Review* (1 May 1997), noting the metafictional aspect of her work. "I hope you go into my book one way and come out another, that it touches your life and makes you think you are alive."

As in *The Lover of Horses,* topics established in Gallagher's poetry—misplaced selves, damaged relationships, losses incurred through time and death—provide the subject matter of *At the Owl Woman Saloon.* Explorations of selfhood include a lyrical study of dissociation, "She Who Is Untouched by Fire," in which the central character's "strange loss of herself" adds new dimensions to her life. "Venison Pie," subtitled "from the Journal of a Contemporary Hybrid," reveals "how life overlaps its own footprints with question marks" as the narrator, "a bearer of legends," recounts her hybrid ancestry in the florid mode of magic realism. Strange disruptions of the ordinary pervade "The Leper," a darkly comic tale. There, the assaults on the narrator's equanimity include the invasion of her house by a funeral party and the spectacle of a herd of horses plunging into the sea. Through it all, her self-possession never falters, thanks to a well-developed sense of wonder.

Gallagher devotes the bulk of her stories to human relationships, focusing on the sexual, social, and familial conflicts they inevitably entail. The unisex clientele of her salo(o)n is exemplified by her telling nearly a third of the stories from a man's point of view. These include a stinging satire on academic megalomania, "The Poetry Baron," as well as two stories of vengeance tempered by compassion, "I Got a Guy Once" and "To Dream of Bears."

The remaining stories are told from a woman's viewpoint. Rivalry gives way to reconciliation in "The Mother Thief" when the central character steps into her adoptive cousin's shoes. Red-hot anger roils beneath the surface of "Creatures," one of the strongest stories in the book. In "Creatures," as in "The Red Ensign," the female sanctuary of the beauty parlor has been disrupted by a man. In this case it is the proprietor's husband, whose fecklessness and infidelity have driven her to an aggressive act of cruelty, the needless euthanizing of two of the beloved salon cats. When a third cat is driven to violence by a spate of teasing, it is as though the owner's anger at her husband has exploded in the room.

The transformative effects of time and death, themes foregrounded in *Willingly* and *Moon Crossing Bridge,* figure prominently in *At the Owl Woman Saloon.* True to the inclusive spirit of the book, widowers as well as widows are among the focal characters. Taking a cue from her essay "The Poem as Time Machine," Gallagher treats temporal consciousness as a fluid medium in which past, present, and future events comingle in an ever-changing stream of possibilities. In "A Box of Rocks" and "Coming and Going," a widower and a widow, respectively, discover that loyalty to a deceased spouse, however imperfect he or she may have been in life, offsets the isolation of bereavement. Gallagher's mordant wit flashes in the latter story when the widow

with a catch in his voice. Her girl friends said it didn't sound like your regular excuse.

He'd also started bringing home single rose buds wrapped in cellophane from the supermarket. Out of the blue, he'd call Elna from a pay phone to say things like, "Hi Honey, just wanted you to know I love you."

It had been hard for Elna to believe Eugene had somebody on the side, and even harder to admit it, once she believed it. Shelly had been all too willing to confirm the diagnosis. She'd had her own experiences with cheating men and had even shared an article out of a women's magazine that told all the signs. "Constant irritability and fault-finding"—those were two they'd agreed especially fit Eugene.

Shelly called for the cats by name, and Elna, who'd been methodically swivelling the curling rod to the teenager's head, withdrew the rod and stepped over to Shelly. She bent and in a confidential tone said, "Lucky and Lightning are no longer with us. They've gone where all good but sadly flawed creatures go." Then she moved back to her client as if she'd dispensed with a very unpleasant matter.

Shelly tried to take this in, that the cats were never to be seen again and, further, that her friend had intended, even arranged this. The respite Shelly had looked forward to suddenly seemed out of range. She consoled herself by noticing that the remaining young black cat, Veronica, was basking in the last rays of afternoon sunlight. Shelly nudged her with the toe of her shoe and the cat blinked her eyes open and shut several times, as if completing some coded message from her dream-filled interior, then shut them again.

"I wish I could have gone with them, straight to Kitty Heaven," Elna said. "Do not pass Safeway or Twelve-Star Video. One minute the needle,

Page from the revised typescript for "Creatures," a story collected in Gallagher's 1997 book, At the Owl Woman Saloon *(Charvat Collection, The Rare Books and Manuscripts Library of the Ohio State University Libraries)*

informs a process server that her husband has "relocated," directing him to the graveyard. "My Gun" likewise takes a comic turn. There, a widow uncertain whether to find a new mate or buy a gun for self-protection discovers that an attractive man, "loaded and ready," may fulfill both needs. The characters in "Mr. Woodriff's Neckties" include a kindly widower, his widowed neighbor, and her recently deceased husband, a well-known writer much like Carver, whose gratitude sustains the others even after he has died.

Healing of the spirit by story, poem, or prayer is the subject of the three remaining tales. "Rain Flooding Your Campfire" is Gallagher's wryly metafictional version of Carver's best-known story, "Cathedral." Like his version, hers concerns an evening spent with a blind man during which several characters come to see their lives anew. In "A Glimpse of the Buddha," as in the poem "Linoleum," Gallagher's theme is the holiness of the ordinary, difficult as that sanctity may be to find in modern life. The final story in the book, "The Woman Who Prayed," movingly evokes the healing force of sacred speech. Believing herself betrayed by her husband and a girlhood rival, Dotty Lloyd finds unexpected strength and comfort in "the calm space of prayer." Instead of withdrawing into bitterness, she expands her prayers to include refugees, accident victims, "anyone, anywhere betrayed, bereft, and lonely." Her prayer becomes her letter to the world, and in the final lines she gets a reassuring answer.

The eclectic spirituality of *At the Owl Woman Saloon* bothered some reviewers, but the majority followed Sherri Hallfren of *The San Francisco Sunday Chronicle Book Review* (31 August 1997) in praising Gallagher's fusion of "plain speech and large vision." Perhaps because of its setting and milieu, the book made an especially positive impression on readers in the western states. "Tess Gallagher illuminates the lives of her everyday characters with lyrical prose, deep respect for their small concerns, and joy at their foibles and wisdom," wrote Judy Doenges in *The Seattle Times* (14 December 1997). For Jeff Baker of *The Oregonian* (28 December 1997) the book marked at once a milestone and a turning point: "Gallagher has found her own voice and moved beyond the influence of her late husband, even as she pays tribute to him."

In her essay "A Nightshine beyond Memory," written on the tenth anniversary of Carver's death and included in *Soul Barnacles*, Gallagher voiced a similar thought. "Ray also seems to have moved with me in the accomplishment of *At the Owl Woman Saloon*," she wrote, "for he is an important function of my self-witnessing—though one not confined to me alone, rather a beneficence shared and sustained with others." That sharing has continued in her second book of nonfiction, *Soul*

Barnacles: Ten More Years with Ray (2000) and her foreword to five newly discovered stories by Carver published in *Call If You Need Me: The Uncollected Fiction and Other Prose* (2000).

Artistically, culturally, and spiritually, Gallagher's horizons continue to expand. Her recent teaching appointments include the 1997–1998 Edward F. Arnold Visiting Professorship at Whitman College, a semester as poet-in-residence in spring 1998 at the Stadler Center for Poetry at Bucknell University, and an Ichihara Foundation fellowship that took her to Japan in fall 2000 to meet writers, scholars, and religious leaders.

Like the protean storyteller in "Venison Pie," Tess Gallagher remains "fascinated . . . by any profusion of hybrids." That fascination shapes her lyric-narrative poetry and her magically realistic fiction, all of which appear frequently in magazines and anthologies. Gallgher's hybridity is evident as well in her continuing involvement with international writers and artists. With Liliana Ursu and Adam Sorokin she continues to work on the translation of Ursu's poems from the Romanian. With Hiromi Hashimoto she is preparing a translation of her own short stories into Japanese. With her companion of recent years, Irish painter and storyteller Josie Gray, she is collaborating on a book of oral tales, tentatively titled "The Courtship Stories." As she declared in her poem "Legend with Sea Breeze" (in *Moon Crossing Bridge*): "I just want to ride my black horse, / to see where he goes."

Interviews:

Roxanne Lawler, "Her Poetry Hits Home in Land of 'Faithful Rain,'" *Peninsula Daily News,* 16 September 1984, p. C1;

Lori Miller, "Away from Ego," *New York Times Book Review,* 28 September 1986, p. 9;

Penelope Moffet, "A Poet Who Savors the Elegance of Simplicity," *Los Angeles Times,* 16 October 1986, V6–7;

Nicholas O'Connell, "Tess Gallagher," in his *At the Field's End: Interviews with Twenty Pacific Northwest Writers* (Seattle: Madrona, 1987), pp. 154–177;

Moffet, "An Interview with Tess Gallagher," *Poets & Writers,* 16 (July/August 1988): 19–22;

James McKinley, "An Active Calm: An Interview with Tess Gallagher," *New Letters,* 59 (1993): 57–65;

Jay Woodruff, "'Red Poppy,' 'Two of Anything,' 'Black Pudding,'" in *A Piece of Work: Five Writers Discuss Their Revisions,* edited by Woodruff (Iowa City: University of Iowa Press, 1993), pp. 53–97;

Kay Bonnetti, *Tess Gallagher: A Conversation* (Columbia, Mo.: American Audio Prose Library, 1994);

Katie Donovan, "Controlling the Chaos," *Irish Times,* 21 June 1995, p. 13;

"Influences: Tess Gallagher, Poet," *New Statesman and Society,* 15 March 1996, p. 19;

Peter Monaghan, "Tess Gallagher Shares Her Passions for Poetry, the Precision of Language, and the Prose of Raymond Carver," *Chronicle of Higher Education,* 13 June 1997, pp. B8–B9;

Katie Bolick, "A Conversation with Tess Gallagher," *Atlantic Unbound* (10 July 1997) <http://www.theatlantic.com/unbound/factfict/gallaghe.htm>;

Daithidh Mac Eochaidh, "Tess Gallagher Interviewed," *Rustic Rub,* 9 (1997): 22–31;

Mick Brown, "Untold Stories," *Daily Telegraph Magazine,* 15 July 2000, pp. 58–62;

Karen Gookin, "Pain, Time, and Beauty: An Interview with Tess Gallagher," *Irish Literary Supplement,* 20 (Spring 2001): 23–24;

Daniel Bourne, "A Conversation with Tess Gallagher," *Artful Dodge,* 38/39 (Spring 2001): 4–21.

References:

Paul Andrews, "Epilogue," *Seattle Times/Seattle Post-Intelligencer, Pacific* [magazine section], 30 July 1989, pp. 6–11, 14–16;

Jan Halliday, "Out of the Shadows," *P.S. The Magazine of Puget Sound,* March–April 1994, pp. 32–35;

Patrick Henry, "Introduction: Raymond Carver and Tess Gallagher," *Philosophy and Literature,* 22 (October 1998): 413–416;

Jeanne Heuving, "'To Speak Aloud at the Grave': Tess Gallagher's Poems of Mourning and Love," *Northwest Review,* 32 (Spring 1994): 144–160;

Tom Jenks, "Together in Carver Country," *Vanity Fair,* 49 (October 1986): 115–117, 139, 141;

Vicki Karp, "Two Poets: Several Worlds Apart," *Parnassus,* 12/13 (1985): 415–421;

William Logan, "Poets Elegant, Familiar, Challenging," *New York Times Book Review,* 26 August 1984, pp. 13–14;

John Marshall, "Tess without Ray," *Seattle Post-Intelligencer,* 18 December 1990, C1–C2;

Marshall, "Widow's Work," *Los Angeles Times Magazine,* 12 January 1992, pp. 18–20, 35–36;

Ron McFarland, *Tess Gallagher,* Boise State University Western Writers Series, no. 120 (Boise, Idaho: Boise State University Press, 1995);

Harold Schweizer, "The Matter and Spirit of Death: Sharon Olds's *The Father* and Tess Gallagher's *Moon Crossing Bridge,*" in *Suffering and the Remedy of Art* (Albany: State University of New York Press, 1997), pp. 171–184;

Schweizer, "Tess Gallagher's Poetry: Like a Thing Never Done," *CEA Critic,* 50 (Winter 1987/Spring 1988): 67–78;

Bonne Smith, "Tess Gallagher: Our Lady of Poetry," *Fifty-Something,* 5 (March 1995): 4;

William L. Stull and Maureen P. Carroll, "Two Darings," *Philosophy and Literature,* 22 (October 1998): 468–487;

Robley Wilson, "The Feminizing of the Short Story," *ANQ,* 5 (October 1992): 258–259;

James Wood, "From the Secular Side of the American Miracle," *Guardian* (London), 6 April 1989, p. 22.

Papers:

Tess Gallagher's papers are housed in the Charvat Collection of American Fiction at Ohio State University.

John Rolfe Gardiner

(20 November 1936 –   )

Mary Beth Long
University of Massachusetts

BOOKS: *Great Dream from Heaven* (New York: Dutton, 1974);

Unknown Soldiers (New York: Dutton, 1977);

Going On Like This (New York: Atheneum, 1983);

In the Heart of the Whole World (New York: Knopf, 1988; London: Bloomsbury, 1989);

The Incubator Ballroom: A Novella and Four Stories (New York: Knopf, 1991);

Somewhere in France (New York: Knopf, 1999).

SELECTED PERIODICAL PUBLICATIONS–UNCOLLECTED: "The Magellan House," *American Short Fiction,* 1 (Winter 1991): 78–106;

"Morse Operator," *American Short Fiction,* 2 (Winter 1992): 110–125;

"The Voyage Out," *New Yorker,* 68 (18 January 1993): 84–90.

John Rolfe Gardiner has been writing fiction since the early 1970s. Though he has only begun to gain popular recognition in the 1990s, Gardiner has earned previous critical acclaim for his work. He was a Creative Writing Fellow of the National Endowment for the Arts in 1977 and won the three-year Lila Wallace/*Reader's Digest* Writers Award in 1993. As a Southern writer Gardiner has been unable to escape critical comparisons with William Faulkner. Like Faulkner and other regional writers, he shows an affection for his characters and their faults and has a personal connection with their local culture. His fictional Stilson County, where many of his short stories take place, is grounded in the solid reality of northern Virginia, and in his later work his settings have expanded beyond that geographic range. A reviewer for *Publishers Weekly* (25 February 1983) observed that "Gardiner is gifted in gently searching out the quirky, the unusual person or turn of events and weaving it into a perfectly logical if bizarre tale." His stories indeed involve the "quirky," but his characters tend to fall within the scope of normality rather than that of the Southern gothic grotesque.

John Rolfe Gardiner (photograph by Sarah Huntington; from the dust jacket for Somewhere in France, *1999)*

John Rolfe Gardiner was born on 20 November 1936 in New York City to Emily Delafield (née Floyd) and Arthur Zimmermann Gardiner. The third of four children, he was raised in a household that valued education, the arts, and civic duty. His mother, a 1926 graduate of Vassar, had an early interest in theater and was a member of the Laboratory Theater in New York City. During the 1930s she contributed to *Hound & Horn* magazine and edited several books, including Kurt Sachs's study of the history of musical instruments. Later she volunteered for charitable organizations and worked in children's remedial education.

Gardiner's father earned a B.A. from Harvard and attended the London School of Economics. He was president of Booth American Shipping Lines in New York City until 1941. In 1942 he moved his family—including five-year-old John—to Fairfax County, Virginia, and began working for the United States government in the war effort. In 1955 Arthur Gardiner became a foreign service officer and was soon posted to places such as Pakistan, Vietnam, and Japan. In Vietnam he eventually became chief of the U.S. Operations Mission, the prewar aid program, and spent the later part of his life directing International Voluntary Services, a private peace corps organization.

Gardiner attended public schools in McLean, Virginia, until the third grade. He then transferred to Sidwell Friends School in Washington, D.C., and graduated from high school in 1955. He earned a B.A. in English from Amherst College in 1959. After college Gardiner served in the Army Security Agency in Yorkshire, England, "listening to radio signals on the Yorkshire moors" for two years. After his discharge Gardiner went to work for trade magazines in Washington, D.C., covering business news in the broadcasting industry for several years. After reporting on the riotous 1968 political conventions for *Broadcasting* magazine and finding that his neighborhood in Dupont Circle was vulnerable to both tear gas and burglars, Gardiner began searching for "a less turbulent place to work." He moved to Waterford, Virginia, to write independently, then to Bluemont, where he began doing carpentry to supplement his freelance writing income.

The peace that Gardiner sought in moving out of the city is reflected in his writing style. Several critics have commented on the quiet, unassuming language that he uses to describe people and places. His thematic concerns, particularly in his early short stories, are with the conflicts of class, generations, and rural (as opposed to urban) values. Gardiner also incorporates into his stories traditionally Southern gothic themes such as incest, respect for the land, the psychology of social outcasts, and a sense of history. At its best his quiet prose surprises with its acute observations of historical juxtapositions, as when mall window-shoppers in "A Crossing" (1978) are described as "clicking on red tile over an ancient cornfield." Gardiner's greatest strength is his ability to focus on moments of fundamental cultural change, whether in his early observations of the commercial development of northern Virginia farmland or his later exploration of one family's reactions to World War I. Many of his stories deal with the period of

unstable transition into a new worldview, rather than the cause or effect of the change itself.

Gardiner's first venture as an independent writer took him into the history of the Tennessee coal miners' rebellion in the early 1890s. He was interested in an episode that involved free miners struggling against the coal companies who were using convict labor in the mines. Gardiner intended his research to result in a history of the event, but it became a novel instead, one concerned with the effect of fictional labor organizer Eugene Daniels on the residents of Coal Creek, Tennessee. The book, *Great Dream from Heaven* (1974), was accepted by Dutton after two years on the publishing market. As became typical of Gardiner in later stories, *Great Dream from Heaven* focused on the moment of a great social change and the unstable reaction of a community to an outsider.

The book met with tempered critical praise; critics felt it was well written but that it suffered from a lack of discipline. Roger Sale's analysis in *The Sewanee Review* (January 1975) is representative in its admiration of the strengths of *Great Dream from Heaven* and his willingness to attribute the weaknesses in the book to Gardiner's inexperience as a novelist: "The failures here are all honorable. Gardiner is a writer with a lot on his mind and a flexible idiom well in control and a sense of the kind of novel he wants to write. He just hasn't written it right yet, but that, after all, is what first novels are all about."

At the time *Great Dream from Heaven* came out, Gardiner was still working half-time as a carpenter. He met Joan Gundelfinger, a ceramic artist, while on a construction job at her property in Unison, Virginia. They married in 1976 and had a daughter a few years later. Between writing stints Gardiner built additions to their house, remodeled an old barn for his wife's studio, and built a writing cottage for himself. Thanks in part to his carpentry skills and her low mortgage payments, they were able to live cheaply until their artistic efforts began to make money.

Gardiner's second novel, *Unknown Soldiers*, was published in 1977, the same year he won a creative writing fellowship from the National Endowment for the Arts. He then began to concentrate on writing short stories, many of which appeared in *The New Yorker*. In 1983 he arranged these stories into his first collection, *Going On Like This*. Most of the stories are set in fictional Stilson County, Virginia, an area Gardiner first explored in *Unknown Soldiers*: place names such as Mercer, Renson, Stilson, and Worton recur throughout the book. The stories are organized in sections according to geographical setting, beginning with the Washington, D.C., Beltway and moving westward into suburbs, villages, and rural areas.

The two stories in the first section, "Beltway," concern Dorsey and Lucille, a teenage couple seeking their identities in a prosaic suburban setting. Though they suspect that their commercially developed landscape is indistinguishable from others, they seem only vaguely aware in "The Crossing" that the lack of distinctiveness in their surroundings might affect them. Gardiner, however, makes sure the reader understands the individual history the land holds by making frequent reference to Dorsey's father, whose stories are intricately connected with the land itself. Though they do not discuss it, the teenagers seem to internalize a similar connection. When they search for a place to make out, they reject a parking lot and highway median as being "common" and decide to cross fourteen lanes of heavily trafficked Beltway to get to some woods—the only bit of nature they know.

The second story, "Homecoming," takes place a few years later. Dorsey and Lucille have grown ironic about their surroundings. They drive on the Beltway, "conquering" it: "The Beltway is entertainment" now, rather than a boundary to cross for entertainment. They travel from one high-school football game to another, delighting in their imagined foreignness. The narrator observes that "it might have amused them" to know that band marchers at two different football fields are "simultaneously out of step." They enjoy the sameness of each high school as much as the differences. Jonathan Penner, in a *Washington Post Book World* review (3 July 1983), called the "Beltway" section "the most striking in the book." The problems with commercial development in northern Virginia that Gardiner explores in "Beltway" play a larger role in subsequent books.

Three of the stories in "Village," the second section, focus on Worton, a community that is not sure how to deal with outsiders. In "Going On Like This," the neighbors cannot decide how to react to a drunken "resident prowler." They spy on him from behind curtains at night, but "in daylight the hamlet pretends it has no prowler," loaning him yard tools and selling him beer. They endure his nighttime gunshots, petty thievery, and attempted arson because they feel uneasy prosecuting a neighbor.

In "Worton Doesn't Perc," one of the community members has become an outsider after he was caught shoplifting and sentenced to jail. Reah and Jonah Harrell have a farewell party for him, taking responsibility on themselves to keep him and his parents from feeling alienated. Similarly, the Harrells take an active, "liberal" role in "Shots" by trying to be fair to a white-trash family whose daughter Mossie is a sort of hustler/entrepreneur who gives homemade inoculations to the neighborhood kids, sells the neighbors' belongings

Dust jacket for Gardiner's 1983 book, stories set mostly in the fictional Stilson County of northern Virginia

back to them in a yard sale, and takes bets on the outcomes of her little brothers' footraces.

Penner observed that "Gardiner is fascinated by groups—by how society, apparently inelastic, nevertheless assimilates us all—'misfit' being, ultimately, an important social role." The neighbors in Worton avoid confrontation at all costs, even when "going on like this" means enduring relative chaos. Gardiner accurately portrays the uncertainty of a community that does not know how or even whether to do the right thing about its outcasts.

"Village" is the only section in the book in which the collective opinion outweighs that of individual characters. In the section titled "Town," Gardiner's thematic focus on outcasts turns inward, to the psyches of the outsiders. The tightly woven "Most Trusted Trusty" follows the exploits of Luther, a jail chef whose lives in and out of jail—first for a bad check, and then repeatedly for breaking parole—are virtually indistinguishable ("the thing had been reduced to bookkeeping") until Simpson, a rival chef, ends up in jail with him. When Luther serves as inadvertent accomplice to Simpson's suicide, he tries to hide evidence by switching their fingerprint cards, but soon finds himself prosecuted for his rival's much more heinous crimes.

Gardiner develops the characters in a way that makes them believable and sympathetic despite the outlandish plot. He leaves his mark on a story that might not otherwise fit this collection by reminding the reader that they are still in rapidly changing 1970s Stilson County, where the courthouse and jail have become "architectural curiosities in the midst of nationally known shapes, the facades of fast-food franchises, oil-company signs, two drive-in banks, auto showrooms and lots."

In "A Prior Claim" and the section titled "Near Country" Gardiner explores issues involving outsiders and their family relationships. "A Prior Claim" describes the role-switching of an orphaned delinquent, Dewey, with his elderly guardian, his uncle Ridenour. Their relationship is strained—"they try to drive each other from the house with aggravations"—as they fight over who has the right to loot an abandoned whorehouse, "where women put on the dress-up clothes and it was against the law." Dewey's innocence about the function of the house contrasts with Ridenour's familiarity in a way that intensifies the irony at the end, when the child Dewey has to bring Ridenour home from jail. Gardiner adapted "A Prior Claim" into an unproduced script for the *American Playhouse* series on public television.

Gardiner's interest in the dynamics of family relationships becomes more evident in the section "Near Country," set eight miles from Stilson. "Love Paint" examines a brother's concern about his sister's marriage to an older, class-conscious man who encourages her to cover a facial scar that the family refers to as "love paint." He views the husband as the "man in the wrong church" because he does not embrace the values the family holds dear.

Such conflict is not uncommon in this section. In "Bell Hawk," which takes place in Renson, "on the edge of hunt country," the Carter family heritage turns out to be based on misconceptions. The family's belief in its gentility is manifested most overtly in its maintenance of its own museum and less so in its romanticization of a Native American relative, Bell Hawk. The museum degenerates into a collection of rather ordinary things, and the "Indian" relative turns out to be "Belle Houck," a South Carolinian whose name got drawled by the family into significance. Contributing to the family's downfall, Louise, a sincere anthropology student, discovers the truth about Belle and engages in incest with the narrator, her cousin. In her earnestness Louise is similar to many of the "hippies" who appear in other stories.

Going On Like This introduced many themes Gardiner developed further in his later work. Edith Milton pointed out in a review for *The New York Times* (14 August 1983) that the world Gardiner creates in *Going On Like This* "succeeds in being both specific and mythical and offers itself as a willing metaphor for something larger than meets the eye: for America itself, possibly, and certainly at least for the collision of past and present that the encroachment of an urban society on a rural one has made a commonplace of our time."

Inevitably, events of Gardiner's own life find their way into some of his stories. The partly autobiographical "American Light" (first published in *The New Yorker*, 31 August 1981; collected in *Going On Like This*) documents the excitement that an inherited painting brings to characters who consider themselves part of a new class: the "prosperous poor," with low income, no taxes, and a do-it-yourself attitude—a class that John and Joan Gardiner would certainly have fit into during their early years together. In "American Light" the painting that "always goes to the one with the worst taste" turns out to be worth a considerable amount. Like the fictional family, the Gardiners were able to get a new roof and live for a few years off the windfall they got at auction.

Like the characters in the story, Gardiner and his wife each have working studios on their land. Gardiner retreats to his writing cabin when "the telephone and other noises interfere with writing." Gardiner was a late convert from manual typewriter to computer, switching over gradually in the early 1990s. Elizabeth Weiner in an article for *The Washington Post* (19 May 1988) commented about the Gardiners, "Living simply and working in silence, they are not unlike the couple in John's 1987 short story 'World After Dark,' who 'had come to join this frontier, not as hippies or lay abouts but with a vision of a quiet, honorable success.'" Since he stopped doing carpentry, Gardiner has been a writer full-time, with the exception of one creative-writing class that he taught at the University of Virginia in the spring semester of 1982. Gardiner's third novel, the story of a high-school teacher, is set in a familiar northern Virginia landscape, the fictional Stilson County just beyond the Washington Beltway. The title of *In the Heart of the Whole World* (1988) refers to the Whole World Mall, a huge structure that is built over the property where the narrator, Ray Sykes, grew up. Sykes writes a textbook history of his town when commercial development erases the connection his students might have with the land. The house where Gardiner grew up disappeared much as Sykes's did. Gardiner told reviewer Michael Kernan of *The Washington Post* (15 October 1988), "I saw that countryside change totally. I read about the plan for a neo-gothic Crystal Palace, with its religious overtones, and I said, What does that mean? That was the kernel of the book." Gardiner developed that kernel into a story dealing partly with the uncertainty of one's historical origins, a theme that also ran through the "Beltway" section of *Going On Like This*.

Sykes's immediate concern is with his illegitimate daughter, Sonia. His obsession with keeping up with the events of her life becomes the defining quality of his character, compounded by his strong connection to his hometown. Because he will never move away or even travel, he cannot escape the hold she unwittingly has on him, and his world shrinks to revolve around only her.

Readers were mixed in their responses to *In the Heart of the Whole World*. Peter Meinke of *The St. Petersburg Times* (20 November 1988) complained that it was "full of more coincidences than any Dickens novel," while Susan Kenney in her review for *The New York Times* (2 October 1988) called it a "show of fictional mastery." Though Kenney considered Gardiner's tightly composed writing "genius overwhelming prudery," other reviewers felt that Sonia's activities (which include leading a teenage sex ring, nearly starring in a snuff film, and posing nude for a mall artist with whom she later ran away to Mexico) overwhelmed the quiet prose that worked so well for Gardiner's short stories.

By the time *In the Heart of the Whole World* came out, Gardiner was considered among the most talented of contemporary Southern writers. He acknowledged in print the difficulty of producing a quality story, telling Kernan:

> If I'm close to the end of a story I'll keep going, but the beginning is always slow: Will I ever do a story again? And so forth. When you get the voice of the narrator, things go better, you have more fun, more little acts of discovery and you think maybe it's going to work. Then you go through the anguish of, What the hell is this? And then you like it again and you send it off to see if anybody else likes it.

He was by this time one of an informal group of career writers living in the area. He told Weiner that the writers' group in Loudoun County was "collegial, with a certain camaraderie—but not to the point of conspiring."

Gardiner continued to write short stories for *The New Yorker* and *The New Virginia Review*, eventually publishing a selection of them in *The Incubator Ballroom: A Novella and Four Stories* (1991). This collection focuses on outsiders trying to connect to the land in an era of change and development. It employs many of the themes of earlier stories and novels: class conflicts, family relationships, community values, and incest.

The title novella deals with a Roanoke family with class pretensions who moves to rural northern Virginia to try to farm three hundred acres. The mother and the two older daughters eventually move back to their former social world in Roanoke. The youngest daughter, Grace, and her intellectual father are left to maintain the pretension of "farming" the land. When rapid suburban development raises their property value, Grace's mother sells all but a few acres, and Grace is left rich but miserable. She lets the yard grow into a wilderness (a metaphor for her own body), to the dismay of her new neighbors, and plans to marry a local good old boy. The family reunites for a wedding that ultimately does not happen. Woven throughout the novella is the story of Grace's cousin Michael, with whom she engages in incest. Gardiner raises two related conflicts in the story: the contrast of the family's perception of itself with that of the community, and the contrast of old values—even when they are held by newcomers—with those of "progress" and development.

In a review for *Studies in Short Fiction* (Fall 1993), Christopher Metress observed that *The Incubator Ballroom* relies for its drama on the comings and goings of its characters:

> The arrivals and departures in this collection are quiet ones, but Gardiner is always careful to show us that our quietest gestures, our simplest movements, betray our most compelling desires. . . . The title novella is Gardiner's most expansive treatment of this search for a controlled journey, for a life marked by certainty in the face of utter disorder.

Other critics did not find the plot or characters of the novella believable but expressed strong admiration for Gardiner's prose style.

The other stories in *The Incubator Ballroom* describe different kinds of outsiders in northern Virginia. "Karaghala's Daughter" focuses on the adjustment of a Hungarian father and daughter to the area; they are in hiding from his shady past. "Our Janice" highlights class differences between a West Virginian nanny and her employers. "World After Dark" makes an interesting companion to the title novella. Roma and Abe are also urban refugees hoping to make a living off their land. Like the characters in "American Light," they believe in the "new economics" of low income, no taxes, and animal husbandry. But Roma and Abe—like Grace's family—are not quite experienced enough to make it work perfectly: they try riding stables, vineyards, asparagus, and sheep before finally having some success with a trading newsletter. The story follows Roma's suspicion of her neighbors' attitudes toward her family, the newcomers. She is sure the rural natives think they "profane the land." When two sheep disappear and a cross burns into their field, Roma assumes the neighbors are trying to teach them a lesson. Her ignorance of the cause of the burned cross—nitrates

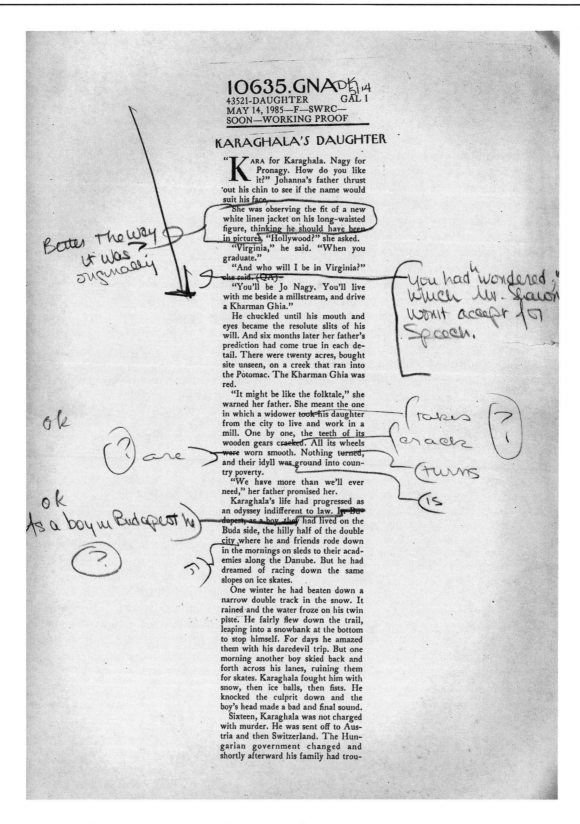

Corrected galley proof for a story published in the 24 June 1985 issue of The New Yorker *and later collected in Gardiner's 1991 book,*
The Incubator Ballroom *(Collection of John Rolfe Gardiner)*

from the sheep droppings—encourages Roma to read too much into a neighbor's comment that the burned cross is the "old sheep business." Always present in the story is the threat of suburban development, a force that makes Roma's attempt to connect to the land all the more desperate. As Metress noted, "Gardiner's Northern Virginia is a place of rapid and disruptive transition; it is a one-time rural but now increasingly suburban landscape where what once was is no longer, where what now is will soon pass." In this volume, as in previous fiction, Gardiner captures the moment of change from one set of values to another.

With this collection Gardiner established himself as the regional writer of northern Virginia. Metress commented that "No other writer today is working with such care and skill to fathom this rich and complex territory, this land that, in the last half-century, has undergone a suburbanization and loss of regional identity typical of many other communities throughout this country. . . . *Incubator Ballroom* deserves to be read by all people who want to understand more fully not only what these communities were once like, but also what it is they are fast becoming."

Having mastered writing about his own territory, Gardiner moved on to less familiar settings. His later fictional landscapes have included Canada, England, Portugal, and France. Most critics agree with Edith Milton's observation in *The New York Times* (14 August 1983) that he "is best when he knows where he is and can speak of the people in terms of place," but few have recognized how skillfully he handles those terms even when they lie outside northern Virginia. In his later stories Gardiner has introduced plots and characters that do not fit into the same categories as his earlier, more regionally based fiction.

In 1989 Gardiner and his family spent eight months in a Portuguese coastal village, a setting similar to one that later appeared in his short story "The Magellan House" (1991). In the story, which takes place on the eve of the Portuguese revolution, the Moura family vacations each year at a cottage on the seaside property of Senhor Carvalho, a prosperous vineyard owner. The narrator is the nine-year-old Polegar, who defines himself against his holier-than-thou sister, Christina, as the family defines itself against the Carvalhos. Most of his perceptions of the family's experience are viewed through the lens of her actions; even his experience of the car trip to the cottage is colored by her infliction of "little cruelties too subtle for the court of family justice."

With the metaphor of family relationships, class conflict becomes the central theme of the story. Polegar recognizes that "it was his sister who made the family different." Her infiltration into the world of the land-

owners ultimately leads to Senhor Carvalho's betrayal of their father's political disloyalties. When the Carvalhos flee the country after the government overthrow, the Mouras move into their house (named for the explorer from whom the Carvalhos claim ancestry), figuring the "moral debt" of the Carvalhos' political betrayal justifies a rent-free stay. Only Christina is able to transcend their class, however, and her actions eventually get them evicted from the Magellan house. Gardiner's affection for Polegar gives the narrative charm, and he skillfully communicates the clashes of the Mouras' politics, class, and family loyalties.

In "Morse Operator" (1992) Gardiner draws from his own experience listening to radio waves in Yorkshire. The main character, Russell, transcribes Morse signals from international business radio for the army during the Cold War. Morse code becomes for him a system to categorize every sound, from common greetings to Beatles songs, into meaningless pattern. While on vacation in Norway, the naive Russell meets Anske, a mysterious Swedish radio operator, and finds that Morse code cannot translate his experience with her. Caught up in the Cold War-era paranoia of the setting, the reader begins to suspect betrayal. Gardiner builds tension in a particularly symbolic scene: atop a too-difficult ski slope, Russell finds that the "only way down" is "sliding on his backside, then pinwheeling out of control until something caught and held." Anske passes him and calls, "Wonderful, isn't it . . . the rhythm of descent?" She skis skillfully down the mountain "to a rhythm for which there was no analogue in his code." He learns soon afterward that another private, Paul, has been spying on him for months, and has presented negative reports of his trustworthiness to their superiors. Russell's discovery of Paul's betrayal instigates for him a return to normality, rather than a departure from it. The real moment of change takes place as Russell observes a television map of the Soviet Union dissolving into multiple states, rendering his years of Morse transcription meaningless.

"The Voyage Out" first appeared in *The New Yorker* (18 January 1993). Through direct narrative, letters, journal entries, and flashbacks, Gardiner describes the sea voyage of British schoolboys to a Canadian boarding school to escape the dangers of World War II. At the insistence of his father and teacher, twelve-year-old Tony Hoskins records his experiences in a daily journal. When his cabinmate, David Rasson-Pier, goes missing (presumably overboard), Tony is asked to turn over his journal as evidence of what might have happened. The pastiche of sources reveals not only that Tony is the last person to have seen David alive, but that the "invitations" to David's bunk after lights-out poison Tony's memory of the older boy. Gardiner achieves a more complicated and convincing plot, particularly in characters' reactions to events, than in previous work.

As do many of Gardiner's stories, this one has its roots in reality. Two English brothers, sons of close friends of his parents, came to the United States to live with Gardiner's family for the duration of World War II and briefly attended a boarding school in Canada. In his contributor's notes for the inclusion of "The Voyage Out" in *Best American Short Stories 1994* Gardiner explained that "The story did not manifest itself full blown. Nor did it arrive in a straight line of discovery. There was backing and filling informed, I suppose, by a couple of shopworn truths—that mystery and suggestion may be more compelling than revelation, and that plot may be advanced by narrators who appear to be busy with other matters." The story also won the 1994 O. Henry Award.

Gardiner's novel *Somewhere in France* (1999) garnered considerable attention and praise. The plot is based roughly on events that happened in his own family, as documented by letters Gardiner found among his mother's papers. In the novel, set during World War I, Major William Lloyd journeys to France to lend his medical skills to the Allies. His nurse, Jeanne Prie, is engaged in her own battle against the trench-fever germs that threaten more soldiers' lives than enemy fire. Her dedication to her experiments intrigues Dr. Lloyd to the point of an obsession, which eventually overrules his other loyalties. His family members, sheltered at their estate on Long Island in refuge from influenza ravaging New York City, read his letters from "somewhere in France" (a description vague enough to pacify military censors) as they work through a box of the letters he wrote his parents while attending boarding school. The plots circle both geographically and chronologically, and eventually all circles meet when both Dr. Lloyd's son and his former enemy from boarding school end up in the hospital he serves, infected with the fever Jeanne Prie is trying to cure.

The novel showcases many of the skills that Gardiner developed as a short-story writer, among them the depiction of the complexities of family relationships and generational struggles, such as those between Emma Lloyd and her mother-in-law. Like "The Voyage Out," it necessarily involves epistolary elements, which serve to illuminate both what Dr. Lloyd has been doing and what he is hiding from his family. Gardiner first utilized this technique in "The Voyage Out" and uses it in *Somewhere in France* to full advantage. The portrayal of a sense of place that he has perfected during decades of storywriting comes to fruition in multiple ways, most strikingly in the experiences of Dr. Lloyd's son, Willie.

Miranda Seymour of *The New York Times* (24 October 1999) noted the "quietness of tone" in the narration, a quality that Gardiner's writing has had throughout his writing career. Gardiner has also maintained his ability to focus on the shift in worldviews as it occurs; as Seymour points out, when one reads *Somewhere in France,* "we are observing the precise moments when a world is changing from old to new." The success of *Somewhere in France* suggests that Gardiner is still honing his skills as a storyteller. As Seymour noted, "Gardiner is a writer worth celebrating."

In spring 2001 Gardiner completed a draft for a novel about identical twin sisters taken into a progressive orphanage during the 1920s. The book follows the girls' tangled lives from age ten into apparently separate paths of young adulthood. Gardiner also continues to write short stories. Another collection is forthcoming from Knopf in 2001.

Allegra Goodman
(5 July 1967 –   )

Ann V. Simon
University of California at Berkeley

BOOKS: *Total Immersion* (New York: Harper & Row, 1989);

The Family Markowitz (New York: Farrar, Straus & Giroux, 1996);

Kaaterskill Falls (New York: Dial, 1998);

Paradise Park (New York: Dial, 2001).

Since her first story was published in 1986, critics have hailed Allegra Goodman as a young virtuoso story-teller. Some scholars identify her often satirically realistic portraits of observant Jews as part of an important new movement in Jewish-American literature. Young authors at the fore of this movement depict religious rituals seriously and sympathetically, instead of breaking from them in a manner more characteristic of writers from a previous generation, from Philip Roth to Norman Mailer (or, more recently, Ehud Havazelet). Other readers both inside and outside Jewish communities applaud Goodman's flair for capturing the shifting identities and overbooked schedules of late-twentieth-century Americans. Whether her stories are set at a makeshift synagogue in Hawaii or a remote college in western Minnesota, skull caps (*kipot*) and prayer books (*sidur*) coexist with airport wheelchairs, vibrating motel beds, and kosher bagel dogs. The characters in Goodman's two collections of short fiction often seem neurotic, self-centered, and only intermittently aware of each other's needs.

Allegra Sarah Goodman was born on 5 July 1967 in Brooklyn, New York. She is the older of two daughters born two and a half years apart to Lenn and Madeleine Goodman, conservative Jews whose lives modeled what can be achieved through judicious blending of intelligence and hard work. When Allegra was only two years old, the Goodmans moved to Honolulu, where both parents worked at the University of Hawaii, her father teaching philosophy and her mother combining a career as a geneticist with a position as chairwoman of the women's studies department.

Goodman developed an early interest in reading and writing. A picture book titled "Choo Choo" that

Allegra Goodman (photograph by Marion Ettlinger; from the dust jacket for Kaaterskill Falls, *1998)*

she wrote and illustrated when she was seven earned not only praise from her teacher but also a profile in *The Honolulu Star Bulletin*. In the fifth grade she tackled *Pride and Prejudice* (1813) not for entertainment, but "to figure out how it was done," her father reminisced to a *New York Times* interviewer in 1997. Both parents took her seriously from the start, reading her work and encouraging her to pursue her dreams. Well after Goodman left Honolulu to study English at Harvard University, both parents relocated to Vanderbilt University in Nashville, Tennessee, where in 1994 Madeleine Goodman had been named the first female dean of arts and sciences.

"Variant Text," Goodman's first published story, appeared in *Commentary* in June 1986, during her freshman year at Harvard. Its contentious, self-absorbed protagonist is Cecil Birnbaum, a stay-at-home father who has recently moved to Oxford, England, where his "lean and brilliant" wife is a professor of abstract math. The story chronicles two days in Cecil's chaotic yet mundane life, during which he prepares burnt oatmeal for three generations; ferries his screaming children to and from school and synagogue; fights with the in-laws who own his ramshackle house; and fields a call from a teacher who announces that his three-year-old has, as Cecil puts it, "peed in the pre-reading center." He also exchanges acerbic words with a rival Shavian scholar he encounters at synagogue, complains to a rabbi about violations of traditional Jewish law, and sidesteps the ongoing maneuvers of a woman who cites Jean Piaget in a thinly veiled attempt to eject Cecil's son from pre-school so that her own child can take his place. Though most of the story traces Cecil's moment-to-moment thoughts and experiences, it also narrates two scenes that occur outside the scope of his consciousness. In these scenes, his certifiably schizophrenic sister-in-law dines with the American expatriate publisher of her experimental poems, then narrowly escapes being hit by a car on her way to an animal rights demonstration.

"Variant Text" showcases several themes that Goodman's later publications continued to explore. It reveals, for instance, that egotistical competition and political bickering are everywhere, even—or perhaps especially—in institutions such as academia and orthodox religion, which claim to promote the rigorous revelation of profound truths. A generous assortment of loud, opinionated characters reminds the reader that a wealth of discord and difference exists even within extraordinarily close-knit communities. The story also underlines that most contemporary souls juggle multiple, overlapping, and sometimes contradictory allegiances. Cecil thrives insofar as he enjoys his contradictions, savoring both the nonnegotiable rigor of ancient Jewish law and the deconstructivist fluidity of secular literary theory.

Over the next three years Goodman continued to publish stories in both *Commentary* and *The New Yorker*. In 1988 a front-page article by Ted Solotaroff in *The New York Times Book Review* (18 December) listed her as one of several young Jewish writers whose observance has restored an "edge" to an ethnic literature dulled by the "diluting and dimming" forces of assimilation. Then, in 1989—on the same day she graduated magna cum laude from Harvard—Harper and Row published her first volume, *Total Immersion*. Critical reception of this collection was almost uniformly positive, both within and without Jewish literary communities. In *The Forward* (8 December 1989) Sanford Pinsker mused that even the word *precocious* failed to do justice to her masterfully realistic dialogue and keen observation of human nature. Though a terse write-up by Randi Hacker in *The New*

York Times Book Review (10 September 1989) complained that Goodman's characters expressed themselves "too academically to elicit much sympathy," Elaine Kendall in *The Los Angeles Times* (27 July 1989) called Goodman a "prodigy" of "astonishing virtuosity," and *Newsday* (20 May 1989) reviewer Francine Prose raved that Goodman "has observed as deeply as many writers can hope to do in a lifetime."

More than half of the stories in *Total Immersion* are set not in Oxford but among conservative and orthodox Jewish communities in Hawaii, where Passover seders are held outdoors among mango trees and thirteen-year-old girls don muumuus to celebrate their bat mitzvahs. By describing in vivid detail the rituals, religious politics, and petty squabbling of an obscure community, Goodman allows non-Jewish readers and Jews outside Hawaii to eavesdrop on the inner machinations of a culture likely to seem both exotic and parochial, at least on the surface. Yet, at the same time, her narratives show that nearly all groups are characterized by divisive feuding of some sort, in addition to shared beliefs and experiences. "One of the themes I explored in *Total Immersion* is that what we imagine as exotic is actually familiar, and what we think is familiar is really exotic," Goodman wrote in a letter that Pinsker published in a 1992 article. "I am interested in the universality of parochialism—the fact that all over the world communities look into themselves/at themselves."

The title story relates the confusion and alienation a traditional Jew named Sandra Lefkowitz feels as she and her husband struggle to adapt to Hawaiian life after years in Washington, D.C. As weeks drag by, Sandra experiences culture shock on many levels simultaneously. As an observant Jew, she struggles to fit in as a French teacher at a congregationalist missionary high school. As a former resident of "the mainland," she tries to find space for herself in a tiny synagogue that meets every other week in the basement of a Unitarian church. Though many characters in this story hope for seamless immersion in just one culture or identity, this dream proves impossible in a time and place where assorted traditions fracture and divide, and nearly everyone is transplanted from somewhere else. Although the head French teacher, "self-appointed guardian of the oral-aural method," bans all English from foreign-language classes, Sandra finds this method of instruction unworkable for her beginning students. They simply do not "pick up irregular verb conjugations from pure idiomatic dialogue." Ginnie, the one student who places in a national French competition, never participates in class.

At the home of an Israeli furniture salesman, Sandra cautiously bonds with the other female members of her synagogue. These women roar with laughter at an overly pious letter from Barbara Ruth, an incompetent dental hygienist who tried to simplify her life by changing her name to Brochah-Ruchel and moving to Israel with her converted Hawaiian husband. These gossipy women reject Barbara Ruth's attempt to erase the contradictions in her life by escaping to a foreign culture and insisting that she is purely happy there. Apparently, they grasp that this strategy of "total immersion" is not a realistic solution to the stressful negotiations and fractured allegiances that characterize life in a mobile, multicultural society. Yet, their own families' attempts to juggle differences in background and opinion ultimately fail. Their synagogue splits into two groups after bitter debate about whether their own services are sufficiently strict and whether women should be granted full participation in orthodox ritual. In the end, the subgroup that refuses to revamp women's roles is so small that it cannot maintain the quorum of ten men required for services.

This phrase, "total immersion," ultimately has multiple resonances within many of Goodman's stories. In addition to the impossible dream of pure acceptance or undivided identity, it may refer to a feeling of being lost at sea, overwhelmed by the nuances of unfamiliar cultures. In an article published in *Studies in American Jewish Literature* (1992) Pinsker defines "total immersion" as "that prospect of being swamped" by the unfamiliar and argues that this disconcerting state, which Goodman's work portrays so vividly, looms inevitably in the background of postmodern lives.

Nearly all of the stories in this collection feature characters who seek spiritual fulfillment or meaningful connection with others. Though they do occasionally achieve moments of transcendence or communion, their satisfaction is tenuous and fleeting, at best. The story "And Also Much Cattle," for example, centers around the Schick family, who have built an ultraorthodox synagogue inside their new home and have invited an unwieldy and highly miscellaneous group for observance of the fast day Yom Kippur. According to Gloria L. Cronin, in this tale even more so than in the others, "Goodman illustrates the intransigence of ordinary consciousness, the stubborn fleshliness of that ordinary life which surrounds all attempts at communion with the holy." For though the Schicks and their guests are sincerely devoted to this holy day, chaos, bickering, and inflamed egos continually threaten to bring down the entire production. Gail Schick runs the show with tremendous (if untidy) energy and generosity but gossips loudly throughout the services and does not notice that her senile mother has fallen from her chair. Mark, her middle child, has recently returned from a year of Talmudic study in Israel, an experience that has filled him with passionate devotion to ritual and tradition. His

zealous attempts to keep the ceremony on track, however, come across as shrill, disrespectful, and insensitive. When his mother chats loudly about her success with an all-pizza, mother-daughter diet, he tells her to "shut up" and barks, "If you aren't going to pray, just leave." He then sarcastically tells his sister when she attempts to hush him, "Oh yes, Pearl, let's be calm. It's only God." Dr. Sugarman, a guest, is tremendously moved by prayers for his deceased first wife but cannot see the stress and fatigue his current wife is experiencing. Just for this day, "the house is clean, we wear our best clothes . . . everyone is praying," the young "baby rabbi" asserts near the end of services. But if he does not intend this claim ironically, he is simply wrong.

Many of the other stories in the volume also feature earnest seekers whose quests are obscured or interrupted by pressure from the workaday world. "Onionskin" takes the form of a long, autobiographical letter that an older student, Sharon, writes to a former professor. She explains that she walked out of his course at the University of Hawaii because it surveyed religious history instead of addressing her big questions about "Life and Truth and God and Freedom." Her nearly penniless journey to Jerusalem and back in search of elusive meaning ultimately seems both bold and naive. In "Young People," the character Henry Markowitz, introduced in "Variant Text," is inspired by brief encounters with individuals who sincerely dedicate themselves to artistic creation. Yet, in the end he cuts off opportunities for future interaction by accidentally giving a gifted young dancer the business card of his Yemenite poet/cab driver instead of his own. In "Wish List"–a spoof of academic culture in which minor characters from several other stories reappear– Henry's academic brother, Edward, briefly sees beyond his formulaic defense of terrorism when a late-night call from public radio informs him that three hostages have just been killed. Moments later he attributes this abrupt insight to indigestion and goes back to sleep.

Admittedly, not all of the opinionated, fast-talking characters in *Total Immersion* are portrayed with equal nuance and complexity. Eccentric intellectuals such as Henry and Cecil who operate outside mainstream academia come across as likable, independent (if abrasive) thinkers. Yet, Goodman tends to use much broader brush strokes when lampooning the social snobbery of minor characters or the simplistically liberal attitudes of intellectuals affiliated with universities. Such seemingly unsympathetic caricatures may be what Sheri Posesoski had in mind when she asserted, in a mostly positive review for *The Baltimore Sun* (16 August 1989), that "Ms. Goodman is young, and her stories lack depth of feeling." Such sketches of shallow people lend Goodman's work an often hilarious dimension of trenchant social

Dust jacket for Goodman's first book (1989), published the day she graduated from Harvard University

satire. They lack the sympathy and possibility for momentary connection and redemption, however, which undergird the characters she explores in more depth.

The summer after her graduation from Harvard, Goodman married classmate David Karger. She spent a year in England writing independently while her husband studied math at Cambridge University. Following this time abroad, both enrolled in graduate programs at Stanford University in fall 1990. Equipped with $30,000 from a prestigious Whiting Foundation Award received in October 1991 for literary accomplishment, Goodman kept writing and publishing short fiction during this period. She also worked steadily on a dissertation comparing the aesthetic ideas of eighteenth-century critic Samuel Johnson and nineteenth-century poet John Keats.

In 1996, nearly eight years after the publication of *Total Immersion,* Madeleine Goodman died of a brain tumor at age fifty-one, slightly before her daughter fin-

ished her doctoral degree and published two more books to a crescendo of critical acclaim. Soon afterward, Farrar, Straus and Giroux released *The Family Markowitz,* a collection of linked stories about the shared history and conflicting values that bind and divide three generations. Though some of its characters appeared in the non-Hawaiian stories of *Total Immersion,* this second volume explores a markedly different culture of urban, liberal Jews, who are observant but not (with a few notable exceptions) orthodox. It rapidly amassed more awards than Goodman's previous work, garnering honors such as a *New York Times* Notable Book of the Year and the first annual book award for fiction from the on-line magazine *Salon.com.* It is "a book that builds upon the considerable achievement of Ms. Goodman's first book of stories . . . and ratifies this 29-year-old writer's impressive talents," Michiko Kakutani wrote in *The New York Times* (22 October 1996). Most other reviewers agreed, applauding the Markowitzes as a scattered clan of exasperating eccentrics ultimately reminiscent of anyone's family. Admittedly, there is a fine line between characters recognizable enough to seem universal and characters so recognizable that they come across as generic, even stereotypical. "To create a family that is quintessential is to sacrifice the incongruities that most truly capture people as distinctive individuals," Claire Messud remarked in an otherwise positive review published in *The New York Times Book Review* (3 November 1996).

Two of the most notable stories in this collection chronicle Markowitz family weddings, occasions that bring together three generations of contentious characters who step on one another's toes, talk over one another's heads, and—at rare, irregular intervals—unite and compromise. In the first story, "The Wedding of Henry Markowitz," Georgetown University professor Ed Markowitz has flown to England with his practical wife, Sarah, and irascible mother, Rose, to attend the wedding of his brother, Henry, to an Oxford University administrator. Since Henry's homosexual leanings had never been precisely secret, his family is astonished to learn that he has stumbled into a happy relationship with a woman who shares his deep love of interior decorating. His mother, though, is most upset that Henry's fiancée is, as Ed puts it, "not a Jewish person."

This story, like most others in the book, traces ongoing, unresolvable conflicts both within and among generations of Markowitzes. It begins with a portrait of the two brothers, who have cultivated a lifelong ability to bicker about anything and everything. Ed is excessively irritated by the aesthetic obsessions and finicky eccentricities of his expatriate brother. "I walk into his apartment and he is still doing *Brideshead Revisited,* with that brocade and those clocks!" he complains to his wife on the eve of the wedding. Henry, for his part, is offended by Ed's unembarrassed American life, with its fast food and slouching teenagers. He also disdains Ed's success as an American professor, dismissing him as "another cog in the grant-getting, TV interview machine." Yet, in the end, this story points out that families contain alliances as well as rebellion. For though Ed disdains Henry's Anglophilia, he leaps to his brother's defense when their mother announces that she is "going to no wedding with priests in it." Similarly, though Rose is perhaps understandably hurt by Henry's flight from her Yiddish culture, her own love of all things British is aroused by his quaint "fixer up" cottage. The story closes with a rare moment of reconciliation. Rose shows up at the ceremony despite her earlier threats; Henry's voice trembles with gratitude as he hands her a piece of his six-tiered cake.

The final story in the book, "One Down," also narrates a Markowitz wedding and likewise showcases an ever-shifting network of feuds and alliances. Through narration of hectic preparation for the wedding of Ed and Sarah's daughter, Miriam, Goodman explores the confusion liberal Jewish parents often feel when their children unexpectedly abandon "pleasant suburban Judaism" for rigid, even strident, orthodoxy. "Religion hasn't come to his daughter gracefully," Ed thinks with consternation. "She refuses to eat in restaurants unless they have rabbinic supervision, refuses to drive anywhere on the Sabbath, refuses to attend services at her own father's synagogues because it has mixed seating and the rabbi uses a microphone." Ed loses his patience when Miriam says she will not dance with him at her orthodox wedding, because she wants separate dancing circles for men and women. He also nearly snaps when he stumbles upon a letter to the editor in which the groom's father argues for a militant, anti-Palestinian position exactly opposed to his own.

Yet, in the end, it is a beautiful wedding. Once again, harmony and compromise conquer discord, however fleetingly. Ed enjoys a moment of "sudden affection" for Henry, who declares that it is "almost anti-Semitic" to print something as "unedited" as the groom's father's letter. Though each father egotistically insists on working his opinion on Israel into his toast to the newlyweds, they discover common disdain for their children's orthodoxy. Ed gets one dance with his daughter after all, and no one disputes that she is deeply in love with her new husband.

With a few exceptions, characters in *The Family Markowitz* are portrayed in a more complex manner and with deeper sympathy than the self-centered gossips and shameless social climbers who frequently surfaced in *Total Immersion*. As point of view shifts from chapter to chapter, readers glimpse each Markowitz through the eyes of a variety of family members. The result is an increasingly complex and ultimately sympathetic sense of each character's strengths as well as weaknesses. Thus, in stories such as "The Persians" and "The Four Questions," Ed's wife, Sarah, comes across as a model of practical efficiency whose own innermost feelings are seldom revealed. In the story titled "Sarah," however, the reader learns she has dreamed of being a brilliant poet or best-selling novelist since high school and ultimately failed to pursue her Ph.D. because "it was easier for her to worry about Ed's career." Readers are also shown the gap between the "warmth and motherliness" attributed to her by creative-writing students at the Jewish Community Center and her actual thoughts about them, "by turns despairing and chortling." With similar double-edged compassion, "Mosquitoes" chronicles Ed's mounting frustration with participants at an ecumenical conference who expect him to speak in the first person "with total honesty and sincerity" instead of delivering the scholarly paper he has painstakingly prepared. "While we laugh along with Ed when he denounces the New Age psychobabble of participants," Kakutani noted, "we are also made to see the genuine pain and loss that these people are trying, in vain, to express."

After completing her doctoral degree, Goodman moved to Cambridge, Massachusetts, with her husband, who teaches theoretical computer science at MIT. Her family continues to reside there and now includes three sons, Ezra, Gabriel, and Elijah. In 1998 Dial published her first novel, *Kaaterskill Falls,* which received the Edward Lewis Wallant Award for Jewish fiction and was a National Book Award finalist. This book, which spans three summers during the late 1970s, portrays daily activities of the Kirshners, an ultraorthodox, non-Hasidic sect who followed their rabbi from Germany to Manhattan shortly before World War II and spend every summer together in the Catskills. Goodman, who describes her current religious practices as somewhere between conservative and orthodox, has not lived a life nearly as strict or sheltered as that of the community she describes. Nonetheless, in writing the book, she drew on her childhood memories of summers spent with her mother's relatives in a similar upstate region. "It's very vivid in my mind because it was so exotic to me as a kid!" she told Ivan Kreilkamp of *Publishers Weekly* (27 July 1998). "If your context is Hawaii, to come to this mountainous place with huge trees, dark forests, cold mornings in the summer, the chill of the evening, was amazing. All of that made a tremendous impression on me."

Like Goodman's short stories, *Kaaterskill Falls* illuminates family life and probes issues central to American Judaism, primarily by narrating simple daily events and routine holiday rituals. As Judith Shulevitz wrote in the on-line magazine *Slate.com* (10 September 1998), "the success of her novel lies in its casualness, the way it makes the extremes of religious practice seem cozily normal." As Elizabeth Shulman, devoted mother of five daughters, gazes with awe at a painting of the region in a traveling exhibition, she is seized with a desire to do or create something all her own. This moment of revelation stirs her in characteristically modest and practical terms: "I want—she thinks, and then it comes to her simply with all the force of her pragmatic soul—I want to open a store." With her husband's reluctant support, she starts a business that imports rabbi-approved kosher foods so that men in the community no longer need to haul in groceries from the city at the end of each working week. Her venture is an unexpected success but is abruptly shut down when word gets out that she catered a young girl's birthday party with kosher food not specifically sanctioned by her rabbi. Instead of protesting, she bears this setback with quiet if anguished grace. Though she grows more conscious of a rift between her beliefs and those of her close-knit community, she remains deeply religious and nurses no real desire to break away. She feels "divided from what she used to be" as if "the tide is in, and she didn't get back in time," but plods ahead with daily tasks and gives birth to a sixth daughter near the conclusion of the book.

Other major characters include: the group's aging founder, whose battle with Parkinson's disease forces him to ponder which of two imperfect sons shall succeed him; a skeptical Hungarian immigrant who escaped the Holocaust with his older sisters; a growing girl who surreptitiously dreams of Israel, though she lives in a staunchly anti-Zionist community; and a restless teen whose friendship with an outspoken Syrian-American girl nudges her toward consciousness of a larger world. Despite the reappearance of Cecil Birnbaum, protagonist of Goodman's first published story, *Kaaterskill Falls* is different from her short fiction. It is not a hilariously arch send-up of contemporary life, but rather a painstakingly researched historical novel whose characters are more earnest than sarcastic. "Where Goodman's stories were steeped in irony and acumen, her novel seems intent on cautionary gravitas," Gail Caldwell wrote in a *Boston Globe* review (9 August 1998).

As American fiction enters the twenty-first century, Allegra Goodman continues to make a name for herself both inside and outside Jewish literary communities. In 1999 she was a winner of the Jewish Cultural Achievement Awards, which are presented annually by the National Foundation for Jewish Culture. Nearly simultaneously, her work appeared in an issue of *The New Yorker* devoted entirely to new fiction by writers no older than forty. She published her second novel, *Paradise Park,* in March of 2001. This novel returns to the spiritual quest of Sharon Spiegelman, the former hippie folk dancer in "Onionskin," the first story in Goodman's first book. "As always, Goodman has a light touch with serious matters," reported Amazon.com shortly after the novel was published. Reviewers agreed that the sincere yet quirky protagonist was just as memorable as Goodman's other characters. Sharon is "naive but not actually stupid, with enough of the smart aleck . . . to make her irresistible as well as maddening," wrote Laura Miller for *Salon.com* (15 March 2001). Because Goodman is still so young, her growing audience can look forward to the further unfolding of her work.

Interviews:

Sara Rimer, "Allegra Goodman: Only Her Characters Are Neurotic," *New York Times,* 26 June 1997, p. B28;

Ivan Kreilkamp, "Allegra Goodman: A Community Apart," *Publishers Weekly,* 245 (27 July 1998): 48–49;

Ada Kabatznick Press, "Talking with Allegra Goodman," *Radcliffe Quarterly* (Spring 1999);

Dave Weich, "Powells.com Interviews: Allegra Goodman," *Powells.com* (27 March 2001) <http://www.powells.com/authors/goodman.html>.

References:

Gloria L. Cronin, "Immersions in the Postmodern: The Fiction of Allegra Goodman," in *Daughters of Valor: Contemporary Jewish American Women Writers,* edited by J. L. Halio and Ben Siegel (Newark: University of Delaware Press), pp. 247–267;

Sanford Pinsker, "Satire, Social Realism, and Moral Seriousness: The Case of Allegra Goodman," *Studies in American Jewish Literature,* 11 (Fall 1992): 182–194.

Lester Goran

(16 May 1928 –)

Patrick Meanor
State University of New York at Oneonta

BOOKS: *The Paratrooper of Mechanic Avenue* (Boston: Houghton Mifflin, 1960; London: W. H. Allen, 1961);

Maria Light (Boston: Houghton Mifflin, 1962);

The Candy Butcher's Farewell (New York: McGraw-Hill, 1964);

The Stranger in the Snow (New York: New American Library, 1966);

The Demon in the Sun Parlor (New York: New American Library, 1968);

The Keeper of Secrets (New York: McCall, 1971);

Mrs. Beautiful (Far Hills, N.J.: New Horizons Press, 1985);

The Bright Streets of Surfside: The Memoir of a Friendship with Isaac Bashevis Singer (Kent, Ohio & London: Kent State University Press, 1994);

Tales from the Irish Club (Kent, Ohio & London: Kent State University Press, 1996);

She Loved Me Once and Other Stories (Kent, Ohio: Kent State University Press, 1997);

Bing Crosby's Last Song (New York: Picador, 1998);

Outlaws of the Purple Cow (Kent, Ohio: Kent State University Press, 1999).

OTHER: Isaac Bashevis Singer, *The Image and Other Stories,* translated by Singer and Goran (New York: Farrar Straus Giroux, 1985);

Singer, *The Death of Methuselah,* translated by Singer and Goran (New York: Farrar Straus Giroux, 1988).

Lester Goran (photograph by Peter Townsend; from the cover for Tales from the Irish Club, *1996)*

Lester Goran is one of the most prolific short-story writers of contemporary American literature. The author of noteworthy mythopoeic fiction, Goran fictively re-creates Oakland, a working-class neighborhood of Pittsburgh, Pennsylvania, in the same way that William Faulkner based his Yoknapatawpha County on Lafayette County in Mississippi, or John Cheever based his Bullet Park or Shady Hill on the suburban towns of Westchester County in New York State. Though Faulkner and Cheever gave new names to their geographical locations, Goran uses the real names of streets, buildings, schools, universities, and churches in Oakland. Within that attenuated world, his stories of fictional residents treat such universal themes as the return of the hero from war, the portrait of the artist, the fall from innocence into experience, the painful plight of the marginalized, sexual desperation and celebration, alcoholism, the agony of the inarticulate, and the necessity of fiction as redemption from existential emptiness. Hope and the promise of a better life constitute the major quests throughout many of Goran's stories.

The child of Russian-Jewish immigrants, Lester Goran was born on 16 May 1928 in Pittsburgh, Pennsylvania. His father, Jacob, had immigrated to the United States in 1895 and was a tailor for most of his life in the Hill District of Pittsburgh. Goran's mother, Tillie Silverman Goran, was born in Bialystok, Poland.

Lester Goran attended Miller Elementary School and played varsity basketball at Fifth Avenue High School in the Hill District of Pittsburgh and Schenley High School, from which he graduated in 1946. He enlisted in the U.S. Army in 1946, where he served in the Corps of Engineers and in the Military Police at Fort Belvoir, Virginia. After a year and a half in the military, he enrolled with the aid of the G.I. Bill at the University of Pittsburgh in 1948. He graduated in 1951 with a B.A. in history and English.

Goran is married to Edythe (Deedee) McDowell. They have three sons: Robert Eliot, William Thomas, and John James. Goran sold construction materials door-to-door while working at his writing, until he entered the M.A. program at the University of Pittsburgh in 1958. He wrote his thesis, "The Fraudulent Artist in the Works of Henry James," under the direction of Charles Crowe and graduated in 1960.

Since 1960 Goran has been teaching English and creative writing at the University of Miami in Coral Gables, Florida, where he founded and became director of the undergraduate creative-writing division in 1965 and initiated the master of fine arts program in 1992. He became a full professor in 1974. He was also responsible for bringing the Nobel Prize–winning writer Isaac Bashevis Singer to teach at the University of Miami for ten years. They team taught a creative-writing seminar from 1978 to 1988, an experience Goran wrote about with wit and insight in *The Bright Streets of Surfside: The Memoir of a Friendship with Isaac Bashevis Singer* (1994).

Goran's literary reputation rests mostly on his three critically acclaimed short-story collections, all published since 1996 by the Kent State University Press and edited by Julia Morton. These books comprise fifty stories: eleven in *Tales from the Irish Club* (1996), twenty in *She Loved Me Once and Other Stories* (1997), and nineteen in *Outlaws of the Purple Cow* (1999).

All but one of the stories are set in working-class Oakland, adjacent to the gritty, lower-class Hill District of Pittsburgh. Goran told Mubarak S. Dahir that during World War II he lived in Terrace Village, a public-housing project on a hill between the two neighborhoods: "I remember the streets of my childhood as a bustling place, filled with all kinds of strange and interesting people to meet, and see, and talk to. . . . Where we lived in Oakland was right near the University of Pittsburgh, but culturally it was a thousand miles away." The most important location in that neighborhood for the impressionable young man was the Irish Club, the central, fraternal drinking organization of the Ancient Order of Hibernians, Division No. 9. The large club was filled with dozens of small, square tables and had big windows overlooking the neighborhood. For years a three-piece band and a jukebox supplied the entertainment. As Goran later explained in *Tales from the Irish Club,* the place was more than a bar: "It was a kind of unofficial community center, and you were just as likely to find a grandmother or a baby in a stroller as you were to find young men and women courting romance. It was nothing to see three generations at one table." Though the club was in a predominantly Irish-Catholic neighborhood, occasionally boys of other ethnic and religious backgrounds frequented it and were eligible for social membership. Goran visited the club until it closed in 1965.

When Goran was invited to Lasek's Bar and Grill—the new home of the Ancient Order of Hibernians—in June 1996 to talk about *Tales from the Irish Club,* he explained the relationship between his stories and his life:

> I sensed disappointment at Lasek's when I confessed that most stories in my collection had been made up, rarely much in them being connected to anything I recognized as having happened back then. But that's what fiction writers do: they imagine stories that later may become more real than what really happened to people of blood and bone. And as for the stories with a kernel of the actual in them: I had brought from the well of the past tales so wild and pure that they may have been inventions.

The most important activity at the Irish Club was the telling of stories. In that sense all three of Goran's story collections are structured like John Steinbeck's *Tortilla Flat* (1935) and *Cannery Row* (1945), which are organized around connecting narratives about the local citizenry, and Sherwood Anderson's *Winesburg, Ohio* (1919), a series of linked stories organized around young George Willard's consciousness and memory. The redemptive power of narrative that temporarily creates a timeless, Edenic realm of hope and promise saves both the tellers and the listeners in all these collections from the fallen world of time, a continuous theme in much of Goran's short fiction. The spiritually sustaining power of such stories resides in the narrative act itself: fiction as absolute necessity, or what Wallace Stevens called "the necessary angel." Goran shares close aesthetic and spiritual affinities with not only Stevens but also with Henry James and Marcel Proust and their use of the energies of the local.

In the first story in *Tales from the Irish Club*, "The Other Thing," the reader is introduced to Johnny Farley, a charming but chronically indolent layabout, who has acquired a solid janitorial job with benefits at a local school and is proud to be seen with his wife and beloved daughter at Irish Club events. When he was a child, the nuns at St. Agnes School had told him stories about saints receiving divine calls, and he began to think of himself as one of those specially blessed people: "But he knew with certainty that he would one day do what he thought of as 'the other thing.' It would be something other people would admire, notice him, talk about. . . . He decided it would be long in coming but sure and he would know it when it finally came."

One night a mysterious character, Finn Mooney, becomes enraged at Johnny's winning streak in a game of penny pitching and beats him almost to death. After four weeks in the hospital, Johnny returns to the club as a local hero and is treated with great respect and deference. The community recognizes him as "a model of courage. . . . Johnny sat in the center of a golden circle, people entering it to tell him he was lucky to be alive and admired his health and courage." Johnny's hidden hope to do "the other thing" has been fulfilled in a completely unexpected way; his call has been to bear agony heroically: "Though the eye covered by a patch, the streamers of lights over the bar and the people dancing in the long mirror looked like everything as it should be. He could take a beating and the world knew it."

As is often the case at the conclusion of a Goran story, the memory of a past event connects the present. Johnny recalls the lights of a carnival scene from his youth: "The Ferris wheel lights were spinning in his battered brain as he saw before him in the mirror his father dead too young and his brother the criminal postman, all dancing." Johnny's apotheosis as local hero unifies the past and the present, the living and the dead, in a redemptive moment outside time. He recognizes the transforming power of his suffering—"he could take a beating"—as that event that makes his life heroic. Using the metaphor of a loom, Goran interweaves the personal and the mythic, past and present, and the living and the dead. The story becomes more than one specific instance of how someone becomes a hero. Another recurring pattern throughout Goran's fiction is that of a character moving from isolation to community or from community to isolation. All the stories in his three collections follow one or the other of these patterns.

The second story in *Tales from the Irish Club*, "Now that Maureen's Thirty," details the painful life of a young, rather unattractive, thoughtful woman named Maureen Scanlon, a librarian at Taylor Allerdyce High School. When she begins to receive short letters from

TALES *from the* IRISH CLUB

A Collection of Short Stories by Lester Goran

Cover for Goran's first collection of short stories (1996), all set in the Oakland neighborhood of Pittsburgh, where Goran grew up

an anonymous admirer, she immediately suspects that they come from the new assistant principal, Bob Donegan, whom she began to have romantic feelings for shortly after his arrival. She begins to pick up signals from him that point to him as the overly shy letter writer: "She felt speech trapped in him. . . . on some days he wore a blue suit, almost as pale as the envelopes, and a darker blue tie. . . . His melancholy eyes betrayed his words." Finally her admirer sends a note that designates a meeting place, where she encounters a student from her school, an awkward teenage boy named Tim Mullaly. Refusing to believe that he could have written the sensitive, mature letters, she rushes to the nearest phone and calls Donegan "a bastard." Maureen's lonely life has fostered fictions that she mistakes for reality. Her frustrated yearning for love has cut her off from any redemptive participation in the common life, and she vents her frustration through rage at an innocent man whose solicitous remarks were meant only to brighten her day.

Not all the stories in *Tales from the Irish Club* are as darkly poignant as the opening two. "Mortality," though ostensibly about death, is really a comic treatment of an Irish-Catholic fatal woman. Pauline Conlon seeks out dying lovers and eases them comfortably into their graves. As the story opens, the reader is introduced to Pauline and her succession of dead husbands: "She was not yet fifty in 1938; still her years weighed on her face and in her eyes. . . . She had buried three husbands respectively to tuberculosis, kidney failure, and heart seizure. . . . People died around her: the mother at birth, her father when she was a child, her two eldest sisters, and her three husbands."

Pauline has become a fatalist, and her negativity is reinforced when her prospective fourth husband, Duffy Kiernan, drops dead two months before their wedding. Then Duffy's brother, Sailor, returns to Pittsburgh after miraculously surviving the Japanese bombing at Pearl Harbor. Having been so drunk that he cannot recall how he escaped the sinking *Arizona,* Sailor has given up all alcohol and taken up strenuous daily exercise. Pauline and he marry. He rebuffs her dour negativity, and she becomes increasingly irritated by his consistently positive, life-affirming attitude and his rigorously enforced health regimen. Falling into a depression because she thinks Sailor might outlive her, Pauline tries to cause his death by locking him outside when the temperature is five degrees below zero. When she finds him alive but nearly frozen on the porch an hour later, she pretends that she did not hear his calls for help and resigns herself to living with him. Decades later they "sat on their porch in summer, smiling at neighbors, he thinking how life had been kind, she thinking things made no sense." In this story, as in so many of his other pieces, Goran uses one of Cheever's favorite techniques, mythologizing the commonplace: With her well-known Irish attitude toward death, Pauline becomes the mythic fatal woman. At the same time, the story satirizes the fatal-woman archetype by placing her in direct contrast with the *elan vital*—the life force—of her last husband. Sailor Kiernan becomes a resurrected Osiris figure who prevails in spite of any and every obstacle placed before him. Goran has built many of his seemingly simple stories on such sophisticated mythic patterns.

In the longest story in *Tales from the Irish Club,* "The Last Visit," Goran has created a classic portrait of the artist in his narrative of the life of high-school art teacher Jack Lanahan. Many members of the Ancient Order of Hibernians, Division No. 9, view Jack as a contented, middle-class human being, but they are not sure why he seems so satisfied. When the story opens, Jack, a widower, is sixty-two years old, has taught art at Schenley High School for more than thirty years, and is living with one of his daughters, Alice. The title of the story alludes to a pattern of recurring, ecstatic, visionary experiences Jack has had since first grade:

> He had visits from moments in his past, moments of such pure transformation that the ecstacy of their having happened stayed with him for years.
>
> . . . Unbidden, each transformed experience reoccurred, four in all, coming at unanticipated times and allowing him to relive them again before they vanished as abruptly as they had come. They were intoxicating. . . . He filled idle moments with the anticipation of their return. Sometimes years passed, but he waited.

The story is also about Jack's recent transformation into a local artistic hero. For thirty years he carved one subject—hundreds of wooden roosters with "wings spread, claws thrust and beaks poised for love or combat or flight"—never deviating from his constant subject, "but there had been no significant artistic progress . . . no movement to indicate growth or promise, aesthetic consummation, or even that a self-conscious artist had been at work." The mysterious connection between his creative impulses and his infrequent visionary experiences, which have filled him "with a transport of sudden joy, that none of it was separate from anything else," has sustained him in what his wife saw as a failed career. That situation changes, however, when Jack meets Mrs. Freiheit, a woman knowledgeable about the New York art world who arranges a highly successful show of his roosters at which he makes $35,000. The story ends as Jack celebrates his belated artistic success at the Irish Club. A bit drunk, he remembers an experience from his childhood, an occasion during which his kindly father had dismantled a hall rack that cast a terrifying shadow on Jack's bedroom wall. Because of his father's loving act, the child Jack felt free and unafraid and knew that "the place of absence" where the shadow used to fall "was where the angels dwelt, light and floating, airbound and boundless. He was at one with things that lay behind hard things seemingly permanent and all that people ordinarily sense." The adult Jack now wishes that "his father would come tonight and tear up the victory that now lay on him . . . so the boy could sleep like angels in a place absent of harm."

"The Last Visit" probes deeply and sensitively into the roots of the artist's creative energies. The rooster is a rather obvious—even humorous—symbol of the connection between the raw vitality of life and the artistic impulse, and may remind the reader of D. H. Lawrence's *The Escaped Cock* (1929), in which Lawrence replaces the Christian dove with the Dionysian rooster as the Holy Spirit. Goran arranges these literary and religious symbols within the context of a Proustian redemption of lost time, transforming them into visionary moments of pure joy, Wordsworthian "spots of time." Because these visits transport Jack out of time and into a condition of oneness with an atemporal, eternal world, the story defines quite acutely Goran's sense of the "sacred" or "holy." The original archaic use of the word *holy* harkens back to the word *whole*, when *holy* meant *wholeness*. Another literary connection is to the Arthurian legends. The Irish Club as a location in which stories unite listeners and tellers parallels the Round Table, where the narratives exchanged within the fellowship of knights formed the basis of the sacred bond—the Word—of the group. The sustaining narratives recited at the Irish Club define and hold the community together over the years. The magic of their telling allows the stories to heal the breech between the past and the present and permits the participants to look to the future with hope.

"Grady's Sister" records a mysterious eruption of the erotic that takes place in the daily life of Oakland in April 1941. Seventeen-year-old Anna Marie DeForrest's transgressive behavior one night in April suggests her connection to Christian and ancient, mythic, female figures. Throughout her adolescence Anna Marie

had read of love in *Photoplay* and *True Confessions* and thought the boys who accumulated around her for a soda at the Sun Drug were characters played in movies by Van Heflin or Robert Taylor. When one asked, she agreed, then another, and another. She saw no reason to draw the line on two or three at a time—or ten—until she appeared again in Oakland on the spectacular evening in April 1941 that tried Dick Best's soul.

By the time Dick Best hears rumors that the sister of his closest friend, Grady DeForrest, is permitting anybody to have sex with her in a room at the back of the Strand Bowling Alley, a long line has formed: "down the stairs to the street and in twos and threes young men stood around on the sidewalk waiting their turn to climb the stairs and mount Anna Marie, who was lying upstairs on an old mattress." Anna Marie's behavior threatens the social and moral order of the community, but the author suggests that she is a symbolic conglomerate of religious figures. Anna Marie's first two names allude to the Virgin Mary and Mary's mother, St. Anne, while the name DeForrest refers to earlier, pre-Christian fertility divinities such as the Norse goddess Freya or the Roman goddess Demeter, making the story a modern version of the Rite of Spring myth. The appropriately named Dick Best views Anna Marie's behavior as a kind of moral transgression that weakens the stability of the commu-

nity: "It was a violation of things in orderly place. It was an anarchy to all he understood."

At the same time, however, he realizes, "It was the opportunity of a lifetime," and he goes to stand in the line. What finally causes him to remove himself from the line is not the conviction that he is committing a sin but the realization that Anna Marie is the sister of his closest friend:

He was taken by a terrible vision—but not of anything he could see; instead, a spectacle of emptiness in the long line. It was a line that could hold all the young men in the world he had ever known except one. . . . Grady was excluded.

It was shadowed by the worst thing that could swim before a person's eyes, Dick thought: emptiness. It was a world without fullness or a promise of the future.

This scene is, for Goran, the fallen world at its emptiest. For Dick the more serious sin is not public fornication but Grady's exclusion from the community: "Exclusion from things: there's no worse sin." Dick redeems himself by remaining loyal to his friend. The sacrifice of oneself for the good of the fellowship is a redeeming act, and Dick realizes that he has acted as a virtuous human being: "He never expected to feel so right again. He loved Grady's sister at that moment." As he returns home that night, he also understands in some vague way the mythic significance of the orgy taking place at the Strand Bowling Alley: "Nothing but morning light now and nothing here to recapture last night's springtime wonder of a woman veiled in ardor and mischief, ease in a complicated life." Ancient Dionysian energies have erupted unexpectedly in his Irish-Catholic neighborhood, suggesting that the rites of spring, though disturbing and transgressive, are necessary for the spiritual sustenance of a community.

The characters in *Tales from the Irish Club* are almost Chaucerian in their variety: returning heroes, virgins, the sexually desperate and obsessed, brutal fathers, emotionally smothering mothers, dependable and virtuous priests, hopeless alcoholics, and most of all, bardic storytellers. The psychological and emotional depth of the stories fully justifies Paul West's blurb on the dust jacket of *Tales from the Irish Club* that Goran's permanent subject is "the lunatic sadness of things." Goran continued to expand his range of characters and deepen his thematic concerns in later collections. Though the setting remains the same, Goran's mythopoeic world becomes darker and more poignant because his characters become increasingly complex.

Most of the twenty stories in *She Loved Me Once* (1997) are much longer than those in *Tales from the Irish Club;* a third of them are the size of novellas. The

7049-39397K-2A
7599-39397K-2-B

school. Mark Carney would have commited suicide rather than let pneumonia blessedly take him had he forseen the fate of his immediate descendants. Mark, once aspiring to be a lawyer like Daly and his father, had become an honest pharmacist, never owning his own shop, travelling vast distances to work in hospitals the other side of the county. He drank next to nothing with alcohol in it, and held as his highest promise of a life well lived the prospect of getting his son one day into Law School or at a point of settlement the Pittsburgh Fire Department and the daughters safely and securely married. As he brushed his white hair, each in place, Daly thought he would rather clean out a hundred stables than try to meet even Mark Carney's modest dreams with that impossible clan.

There is a bar near the Carney family apartment where Daly occasionally stops, and he hurries toward it. Two glasses of wine before the fray.

Tonight he must enjoy in solitude two glasses of white wine, a matter of nerves and remembering the first Right Racklin too strongly. The bartender there is a man named O'Malley and O'Malley speaks often of Daly's father, seeming to have noted every good deed forgotten by the world. O'Malley had been in any number of saloons in Oakland in his time, and from one or another he came to know everyone. Daly would like to hear about his father tonight; he wants to feel like a good man's son, that things that his father represented, no need for fine words on the subject, were not buried with old-fashioned popes or the Latin Mass. But O'Malley is busy with a baseball crowd in the bar and can only wave to Daly as he mixes drinks. Daly salutes him and goes to the door, not ordering anything in the jammed bar.

He is pensive on the sidewalk. He climbs the steps to Mark Carney's old apartment and tries to assemble the women and the boy. He has in mind a festive dinner. Feeling forlorn, he will raise the spirits of his woeful charges. Who else would serve them anything but dog food? And that is where kindness must begin: where it is least expected and unwarranted. No one holds back charity and love from the beautiful and graceful and

20

Page from the revised typescript for Bing Crosby's Last Song *(1998), a novel drawn from "Evenings with Right Racklin,"*
collected in Goran's 1997 book, She Loved Me Once and Other Stories *(Collection of Lester Goran)*

themes remain generally the same: hope and promise, forms of heroism, sexual desperation, loneliness, isolation and community, and the necessity of fiction.

Four characters reappear frequently throughout *She Loved Me Once:* Pal "the Last Word" Mahoney, a former Jesuit with impressive gifts for casuistic argumentation and an all-purpose wise guide; Father Farrell, pastor of St. Agnes Catholic Church; Clifton Clowers, Jewish outsider and Goran's alter ego; and Paul Kerry, bartender at the Irish Club, an ever-present commentator on the foibles of human nature. Goran's introduction to *She Loved Me Once* delineates how he connects local energies with the defining powers of the imagination to transform the temporal into the timeless:

> In the old days, of course, people went their own ways as they do now, disappeared, died in strange places, were even almost lost to memory, but that was not the truth of it then. The fact that all of history and futures of the men and women in those years born to Dunsieth, Terrace, Robinson, Chesterfield Road, and Darraugh Street were known to start here on the old cobblestones and culminate here somehow as if all judgment that was and was to come lay only in the old houses, the stones, and the memories of the old people on their porches on Robinson. There was the Word too, and it was all—the Trinity, the Eucharist, Communion, and the Mass—eternal, luminous, concrete like an Egyptian pyramid or a mountain beneath the seas never to be altered by time or humanity.

In his talk at Lasek's in June 1996 Goran further expanded on his theories about the connection between the past and the function of literature. When he went to a copy center to have his old, crumbling Irish Club membership card duplicated and laminated, the young clerk was hesitant to make copies, fearing that he would be creating fake IDs. Goran explained:

> We have to go back in time fifty years for the card to be valid, and that is impossible except by the words we write and our blessed memories, and he relented. I think of the young man at the duplicating machine as an agent of history, because memories are after all, no matter how real to us, facsimiles, and so is fiction a fabrication, representations of life. . . . Only through imagination now can we look once more . . . over the rim of the well of the past.

For Goran it is the imagination as a loom weaving a tapestry—a fabric of fictions—that transforms the transitory into the timeless: art.

The opening story of *She Loved Me Once,* "Evenings with Right Racklin," demonstrates better than any of the other stories in the collection the way fiction becomes reality through words. As David Willis McCullough explained in *The New York Times Book*

Review (26 October 1997), "a lonely lawyer finds comfort on the anniversary of his father's death in a bartender's reminiscence about the old man even though it soon becomes obvious that the one being remembered so fondly is someone else entirely. It's the stories themselves that count and heal." The sustaining power of the narrative itself to make permanent an event from the past redeems the transitory nature of time.

The main character in the story, Daly Racklin, bears the burden of, and is frequently mistaken for, his legendary father, who became a local hero of sorts. On the fifteenth anniversary of his death, Daly's father's presence is palpable, and when Daly realizes that O'Malley, the bartender at the Metropole, has confused Daly's father with another fondly remembered character, his realization opens the world up in a completely unexpected way: "Why, the two of us are celebrating goodness that doesn't need a man attached, goodness so pure in the air that it inhabits one man or another, no matter." As fine a man as his father was, Daly decides, "There was another somewhere just as good. . . . Outside the night wears shoes of iron, but in here there are good men to spare." Daly discovers within himself a spiritual generosity that he has never before encountered. This insight is certainly one of the reasons that Goran made Daly Racklin the hero of his novel *Bing Crosby's Last Song* (1998).

One of the phases of the mythological journey of the hero in Joseph Campbell's scheme of the hero's transformations is what he calls "father atonement"; that is, the hero becomes one with his father, a process of "at-one-ment" at the end of his journey. Daly Racklin has this sort of experience, a visionary moment that defeats time in redemptive memory and connects him and his father to the larger world of virtuous men, living and dead.

In the title story of *She Loved Me Once* the character Ada has a disfiguring birthmark on her cheek: "She was no prize at first, young and carrying burdens of no great beauty and difficulty of personality." The male protagonist, Barry Whelan, marries her for what he considers the most noble of reasons and envisions himself as "a knight riding up to save her on a white horse or better, marrying her, blemish and all, expecting to be recognized, at least by her, for the charity in his heart for a misfit girl." Ada's blemish has caused many people to turn away repulsed, and so, since he married a woman whose appearance disgusts others, Barry believed that "she owed him something" because he has made "a great sacrifice, to be rewarded by her loyalty forever." The story begins six years after their marriage has ended in an amicable divorce. Barry is still mystified about why the marriage did not work and hopes that they might somehow be reunited. Since his mother died and left him with a substantial inheritance, he could now offer Ada an easier life of travel and freedom from financial pressures; yet, she refuses to be reconciled to him. The story illustrates Barry's confusion of his fictions about life with reality. Eventually falling into disillusionment, Barry is angry at Ada for causing it: "She made me sour on miracles and for that I'll never forgive her." Barry's consolation is the idea that, in spite of her rejection, "she loved him once, and wasn't that on record somewhere?" He finally realizes that there are no answers, that he will never understand why the Edenic future life he has imagined for them will never take place.

Frankie Dodge in "An Excess of Quality" views himself in unmistakably heroic terms. His heroism, however, takes the form of a narcissistic elitism: no one, he believes, has suffered so deeply, or so unjustly, as he: "nobody would really understand, unless they were people with the kind of innate good sense, and maybe refinement, he possessed by birth. He was quality. He was a knight with ideals forced to live with ignorant peasants." As the title suggests, he possesses "An Excess of Quality." The story is a psychological study of the making of a reactionary bully who revels in the pain of the less fortunate. Expelled from law school for cheating on an examination, he works as a law clerk but so often tells people he is a lawyer that he begins to believe his own lie. He also fine-tunes his unconscious life narrative with his role as victim most prominent.

Frankie detests and becomes obsessed with a poor neighbor named Micki Aukland and her abusive, alcoholic husband, Kurt. When he discovers Micki is involved in a bingo operators' flimflam game, he surreptitiously reports her activities to the police, the local newspapers, and radio and television stations. He is delighted when she is sent to jail for a month. When Micki returns to the Irish Club, however, "she was treated like a monarch returning from exile. . . . people came as if paying court to a wise woman." Frankie feels cheated because he thinks the community should be honoring him as a moral champion for exposing her corruption. Hypocrite that he is, however, he joins in a protest over the eviction of the Aucklands from government housing, prompting the drunken Kurt to embrace the horrified Frankie. Kurt sums up Frankie's spiritually empty life with keen precision: "You ain't such a bad guy—you got your own ways. . . . Just loosen up a little, don't let the little things get to you. You got to see the big picture."

Frankie Dodge is certainly one of Goran's most repulsively cruel characters, primarily because he celebrates the agony of the less fortunate, but he is still a complex human character, and there are plausible explanations for his behavior. Frankie's sensitivity to class distinctions and his debilitating sense of isolation reduce him to a life of unearned arrogance, spiritual emptiness, and tormenting envy of others' good fortune.

The major theme of "Build Me a Castle" is the process by which a seemingly ordinary human being becomes a hero and is betrayed by those who profess to love him. The story is also about the fictions people create in order to survive, and it mythologizes the commonplace with great subtlety. Michael K. Horner, the seventeen-year-old nephew of Harold "Fabulous" Flynn, has made his uncle the heroic center of his life. Fabulous Flynn is the classic example of someone whose personality and creativity have made him a powerful millionaire, and Michael, who wants nothing more than to follow his uncle's path from "rags to riches," imitates Fabulous's smile and his way of carrying himself. He loves his uncle because he has "shared good luck with his brothers and sisters, all living more or less on his generosity." Because Fabulous and his wife have no children, Michael, who works for Fabulous, believes he is the heir to his uncle's many businesses. Michael loves his uncle's indefatigable optimism: "the best of it was that there were always better things ahead."

Michael's life becomes complicated when he begins a long-term affair with his uncle's wife, Vonine. After Fabulous loses $200,000 at the gaming tables, he dies from a fall—or a leap—from the balcony of a Las Vegas hotel. Michael assumes that he and Vonine can now live together as man and wife. Yet, while she promises to support him and help him find a new, equally rewarding profession, Vonine, who has inherited the fortune, informs Michael that their relationship is over, explaining: "You're wrong to think you meant as much to me as my husband, never was, never can be. . . . It's something people do, and now it's something I'm not doing." The major revelation for Michael is that he miscalculated the importance of their physically rewarding affair. At the cemetery after the funeral Vonine orders Michael out of the limousine, and he experiences a profound revelation as he confronts the destructive nature of time:

The sky was bright, mocking the sobriety that Michael felt about all living things soon to perish, dry away one day and leave below only the ground and grass the same. Only us after death will be absent from rain, sunshine, and the possibilities in yesterday's pie at formica-counter restaurants and the time of an endlessly racing heart.

Michael cries out in the empty graveyard: "you can't be dead, not you. Not alive and walking doesn't mean a man isn't here." The story concludes by showing the apotheosis of Harold "Fabulous" Flynn into another form of fabulousness, a legendary hero or informing spiritual presence who will continue to inspire and accompany Michael for the rest of his life. In spite of Michael's betrayal, he has also loved Fabulous more than anyone else on earth.

In the stories of *She Loved Me Once* Goran developed his Pittsburgh characters in greater detail than in earlier stories and probed more deeply into their psychological and emotional origins. The stories are more complex, darker, and more disturbing. As McCullough wrote, "To read them is to enter a lost world, like stepping into the seductive shadows of one of Raphael Soyers' or Isabel Bishop's moody paintings of street life during the great depression." While deepening the mythic dimensions of his characters, he also made room for ghosts, spirits, and even sorceresses. Some of the characters painfully reach for mystical explanations to exorcize their morbid sense of emptiness. The reader can understand Pal Mahoney's fearful exclamation in "Our Billy": "It's either ghosts leaping about and howling on their mysterious business or nothing here at all down below but wind and snow. Now, give me a ghost every time."

Writing for *The Miami Herald* (14 November 1999), Paula Friedman opened her review of Goran's third collection, *Outlaws of the Purple Cow* (1999) with the observation that Goran "conjures with humor and poignancy the sometimes wild aspirations of Irish Americans living in Pittsburgh." Friedman also pointed out how many of the stories in this collection are about people seeking refuge from the intrusion of the external world into their personal lives, noting "how many of his characters are unable to waken from their fantasy lives. . . . people get caught in the fantasy worlds of others as well as in their own." In *Outlaws of the Purple Cow* moral dilemmas become less important than phenomenological ones, and the questions that some characters ask themselves no longer concern issues of right and wrong but rather: "did this really happen or am I making it up?"

In the first story, "Jenny and the Episcopalian," Jenny McAvoy, a marginalized and desperately lonely young cleaning lady, begins to feel that "something soul-stirring could happen at any time." Her isolation is so profound that she begins to confuse

Dust jacket for Goran's 1999 book, stories about people whose fantasies provide respite from what one reviewer has called "the lunatic sadness of things"

appearance and reality: "She fancied she'd see a gigantic tank driving up the middle of Center Avenue." Her mother and her few friends consider her "harmless and hopeless."

As Jenny is walking by St. Peter's Anglican Church, she encounters its former pastor, the Reverend Woodrow Carter-Batterman, who has been dead for five years. Though Jenny is somewhat taken aback at meeting a ghost, she is thrilled by the obvious affection that he shows her. They begin a passionate affair at the Chateau Hotel, where they meet once a week for ten months. She has told her mother and a few friends about her affair, but they dismissed her story as Jenny's overwrought imagination. Her ghostly lover stops showing up at the hotel in August 1945, on the day the United States dropped the first atomic bomb on Japan. Jenny trusts that he will reappear someday, and if he does not, they will continue their highly satisfactory affair in the afterlife.

This story could be considered Goran's first foray into magical realism, and it also suggests the influences of Henry James and Wallace Stevens. In one of Stevens's letters he explains, "The imagination creates what it seeks"; that is, human beings unconsciously—or in some cases consciously—create what they need to survive emotionally and spiritually. Jenny's conviction that she has met the object of a true love that nothing can ever destroy is the result of her faith that love conquers all. The possibility that he could be anywhere and appear to her at any time—that he is both imminent and immanent—is enough to sustain her in a condition of permanent bliss. Jenny has unconsciously created a fiction that redeems her from the existential emptiness of her pathetic life. As long as she can live in a kind of visionary expectation beyond time and physical place, she can function and feel a part of a commonly shared world. Her harmless solipsistic condition becomes her redemptive agent. This casual acceptance of the psychopathology of everyday life is a new development in Goran's stories.

"Keeping Count" also deals with the same problem of grounding experience in a knowable reality. The main character, James Thierry, is in many ways an opposite of Jenny McAvoy. James is a genuine hero: a highly decorated police captain who, as the story opens, has just saved the lives of five people in a bus accident. His near-death experience during this act of heroism has caused him to become obsessed with his own death. During his ruminations on the subject, James unconsciously reconstructs his life in terms of its most significant events. Seeking redemption from mere destructive duration, he makes a list of the women he has made love to, an act that validates his manhood and proves to him that he has led a passionate, fulfilling life. The list reaches ninety-nine women, and he becomes obsessed with adding a one-hundredth name. In his official capacity as an officer of the court, he meets an attractive, married woman, Irene Dubrinia, while in the process of determining whether her troubled daughter should receive prison or psychiatric care. Irene is more than willing to go to bed with the attractive James, but when she has undressed, James experiences a shattering revelation: he "realized for fleeting seconds now that he was counting again, tumbling, but now with a miser's passion, coins piled up as foolish treasures, women numbered, days left till retirement and till death itself. . . . This was a place without him at all in it and no promise that there was the remotest quality of love there." James realizes that he is only involved

in "the ceremony of counting," that he is "keeping count" of his sexual conquests for the most narcissistic of reasons. He cannot go through with the seduction, and departs from the mystified Irene with the assurance that James will treat her daughter with fairness. As with Dick Best in "Grady's Sister," James Thierry's resistance to temptation transforms the commonplace into something sacred: "The air on the north side as James walked to the bus stop was ripe with the promise of the coming summer. Light and soft, it shone on the porch railings and brass ornaments on the front doors of the houses he observed, the day not bowed under age or failure or remorse, on the air only the innocent pleasures of things beginning to bloom with the season." James's virtuous and selfless behavior opens a visionary moment in time, which he discovers is the only thing that really "counts." In his later stories Goran has combined motifs that have before seemed mutually exclusive: venerable characters finding their true selves through disgrace, mythic figures moving from Apollonian to Dionysian levels, and sexual obsessions becoming agents of spiritual revelations.

"O'Casey and the Career," like "The Last Visit," is a portrait of the artist. Clarice Cunningham's favorite aunt, Aunt Olive, has left Clarice $12,000 so she can attend the University of Pittsburgh and escape her lower-class roots. There, in a literature class, she discovers some of the great Western writers: Tennessee Williams, Sophocles, Noel Coward, Federico García Lorca, and especially dramatist Sean O'Casey. Inspired by O'Casey probing examinations of class in early twentieth-century Ireland, Clarice begins to write her own play. Imitating O'Casey, she takes her neighborhood and its people as her subject matter: "The voices rising in noble foolishness at the Irish Club nightly . . . so long recited they had become more fixed than the truth of certain matters." The most mysteriously troubling voice for her creative development comes from her father's drunken monologues: "Whatever had died in the man, extinguished by drink, had come to reside in the voice which orated tales of the cabdriver's life all night long. . . . The old man holding on, continued narrating, sometimes alone at the kitchen table with phantoms who came unbidden to the empty kitchen." In spite of her disgust with her father's habitual drunkenness, Clarice recognizes the preternatural bardic power of his narrative, coming from some ancient archetypal well and having little to do with his wretched life. Like O'Casey, who mythologized lower-class Dublin life by transforming it into great art, she also realizes that her creative energy comes from her everyday life.

Though she takes great pains to conceal their identities, Clarice uses members of her family and friends, especially characters from the Irish Club, as the source of her material: "She knew that she embraced them most when she wrote about them, loving each lie and vision and invented history, putting it down so that someone else could hear it, love the teller and the one who had become the teller's story teller. She held her mother close in her writing, forgave her father." Yet, after the production of her first play almost all the members of her family and the community turn against her for humiliating them publicly: "It's the way an enemy would see us, boozing, talking about fighting, foolishly daydreaming. Bearing old grudges. . . . Like old ladies washing clothes at a mountain stream." Clarice's mother deals the cruelest blow: "You've failed your heritage."

Clarice presented her family and community accurately, mistakenly assuming that they would recognize and be grateful for her obvious affection for them. The story shows how an artist—or anyone who speaks the truth—is exiled from the community. The one hope for the artist trapped in a dead-end existence is to write herself out of it and into a fuller life created from her own imagination. Though rebuffed by the community, Clarice—like her models O'Casey and García Lorca—bravely moves on, and the story implies that she will probably seek her fortune in a less hostile environment.

All but one of Goran's fifty published stories take place in and around Oakland. In his stories Goran makes the world of Oakland mythopoeic through the sustaining power of narrative to create order from chaos, Eden from the wasteland, and community out of isolation. He peoples his stories with a range of personalities: fatal women, drunks, priests, ghosts, mad people, evil people, the sexually desperate, artists, and most of all, heroes of all varieties, redeeming them from the ravages of time. The hope and promise of a better life keeps his fictive world and characters alive, as the power of his narrative enchants his readers and transports them to the timeless realm of a caring community in spite of "the lunatic sadness of things." Goran is currently preparing another collection of short stories, tentatively called *The Fall of the Blond Sailor*.

Reference:

Mubarak S. Dahir, "Oakland Writ Large," *Pitt Magazine,* 13 (June 1998): 22–25.

Alyson Hagy
(1 August 1960 –   )

Cynthia A. Davidson
State University of New York at Stony Brook

BOOKS: *Madonna on Her Back* (N.p.: Wright, 1986);
Hardware River (New York & London: Poseidon, 1991);
Keeneland (New York & London: Simon & Schuster, 2000);
Graveyard of the Atlantic (St. Paul, Minn.: Graywolf, 2000).

OTHER: "Where Men Go to Cry," in *"Eric Clapton's Lover" and Other Stories from the Virginia Quarterly Review,* edited by Sheila McMillen and George Garrett (Charlottesville: University Press of Virginia, 1990), pp. 82–99;
"The Field of Lost Shoes," in *That's What I Like (About the South) and Other New Southern Stories for the Nineties,* edited by Garrett and Paul Ruffin (Columbia: University of South Carolina Press, 1993), pp. 159–171;
"The Nymph of the Lo River," in *A Visit to the Gallery,* edited by Richard Tillinghast (Ann Arbor: University of Michigan Press, 1997), p. 21;
"A Recipe for Influence," "Notes from a Regional Writer," and "Grits and Glitter," in *Deep West: A Wyoming Literary Guide,* edited by Michael Shay (Cheyenne: Wyoming Center for the Book, forthcoming 2001).

SELECTED PERIODICAL PUBLICATIONS–
UNCOLLECTED: "Rebecca," *Shenandoah,* 42 (Winter 1992): 61–74;
"Keeneland," *Story,* 41(Summer 1993): 100–108;
"My Back Pages," *Boston Globe,* 27 October 1996, p. 20;
"Snagged," *Bulletin of Miss Porter's School* (Fall 1996);
"The Examiner," *Crania,* 1 (Winter 1997) <http://www.crania.com/issue1/hagy.html>;
"Spring Meeting," *Idaho Review,* 2 (Fall 1999): 161–172.

Alyson Hagy is a writer of lyrical and emotionally rugged fiction in which psychologically complex characters confront the realities of their lives, often within a rural and decidedly American landscape and culture. Born Alyson Carol Hagy on 1 August 1960, she grew up on a farm

Alyson Hagy (photograph © Adam Jahiel; from the dust jacket for Graveyard of the Atlantic, *2000)*

in the Blue Ridge Mountains of Virginia, the child of country physician John Albert Hagy and homemaker Carol Elaine Lindsay. Her grandparents were ministers, blacksmiths, and schoolteachers. A preoccupation with vocation frequently enters Hagy's work, possibly because of her early exposure to traditional professions. Hagy said in an unpublished 25 April 2000 letter, in regard to the Kentucky racetrackers, retired Merchant Marines, and female Coast Guard members in her stories, that "I was drawn to these occupations, these intricate vocations, and I

164

wanted readers to see and smell and taste these very physical laborers at work. I wanted to translate those weather-worn occupations into stories." She also is interested in the relationship between people and nature; at the heart of this interest seems to be a quest to discover what human nature is and how the variations in it might be expressed. She said, in a statement published in *Contemporary Authors* in 1992, "As a storyteller I suppose I am obsessed with others' obsessions. I write to discover why humans desire what they desire and how they survive the consequences of their passions."

Hagy's interest in writing developed early. By the age of eight she had written three detective "novels" in imitation of the Nancy Drew mysteries she loved. By nineteen her interest in writing had become serious. Halfway through her undergraduate studies at Williams College in Massachusetts, Hagy believed her writing could become her vocation. She amassed a "swift and intense study of literature in my college classes" and filled reams of notebooks with "superheated" journal writing, poetry, and fiction. "Words began to fill my head in a way they never had before," Hagy wrote in an unpublished letter. "I had to, somehow, cope with the words. Was their source the swift and intense study of literature in my college classes? Or did they arise from the turmoil of being a Southerner who no longer lived in the South, a farm girl who no longer lived on the farm?" She graduated with a B.A. in English in 1982 and then entered the M.F.A. program in creative writing at the University of Michigan, where she won the prestigious Avery and Jule Hopwood Award for short fiction in 1984, the year before she graduated. On 25 May 1986 Hagy married Robert Wroe Southard, a lawyer, with whom she has since had a son, Connor. Also in 1986 Stuart Wright published her first collection of short fiction, *Madonna on Her Back.* The book was praised in *The Los Angeles Times Book Review* (25 January 1987) by William Price Fox. A story from the collection, "Where Men Go to Cry," later was collected in the anthology *"Eric Clapton's Lover" and Other Stories from the Virginia Quarterly Review* (1990).

Madonna on Her Back is an eclectic mix, showing the range of Hagy's interests and imagination in her early work. In these eight stories Hagy develops a trait that appears in her later work: the voicing of sexual differences and the evolution of gender roles in a changing world. These stories have a more overtly feminist tone than the later work; many of them concern women who are learning to live without men or who would be clearly better off without them. Hagy is mainly interested, however, in the nuances of personality, often expressed through relationships and sexuality. The locales are varied, ranging from the rural South in "No Kind of Name," about the invasion of a gentle farm worker's private world, to Africa in "Where Men Go to Cry," about an affair between mis-

matched art students. Mothers and children play a central role in two stories, the title story and "Mister Makes." A welfare mother is scapegoated by the system as she attempts to care for a handicapped child in "Mister Makes." In "Shoreline" a woman obsesses about the would-be male lovers to whom her husband has professed attraction. "Stadia" is a gentle *danse macabre* between an alcoholic and the wife who would save him. On the dust jacket for *Madonna on Her Back,* George Garrett described this collection as "highwire daring" fictions "of amplitude and resonance."

In the title story a young, female artist, Joelle, creates a personal body of work out of sketching her nursing sister, Ellis, with whom she shares a house. Although both women are recovering from failed relationships with men, they are developing different attitudes about their pasts: Joelle becomes increasingly independent and female oriented, while Ellis desires to recapture her youthful, triumphant figure. Joelle iconizes Ellis's nude body in her art and in her general attentions, not because of its adherence to a cultural ideal but because of its history, marked by poignant, graceful aging. In the images she creates of her sister's body, Joelle escapes Ellis's desperation for a male-sanctioned physique and finds a budding, intuitive feminism: "There was real passion in the quiet of a girl's loss, a mama's gain, she thought." Ellis, however, cannot appreciate her personal history and its physical manifestations, which Joelle finds so moving, because her past is wrapped up in the pain of abandonment. Her main desire is to curtail the toll of time and regain the body she once possessed. Ellis believes she must see herself reflected in the eyes of a desiring male in order to be assured of the physical transformation she seeks. To see herself as her sister does, she would have to be "different," an option she refuses.

Another story, "Infrared Signature," humorously explores the evolution of gender roles in a relationship. It concerns a man involved in a Walter Mittyish project and the woman who tries desperately to support him, physically, financially, and emotionally. Pete decides to capture a B-52 in a large net made of fishing tackle, hoisted by hot-air balloons. Wheeling, his partner and lover of seventeen months, has a plethora of domestic talents that she uses to keep the household afloat economically while Pete teaches grade school (a job he seems to take none too seriously) and cooks up wild, expensive schemes on his days off. Pete barely notices Wheeling's contributions, taking her presence for granted. His confidante is a former marine named E. Drake, who eventually moves in with Pete and Wheeling, bringing his dog.

In an increasingly animated effort to reach Pete on any level at all, Wheeling heads off to the public library to learn all she can about the chances for the success of their project and to be a better informed, more involved partner.

After she finds that his idea was originally conceived by Canadian peace activists as a protest against military aggression, she develops greater political awareness and a sense of connectedness not only to Pete but to a larger community comprised of like-thinking individuals. Her personal contribution to the project is to create an "infra-red signature" made of treated cloth letters that will identify the net as "theirs"—meaning not just Pete and Wheeling, but their community. Psychologically, the infra-red signature signifies the structure of limits that separate reality from fantasy and allow fruitful connections to flourish. In this sense Wheeling is mothering Pete, but she is also finding herself to be a mother of humankind at large, a person with power. Yet, there is a mundane aspect to her actions. The infrared signature may also symbolize Wheeling's desire to territorialize her relationship, to make it meaningful and lasting to herself alone—"signed off"—like the suburban weddings that she caters. She is clearly trying to "catch" her man as he tries to catch something that barely necessitates, in his eyes, her participation. After the rig fails to snare a B-52 and Pete shrugs off the failure by stating that "Maybe the sky's not my bag," Wheeling explodes, "That mess belongs to all of us. You can't act like it's your personal toy." By the end of the story it seems doubtful that the relationship will adapt to Wheeling's social and psychological growth.

Another story in this collection, "Where Men Go to Cry," is the story of a doomed romance that reverses the typical, gendered roles of "beast" and "beauty." Paul, a handsome doctoral student in anthropology who dabbles in art, is preparing to leave Portland to do fieldwork in Africa, and encounters an older, brilliant, remarkably ugly female art student, Linnea, who is dying of a neuromuscular disease as quickly as her reputation and the value of her work are rising. Despite Linnea's limitations, Paul is emotionally and erotically fascinated by her. He is a rather directionless person who is drawn into the "heart of darkness" provided by Linnea's relentless focus on his body, which she iconizes, and its contrast to her own. At the same time she is able to present herself as a profoundly superior individual mentally, able to see into Paul's mind and understand things that he "can only begin to feel." The evidence for this claim rests solely with Linnea herself, but Paul is completely mesmerized, depicting an almost humorous reversal of the ugly but articulate male who convinces beautiful younger women of his charm and power. Linnea, however, is never charming, despite her power, and does not triumph in the situation, for her real desire is not to conquer beautiful men but to be beautiful herself. Despite efforts to convince himself that he is merely filling time before leaving for Africa and being kind to a sick woman, Paul finds that Linnea has touched his heart and, finally, betrayed his trust when she abruptly attempts to dismiss him before his departure. Linnea is also wounded by Paul despite her efforts to keep him at arm's length and treat him as an object. Neither one can escape the fact that they have allowed themselves to love the other despite the other's perceived limitations.

More attention has been focused on Hagy's second collection of short stories, *Hardware River,* which came out five years after *Madonna on Her Back*. Hagy asserts that her first two collections were influenced by Flannery O'Connor, Eudora Welty, Katherine Anne Porter, and Carson McCullers. Described by Michael Harris in *The Los Angeles Times Book Review* as "seven stories about violence and desire in the rural Midwest and South," this volume opens and closes with two tales of love and betrayal of young men: "Hardware River," the gothic tale of a rather forgettable young man driven to an unforgettable suicide by a cruel female lover and her waiflike sister, and "Kettle of Hawks," a character study of a doomed and complicated relationship between a lonely bisexual farmer, an emotionally insulated widow, and her beautiful, free-spirited teenage son. David Finkle of *The New York Times Book Review* (31 March 1991) marked this last story as "the best of the lot" because "Ms. Hagy is true to the natures of the people she's created." It illustrates a recurrent theme in Hagy's work: the exploration of gender identity and sex-role transgression and the expression of sexual differences. Finkle also noticed a propensity for love triangles in the collection and pointed out that the author "seems to be suggesting . . . that bungled three-way relationships are the most common way in which people play out attempts at communication." This pattern was also present in *Madonna on Her Back,* especially in the title story and in "Infrared Signature."

Most of the stories in *Hardware River* include some kind of relationship triangle. In "Ballad and Sadness" a young American woman traveling in Scotland takes a lover while thinking of her brother, a convicted child molester. In "The Field of Lost Shoes" a young academic conflicts with his married, female lover while forging a connection with her ten-year-old son. "A Seeming Mermaid" concerns the haunting memory of an absent woman as discussed by two close friends or lovers. "The Grief is Always Fresh" relates the intersection of two triangles, one between brothers and the girl they murder and another between a young artist, her absent journalist husband, and the local policeman who substitutes for him during a troubling season. Only "Native Rest," an anecdotal tale about a man's memories of "different" German Baptist neighbors and the present dying of one of them, escapes the three-pronged relationship intensity, which reaches its pinnacle in the concluding story.

"Kettle of Hawks" is an effective midpoint of Hagy's strengths and concerns, which she has developed in her later books, the novel *Keeneland* (2000) and the story collection *Graveyard of the Atlantic* (2000). These concerns include the placement of human intimacy within various social structures (the family unit, the community) and its relationship to external, natural forces that are unflinching and unyielding, such as nature as predator or unstoppable force. The story is about Tom Price, a sensual but emotionally remote farmer who hires an attractive young neighbor, Abraham, to work for him. Abe's closest friend is his mother, Miriam, a widow, who raised him "solo and free." Her emotional life is dominated by Abe and by memories of her husband, Michael, who died in Vietnam when Abe was a baby. Abe begins to hero-worship Tom and fantasizes about bringing together Miriam and Tom to create the close family unit he has always dreamed of. Against her desire for isolation, Miriam invites Tom to dinner, where she sees immediately that he is falling in love with Abe. Taking him aside, she tries subtly to create a pact with Tom that will "protect" Abe. Although Tom agrees and at first tries to honor the pact, he feels overwhelmed by the boy's presence, which reminds him of his long-suppressed love for his brother, Quint. Tom temporarily sublimates his desire by building a shelter for hawks, as he means to resurrect an occupation that he shared with his brother many years earlier. Eventually he seduces the younger man, who has been made vulnerable by a farm accident, and forces Abe to realize his completely unconscious attraction to Tom and the insupportability of his own ideal family image. Afterward, Abe returns home to Miriam in pain and confusion. Miriam leaves Abe alone while she searches for Tom in the night, planning revenge. When she finds him, however, he undercuts the power of her revenge by making her realize that she herself is partially to blame, because she never found out what the boy really wanted.

Hagy presents these characters with sympathy but not sentimentality. All three bring a mythical persona into play that grows out of a combination of an uncertain relationship to the community and their own dreams of love, security, and mastery over the environment, as well as their fantasies about the fulfillment they might bring to one another. In this story and others in the collection Hagy's lush prose can be a bit heavy-handed, with overt symbolic imagery: for example, a handsome horse named Ragged Time, with "the temperament of a bad and jealous boy," initializes the closeness between Tom and Abe. The prose tends to lean on literary tropes that are conventional, although elegantly executed.

Interested in the translation from sensuality to language and the connections between humans and animals, especially horses and birds, Hagy often represents these themes in her work. Lute's passionate attachment to a bird in "Hardware River," Tom's wild yet obedient hawks and half-broken horse in "Kettle of Hawks," and later the dance between racehorses and their human entourage in *Keeneland,* all mark a territory of communication between

Dust jacket for Hagy's first book (1986), a collection of what George Garrett called "highwire daring" stories

human and animal that is not clearly defined, even metaphorically, by human social reality, except for that which is secretive, sexual, spiritual, sacred, or taboo in nature. These relations illustrate another important theme in Hagy's fiction, unconventional or private communication between people that forces human history forward in private, unrecorded ways. If these events do translate to the public record, they often do so as "senseless" or "irrational" acts that stun the community.

A similar, though more troubling, type of communication occurs when the psychotic or asocial human tries to deliver his experience—with hostility or not—to other people. Hagy relates these situations to creativity in general, which is not rooted in words and law but raw, natural desires and action. With his suicide act, Lute in "Hardware River" seems to be staging some kind of statement on the failure of society to support his dreams. Lute lashes himself to a mill wheel and exposes himself to the elements, a clear symbol of desperation, yet the narrator can only speculate on "what that boy meant to create." In another story, "The Grief is Always Fresh," two teenage boys face the legal and social consequences of killing a young woman they were sleeping with. Until the time of Marilyn Height's death, Nick and Tony were "assholes," according to their younger cousin Fulton, but Nick, at least, was known for his honesty: "If you didn't lie to him, he'd treat you fair." Nick's personal system of justice is upset later, when he is being interrogated by the police and finds that he is expected to lie about his lack of remorse:

> The stories you told eventually wore themselves out until the real way you'd moved and thought was lost forever, even to you. A man was never direct. If that were so, he'd probably still be out there, shifting and tight, capable of sticking to a promise and a threat full of quiet, rushing blood. Instead, he was here where it was hot and dull, where they'd make him remember their outrage, make him imagine a made-up pain and confess to a mouthful of thick, sloppy lies.

Nick simultaneously loses himself to society as he finds the essence of his vibrant self. To communicate successfully this experience to others, he must threaten the foundation of human society—and he will not be allowed to do so, unless he becomes a sociopath. He realizes that there are levels of death that are a part of survival and of submission to the system, which is made not of men and their actions but of words. At the other end of the spectrum in this story is Sarah, who is totally enmeshed in her human attachments but feels unrelated to place; as a result, even her human connections lack depth, and she searches for meaning in the tragedies of others. On finding the spot where the young woman was murdered, she realizes that even this close approximation to mayhem cannot vivify her life. The "scars and flaws" of Sarah seem to be those traits that have not allowed her to reconcile her material and psychological resources with her dreams. Sarah's ineffectual husband, Parker, is a man of words, a journalist, but he cannot convey the kinds of terrible empowering truths that his wife needs to hear to feel alive, or that Nick needs to say to feel like a man. Sarah further compromises her need to feel close to the center of natural power when she has a passionless affair with Jack, a policeman.

Between 1986 and 1996 Hagy worked at establishing a career in higher education, teaching fiction-writing workshops at the University of Michigan, while still publishing a steady stream of short fiction in journals. In 1996 she relocated to Laramie, Wyoming, where she is an assistant professor of English at the University of Wyoming.

Hagy's first novel, *Keeneland,* garnered a different level of critical attention than her earlier collections with their gothic, literary tenor. "Even readers who don't give a dang about horses should love Hagy's fresh, funny, brilliantly made and irreducibly twangy debut," said a reviewer for *Publishers Weekly* (7 February 2000), adding

that the "sassy but chronically unlucky heroine shows us the hardscrabble underside of the glitzy horseracing world." In *Keeneland* Hagy's prose moves at a racer's clip, and clearly she has worked at toning down the literary tropes that appeared frequently in *Madonna on Her Back* and *Hardware River.* Certain issues reappear that were central in those collections—the difficult translation between language and nonverbal experience, the discrepancies between resources and expectations, the mysterious connection between humans and animals, and the invisible nuances of human sexual relations that affect public reputation.

Keeneland is the story of a twenty-seven-year-old exercise rider named Kerry Connelly. When the story opens, she has bolted from her abusive husband, Eric, a New York breeder plagued by loan sharks. Kerry has pocketed $10,000 and some heirloom jewelry, gifts from Eric. She brings nothing else of value to the Lexington racetrack community except the memory of her true love, a fast and beautiful mare named Sunny. It is an inauspicious return for the Kentucky-bred woman who had only a few years before left a good job exercising horses for Billy Tolliver, one of the few honest roulette dealers and horse trainers, to marry wealthy and handsome Eric, with whom she shared dreams of conquering the racetrack circuit. Kerry considers her marriage to Eric a "bad choice," and she continues to make bad choices that are clearly masochistic attempts to recover her lost sense of self through pain. Kerry alienates three bosses, including Alice Piersall, a tough but honest horse trainer who wants to help Kerry learn to survive without pulling herself down. Kerry instead gets involved with a groom named Danny, who helps her win $35,000 to pay off the loan sharks threatening to harm the mare. Danny, however, then steals the money after seducing her. Devastated, Kerry scrambles to find a backup scheme for saving Sunny while she continues to battle demons of her past. She is also training Twilight Flare, Alice's prized horse, for an important stakes race. An unethical trainer, Roy Delvecchio, attempts to bribe Kerry into helping him obtain Twilight Flare. Although Kerry is loathe to pledge loyalty to Alice, she is disgusted by Delvecchio's strong-arm tactics. She needs to find solutions to her financial woes without selling her own soul or selling out Alice. A combination of wit, wiles, and mostly sheer endurance allows Kerry to survive a final round of difficulties before she can close this chapter of her life and begin again.

A new collection of short stories, *Graveyard of the Atlantic,* was released by Graywolf Press shortly after the appearance of *Keeneland.* In this third collection the tales are united by common geography—the Outer Banks of North Carolina. The ocean shows a different side of nature than the unyielding loam or woodland of the earlier stories; the sea allows quicker changes, and more of them. The sea is the first cradle of life and, traditionally, a symbol of the Great Mother of the collective mind. The characters in these stories tend to be mature men and women who are confronting mortality; this theme absorbs the concerns of identity found through transgressive desire and sexual differentiation that marked Hagy's earlier work. The stories tend not to have much plot, and the deep gothic quality of *Hardware River* or the clipped activity and smart observations of *Keeneland* are replaced by narrators who sort through their losses. There is less folklore and more sheer physical detail, less overt cruelty and more sheer endurance. In "Sharking" a veteran shark fisher bonds with a woman recovering from cancer while barely rescuing some novice sharkers. "The Snake-Hunters" follows a local boy's relationship with visiting scientists looking for an elusive specimen. "Graveyard of the Atlantic" examines a man whose emotions and creativity are inhibited by marriage to a formidable but fragile poet. In "Semper Paratus" a woman copes with deep-sea rescues and the men she works with. A woman sorts through changes, and the lack of them, in a sibling relationship in "Brother, Unadorned." In "Search Bay" an aging loner caught between a gentle Indian woman and her prideful young son makes an angry mistake that will come back to haunt him.

In these stories so much occurs in the subtle currents of setting that the human element is absorbed nearly as quickly as it is revealed. Connections between people, when they occur, seem as old as the ocean itself, and not related to the more landlocked American psychoscapes of William Faulkner or O'Connor, where passions tend to nest, take root, and fester. The narration, even when first person, seems distanced from the scenes described. Characters frequently measure themselves against nature itself or those who have worked in or around it the longest, or those who have suffered the greatest losses in, around, or because of it. Loss emerges as Hagy's most enduring and persistent theme.

Many of the people in these stories are long-married couples or long-abandoned lovers, divorcées, widows, and widowers caught between washed-away memories and painful recurrent remembrances. Such a character is Thalia in "North of Fear, South of Kill Devil." A furiously angry, grieving widow who haunts the Cape Hatteras Sound she used to frequent with her soulmate husband, Ben, she is courted tirelessly by a vacationing writer, Bill, whose encouragement she mistakes for love. She turns on him in rage but gives way to the realization of her buried rage toward her husband for dying, and finally, an acceptance of his death.

In the title story, perhaps the most effective of this collection, an unhappy husband faces the realization that he will never fulfill his dreams of romance and creative achievement because of choices he has made in his youth. Chris has been married for fifteen years to Lucy, "A poet

who, in cruel and important ways, was becoming lovelier and more gifted as she aged." Wrapped in a dark fist of creative reverie, she leaves him to his own devices along the coast in Frisco, North Carolina, where he tentatively pursues other women who might be able to give him the tenderness he craves. The dysfunctional intimacy of their partnership is displayed in a confrontation during which he realizes that he wants to leave her and assert his own creative powers, but he never will because they are "twined together, throbbing, and he could not resist" her dependence on him, as well as the painful realities that she expresses through her gifts "in a language more lovely and terse than he could speak." Again the familiar theme of private communication emerges.

"Search Bay," chosen by Annie Proulx for inclusion in *Best American Short Stories 1997,* is a lyrical tale of an aging mariner haunted by memories that confront him in the shape of his lonely present. The protagonist, Hansen, is now retired and living alone in the woods near Lake Huron, half-consciously preparing for death, when he encounters a teenage Indian boy. The boy's mother is a local barmaid for whom he had once had feelings, although the connections seem to have been marginal and wrought with fantasy. The meeting with her son resurrects memories of a sea cook named Henderson, an Indian whom Hansen had liked who had possibly killed a passenger on a ship where they had worked together. Hansen's memories of this event are distorted, but as he is drawn against his will into the society of people in the present, he is forced to confront his past. Indians and seaman both connect to the world in a manner that eludes words and man-made laws but unfolds in fluid action, which may transgress these laws and may prevent immersion in society. The protagonist visits the boy's mother after the teenager's accidental death and is disturbed by her grief; he is unable to know how to react properly in a social context. Instead, to cope with the loss of the boy and of his own youth, in a private memorial he launches a buoy near the place where the boy's body has fallen to the lake floor. Again Hagy depicts the private communication of an individual who is poorly adapted to modern society but nonetheless realizes his connections to human life and nature on his own terms.

In her relatively short career Alyson Hagy has captured the attention of critics as a serious artist—one who, as George Garrett said, "takes very real risks" writing about subjects which are "at heart, deeply complex, difficult, even dangerous" with "impeccable care and craft." In a time when writers nurtured in academe are frequently dismissed as safe and formulaic, and experimental writers frequently seem inaccessible to mainstream readers, Hagy combines the best traits of traditional genre with edgy subject matter and a shrewd, eclectic political awareness.

Pam Houston

(9 January 1962 –   )

Kathryn West
Bellarmine University

BOOKS: *Cowboys Are My Weakness* (New York: Norton, 1992; London: Virago, 1993);

Waltzing the Cat (New York: Norton, 1998; London: Virago, 1999);

A Little More About Me (New York: Norton, 1999); republished as *A Rough Guide to the Heart* (London: Virago, 1999).

RECORDINGS: *Cowboys Are My Weakness,* read by Houston, Englewood Cliffs, N.J., Publishing Mills / Media Books, 1992;

Waltzing the Cat, read by Houston, Englewood Cliffs, N.J., Publishing Mills / Media Books, 1999.

OTHER: Harriet Fish Backus, *Tomboy Bride: A Woman's Personal Account of Life in the Mining Camps of the West,* introduction by Houston (Boulder, Colo.: Pruett, 1991);

"A Hopeful Sign: The Making of Metonymic Meaning in Munro's 'Meneseteung,'" *Kenyon Review,* 14 (Fall 1992): 79–92;

Women on Hunting: Essays, Fiction, and Poetry, selected, with an introductory essay, by Houston (Hopewell, N.J.: Ecco, 1995);

Men Before Ten A.M., photographs by Véronique Vial, text by Houston (Hillsboro, Ore.: Beyond Words, 1996);

B. M. Bower, *Lonesome Land,* introduction by Houston (Lincoln: University of Nebraska Press, 1997).

Pam Houston (photograph from the dust jacket for Waltzing the Cat, *1998)*

Pam Houston attained critical and popular success with the 1992 publication of her first short-story collection, *Cowboys Are My Weakness.* The volume garnered its author not only impressive sales and reviews but also media attention in the form of magazine profiles, interviews, and several talk-show appearances, suggesting that her stories of adventurous women rafting through white-water rapids, guiding Dall sheep hunters in Alaska, and attempting to establish relationships with men of the American West tapped a little-explored but ripe territory in contemporary consciousness. *Cowboys Are My Weakness* was named a *New York Times* Notable Book in 1992, won the 1993 Western States Book Award, and was later translated into at least nine languages. A review in *The New York Times* (15 July 1992) stated, "Her collection of short stories is an odyssey of a young woman who develops a habit of bad love and uses adventure both to recover and carve a place for herself in the American West. . . . In the last

170

six months, it has been critically acclaimed, climbed best-seller lists, garnered Hollywood offers, and turned its author–also a licensed river runner, hunting guide, horse trainer and ski instructor–into a cult figure."

Houston's second collection, *Waltzing the Cat* (1998), also a best-seller, received the Willa Cather Award for Contemporary Fiction. Houston has published fiction in a variety of magazines and journals, including *Mademoiselle, Mirabella, The Mississippi Review, Ploughshares, Redbook, Vogue, Cimarron Review,* and *The Gettysburg Review,* while her essays have appeared in equally wide-ranging outlets: *Condé Nast Sports for Women, Outside, House and Garden, Travel and Leisure, Elle, Food and Wine, Ski, Mirabella, Mademoiselle, Allure, Los Angeles Magazine,* and *The New York Times.* Her stories are becoming widely anthologized. "How to Talk to a Hunter" was collected in *Best American Short Stories 1990,* and "The Best Girlfriend You Never Had" was collected in the 1999 edition of that same series. "The Best Girlfriend You Never Had" was also the only story to be added to John Updike and Katrina Kenison's selections for *The Best American Short Stories of the Century* in its transition from hardback to paperback. Judith Freeman, reviewing *Cowboys Are My Weakness* for *The Los Angeles Times Book Review* (23 February 1992), encapsulated what many find so appealing in Houston's work. She called the volume a "brilliant first collection" in which "Houston claims for women the terrain staked out by male writers from Hemingway to Richard Ford" and ends up "revealing much about the complex state of relations between men and women."

Born Pamela Lynne Houston on 9 January 1962 in Trenton, New Jersey, to Catherine Louise (Hoff) Houston, an actress, and Beverly Ord Houston, an unsuccessful businessman, Houston grew up in Bethlehem, Pennsylvania. She learned to read at two and a half under the guidance of a baby-sitter named Martha Washington (who, Houston reports, had a brother named George). In many essays and interviews Houston has described the atmosphere in her childhood home as one full of fear and insecurity, shaped by alcoholism and resentment. In "The Long Way to Safety," an essay appearing in her collection *A Little More About Me* (1999), she said, "By my sixteenth birthday I had walked away from sixteen serious automobile accidents. In more than half of them, a great deal of alcohol was involved. My mother drove a Plymouth Fury right through a 7-Eleven, my father rolled a Cadillac Seville nine times on Christmas Eve, my best high school girlfriend put us and her Ford station wagon under a semi, right at decapitation level."

Houston survived these dangers and completed a B.A. with honors at Denison University in 1983. After bicycling across Canada and south to Colorado, work-

ing such odd jobs as bartender and flag person on a highway crew, she entered the Ph.D. program at the University of Utah in 1986 but chose to leave it in 1992, five months before completing the program. While in graduate school, Houston moved to Park City, Utah, where she made her home for several years; she has described her experiences with the changes in the area from rugged Western town to resort-oriented tourist center in the essays "The Bad Dogs of Park City," "The Pit Bull and the Mountain Goat," and "Growing Apart: Leaving Park City" (all collected in *A Little More About Me*). Her reactions to the various incarnations of the area reveal much about how she sees herself. As she wrote "I know people who wind up leaving a place they've lived in a long time because they say they've outgrown it" in "The Pit Bull and the Mountain Goat," an essay collected in *A Little More About Me.* "But I'm leaving Park City because it's outgrown me. . . . We have espresso now, and sushi, and bars with bands that are actually worth paying money to see. . . . Park City is a world-class resort now; it's me who's still a little rough around the edges, and I'm bound to find someplace new that's at least as scruffy as I am."

The Park City years were interrupted by one spent in Ohio, where Houston taught creative writing at her alma mater, Denison University, during the 1991–1992 academic year. A licensed river guide, Houston has also worked as a hunting guide, horse trainer, ski instructor, and instructor in literature and creative writing, and has been a recurring guest on *CBS-TV Sunday Morning* with a segment titled "Postcards from Colorado." She has taught creative writing at St. Mary's College in Moraga, California, and at various workshops and festivals across the country. She now holds a permanent teaching position at the University of California, Davis, where she spends half the year.

Experiences of adventure, travel, wilderness, danger, of following men into and connecting with them in such situations, characterize–and drew the most attention to–Houston's early writing. In the essay "In the Company of Fishermen" Houston related her reaction to being asked to accompany a group of late-night fly fishermen to a Michigan lake site:

> I have always said yes, and as a result the shape of my life has been a long series of man-inspired adventures, and I have gone tripping along behind those men, full of strength and will and only a half-baked kind of competence, my goal being not to excel, but to simply keep up with them, to not become a problem, to be a good sport. It is a childhood thing (I was my father's only son), and I laugh at all the places this particular insecurity has taken me: sheep hunting in Alaska, helicopter

skiing in Montana, cliff diving in the Bahamas, ice climbing in the Yukon territory.

Yet, she described herself as not at all athletic:

> For all the things I undertake—whitewater rafting, back-packing, rock climbing, skiing, scuba diving, tennis, kayaking, horseback riding, softball, sailing, etc.—I have not one ounce of natural ability. God gave me brains, a good ear for language, a face that most people think they can get along with, and my mother's strong legs. Grace, finesse, timing, and all the other things that make an athlete an athlete didn't come in my package.

She noted that therapists suggest that her penchant for dangerous, even life-threatening, situations stems from a determination to re-create the daily danger of her childhood in order to gain some retroactive feeling of control. While she accepts this interpretation and refers to it more than once in writing about her life, she also does not want the theory to "explain why I love a good adventure. I don't want it to explain why I love to be outdoors."

Whatever else is happening in a Houston story, love and appreciation for the outdoors and a seemingly innate sense of how it works are always present. The lead story in *Cowboys Are My Weakness,* "How to Talk to a Hunter," typifies the themes of many of the stories in the collection—a young woman negotiating the rugged weather and terrain of the American West while negotiating the equally rugged terrain of a relationship with an emotionally unavailable and unfaithful man. One of only two stories in the collection that does not feature a first-person narrator, "How to Talk to a Hunter" employs the unusual second person; this approach and its ironic tone have invited comparisons to Lorrie Moore's *Self-Help* (1985) which Houston has admitted to trying to imitate. The protagonist of "How to Talk to a Hunter" works through her feelings about this relationship in a series of observations aimed as much at herself as at her listeners: "You will spend every night in this man's bed without asking yourself why he listens to top-forty country. Why he donated money to the Republican Party. Why he won't play back his messages while you are in the room." The story is set in December, in the time of the longest nights of the year just before Christmas, with thirteen straight days of snow and then temperatures at sixty degrees below zero. The narrator finds herself wrapped in the skins of animals her lover has killed, talking to a man who, although claiming to be always better at math and not so good with words, "will form the sentences so carefully it will be impossible to tell if you are included in these plans" he is making, and who "will manage to say

eight things about his friend without using a gender-determining pronoun."

None of the lessons of college ("A man desires the satisfaction of his desire; a woman desires the condition of desiring"), of graduate school ("In every assumption is contained the possibility of its opposite"), or of the pop psychology books ("Love means letting go of fear"), nor the advice of "your best female friend" and "your best male friend," whose responses are scattered throughout the story, provide epiphanies or solutions. Yet, these remembered words and the act of talking herself through the hunter/lover's nights with the other woman, the "coyote woman," bring her by the end to a metaphor that suggests she will break away soon. The final paragraph centers on her dog, whose "long low howl" sounds in the night. Although the hunter is with her this night, she identifies with the situation of the animal: "chained and lonely and cold. You'll wonder if he knows enough to stay in his doghouse. You'll wonder if he knows the nights are getting shorter now."

It is an engaging narrative, with enough wry humor to banish any tone of self-pity. Yet, the narrator/addressee seems immature throughout and a bit jarring against some of Houston's other heroines. She professes to love dogs, but she not only banishes her dog to the dangerously cold outdoors when the hunter comes over but also feeds her pet the chocolates that the hunter has sent. "How to Talk to a Hunter" was originally published in *Quarterly West* (1989) and was chosen by guest editor Richard Ford to be included in *Best American Short Stories 1990.*

While "How to Talk to a Hunter" gives no information as to how the protagonist came to be in the wintry West with her lover, "Selway," the second story in *Cowboys Are My Weakness,* makes plain that the protagonist is running the rapids of the Selway, one of the roughest rivers in North America, at its most extreme high water in several years, in order to be with Jack, her latest "wild" lover. Somewhat predictably, their boat turns over at one of the most dangerous points, and, as seems to be their half-unconscious purpose in making the trip, they face death. Both survive, and Jack contemplates taking on the tamer desert rivers from then on, while the narrator finds such a stillness in the mountains she can "imagine a peace without boredom." Although the plot does not surprise, the descriptions of the river—and of the physical exertions the people must produce in order to survive it—feel authentic and engaging.

In the course of "Selway" both main characters voice several opinions about the differences between men and women and the possibilities for relationships between them. In a line frequently quoted in reviews of *Cowboys Are My Weakness,* the narrator says, "I've been to four years of college and I should know better, but I love it when he calls me baby." Jack thinks of the narrator as naturally "life-protecting" because she is a woman; the narrator in turn believes the "old southern woman" who has told her "men can't really live unless they face death now and then." At first believing she has come along on the trip because she enjoys danger, she decides she is actually there to be with Jack:

> And even though I knew in my head there's nothing a man can do that a woman can't, I also knew in my heart we can't help doing it for different reasons. And just like a man will never understand exactly how a woman feels when she has a baby, or an orgasm, . . . a woman can't know in what way a man satisfies himself, what questions he answers for himself, when he looks right at death.

These ideas echo those in a critical article Houston published in *Kenyon Review* (Fall 1992), written while she was still in the Ph.D. program at the University of Utah. "A Hopeful Sign: The Making of Metonymic Meaning in Munro's 'Meneseteung'" articulates some of Houston's key assumptions about gender. She describes a conversation with a class in which she suggested that there are masculine and feminine thought processes, with the masculine thinking in a straight line ("this strict limitation on the context and consequences of his actions, and the sharpness of his focus allows a man a certain freedom to act in ways that continually baffle women") and the feminine defined by circles, with every circle containing the next one and the one before ("Context is not just a small part of the system, it defines the system"). Houston continues her speculation by drawing on the work of Jacques Lacan and Jane Gallop in order to discuss the association of metaphor with the male sensibility and metonymy with the female, carefully describing these as matrices and sensibilities that may be taken on by a person of either gender. She ends her analysis of Alice Munro's "Meneseteung" (collected in *Friends of My Youth*, 1990) with the argument that metonymy (and thus the female principle) is not one of dependence and lack, as Lacan would have it, but of "unlimited generative potential and creative possibility." Thus, the article provides some interesting insight into the way Houston thinks about fiction and about gender and also demonstrates why some feminist critics see stories such as "Selway" as too essentialist.

In the third story in *Cowboys Are My Weakness,* "Highwater," first published in *The Gettysburg Review,* two friends, Millie and Casey, both thirty years old, are dating men ten years older. The story opens with Casey telling Millie, the narrator, that she is pregnant. Her live-in boyfriend, Chuck, is a frequently stoned,

happy-go-lucky musician, while Millie's Richard is a fastidious stockbroker who still regularly visits his old girlfriend halfway across the state. By the end of the story Millie marvels over how two men who seemed so different could have been so much alike—both have left, Chuck to avoid the responsibility of the baby and Richard for a weekend trip with the old girlfriend. Yet, visiting Casey in the hospital, Millie decides the thing truly worth marveling over is the new baby.

"For Bo," which first appeared in *Cimarron Review,* turns the focus from male/female relationships to a young woman negotiating her finicky mother's visit to her own somewhat scruffy household consisting of three dogs and a tattooed, guitar-playing husband. Humorous in tone, the story includes moments delineating the tensions that arise when children develop tastes and lifestyles different from those of their parents. "What Shock Heard" continues the theme of an emotionally damaged woman, Raye, trying to connect with Zeke, a cowboy. Zeke can calm animals with the touch of his hands and with the noises he makes in his throat, which implies that he would be equally capable of soothing Raye, who has experienced both her husband's suicide and a rape. Actually, she feels that her horse, Shock, better shares her sense of trauma over these events. When she tries to explain these things to Zeke, she realizes that her words only widen the gap between them.

"Dall" appears to be one of the most closely autobiographical stories in *Cowboys Are My Weakness.* In her introduction to the 1995 collection *Women on Hunting: Essays, Fiction, and Poetry,* Houston wrote:

> When I was twenty-six years old, and just catching on to the fact that my life wasn't going to be something that came at me like opposing traffic, but something I actually had to take control of and shape, I fell in love with a man who was a hunting guide for a living. We didn't have what you would call the healthiest of relationships. He was selfish, evasive, and unfaithful. I was demanding, manipulative, and self-pitying. . . . Yet somehow we managed to stay together for three years of our lives, and to spend two solid months of each of those three years hunting for Dall sheep in Alaska.

The fictionalized version of this experience is one of the strongest stories in *Cowboys Are My Weakness.* The narrator experiences internal conflict over hunting (she describes herself as responsible for the death of five animals, through acting as a guide, but insists she has never killed an animal herself and will not); external conflict in her relationship with Boone, the hunting guide, which escalates into physical violence; and the wonder and fear of facing the northern lights and, immediately after her worst fight with her lover, facing a mother grizzly bear.

"Here is a powerful new voice in the short story, in twelve tales about wildness. In Pam Houston's wonderful stories sex and hunting are somehow confused, as are humans and animals. People wear skins, the animals speak, and those guys—the ones we all thought were extinct, the ones who once defined what a man was—turn up, very much alive, and up to their usual tricks. Pam Houston's women know they should know better, but they don't, and the result is a beautiful collection about sexual politics, old and new."
—Charles Baxter

W·W·NORTON

NEW YORK · LONDON

ISBN 0-393-03077-6

Dust jacket for Houston's first book, selected as a New York Times *Notable Book of 1992*

As assistant hunting guide the protagonist occupies an interesting position between Boone and the men they guide through the Alaskan wilderness; it provides her with insights into the relationship between hunters and nature, and between men and men. Early on she muses, "I thought how very much like soldiers we looked, how very much like war this all was, how very strange that the warlike element seemed to be so much the attraction." Later, after one of their clients has successfully killed a ram and is celebrating and posing for pictures with Boone and the carcass, she sees the activity in a larger context: "I understood that what we had accomplished was more for this moment than anything, this moment where two men were allowed to be happy together and touch." Houston puts into play a thought-provoking array of gender reflections in "Dall." Before turning away to leave with her cubs, the grizzly bear gestures at the narrator with a huge paw, who sees it as "both forbidding and inviting," perhaps the invitation from one female to another to be a different kind of participant in the natural world. The one time she sees the northern lights, they are:

a translucent green curtain . . . on the horizon. Then the curtain divided itself and became a wave and the wave divided itself and became a dragon, then a goddess, then a wave. Soon the whole night sky was full of spirits flying and rolling, weaving and braiding themselves across the sky. The colors were familiar, mostly shades of green, but the motion, the movement, was unearthly and somehow female; it was unlike anything I'd ever seen.

Thus, the grizzly bear and the northern lights, both figures of awe, are markedly female, while Boone and the hunters are male. As they are packing to leave Alaska and go their separate ways, Boone notes that she "really hung in there" but goes on to add, "But it made you stop loving me." He believes it is the activity of hunting that has come between them, when in fact her connections with the grizzly bear and its wave, with the northern lights–"a goddess, a wave . . . unearthly and somehow female"–suggest instead that she has found a strength inside herself that will not allow her to stay with a man who is physically abusive. With "Dall," the stories in *Cowboys Are My Weakness* begin to feature more self-confident heroines.

The title story, "Cowboys Are My Weakness," finds its narrator (unnamed, born in New Jersey, now a resident of the West for ten years) on a ranch in Grass Range, Montana, accompanying her boyfriend, Homer, to observe whitetail-deer mating season. She has been in search of a real cowboy to fit in her picture of her ideal life on a tiny ranch, but as the story opens she has already begun to come to terms with the fact that "even though Homer looked like a cowboy, he was just a capitalist with a Texas accent who owned a horse." Enter Montrose T. Coty, known as Monte, described by his friends as the "real thing" because he was once spotted by a director in a laundromat and offered two thousand dollars to be in a Wrangler commercial. Monte invites the narrator to the Stockgrowers' Ball. During their night of dancing she decides she has finally gotten where she had set out to go; she could be a Montana ranch woman and Monte could be her man. When he takes her home early in the morning, he says, "I'd love to give you a great big kiss, but I've got a mouthful of chew." There is a third man present, David, the owner of the ranch, a poet and vegetarian, who undergrazes by almost 50 percent and is raising the "fattest, healthiest, most organic Black Angus cattle in North America," a "sensitive, thoughtful, and kind" man, the type "I always knew I should fall in love with, but never did."

As the narrator packs to leave the ranch earlier than planned, Homer tells her he has decided she is the woman he wants to spend the rest of his life with "after all"; David offers compliment after compliment; and Monte rides after her to ask if she will write to him and come back for another date someday. As she drives toward Cody, Wyoming, listening to country music in which the women are all victims and the men "brutal or inexpressive and always sorry later," she reflects on stories, how people invent themselves through their fictions and how the stories "come to put walls around our lives." She decides, "there really isn't much truth in my saying cowboys are my weakness; maybe, after all this time, it's just something I've learned how to say." As Krista Comer noted in *Landscapes of the New West* (1999), halfway through the story the protagonist is on the verge of obtaining her deepest desire, the love of a "real cowboy," but "realizes she has allied herself with an incompatible script."

The story ends with the narrator declaring that the narratives offered by country music—and, by extension, those offered by Homer and Monte—are "not my happy ending. This is not my story." Earlier she has recognized her addiction for certain overly simplistic plots but has felt inevitably tied to them: "I've been to a lot of school and read a lot of thick books, but at my very core there's a made-for-TV movie mentality I

don't think I'll ever shake." The ending offers hope that in fact she is ready to begin writing her own narrative. The humor and spare but descriptive language of this story, added to a cohesive and stronger ending than many of the others, show Houston at her best. "Cowboys Are My Weakness" has been anthologized in the second edition of *The Norton Anthology of Contemporary Fiction*, edited by R. V. Cassill and Joyce Carol Oates.

"Jackson is Only One of My Dogs" is one of the most humorous stories in the collection. First appearing in *Mirabella*, it describes the narrator's two dogs: Jackson, constantly active, in trouble with dogcatchers and police, "athletic, graceful, obnoxious and filled with conceit," and "the other dog, the good dog," Hailey, who is "slow, a little fat, and gentle to her bones," and never in trouble. As with the men in her life, the narrator finds she has a better relationship with Jackson, "the charm machine," than with Hailey, "simply a low-maintenance dog." Yet, by the end she finds herself in a relationship with a kind, gentle, "low-maintenance" but "high density" man and discovers it offers complexities and "a kind of flying" beyond her imagination. Not all the metaphors in the story are convincing, but the writing is sprightly and humorous, animated by Houston's love for dogs.

In "A Blizzard Under Blue Sky" the narrator is told she is clinically depressed and rejects drugs in favor of a weekend of winter camping in high country at thirty-two degrees below zero. Accompanied only by her dogs (Jackson and Hailey of the previous story), she discovers at the end of a freezing fourteen-hour night that she has not spent any of it thinking about deadlines or bills or her unfaithful lover. "The morning sunshine was like a present from the gods . . . I remembered about joy." She admits it would be a movielike oversimplification to pretend a few nights in nature solved all of life's problems, but "On Sunday I had a glimpse outside of the house of mirrors, on Saturday I couldn't have seen my way out of a paper bag." One of the shortest pieces in *Cowboys Are My Weakness*, "A Blizzard Under Blue Sky" draws much of its power from the detailed descriptions of the necessities of winter camping and Houston's ability to communicate the physicality of the experience as a metaphor for her emotional needs. The story first appeared in *Lodestar*.

The only story aside from "How to Talk to a Hunter" to employ second-person narration, "Sometimes You Talk About Idaho," takes the narrator, a writer, to Manhattan, where she has a blind date with a soap-opera star, set up by the man she calls her "good father." The story explores the blurred line between performance and lies and performance based on true feelings, finding no satisfactory resolution. It was first published in *Mirabella*.

"Symphony" is a four-page recitation of the narrator's lovers. Here, Houston indulges a concentration on sensuality that tends to appear only briefly in the other stories, making this piece the most lyrical she has produced. Aware of the danger of how she might be labeled for admitting to having more than one lover ("I'm afraid of what you might be thinking. That I am a certain kind of person"), she balances the tightrope she admits to creating by interspersing dreams that reveal her needs and by an almost chastening tone: "I could love any one of them, in an instant and with every piece of my heart, but none of them nor the world will allow it, and so I move between them, on snowy highways and crowded airplanes." The voice created in this story is intimate and personal, almost uncannily drawing the reader into its sensuality: "I was in New York this morning. I woke up in Phillip's bed. Come here, he's in my hair. You can smell him."

The final story of *Cowboys Are My Weakness*, "In My Next Life," centers on the relationship between two women, one of whom sounds much like the other narrators in the collection. The opening line informs readers, "This is a love story," going on to explain that, while the narrator and Abby were never lovers, it "would have been possible." Abby, a horse trainer with strong New Age tendencies, develops breast cancer and dies. As Comer argued in *Landscapes of the New West*, it is not an unhappy ending, however, for "female solidarity and companionship has infused the protagonist with a new sense of self-worth. . . . This is a curious ending for a book that tantalizes readers because of its appeal to an ostensibly widely shared cultural experience: attraction to the rugged American cowboys." While Comer is not entirely accurate in claiming there are "no men" in this final story (both women have had troubled relationships with men), she astutely notes that with this ending and in the volume as a whole, "Desire, finally, is variable, open-ended, adventuring, without conclusion."

The essay "Breaking the Ice" (in *A Little More About Me*) reveals that "In My Next Life" developed from Houston's relationship with a friend named Sally Quinters, who died of breast cancer. Houston revisits this relationship in more than one essay and again in fictional form in "Like Goodness Under Your Feet," collected in *Waltzing the Cat*.

A best-seller (an unusual accomplishment for a short-story collection), *Cowboys Are My Weakness* drew favorable reviews from most major publications, including *The New York Times Book Review, Library Journal, Publishers Weekly,* and *The Los Angeles Times Book Review,* and mixed reviews from *The New Yorker* and the *Women's Review of Books*. The paperback edition of *Cowboys Are My Weakness* appeared in February 1993 under the Washington Square Press imprint.

In 1992 Houston married Michael Elkington, a safari guide from South Africa; they later divorced. In the essay "Pregnancy and Other Natural Disasters" (originally in *Condé Nast Sports for Women,* reprinted in *A Little More About Me*), she writes of finding herself pregnant and becoming deeply depressed over the prospect of having to give up her adventurous, often dangerous lifestyle, as well as her anxiety over weight gain and lack of control over her body inherent to pregnancy. She recalls her mother's saying, "'A fat girl is nothing but a *fat girl,*' . . . as she squeezed herself into her girdle every morning, '*no matter what else she accomplishes in her life.*'" Houston adds, "Of all the misguided rules for living that my mother handed down to me, that is the one I think about most often, every time a bite of food leaves the fork and enters my mouth." She also discusses having had an abortion many years earlier, at her mother's urging. The pregnancy ends in a miscarriage, and Houston ends the essay remaining unsure whether she wishes to have children, aware that this position is still viewed with some suspicion by many in the contemporary United States. The issues of a woman's control over her body, and the national—and her personal—obsession with thinness and traditional notions of beauty, appear in many of Houston's nonfiction pieces, such as "Out of Habit I Start Apologizing," "The Morality of Fat," and "In Pursuit of What I Don't Do Well" (all collected in *A Little More About Me*). These topics frequently occupy her fictional protagonists as well.

In 1995 Houston edited and provided an introduction for the collection *Women on Hunting: Essays, Fiction, and Poetry*. It includes forty-seven new and previously published stories, poems, and essays by writers such as Joyce Carol Oates, Margaret Atwood, Louise Erdrich, Annie Dillard, Terry Tempest Williams, Tess Gallagher, Francine Prose, Jane Smiley, Alice Hoffman, and Ann Beattie, as well as pieces by several lesser-known authors. Houston contributed "Dall," from *Cowboys Are My Weakness*. The dust jacket suggests the purpose of the collection is to awaken readers to the "notion that the chase and the kill reflect many of our archetypal human experiences—that our relationships are almost always based on elements of the hunt, the constant interplay of power, desire, and need." Houston chose to include selections that present the perspective of women who are fervent and enthusiastic hunters, women who detest the practice, and those who are—as she describes herself—somewhere in the middle.

In her introduction Houston writes that hunting "in this anthology, is neither a sport, nor a philosophical dilemma, as much as it is a metaphorical framework from which to tell a tale." J. Z. Grover, reviewing the volume for the *Women's Review of Books* (February 1996), noted that *Women on Hunting* "collects some terrific material" but seems to have "no central focus," given the different ways in which the stories, poems, and essays incorporate hunting–from delight to disgust with the activity, as metaphorical or formal structure, with anger and polemicism, humor and angst. While praising Houston as a writer and for the quality of her choices, Grover does take issue with what she perceives as Houston's belief that women and men experience the world differently, citing Houston's assertion in the introduction that, "While a man tends to be linear about achieving a goal, a woman can be circular and spatial. She can move in many directions at once, she can be many things at once, she can see an object from all sides, and, when it is required, she is able to wait." For Grover this statement is the "primitive backcountry of essentialism," though Houston was writing in terms of tendencies rather than absolutes.

Houston collaborated with French photographer Véronique Vial on a volume of photographs titled *Men Before Ten A.M.* In the introduction Houston described a telephone call from Vial, proposing the project: "I have an idea that men put their masks on by ten o'clock in the morning, that if you want to capture what is inside a man, you have to catch him when he first wakes up. . . . I always go alone, without an assistant. I shoot for ten or fifteen minutes. I use only available light. It is very intense, very intimate." The volume features photographs of ninety-nine different men from several countries and professions. In addition to the introduction, three essays by Houston are interspersed through the work: "The Things That Men Do in the Morning," "Why We Still Love Men," and "The Man I Love in the Morning."

In 1997 Houston provided an introduction for a reprint edition of B. M. Bower's 1912 novel *Lonesome Land*. Bertha Muzzy Bower was a prolific author in the first decades of the twentieth century, writing Westerns under her initials only; thus her (often male) fans believed her to be a male cowboy. Many of her protagonists were, however, women of action in the West.

In 1993 Houston moved to Oakland, California. Out of her time there she produced an essay that details being mugged and meditates on the differing dangers of cities and wilderness areas. Her experiences in Oakland are also reflected in the opening story in *Waltzing the Cat*, "The Best Girlfriend You Never Had." Also like the protagonist in *Waltzing the Cat*, Houston settled on a one-hundred-and-twenty-acre ranch in southwestern Colorado, where she makes her home–as she describes it–nine thousand feet above sea level, near the Continental Divide and the headwaters of the Rio Grande.

Waltzing the Cat is much more of a short-story cycle than is *Cowboys Are My Weakness*. The stories in this sec-

ond collection feature the same protagonist throughout, Lucy O'Rourke, a photographer, and the volume ends with a piece titled "Epilogue." It also works as a cycle thematically, with each story a progressive episode in the life and emotional development of Lucy. The ties between author and protagonist are unmistakable, especially when one turns to *A Little More About Me*, the essay collection published a year later, in 1999. Just as Houston has a good friend named Henry and a not-quite-lover named Carter, similar figures named Henry and Carter appear as friend and not-quite-lover of Lucy in *Waltzing the Cat*. Houston and Lucy both make their living in large part through work for magazines and travel a great deal as a result of that work. Yet, it would most likely be a mistake to read the fictions–or the essays–as literal renderings of Houston's experiences. "Stories always change in their telling. Does anybody ever tell something exactly as it happened?" Houston noted in an October 1996 profile in *Writer's Digest* titled "The Emotional Truth." The author of that piece, Julie Fanselow, wrote that Houston claimed she attempts to write the truth, "not necessarily the truth as it happened, but the emotional truth, the truth of the world as I see it."

Yahlin Chang, reviewing *Waltzing the Cat* for *Newsweek* (19 October 1998), called Lucy "more mature, more honest, and more afraid" than the heroines of Houston's first collection: "Lucy sees her death-defying adventures for what they are: compulsive acts of self-destruction. And she realizes she's pathetic about love–but that she'll grow out of it." In "The Best Girlfriend You Never Had" Lucy describes life and friends in Oakland, where "all the people you know–without exception–have their hearts all wrapped around someone who won't ever love them back." Houston proved herself as adept at rendering the dangers and emotional atmosphere of the cityscape–muggings, boyfriends who turn into stalkers, the homeless man who baptizes her with urine, a jumper who changes his mind about leaping from the bridge when he discovers he would be the undistinguished number 251 of the year–as she is at depicting the challenges and emotional realizations found in wilderness landscapes and adventures. Much of the story takes place in a series of dialogues between Lucy and her various male and female friends. Interspersed are memories of a troubled childhood: being thrown into the New Jersey surf at the age of two by her father, having been in sixteen serious car accidents by the age of fifteen, fantasizing about being hospitalized after one experience there led to visits from her parents who showed up, for once, sober and "happy to see me." Thus, "The Best Girlfriend You Never Had" is individually the story of a young woman negotiating

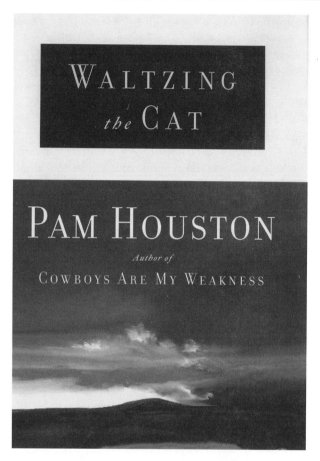

Dust jacket for Houston's 1998 book, a collection of linked short stories about a photographer named Lucy O'Rourke

women give up some of their rights and privileges. Following Josh's instructions, Thea and Lucy end up falling over a seven-story rock into the worst of the rapids. As the men later exult over Josh's skill and the "perfect day" he has given them, Lucy says to Thea, "What I wanted one of them to say is *tell me what it felt like under there.*" Gender differences are highlighted again at the end of the story as, on the way home, Thea and Lucy sleep together in a womb-like space in the back of the truck while Josh recklessly passes semi-trucks, goaded on by the other men. While suggesting that men and women often value different goals, Houston avoids despair by maintaining a wry tone and a focus on the physical challenges both genders assay.

"Waltzing the Cat," the title story, takes the adult Lucy home after the unexpected death of her mother. The household is ruled by a fat phobia and an inability to express love, resulting in Lucy's parents lavishing emotions and food on the family cat, so much so that it has reached an astonishing twenty-nine pounds. With a mother who is both her harshest critic and her biggest fan, and a father who is by turns bullying and needy, both alcoholics, Lucy's family's only originality in contemporary fiction may be in their extreme terror that their daughter will grow up overweight. Yet, Houston's delineation of the communication (and lack thereof) among the O'Rourkes is so concrete, understated, and exquisitely nuanced as to create a heartrending psychological portrait. Carolyn See, reviewing for the *Washington Post Book World* (6 December 1998), declared that the "title story deserves to be anthologized into eternity." Earlier versions of "Waltzing the Cat" appeared in *The Mississippi Review* and *Redbook* and in the anthology *These Are the Stories We Tell.*

A reviewer for *Booklist* (1 September 1998) argued that "Lucy acquired machismo both to prove her worth and to protect herself, but she's realizing that while she's learned to be strong, she doesn't know how to be happy." Coming off the emotional turmoil of "Waltzing the Cat," Lucy heads for a machismo adventure in "Three Lessons in Amazonian Biology." She travels to Ecuador for New Year's and the week before her thirty-third birthday, attracted by the notion of balance, of twelve hours of darkness and twelve hours of light. She explores the highest point on earth along the equator, nineteen thousand feet above sea level, visits the north coast to see the ruins of the ancient culture of Agua Blanca, and sojourns to the Isla de la Plata and the cloud forests near Mindo—all necessary, her guide tells her, to be ready for the experience of the Amazon Basin. A series of horrible dates after she returns to the United States are then understood through the metaphors offered by the phenomena she observed in Ecuador. "Three Lessons in Amazonian Biology" appeared

internal and external emotional obstacles in order to find the courage to look for something "that will last." As the opening story in the cycle, it establishes the current emotional challenges of the protagonist by showing scenes from her oppressive childhood and scenes delineating how she copes as an adult.

In many respects the second story, "Cataract," revisits the territory of much of *Cowboys Are My Weakness.* Lucy runs the hazardous rapids of Cataract Canyon in the Colorado River with her boyfriend, Josh, one female friend, and two other males. Lucy struggles as much with gendered behaviors as with the challenges posed by the river, as she tells readers, "It had been three years since Josh had come into my life wanting to know how to run rivers, two years since I taught him to row, six months since he decided he knew more about the river than I did, two weeks since he stopped speaking, since he started forgetting indispensable pieces of gear." While the connection between Lucy and her friend Thea is strong enough that Thea reads her mind "a couple of times daily," the men have conversations about how things will never be right in the world until

in the Fall 1998 issue of *Ploughshares,* guest-edited by Lorrie Moore.

"The Moon Is a Woman's First Husband" is also an adventure story. Lucy finds herself on a boat heading for Bimini with friends Henry and Carter, caught up in Hurricane Gordon. Storytelling plays a significant thematic and literal role in this piece, as the men talk about their engagements and the three trade stories from cultures around the globe, revealing through their choices their differing beliefs about love and relationships.

The terrain being explored moves from the physical and the emotional into the spiritual and mystical in "Moving from One Body of Water to Another." After missing a plane at LAX, Lucy runs into Carlos Castaneda, who tells her she should "spend at least an hour a day in the sight of open water" and move to a house with hardwood floors. He announces that her life is about to open up in ways she could never imagine and that she will meet a man who thinks with precision, whom she would do well to love. As Lucy has grown increasingly homesick for the Rocky Mountains and found her attempts to nest with "world class pots and pans" in Oakland to be futile, a series of uncanny events culminates in the news that her grandmother has died and left her a ranch near Hope, Colorado, by the Rio Grande. Despite warnings about back taxes and the dilapidated state of the property, as well as her fears of going to live in a place where she knows no one, Lucy finds the strength to give up on the unsatisfactory "virtual love" of Carter, to make the move to the ranch and be alone for a while, after which, she is convinced, "I'd be way too smart . . . to settle for anybody's virtual love."

"Like Goodness Under Your Feet" takes the traditional Western settlement story and preserves the trope of the lone figure setting out to carve a new life in a new place but changes the typical gender of that protagonist. Lucy finds the ranch "is not a house that sits on the land as much as one that sits in it," raising another trope of the West, of the land as pristine and still in charge. While appreciating the naturalness of the landscape and the prairie grasses and flowers, Houston also acknowledges the history that has taken place there; there is a family graveyard and a town history she learns from B. J., a friend of her grandmother's. Lucy discovers connections to that past; she uncannily resembles the grandmother who left her the ranch, a woman she has not seen for thirty years thanks to a fight between the grandmother and Lucy's parents. Yet, Houston diverges from the Western settlement story: rather than working to tame the local animals, Lucy adopts and makes friends with a dog that may have more than a little coyote blood. Instead of conquering

the land in order to "civilize" it, Lucy finds it a fertile place for getting in touch with the elemental: "People are supposed to accumulate, I thought, as they get older, but I seem to be sloughing off, like a person wrapped in a hundred layers of cellophane, tearing one layer off at a time, trying to get down to me." It also proves a fertile place for making new friends–B. J. and the dog, named Ellie–as well as land to which she can finally relinquish the ashes of her best friend, Ellie, who had died of breast cancer five years before. As an individual story "Like Goodness Under Your Feet" provides a fascinating revision of the independent loner striking out to build a new life in the West. A key moment in the short-story cycle, it brings Lucy to a place where she has "written myself a full-time prescription" for being alone, something "necessary" and she hopes "temporary," a place from which she can both move forward emotionally and "hold our ground."

Yet, the next two stories find Lucy involved with one unsuitable man after another. In "Then You Get Up and Have Breakfast" Lucy finally breaks off her relationship with the sexually and emotionally unavailable Carter and begins living with Eric, an alcoholic who likes to shoot bowling balls from a cannon. He quits drinking and redoes the foundation of her house, eliminating the risk that it will slide into the river. Yet, in "The Kind of People You Trust with Your Life," Eric has started drinking again, and Lucy, aware from her childhood of the repercussions of living with an alcoholic, sends him away. Most of the story takes place with Lucy in a glider plane, remembering moments of fear and experiencing the exhilaration of feeling fear and then letting go of it as the glider swoops and dives through the mountains. "Then You Get Up and Have Breakfast" previously appeared in *Elle* and in *Fish Stories.*

As does the final story of *Cowboys Are My Weakness,* the final full story of *Waltzing the Cat,* "The Whole Weight of Me," turns its attention to female friendship. In Provincetown to teach a workshop, Lucy has dinner with one of her students, Marilyn, and they discover they both grew up in families obsessed with the fear of being overweight. In perhaps the most emotionally resonant passages in the story, as they share memories they have never told before, Marilyn says, "We had very complicated rules when we went out to dinner. . . . No appetizers or dessert ever, and if you wanted extra credit you could order. . . ." The sentence is finished by Lucy, "An appetizer instead of dinner. And no bread." She goes on, "I always think, if I never spent another minute feeling bad about the shape of my body, what would I do with all that space in my brain." Lucy quickly becomes involved with a man she meets in Provincetown, in spite of Marilyn's warnings. When he turns out to be married-but-soon-to-be-divorced, Lucy turns back to Provincetown to spend more time with Marilyn instead of going to visit her emotionally abusive father as planned. Again, the story is one of a protagonist on the verge of shedding old habits and becoming a new person: "I would go back to my ranch and see if another round of seasons would make me any smarter, and wait there by the river for the new Lucy to come home."

"Epilogue" continues the spiritual/mystical tone introduced halfway through the volume as Lucy, out walking with her dog on the ranch, meets up with a seven-year-old girl who shows her photographs from her own past. As she finds the courage to face the memories of the abuse she lived through, Lucy–and Houston– reflect on the nature of stories and lives, how they repeat themselves and how to make them move forward.

Waltzing the Cat was greeted with largely favorable reviews in most major publications, with a few objecting to the thread of mysticism as New Age and unconvincing. Sybil S. Steinberg, reviewer for *Publishers Weekly* (13 July 1998), believed "Houston describes Lucy's sporting adventures with cinematic detail, conveying both her technical prowess and the exhilaration of physical daring." In *The Spectator* of 20 February 1999, Jessica de Rothschild tempered her positive review with "If *Waltzing the Cat* lacks anything it is pace. Waiting for Lucy's moment of reckoning is rather like waiting for a night bus in the rain in a dodgy part of town. It takes forever. However, just as Houston's softly, softly approach becomes irritating, she redeems herself with unexpected insight and a strong sense of humor." One of the most enthusiastic reviews came from Mary Loudon in *The London Times* (30 January 1999): calling Houston a "stunning, stunning writer," Loudon wrote that "*Waltzing the Cat* is bold, energetic and exhilarating; its laconic tone and meandering structure perfectly reflect the contradictions of the life contained therein. . . . Her feel for landscapes both actual and metaphorical is so accurate and acute that you feel you could reach out and touch every part of her stories."

Just a year after *Waltzing the Cat,* Houston published *A Little More About Me,* a collection of twenty-four essays, all but six of which were previously published. The essays cover approximately five years of her life, during which she visited forty-three countries and five continents. In addition to pieces on traveling through the

Teton Range, Botswana, France, the Andes, and Bhutan, Houston writes on various sports, body image, notions of success, and, perhaps most charmingly, her relationships with her dogs and horses. While reviewers have praised Houston's writing in *A Little More About Me,* it has been less well received than have the short-story collections, with reviewers such as Elizabeth Gilbert in *The New York Times Book Review* (12 September 1999) finding parts of it too self-absorbed. Many essays relate events that correspond to occurrences in the fictions, thus making them a useful source for those wishing to trace autobiographical connections.

Certainly a key element in Houston's fiction is the woman who follows the man she is attracted to into wild and rugged territory. Yet, easily as important, and increasingly present as her career has progressed, are the women in Houston's fiction who test themselves in and against the wilderness, the support they offer one another as friends and confidantes, women and men as friends and confidantes, relationships between parents and children (in particular, the outcomes of having had alcoholic and neglectful or abusive parents), and women and their relationships with animals–especially horses and dogs. Houston is praised for bringing a female perspective to the story of the loner facing down nature and the outdoors, a perspective that engages the wilderness as much as it challenges it. In a description of a short-fiction workshop Houston offered in 1999 at the University of California, Davis, she stated what she believes to be the "real artistry of fiction": "the translation of the emotional stakes of the story onto its physical landscape." In this statement she articulated her own best achievement.

Interview:

Randall Osborne, "Kissing the Cowboys Goodbye: Pam Houston Talks about Dangerous Love and the Unnavigable Gap Between Men and Women," *Salon.com* (8 January 1999) <http://www.salon.com/books/int/1999/01/08int.html>.

References:

Krista Comer, *Landscapes of the New West: Gender and Geography in Contemporary Women's Writing* (Chapel Hill: University of North Carolina Press, 1999);

Julie Fanselow, "The Emotional Truth," *Writer's Digest,* 76 (October 1996): 6–7.

Josephine Jacobsen

(19 August 1908 –   )

Ned Balbo
Loyola College, Maryland

BOOKS: *Let Each Man Remember* (Dallas: Kaleidograph, 1940);

For the Unlost (Baltimore, Md.: Contemporary Poetry, 1946);

The Human Climate (Baltimore, Md.: Contemporary Poetry, 1953);

The Animal Inside (Athens: Ohio University Press, 1966);

The Shade-Seller: New and Selected Poems (Garden City, N.Y.: Doubleday, 1974);

A Walk with Raschid and Other Stories (Winston-Salem, N.C.: Jackpine, 1978);

The Chinese Insomniacs: New Poems (Philadelphia: University of Pennsylvania Press, 1981);

Adios, Mr. Moxley (Winston-Salem, N.C.: Jackpine, 1986);

The Sisters: New and Selected Poems (Columbia, S.C.: Bench, 1987);

On the Island: New and Selected Stories (Princeton: Ontario Review, 1989);

Distances, edited by John Wheatcroft (Cranbury, N.J.: Bucknell University Press, 1991);

In the Crevice of Time: New and Collected Poems (Baltimore, Md.: Johns Hopkins University Press, 1995);

What Goes without Saying: Collected Stories of Josephine Jacobsen (Baltimore, Md.: Johns Hopkins University Press, 1996);

The Instant of Knowing: Lectures, Criticism, and Occasional Prose, edited by Elizabeth Spires (Ann Arbor: University of Michigan Press, 1997).

OTHER: *The Testament of Samuel Beckett,* by Jacobsen and William R. Mueller (New York: Hill & Wang, 1964; London: Faber & Faber, 1966);

Ionesco and Genet: Playwrights of Silence, with Mueller (New York: Hill & Wang, 1968);

From Anne to Marianne: Some Women in American Poetry (Washington, D.C.: Library of Congress, 1973);

The Instant of Knowing (Washington, D.C.: Library of Congress, 1974);

One Poet's Poetry (Atlanta, Ga.: Agnes Scott College, 1975).

Josephine Jacobsen, 1987 (courtesy of the author)

When Josephine Jacobsen was appointed to the first of two consecutive terms as Poetry Consultant to the Library of Congress (now Poet Laureate) in 1971, she was acknowledged, at sixty-three, as a poet of the first rank, the author of four collections of verse that had earned an admiring audience. Her work in criticism, the essay, and short fiction, however, was less well known. The last form she especially loved, and early in her career she had produced stories good enough to attract an agent. Discouraged when none were published, though, she abandoned the form for two decades but found success when she resumed her efforts in the mid 1960s. "On the Island," the first of her new stories, was accepted by *Kenyon Review* and reprinted in the *Best American Short Stories of 1966.* Her first collection, *A Walk with Raschid and Other Stories,* appeared from the Jackpine Press in 1978. After a promising start and a nearly twenty-year delay, Jacobsen's career as a fiction writer was under way.

Like her poetry, Jacobsen's fiction vividly evokes exotic locales; yet, her emphasis always remains on character. She selects precise words or subtle actions that reveal the inner life of her characters. Influenced by Joseph Conrad, J. D. Salinger, and Flannery O'Connor, Jacobsen's stories are beautifully written, examining themes such as the effects of sorrow, the conflicts within love and marriage, and the ethical/moral dimensions of human conduct. Often drily ironic, Jacobsen captures her characters' foibles as revealed through physical danger or the prospect of sudden loss. Her most admired stories, however, center on a destructive impulse discovered in some unexpected place or person. A skilled poet and literary veteran, Jacobsen brings to her fiction a wealth of life experience and a mastery of craft. Her subsequent collections, *Adios, Mr. Moxley* (1986), *On the Island: New and Selected Stories* (1989), and *What Goes without Saying: Collected Stories of Josephine Jacobsen* (1996) show not so much an evolution in technique or conception as a determined and successful effort to broaden her range of characters and to refine ideas long central to her work. By the time *What Goes without Saying,* a collection of her best short-fiction work, was published, Jacobsen's short stories had appeared in six O. Henry Prize collections, a volume of *Best American Short Stories,* a Pushcart Prize anthology, and periodicals from *McCall's* and *Mademoiselle* to *Commonweal.*

In an essay for *Contemporary Authors Autobiography Series* (1994) Jacobsen wrote of her early years, "I believe that for any writer it is these years which are the true seed, however disguised, of the subsequent work—strained through the mesh of time, colored by a growing perception of depths and alchemy, but already determining the texture and direction of the work." Josephine Winder Boylan was born prematurely on 19 August 1908 in Coburg, Ontario, Canada. Shortly after her birth, the family moved to Long Island, New York. Her father, Joseph Boylan, was a retired American doctor educated in Heidelberg and Bonn; her mother, Octavia Winder, was a North Carolina native with an eleven-year-old son from a previous marriage. Joseph Boylan was athletic and gregarious, his wife "capable of

great gaiety" though "mercurial," Jacobsen wrote. Boylan died when his daughter was five—a stroke had paralyzed him two years earlier—and so a long, unsettled period began for her. She and her mother, along with Jacobsen's adored nurse, Alice, left Long Island and lived at various times in New York City; Pinehurst, North Carolina; Sharon, Connecticut; and, during the winters, Atlantic City, New Jersey. John Skinner, Jacobsen's brother, attended boarding school and college as the family moved around. Eventually her mother settled in Baltimore, Maryland, and Josephine Boylan received her only formal education at the Roland Park Country Day School. Tutored at home throughout her childhood, she proved an outstanding student and took enthusiastic part in school activities.

Long before adolescence Boylan thought of herself as a writer. She wrote her first poems at eight or nine and published several in *St. Nicholas,* a magazine of children's writing. At this time she also wrote her first "little tales," having always felt surrounded by stories, "a welter of small events" with "roots that ran in unexpected directions." As a young woman during the 1920s Boylan became a member of the Vagabonds, a semiprofessional theater company in Baltimore. By 1932, however, she gave up the thought of a dual career as writer and actress when, after a brief courtship, she married Eric Jacobsen. They had one son, Erlend. Josephine Jacobsen credited the theater with influencing her fiction and poetry, and she later collaborated with William R. Mueller on two books of dramatic criticism, *The Testament of Samuel Beckett* (1964) and *Ionesco and Genet: Playwrights of Silence* (1968). For most of her adult life Jacobsen settled into a pattern that combined what was by all accounts a fulfilling marriage with family life, her cultural interests, various travels with her husband, and the pleasures and demands of literary work.

Thematically mature and technically proficient, *A Walk with Raschid,* Jacobsen's first collection of short stories, includes eleven pieces that reflect Jacobsen's characteristic preoccupations, such as the subtle power shifts of intimate relationships, an acute awareness of mortality, and a fear of isolation or entrapment. Dedicated to Elizabeth Otis, the agent who had advocated for Jacobsen's early fiction, the volume introduces a writer already fully formed: a voice familiar with the small deceits and heroisms of everyday life, an acute observer of the physical world, and a storyteller who can shift perspective or tone with ease. After Eric Jacobsen's retirement, the writer and her husband had traveled widely to destinations that included Guatemala, Mexico, Ireland, Italy, Greece, Morocco, and the Caribbean, especially Grenada, where, by her own estimate, Jacobsen produced a full third of all she wrote. In reviewing *A Walk with Raschid* for *New Letters,*

Nancy Sullivan took note of Jacobsen's talent for evoking locations–of the stories in that collection, "Each one, because of Josephine Jacobsen's profound sense of place and character, has a life and geography all its own." Jacobsen's essay "The Meaning of Arrival" (collected in *The Instant of Knowing: Lectures, Criticism, and Occasional Prose,* 1997) offers insight into how that talent operates: "I find that what really sticks with me most permanently from a visit to a new country . . . is a person or an event . . . which is so tinctured with the essence of a place that afterward that person, that moment, becomes a sort of quintessence." Jacobsen also cautioned, "If you remember such things of a place with sentimentality . . . they will shrivel up and change into something to throw away."

Both the title story and "On the Island" are classic examples of Jacobsen stories set abroad. Both stories feature a similar narrative progression: a vacationing American couple faces the gulf dividing them from another culture, and friendship with a local boy provokes the central conflict. Both stories make use of surprise endings, a favorite strategy of Jacobsen's. "On the Island" and "A Walk with Raschid" depend on defining realizations: that ignorance of another culture holds inherent risks; the impulse to transcend cultural difference is fraught with danger; and, travel abroad exerts a revealing pressure upon relationships.

Like several other other Jacobsen stories, "On the Island" explores racism as a cultural construct and pretext for brutality. Henry and Mary Driscoll, on holiday in the Caribbean, are an appealing couple–tourists who value the nearness of "real jungle" and are also attentive to each other and suitably outraged by their host, the racist hotel owner Mr. Soo. Ignorant of his restrictions on the use of adjacent areas, the Driscolls casually mention Victor, a black child whom they met on a nearby beach. Mr. Soo reacts with rage, and although the couple defend Victor, their host remains obsessed with what he considers the boy's trespassing. The next day the couple hears that Mr. Soo has threatened Victor, even though, as they also learn, he holds no legal claim to the beach. The Driscolls are frustrated, well intentioned, but ultimately helpless. Worse, by staying at the hotel, the couple are part of the corruption: they share in the privileged position of their host, and their presence is the catalyst for action against Victor.

These minor conflicts prefigure a greater danger that the Driscolls only partly comprehend. Mary ponders leaving the island early, but a previous decision determines their fate. Because of a plumbing problem, the Driscolls have moved to Mr. Soo's quarters where, on their last night, they retire after news of Victor's death–presumably at the hands of someone working for Mr. Soo. Hours later, as Mary wakes, Victor's

Jacobsen in Baltimore, 1933 (courtesy of Josephine Jacobsen)

brother, machete in hand, flees the room. Henry, mistaken for Mr. Soo, has been decapitated. In exchanging rooms, the couple exchange their fate with Mr. Soo's: they shared his status and now suffer the vengeance meant for him. At a public reading covered by the *Washington Star-News,* Jacobsen described the genesis of "On the Island": "One of evil's greatest habits is choosing a trivial incident in which to manifest itself. We tend to see the incident as accidental, but . . . evil is always there waiting for that accident."

Alone with Mary in Mr. Soo's room, Henry had said of Victor's death, "It's a pattern . . . We saw it happen all the way from the beginning, and now it's ended. It had to end this way." Henry speaks in words that resonate for Jacobsen's readers: her stories follow a fateful course, as human actions, for good or ill, fall into place. On their first night Mary Driscoll had observed that Mr. Soo had "appeared almost as though he had been decapitated and then had his head with its impassive face set, very skillfully, back upon his shoulders." Here, laid into the fabric of "On the Island," is the all-important clue, the omen Mary cannot recognize. Jacobsen's use of surprise endings depends on such skillful foreshadowing.

In "A Walk with Raschid," foreshadowing is also used to suggest aspects of character. The story concerns James Gantry's displacement of feeling for his absent son onto a Moroccan boy. After some sightseeing in Fez, Raschid invites the Gantrys on a private tour and dinner: although suspicious of Raschid's "angle," James urges his wife, Tracy, to accept; later, a second invitation conflicts with these plans. In the final scene the Gantrys wait in vain for Raschid's arrival, spending the afternoon with the Neesons, whose invitation Tracy still hopes to accept. Finally, at his wife's suggestion, James checks for Raschid outside the courtyard. A taxi driver tells him about an altercation he had witnessed, praising Tracy as her husband realizes she deceived him: Raschid did keep the appointment, but an argument broke out when he refused Tracy's bribe to cancel the outing.

Jacobsen's approach to character is remarkably astute, especially in light of the whole story. James, "like Tracy," considers lying "the meanest of the vices. 'Know the truth, and the truth shall make you free.' It was Tracy's only biblical quotation." The irony becomes apparent after the argument with Raschid; yet, Jacobsen's tone captures how a lie may seem convincing. Equally strong is Jacobsen's dialogue. In explaining why Oliver, their son, chose his mother over James, Tracy says, "A child that age, even a *frank* child . . . can't get words around huge things, the things its life is made of. . . . That's where, perhaps, I helped . . . Christ, the things people do in the name of loyalty." Tracy's empathy sounds genuine enough until the reader discovers she manipulates father and son to her own ends. James Gantry, too, is ambiguous: "The future, now, was Tracy. He had never been truly equipped to love Oliver, if love entailed satisfaction. But . . . he would have offered as fine substitutes as his nature would provide and guilt could prompt." James Gantry cannot love his own son, a fundamental failing and catalyst for the story, and so he is scarcely to be pitied when he discovers his wife's deceptions. Unlike the Driscolls, good people helpless before an unforgiving culture, the Gantrys are strangers to each other, superficially attractive but incapable of love.

In "A Walk with Raschid" the differences of another culture are nothing compared to those a human heart conceals. In "The Glen" Jacobsen explores similar themes against an American backdrop. When Jessie realizes that Harmon married her chiefly so she would care for Cora, the "speechless, defective" child of his first marriage, she refuses to accept her lot, instead deciding to take action: she lures the child to the glen behind the house where "the rock, the rotting log, the tangle down toward the stream, the whole small lucid slope" wait precariously. In the final scene, her plot in motion, Jessie watches from a window, then turns away to light the fireplace. Of her approach to fiction Jacobsen has written, "My stories must continue beyond the end of the storyline, and the story life must have had a beginning long before the first word; the stories intercept something at a definitive moment." Jessie's flash of inspiration provides the definitive moment of this story when, walking alone in the glen, she formulates her scheme. Jacobsen never states explicitly what will happen but suggests each step of Jessie's evolving plan. Jessie carefully considers the "fresh inevitabilities" from every angle: out in the cold, unsupervised, Cora will surely fall; if she injures herself, Harmon will agree to commit his daughter; if she dies, Jessie's purpose will be even better served. In this denouement Jacobsen captures all that is essential: having shown what soon must happen, she ends the story before the fall, the fatal plan already inexorably in motion.

Essential, too, are the personal histories of characters prior to moments the narrative "intercepts." Like Tracy Gantry, Jessie appears acquiescent, even as she plots to eliminate a stepchild. The difference in point of view, however, is crucial: where "A Walk with Raschid" closely follows the husband's outlook in order to surprise the reader with Tracy's deception, "The Glen" centers on Jessie's viewpoint, the better to trace her path from caretaker to killer. The reader learns, therefore, that "Jessie came of people who were Wonderful . . . She admired wholly the women in her family." These women include an aunt whose young husband died in a car wreck, and Jessie's own mother, "whose . . . husband, faced with a long and unpromising illness, had died from an overdose of his carefully regulated medicine." Family hardship may have soured Jessie's taste for martyrdom; yet, one could speculate that Jessie's mother may have murdered her husband. Is seeming "Wonderful" only a tactic meant to divert suspicion? The source of Jessie's scheme may lie in her own family tree, in murders practiced by her mother and her aunt.

Given Cora's intellectual limits and lack of voice, her portrayal poses the greatest challenge of the story. As Harmon reads from an illustrated *Alice's Adventures in Wonderland* (1865), he shows Cora the mushroom that causes Alice to grow and shrink. Later, when Jessie finds a similar mushroom in the glen, she sees its value as bait. Her final words to her stepdaughter are therefore all the more chilling—"I *saw* the mushroom . . . It's here, it's right *here*. At the top of the glen, near the rock" as the deception that dooms the child gives dramatic confirmation of her human faculties.

In "A Walk with Raschid" and "The Glen" Jacobsen deals with characters whose consciences are flawed or eerily absent. "Late Fall" depicts the opposite extreme: an overactive yet misdirected conscience. Father Considine, guilt stricken about his distaste for his parishioners, punishes himself with visions: the lion, his private metaphor of death, disgrace, and doubt, and the desert that, for the priest, will hold "the ultimate encounter," a final, solitary moment under "the high wheeling vulture." The priest wants to recapture his lost grace and somehow reconnect with God. Instead, he reverses his car too quickly and crashes into the local dump where, ejected, he lies at the bottom with the trash. The accident answers the priest's own longings: instead of dying quietly, "anointed, and murmured to rest," he inhabits his own vision, though, as Jacobsen adds wryly, "nothing large moved in the Dump"–no lion he must face down–"and the bird wheeling above was an autumn starling." The priest's "climactic encounter" reduced to the mundane, his "late fall" a comical car wreck, Father Considine finds no relief from his essential isolation.

In the two stories that frame *A Walk with Raschid,* "Nel Bagno" and "Jack Frost," isolation is the key dramatic element. In "Nel Bagno" Mrs. Glessner, preparing to leave for Italy, accidentally locks herself in the bathroom; there, she tries to cheer herself with gallows humor, but wit cannot fully quiet her sheer terror at her predicament, trapped and inaudible to the outside world. At one point she flushes away a vial of sleeping pills, either a "melodramatic gesture" or one of "involuntary self-knowledge." Beneath the light touch, "Nel Bagno" explores ultimate aloneness, those boundaries that may close and cut life off at any time: "Never did she say in her mind, *starvation . . . death.* She was saved by the low comedy of the situation." Of course, a writer herself, Mrs. Glessner knows how swiftly comedy may turn to heartbreak: "Still torn between a sort of abashed amusement–she would dine out on this yet–and what she was afraid was the onset of fear, she said aloud: 'All right, how would I sum it up? My immediate chances?'"

In "Jack Frost" these chances run out, and the query becomes more pointed. Mrs. Travis lives on the outskirts of a small New Hampshire town, dedicated to the flowers that she raises every summer. Despite a forecast of sudden cold and her solitary, single-person household, she ignores the priest concerned about her welfare. He departs with an offhand reference–"don't let Jack Frost get your flowers"–but his remark returns to haunt her, transformed during a dream into the figure of Jack the Ripper. Her garden threatened, Mrs. Travis wakes and ventures out to save her flowers, not least the rose begonia with "its ruffled heavy head, the coral flush of its crowded petals," a passage that conveys Jacobsen's gift for describing flora. "Jack Frost"

concludes with Mrs. Travis's death, but not before she succeeds in crawling back to her warm kitchen, her ankle broken but her will unbowed.

What might prove a saddening narrative in another writer's hands becomes, in Jacobsen's, a story of affirmation. As the author noted in an *Image* interview (Summer 1999) with A. V. Christie, "One of the stories that ends with death I think is one of the happiest stories–'Jack Frost' . . . To me, that is not a sad story at all." There is much to admire in Mrs. Travis's stubborn commitment: she dies at home in extreme old age, her final moments an act of rescue in defiance of the cold and her own mortality. Although, as Jacobsen conceded, "there's a great preponderance of death" in the stories, given her overall vision, this emphasis, too, makes sense. As Doris Betts noted in the *Winston-Salem Journal* (13 August 1978), Jacobsen "understands her characters against the falling of mortality. As a Catholic, she has hope of grace, but none of her realistic work denies the grief, pain, or loss of ordinary human life in the here and now." A practicing Catholic, Jacobsen carries the imprint of her faith, the eschatological bent of a distinct religious culture.

In *The Hollins Critic* Sullivan mentioned the importance of Jacobsen's 1 May 1972 Library of Congress lecture, "From Anne to Marianne: Some Women in American Poetry." Reflecting on women and power, Jacobsen observed, "in the past, where they had native intellectual and artistic power, it was all too often cut off from implementation. No group oppressed . . . ever frees itself or flowers without the traces of that oppression." With their large number of trapped or isolated women, Jacobsen's stories confront the politics of gender. With a range of settings that frequently include a clash of cultures, they squarely face various aspects of race and class. In many cases these strands intertwine, as in "Taxi," from *A Walk with Raschid,* in which a cabbie's racism first offends and later frightens his passenger: suddenly aware that her apartment is not secure, Mrs. Mayberry fears how far the driver's anger may extend. Despite advantages of class and education, Mrs. Mayberry lives alone and is therefore vulnerable to violence. Her fear originates in the driver's words and her painfully injured arm, but also in realities of gender. In other stories, too, such figures play a central role: a man (frequently racist) shows an arbitrary cruelty that drives the story forward, often to a tragic end.

A new appreciation of Jacobsen's work and importance began to emerge in the mid 1980s, just before the publication of *Adios, Mr. Moxley* (1986), her second volume of fiction, and the Lenore Marshall/*The Nation* prizewinner *The Sisters: New and Selected Poems* (1987). In April 1985 *The Hollins Critic* ran Nancy Sullivan's in-depth essay "Power As Virtue: The Achievement of Josephine Jacobsen" as the cover article. In seeking connections between Jacobsen's work in all genres, Sullivan argued for the "classic" status of the stories. A few months later Stephen Goodwin, in *The Washington Post* (30 November 1986), praised "the poet's touch" in *Adios, Mr. Moxley,* noting that Jacobsen's gift for the "deft turn of phrase is also, obviously, a turn of mind." A year later Marilyn Hacker's extensive, scholarly appreciation, "Mortal Moralities," appeared in *The Nation;* this essay-review, encompassing the volume of selected poems and *Adios, Mr. Moxley,* discussed the full range of Jacobsen's achievement. Jacobsen, Hacker wrote,

> is a coeval of Auden and Roethke, Bishop, Miles and Rukeyser . . . She shares with Bishop a passion for travel and a sense of being most at home somewhere radically else; with Miles, moral imperatives expressed through the quotidian, the anecdotal; with the later Auden, an aesthetic informed by faith; with Rukeyser, the theme of human interparticipation . . . ; with Roethke (and James Wright), the love for the human creature others would find grotesque, merely pitiable, or fatally boring.

Hacker touched on Jacobsen's interest in "places of passage," where encounters or epiphanies occur—the beach, hotel, automobile, or hospital. Whatever the setting, Hacker argued, Jacobsen's is "a woman's art . . . committed to survival."

This praise is borne by the ambition and achievement of *Adios, Mr. Moxley.* Simon Jarvis, protagonist of the title story, is seriously, perhaps terminally, ill, and while awaiting surgery must endure the over-friendly Mr. Moxley and his wife. Essentially powerless, Simon concentrates on his wish for a private room; his wife, Emily, offers comfort but no false hope of recovery. Eventually, on the eve of the operation, Emily is required to leave. The next day Simon wakes, still faced with Mr. Moxley. Wheeled to surgery Simon catches a near glimpse of his wife but then arrives in the hands of the anesthesiologist. The story ends as Simon forces routine conversation, the anesthetic taking effect as he inwardly calls for Emily.

Like "Nel Bagno" and "Jack Frost," "Adios, Mr. Moxley" belongs to the subgenre of Jacobsen stories in which isolation serves as a metaphor for death. Outwardly calm but inwardly frightened, Simon longs for solitude, a "fine and private place" beyond the requirements of civility. In the literal sense Simon is seldom alone, with an unwanted roommate and various hospital personnel. Yet, the identity of "patient" is isolating in itself: the hospital staff maintains a clinical distance, and Simon's devoted wife stands separate from his fate. As he surrenders to greater losses of privacy and independence, a disconnection grows between Simon's polite replies and inward panic. Yet, both the swift pacing and Jacobsen's control of tone offers more than a dark vision in "Adios, Mr. Moxley." Mrs. Moxley, for example, suffers from a cold, her Kleenex and reddened eyes a running parody of sorrow. A motel flashback is used to convey a sense of erotic wonder, the promise of life against the threat of illness. Finally, the title of the story is drawn from Simon's trip to surgery as he nervously reexamines the words *farewell* and *goodbye.* Never uttered in the story, the phrase "Adios, Mr. Moxley" conveys Simon's final flourish before departure. If, as H. Susskind wrote in *Choice* (October 1989), Jacobsen's fiction includes "few heroes and even fewer happy endings," Simon's stubborn poise before the oblivion of anesthesia, metaphor of the final darkness that takes all people, is admirable.

In "Vocation" a doctor tries to weaken a patient's confidence in her surgeon: "I just think it's fairer that you shouldn't count on anything." Despite her fear, Mrs. Curtis recognizes the doctor's sadism, connecting his look—"the lazy yet eager look of total power"—to that of a security guard she once saw bully a homeless man. As a patient, Mrs. Curtis is vulnerable by definition, subject to her doctors' whims; yet, she keeps her wits and, after a difficult convalescence, confirms her suspicions with the supportive Dr. Logan: his colleague's "vocation" is cruelty, his "siblings . . . steadfast, unsmiling; ancient."

In "Protection," also from *Adios, Mr. Moxley,* small cruelties gather an unpredictable momentum. The protagonist, Mr. Maris, faces several petty conflicts, most memorably with a stranger who exclaims in a New York City rainstorm, "God damn you to hell, get out of my way!" The explosion of rage haunts Mr. Maris and returns in other guises, most vividly in the person of his building security guard: "Beverly knows: muggers, rapists, vandals—invasion. Beverly lives to thwart these—invisible, but surrounding the brief grounds of the Avon." The story unfolds over many months and brings Mr. Maris to several cities, and these encounters come together at his home in Baltimore. When a black, teenage skateboarder trips Mr. Maris near the Avon, Beverly shoots the boy, acting on his long-held fears and out of racism, which largely determines what he sees. Like the security guard in "Vocation," Beverly revels in petty authority. Yet, Mr. Maris, too, is implicated: the New York stranger, differently dressed, "might have been his mirror," while his mistaken shout, "Stop, thief!" gives Beverly an excuse to shoot. His recent encounters have led Mr. Maris to expect random cruelty. He has found his world changing, its mood turned subtly hostile; the teenager had yelled an insult as he tripped him. As "Protection" examines cruelty in set-

Jacobsen in her attic workroom, 1971 (courtesy of Josephine Jacobsen)

tings seemingly benign, the role of accident is crucial, as Jacobsen herself has noted: it is the catalyst through which trivial evil gains destructive force.

Also through accidental encounters that involve petty crime, "Sound of Shadows" and "A Criminal Career" further explore human nature, with gender and class a disadvantage for both protagonists. Both stories feature a working-class woman facing financial struggle, although Mrs. Bart in "Sound of Shadows" is by far the more hopeless character. Living alone on a fixed income, in a phoneless "little pit," she watches television for hours at a time, the people on the screen her only "friends." Increasingly resistant to ordinary human contact, Mrs. Bart retreats into fantasy, trying to lock out the real world. This world intrudes in the form of a girl (an implied drug addict) who breaks into Mrs. Bart's home and threatens her with a switchblade. Forced to wait out a storm, the two converse tensely until the girl escapes with Mrs. Bart's cash. Although Mrs. Bart is the obvious victim, the girl, too, seems pitiful, her bullying manner a failed mask for weakness and addiction. Against this anxious background of urban crime and anomie, neither woman is truly independent. Their failed choices partly determined by the

poverty they share, both are trapped in ways they cannot comprehend.

By contrast, Maybelle, the cleaning woman of "Criminal Career," is energetic and resourceful. A widow reliant on her earnings and "a little insurance," Maybelle is raising a son, Samuel, whose "extraordinary" mind has surpassed the resources of his school. His teacher urges Maybelle to send him to the exclusive Hill House School, but even if he won a scholarship, Maybelle could never afford the balance of the tuition. Chance, however, takes a hand. Having accidentally glimpsed her employer in bed with the au pair, Maybelle conceives a plan: for fifty dollars a month, she will keep Mr. Guntz's secret from his wife. Maybelle acts decisively, confronting the husband with her terms: elated at first by her own daring and impatient for tangible reward, Maybelle feels "God had delivered Mr. Guntz into her hands." After the first payment, however, Maybelle's resolve wavers, her conscience reasserting itself when she lies during Confession. Eventually, the reader grasps the poignancy of her dilemma: Maybelle is too much the believer to sustain blackmail over time; she is unable to numb her conscience. Her faith, though admirable, paralyzes and entraps her: "She sat back down at the table, and . . . saw her hours unchanged. Her brilliant, audacious move, Mr. Guntz's deserts, Miss Halsted's judgment, Samuel's swelling future melted, were gone." Beyond constraints of class and gender that leave her struggling to raise a child, Maybelle remains "contained and controlled by . . . the unpitying power of love"–both the love that is the basis for the moral vision of Christian doctrine and Maybelle's love for her own child. Her belief that Samuel, if he knew, would condemn her actions on his behalf delivers the final blow to Maybelle's "criminal career."

In an article in *The Maryland Poetry Review* (Spring/Summer 1992), Nancy Norris engaged the "Anatomy of Evil in Josephine Jacobsen's Work" by pointing out that crimes by legal definition occupy only a small part of Jacobsen's attention: "Evil can characterize sadistic authority figures, prejudiced acquaintances, manipulative relatives, and enraged strangers, but also . . . the destructive consequences of innocent intentions. On occasion, it infects the atmosphere of a place like a virus and generates despair about not only the reality of goodness, but the very possibility of meaning." The closing story of *Adios, Mr. Moxley,* "The Mango Community," is an example of the destruction brought about by laudable intentions. A close descendant of "On the Island," it also provides a case study in Jacobsen's growth as a writer. Unlike Henry and Mary Driscoll, whose first suspicions of danger are ill defined, novelist Harry Sewell and painter Jane Megan are explicitly advised to leave St. Cecile: "the U.S. government simply cannot be responsible for your safety," the vice-consul warns in the opening scene. Also unlike the Driscolls, Harry and Jane are at odds: early on Jane points out the dangers of the imminent coup, but her husband responds with blind conviction: "The place is beautiful. The people are marvelous. I'm working, you're painting. Dan's happier than I've ever seen him." Harry's stubbornness and the presence of Jane's son, Dan, create circumstances more complex than those of "On the Island": while the Driscolls merely attempt to run out the clock on an anxious week, Harry and Jane must break arrangements originally meant to last a year. Dan's "united front" with Harry must also be taken into account: "Harry's need to proselytize, and Dan's to be stable, were locked into a kind of dogged intimacy. Why this should frighten her, she had no idea." A further complication, and particularly well rendered, is the family's relationship with their indigenous neighbors, the Montroses: the distances negotiated and maintained on both sides are essential to the exploration of cultural conflict. Eventually, "The Mango Community," too, ends with violence. Harry's influence over Dan bears unwanted fruit; marching with Dan in a pro-

test, Alexis Montrose, the neighbors' son, is assaulted by police, leaving him paralyzed. Only after tragedy do Jane and Dan escape the island, Harry staying back to offer (unwanted) help to the neighbors and, presumably, to keep writing.

"The Edge of the Sea," one of Jacobsen's most deeply skeptical narratives, resembles "A Walk with Raschid" in remaining confined to one character's viewpoint, the better to surprise the reader with a shocking revelation; but the narrative implications are darker. Caddy, a college student, joins second cousin Dan and his wife, Lily, on vacation in Acapulco. Her family hopes Caddy will complete her long recovery after a painful breakup and suicide attempt. Also along is Gina, Lily's wealthy sister, still getting over a divorce. By the last night of the trip (the opening scene) all are "a little in love with each other," in Caddy's view, "good, beloved, and loving." Caddy is aware that Dan's first wife killed herself. She imagines "unknown Eloise, forever clutching her empty vial," but intelligent and fragile, Caddy appears near stability, calmed by her companions' "golden ease." The story turns on Dan's plan for the party to visit Recuerdo Beach, but as Norris observed, "The reader knows that the waves are big, Lily's asthma has worsened, the Mexican children warn 'Tiburones,' and Dan lies about the 'fake shark alert' to 'his monolingual women.'" By the time the excursion is over, Lily is dead, caught by the undertow, and the four's "circle" of friendship is permanently "broken."

Even more upsetting is Caddy's discovery of the truth about her cousin. Mrs. Brounlow, Lily's great-aunt and Caddy's friend, had arranged for Caddy to join the couple on their trip. In the last scene, now a successful student who has gained a "steadiness," Caddy revisits the ailing, old woman. From Mrs. Brounlow, Caddy learns that Dan and Gina have married, but Mrs. Brounlow is so frail that family and friends have concealed the drowning, preferring that she believe Lily died of a heart attack. When she brings out an album of old photos from a vacation Dan had spent with the Brounlows, Caddy is shocked to learn that they had stayed at Recuerdo Beach, which Dan professed he had never seen before the outing.

In one instant, all Caddy believes she knows comes into doubt. In retrospect her cousin's every action seems a clue, his every word part of the plan to murder Lily; yet, Caddy missed the signs, even though obsessive watchfulness had characterized her breakdown. Caddy feels the force of disconcerting identifications, the boundary between herself and others thrown abruptly into question: in the photos Dan, close to her own age, is himself cast as the invalid, recovering from Eloise's recent death. But was Eloise truly a suicide? As horrifying as the thought that Dan had murdered before, or that he could murder at all, is the length of time he carried his knowledge of Recuerdo Beach before turning the information to deadly purpose. Ultimately, the story offers little consolation. Mrs. Brounlow survives in ignorance, her own years running out; Caddy loses the illusion that protected her from pain; Lily's death is transformed from tragic to grotesque. With such knowledge Caddy even stands to lose her "steadiness," the question of whom or what to trust once more painfully in doubt. "The Edge of the Sea" takes the reader to the edge of meaning, where appearance is fatally deceptive, where "steadiness" of self is only an illusion, where language lacks connection to intention.

Impressive in her longer stories, Jacobsen excels also in the expert miniature, and two more resort stories–"The Couple" and "Atlantic City"–provide her second volume with portraits of a vanished time. In "The Couple," set at a small hotel in St. Cecile, Major Drayton and Melissa, his eleven-year-old daughter, become subjects of fascination, their past a mystery that provokes much speculation. Drayton claims friendship with the Bronsons, established guests not yet arrived, and on that basis obtains their usual suite "looking straight out to sea." He expects he and his daughter will be gone by the time they come, but, after a change of plans has the Bronsons expected shortly, the Draytons abruptly disappear, Major Drayton leaving a large, unpaid bill. Jacobsen leaves much to the reader's imagination: the two are probably swindlers and certainly no friends of the Bronsons, but the extent of their deceptions remains uncertain: "Mystery being hard to shake off, and mystery always ending Mrs. Lupin's speculations, Melissa and her father remained, unaging, and unwilling to answer." Especially touching is Melissa's farewell gesture to Mrs. Lupin: she leaves the brooch she believes "valubel" (and which may be stolen) as a present and partial recompense, having connected with her host and tired of her itinerant life. Indeed, the purpose is, in part, to examine types of solitude: father and daughter essentially isolated from fellow guests, Mrs. Lupin loath to transgress their carefully calibrated distance, the loneliness of having to flee from place to place.

"Atlantic City" is explicitly drawn from Jacobsen's childhood experience, as she recounted in the essay for *Contemporary Authors Autobiography Series:* "We were in Atlantic City–as ever at the Dennis–when America entered the First World War, and my memories of that time are totally tangled in the confusion of emotional highs." The story "Atlantic City" captures that time with skillful economy through loving description of people and places along the boardwalk: the "stocky Japanese" who are keepers of a game called ping pong (not the familiar version); the Sand Artist, whose likenesses were "truly recognizable"; the narrator's nurse, Bertha; "the Apollo's live theater, where I had seen Pavlova . . . advance on points toward the footlights." Jacobsen also captures the mood of patriotic fervor, as well as an early encounter with ethnic prejudice when one of her mother's suitors, "Mr. Zubach" in the story, is fired from his job because he is German. The closing description of the dark sea visible from a balcony–"The last, the final war was out there, on the black water"–is compelling in its fusion of a child's wonder before a half-understood world with the adult narrator's regret over a vanished past.

The publication of *On the Island* in 1989 and *What Goes without Saying* in 1996 brought continued accolades and critical notice, as did the appearance of her much-lauded *In the Crevice of Time: New and Collected Poems,* a 1995 National Book Award finalist. During this period critics began to see Jacobsen not merely as a good poet dabbling in short fiction but as a major literary figure whose accomplishments in both genres are invaluable. In 1994 she was elected to the American Academy of Arts and Letters and in 1997 received the Robert Frost Award of the Poetry Society of America in recognition of her lifetime achievement, with her work also appearing in several *Best American Poetry* and *Pushcart Prize* annual volumes. Jacobsen's fiction also received acclaim: *On the Island* was one of five PEN/Faulkner fiction award nominees, a recognition that, she said to Christie, "gave me a sort of feeling–well, I must be doing something right." Steven Kellman, writing in *The New York Times Book Review* (27 August 1989), praised the "20 exquisite stories" and the "narrative haiku" of *On the Island,* while Michael Upchurch, in *The Washington Post* (18 June 1989), wrote that Jacobsen was "news to me–and she's very good news," concluding that *On the Island* was "superb."

Though Jacobsen's later stories reflect her traditional concerns, they also show a mature artist applying new techniques as she examines the finer shadings of human conduct. Among the stories first collected in *On the Island,* "The Inner Path" is a classic Jacobsen story stripped down to its absolute essentials. Peter Vail, an American journalist, tries to fathom the culture of politics and violence of Guatemala; instead, he becomes a victim, his fingertip cut off when he offers to purchase a carving from a stranger. The politics that serve as backdrop for so many Jacobsen stories here become the principal focus of the narrative; no domestic conflict intercedes. "The Night the Playoffs Were Rained Out," another streamlined narrative, returns to the issue of racism: Mr. and Mrs. Plessy, staying in a motel, lose their television reception and so, reluctantly, join the Gombrechts in their room. Mrs. Gombrecht's racist

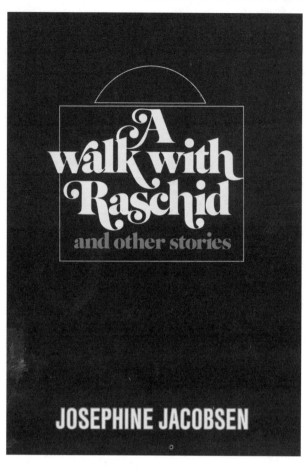

Dust jacket for Jacobsen's first collection of short fiction (1978), in which the title story examines the risks inherent in tourists' ignorance of another culture

George suffers a mild stroke, and the story turns its focus to his convalescence at home, assisted by David and Quincy, his longtime servants. A stilted visit by the rest of "the company" ensues. Five days later George suffers a second stroke, his speech impaired but not his mind: soon the realization dawns on George and those around him that he may never recover. Small touches signal George's declining state, such as Quincy's altered duties and David's tactful exit after a hospital visit. Jacobsen keeps the action smoothly flashing back and forth from conversation among "the company" to the sickroom. After George's funeral the remaining "company" return to the club, their sentimental praise signaling their friend's transition from disquieting reality to comfortable memory. The most effective passage comes when Jacobsen pinpoints the dilemma with a ruthless yet compassionate precision:

> But there was a period, mused George . . . in which those who were neither in nor out of the living number waited . . . What did they have to have in common . . . ? . . . They must be people so lodged in life and its minutiae, so enmeshed in it, that their disappearance into some sort of immobility left tangled shreds, ruptures . . . What a number they must be, constantly deserting, but constantly replenished: his peers.

Jacobsen examines homosexuality in "The Squirrels of Summer," first collected in *What Goes without Saying*. Eight-year-old Jenny, who is staying with her paternal grandmother, Sophie, reveals in passing that she has seen her mother kiss Priscilla, the friend who "brings in the wood, and lays the fire" at their house. The child, wholly unaffected, does not realize her grandmother is seeking such "evidence" of homosexuality in her daughter. Armed with this information, Sophie intends to "take steps to change a disgusting . . . situation"—to take Jenny from her mother—and consign her to boarding school or camp, as the season dictates. Unexpectedly ill, Jenny is brought home from a party and from her bedroom overhears her grandmother's plans. Shocked by the revelation and helpless to take action, Jenny withdraws to bed again in abject fear.

Jacobsen's child characters usually play a secondary role or serve as a version of the author; Jenny, by contrast, is a convincing, fully rounded child protagonist with a distinct personality and voice. Furthermore, beyond the specifics of mere plot, Jacobsen carefully weaves her themes into the fabric of her story, archly gesturing toward the homoerotic side of heterosexual institutions. Sophie, for example, does not see the contradiction of placing a child she fears "warped already" into same-sex living arrangements with other girls. In "The Squirrels of Summer" childhood itself appears to be a world in which same-sex relationships without

remarks highlight the couples' differences, and tempers, aggravated by drinking and the playoff game being interrupted by rain, flare, with Mr. Gombrecht finally fuming, "You lap up our Chivas Regal. And then you—you *sneer!*" The balance of the narrative asks what separates different "clans." Mr. Plessy concludes that the Gombrechts were "dogs looking for cats," and the narrative ends ambiguously, Mrs. Plessy meeting Mrs. Gombrecht's "blue . . . ceramic gaze" that sends "a look straight into Mrs. Plessy's tentative eyes." Through this not-mistaken glance across a motel dining room, Jacobsen acknowledges the racist's frightening certainty.

"The Company," one of Jacobsen's best stories, is a touching account of how the elderly or ill are forced to watch themselves painfully fade from notice. The story opens at "the Club" as three "old friends," businessmen and solid citizens, gather for George's sixty-seventh birthday. "Childless, wifeless," in "voluntary retirement" and apparent good health, George keeps "a paternal eye" on various "board presidencies, trusteeships," and the like. Before the celebration ends

overt eroticism offer a refuge from the threat of adult sexuality: from the quarrelling Jenny associates with her parents' marriage or from the screen kiss Jenny believes resembles her fish "eating seaweed." Most painfully for Jenny, her love for Sophie is intense, a blend of feeling for the woman and her household– "Sophie's house was a little like a fairy tale, made up of treats and surprises, and beautiful, beautiful Sophie"– so Jenny's shock at overhearing her grandmother's dismissal of her "character" holds a crushing impact. Jacobsen ensures that any guess about Jenny's adult sexual preference is inconclusive; still, it should be noted, the only mutually loving relationship in the story is that between Jenny's mother and Priscilla. Sophie's morbid vigilance and her use of her granddaughter as a means of exacting revenge against her own daughter are appalling. Sophie's attitudes and actions provide one of the cruellest domestic encounters of Jacobsen's fiction.

In her essay "The Instant of Knowing," Jacobsen described an epitaph that she and her husband once found in a New England cemetery: "It is a fearful thing to love / What Death can touch." Using the epitaph as example, she defines the title phrase: "A knowledge of what we already knew becomes for an instant so devastatingly fresh that it could be contained no more than a flash of lightning." Although in this essay Jacobsen addressed the source of poetical power, her words apply equally well to her stories. If her poems show, as Eliza-beth Spires wrote in *The New Criterion* (November 1995), "an unnervingly pure lyric intensity," so, too, do her narrative epiphanies. Her flashes of insight strike readers with the force of long-held knowledge abruptly fused with the brilliance of first experience. In the introduction to the collected prose Spires wrote that for Jacobsen, "the making of art . . . is a form of consolation in a time-bound world." If so, Josephine Jacobsen has written stories of permanent value.

Interview:
A. V. Christie, "A Conversation with Josephine Jacobsen," *Image: A Journal of the Arts and Religion,* no. 23 (Summer 1999): 45–61.

References:
Marilyn Hacker, "Mortal Moralities," *Nation,* 245 (28 November 1987): 644–646;

Nancy R. Norris, "The 'Terrible Naive' and Others: Anatomy of Evil in Josephine Jacobsen's Work," *Maryland Poetry Review,* no. 11 (Spring/Summer 1992): 19–24;

Elizabeth Spires, "Joy & Terror: The Poems of Josephine Jacobsen," *New Criterion,* 14 (November 1995): 28–33;

Nancy Sullivan, "Power as Virtue: The Achievement of Josephine Jacobsen," *Hollins Critic,* 22 (April 1985): 1–10.

Ha Jin

(21 February 1956 –   )

Paula E. Geyh
Southern Illinois University, Carbondale

BOOKS: *Between Silences* (Chicago: University of Chicago Press, 1990);

Facing Shadows (Brooklyn, N.Y.: Hanging Loose Press, 1996);

Ocean of Words: Army Stories (Cambridge, Mass.: Zoland, 1996);

Under the Red Flag (Athens: University of Georgia Press, 1997);

In the Pond (Cambridge, Mass.: Zoland Books, 1998);

Waiting (New York: Pantheon, 1999);

The Bridegroom (New York: Pantheon, 2000);

Wreckage (Brooklyn, N.Y.: Hanging Loose Press, 2001).

Few writers have appeared on the American literary scene to such sudden acclaim as the Chinese émigré, Ha Jin. His first short-story collection about life in the Chinese People's Liberation Army, *Ocean of Words* (1996), won the Hemingway/PEN Award for First Fiction in 1996; his subsequent short-story collection depicting village life in China during the Cultural Revolution, *Under the Red Flag* (1997), won the 1997 Flannery O'Connor Award for Short Fiction. His stories have also garnered three Pushcart Prizes, and four were selected for inclusion in *Best American Short Stories* volumes for 1997, 1999, 2000, and 2001. Along with three books of poetry—*Between Silences* (1990), *Facing Shadows* (1996), and *Wreckage* (2001)—Jin has published two novels: *In the Pond* (1998), a dark comedy about a man's rebellion against unfair policies within his village commune, and *Waiting* (1999), the story of a couple forced to wait eighteen years to marry, which won the National Book Award for Fiction in 1999 and the PEN/Faulkner Award in 2000.

Xuefei (pronounced shu-FAY) Jin, who writes under the pen name of Ha Jin, was born on 21 February 1956 in Liaoning, China, where his father, Danlin, an officer in the Chinese People's Liberation Army, was stationed. Jin went to boarding school when he was seven but returned home to his father and mother, Yuanfen, two years later when Chairman Mao Tse-tung launched the Cultural Revolution and closed schools

Ha Jin (photograph © Jerry Bauer; from the dust jacket for The Bridegroom, *2000)*

throughout mainland China. In the years that followed, young Jin became a member of the Little Red Guard and spent his time, as he recalled in a 6 February 2000 interview with Dwight Garner of *The New York Times,* "wearing red armbands, waving flags and singing revolutionary songs." At age fourteen, amid rising tensions between the People's Republic of China and the Soviet Union, he lied about his age and enlisted in the People's Liberation Army. "Like everyone else," Jin told Garner, "I wanted to be a hero, a martyr." His army service lasted five and a half years, one of which he spent on a frigid outpost on the border of China and Soviet Russia. He eventually developed an affinity for Russian literature that remains a strong influence on his work today. "The reason I'm drawn to the great Russians," he explained in an interview with Jesse Berrett of

BayAreaCitySearch.com, "is that the world they described reminded me of the world I experienced–quite a harsh life."

Jin left the army when he was nineteen and became a telegraph operator in a remote city in northern China. He spent three years there, learning English from a radio program and reading literature. His facility with English helped him to be selected to enroll as an English major at Heilongjiang University, from which he graduated with a bachelor's degree in 1981. During a subsequent period of relative cultural openness to the West, Jin continued his studies in American literature at Shandong University. "Like everyone else," he told Garner, "I became obsessed with Faulkner, with Roethke, with Bellow. It was finally O.K. to read these writers." In Shandong, he met Lisha Bian, a mathematics teacher; they married on 6 July 1982 and have one son, Wen. Jin completed his master's degree in 1984. Leaving his young wife and son behind in China, Jin came to the United States the next year to begin doctoral work in American literature at Brandeis University. His wife joined him in 1987. His plan was to complete his Ph.D. and return to teach at a university in China, but that changed with the Chinese army's massacre of students demonstrating for democratic reform in Beijing's Tiananmen Square in early June of 1989. "I was not prepared for what happened," he said to Garner. "I had always thought that the Chinese army was there to serve and protect the people." Certain that he could not return to China, Jin began making arrangements for his son to join him in the United States.

While working at Brandeis on his dissertation on modernist poetry (the works of Ezra Pound, William Butler Yeats, T. S. Eliot, and W. H. Auden) and its relationship to Chinese literature and culture, Jin also studied creative writing at Boston University with Leslie Epstein, Frank Bidart, and Allen Grossman. Jin's first book of poetry, *Between Silences,* was published in 1990 and was hailed by Bidart as "a profound book, an event." Jin finished his Ph.D. at Brandeis in 1992 and began teaching creative writing and literature at Emory University in 1993. His first book of poetry was followed by *Facing Shadows* in 1996. That same year, Jin also published *Ocean of Words,* a highly acclaimed collection of short stories based on his experiences in the Chinese army.

Jin's prose is remarkable in its clarity, precision, and grace. While English is not his native language, all of his published literary works (with the exception of the characters' dialogue) have been painstakingly conceived and composed in English. Nonetheless, they bear strong signature traces of the Chinese worldview and its metaphorical structures. For example, in the story "Love in the Air," one of Jin's characters captures

the nuances of the Chinese view of "bad" women in the vernacular: "He thought of her as a 'broken shoe,' which was worn by everyone, a bitch that raised her tail to any male dog, a hag who was shunned by all decent men, a White Bone Demon living on innocent blood."

Writing in English, Jin is quoted as saying in a 24 December 1996 review by Jocelyn Lieu for *The Chicago Tribune,* has "meant a lot of labor and some despair–but also, freedom." "The [written] Chinese language is very literary and highbrow and detached from the spoken word," he observed to Garner. "It doesn't have the flexibility that English has." Expanding upon this topic in the interview with Berrett, he argued that "the language of the common people in English is very expressive, and there are all kinds of possibilities in writing–different levels of diction that are so close to the spoken word. . . . In Chinese, especially if you write literary fiction, you don't write in plain speech: a lot of words and phrases would have a long history of allusions, so it's very different. . . . It's not just language, you have to see the work in the context of the literature written in the tradition." Jin's adjustment to writing in English required a new way of thinking: "I slowly began to squeeze the Chinese literary mentality out of my mind," Jin remembers. The experience of exile, however, has not been easy. "For the initial years," he told John D. Thomas in *Emory Magazine* (Spring 1999), "it was like having a blood transfusion, like you are changing your blood."

While all of Jin's stories take place in China, he told Berrett that he believes they are marked by his experiences of "living in America–the distance in time, the space" has changed his perspective. At the same time, though, stories can serve, he said, "to enrich the writer's own life and at least recover some loss, preserve some things that have been lost." Jin's stories and novels are not autobiographical, but they draw deeply upon his experiences as a child growing up during the Cultural Revolution and as a young man in the Chinese army.

Jin's writing is indebted to the great Russian masters of literature. Isaac Babel's episodic novel composed of powerful vignettes about the Russian Civil War, *Konarmiia* (1926; translated as *Red Cavalry*), convinced Jin that he might be able to write a similar book about the lives of Chinese soldiers. In a review of *Ocean of Words* Lieu noted the resemblances between Jin's technical mastery and Babel's. In this book, she wrote, "the voices of young recruits, Communist Party secretaries and officers are beautifully knit together in a way that, like Isaac Babel's *Red Cavalry* stories, makes the most of irony." Jin's restrained and concise prose, too, is indebted to that of Babel, who once wrote, "There is no iron that can enter the human heart with such stupefying effect as a period placed at just the right moment." Another clear influence is Leo Tolstoy: the words Jin uses to describe Tolstoy's style—"straightforward, honest, simple"—are equally apt descriptions of his own prose. His sense of what is essential in a piece of writing has also been shaped far more by classic authors than by his contemporaries. Saying that many of his students' stories "feel so ephemeral," Jin commented to Garner: "They are full of references to TV shows and movies. What's important is to get human feeling onto paper. That's what is timeless, and that's what you get from Tolstoy and from Gogol and from Chekhov." Jin's subjects and themes frequently parallel those of these writers, from Tolstoy's intimate dramas of individuals caught up in the maelstrom of war, to Nikolai Vasil'evich Gogol's sudden eruptions of the absurd, to Anton Pavlovich Chekhov's haunting portrayals of the emotional turbulence of village life.

The stories in *Ocean of Words* are set on the border between Russia and China in the early 1970s, a time when the two countries frequently seemed to be on the verge of war. The soldiers in these stories are always on the alert for signs of imminent enemy attack or for eruptions of "bourgeois liberalism" (a term that indicts a broad range of ordinary human emotions, including love, lust, and longing) in themselves and their compatriots. "Warily eyeing Soviet troops from their watchtowers, the characters in these stories believe that the Soviets 'were barbarians and Revisionists, while we were Chinese and true Revolutionaries.' But what they are all revealed to be is achingly human," Andy Solomon observed in his 2 June 1996 review of the book for *The New York Times*.

Many of the stories deal more or less explicitly with the conflicts between Communist Party ideology, which officers try to enforce and which their troops try to obey, and the imperatives of human nature. "A Report," the first story in the collection, recounts an event in which a company of soldiers marching through a city en route to exercises breaks down in tears while singing a patriotic song. In his official report to a divisional commissar, the "Loyal Soldier and Political Instructor" Chen Jun struggles to account for "the surprise of bourgeois sentiment" that seized the men in his company. The report denounces the song, which begins "Good-bye, mother, good-bye, mother," as "a counterrevolutionary one" as evidenced by its effect upon the soldiers. The story sustains the ironic tension created by Chen's attempt to create a politically acceptable interpretation of his troop's reaction to the song through the very end, in which he dutifully supplies "the lesson we have learned from the reported event": "Our class enemies are still active, and they never go to sleep . . . We must grow another pair of eyes in the backs of our heads so that we can keep them under watch everywhere and at all times."

In "A Lecture" another patriotic exercise goes awry. Hoping to begin a yearlong study of the history of the party "with a vivid lecture that would at least arouse the soldier's interest," the secretary of the Radio Company, Si Ma Lin, invites a veteran of the Long March (the Red Army's grueling but victorious yearlong trek across mainland China that culminated in the defeat of Chiang Kai-shek's forces) to speak to them. The secretary expects an inspiring narrative of epic and heroic deeds. "Tell us something about the battles and victories," he urges the veteran, Liu Baoming. Old Liu's version of the march, however, begins with his joining the Red Army in order "to have something to eat," and continues on through the would-be revolutionaries getting caught in a terrible hail storm, sinking in mud in the grass marshes, hiding and fleeing from enemy attack, and finally, eating a captured enemy officer (an event that prompted Liu's desertion). Eventually he joined a medical unit and so finished out the war, he gleefully explains, carrying "not a gun but a large chamber pot." As the lecture concludes, the disconcerted troops are requested to turn in their notes and not speak of what they have heard, lest the truth brand them all as "Current Counterrevolutionaries."

The narration of this story, which is told in the third person but seems to be from the carefully muted point of view of an observer at the lecture, is brilliantly understated. Lines such as "Secretary Si Ma Lin of the Radio Company had to rewrite his lectures, because the significance and nature of some events in the textbook changed each year. For example, the year before, Lin Biao had been 'the Wise Marshall,' but the next year he became a traitor throughout the history of the Chinese Communist Party," are presented matter-of-factly, with no indication that the narrator recognizes their absurdity. Much of the humor of Jin's stories results from such disjunctions between the narrator's and the reader's viewpoints. "Good writers should observe and tell the story, try to reveal the complexities, the subtleties, to tell what's happening," Jin said in a 2 February 2000 interview with *Powells.com*. "The narrator shouldn't be intrusive. You have to respect the intelligence of the reader."

Jin's first-person narrators, such as those in "Too Late," "Dragon Head," "The Russian Prisoner," and "My Best Soldier," are often midlevel army functionaries or bureaucrats in charge of enforcing party doctrine and discipline. Surprised or bewildered by the waywardness of their subordinates, they are the perpetual straight men to the comedy of human errors in the face of this inflexible doctrine and discipline. In "Too Late," the narrator finds himself unable to comprehend the soldier Kong Kai's persistence in a love affair with an orphaned young woman whose parents were capitalists before the Revolution. Convinced that "if he knew her family background, Kong must have lost his senses and ignored the class distinction," the narrator takes a polemical tack. "Chairman Mao has instructed us," he reminds Kong, "there is no love without a reason, and there is no hatred without a reason; the proletariat has the proletarian love, whereas the bourgeoisie has the bourgeois love. As a Communist Party member," he continues, hoping that the irrefutable logic of the situation will become clear to Kong, "to which class do you belong?" Yet, Kong stubbornly refuses to abandon his "abnormal affair," as his superior officers term it, and finally flees to the countryside with his lover, a "counter-revolutionary" act that transforms the two lovers into "criminals at large."

In one of the most haunting of Jin's stories, "Love in the Air," another "irrational" love changes the life of a young army telegraph operator, Kang. An "awkward giant" of a man, Kang has no experience with love until he encounters the "excellent hand" of another operator's call sign. Discovering that the "hand" belongs to a young woman, he grows entranced with its "elegance and fluency," the dots and dashes of the military messages becoming like "tender, meaningful words the young woman sent to him alone . . . amorous messages inviting him to decode their secret meanings." The young woman, Lili, knows nothing of his fantasies, and Kang is devastated to learn that she has in fact been carrying on "a love affair in the air" with another operator in his company. Unable to "forget that woman's voice and her telegraphic style," and so unable to cure himself of the "bourgeois liberalism" of his feelings, Kang finally concludes he has destroyed his future and asks to be reassigned to manual labor.

In nearly all of Jin's fictions, the high-minded precepts of party ideology prove to be utterly unavailing against the exigencies of human emotions and drives. In "My Best Soldier," lust, rather than love, causes the fall of the priapic Liu Fu. Despite his commanding officer's exhortation that "we must not lose our fighting spirit by chasing women" and his orders that Liu carry out an examination of "the elements of bourgeois ideology in his brain," he cannot restrain himself. In the end, Liu is shot by his commanding officer while trying to desert.

While Jin's shortsighted and unimaginative officers and bureaucrats have a somewhat generic or stereotypical feel to them, generally appearing as detached and rather naive observers of the events in the stories, the individual soldiers on whom many of the narratives focus are always sharply drawn. One of the best stories in *Ocean of Words* is "Dragon Head," a portrait of a wily,

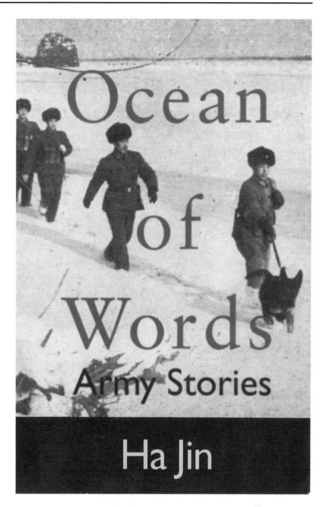

Cover for Jin's 1996 collection, stories set on the Russo-Chinese border during the 1970s

charismatic militia leader, of whom one character observes, "If this were the Old China, no doubt Dragon Head would become a small warlord." The story traces the progress of the uneasy relations between Dragon Head and his men and the regular army battalion commander, Gao Ping, and the soldiers under his command. When Gao arrives in the village with his troops, he meets Dragon Head and, "amused by this young man," he proposes that "from now on, we are friends and comrades-in-arms." As in so many of Jin's stories, a small, telling detail conveys a crucial supplement or subtext to this conversation: as Dragon Head smiles and enthusiastically agrees, the reader is told that "he inserted his hands behind the holsters of his pistols," a gesture that simultaneously undermines the amicability of his words and foreshadows the trouble that will soon erupt between the militia and the regular army.

In "A Contract," a squad leader with a quick wit disarms a bully who has challenged him to a fight by offering him a contract that states that "All having been considered, we realized that a melee does not suit the style of revolutionary soldiers, so we have decided to do it with weapons. Also having considered bullets must be saved for the Russians, we have chosen to use bayonets"–a stratagem that effectively trumps the bully's physical strength and leaves him with his head "buried . . . in his quilt." The nature of comradeship among men and the often harsh ways it is expressed are the subjects of another story, "Miss Jee." Told in a voice that alternates between the first-person singular of one soldier and the plural "we" of the Thirteenth Squad, "Miss Jee" is about Jun Jee, a patriotic young soldier who becomes the butt of an entire squad's humor for his effeminate looks and voice. Over the course of their training, the squad creates a series of doggerel verses about Jee's feminine allure and technical incompetence. Before the squad sets out for its new units at the end, the narrator says, "we all wrote the poem down in our notebooks, as though it was our common heritage, which we would carry to the battlefield."

In "The Fellow Townsmen," the bonds of kinship and the obligations of hospitality are tested against individual animosities when Chen Jun, a soldier, is confronted with his archenemy from his hometown, Chu Tian, who jilted Chen's sister and disgraced his family. Destitute and on the run from his unit, Chu brings his sick son for treatment to the army infirmary where Chen works. Throughout the story, even as he makes small concessions to aid Chu, Chen plots revenge. In the end, however, in spite of all his plans and intentions, he helps Chu and sends him off with medicine and money.

Despite its overtly Manichaean logic of "us" versus "them," few other circumstances in life seem to spawn so many moral ambiguities as war. In "The Russian Prisoner," a squad of Chinese soldiers is assigned to guard a captured Russian soldier, Lev Petrovich, while they try to determine whether he is a deserter or a spy. A change of clothing leads one of the soldiers to observe that "you could easily take him for one of us if you looked at him from behind." Yet, Lev's writing and gymnastics skills render him suspicious: "No one would believe that a common Russian soldier could write an article the length of a book and could use the horizontal bar like a professional athlete. The more you thought about him, the more he looked like a well-trained agent." The hapless Lev is finally returned to the Russians, who, the narrator muses, "would suspect him of being either a traitor or a Chinese agent."

In his second short-story collection, *Under the Red Flag* (1997), Jin turned his attention to depicting life in the small Chinese village of Dismount Fort during and after the Cultural Revolution. Mao's Cultural Revolution, which began in 1966 and lasted virtually up until his death in 1976, was a movement that aimed at destroying "bourgeois" influence and "capitalist roaders" in the Communist Party and across China. To launch it, Mao appealed directly to the "revolutionary masses" to restore the original ideals of the Communist Revolution and root out "rightist tendencies," both inside and outside the party. The Cultural Revolution commenced with three years of widespread mob violence, during which the Red Guards (aided by many peasants and workers) attacked a vast range of "rightist" targets. Anyone or anything associated with pre-Revolutionary China and its social and cultural hierarchy was suspect. People whose families or ancestors had owned property or operated businesses were ostracized and mercilessly persecuted, as were professionals and scholars, many of whom were sent to the countryside to be "reeducated" through backbreaking labor. In an attempt to sweep away all vestiges of the Old China and its thousands of years of feudal and "bourgeois" culture, books were banned and burned; priceless art was destroyed; and temples and other historic buildings were razed.

Jin was nine years old when the Cultural Revolution began, and his family, like the rest of China, was caught up in the events of the time. "Because my grandfather had been a landowner, my mother was criticized very severely," Jin recalled in the Garner interview. "People did terrible things to her." While the family was afforded some protection by his father's position as an army officer, Jin's father's books were nonetheless confiscated and flung into a bonfire. Jin's education was interrupted for several years when all the schools were closed. His experiences during these formative years of his childhood and adolescence left a deep mark upon him and no doubt are the source of much of the emotional intensity that characterizes these later stories. The stories in *Under the Red Flag* (a phrase that refers to the time period following the overthrow of Chiang Kai-shek and the creation of Communist China) capture a fuller range of human experience than those of *Ocean of Words*. While most of the stories focus on men's lives, the bleak experiences of women are here, too, and several of the most memorable stories are about boys.

The Cultural Revolution functions, Jin commented in the Berrett interview, as "a set of basically external forces" that are used to provide context. "Mainly," he continued, "I focus on how these people behave in these situations." While Jin may not have intended these stories to be read as political polemics, they do reveal how high-minded political rhetoric is frequently used as a justification or a cloak for base human actions and emotions. The story "In Broad Daylight," which opens the collection, concerns the public repudiation and tormenting of a prostitute, Mu Ying, by the Red Guard and inhabitants of the village of Dismount Fort. She is interrogated, forced to make a public confession, beaten, and forced to wear a placard reading "I am a Broken Shoe. My Crime Deserves Death," as she is paraded through the village in a punishment that leaves her husband dead and herself abandoned at the bus stop by the mob, pleading for help that will not come. While the "trial" is accompanied by the proper political rhetoric–"Why do you seduce men and paralyze their revolutionary will with your bourgeois poison?"–it is clear from the village history of burning prostitutes alive on a hill called Heaven Lamp that this latest persecution is merely a new variation on an old custom. That the story is told from the point of view of a young boy who, along with his friends, becomes caught up in the excitement of the persecution, makes it all the more disturbing. In "Emperor," another story narrated by a young boy, Jin shows how the boys' rivalries and war games mirror those of their elders and their society. The connection is made explicit in the resonant ending: "As time went by, we left, one after another, to serve different emperors."

In "A Decade" a young woman returns to the village where she lived as a child and decides to visit her former teacher, Zhu Wenli. She reminisces about Wenli, who came to the village as a shy, pretty young woman right out of college. When the children in her class spy her kissing another teacher with whom she has fallen in love, they turn her in to the school authorities, setting off a full-scale persecution. The school fills with billboards and signs such as: "Root Out the Bourgeois Lifestyle," "It's Shameless to Open Your Pants in the Office," "Why Do You Still Behave like a Hoodlum?," "Zhu Wenli: the Stinking Bourgeois Miss," and "New China Does Not Tolerate the Incorrigible Progeny of Capitalists." Both teachers are subsequently sent to the countryside to be reformed through labor. Convinced of the rectitude of their own actions, the children feel no guilt. When the young woman approaches her former teacher, she is surprised to find her changed, coarsened: "All the tenderness and innocence which had marked that face was now replaced by a numb, stony look. Even her voice had changed too, full of scratchy metal." She was, the young woman realizes, "no longer the person I wanted to meet." There is no indication, however, that the narrator recognizes that she herself bears some responsibility for her former teacher's state. As in so many of Jin's stories, as Lieu observed, he "lets silence speak for him allowing the sometimes hilarious, sometimes terrible truth to sink in without commentary." This story and others make clear that Jin came to see the Cultural Revolution and those participating in it as mindlessly destroying human qualities that remain necessary, perhaps more than ever after the Revolution.

Yet, they will take a long time, perhaps even needing new generations, to rebuild.

Political justifications for persecutions of those who incite the anger, guilt, or resentment of their fellow citizens are also deployed in "The Richest Man," the story of Li Wan, the richest man in Dismount Fort, who is the object of the envy of the other villagers. When an inadvertently broken Mao button is found by his neighbors in his trash heap, he is jailed, and all of his belongings are confiscated and distributed among the villagers. Six years later, he experiences another reversal of fortune and is acquitted. He returns to being the richest man in the village, and "people went on talking about his stinginess and arrogance." "In secret," readers are told, "some were looking forward to another political movement."

While many turn the climate of political turmoil and persecution to their own advantage, other characters in Jin's stories find themselves caught in heartbreaking conflicts between political dogma and private devotion. In "Winds and Clouds over a Funeral" the chairman of the commune experiences such a dilemma when his mother dies after making him promise that he will not cremate her. Shortly thereafter, he is reminded that "to prevent burials is a major political task this year." His insistence on burying his own mother, he is reminded, would set a bad example for the other members of the commune. Yet, if he cremates her (and he finally does), he will be condemned as an unfilial son. He finds a way out of this conundrum by putting out the story that the old woman had actually volunteered to be cremated in order to preserve "clean" ground for future generations, thus making himself appear both patriotic and properly filial. In this way, too, he ensures the future of his own son, who will benefit from his father's station and power.

Despite attempts by the "New China" to sweep away vestiges of the "Old China"–among them its Confucian traditions of filial piety, patriarchy, ancestor worship, and its many superstitions, Jin's stories suggest that the Old China still endures. In "New Arrival" the lives and unhappy marriage of a couple, Jia Cheng and his infertile wife, Ning, are transformed with the arrival of a young boy whom they agree to care for while his parents are away. As they grow to love the boy they are fostering, their marriage is restored, and they find contentment. Familial relations of a different tenor are explored in "Fortune," the story of a middle-aged man named Tang Hu, who is told by a fortune-teller that he is destined for a "mighty life," but that his ascent has been hindered by his son. "You were born to be a big general," she says, but he has failed to achieve his intended greatness because he unwisely named his son Da Long, which means "great dragon." "Your son's life is too strong," the fortune-teller advises him. "His fortune reduces yours and he is the evil star over your head. . . . His life has overcome yours." Tang becomes obsessed with the "jinx" of his son and the possibility of "wealth, rank, splendor" in his own future, if only he could rid himself of his son. In the end, he is totally consumed by his obsession; he descends into madness and kills his son.

The cruelty of events in Dismount Fort and the restrained matter-of-factness with which they are narrated in these stories often make for deeply disturbing reading. "Man to Be" is the story of Hao Nan, a young man who is engaged to marry a rich, pretty girl. Along with four other men, he is invited one night by a man known as "Cuckold Sang" to gang-rape Sang's unfaithful young wife, Shuling. Despite misgivings and feelings of unease, Nan joins the other men, but after the act, he finds that he has "lost his Yang" and becomes completely impotent. The story is told as if it were his tragedy (it concludes with him wistfully watching his former fiancée from afar). Recalling the controversy Jin's graphic narratives often generated in the creative-writing seminars at Boston University, his former classmate, the writer Jhumpa Lahiri, recalled in Garner's *New York Times* profile of Jin that "his stories really pushed people's buttons." Jin himself acknowledged in the same piece that his stories "are not gentle stories." "The question for me," he said, "has always been, How do you write about terrible things without resorting to vulgarity? I think I might push things farther than people expect. But that's how you test yourself as a writer."

As depicted in Jin's stories, the lives of women are determined by convention and their frequently grim circumstances. Told that "Every woman ought to marry; if she didn't, people would think her abnormal," Hong Chen, a young woman who is the protagonist of "Taking a Husband," tries to decide between two men, neither of whom she loves or even likes. She finally resorts to drawing lots in order to choose, but then, to her dismay, finds that she has made the wrong choice by selecting the one who does not receive the coveted promotion for which the two suitors were vying. In "Again, the Spring Breeze Blew," another young woman, Lanlan, finds herself subject to the vicissitudes of fate. Shortly after she is widowed, Lanlan is attacked by a man intent on raping her. She manages to get hold of his knife and stab him but afterward is not believed by the villagers, who suspect her of having known the man. Pressed to marry an old widower in the village, she decides to wait, certain that "things would change as long as she waited patiently." When her attacker turns out to be an escaped, convicted rapist, she becomes a local hero, in the words of the newspapers, "a brave woman and a good wife," "a young woman

[who] subdued a violent criminal." Her misfortune eventually becomes the engine of her good fortune: as a result of her newfound fame, she is given a good job and becomes a city dweller.

"Resurrection," another story in the collection, also features a reversal of fortune, but one that is disturbing rather than heartening. Lu, a man who has slept with his pregnant wife's sister and been discovered, is told by his village brigade leaders to write out a detailed confession of his crimes. Unable to create a narrative that will satisfy them, he finally castrates himself in despair. Afterward, "nobody thought of pressing him for the confession again, since his act had indeed proved his remorse and sincerity." The story has a peculiarly happy ending: Lu is reconciled with his wife and elected an exemplary commune member. And, "most significant of all, he had a new, normal life."

Jin's most recent collection of short stories, *The Bridegroom* (2000), revisits many of the themes from his earlier fictions, including clashes between political doctrine and human nature, the capriciousness of the powerful, the cruelties of everyday life, and the strange exigencies of love and fate. Yet these stories, which are set in Muji City during the recent past and present day, also depict in sharp relief the conflicts and contradictions of the New China as it attempts to change its economy to allow for capitalist or entrepreneurial initiatives while still maintaining good "party discipline" among the populace. Many of these stories are far more marked by a sense of disillusionment and rage toward those in power than Jin's earlier stories (in which the powerful were more likely to be unintentionally obtuse than deliberately malevolent). "Saboteur" is a Kafka-esque story in which Mr. Chin, a university professor and faithful member of the Communist Party, has a disastrous encounter with two railway policemen while he and his new bride are waiting to catch a train. When one of the policemen tosses away his leftover tea, splashing the professor and his wife, Chin chides him: "Comrade Policeman, your duty is to keep order, but you purposely tortured us common citizens. Why violate the law you are supposed to enforce?" They respond by taking him into custody and charging him with being a "saboteur" for disrupting the public order. Chin's former law student, sent by his university to secure his release, is also imprisoned and cruelly interrogated. When Chin threatens the authorities with exposure, they remind him that it is they, not he, who determine the "truth": "We are not afraid of any story you make up," they tell him. "We call it fiction." Defeated, Chin signs a confession, but before leaving town he retaliates against the whole city by going from restaurant to restaurant, spreading the hepatitis that has been made acute by his imprisonment. When an epidemic breaks out a short time later, Chin, who has indeed become a "saboteur," is long gone.

The complexities of power and language are further explored in "A Bad Joke," in which an offhand joke told by two peasants is retold by others and comes back to haunt them in "monstrous form." In the process of dissemination, the joke is transformed into one critical of Chairman Deng Xiaoping, and the police arrest the two peasants for slander. That the two peasants do not even know who Deng Xiaoping is (their joke concerned their commune chairman), is immaterial to the police, for "how could there be a crime without a criminal?" Now cursing the authorities in earnest, the two peasants are led off to prison. In "In the Kindergarten," one of Jin's most-successful and best-known stories, a young girl also experiences the disillusionment and rage of the weak, but unlike the peasants in "A Bad Joke," she does not remain powerless. Shaona and her classmates spend days in the hot sun picking purslane, which their teacher promises them will make a dish that "tastes great, different from anything you've ever had." Yet, the purslane is never served, and Shaona discovers that her teacher has sold the plants to pay a debt. On the last day the children gather purslane, Shaona secretly urinates on their harvest. That evening, empowered by her revenge, "she was so excited that she joined the boys in playing soldier, carrying a water pistol, as though all of a sudden she had become a big girl. She felt that from now on she would not cry like a baby at night again."

The vicissitudes of love, particularly when in conflict with the puritanically strict morality of Communist China, is one of Jin's favorite themes, and he explores it in several of the stories in *The Bridegroom*. In "Broken" Manjin, a young worker at the Muji Railroad Company, becomes enamored with a beautiful typist, Tingting, who is the object of all the men's sexual speculation. When the men begin to suspect that she is carrying on an affair with a married man, they lay a trap to catch her in the act. Despite his reluctance, Manjin joins the men in exposing her and then is forced to take part in her interrogation and in writing the report on the incident. Years later, he has a sexual encounter in a dark movie theater with a woman he thinks is Tingting. When she hurries away before he can speak with her, he pursues her out into the courtyard, where he mistakenly embraces a woman who turns out to be the vice mayor's daughter. Even though he is not certain that the woman in the theater was Tingting, he betrays her to the police to save himself from being accused of assault. Haunted by her subsequent suicide, Manjin withdraws from the companionship of his fellow workers: his only comfort is a pair of butterfly panties that

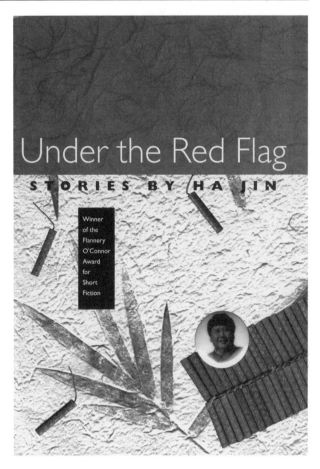

Dust jacket for Jin's 1997 book, stories about village life in China during Mao Tse-tung's Cultural Revolution

were taken from the unfortunate Tingting on the night Manjin and the other men caught her with her lover.

In the title story a forbidden love of a different sort destroys the life of a young man named Baowen. The story is told from the point of view of Old Cheng, a factory security manager whose close friend has died, leaving a daughter in Cheng's care. In time, to the puzzlement of Cheng and the rest of workers, his rather plain foster daughter, Beina, becomes engaged to Baowen, the most attractive young man at the factory. They marry and are happy together, but Beina does not become pregnant. One day, Cheng is informed that his son-in-law has been arrested for homosexuality. Sentenced first to a mental hospital, where he undergoes shock treatment, and then to prison, Baowen is condemned for a form of sexuality that the Chinese regard as having "originated in Western capitalism and bourgeois lifestyle . . . a kind of hooliganism." Despite the words of the doctor who admitted to him that Baowen's "disease" is really only "a sexual preference . . . like being left-handed," Cheng remains doubtful. "If homosexuality is a natural thing, then why are there men and women?" he wonders. When Beina, who insists she still loves her husband, refuses to divorce him, Cheng, fearing the loss of his job, abandons her, betraying his old friend's trust. "It's impossible," he tells her, "for me to have a criminal as my son-in-law."

In "Flame" a married woman's steadfast love for a former suitor she has not seen in seventeen years transforms her life and that of her husband. Having been forced to marry a man she does not love to save her family from starvation during a famine, Nimei has never forgotten the man she truly loved. One day she receives a letter from him, asking if he can come to see her. Contemplating his visit, Nimei assesses her life and sets about transforming it in order to make a better impression on him. She successfully campaigns to get her husband a better job, paves the yard of their house, dyes her hair, and loses weight. In the end he does not come.

Fate is the transforming force in "Alive," in which the life of Tong Guhan, a middle-aged cannery manager, is forever altered when he is among the victims of a massive earthquake in a city where he has been sent by his factory to collect a debt. Seriously injured, he recovers his health, but he has lost all memory of who he is or of his former life: he is one of the many "unidentifiables," including orphaned children, the senile, and people too injured to tell the authorities who they are. Faced with tens of thousands of widowed adults, parentless children, and childless old people, the government launches a movement called "Form New Families" to encourage people to marry again and provide families for homeless children and old people. Unaware that he already has a wife and children, Guhan marries a woman who has lost her husband and two children, and they are assigned an orphaned boy. Years later, Guhan is reminded of his previous life by the aroma of leek dumplings. Leaving his new family behind, he returns home only to find that he is "back as a mere ghost." Guhan's wife, now living with her brother, has been husband hunting; their son has married and taken over the family apartment; his job has been taken by his rival, and the cannery cannot rehire him. although he decides to remain there, Guhan is not sure he should have returned at all. His family's surprise and joy upon seeing him alive, he realizes, was irrevocably "mixed with confusion, shame, and sadness."

Ambivalence is the primary emotion of "An Offical Reply," a story written in the form of a recommendation letter that ultimately reveals far more about the recommender than the recommended. In response to a request from a professor at Beijing University, a young professor writes a lengthy letter of recommendation for a senior colleague who was once his teacher. The writer of the letter details the brilliance of the professor, but then opines, "although he was a promising late bloomer, he has not blossomed fully." As he discusses the professor's attractiveness to women, it appears that he is simultaneously disapproving and envious. Seemingly oblivious to the possiblility that it might be read as a commentary on himself, the professor closes his letter with the admonition that his colleague "can be used but should never be trusted, not unlike the majority of intellectuals, who are no more than petty scoundrels."

Self-delusion of a more severe type can be found in "A Tiger Fighter Is Hard to Find," a story about the fate of a young movie star filming a polemical television series based on an old Chinese folktale, "Wu Song Beat the Tiger." The series is praised by the provincial governor, who tells its makers: "We ought to create more heroic characters of this kind as role models for the revolutionary masses to follow. You, writers and artists, are the engineers of the human soul." When the governor decides that the crucial scene in which the hero kills the tiger is insufficiently convincing, the director decides to reshoot it. In the course of the filming, the young star becomes convinced that he is the legendary tiger-slaying hero, a delusion that persists even through a scene in which the part of the tiger is played by another man, whom he nearly kills. The story may be read as a warning of the perils of propaganda for those who, like the young actor, come to believe in it and for those who suffer at the hands of the believers.

Among the most interesting of the stories in *The Bridegroom* are those of the increasingly capitalist New China, in which "the government was encouraging people to find ways to get rich," and peasants who make fortunes are hailed as "model citizens" and given membership in the Communist Party. In "An Entrepreneur's Story," Liu Feng, a man who "never thought money could make such a difference" finds his life is transformed once he starts a successful importing business. Although he is now treated as a person of consequence and is finally able to marry the woman who refused him when he was poor, he cannot forget that his neighbors used to treat him "like a homeless dog," while his wife treated him "like a bedbug." In the end, all his good fortune cannot overcome his disgust and lingering resentment. In "The Woman from New York," a young mathematics teacher returns from an extended trip to New York to find that she was mistaken when she thought that she "could always come back." In her absence, neighbors have spread the rumor that "she had become the fifteenth concubine of a wealthy Chinese man in New York City"; her husband has grown disaffected and sent their daughter to live with his parents; and her job has been filled by someone else. Her attempts to fit back into her old life are thwarted by the distrust and resentment of her family and neighbors, and eventually she disappears, leaving them to carry on again without her.

Like "An Entrepreneur's Story," "After Cowboy Chicken Came to Town" depicts the personal and social upheaval created by the arrival of capitalism in Communist China. The story is told from the point of view of Hongwen, a young man who works in the newly opened Cowboy Chicken and struggles to adjust to the precepts and practices of flexible capitalism. Despite some customers' opinion that "This Cowboy Chicken only sounds good and looks tasty. In fact it's just a name," the franchise is successful. The owners of nearby chicken handcarts respond first by moving farther away, and then by introducing "PATRIOTIC CHICKEN . . . 30% CHEAPER THAN C.C.!" They curse Hongwen and his fellow employees as "American Dogs" and "Foreign Lackeys." Hongwen is simultaneously admiring and resentful of the Australian "white devil" Mr. Shapiro, who owns Cowboy Chicken, and of his assistant manager, Peter, an ambitious young Chinese man who has studied in America. While Hongwen is well paid, he has to work hard at the restaurant and wishes that he could "be like some people who go to their offices every morning for an eight-hour rest." When he and his coworkers discover that Peter burns each day's leftover chicken on Mr. Shapiro's orders, their resentment and envy come to a head. They decide to go on strike and demand that Peter be fired. Their plan backfires when Mr. Shapiro responds by "terminating" them all and hiring new workers to take their places. It is their first experience of the true power of the capitalist boss, and the story concludes as they plot their revenge: "This was just the beginning."

While there has as yet been little scholarly study done of Jin's work, the critical acclaim it has received in the popular press, the prizes it has garnered, and Jin's ascent to the position of a major Chinese American writer guarantee that such work will be forthcoming. In the meantime, to understand his work as a writer and his view of literature and the world, readers can turn to his own thoughts. "I have more of an aesthetic ideal than a political or a commercial one," Jin told Berrett:

Commercial success doesn't interest me. We can't worry too much: all we can do is give a book a strong heart, give everything we can to it. After I finish a story, I usually feel a lot more calm. Before finishing the work, I feel terribly bothered–I need to finish it to calm the ghost down, or myself down. If you write a good story or a good poem, you've done the work, the ghost won't bother you anymore. But there are other kinds of demons that begin to bother you. That's a good feeling–if you feel terribly bothered by something, that's a very good impulse. A book's function very often isn't to answer, but to present the vitality of, a question.

Interviews:

Jocelyn Lieu, "Beating the Odds," *Chicago Tribune Books,* 24 November 1996, p. 14;

John D. Thomas, "Across an *Ocean of Words*," *Emory Magazine,* 74 (Spring 1998);

Dave Weich, "Powells.com Interviews: Ha Jin Lets It Go," *Powells.com* (2 February 2000) <http://www.powells.com/authors/jin.html>;

Dwight Garner, "Ha Jin's Cultural Revolution," *New York Times Magazine,* 6 February 2000, pp. 38–41.

Thom Jones
(26 January 1945 –   )

Denis Hennessy
State University of New York at Oneonta

BOOKS: *The Pugilist at Rest: Stories* (Boston: Little, Brown, 1993; London: Faber & Faber, 1994); *Cold Snap: Stories* (Boston: Little, Brown, 1995; London: Faber & Faber, 1996); *Sonny Liston Was a Friend of Mine: Stories* (Boston: Little, Brown, 1999; London: Faber & Faber, 1999).

Thom Jones's first collection of short stories, *The Pugilist at Rest,* was published in 1993 and brought almost instant critical attention to its author. While many critics admired Jones's talent and praised his short fiction, there was an overall sense of uncertainty about how best to measure the author's unusual imagery, scenes, and inchoate ideas. Part of this confusion lay in Jones's background. The Thom Jones who became well known overnight was drawn variously as a former Marine, a beclouded former boxer, an occasional janitor, and ad writer, who stumbled into writing while on various drugs and after reading too much Friedrich Nietzsche and Arthur Schopenhauer on his breaks. Some reviewers simply seemed unwilling to take a forty-eight-year-old janitor seriously. Publishers' blurbs and newspaper book reviews were many times ambiguous and mixed biographical misinformation with unfounded suppositions. Since the publication of two more collections, *Cold Snap* in 1995 and *Sonny Liston Was a Friend of Mine* in 1999, critics have yet to come to a consensus regarding Jones's ability. Yet, Jones received the Best American Short Stories Award from Houghton Mifflin in 1992, was nominated for a National Book Award and given an O. Henry Award in 1993 for *The Pugilist at Rest,* and was made a Guggenheim Fellow in 1994–1995. His story "I Want To Live" was included in *The Best American Stories of the Twentieth Century,* edited by John Updike. Clearly, he is a noteworthy American writer; less clear is his place in the evolution of the American short story.

Thom Jones was born in Aurora, Illinois, on 26 January 1945, the son of Joseph Thomas Jones and Marilyn Faye (Carpenter) Graham. His father's boxing career never grew beyond the journeyman's class but

Thom Jones (photograph by Marco Prozzo)

provided Jones with not only the motivation for his own career in the ring but also the subject matter for several of his best stories. In 1963 Jones was honorably discharged from the Marines after having been injured in an amateur boxing match, triggering epilepsy. In subsequent years the epilepsy caused Jones to spend much time in hospitals, sometimes in mental wards. He was married on 28 September 1968 to Sally Laverne Williams, and they have one daughter, Emily. In 1970 he earned a B.A. from the University of Washington and in 1973 an M.F.A. from the University of Iowa. Jones and his family live in Olympia, Washington. He teaches writing and gives readings throughout the country, while also working on current projects and pursuing his interest in philosophy.

His first published short story, "The Pugilist at Rest," was picked out of the unsolicited pile at *The New Yorker* and accepted. Appearing in the December 1991 issue, this story brought him immediate attention as an original talent as important as Raymond Carver and Denis Johnson, two of Jones's colleagues at Iowa. Other stories followed. The critical praise was tempered only by the nagging doubt expressed by some critics that the machismo, violence, and misguided pessimism made Jones just another writer pandering to a male-chauvinist audience, criticism that followed his next two collections of short fiction. One critic, Ted Solotaroff, assumed that Jones's rage was probably the effect of his war experiences in Vietnam, though Jones never saw combat. These misperceptions were not entirely without provocation, for Jones's narrators and most of his characters are traumatized by the horror of life and by the effects of a pharmacological crisscross of drugs, prescribed or otherwise. Only a close look at the stories as fiction can reveal their true contribution to late-twentieth-century writing. As the critic Matt Barnard reminded readers in a 26 February 1999 *New Statesman* review of *Sonny Liston Was a Friend of Mine,* even as the media dwelt on the more-dramatic facts of Jones's life, "The one autobiographical subject that does not make it into his fiction is the master's degree in creative writing. . . . It is not something that sits comfortably with the man-on-the-wild-side myth." The media has made it difficult to assess Jones's work by helping readers forget that they are being entertained by a skilled artist.

The title story of *The Pugilist at Rest* begins by offering readers a glimpse of Jones's aesthetic beliefs; the paragraph is a statement not unlike James Joyce's own aesthetic in *The Portrait of the Artist as a Young Man* (1916). Jones describes the pugilist of the title, the statue, perhaps of Theogenes, as a fighter who had survived many battles. The details of the seated boxer are realistic and accurate, the figure's head turned, looking over his shoulder. The gaze of the statue leaves the viewer imagining the cause of the turn. That gesture, says Jones, is art. The pugilist's face and posture seem to mirror his wonderment. The pugilist's thoughts at the time, his puzzlement as to how he became the center of such violence, his curiosity as to who might be trying to get his attention are all unknown to the viewer. Readers of this collection of stories are curious

about the contingencies that have brought Jones's characters to their state in life, but the author provides only enough detail to imagine and empathize with their misery and joy. These several paragraphs in the first story seem to act as a guide to reading all of Jones's work.

The Pugilist at Rest includes fourteen stories grouped into four parts. The three stories in the first part are about the horrors of Vietnam; the second trio are about men at war with women; the third set concerns people fighting the difficulties of divorce, mental defects, and the ravages of cancer; and in the fourth section characters battle against epilepsy and alcoholism. The art in these tales shines through the overwhelming pessimism to present characters believable and even recognizable to the careful reader. The tone is more stoical than glum. The recurring theme is courage in all its protean forms, from the manic bravery of the Medal of Honor winner Baggit in "Break on Through" to the quiet, undaunted will of Mrs. Wilson, the doomed cancer patient in "I Want to Live."

In *The Pugilist at Rest* the first three stories adumbrate the sensibilities of the personae who appear in the rest of the collection. The narrator of the title story, the character Hollywood in "Break on Through," and the narrator of "The Black Lights" seem to be the same young man, the person whose consciousness is present in all eleven stories that follow. His language and ideas reflect a high-school education and a naiveté incongruent with the mature and hardened philosophy he has formed out of his horrific experiences preparing for war and being in the middle and aftermath of dehumanizing battle.

In "The Pugilist at Rest" the narrator recounts his experiences in Camp Pendelton with his two companions, Hey Baby and Jorgenson. The former is a bully, the latter a disaffected hippie-type. When Hey Baby continues to persecute Jorgenson, the narrator clubs Hey Baby with the steel buttplate of his rifle, nearly killing him. Jorgenson changes into a "gung ho" Marine and saves the narrator's life in battle, only to lose his own. Jones frames his story by having the narrator recall these events from his home. While cleaning out the attic he reminisces about the events in Pendelton and Vietnam, the medals for bravery he has won, and the head injury he sustained in a desperate prizefight that caused him to become a "neuropsych." The events closely reflect Jones's own experiences—except for the scenes in Vietnam—and the narrator's voice tries to ascribe meaning to it all by piecing together bits of quotations from Schopenhauer, Jones's own favorite thinker. Yet, the fictional narrator's conclusions are patently jejune in crucial places, and Jones's own voice seems to intervene, especially in describing Theogenes and the work of art. This shift of viewpoint from narra-

Dust jacket for Jones's first book (1993), which was nominated
for a National Book Award

tor to author is subtle but telling. The artistic merit of the story is not in the morbid and macabre glimpse into the unregenerate consciousness of a tormented war veteran but in the hard-won wisdom of an author coming to terms with the inevitability of violence in human existence. There is also in the story a more complex intertwining of this violence with love. More than once the narrator refers to the blue eyes of Jorgenson; they seem to transfix him. Jorgenson responds to the narrator with an unspoken affinity, which at least one critic suggests might be a homoerotic attachment between the two Marines.

In the next story, "Break on Through," the relationship between Baggit, the half-crazed Navy Seal, who is likely a murderer, and the narrator, Tommy "Hollywood," also is tinged with love. Baggit saves Hollywood from certain death in a firefight, and Hollywood subsequently saves Baggit from a savage beating from one of their fellow Marines. He comforts Baggit and thanks him for his rescue, reassuring him that he is a great fighter. Baggit responds warmly, but once discharged and sent home, he lives only a short while before killing himself and his wife during a violent kidnapping attempt. This faint hint of camaraderie or love can only flower, in Jones's stories, in an atmosphere of danger, violence, and death.

In the third story in part 1, "The Black Lights," there is the same theme of tenderness among warriors, warriors now hospitalized for mental care. Gothia, a giant of a man, manic and potentially dangerous, has a calming effect on the narrator, advising him and settling him down. Another patient, Chandler, helps the narrator with his reading. The pugilists at rest in this story are becalmed temporarily by drugs but trying to connect with one another without knowing why, governed by inner instincts that the horrors of the world cannot extinguish. Commander Andy Hawkins, the psychiatrist in charge of the unit, a man also touched by horror, has had his nose bitten off by a Marine gone mad. Eagle, as Hawkins is called by the men in his ward, triggers two positive changes in the narrator's life: he suggests that the narrator take notes in a diary, and he gives him his freedom–a discharge and pension. Although the narrator, after his discharge, speeds off with an AWOL escapee, feeling "in the zone" again as they crash through the gate, the reader wonders whether he can interpret "the zone" as a result of the violent smash through the gates or the feeling one gets when experiencing real freedom. There would be some optimism possible in the latter, except that violence and danger seem necessary for this feeling to take hold.

The stories in part 2 of *The Pugilist at Rest* seem to be a conscious effort on Jones's part to expand his thematic range, and although none deal directly with war, the characters are disaffected, adrift; battle has not scarred them, but the anomie of the late 1970s and 1980s that affected post–Vietnam America is evident in the characters of these stories. Herbie, the narrator of "Wipe Out," boldly but ingenuously describes his method of dealing with life, especially with women, in terms stolen from a combination of the *Playboy* philosophy and the beliefs of Jean-Paul Sartre. Perhaps the name of the woman who is the target of his existential ploys, Simone, is supposed to remind the reader of Simone de Beauvoir and her companionship with Sartre. Herbie artlessly proclaims his motivations in seducing this woman whom he has picked up in the philosophy section of the library, and his only goal is conquest, the satisfaction of his sexual desires. He successfully woos her, but when the passion begins to turn to love and caring, Herbie stays true to his code and leaves Simone. The reader is left with revulsion and contempt for the narrator and ponders the despair and emptiness of life in an era of existential doubt that particularly characterizes post–Vietnam America.

Humor, a mere passing form of communication in the collection, takes center stage in "Mosquitos." The narrator is Dr. Bob, a surgeon visiting his brother, Clendon, an English professor at Middlebury College who is married to a beautiful harridan, Victoria, who is cheating on him. The contrast in the brothers' lives, the narrator's darkly existential views on the phoniness of academic communities, and his criticism of the uxorious lives of men such as his brother are the sources of the wry humor in the story. Bob's diatribes on middle-class hypocrisy seem to be an attempt by the author to make the reader laugh with politically incorrect glee. The consciousness of Dr. Bob, perhaps, is being held up for ridicule: his life is no more meaningful than the lives of those he is criticizing. Like the others in the story, he cannot tolerate the mosquitoes, the annoying contingencies of ordinary life. Yet, Victoria and Clendon, despite their errors and weaknesses, are more noble than the doctor simply because they are living with one another, raising children, and dealing with their shortcomings instead of running from them, as rebellious Bob is doing in his speedy Jaguar V-12. The narrator interrupts his story to re-tell a revisionist interpretation of Daniel Defoe's *Robinson Crusoe* (1719), treating it as a parable for the necessity to turn away from civilization and embrace Nature. Readers of "Mosquitoes" might well ask at the end of the story if Bob is not the one who, because of his cynicism, is running away from things.

Critics who see Jones as a writer appealing to macho misogynists use the story "Unchain My Heart" to support their claim. Ostensibly the story deals with a woman, a fiction reader for a publishing house, who loves and lusts after a deep-sea diver whose sexual powers are enhanced by the deadly gases he breathes in his work. The story is narrated from the first-person viewpoint of this woman, and Jones handles this technique with chilling success. A basis for accusations of sexist stereotyping can be detected: the narrator is attracted to this man because she feels safe in his protective grasp; she fears and is awed by the danger he represents and is generally and sexually submissive to this brute. She is, however, also intelligent and honest, telling the story with a breathless passion. Her male coworkers belittle her obvious submission to this sex titan and leave her humiliating notes and obscene drawings. Her bosses and colleagues at the firm are all male, and the competition for recognition and promotion is furious, underhanded, and tawdry. Jones seems to be holding up for comparison the ferocity of the urban climber to the courage of the diver; having the intelligent woman as narrator makes the point even more dramatically—it is not his brutality she feels attracted to so much as his honesty and innocence.

"I Want to Live" is told by a limited omniscient narrator that gets into the mind of Mrs. Wilson—the name suggesting Schopenhauer's main theme, will—who is dying of cancer. Jones's mother-in-law was the model for the tale, which recounts the last sufferings of a courageous woman fighting a losing battle with cancer, the last efforts of the medical procedures and chemical dosages. At the center of the story is this woman's powerful will, not only to live but to find the truth about life. Her son-in-law gives her Schopenhauer to read, and she devours his work, angry that she had not come to this pessimistic but tough-minded thinker sooner in life. Jones covers the same philosophical ground, but this time from the point of view of a human being facing certain death, a human being thirsty for a kind of truth denied to her in her lifetime.

One childhood memory, of her family's rooster, Mr. Barnes, keeps coming back to Mrs. Wilson. To her he represents the perfect Schopenhauer creature: fierce in his protection of what is his, steadfast in his search of what he needs to please himself, oblivious to complaints of neighbors about his intrusive travels to their turf in search of females. She hopes that maybe she will meet him in the hereafter and be able to bask in the glory of his strong-willed appreciation of life. Mrs. Wilson never had the chance to live a life of freedom and pursuit of adventure. The reader is left to wonder, though, which life is worth more, the free-as-a-bird fiction reader's or the one of sacrifice and family Mrs. Wilson lived.

At the University of Iowa in the mid 1970s, Jones's mentors suggested that he find a mentally undemanding job while he was writing. Jones subsequently spent eleven years working as a janitor at North Thurston High School, providing him "sanctuary" in which to think and write. Jones used his experiences as a janitor in his story "Silhouettes." This story demonstrates his artistic sensitivity at work, trying to make sense of some of the desperate lives he saw. Window is a mentally handicapped student who does chores for the janitorial staff and shares his woes with them. One of the janitors, Meldrich, a philosophy reader, tries to dissuade Window from becoming seriously involved with Catherine, a Native American girl of bad reputation. Window stubbornly falls into a marriage in which one pregnancy is aborted and another produces a child whose father is not Window. The book-wise Meldrich does not save Window; rather, Josie, another janitor and the only other woman in the story, urges him to have a blood test proving the baby is not his, thus relieving him of the overwhelming burden of the child-support payments. The rest of the janitorial crew helps Window from there, especially in escaping from the rapacious Catherine. With their advice and the satisfaction of hard janitorial work, Window gains a stubborn self-respect and sense of independence. The reader is left to wonder how the academic staff at the school could have helped this "special education" student any better. The story shows how the "special" part of his education comes from these practical, simple, and

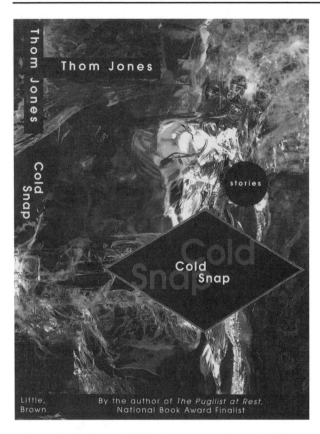

Dust jacket for Jones's 1995 book, whose stories Joyce Carol Oates compared to "the paintings of Bosch and Goya, the terrifying portraits of Francis Bacon"

The second story, "Rocket Man," tells of another bond of love, one based on the violence and angry revenge of a fighter, identified only as Prestone, and his trainer. The denouement finds both men, strongly bonded with a mutual respect and loyalty, eager for the upcoming bout where, Jones makes it clear, Prestone will be outclassed and beaten. The fighter is seen leaving his mentor, who is in a mental ward, seething and raving. Prestone is showing a bravado and optimism clearly transparent to the reader. Part 4 then leaves the reader with this fork in the road to happiness: one through love—aided by seemingly magical drugs; the other, a futile path of hatred and wounded pride toward certain defeat.

Two years after the publication of *The Pugilist at Rest,* critics were again divided in their reaction to Jones's second collection, *Cold Snap.* Benjamin Wiessman in the 6 August 1995 edition of *The Los Angeles Times* dismissed Jones's new efforts as macho fiction, formulaic stories that pass off violence and confusion as mystical insights, stories designed to please the same morbidly curious audience. Joyce Carol Oates in *The New York Times* (5 June 1995), however, compared the scenes in *Cold Snap* to "the paintings of Bosch and Goya, the terrifying portraits of Francis Bacon" filled with "the walking wounded, 'characters' in the fullest sense of the term." Oates summarized her review by saying that Jones's voice "transcends his subject," which is man's choice or lack of choice to be himself, free to choose his own destiny. She praised the "thrilling urgency of his voice," a voice that is heartrending. Most reviews were in between these extremes, often praising some stories and disparaging others in the collection. Jones shifted his focus and setting from warriors caught in the manic elation of war in Vietnam to the thrilling but mind-numbing, body-wasting terrors of doctors fighting disease and starvation in Africa. The first three stories involve doctors who are in Africa or have returned to the United States from that continent. Names of drugs used for depression, or for somehow altering mental states, abound. Nihilism, as an inevitable last resort or a disease to be medicated, pervades the stories.

The title story is narrated by Richard, a doctor who has returned from Africa to California, which is experiencing a cold snap. He is paranoid about the pipes freezing and doubtful about the antifreeze in his car. Most critics ignore the story or dismiss it as one of the weakest, failing to see it as a link to the thematic development that Jones began in *The Pugilist at Rest:* the power of love to transcend the agonies of mental illness. Richard, a manic depressive, loves his sister, Susan, and visits her frequently in her mental hospital. She had attempted suicide but the bullet lobotomized

wise people working in menial jobs, taking the problems of life as they come.

The last two stories make up part 4 and can be seen as Jones's summary of what he has wanted to say in the collection, not really as a moral but as an attempt to see ordinary man's choices to achieve happiness. In the first, "The White Horse," the main character, Ad Magic, is lost and gradually realizes he is in Bombay. Jones himself was, like his protagonist, an advertising writer, troubled by bouts of epilepsy that left him in pain and confusion. The mood of the story is partly surreal, Kafka-like in its realistic improbability. The story unfolds like a fable in which Ad Magic focuses all of his attention on a white horse, old, dying, obviously in pain, ignored by the tourists and locals of the little hamlet. He pays a doctor to relieve the animal's pain and take care of it, keeping it alive as long as he can. The doctor complies and also gives Ad Magic some pills that relieve his own pain, so that back in his hotel he finds peaceful sleep, remembers his identity, and calls his loving wife. Love for a creature and helping it out of pain has given him the power to find his way back to reality.

her, leaving her somewhat relieved but helpless. The patent absurdity of this story line is counterbalanced by Richard's loving and tender bantering with Susan, perhaps being helped in his therapeutic understanding of her by his own mental battles, won or lost. The two siblings at the end of the story share lunch outside, taking refuge in Richard's car, spinning a dream of a nirvana where there is "perfect health, no wars, no fighting, no discontent."

In the next two stories, "Superman My Son" and "Way Down Deep in the Jungle," the surrealistic mood, that seems patterned on T. Coraghessan Boyle's more flamboyant stories, is dark and ominous. The light of optimism that shines through at the end of each seems forced, ironic. The omniscient narrator is fully engaged with his characters' inner thoughts, taking on the voice of their unconscious minds at times. In "Superman My Son" Blaine, a failing businessman whose material possessions are fading quickly, is visiting his manic-depressive son, Walter. A cousin named Freddy, who is also visiting, bears striking resemblances to several of Jones's protagonists. A doctor just arrived home from Africa, he is an epileptic and has almost gotten arrested for fighting on the homeward-bound plane. The whole family, including Walter's wife, Zona, seem to be on the edge of insanity, except for Blaine. Walter is an adopted son, had been an outstanding athlete in high school, and had miraculously survived a terrible auto accident. Presumably he is the superman of the title, and he is upstairs during the story, where he appears to have been saved by reading a passage from the Bible, a promise that those who take refuge in God will be saved from the "terror of the night." The father-son hug at the end and Blaine's tears seem to be a hollow, sardonic denouement, the reader foreseeing a short-lived hiatus in Walter's desperate condition.

"Way Down Deep in the Jungle" resembles Boyle's story "The Descent of Man," hinting at the analogous relationships between man and brute animal. Jones allows human frailty and capacity to love shine through more warmly. Koestler, the hero, is more fully drawn as a kindly man than any of Boyle's allegorical stick figures. Altruism, especially of the doctors trying to help in the impoverished jungle communities in Africa, is seen as short-lived, fading as the majority fade and burn out, taking refuge in despair and nihilism. The main animal "character" in the story, a baboon named George Babbitt, depends on Dr. Koestler for mood-altering drugs; Koestler avers that his aim is to turn the baboon into a "full Cleveland," a human with all of the idiotic appointments of middle-class, middle American complacency. The doctor's blind affection for the animal is compared to Philip Carey's obsession with the pale Mildred in W. Somerset Maugham's *Of Human*

Bondage (1915). Jones's literary allusions are usually jarring, making the reader feel that they have hidden significance; but they are opaque, not intellectually helpful, yet striking emotional chords. Babbitt, for example, is likened to Faust, having sold his soul to Koestler and his drugs. Koestler disappears into the jungle with a dimming flashlight, much like Joseph Conrad's Marlow looking for the errant Kurtz.

Although Jones seems to be writing some of these stories to satisfy an urge to vary themes and setting, to stretch his fictional world beyond the mundane, his creative imagination allows him to stray far from reality without losing the human touch. "Quicksand," for example, is another story that seems preposterous when summarized, silly in mood and tone; yet, in Jones's execution there is humor, entertainment, and a good measure of real meaning. Ad Magic reappears, this time in Africa; his copywriting has reaped huge benefits for the charitable food fund Global Aid. His direct-mail promotional letters have stirred the "donor-weary" philanthropists to part with their charitable contributions. In a state of agony, with dysentery, malaria, a broken thumb, and the dementia that accompanies such horrors, he meets a fantasy-realization, a beautiful woman doctor who admires his letters and wants to relax and cure him, to sleep with him, and to flatter his writing and other abilities. The Pastor and other comical characterizations, satirical dialogue, and explicit sex help Jones wryly express the same message as in the other Africa stories: altruism wearies the mind and spirit.

"Ooh, Baby, Baby" continues with this theme, using another exhausted doctor, Galen, a former volunteer worker in Africa who gave up charitable work for a lucrative practice in cosmetic surgery in California. He is first introduced in a traffic jam. He is a diabetic, and his low blood sugar has caused him to be in a rage that almost leads to an altercation with a policeman; his girlfriend, Linda, is also fast losing patience with him. In moments of silent thinking during the traffic jam and the labored sex with Linda afterward, he goes over his experiences in Africa: his saving the life of a boy, then financing this boy's education; his souring attitude about the comfortable but continually dependent boy; and the emptiness of his medical work since then. In the end he welcomes the death from a heart attack that releases him from his empty life. Jones's style in this story is straightforward, his tone whimsically ironic, and his theme is a questioning analysis of the commitment of doctors to do the work most needed from them. Galen is seen more as a man than a caricature or freak, and his surrender to reality is more believable and more readily understood than in other stories.

Jones is effective with the first-person narrative technique, and he uses it in different ways to delineate

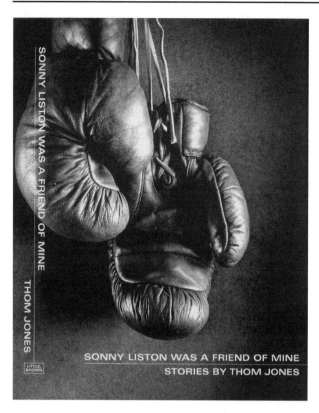

Dust jacket for Jones's 1999 book, in which the title story is one of several for which Jones drew on his experiences as an amateur boxer

character. In "I Need a Man to Love Me" he is describing the protagonist, who has muscular dystrophy, but characterizing the narrator at the same time:

> She was not Stephen Hawking yet, or like that guy with the left foot, Christy Brown, but close. That's why she liked to keep everything about her the same—the environment the same. . . . The doors and windows were now secured with metal bars, a little crack action down on the corner, but hey!—that's New Orleans for y'all.

Jones's narrative persona is "hip" and knows the lower-working class, yet has more than a touch of literary allusions that make him seem bright and well-read, if not well-educated. The illusion he can create with this technique becomes part of enjoying and getting the point of the story. The woman in this story becomes another of Jones's prisoners, fighting off the tragedy of life, using all the drugs and medications that can stave off the final drop into death.

"Dynamite Hands" is the last story and the weakest in the collection. Once again Jones uses boxing as the backdrop, and this time the story is told by Angel, a Chicano journeyman fighter. The familiar themes are forced into play with little detailed development.

Johnny meets a bear on one of his roadwork runs and contemplates the peace that could come with death; Chester, a gym rat since the narrator caught him with a blow that caused temporal lobe epilepsy, is bested in the ring by a walk-in nobody; both Johnny and the narrator reach that state of mind where they feel "in the zone," invincible and filled with supernal energy. The reader and the critics are left with hopes that the next collection will maintain a more consistent level of excellence. Akin to the "outtakes" at the end of some movies, the acknowledgments following *Cold Snap* offer another look at Jones's irreverent and eccentric style and wit. He thanks members of his family, his editors, friends, and teachers, but includes a nod of gratitude to the specific pharmaceutical companies for "further expanding that narrow channel of joy by manufacturing Effexor and Elavil; drugs so good they feel illegal. Thanks to my dog Shelby who also makes me feel pretty good."

The appearance of the short story "Sonny Liston Was a Friend of Mine" in the 17 November 1997 issue of *The New Yorker* signaled Jones's return to telling his stories of warriors and prizefighters. It became the title story and opens his 1999 collection, a more human, personal, and real body of work than all his previous stories. The book was received with more praise and with fewer reservations by the critics. In the Sunday *New York Times* review (14 March 1999) Dwight Garner pointed out that the humor in several stories in *Sonny Liston Was a Friend of Mine* "comes out of nowhere and knocks you silly." He also claimed that Jones's war writing is as good as any in American literature. Simon Carnell, writing in *The London Sunday Times* (28 March 1999) also praised his wit and inventiveness. Bruce Culp in *The Montreal Gazette* (15 May 1999) lauded the stories as unabashedly entertaining, for all their morbidity and violence. Yet, according to most, the same shortcomings persist: the lack of focus in the longer stories, the stereotyped roles given to his women, and the frenzy of his narrative.

The title story is another semi-autobiographical coming-of-age story. The protagonist is Kid Dynamite, who is being raised by his mother and her husband, Frank, a steady smoker suffering from cancer. The omniscient narrator has a markedly different tone in this story, a milder, more gentle one, unusual in Jones's stories. As a result, the mood of the story is less frenetic, more controlled, more like a piece of "young adult" fiction, but with a more ominous sense of urgency.

The story line is trite: the Kid hates his stepfather, who is always criticizing him and making raucous love to his mother in the next room. Motivated by the example and wishes of his absent father, hospitalized for mental problems probably caused by his own boxing career, Kid Dynamite fights in his final tournament for revenge, love, and a raft of reasons unexplainable on the surface. Jones takes this threadbare narrative, however, and transforms these ordinary ideas into the same drama as in all his combat tales. His style is deceivingly straightforward, with little or none of the profanity or scatological language some critics have charged to his macho rantings. The boy is honest and frank, troubled but trying to sort out his problems, and Jones makes a story that could explain his older heroes' wasted lives. They too are tortured by the crass incompetence of people in charge, faced with a life that seems impossible without witnessing violence and injustice. The title of the story comes from a visit the Kid makes to Sonny Liston's training gym. He is awed by Liston's strength, speed, and assurance, and he accepts an autographed picture from the champion. The reader wonders how the boy felt later on when this invincible hero was "knocked out" by a phantom blow by a more marketable heavyweight in a fight almost certainly rigged. The Kid is coming of age, but into a troubled world.

If the reader could imagine the Kid grown and enlisted in the Marines, the next two stories (which read more like one story with two parts) show the world he has inherited. The naive but tough young Marine who acts as narrator of "The Roadrunner" and "A Run Through the Jungle" tells of a rowdy group in boot camp coming home from a night of drunken fighting and whoring in the first story. A roadrunner is spotted and captured by one recruit and the rest try to help it. Felix, a hapless and wild Marine, finally burns the bird to death, shocking even his hardened buddies. In the second story, the same men, now in Vietnam as a reconnaissance group, make a fierce foray into enemy territory to assassinate an important enemy general. The mission is a success and all are returning to base when Felix trips and is burned to death by his own phosphorous grenade.

Ondine, a familiar character in many of the war stories, is the narrator in "Fields of Purple Forever." In this piece he is out of the fray and swimming all over the world, especially in dangerous stretches of water, alone. The story is another unsuccessful attempt by Jones to use a narrator too distant from his own background and experience. The story covers the same thematic ground as most of the war and boxing stories, and it suffers from the same problem critics point out frequently in his work: how could a character of so little education possibly be making the literary and philosophical allusions that Ondine makes? Finally, it seems, Jones is making clear that verisimilitude is not his goal; having a "grunt" use the ideas and words of great thinkers to express what in real life is pent up within them is worth the attempt.

Jones said in an interview with Amazon.com that the story "40, Still at Home" is based closely on the life of his brother. His mother complained about this invasion of the family's privacy, as she did with others of his stories, especially "Sonny Liston Was a Friend of Mine." His brother, on the other hand, wanted copies of the story to show to friends. The omniscient narrator delves into the conscious and unconscious mind of the protagonist, Matthew, and the result is a revealing peek at a Jones character untouched by any of the life-threatening experiences the evil world can provide. The idle Matthew, scorning the world that treated him so badly, finds evil on his own, resorting to stealing his mother's medication to get the high he needs. The "whole game of existence" becomes clear to him; he feels bliss and realizes that love is the answer. The reader sees Matthew's callow euphoric glow as empty, a trick of the drugs, not the hard-earned wisdom that can only come from experience, a wisdom that Jones's other protagonists have at least partially won.

"Tarantula," like "Silhouettes," is taken from Jones's experiences as a janitor in a high school. The story is a harrowing and hilarious chronicling of a vice principal's career demise at the hands of a scheming and vengeful alcoholic janitor. The idealistic and dreamy Hammermeister is no match for the flush-faced Duffy and the crew of janitorial realists. Although the high-minded administrator, whose forte is discipline, keeps a tarantula caged on his desk to remind adolescent miscreants of the harsh nature of his rule-keeping, Duffy is the one who exemplifies the Machiavellian ferocity of a threatened underdog. As Hammermeister walks alone in the all-black neighborhood around the high school that just fired him, the reader sees again the futility of the idealist, afraid of reality, a stranger in it really, wandering lonely and disabused.

Even more Darwinian in philosophy is "Mouses," in which an out-of-work engineer experiments with mice he has captured in his apartment. He gains some affection for them as he keeps them alive, but he begins hormone experiments on them and ends killing them all. The parallel of his own career, looking for work where there is not any—and being turned down, he suspects, just because of his diminutive stature—is all too obvious, another forced metaphor that does not move the reader or satisfy intellectually. The humor, though, is silly but sidesplitting.

Humor does more than just entertain in "A Midnight Clear"; it is the theme and raison d'être of the story. A doctor, Freddy, drives his stepmother to make a Christmas visit to their cousin Eustace in a mental hospital. Freddy's bitter wit energizes the visit, exposing and criticizing the emptiness and hypocrisy of the mental health establishment, the feasibility of institutionalizing mental patients, and any meaning one could ascribe to life in general outside the love shown to one another on a zany Christmas visit. This story is a summary of all of the psychiatric and medical stories he has written so far. Like Freddy, Jones takes solace only in the tonics of humor and goodwill. In "My Heroic Mythic Journey," one of the last in *Sonny Liston Was a Friend of Mine,* the narrator/protagonist summarizes the boxing stories in Jones's work to date. After rising and falling in the fight game, he says to his detractors:

> He didn't know nothing. He didn't know better.
> I knew better. I knew myself. I experienced clarity. It's just that it's gone now, and it's not going to come back.

Before the last story in the collection, which is close to a novella in length, Jones puts in a grisly story that appears to be antithetical to the title story in plot and theme. In "I Love You Sophie Western" Frankie is the young protagonist pitted against all the adolescent problems that the Kid battled. He loses a fight in the street over a girl, is humiliated, and is then co-opted into performing fellatio on a weird movie projectionist who promises money to help Frankie purchase a car to attract girls.

"You Lied, You Cheated" is the last story in the collection, and it is unusual in its lack of typical Jones themes: no war, little boxing, but a great deal of sex, some of it explicit. A character named Molly Bloom recalls James Joyce's, and this Molly just as much a symbol of the libido as a life force. William O. Smith, the narrator, is waiting in the doctor's office, a notoriously long wait in a small town outside Chicago. He is reading Schopenhauer to pass the time when Molly Bloom walks in. The rest of the story is a fantasy. Molly flirts with William, as she does with everyone, and soon the young couple is launched on an adventure to Hawaii, filled with almost nonstop sex, some of it blissful, some violent and irascible. Soon William discovers that Molly and the sexual dreams and beauty represented can only be illusory, whether lived in reality or fantasy, just another "decoy," he thinks to himself. So the boy, pulled from his Schopenhauer by the temptations to joy that can pull any boy back from depression, finds himself back in reality. The local doctor for whom he had been waiting scolds him for taking a temporary leave and advises him, "You go on. You ride it out. You have a lot of hidden strength in you. . . . A person can't control how he feels, but he can control what he does. Do right and your life will work out for you."

Perhaps this last story is the precursor of the novel that is promised from Jones. The length, the complexity, the explicit sex, and seemingly endless possibilities for development make it unlike his short stories so far. Although violence and revenge are there, they are not center stage. One could say that the story shows that Jones is listening to his critics, but that seems doubtful. More certainly, it is clear that he is maturing as a writer.

Interviews:

Mary Park, "Assault with a Deadly Weapon," *Literature and Fiction@Amazon.com* (January 1999) <www.amazon.com/exec/obidos/tg/feature/=/10335|107-8528159-4339727>;

Jim Schumock, "Thom Jones," in *Story, Story, Story: Conversations with American Authors,* edited by Schumock (Seattle: Black Heron, 1999), pp. 248–267.

William Kittredge

(14 August 1932 –   )

Norma Tilden
Georgetown University

See also the Kittredge entry in *DLB 212: Twentieth-Century American Western Writers, Second Series.*

BOOKS: *The Van Gogh Field and Other Stories* (Columbia: University of Missouri Press, 1978);

Cord, by Kittredge and Steven M. Krauzer, as Owen Rountree (New York: Ballantine, 1982);

Cord: The Nevada War, by Kittredge and Krauzer, as Rountree (New York: Ballantine, 1982);

Cord: Black Hills Duel, by Kittredge and Krauzer, as Rountree (New York: Ballantine, 1983);

Cord: Gunman Winter, by Kittredge and Krauzer, as Rountree (New York: Ballantine, 1983);

We Are Not in This Together: Stories, edited by Raymond Carver (Port Townsend, Wash.: Graywolf, 1984);

Cord: Hunt the Man Down, by Kittredge and Krauzer, as Rountree (New York: Ballantine, 1984);

Cord: King of Colorado, by Kittredge and Krauzer, as Rountree (New York: Ballantine, 1984);

Cord: Gunsmoke River, by Kittredge and Krauzer, as Rountree (New York: Ballantine, 1985);

Cord: Brimstone Valley, by Kittredge and Krauzer, as Rountree (New York: Ballantine, 1986);

Cord: Paradise Valley, by Kittredge and Krauzer, as Rountree (New York: Ballantine, 1986);

Owning It All: Essays (St. Paul, Minn.: Graywolf, 1987);

Phantom Silver (Missoula, Mont.: Kutenai, 1987);

Hole in the Sky: A Memoir (New York: Knopf, 1992);

Lost Cowboys (But Not Forgotten) (New York: Whitney Museum, 1992);

Who Owns the West? (San Francisco: Mercury House, 1996);

Taking Care: Thoughts on Storytelling and Belief (Minneapolis, Minn.: Milkweed Editions, 1999);

The Nature of Generosity (New York: Knopf, 2000).

PRODUCED SCRIPT: *Heartland,* motion picture, additional scenes and dialogue, Wilderness Women, 1979.

William Kittredge (photograph from the cover for Owning It All, *1987)*

OTHER: *Great Action Stories,* edited by Kittredge and Steven M. Krauzer (New York: New American Library, 1977);

The Great American Detective, edited by Kittredge and Krauzer (New York: New American Library / London: New English Library, 1978);

Stories into Film, edited by Kittredge and Krauzer (New York: Harper & Row, 1979);

TriQuarterly, special contemporary Western fiction issue, edited by Kittredge and Krauzer (Spring 1980);

"Stoneboat," in *The Available Press/PEN Short Story Collection,* edited by Anne Tyler (New York: Ballantine, 1985);

"Agriculture," in *The Pushcart Prize Ten: Best of the Small Presses,* edited by Bill Henderson (Wainscott, N.Y.: Pushcart, 1985), pp. 215–223;

The Last Best Place: A Montana Anthology, edited by Kittredge and Annick Smith (Helena: Montana Historical Society Press, 1988; Seattle: University of Washington Press, 1991);

Montana Spaces: Essays and Photographs in Celebration of Montana, edited by Kittredge, photographs by John Smart (New York: Nick Lyons, 1988);

"Phantom Silver," in *Graywolf Annual Four: Short Stories by Men,* edited by Scott Walker (St. Buli: Graywolf, 1988);

R. M. Rylatt, *Surveying the Canadian Pacific: Memoir of a Railroad Pioneer,* foreword by Kittredge (Salt Lake City: University of Utah Press, 1991);

The Best of the West 5: New Stories from the Wide Side of the Missouri, edited by James and Denise Thomas, introduction by Kittredge (New York: Norton, 1992);

"Three Dollar Dogs," in *Fathers and Sons,* edited by David Seybold (New York: Grove, 1992), pp. 91–97;

A. B. Guthrie Jr., *Murders at Moon Dance,* introduction by Kittredge (Lincoln: University of Nebraska Press, 1993);

"Looking Glass," in *Listening to Ourselves,* edited by Alan Cheuse and Caroline Marshall (New York: Anchor, 1994), pp. 113–118;

The WPA Guide to 1930s Montana, foreword by Kittredge (Tucson: University of Arizona Press, 1994);

The Portable Western Reader, edited, with an introduction, by Kittredge (New York: Penguin, 1997);

"Thirty-Four Seasons of Winter," in *The Workshop: Seven Decades of Fiction from the Iowa Writers' Workshop,* edited by Tom Grimes (New York: Hyperion Press, 1999);

Balancing Water: Restoring the Klamath Basin, photography by Tupper Ansel Blake and Madeleine Graham Blake, text by Kittredge (Berkeley: University of California Press, 2000).

SELECTED PERIODICAL PUBLICATIONS–
UNCOLLECTED: "Performing Arts," *TriQuarterly,* 48 (Spring 1980): 144–165;

"Balancing Water," *Paris Review,* 104 (Fall 1987): 14–27;

"Be Careful What You Want," *Paris Review,* 97 (Fall 1985): 192–214;

"Do You Hear Your Mother Talking?" *Harper's,* 282 (February 1991): 62–69.

"Give some people the world," complains a stubborn old rancher in William Kittredge's story "Flight" (in *We Are Not in This Together: Stories,* 1984), "and they wouldn't use it as nothing more than a place to read books." Despite Kittredge's prolific contributions to the world of books as essayist, memoirist, short-story writer, editor, and teacher, his character's words underscore the dual allegiance to literary art and the living world that distinguishes his career. Few writers have worked harder to make a connection between books and the "world," and few practitioners of the short story have done more to frame and defend an activist theory of storytelling.

Kittredge has been unusually open in describing his development as a writer, re-examining his practices and beliefs in such nonfiction works as *Hole in the Sky: A Memoir* (1992), *Who Owns the West?* (1996), and *Taking Care: Thoughts on Storytelling and Belief* (1999). In discussing the writing life, Kittredge consistently attaches to stories words such as *useful, sustaining,* and *cautionary.* Kittredge claims importance for stories as "consoling agents" and "mythologies" that readers "inhabit." In *Taking Care* Kittredge articulated what Scott Slovic described as "first and foremost . . . the 'credo' of a storyteller." To trace Kittredge's life as a writer is, at the same time, to track his evolving belief in the power of stories to shape and reshape community.

In his essay collection *Who Owns the West?* Kittredge explores the connection between stories, both fictive and nonfictive, and the complexities of what he calls the "actual." He suggests that "stories, when they are most valuable, are utterly open in their willingness to make metaphor from our personal difficulties." Having connected the writer's life and the written story, Kittredge then frames a tribute to Raymond Carver's stories as "masterworks of usefulness," which could also serve as an apology for the genre itself: "they lead us to imagine what it is like to be another person, which is the way we learn compassion. . . . Nothing could be more political." In the epilogue to *Who Owns the West?* Kittredge develops this idea into the essay "Doing Good Work Together: The Politics of Storytelling": "We figure and find stories, which can be thought of as maps or paradigms in which we see our purposes defined." These two activities–finding stories and "figuring" them–suggest the powerful social and political impulse from which Kittredge writes. Stories, he believes, do vitally important work; they have the capacity to "drive us to the arts of empathy, for each other and the world."

William Alfred "Bill" Kittredge was born on 14 August 1932 in Portland, Oregon, the oldest of three children of Josephine Miessner and Oscar Franklin Kittredge. The Kittredge family traces its American ancestry to an English sea captain, John Kittredge, who settled in Massachusetts in 1660; their migration westward began in 1826 when Dr. William Kittredge traveled with his wife to Michigan. Two years later, Kittredge's great-grandfather, Benjamin Franklin Kittredge, was born. By the time he was twenty-two, in 1850, he was heading westward for the first of two disappointing ventures in the goldfields. In 1875, while Benjamin Franklin was teaching school near Yakima, Washington, Kittredge's grandfather and namesake was born, a person Kittredge describes as "the most powerful figure" in his early life. By 1911 Kittredge's grandfather had begun accumulating property in the salt-grass meadowlands around Silver Lake, in southeastern Oregon, a landscape that figures prominently in his grandson's essays and stories. In 1937, when Kittredge was five years old, his grandfather bought the MC Ranch in the Warner Valley near Lakeview, Oregon. Kittredge's father and the family joined him in what eventually became a huge agribusiness, raising cattle and grain. Early in 1938 Kittredge contracted polio, from which he recovered completely, but his convalescence gave him time alone to explore his new territory, wandering the valley "like a small stalking beast" before he started school in nearby Adel.

In the 1993 introduction to A. B. Guthrie Jr.'s *Murders at Moon Dance,* Kittredge stated that his first impulse to write came at sixteen, when he read Guthrie's *The Big Sky* (1947) and discovered "that the place where I lived *had* a history, which connected to larger stories." Throughout his writings, Kittredge returns to the people and places of Warner Valley, which he described as the "main staging ground for my imagination." Most of his stories center on a rural American life of small towns and big distances, many set in what Kittredge calls "our outback," the landlocked deserts and oasis valleys of southeastern Oregon, where he grew up. Some of the later stories are set in and around western Montana, where Kittredge has lived and taught since 1969. His working-class characters earn their money in the sorts of jobs that such places offer: driving combines, collecting garbage, breaking horses, cutting timber, and tending bar. Many characters parallel people from Kittredge's early life: old men like his grandfather, who derive their identity from owning property; farmers and ranchers like his younger self, working hard while trying to distance themselves from some trouble that keeps them drinking and running the roads at night; and a series of enigmatic, strong women who seem to know more than men, but keep their wisdom to themselves. In the historical fictions, readers encounter the ancestors of these people, enacting the sometimes violent individualism at the heart of the Western myth.

In the introduction to Kittredge's second collection, *We Are Not in This Together,* Carver described Kittredge's characters as "light-years away from the

American dream." Still, these stragglers have dreams of their own, poignantly revealed in what they say and do. Through rough words and clumsy gestures, Kittredge's people unwittingly act out deep-seated mythologies that are telling them how to live. What community they enjoy is found in bars, cars, and hotels, or sometimes in a house surrounded by isolating distances where the male protagonists live out what Carver calls "a certain terrible kind of domesticity." A Kittredge story is always rooted in a place, and that place is insolubly wedded to the people and events that unfold.

While his father and grandfather transformed the Warner Valley properties into an agricultural empire, Kittredge set off in 1949 for Oregon State University in Corvallis, where he majored in agriculture. Early in 1951 he met his first wife, Janet, also a Corvallis student; by December they were married. Both were nineteen.

In college Kittredge discovered writers such as Henry David Thoreau and Walt Whitman, who "began rural" and "made lives as writers." More important, he discovered Ernest Hemingway, whose "Big Two-Hearted River" (*This Quarter,* May 1925) invoked landscapes similar to those of his own childhood. Kittredge most admired Hemingway's "ringing accuracy." Kittredge's reading prompted him to enroll in a creative-writing class with Bernard Malamud, who had just published *The Natural* (1952) and was then teaching at Oregon State. Malamud "hooked me, him and Hemingway," Kittredge said in his memoir. At first, though, he balked at his teacher's advice. Malamud stressed to his students the importance of writing a story that "turned on recognitions, moments of enlightenment," but Kittredge found the notion "utterly false." Resisting Malamud's insistence on change as the essential mechanism of plot, Kittredge was determined to document timeless moments. He calls his early attempts "anecdotal celebrations." Remembering the familiar stories he had heard among ranch hands in the cookhouse, he wrote descriptive vignettes about people "doing what they always did," rooted in age-old rituals of life in his part of the West. Thus began a continuing and productive tension between two strains in Kittredge's fiction: on one hand, an elegiac celebration of a lost way of life, lived in intimate connection to land and animals; and on the other, a sad critique of the cost, to nature and community, of the worn-out pastoral mythology that supported this traditional culture.

In a 1989 interview with Gregory L. Morris (published in 1994), Kittredge provided a frank and self-critical summary of his early forays into fiction writing. He confesses that by the time he graduated from Oregon State he was gripped by "that idea of being a writer." In *Hole in the Sky* he speculates briefly on the motives

Pat, Roberta, and William Kittredge during their childhood in the Warner Valley of Oregon (courtesy of the author)

behind this unlikely career choice: "Maybe I wanted a world in which I was the one who made things up." Immediately, though, he rejects this explanation as too simple and focuses instead on "poor lost Hemingway," who first gave him the sense that storytelling might be a "useful thing to do."

Immediately following his graduation from Oregon State in December of 1953, Kittredge joined the U.S. Air Force, where he was trained in photographic intelligence. He served four years, moving with his growing family from Colorado to California to Guam. His daughter, Karen, was born in 1954 and his son, Bradley, two years later. Near the end of Kittredge's tour in Guam, his family in Oregon began to break apart. Kittredge's grandfather had broken with his father, who was no longer working at the ranch, and his parents divorced. Following his discharge, Kittredge and his young family returned to Warner Valley where, after his grandfather's death in 1958, he became "farming boss," managing the grain camp that had been his father's main project. He did this work for eight years, at first loving it as "craftsmanlike," but finally driven to

"craziness" as he agonized over the human and environmental costs of industrial farming. In his memoir Kittredge marks the return to Warner as "a grand turning point in my life, and a mistake that cost me a decade."

Despite his growing responsibilities, Kittredge did not abandon the idea of being a writer. During the air-force years he had completed a novel that he dismissed, in his interview with Morris, as "terrifically silly." In *Taking Care* Kittredge described the moment when years of "slowly accumulating intention" became resolve: "On the day after Thanksgiving in 1964, hungover and thirty-two years old, I sat down and told myself that I would write each day, giving it a lifetime of effort whether it worked or not." He wrote early in the morning before going off to run the grain camp. After eight or nine months of this regimen, Kittredge dug up the once-abandoned novel and "made a short story out of it." This piece was his first published fiction, "Society of Eros," which appeared in *Northwest Review* (1965/1966). The initial foray into short fiction was followed immediately by "The Waterfowl Tree" (*Northwest Review,* 1966/1967), one of his best stories and later the lead piece in his second volume of fiction, *We Are Not in This Together.*

In a succession of autobiographical essays and books, Kittredge has retraced the series of "crimes" against the natural world that brought about the decline of the MC Ranch. In *Taking Care* Kittredge connects that bleak vision to the stories he was writing at that time: "I saw no dynamic working in the world except for the one in which people were ruined by time, which I took to be the master story of all creation." Kittredge's second published story, "The Waterfowl Tree," shows him tracing the arc of that "master story," witnessing the ruinous effects of time on his own family and region. Like most Kittredge stories, this one grows out of real incidents, in this case an occasion when Kittredge's father, after suffering a stroke that left him partially disabled, revisited the Warner Valley in order to go duck hunting with a friend. Kittredge and his father's friend tried to follow through on this longstanding ritual, but ended up just standing in the swamp, marveling at the fifty thousand birds they found there. "It would have been like shooting off your shotgun in a cathedral," Kittredge told Morris, so they "turned around and walked out."

The autobiographical incident remains central to the finished story, echoed in the underlying trope of a father returning to a familiar landscape to hunt waterbirds, although the son in the story is a seventeen-year-old boy and the father a widower who is "long estranged from this remote and misted valley of his childhood." At first glance, the story seems indebted to the initiation stories of Hemingway and William Faulkner: a boy on the verge of manhood accompanies his father on a trip to the father's childhood home for a hunt, freighted with ritual significance. Like other initiation stories, this one has a mysterious woman at its edges–Eva, a "gentle" farm woman who is involved with the father–as well as a trusty male companion, Charlie Anderson, the father's hunting partner "from the old days." Kittredge focuses on the boy as he tries to understand "the different man his father had become" in this place. As they huddle among the reeds, waiting for the birds to regroup, wheel, and drop in their great formations, the father recalls other days of hunting, especially one afternoon when he and Charlie, both fourteen years old, killed 150 water birds. "I guess that was the best day, the tops in my life," the father remembers. The boy invokes the master story when he wonders: "Had everything been downhill since?"

True to the Hemingway model, the foray into wild nature involves sexual awakening and violent death. Ultimately, though, Kittredge's concern is less with the boy's progression to manhood than with his awakening to the complex, ethical responsibilities of caring for the material world. Kittredge uses the emblematic image of the title, a tree hung with the frozen remains of dozens of geese and ducks, to lift the story out of the familiar naturalistic obsession with time and ruin. Mary Clearman Blew cited the first version of "The Waterfowl Tree" to show that as early as 1966, Kittredge was addressing what became his central theme: "human alienation from the natural world and its consequence in alienation of feelings." Kittredge reinforces this reading in *Hole in the Sky* when he recounts a second duck-hunting incident from his ranch days, an afternoon when his father, "like a crown prince of shotgunning," dropped more than a hundred ducks for an Elks Club feed. After describing an old crabapple tree hung with frozen waterbirds, Kittredge reflects on the "style of going at the world" that he learned from such incidents and considers his family's complicity in "a long string of crimes" against nature. In "The Waterfowl Tree," Kittredge transforms the image into a narrative meditation on this theme. Near the center of the story, as the boy helps his father twist the necks of the dead birds to tie them into bunches, Kittredge weaves conflicting emotions into a wrenching, two-hearted moment: "They were heavy and beautiful birds and the boy twisted their necks the way his father did and felt sorry that they could not have lived and yet was glad that they were dead. They were trophies of this world, soft and heavy and dead birds."

Near the end of his ranching career, Kittredge's life, too, seemed to be following the curve of that pessimistic master story. By 1967 the family was selling the ranch; Kittredge's marriage was over; and Janet had moved to California with the children. By late summer he met Patricia, who became his second wife in spring 1968. Eventually, Kittredge came to see this period as a "clean break" that gave him the courage to pursue a different course. In the spring of 1968 he and Patricia moved to Eugene, where he studied creative writing at the University of Oregon for one semester, and by late summer they were driving east toward the Iowa Writers' Workshop. When Kittredge completed his M.F.A. in the fall of 1969, he accepted an offer to join the English department of the University of Montana. He and his wife moved to Missoula, where he taught for almost thirty years. In the fall of 1973 he left for a year at Stanford on a Stegner writing fellowship. When he returned to Missoula, the marriage ended.

At Iowa Kittredge had worked with Richard Yates and Robert Coover at a time when there was a great deal of interest in reinventing narrative. He began to explore the possibility of a master story grounded in responsibility. In the interview with Morris, Kittredge observed that while the then-fashionable idea of a "self-reflexive narrator" would probably prove a short-lived phenomenon, a more lasting process of "reinvention" was also under way–one that stressed the power of personal voice in storytelling and the impulse to "have some say about your culture, about your part of the world." In a Coover class called "Exemplary Ancient Fictions," Kittredge was drawn toward the role of fictions in critiquing and reinventing cultural mythologies.

The mandate to shape new narratives out of worn-out traditions figures strongly in some of the stories in Kittredge's first collection and received a boost in the mid 1970s, after Kittredge had returned from Stanford. In *Who Owns the West?* he describes how in the summer of 1976, "defeated and drinking the days away," he "drifted down" to Sun Valley, Idaho, for an academic conference on Western movies, along with fellow writers James Crumley and Steven M. Krauzer. At the conference he found "serious people talking about the prime mythology of my homeland." Kittredge marks this event as a turning point in his career, the beginning of his education in the political ideology of the West: "I was on my way toward being able to name my story, which is to say, my work." Kittredge had found his theme in the seductions of the Western myth and the need to fashion an alternative story.

This sense of purpose revitalized his fiction, resulting in stories such as "Phantom Silver," first published in 1977 in the *Iowa Review* and republished in 1987 in a limited edition chapbook of 150 copies. Coover, who had encouraged his Iowa students to examine and reinvent their "exemplary fictions," edited a special issue of the *Iowa Review* on the theme of American mythologies. Kittredge's "Phantom Silver" appears in the section titled "Dreamtime U. S. A.: Confrontations with American Myth." Kittredge locates the story within the confrontational, deconstructive framework suggested by the section title. Speaking to Morris, he described "Phantom Silver" as an effort to turn the Lone Ranger myth "back on itself" in order to say: "this mythology, however useful it may have been fifty or a hundred years ago to a people who were intent on conquering a part of the world, isn't even useful anymore, it's destructive."

"Phantom Silver" opens with a dreamy image from the old television show: a "great white horse" rearing above the horizon, "golden and simple in the sunset." In its familiarity the image reminds us of the universal appeal of the Lone Ranger romance; but the picture soon fades, and "we are left in that dreamed yesteryear" as the Lone Ranger rides away. Immediately, Kittredge begins to humanize the myth by constructing a life for the masked man before and after he rode with Tonto. This expanded focus reaches behind the myth to uncover whatever secret desires might have created the demand "to be austere and distant if you were to be great and right." The narrative also presses forward to the end of the trail. The narrator asks, "Could there have been a mortal family" behind such a mythic figure? Then he answers, "Of course." The rest of the story explores a tangled course of all-too-mortal troubles in an ordinary family, a fiction that intersects powerfully with facts of Western history. Like all Kittredge's stories, "Phantom Silver" gains power from his willingness to confront both sides of the questions he raises, including, in this case, both the dangers and the appeal of the seductive simplicities that foster such a myth.

The years following the Stegner Fellowship and the Sun Valley conference were decisive for Kittredge's career. Back in Missoula, he taught a course on Western movies that reconfirmed the pervasive presence of the myth of conquest in popular culture. With Krauzer he edited a series of collections of well-known stories: *Great Action Stories* (1977), *The Great American Detective* (1978), and *Stories into Film* (1979). In the spring of 1980 Kittredge and Krauzer edited a special issue on contemporary Western fiction for the journal *TriQuarterly* (Spring 1980). Their introductory essay, "Writers of the New West," probes the double burden of a generation of Western writers "cut loose" from the simplicities of the old mythology while trying to repossess their actual lives in the West. The collaboration with Krauzer then moved into writing popular fiction. Between 1982 and 1986 Kittredge and Krauzer wrote the "Cord" series of nine genre Westerns under the pseudonym "Owen Rountree." Kittredge claims that these formula Westerns represented, in part, an attempt to pose an alternative and feminist reading of Western myth. Still, despite

their subversive intent, the novels were "never read that subtly" and were "thin as gauze."

During these years Kittredge also began a personal and professional relationship with Montana writer and motion-picture producer Annick Smith, whom he consistently describes as "the luck of my later life." Since 1978, when Kittredge served as consultant to Smith and her partner, Beth Ferris, on the script of the movie *Heartland,* Kittredge and Smith have worked together on many motion-picture projects. In addition, an anthology they edited, *The Last Best Place: A Montana Anthology* (1988), has established them as respected and effective champions for the many literary voices of their region.

Early in 1979 another push toward refining an ethical and political mission for writing came from editor Terry McDonnel, who was putting together the new *Rocky Mountain Magazine* and asked Kittredge to write an essay for it. Kittredge claims that he did not know how and that McDonnel walked him through the basic process over the phone. The result was Kittredge's classic essay "Redneck Secrets" and the start of a career as author of some one hundred essays. In *Taking Care* Kittredge described the approach he learned from McDonnel in terms that reveal how his "stories," whether short fiction or essays, are shaped by similar techniques. "What he wanted," Kittredge said, "was a series of scenes in what constituted an emotional progression, witnessed by a figure . . . who is trying to fathom their meaning." McDonnel called for an essay beginning in real experience but ultimately "gesturing toward social implications." His advice remains a fair description of Kittredge's artistry as both essayist and fiction writer.

Kittredge's first collection of short fiction, *The Van Gogh Field and Other Stories,* was published in 1978. In the jacket notes he said of the two narrative strains at work in these eight stories: "I try to operate in the interface between myth and reality, sometimes overtly dealing with the mythological, at times trying to render life in a quiet, realistic manner." In certain of the stories—especially "The Mercy of the Elements" and "The Stone Corral"—he experiments with refiguring Western myth and history, at times approaching an American version of magical realism. Others, such as "Thirty-four Seasons of Winter" and "The Van Gogh Field," come closer to what Kittredge describes as the "social story": quietly realistic renderings of ordinary people doing the best they can and then living out the consequences. Of the remaining stories, "The Underground River" and "The Soap Bear" most successfully enact the social/metaphysical "interface" to which Kittredge alluded in the jacket notes and in his conversation with Morris.

In *Taking Care,* when Kittredge revisits his reasons for leaving the family ranch, he speaks of the sorrow of entering rooms in the bunkhouse where "old working men were dead" and the horror of having "to acknowledge the degree to which they had been used and abandoned." In different ways the specters of these old men haunt the first two stories of *The Van Gogh Field*. In the possibly autobiographical title story, Robert Onnter, a fugitive from some crippling "stasis" in his life, gazes at a Vincent van Gogh self-portrait in the Chicago Art Institute, "trying to see through" the portrait, as if it holds some secret. The van Gogh landscapes remind Onnter of the wheat-field prints his mother had cherished back in their home in the Oregon valley. They evoke memories of childhood trips into the fields to look at the ripening crop, especially a particular field of barley that she had named "the van Gogh field." Onnter's museum visits are intercut with a series of meetings with a woman with whom he is having a casual affair. The more-important encounters emerge from his visits to the self-portrait, which finally returns him to memories of Clyman Teal, an old man who worked at harvesting the family's van Gogh fields until he died on the job.

The second story, "Breaker of Horses," also reads as homage to a life lived in harmony with the processes of the natural world. As is often the case, Kittredge shapes an act of imaginative empathy with a character who faces death. In the spring of his eightieth year, Jules Russel, a horse breaker, suffers a stroke and wakes "to immobility, muteness, blindness" in his isolated cabin, "imprisoned to await cessation like a living rodent within the darkness of a snake's digesting length." Through an extended interior monologue, Kittredge probes Jules's surprising discovery that even at this extreme moment, consciousness of death is supplanted by "habitual concerns" and reveries of a life lived within what Kittredge elsewhere calls a "horse culture." Within that culture, a man "had to die on horseback and working" to inspire ceremonies. Jules, who has outlived his usefulness, recalls the long-ago burial of Ambrose Vega, who died working. Although the story is darkly naturalistic, the dying Jules finds some pride in his intimate knowledge of animals "gentled firmly and slowly." He remembers reading the *Iliad* as a child, where Hector is eulogized as "a breaker of horses." Kittredge's story serves as the eulogy that Jules thought he had outlived.

"Thirty-four Seasons of Winter," first published in *Quarry* in 1972 and included in both short-story collections, has also been anthologized in *The Workshop: Seven Decades of Fiction from the Iowa Writers' Workshop* (1999), where Kittredge introduces it as an example of "the way stories, at least for me, were always going to figure themselves out." He describes how this piece, an early story begun while he was still on the ranch, grew

out of an "emblematic" childhood memory of two boxers battering one another in "the fights" at the Klamath Falls Armory. Not until he was working with Yates at Iowa was Kittredge able to stop reworking the episodes and consider the story "as finished as it's going to get." He came to realize that for him, plot would never be a matter of "thinking it through." Rather, "events had to be felt, response by response," in a process of trying to "intuit what my people would do."

This sense of an organic, "felt" structure characterizes "Thirty-four Seasons of Winter." The story recounts the uneasy history of two stepbrothers: Ben, who always "remembered years in terms of winter," and Art, a former boxer who is already dead when the story begins, shot from his barstool by a pregnant high-school girl while the jukebox plays "That's What You Get for Loving Me." As Ben tries to make sense of Art's death, he retraces a downward trail of small-time, roadhouse face-offs, tempered by early memories of working together in the fields. Kittredge uses the emblematic image of the boxing ring to develop an agonistic narrative that forges, through a series of violent blows and shocked recoveries, a solid redefinition of brother-love.

Juxtaposed against the harsh realism of "Thirty-four Seasons of Winter," the next two stories of *The Van Gogh Field* embody a surreal narrative technique that mixes naturalistic detail with elements of dream and myth. First published in *TriQuarterly* (Spring 1976), "The Mercy of the Elements" opens with an unidentified "we" who "remember Venuto, who died." This collective voice then places Venuto and his son, Bowman, in a series of vivid landscapes within a valley defined by a steep, geologic fault ridge. While working away at an obscure digging project, a kind of archaeology that he only dimly understands, Bowman has surreal fantasies involving a series of otherworldly, heartbreaking women. These episodes move him through layers of family history. His progress toward defining "a history of his own" reflects a dreamlike reworking of episodes from Kittredge's life.

First published in the Winter 1974 issue of *TriQuarterly*, "The Stone Corral" mixes historical fact with fictionalized narrative to reexamine certain complex threads—religious, racial, and sexual—that underlie the paradigm of westward expansion. A Nevada state historical marker, mounted at the entrance to a stone-walled circle, supposedly "documents" the 1892 Indian massacre of a wagon train of religious zealots on their way to California. In some details, this "Sleeping Child Massacre" resembles the Mountain Meadow Massacre of 1857. The historical event may have suggested to Kittredge the notion of a fictional critique of the destructive templates underlying the settlement of the West. Through the device of a journal kept by Jerome Bedderly, leader of the wagon party, Kittredge

Cover for the special contemporary Western fiction issue that Kittredge edited with Steven M. Krauzer

once comic and revelatory. Drunken barroom conversations reproduce a seemingly aimless vernacular realism in which speech propels the action.

In "The Underground River," which first appeared in *The Atlantic* in 1971, Kittredge moves easily between gritty naturalism and a ritual symbolism derived from Native American ceremony. Like "Thirty-four Seasons of Winter," the story concerns two dissimilar brothers bedeviled by troubles only partly of their own making. The brothers, Native Americans named Lonnie and Cleve, have recently collected their shares of the tribal money. As the story opens, Red Yount, the Indian deputy, arrives at Cleve's place to break the news that Lonnie is dead of alcohol poisoning, just 123 days after coming of age. "Leastwise," Yount says, thinking of the tribal allowance, "you can afford to bury him." The story that follows, a violent clash of cultures and laws, grows out of Cleve's determination to give his brother what he perceives as a fitting burial, piecing together a ritual from memory and a series of dreams in which he imagines himself a part of ancient Indian rites.

The volume concludes with "The Soap Bear," a three-part story that combines careful narrative shaping with the random feel of real life. Like many of Kittredge's stories, "The Soap Bear" begins with a scene of violent death: "So now Grace was dead, and Danzig was dead, and they all were dead. Someone would have to clean up the mess." Virgil Banta, a young man "gone rotten," has murdered his sister, Grace, along with all the other members of a commune, including the fifty-year-old leader, Danzig. He reports the crime to Sheriff Shirley Holland, then waits at home with the sheriff's wife, Doris, while Holland and his deputy investigate. In the foreword to Kittredge's second collection, where "The Soap Bear" is reprinted, Carver observed that Kittredge "gives us characters . . . whose high hopes have broken down on them and gotten left behind like old, abandoned combines." The arc of "high hopes . . . broken down" characterizes this darkly comic take on domesticity "gone rotten." The story is filled with ironic images of aspiration: the motto that Sheriff Holland hired someone to paint across the outside wall of his jailhouse ("A NEW WORLD EVERY MORNING"), Danzig's display of seven backpacks and seven automatic rifles under a yellow-painted slogan ("THE SEVEN DWARFS"), the rhinestone-cowboy regalia of the deputy, and the soap bear of the title, lovingly carved by the murderer's sister. Walking through the house full of bodies, Sheriff Holland remarks on a familiar pattern, Kittredge's master theme: "whatever these kids thought they were going to force toward perfection . . . now there is this same old trouble."

tracks a collision of social and sexual forces that explodes in violence. Kittredge mixes historical personages with allegorized figures, such as the Shoshone woman who "simply materialized . . . a small dark figure holding her swaddled child" to lead the desperate pilgrims through the desert to their martyrdom in the stone corral.

With "The Man Who Loved Buzzards," first published in *Carolina Quarterly* (1974), Kittredge returns to the realistic social story, but in a form that acknowledges and incorporates the unseen. The protagonist, a military veteran named Ringman, is visited by dreams and memories that lend a surreal dimension to the "simple life" he tries to maintain. Ringman is a damaged man, dogged by an atrocity he experienced in Laos. He wants to identify with buzzards, which he sees as "invulnerable birds," emblematic of his effort to anesthetize himself by hard work, gin, casual sex, and tedium. The story provides one of the best examples in the collection of how Kittredge uses dialogue that is at

The downward curve of the plot is echoed in the language of the characters. In rendering their thoughts, Kittredge retains the clipped idiom of people working hard to make complicated things simple. "Rule number eleven," Banta remembers from his days in the commune, is to keep your head warm: "You got to do lots of things this way . . . with your head turned off." The four characters interact in a constantly shifting balance of affiliations that works like an intricate system of weights, a pattern that also characterizes such stories as "Be Careful What You Want" (1985), "Balancing Water" (1987), and "Do You Hear Your Mother Talking?" (1991).

With its authentic dialogue and sure sense of form, "The Soap Bear" anticipates Kittredge's second collection, *We Are Not in This Together* (1984). Three of the strongest stories from *The Van Gogh Field* are reprinted—"Thirty-Four Seasons of Winter," "The Soap Bear," and "The Underground River"—along with five newly collected pieces, some of which, such as "The Waterfowl Tree," first appeared early in Kittredge's career. The title page describes the volume as "edited and with a foreword by Raymond Carver." Kittredge told Morris that when the stories were collected, "Ray Carver went through them all again and marked them up." Kittredge acknowledges that he "took all his changes too, pretty much," although they were "lines changed here and there . . . nothing to do with intent."

Technical sureness is matched by the strong sense of purpose exhibited in this volume. In *Taking Care,* Kittredge describes the writer's job as "trying to see through to coherencies," and the eight stories of *We Are Not in This Together* show Kittredge in the process of "trying to see through" the distinctive idioms and artifacts of his characters' lives to expose the cultural contexts in which these gestures cohere. He made these coherencies more explicit in the almost one hundred essays he published since "Redneck Secrets."

A passage in *Hole in the Sky* illustrates how Kittredge's stories, whether fictive or nonfictive, arise from the same pressing questions. Kittredge describes his grandfather and namesake, who lived out the romance of "owning it all" until he died playing cards in 1958. "I wish I could at least guess at what he thought as the light vanished," Kittredge said of his grandfather. "Life had given him great properties. What were they worth in the end? I wish I had talked to him before he died." The heavily autobiographical third story in *We Are Not in This Together,* "Flight," serves as a fictionalized meditation on the same questions. In telling the story of "Old Man" Carl Fuller and his grandson and namesake, Kittredge attempts to work out the complexities that motivated those old Westerners "who'd opened the country" and then

resolved to own it. In its proximity to essay form, the story is experimental. As if to signal the blurring of genres, Kittredge divided the action into four parts, each marked with a title that signals a new movement in the developing theme. "Flight" refers to the first section of the story, an aerial description of the approach to the valley where the story is set. A small plane flies low over croplands and geologic fault ridges—landforms that, as Kittredge says in *Hole in the Sky,* "confront us with both geologic time and our own fragility." The second section, "Owning It All," describes Carl Fuller's history of buying up property in the valley, followed by a segment in which the grandson has a violent dream that conflates the strata of family history contained within this place. All four sections work together to achieve an effect that Kittredge suggests in the title to the fourth section: "Broken Film" or *Ekphrasis, the still movement.* In this section the grandson recalls Fuller's funeral as a "series of tableaux which . . . contained the past and implied the future," an apt description of the four-part structure of the story. Ultimately, the title "Flight" offers an aerial perspective on the history of both family and place, another image for the distancing that young Fuller represents as *"ekphrasis."* Kittredge uses the motif of an aerial perspective in a similar way in the 1984 story "Agriculture," in which a young ranch wife, after wrangling a ride in a crop duster's plane, begins to imagine her way out of a dead-end marriage.

Kittredge collects random conversations and revealing gestures discovered in unlikely places, holding them up to illuminate the latent values, desires, and fears they contain. "Blue Stone," first published in *Ohio Journal* in 1973, reads like a "found" story, a serio-comic look at another rich old man who is accustomed to having it all. "Old Man" Trainer, who has "gone loopy" in old age, pedals his ten-speed bicycle to his favorite bar each day, wearing tennis whites. A former actor who starred in Westerns, Trainer now lives in fantasies, making absurd pronouncements about a circus he plans to start: "Going to fill it up with crazies," Trainer says, "Bring in people from California to see it." Kittredge spins "Blue Stone" out of a drunken barroom conversation that rides on a wild logic of its own, each new phrase offering a possibility of new purpose: "What I'm after," Trainer improvises, "is a syndicate. . . . the word soothing, a name for what they will be." "Blue Stone" represents the first of several stories, including "Performing Arts" (1980), "Phantom Silver," and "Looking Glass" (1993), in which Kittredge explores the hazards of "performing" a make-believe version of Western experience.

"Momentum Is Always the Weapon" is another social story, told in an open and exploratory vein that echoes the voice of Kittredge's essays. The maximlike title suggests that this piece will be a story that probes the consequences of a heedless act. It begins darkly as Ambler, an old rancher, rides into a rainstorm, trying to absorb the fact that his daughter, Christy, is dead at twenty-three, shot by mistake in a bar fight. Kittredge traces Ambler's efforts to place the blame for her "spoiled" life on Eddie Matson, "the boy who had started her." Despite the naturalistic tenor of this theme, the action unrolls in a series of gently swerving plans and revisions of plans that take the characters by surprise. As in "Blue Stone," the dialogue rides on its own momentum: "This talk, as it came from him, was forming, and Ambler wondered how much he meant what he was saying as he listened to himself." Ultimately "Momentum Is Always the Weapon" turns its aphoristic title back on itself to affirm community, rather than to level blame.

In the last story in the collection, "We Are Not in This Together," Kittredge expands the notion of community to encompass animals and the wilderness they inhabit. In "Grizzly," one of the best-known essays in his 1987 collection *Owning It All,* he explores the "tangle of feelings toward the grizzly" that dates back to Lewis and Clark. Both essay and story begin with a graphic reconstruction of a real incident in which a girl Kittredge knew, a Montana student working in a local bar, was killed by a bear in Glacier National Park. In his conversation with Morris, Kittredge speaks of the killing as something he "could not resolve," and this lack of closure may account for the open, associative way he plots the fictional narrative. The story begins with the protagonist, Halverson, lying awake imagining the attack and trying "to understand the feeling of knowing you were killed before you were dead." Through an emotional chain reaction, Halverson's clumsy efforts to "center himself in that frail girl" eventually connect him to other people in his life: his long-dead father, his girl-friend Darby, the dead girl's companion who survived the attack, and even the bear that he kills in a confused attempt to even the score. "Thinking was beside the point," Halverson concludes early on, and so his resolve to hunt down the grizzly is less a matter of logical motivation than an instinctive need to act. Kittredge interweaves Halverson's stalking of the bear with the darkly comic story of his troubled relationship with Darby who insists on going along when Halverson decides "to get things even." By the end of the story,

the phrase "we are not in this together," a thought that Halverson directs toward some rangers who are looking for him, becomes an ironic comment on his failed attempts to detach himself from other peoples' troubles. Despite Halverson's best efforts, "We Are Not in This Together" enacts a hard-won celebration of community.

In the 1980 essay "Writers of the New West," which introduced a special issue of *TriQuarterly* devoted to contemporary Western fiction, Kittredge and Krauzer praised Wallace Stegner for portraying "the life considered," a past that is "personal, and possessed." This description is also applicable to Kittredge's writing life. In stories of many kinds, Kittredge continues to render what he called in Stegner an "emotionally possessed life." For Kittredge, such a life is lived solidly in community.

Interviews:

David Long, "A Talk with William Kittredge," *Poets & Writers,* 15 (March/April 1987): 5–10;

Ray Gonzalez and Ida Steven, "The Myth of Ownership: An Interview with William Kittredge," *Bloomsbury Review,* 8 (July/August 1988): 4–5, 14–15;

Gregory L. Morris, "William Kittredge," in *Talking Up A Storm: Voices of the New West* (Lincoln: University of Nebraska Press, 1994): 167–184.

Bibliography:

Scott Slovic, "Bibliography of William Kittredge's Work," in *Taking Care: Thoughts on Storytelling and Belief* (Minneapolis, Minn.: Milkweed Editions, 1999), pp. 101–125.

References:

Mary Clearman Blew, "William Kittredge," *Updating the Literary West,* edited by Thomas J. Lyon (Fort Worth: Texas Christian University Press, 1997): 764–771;

Scott Slovic, "William Kittredge: A Portrait," in Kittredge, *Taking Care: Thoughts on Storytelling and Belief* (Minneapolis, Minn.: Milkweed Editions, 1999): 81–99.

Papers:

William Kittredge's papers for 1954–2000 are in The Southwest Collection, Special Collections, Texas Tech University.

John L'Heureux

(26 October 1934 –   )

J. V. Long
Portland State University

BOOKS: *Quick as Dandelions: Poems* (Garden City, N.Y.:
Doubleday, 1964);

Rubrics for a Revolution (New York: Macmillan / London:
Collier-Macmillan, 1967);

Picnic in Babylon: A Jesuit Priest's Journal, 1963–1967
(New York: Macmillan, 1967);

One Eye and a Measuring Rod: Poems (New York: Macmillan / London: Collier-Macmillan, 1968);

No Place for Hiding: New Poems (Garden City, N.Y.: Doubleday, 1971);

Tight White Collar: A Novel (Garden City, N.Y.: Doubleday, 1972);

The Clang Birds: A Novel (New York: Macmillan, 1972);

Family Affairs (Garden City, N.Y.: Doubleday, 1974);

Jessica Fayer (New York: Macmillan, 1976);

The Priest's Wife: 13 Ways of Looking at a Blackbird (Stanford, Cal.: Goodmorrow Press, 1981);

Desires (New York: Holt, Rinehart & Winston, 1981);

A Woman Run Mad (New York: Viking, 1988);

Comedians (New York: Viking, 1990);

An Honorable Profession (New York: Viking, 1991);

The Shrine at Altamira (New York: Viking, 1992);

The Handmaid of Desire: A Novel (New York: Soho, 1996);

Having Everything: A Novel (New York: Atlantic Monthly
Press, 1999).

John L'Heureux (from the dust jacket for Having Everything,
1999)

John L'Heureux's fiction is important both for its
substance and its style. His undertaking is contrarian
and ambitious: to map the presence of God in a world
hostile to the sacred. His writing is committed, complicated, frequently witty, and sometimes unpleasant in
its unflinching accounts of the violent and their behaviors. With prickly discernment, he excavates the mysterious in ordinary experience. L'Heureux has an
instinct for locating and exposing the absurd in the
choices men and women make or have thrust upon
them; yet, he refrains from surrendering to easy reso-
lutions and eschews sentimentality of any kind. He
relies neither on superstition nor miracles but has
staked out the tense frontier between the serious
claims of faith and the partisan demands of belief. In

an unpublished interview conducted on 25 April 2000
he said, "I heard a nice description offered by Graham
Greene in his last days: 'I'm a Catholic Agnostic,' he
said. 'I have faith but not belief.' I rather like it for
myself, though I'd change the last part to 'I'm not sure
I have Faith, but I do have Hope.' Catholic Agnostic,
though, perfectly preserves the two things that matter
to me most."

John Clarke L'Heureux was born in South Had-
ley, Massachusetts, on 26 October 1934; his parents
were Wilfred and Mildred L'Heureux. After two years
at the College of the Holy Cross in Worcester, Massachusetts, he entered the Society of Jesus (the Jesuits) at
the age of nineteen and began the arduous intellectual
and spiritual journey that led to his ordination as a
priest in 1966. During these years of religious formation he published several books of poetry and a jour-

221

nal, *Picnic in Babylon: A Jesuit Priest's Journal, 1963–1967* (1967), which chronicled his final years of seminary study. The latter part of L'Heureux's life as a Jesuit coincided with the upheaval the Roman Catholic Church experienced in the wake of the Second Vatican Council (1962–1965), which was convened to "open the church's windows" more widely to the complicated aspirations of the modern world. The turbulence that accompanied engagement with the world proved to be both exhilarating and disruptive for an entire generation of priests and nuns. L'Heureux's career as a priest, which included time as a graduate student in English at Harvard and a stint as a staff editor at *The Atlantic Monthly,* was fairly conventional for an unconventional time.

L'Heureux left the priesthood and was laicized in 1971; that year he also married Joan Polston, the dedicatee of most of his subsequent books. He wrote in *Picnic in Babylon,* "I became a Jesuit, paradoxically, on the grounds of coldest reason: I felt God wanted me to, I could, and therefore I should. So I did." He explained some of the reasons behind his leaving the priesthood to *The National Catholic Reporter* (*NCR*) in an article published on 11 May 1990 to coincide with the release of his short-story collection *Comedians.* During a period when Jesuits were deeply involved in the anti–Vietnam War movement, and sometimes went to jail as a consequence of their commitments:

> I wasn't involved in that. It's one of the reasons I left the Jesuits, in fact–a feeling of guilt began to set in, that I wasn't as selfless and as generous and as dedicated as Daniel Berrigan. . . . That seems to me what a priestly task is. And as long as we're going to have the monsignori, we're never going to have the kind of Christianity you can find evinced in the work of Berrigan and company.

L'Heureux published three collections of poetry before he began to write fiction. His poem "*from* St. Ignatius Loyola, Founder of the Jesuits: His Autobiography [with directions for reading]" (in *No Place for Hiding,* 1971) seemed a bridge from verse into narrative prose. L'Heureux said later in an unpublished interview that he "never looked back. It became more satisfying to explore consciousnesses different from one's own." His short fiction began appearing in *The New Yorker, The Atlantic Monthly, Harper's, Esquire,* and several literary journals, and has been included in *Prize Stories: The O. Henry Awards* and *The Best American Short Stories.*

After several visiting academic appointments, L'Heureux moved to the English department at Stanford University in 1973 and began his association with the creative-writing program there. He served as its

director from 1976 through 1989 and is a professor of English. At Stanford he has taught and worked with some of the most interesting and successful American fiction writers, including Tobias Wolff, Kathryn Harrison, Allan Gurganus, Tom McNeal, Harriet Doer, Michael Cunningham, Ron Hansen, Michelle Carter, and Stephanie Vaughn–as well as playwright David Hurang. He regards teaching as being a complement to, rather than competition for, his writing: "It forces oneself to specify to young writers what it is that is missing . . . what's preventing the full resonance of a story's psychic and material freight from being realized in its own terms. To do that I have to exercise my own imaginative muscles."

L'Heureux's fiction is risky, learned, and witty. His short stories and the best of his novels undertake to expose the architecture of faith in the structures of human behavior. He answers in the affirmative a rhetorical question Graham Greene once posed in response to a question about his own work: "Mustn't we illuminate God's infinite mercy to men, and can't it be done by using indirect lighting?" L'Heureux maps the presence of God in a world ill disposed to intrusion by the divine and thereby locates irony as one of the unnamed and intractable gifts of the Holy Spirit.

The experience of being a priest provided L'Heureux with both the material and the vocabulary to shape a body of fiction that remains intricate, compelling, and deeply religious even as it eschews the conventions of dogma and practice. L'Heureux's writing exposes the futility of attempting to corral faith with doctrine. He uses language to shape lives complicated by the discovery that grace is as inescapable as pettiness or mediocrity. In the 1990 *NCR* interview L'Heureux admitted that his

> preoccupation happened to be, for a long time, theological . . . not religious in the sense of organized religion, but theological in the sense of questions that have to do with the meaning of one's life, if it has any meaning, with God if there is a God, and who he or she is . . . the notion that there is such a thing as grace, and I have no doubt there is such a thing as grace, and I do believe there is a God. All my characters agitate because they are not as convinced as I.

The Jesuit Order is organized on a military model. The head, who resides in Rome, is called the General, and the solemnly professed Fathers are, ostensibly, bound by a special vow of obedience to go wherever the pope sends them. As a reaction to the Jesuits' vaunted authoritarianism, it is not surprising that L'Heureux's preoccupation with the attributes of God works itself out by focusing on the consequences of power in the dynamics of human relationships. His

Dust jacket for L'Heureux's 1981 collection of short fiction, which prompted novelist John Gardner to comment, "L'Heureux builds stories the way the Shakers built chairs"

fictional clergymen frequently belong to a Jesuit-like order called the Thomasites. They clearly evoke not the cool certainty of Thomas Aquinas's scholasticism but the edginess of Jesus' doubting disciple who refused to believe in the Resurrection until he could touch the physical wounds in Christ's crucified body.

L'Heureux's fiction probes human experience. He wants to know both how things work and why they work the way they do, but he is too smart to expect a convincing answer. He takes God to task, especially for the vulnerability of the innocents—children, students, and simpletons among them—and associates himself with the most ancient narratives that describe the tension between the demands of faith and the demands of God. The sacrifice of Isaac, for example, echoes frequently in this modern storyteller's work. His characters inhabit a world where the only mystery deeper than violence is love.

L'Heureux's first collection of short stories, *Family Affairs,* was published in 1974, a year after he began his association with Stanford. The title seems to point to an innocuous psychological landscape, but the

reader is immediately alert to the strange intensity of L'Heureux's imagination. The opening story, "Something Missing," is about parents and children, teachers and students—familiar protagonists in both his short fiction and his novels—but the freight these characters bear is apparent from the beginning. The compelling biblical drama of Abraham and Isaac is built into the story. The opening sentences of the first two paragraphs introduce the violence that frequently erupts in L'Heureux's stories: the reader knows there has been a "fire in the school" and that "Avram Goldfarb was a child prodigy of seven, a pianist, when a drunken Nazi broke his hands." The reader then experiences the inexorable trajectory that leads to Avram's son's immolation. In this version of the Old Testament story, there is no ram to sacrifice instead of the son.

Isaac is a beautiful boy with talent short of genius, and he is, therefore, unable to fulfill his father's transferred ambitions. The normal psychological and physical awkwardness that attends adolescence is amplified by a move to a new high school, where Isaac hopes mainly to remain unnoticed. He is a preternatural exile, however–a Jew, an artist (with talents his father cannot recognize), and a likely homosexual–in a world built around the conventions of belonging. Isaac withstands the impatience of his father, who "spent much of his day trying to infuse his own genius into his angry, despairing son. Neither understood who the other was." His alienation is reinforced by the taunts of a bullying, anti-Semitic football coach who feels sure he can provide appropriate instruction about "what a real man can do," and by the empathy of an English teacher, who recognizes both his problems and his pain and recommends dermatology to address one of Isaac's obvious and remediable problems.

Isaac, however, remains isolated and unappreciated. When he cuts gym class and finds refuge in a room with a piano and "played a Schubert sonata, but softly, softly," the football player sent to find the truant overhears Isaac. Ed LaCroix (whose name is significant), "pleased for some reason he himself did not understand," covers for Isaac. Both LaCroix and his girlfriend begin to penetrate Isaac's loneliness, and he imagines "it was still possible. Perhaps he could still have friends and be like the others." With nascent inner resources, Isaac performs impressively when, as a punishment for skipping class, the coach puts him through a grueling physical workout with the football team. In the locker room afterward, "He was at once conscious of his exhaustion and of an exhilaration at being a man among other men, naked and accepted." Then LaCroix offers a gesture of friendship that dooms Isaac: "He turned large, frightened eyes up to Ed LaCroix's wide grin as the quarterback tightened his grip on Isaac's shoulder, shook him a little, and said, 'Nice going man. You done real good.'" Isaac's body involuntarily responds to the touch, and he is exposed, though his unmasking is more than simply the articulation of desire.

Isaac's nakedness is spiritual as well, and as he begins to grapple with the consequences of this new, unimaginable isolation, he finally finds the passion that imbues genius:

> Having struggled endless hours with the Art of the Fugue, Isaac knew Bach, but his father did not like the cantatas, and so he had never played them. Sitting down to No. 57, 'Seilg is der Mann,' Isaac felt he was recognizing a piece he had learned ages ago . . . the four arias spoke through Isaac's fingers of exile and the desire for death, death's sweetness and its joy, delivery from the martyred body.

His genius, however, is evanescent. Isaac takes time only to taunt his father with it before he lights the fire with which the story begins.

The author conveys these horrors with a detached, almost icy precision, as if acknowledging the futility of intervention. There is a feeling of helpless fascination in being unable to confront evil: to define it and to fight it. What if unseen and unknowable forces are not controlling the spiral of violence that engulfs Isaac? What if his suffering simply makes no sense? The Nazis are insufficient as the prime movers of Isaac's tragedy, and neither Schubert nor Bach can assuage his despair.

L'Heureux employs the same hard, flat tone in the other stunning story of the collection, "A Family Affair." Once again he takes on the dynamics inherent in family life, and he makes it clear that procreation is unpropitious. While the opening verses of Genesis describe a divine wind blowing over the void, L'Heureux's story pointedly begins, "In that country there was never a wind." The characters are all stillbirths who inhabit a world so exhausted and taut that any seed thrown hits rocky ground.

An army base has brought the semblance of prosperity to a dusty, barren town. The inhabitants' desiccated spirits mimic the arid geography. Beryl Gerriter, as the story opens, is in the throes of a difficult birth that produces a mongoloid baby. Her husband, Luke, responds to the birth of his son in an appalling manner. "'So you had to do this to me, too,' he says to his wife; 'One lay in three years, and you had to produce this. You bitch.'" Their twelve-year-old daughter, Elissa, is emotionally stunted, and within a couple of years–after she has cared for her baby brother until he dies–inherits her parents' inescapable patterns, simply because she has no way of knowing any better.

The brutality, chronic abuse, and futility in the narrative are as inescapable as the desert sun. Soldiers from the base come to town to drink on weekends and seduce whoever is available. Elissa is a predictable and ready victim. She is like a desert creature that must adapt to long periods without water. Nothing in her environment is nourishing, and, aside from her dog and her dead brother, Elissa has never had any experience of love. She borrows beauty tips from a sexually precocious friend. The act of "making up" is horribly telling. Willing to mistake desire for tenderness, she responds to a soldier's physical entreaties and, predictably, suffers the consequences. To punish her for her pregnancy, her father insists on returning to the desert spot where the sexual encounter had occurred. The Gerriters' fictional world finds the prospect of birth totally insupportable. Although Luke intends to make Elissa shoot her dog, the story ends with Elissa pointing the gun at herself, and the real horror of the story is the realization that even a fatal shot is superfluous to someone who has never really come to life. In "A Family Affair" Elissa becomes a sort of sacrificial ram to her dog's Isaac.

L'Heureux's language in the story once again creates an unsparing tone, yet, he withholds judgment. There is a moment of surprising tenderness when Luke picks flowers and asks Elissa to carry them as a gesture of reconciliation to his wife, who refuses them. These men and women, incapable of creation, are desperately searching for their hearts. It is an exhausting search, however, and exhaustion insures that the desert will ultimately prevail.

Carolyn See, reviewing L'Heureux's second collection, *Desires* (1981), in *The Los Angeles Times* (28 April 1981), warned readers about the stories: "You either get them or you don't. But their demands are refreshing. They are the opposite of 'a good read.' They are difficult, cranky, beautiful works of art." L'Heureux exhumes the haunting, neurotic oddness lying beneath seemingly benign surfaces. In "The Anatomy of Bliss" an academic's wife covers the walls of their home with writing but cannot convincingly articulate the unhappiness behind her compulsion. "Departures" is one of L'Heureux's most disturbing stories about the priesthood. A young priest on a visit home greets his parents, who have come to meet his train, and responds to his mother's embrace, "I'll just kiss you on the cheek—don't touch me—and I'll shake hands with Dad, and then we'll turn and walk out of here." The frigid restraint, highlighted by the priggish "don't touch me," metastasizes throughout the clergyman's career and shadows all of his approaches to transcendence.

"Brief Lives in California" is a story situated in a specific place (the Stanford University campus, its environs, and San Francisco) and time (the late 1970s). L'Heureux plays with that specificity and turns the readers' and characters' expectations inside out. He once again eviscerates the tense dynamic of authority and ambition between parents and their children.

Leonora, the protagonist, is an unremarkable child to everyone but her mother. "She could be a photographer's model," her mother imagines. "She could be on all the covers." The structures of the mother's sentences are characteristic of L'Heureux's style. The repeated phrases and deceptively simple construction convey a particularly unexpressive impression. Though Leonora gives every indication of being ordinary, she is cursed with the self-imposed burdens of the overachiever. In refusing to gratify her high-school boyfriend's sexual urges, she simply asserts, "'I think I was meant for better things,' . . .

not really knowing what she meant." The girl moves from the waiting list into the freshman class at Stanford and is crushed when she receives her first C in a freshman English class. Her instructor, a fledgling novelist named Lockhart, explains that it is a perfectly average grade, and Leonora acts as if she is being addressed in a foreign language. In Leonora's character L'Heureux dissects the unnerving gall of the callow and their demands. It is an acute indictment against Americans in general and Californians (especially in L'Heureux's world) in particular. Leonora is simply convinced that her teacher is neither equipped nor willing to appreciate her abilities. The gap between Lockhart's judgment (her essay "was covered with little red marks—diction? antecedent? obscure, no no no—and there was a large black C at the bottom of the page") and Leonora's self-image is a vacuum that L'Heureux's readers will not expect to be filled happily. This narrative also ends with gunshots.

The girl's university career is characteristically compressed into a series of vignettes that reveal her spirit as essentially formless. L'Heureux is particularly deft managing history as a component in "Brief Lives in California." There was a compressed horror to that era, particularly in the Bay Area—the background of Leonora's story includes Patty Hearst's kidnapping, capture, and incarceration, the Jonestown massacre, as well as the murders of San Francisco mayor George Mascone and Harvey Milk, the first openly homosexual city supervisor—that subverted the balmy, blonde, healthy image of life in California. The world seemed like a black hole; a cipher like Leonora did not stand a chance.

Without L'Heureux's spiritual investment in his characters, they might seem merely a pageant of odd neurotics. There is evidence, however, in *Desires* of a maturing imagination, one that turns more deeply inward even as it becomes more seriously playful. "Roman Ordinary," for example, is a mordant tale that speculates on the complexity of papal relaxations: "His Holiness Pope Paul VI is an ordinary saint. All day long he does what he has to do, and at night he dances." It is a macabre dance, indeed. The Pope's bones are housed in an antique armoire and viewed surreptitiously, after hours.

"Witness," the longest story in the collection, is a particularly harrowing narrative about "a model California woman" named Morgan Childs. The reader knows from the start that she is "a born manager" and is thus certain that things will quickly spin out of her control. She is a successful academic, intensely secular, sexually promiscuous, and completely self-possessed. At a faculty party she seduces

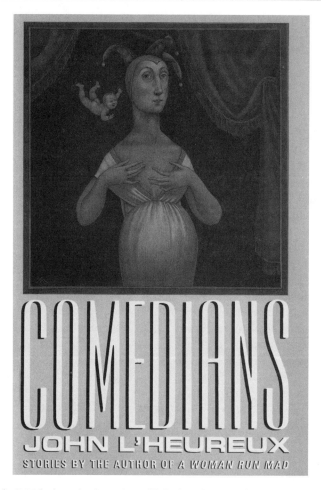

Dust jacket for L'Heureux's 1990 book, stories that reviewer Linda Gray Sexton praised for "providing a bridge across the gulf of such treacherous subjects as God, death and man's failure to live with integrity"

a married graduate student, a former seminarian. During Lent the young man's scruples arrive and he breaks off the affair. At the same time, Morgan begins to experience strange, painful sensations in her wrists. The pain intensifies without having a discoverable cause and, within a month, wounds appear. That Morgan could be experiencing the stigmata—the physical impressions of Christ's wounds on hands, feet, and side—appears at first outlandish (when she tells her son that she is a stigmatic he responds, "You need glasses?") and then increasingly likely.

For a divorced, Jewish atheist this realization is understandably discomfiting, and she attempts to escape by engaging in behaviors unrecognizable to the saintly. Morgan can anticipate the arrival of her ordeal on Fridays: "She found she could locate the precise point of . . . of what? Of entry, she was thinking, as if she had been violated somehow." This point is a quintessential moment in L'Heureux's fiction.

There is both the literal probing that recalls Doubting Thomas, and, more significantly, a description of God's uninvited, unwelcome, thoroughly mystifying intrusion. Jamie O'Hara, the pliable graduate student, gives Morgan a theological explanation for the phenomenon: "You can't earn grace. . . . You can't escape it either."

Morgan looks for an explanation. She goes to the emergency room, where the attending physician is a former sexual partner named Underhill (recalling the preeminent historian of mysticism, Evelyn Underhill); she sees a psychiatrist; and she consults a distinguished hematologist. Ultimately, there is no recourse but to surrender. In an early attempt to rationalize the pain Morgan had thought, "It was mysterious but not meaningful." As she disintegrates into a kind of holiness, attended by its own peculiar humiliations, Morgan realizes the truth that underlies all of L'Heureux's thoughtful fiction: mystery always has meaning.

There is a clear progress from L'Heureux's first collection to his second. The characterizations are more intricate, and the self-consciousness of the act of writing itself is explored in stories such as "The Priest's Wife" and "Love and Death in Brighams." The author's work is built at angles, some of which are jarring indeed, but his voice is singular. It is easy to understand the late John Gardner's meaning in the critique of *Family Affairs* he sent to an editor at Doubleday: "In an age of tour-de-force technique, three-ring-circus virtuosity, L'Heureux builds stories the way the Shakers built chairs; in an age which has cut the imagination free, an age of hippogriffs and seven-legged maidens, L'Heureux sits, stodgy as old Chekhov, observing real human beings and putting them on paper, pore by pore."

Comedians (1990), L'Heureux's next collection, includes evidence of a more expansive imagination. While his stories are never buoyant, there are luminous moments in this book that the earlier collections did not predict. The book was reviewed favorably across the United States. Linda Gray Sexton of *The New York Times Book Review* (18 February 1990) began her notice, "With his elegant, spare prose providing a bridge across the gulf of such treacherous subjects as God, death and man's failure to live with integrity, John L'Heureux finds and expertly maintains his footing."

The story titled "Themselves" in this third collection is characteristic of L'Heureux's style and representative of his themes. The narrator, a Catholic "of a sort," is posthumously describing and commenting upon the conversation at his last dinner party, which immediately preceded the stroke that has killed him: "my brain simply burst with the effort of accommodating all the new things that were going on, and, well, here I am." Margaret, "an atheist, but like all atheists she's fascinated that some people believe in God" at the end of the meal "just sort of wailed, 'Oh, I'm so tired of Jesus and God.'" The distinctive character of L'Heureux's stories depends upon the skillful orchestration of these three experiences—fascination, exhaustion, and wailing—as responses to the presence of God in a world where death is capricious.

These stories display a fresh encounter with the complexity of creation in all its forms and also encompass the political realm. "The Comedian," in which an abortion is under consideration, implicitly exposes the shallow facileness with which contemporary politics has appropriated the most intimate preserves of human personality and choice; as if to make the point inescapable, the story is told in the present tense. More overtly, "María Luz Buenvida" depends upon and excoriates readers' memories of the terror and civil upheaval in countries such as El Salvador in the 1980s.

These two stories, which open and close the collection, are particularly rewarding. Corinne, the comedian, is a thirty-eight-year-old woman, unexpectedly pregnant, who vacillates about the wisdom of aborting her fetus, who sings to her. Corinne and her husband know there are genetic abnormalities; the comedian is high-strung; practical considerations would seem to make it a clear decision. From the moment the choice is made, the baby stops singing. As the procedure gets under way, "Corinne closes her eyes and tries to make her mind a blank. Dark, she thinks. Dark. She squeezes her eyes tight against the light, she wants to remain in this cool darkness forever, she wants to cease being." Yet, she resists: "instead of surrendering to the dark she pushes it away . . . there is no abortion after all." Corinne, a cradle Catholic, understands that her baby's singing includes "some revelation, of course, but she does not want to know what that revelation might be." Corinne suddenly, intuitively understands and accepts that her baby will be born mute. This surrender allows her to be penetrated by revelation. "The light envelopes her, catches her up from this table where the doctor bends over her and where already can be seen the shimmering yellow hair of the baby. The light lifts her, and the singing lifts her, and she says, 'Yes,' she says, 'Thank you.'" The combination of mysticism and lyricism makes this moment particularly intense. It is seriously inventive fiction.

"María Luz Buenvida" is no less moving. Once again L'Heureux upends the conventional development of narrative: María begins her story by describing how she has been raped and mutilated by the soldiers who have arrested her: "And of course I will be dead in minutes." This story takes place in a Latin American oligarchy where the military has become increasingly protective of its prerogatives and suspicious of anyone whom they think capable of subversion. María's father is a distinguished movie director, whose current project is *Ifigenia;* her mother is an alcoholic American incapable of coping with the tragedy engulfing her family; and María's brother is associated with the revolutionary party.

Art is the true agency of subversion, and María's father is an artist:

> He cannot indict the military and the aristocracy and, yes, the clergy except under the cloak of ancient history. And to that history, which he cannot alter, he brings his own mystical belief: that from all this suffering there must eventually come some kind of redemp-

tion. And so his movies seem to be mythological, even fantastic, to some critics. But always they are a metaphor for our lives today. My father was very much a political man.

He is all but living through a contemporary production of Euripides, though he is not to blame for the family's horrible fate. María's sacrifice is unencumbered and not propitiatory. All responsible men and women, whether artists or not, both parents and children, are implicated in the struggle that results when power is asserted without justice.

The only fuel that will sustain such a struggle is love, and María is unwilling to abandon its possibilities even if it means passion lasts only an instant. To abandon that possibility is to give victory to despair. María's death is a surrender to light–it is her name–in much the same way that Corinne experiences it in "The Comedian." Their apotheoses link birth and rebirth:

> Cleansed in my own blood, my breasts lucent, and in my throat a triumphant cry, I will sprout wings of bronze and I will course throughout the night; at dawn I will hover above them, the murdered, the defiled, the dying; I will draw them to me; and I will draw the evil and the sick and the depraved and I will assume them, in my breast, in my loins, in the star they carved on me and in the cross upon my face; I will take them into myself and they will be transformed, made whole, all one.

In the maelstrom of violence that has sucked the life out of her culture, just as surely as breath is leaving her body, her heart is enlarged. Like a re-envisioned Guadalupe, María offers protection and consolations to all the abandoned, even the torturers.

Between these stunning frames, L'Heureux's stories, including an intricate and interesting novella, "The Terrible Mirror," all trace God's "meddling in our lives." Besides birth and rebirth, L'Heureux remains focused on the complexity of vocations, whether artistic or religious, and the inevitability of death. The stories in *Comedians,* however, are more generous; inevitabilities are less grim.

There are sharp edges throughout John L'Heureux's fiction. His imagination, even when it seems severe, is relentless in trying to articulate the difficulties men and women encounter when they try to make sense of themselves and of each other. The usually unwelcome arrival of God in these dilemmas is a catalyst that L'Heureux traces and describes with an unmistakable voice. His fiction invites readers to reflect on the depths and wonders of their own predicaments from perspectives as old as Genesis. One of this author's indisputable acts of faith is that the hardest questions endure. Everyone, finally, is a citizen of mystery. L'Heureux is at work on a novel, *The Miracle,* to be published by Grove/Atlantic in 2002. A screen version of *A Woman Run Mad* is being filmed by Highwire Productions.

Interviews:

Michael J. Farrell, "L'Heureux's People Perplexed by Ironic God," *National Catholic Reporter,* 25 (11 May 1990): 21, 30;

Diane Manuel, "Suffering Fools Gladly: John L'Heureux 'Does His Thoughts,'" *Stanford Report,* 29 (9 October 1996): 7;

Yvonne Daly, "Satire under the Palms," West Magazine, *San Jose Mercury News,* 3 November 1996.

Papers:

Some of John L'Heureux's manuscripts are housed at Boston University and at Stanford University in California.

David Long

(6 March 1948 –   )

Dennis Held
Lewis-Clark State College

BOOKS: *Early Returns* (Waldron Island, Wash.: Jawbone Press, 1981);

Home Fires (Urbana: University of Illinois Press, 1982);

The Flood of '64 (New York: Ecco Press, 1987);

Blue Spruce (New York: Scribners, 1995);

The Falling Boy (New York: Scribners, 1997);

The Daughters of Simon Lamoreaux (New York: Scribner, 2000).

David Long is the only child of John H. Long, a corporate lawyer specializing in labor relations, and Jean (Dimond) Long, a cellist and homemaker. Long was born on 6 March 1948 and raised in Lunenburg, Massachusetts, a small town about an hour west of Boston. He attended Pomfret School, a private high school in Pomfret, Connecticut, and went on to Albion College in Michigan, where he majored in English and studied with Paul Loukides. "Paul was a great influence," Long said in an unpublished interview. "It was my first experience with Iowa-style writing workshops." He met his future wife, Susan Schweinsberg, in a history class, and they married in December of 1969.

In 1970 Long attended the Hartford Seminary Foundation, graduating with a master of arts degree in religious studies in 1972. He also took classes in poetry with Terry Stokes at the University of Hartford. Long applied to graduate schools in creative writing and was accepted at the University of Montana, where he began studying in the fall of 1972. His first classes were in poetry, with Madeline DeFrees and Richard Hugo. In the summer of 1973, at the urging of essayist and fiction writer William Kittredge, he began to write short stories. "I'd been writing fiction in high school, a little in college, but I'd stopped, and I hadn't read a lot in the way of contemporary short stories up to meeting Bill," Long said in the unpublished interview: "It was a combination of reading and Bill's encouragement that led me into fiction."

In the fall of 1973, Long was hired by the Poets in the Schools program, sponsored by the Montana Arts

David Long (photograph by Marshall Noice; from the dust jacket for
The Daughters of Simon Lamoreaux, *2000)*

Council. He recalled the ways this job affected his creative work:

It kept me writing poetry, kept me reading other poets. It also got me out, into the small towns of Montana—I began to hear people's stories, and to imagine other stories that could take place in that landscape.

I was constantly looking for good models to use, and I asked the students to write real literature—not just busy work, but writing that was important to them. That helped me understand some things that became important in my own work—clear speech, people talking about what mattered to them, and that philosophy of teaching developed into a philosophy of writing.

Long received the master of fine arts degree in the spring of 1974, and by that time he had already published stories and poems in small magazines. His first short-story publications appeared in 1974 and 1975 in *Nimrod, Epoch, Confrontation, fiction international,* and the *North American Review.* In the summer of 1975 Long moved to Kalispell, Montana, when his wife accepted a position as medical librarian at Kalispell Regional Hospital, where she worked for the next twenty-four years.

The couple's first son, Montana, was born in January of 1976, and their second, Jackson, in March of 1981. Long was writing full-time and began teaching at Flathead Valley Community College as a part-time instructor in 1976. His first book—a collection of poems, *Early Returns*—was accepted in the summer of 1978 by editor Sam Green at Jawbone Press of Seattle, and it was published in 1981.

Also during this time, Long's fiction began to be recognized by a wider range of editors and readers, and more stories appeared in magazines and anthologies, including "Eclipse," which appeared in the Pushcart Prize anthology of 1981. In 1982 the University of Illinois Press published Long's first short-story collection, *Home Fires.* Stories from that collection had appeared in such periodicals as the *Carolina Quarterly,* the *Denver Quarterly,* and the *Sewanee Review.*

Home Fires introduces Long's major concerns as a writer: the need for people to pay close attention in their lives, because things happen only once and a defining moment may occur at any time; and the life-changing effects of chance, of small but substantial moments that can unsettle people's lives, but which also allow them to redeem the past through acts of grace in the present. In an interview with *Contemporary Authors* (1997), Long said, "If I have a theory of fiction, it's that something of consequence must be at stake in a story. People must make choices and live with their decisions."

The first story in the collection, "Eclipse," takes place in a western Montana town that is not named, but which resembles Sperry, a fictional re-creation of Kalispell. The unnamed narrator comes home "on borrowed rides" after a dissolute life. He finds that the "wave that had carried off so many of us who grew up here had left only the stubborn." The narrator has married and had a son, but he seems unable to love, and his family has left him.

The story illustrates the difficulty of finding connection in a hard land, in a world where the old order no longer works, and whatever will replace it has yet to arrive. "I felt born to no work in particular," the unnamed narrator says, and that sense of dislocation goes to the core of who this man is. In the unpublished interview Long said that "Eclipse" was "a Kittredge story—the content, all the details of the western life—that was outside of my experience, up to that point, so it was a kind of a breakthrough."

"Eclipse" introduces Long's style—crisp and spare prose, with moments of transcendent clarity: "So Mr. Tornelli and I drank the brandy. It worked on me as it does in the high timber, back to the wind. I stopped shivering. The cipher of ice in my middle began to melt under its heat." The story also includes moments of Long's deadpan humor. Searching for a neighbor, the narrator rattles the doorknobs of other tenants of the beaten-down hotel he is living in: "Mrs. Bache hadn't seen him. No one answered in 312. Mr. Karpowicz in 309 offered to break my jaw again."

The ending of the story offers the suggestion of hope that so often tinges even the most desolate of Long's work. After the narrator watches an eclipse, he notes that "the darkness began to ease; there was the slightest lightening visible at the edge of things." It is a haunting story of surprising connections and missed opportunity, of love and loss.

"Border Crossing" is a crime story that does not explore as fully as Long's other stories the interior workings of his characters' lives. Long revealed in an interview for *Talking Up a Storm: Voices of the New West* (1994), "I had been knocked for not having enough 'plot' in my early stories, so as an experiment I took the material for 'Border Crossing,' as well as for a few other stories, straight from the newspaper, and let the facts provide the armature. I wrote it with the same three-act structure that a screenplay would have." A reviewer for the *Missoulian* newspaper (2 November 1984) found it "a powerful story, no less for its suspense than its insight" into the mind of Carver, a small-time criminal who is swept into events that quickly get out of his control.

In "Saving Graces" Long reveals an affinity for writing from the female point of view that is evident throughout his career. One engaging aspect of this story is the gruff humor of the narrator, LaDonna: "Pert, she thinks, deliver me from pert."

One of the most substantial pieces in the collection is also the most ethereal. "Like Some Distant Crying" is about Celestia, a woman on the road who "generally . . . tries to expect nothing," to keep her disappointments at a minimum. She runs into a brittle old innkeeper (with no inn to keep) named Murphy, who also runs a cafe that no longer serves food and a hot spring that has apparently dried up. It is an odd, slow-moving story of the search for grace and redemption in a land hard-used, by people whose lives are also damaged by abuse or neglect. Against Murphy's orders that she clear out, Celestia decides to stay: "Later, in the dark, she unrolls the down bag on top of the mattress, smooths the wrinkled nylon with the gentle distraction of a woman straightening a child's hair." Only later do readers learn why Celestia is running: "Her boy is dead." Her husband, crushed by the loss, has turned to other women, and "Her choice was movement instead of bitterness." It is the kind of choice many of Long's characters are forced to make, limited by damage from the crushing blows to the spirit that human beings must endure. At first, Celestia struggles to get Murphy to re-enter the land of the spiritually alive. By the end, she realizes that her choice of flight is a kind of turning away, too. Her desire to fight the loneliness and isolation of the human heart eventually wins and offers them both a way out.

Another story in which a woman is the focus, "Morning Practice," reveals Long's understanding of the power of music to shape lives. (For many years, he played rhythm guitar and harmonica in "Tut and the Uncommons," a Kalispell rhythm-and-blues band.) Kate Wolf has come home "to be with her father in his grief" over the death of Kate's mother, a cellist. They will not even build a fire in the fireplace, for fear of conjuring the woman's memory. The fresh and original language is attuned to the telling detail that carries the story into a higher imaginative realm, as when Kate sees her father's legs as he sleeps, "blue-white and smooth as potato shoots."

The pair embark on a quest to find the mother's damaged cello, and when it turns up at a repair shop, the luthier reveals that the mother "had never told him about a husband or grown daughter." The father is crushed; he had hoped to recapture a connection to his lost wife, but instead their separateness is further emphasized. Long's critics have pointed to such moments as evidence of a "bleak vision," but the ending, like Long's vision itself, is much more complex. Like many of Long's characters, Kate has withdrawn, settling for less rather than risking the heartache that accompanies love. But in the last sentence of the story, Long shows Kate's conviction to once again embrace the world in all its aches and splendors: "In the dimness of the hallway the steps down were treacherous, but Kate held her father firmly, and they made their way out to the darkening street, unaccompanied."

The final story, "Home Fires," is fiercely Western, a story of near-death and wide-open possibilities. An internally directed man, solitary, Pack finds himself almost literally embedded in landscape, victim of a truck wreck. In a move that is perhaps a bit too convenient, the point of view shifts to Pack's wife, to a letter she is writing that informs the reader that Pack "*knows his loneliness better than he knows me.*"

The story hinges on Pack's response to the sudden, surprising choices offered him by the accident. His ordeal is firmly locked in the imagination by the lush physicality of the language and the scope of Long's sensitivity to his characters:

> Pack hugged his arms inside the sweatshirt the driver had lent him. This was always a nervous and transitional hour, one kind of thought giving way to the next. Pack remembered how much of his life had disappeared working like the driver beside him, only with less sense of destination than this man surely had. He remembered the few times he had left a woman at that hour, the sadness of strange doorways and words that disappear like balloons into an endless sky, the whine of his engine as it carried him away.

In a review of *Home Fires* in the *Los Angeles Times* (25 November 1982), Art Seidenbaum raved about Long's storytelling and his ability to flesh out the emotional worlds of his characters: "There is plot. And there is resolution. And there is even satisfaction for the reader. Long characters, like Long settings, make natural sense. In his expansive landscapes, there is room for sentiment next to harsh reality." James W. Grinnell, in his review of *Home Fires* for *Studies in Short Fiction* (1983), said the stories "transcend their particular locale and enter the realm of universality" through Long's "warm and human" empathy for his characters. The book won the $1,000 St. Lawrence Award from St. Lawrence University for an outstanding first collection of short fiction.

Magazine editors continued to show their support for Long's work. By 1987 Long had another collection ready, this one broader in scope, with two novella-length stories and a range of historical periods represented.

More frequently, Long began setting his stories in and around Sperry, Montana, a fictionalized version of Kalispell, and the Flathead Valley. In the interview for *Talking Up a Storm* Long explains his relationship to Sperry:

> I've been most comfortable making up a fictitious place, then using whatever real details of Flathead County I wanted to. It's almost as if I have a circle, and everything within the circle is fictitious and everything outside is authentic. There's no attempt to hide the fact that it's Flathead County; it is just a psychological device to make myself feel comfortable about writing about this place. There's an aesthetic distance that's necessary.

HOME FIRES — STRUCTURE

ACT 1

1) PROLOGUE

2) PACK AFTER ACCIDENT [MCE-ONLY]

    1) REALIZATION THAT HE'S ALIVE
    2) EXPOSITION ON HIS RECENT CONDITION
    3) WONDERING WHAT HE'LL DO W/ THIS [#1].

3) CILLIE PACK AT HOME [USUAL]

    1) REALIZING SHE CAN'T BEAR
       HIS HOMECOMINGS
    2) NEW DEFINITION OF "FAITHFUL"
    3) SERIOUS DOUBTS ABOUT PACK

ACT 2

1) PACK LEAVES WRECK
    — HE'S SCARED

COMPLICATIONS
FEAR
FATIGUE
CLARITY
CHOICE

Outline and page from the revised typescript for the title story in Long's 1982 book (Collection of David Long)

of double tire tracks continued straight this morning, through
the chunks of reddish clay, into the dry brush and the feathery
upper branches of the firs.

The truck lay upside down, back end crushed like a soda
can, the cab folded into so dense a bolus of steel it would
take Search & Rescue better than two hours working with weld-
ing torches and hydraulic jaws to discover it contained no
body. Up slope, scattered among the outcrops of shale and
limestone, in the trees and resting here and there on the flaps
of freshly gashed topsoil, were strewn white packages of frozen
fish, still rock-hard, though the exposed sides would be feel
mushy to the fingers of the first county deputy to huff down
the path, midafternoon. The truck had nearly made it to the
river, stopped only by a slug of granite twice its size, where
now the man named Pack squatted, head between his knees, glanc-
ing up every few seconds at the wreckage, that for a reason
he could not get a clear fix on, did not include him.

Maybe he had fallen asleep.

Some drivers fear the graveyard hours, though secretly.
They ride behind the wheel, pumping Dentyne or cigarettes or
Maalox, half-awed by the power of the diesel and the headlamps,
half-terrified by their limitations, eyes narrowed on the
curvature of the road. But for Pack those hours were peaceful, or used to be. He didn't challenge the road or the clock
or the ICC, refused to make a frantic game of it. Most nights
he sang with the radio, familiar C & W choruses on the clear
channel stations from Casper or Yakima...don't have one thing
against you, just wish you were someone I loved...the old

233

When Long began sending the book manuscript around to New York publishers, he found that his attention to the local was not always welcome. He recalled in the unpublished interview, "An editor at Norton wrote to me after *Home Fires* and said she wanted a look at the next book. When I sent it to her, she said oh–it's too western."

Long had begun digging deeper into the stories he was discovering about Montana, and restoring the human dimension to the scraps he found in the historical record. "I was starting to do some historical fiction at that point," Long said in the unpublished interview; "Historical novels were very common, and I hadn't seen a lot of short stories dealing with that kind of material."

Long also began to publish essays in *The Magazine of Western History, Northern Lights,* and *Antaeus,* the editor of which, Daniel Halpern, expressed an interest in Long's book manuscript. Halpern was also the editor of the Ecco Press of New York, which in 1987 published *The Flood of '64,* Long's second collection of short fiction.

The Flood of '64 amplifies the themes and locales of *Home Fires,* with experiments in point of view and shifts in time frames. The inclusive tone continues, and Long reveals a deepening understanding of the ways of the human heart. The second book is framed by two lengthy historical pieces, set in 1917 and 1924, and it is imbued with the specifics of the landscape of a particular place; of the nine short stories and the novella, all but one are set at least partially in Sperry County, Montana. Julia Stein, reviewing the book for the *Short Story Review* (1987), pointed out the cumulative effect of portraying Sperry from various time periods: "Though the characters do not overlap from one story to another," she wrote, "the stories build, one upon another, describing the history of the county, giving us the texture of a place, an intimacy with its inhabitants."

"The Last Photograph of Lyle Pettibone," set in 1917, starts in first person, addressing someone who seems to be a reporter sent to interview the narrator about his career as a documentary photographer: "You asked me how I got started." Long quickly draws the reader into the storyteller's world, and the quality of observation holds him there:

Or picture any of the other (photographs) I dreamed up, still hidden in the lee of the depot, the camera folded against my shirt, not twenty feet from where the sweating out of (union organizer) Pettibone's actual whereabouts continued, the sheriff's shadow obliterating each man's night-beaten face in turn. What they'd have in common, these pictures, would be Pettibone in flight, for I couldn't shake the image of him in the upstairs hallway, face abruptly unleavened by the news

I'd delivered and all the implications wrung from it in a few consecutive instants.

One of Long's strengths is in finding fresh and inventive ways to explore the results of the decisive moments that often anchor his narratives. As is the case in this story, Long's main characters occasionally fail the test in those critical circumstances where they have the chance to be heroes. But even when his characters let themselves down, the narrative voice–which sets the tone–never makes fun of them. Instead, Long helps the reader understand them, and most often his tone offers a kind of inclusive, humane sense of forgiveness toward his characters, offering the reader a reminder to appreciate the humorous and the sublime available in every moment. In an enthusiastic review for the *Los Angeles Times* (19 April 1987) Rena S. Kleiman cited Long's ability to help the reader understand the lives "of real people doing real, everyday things" by using the "informal voice" of "the campfire storyteller–the spinner of yarns about people we used to know and how their lives turned out."

"Cooper Loftus," the next story in the collection, is about another loner, a man who makes no plans for the future, who feels alien wherever he goes. The story traces how one wrong deed can lead to a life gone sour, a common thread in Long's work; and, like many of his stories, "Cooper Loftus" offers a source of redemption, in this case through friendship.

"Clearance," like "Home Fires," offers yet another shot at a new life, wrought by an accident. In this case, a man finds himself in the middle of his life, disconnected from his family; he is camping alone in the backcountry, trying to sort things out, when he hears a plane go down nearby. His responses on the mountain bring him to an understanding about the ways in which he has been careless regarding those he loves.

Long is often referred to as "a Western writer," but in an interview for *Glimmer Train* magazine, he made a distinction between his work, especially the stories set in and around Sperry, and the work of others who write primarily about the High Plains:

Now, I was an easterner. I came to the West from Massachusetts–went to college in Michigan, came here [Montana] after that, 1972. . . . It's also true that I've spent virtually my entire adult life here, so I suppose my viewpoint is as valid as anybody else's. But I've been writing about a different Montana from what you often see. It's not the prairies. It's not ranch life, although there's a little bit of that in the books. But I wasn't nearly so comfortable with that because that's not really my story. My story is about people who live in towns, and the towns are in mountain valleys. They live in a human community.

Long returns to his past in New England in "Alex's Fire," in which two boys head into their senior year in high school, poised to move in opposite directions. The painful, not-yet-arrived-at existence of a teenager is perfectly rendered: "Here we are, stranded between the two chunks of time that make up our lives."

"Great Blue," set in Michigan, is about a boy who overhears something he should not and is abruptly forced to face some truths that even adults find hard to understand. The descriptions of the natural world are lush and vibrant with suggestions of the sublime: "he'd talk himself down the stairs and back toward the outhouse. He'd never make it the whole way. He'd stop beyond the woodpile and go there, then find himself looking up through the blowing limbs of the pines at the stars, so needle-bright and endless that he imagined himself falling out into them until he'd look away and hurry back up the porch steps, hating himself for not being brave."

The boy, Paul, does learn a kind of bravery, however, as the story he has heard in the night is brought to daylight. Since "the camp" is occupied by several family branches, there are the usual struggles and alliances, and much of the texture of this story involves the way the past is invoked: through camp and family rituals and through the stories that are told—stories that encapsulate a truth in a glimmering form that is not easily apprehended.

One such story passes between Paul and his grandfather while they are fishing, and they share a moment of silence: "They'd come out too late and pretty soon they'd need to turn around and go back, but for a few minutes more they sat in the boat together, watching the heron disappear into the darkness of the reeds." The story risks becoming sentimental, but Long avoids overstating his case by trusting the image, the language, to carry the suggestion of the emotion.

The tone shifts quickly with "Compensation," a shorter (twelve pages) look through the eyes of Patsy, who has a way of wrapping herself around everything she says:

This late, the Stockholm's dead, the air's gone out of the meringue, the drunks are still out drinking. We've got a boy and girl tucked elbow to elbow in the last booth, feeding each other fries. Except for Mitch, that's it, everybody's slunked off home. This girl's maybe seventeen. Hours and hours ago it was hot enough for that gauzy thing you can see her tan through. Out in the kitchen, Yvonne has her nose in a romance when

she ought to be running potatoes through a shredder, but Yvonne's not my number-one problem tonight.

"Solstice" is a ranchland story, an interesting exercise in point of view—at one juncture, the point of view moves back and forth between two men, idling in winter, side by side in their pickup trucks. "V-E Day" is set at the end of World War II. "The Flood of '64" alternately tells the story of Sperry County Sheriff Carl Prudhomme and his sister, Carla. The story balances on a question of justice, and the shifting narrative emphasizes the ambiguity of the moral question at hand. Sometimes, Long said in the *Glimmer Train* interview, his characters discover that there is no single right answer to how they should behave: "the stories construct a moral universe. People are worrying about whether they've acted in a way that's moral, although they might not phrase it like that. . . . That's the problem. A lot of times, you want to do the right thing and you just can't figure out what that is."

The final story in the book is a fifty-page historical novella, "The Oriental Limited." In 1924, on a train headed west, Lillian Wallace of Chicago is in search of her two brothers, who have disappeared into the wilds of Glacier National Park. The story is a deeply personal account of the difficult time that follows, layered with the mysterious intricacies of family love and intrigue and the rich physical texture of the period. "The Oriental Limited" won high praise: in *The New York Times Book Review* (5 July 1987) Greg Johnson called it a "superb novella" that "is at once an adventure mystery, a psychological study and a story of courageous self-determination."

The Flood of '64 was reviewed widely, with favorable criticism in the *Los Angeles Times Book Review* and *The New York Times Book Review*. Other reviewers cited the poetic language that is heightened, yet also clear and direct. A reviewer for *Publishers Weekly* (16 January 1987) said Long's prose "is both rugged and nuanced; he can grip the reader with a sense of the vitality and treachery of the Western landscape—every rock, cloud and flood of which is intimately entwined with character."

Following the critical success of *The Flood of '64*, Long considered writing a novel, but never hit upon a plot that sustained him. In the *Glimmer Train* article he said he often begins a story unsure of its plot: "I discover it as I go. Very few stories do I know ahead of time." This approach makes his method of composition slow and meticulous: "These stories take six weeks to three months to draft out some times, and then longer to revise. Often I'll let them sit awhile." Long began writing new stories at the rate of a few a year from 1988 until his next collection, *Blue Spruce,* came out in 1995. His magazine credits began to build: by the time *Blue*

Dust jacket for Long's 1987 book, in which most of the stories are set in Sperry County, Montana

Spruce was published, stories from the collection had appeared in such periodicals as *GQ, Antaeus,* and *Story,* and Long's work had been collected in ten anthologies, including *Writers of the Purple Sage* for Viking Press (1984) and *The O. Henry Awards* anthology (1992).

In 1990 Long sent "Cooperstown," a baseball-oriented short story, to *The New Yorker* editor Roger Angell, who has written widely on the sport. Angell turned the story down but asked to see more, and he accepted the next piece Long sent, "Blue Spruce." In the *Talking Up a Storm* interview Long recalled that event as a "turning point": "I was contacted by my present agent, Sally Wofford-Girand, and that was my access to the world of New York publishing."

"Blue Spruce" appeared in *The New Yorker* in 1990, and "Attraction" followed in 1991. Long was awarded a National Endowment for the Arts fellowship in creative writing in 1993, and when *Blue Spruce* was published by Scribners it won the Richard and Hinda Rosenthal Award for fiction from the American Academy of Arts and Letters.

The first piece in the collection, "Attraction," is another story launched by an accident—in this case, actually a petty act of violence that turns out to have dire consequences. But as so often happens in a Long narrative, the high-drama moment is not what gets the narrator's attention, but rather the lengthier deliberations about the moral choices that inform human lives. Reviewing the collection for *The New York Times Book Review* (23 April 1995), Lisa Sandlin said the twelve stories in the book "explore how we nourish the 'crimp' in ourselves—habits of meanness and fear—and how we manage to expand. Some of the stories explode into meaning, but most require the reader's patient orientation as relationships and consequences shape themselves."

"Perfection" is a narrative about storytelling, with long italicized sections of legal testimony interspersed with the intense memories of a young woman who has witnessed a killing. Michael Upchurch, writing in the *Chicago Tribune* (26 March 1995), called it "a many-layered story" and said "it's astonishing how much Long is able to tell us about her life in a mere sixteen pages." In the widely anthologized "Lightning" a younger son grudgingly returns to a ranch and is made to face his father—and his own sense of failure.

"Talons," and later in the volume, "Josephine," are shorter stories than the others in *Blue Spruce,* and they offer glimpses into the lives of characters who need guidance. "Talons" is a first-person story in which the narrator describes a summer of great change, including his marriage, "the last forced show of family solidarity," and the death of an aunt, which starts a mystery. The story is told from a narrative remove that allows reflection: "I was young enough I'd never lost anyone to death. I was angry, but it was anger I didn't know, raw and chastening as the other feelings consuming me that summer. And mixed with it, like grains of gravel, was something else—I felt betrayed, stiff-armed away from business of wonderful importance."

Such telling observations about the emotional world lift "Talons" and "Josephine" above the realm of anecdote that most "short-short" stories usually offer; still, just as they are gathering momentum, they stop, and readers used to Long's leisurely pacing might feel shorted. Sandlin praised "Talons" for its focused study of the narrator, Frank Leland, who chooses to stay locked inside his self-imposed confines. "Not that taking a chance guarantees anything," Sandlin notes: "In Mr. Long's stories, as in life, reward isn't guaranteed—except by that movement toward spaciousness he describes in various ways."

In the center of the book, "Cooperstown" looks at a man trying to come to terms with the horrifying, defining moment in his life. A former major-league pitcher, Isham visits the man he purposely beaned a dozen years earlier, ending a promising career. The beaning incident is the beginning of the end of Isham's career as well, and he associates it with the start of his twelve-year-long slide: "Then, high summer of that same year (Isham still believing, deep down, he must be on some extended leave of absence), his wife, Janey, packs and is gone, the adhesive between them aged to a gritty powder."

"Cooperstown" is also a story of the breakdown of a man's carefully constructed self-deception. The narrator says, "Picture this, a chain of events," and describes a version of the pitch that is probable and absolves Isham. But the narrator later makes corrections: "This is fraudulent, though, if it starts with Hewitt not ducking." It is another way to increase narrative tension—as readers follow Isham's literal journey to confront the man he has beaned, they also see the stripping away of the rationalizations that he has made to keep himself going during those twelve years. Long often manipulates the point of view or offers alternate tellings of the same incident (as in "Perfection") as a subtle way to reinforce readers' awareness of the importance of storytelling in the waking, "nonfiction" world.

"Blue Spruce" is a story that many reviewers praised for its intense scrutiny of a critical chapter in the lives of two sisters-in-law who share a house in Sperry. For Sandlin it reveals the quintessential arc of a Long story: conflict on the surface between characters mirroring deeper conflicts within the characters. (In a telephone interview, Long said he agreed with William Butler Yeats: "Of conflict with others we make rhetoric; of conflict with ourselves we make poetry.") As always, the details of scenery, the descriptions of landscape, reinforce theme and character. The story begins:

> Laurel is up in the cool shadow on the porch roof, in dungarees and a sweatshirt, scraping off the pine needles with a snow shovel. Below, an old garden hose snakes its way across the knobby dirt, its pinhole leak shooting up a spray that fizzes in a slash of sunlight. There's a breath of wind, a commotion in the lilacs. Down the lane, stones are finally warming in their sockets.

The "commotion" in the flowers suggests the squall to come and emphasizes the change about to happen. Long's poetic yet specific language is often cited as one of his strengths; those passages serve as underplayed reminders of the major themes of each story.

Upchurch wrote that "Real Estate" is "a miniature *Howard's End*": it "uses a house to unveil truths about family loyalty and the disruptive power of sex." *Los Angeles Times* book critic Richard Eder called it "a complex and engaging story." He, too, noted Long's

inclusive tone: "He is with his characters, never above them, and he finds as much redemption on their behalf as he can."

Long's look at a local campaign manager in "The Vote" reveals a man who is offered redemption, but who seems to choose the narrowness he is most familiar with: when the candidate points out how quickly evening falls in November, his handler, Smithlin, immediately thinks, "And still six weeks to the shortest day." Though he recognizes the "wonderful dark joke" at the center of the story—a woman's accidental vote for the opposite candidate—Smithlin's pessimism does not allow him to see his life in any new way. He lacks that ability to engineer one's own rebirth, to shake off the burden of old stories, which fuels much of the affirmation in Long's other work.

"Perro Semihundido" (the half-submerged dog) takes its title from a Francisco Goya painting. The protagonist, Faith, is stagnating in a relationship that is not threatening, but is equally unrewarding. Out of concern about an adored, missing brother, she travels to Seattle and learns some unsettling facts about his life that he has successfully hidden from her for many years. The unveiling continues, as Faith reconsiders her own life after looking back at her brother's. Once again, the story underscores the power of the imagination in leading people into transformation: once their lives are re-imagined, they can reconsider who they are, and who they can become.

Set in Massachusetts, "Eggarine" is a story of fathers and sons, of quiet estrangements and tender moments of reflection. Originally published in *GQ*, "Eggarine" is "perhaps the most personal story" he has written, Long told a reporter for the *Spokane Spokesman-Review* (25 March 1995); "But," he quickly added, "I don't really write very autobiographical stuff." On the larger question of autobiography, Long added:

> I could go through all the stories . . . and I could point to line after line—this came from this place and this came from that place. It's not like you totally invent stuff. When you sit down to write, all these little details slip into your head from your own reading, from the newspaper, from things you remember.

The last story in the book, "The New World," is a "bigger, looser" story than some of his others, Long said in the interview for *Talking Up a Storm*. "The same themes of chance and choice come up in it," Long said, and it "becomes a way of talking about the process of middle age where you're confronted with a world you're over-familiar with, that doesn't give you awe, and how you get beyond that point." Sandlin called "The New World" "the book's loveliest story," in which the main character, McCutcheon, "steps amazed into the vacant room of his own grace."

After he finished work on the stories in *Blue Spruce,* Long faced a dilemma: he had always considered himself a short-story writer, but his contract with Scribners called for a novel, to be published after the short stories came out; and he did not have a novel. But he turned to a longer piece he had written, "Falling Boy Stories," and it became the basis for his first novel, *The Falling Boy,* published in 1997 by Scribners. "That book presented me with a new set of technical problems," Long recalled in the *Talking Up a Storm* interview: "To open it up, I began to share the point of view around among the characters, which was a challenge for a short-story writer. I was used to focusing on a single consciousness." The book was well received, earning a starred review in *Publishers Weekly,* and it was named a notable book by the National Book Critics Circle. Subsequently, Scribners signed him to a contract for a second novel.

Since *Blue Spruce* Long has published just two more stories: "Jokes," in the Spring 1996 issue of the *Talking River Review,* and "Morphine," which appeared in the 20 July 1998 issue of *The New Yorker.* Scribners released Long's second novel, *The Daughters of Simon Lamoreaux,* in May of 2000. In the *Talking Up a Storm* interview Long said that his short-story career is "on hiatus":

> I'm writing novels now. There's that hunger to see books on the shelf. Writing stories takes too long, and it's too hard—it takes much longer for me to write a book of short stories than a novel of equal length. That's because novels are mostly middles—you don't have so many beginnings

and endings, and so many entirely different plot lines to think up. That's the hardest part for me. And the novel is simply the form that interests me most now. So I'd have to say, I don't see myself writing stories in the foreseeable future.

Wherever Long's career takes him, he has had an indelible effect on the contemporary short-story form. He has served as a consultant for the University of Illinois Press and has judged manuscripts for state arts organizations in Arizona, Idaho, Montana, and North Dakota, as well as for the Loft-McKnight fellowships and the Ucross Foundation. He has taught the craft of fiction writing in the graduate program at the University of Montana and has led writing workshops at conferences across the country. But David Long's most lasting legacy is the fiction itself: clear, elegantly written stories that throw the light of compassion and understanding into the lives of his characters.

Interviews:

Linda Davis, "Interview with David Long," *Glimmer Train Stories,* issue 16 (Fall 1995): 119–137;

Gregory L. Morris, "David Long," in his *Talking Up a Storm: Voices of the New West* (Lincoln: University of Nebraska Press, 1995), pp. 185–202.

References:

James W. Grinnell, "Review of *Home Fires," Studies in Short Fiction* (Spring/Summer 1983): 124–130;

Julia Stein, "The Stories of David Long," *Short Story Review,* 1 (Summer 1987): 36–42.

Hilary Masters

(3 February 1928 –   )

Sigrid Kelsey
Louisiana State University

BOOKS: *The Common Pasture* (New York: Macmillan, 1967);
An American Marriage (New York: Macmillan, 1969);
Palace of Strangers (New York: World, 1971);
Last Stands: Notes from Memory (Boston: Godine, 1982);
Clemmons (Boston: Godine, 1985);
Hammertown Tales (Winston-Salem, N.C.: S. Wright, 1986);
Cooper (New York: St. Martin's Press, 1987);
Manuscript for Murder, as P. J. Coyne (New York: Dodd, Mead, 1987);
Strickland (New York: St. Martin's Press, 1989);
Success: New and Selected Short Stories (New York: St. Martin's Press, 1992);
Home Is the Exile (Sag Harbor, N.Y.: Permanent, 1996);
In Montaigne's Tower (Columbia & London: University of Missouri Press, 2000).

OTHER: "Joyce Carol Oates" and "Ann Beattie," in *The Brand-X Anthology of Fiction,* edited by William Zaranka (Cambridge, Mass.: Apple-Wood Books, 1983), pp. 325–326, 327–328;
Wayne Dodd, ed., *Ohio Review Anthology,* includes a contribution by Masters (Athens: Ohio Review, 1983);
Lee Gutkind, ed., *The Essayist at Work: Profiles of Creative Nonfiction Writers,* includes a contribution by Masters (Portsmouth, N.H.: Heinemann, 1998).

SELECTED PERIODICAL PUBLICATION–
UNCOLLECTED: "Italian Grammar," *Virginia Quarterly Review,* 74 (Spring 1998): 234–250;
"Shoe Polish," *Virginia Quarterly Review,* 76 (Summer 2000): 500–512.

Hilary Masters (photograph by Maurice Tierney; from the dust jacket for Success, *1992)*

Best known for his highly acclaimed autobiographical work, *Last Stands: Notes from Memory* (1982), Hilary Masters is an accomplished novelist, essayist, short-story writer, and memoirist. A realist and a regionalist, Masters follows in the tradition of other American realists such as Peter Taylor, Sherwood Anderson, and his own father, Edgar Lee Masters. His two collections of short stories, *Hammertown Tales* (1986) and *Success: New and Selected Short Stories* (1992), as well as his other short fiction, reiterate the themes and techniques often appearing in his longer works. Much of his work is filled with characters longing to recapture lost memories, dealing with relationships, and finding closure by examining their ideals and accepting their situations. Characters, rather than plot, are often the focus of his work. Masters weaves compelling stories and situations into ordinary settings with which his readers can identify. "It seems a sorrowful mystery," wrote Susan

Dodd in *Harvard Review* (June 1992), "that a writer of such magnanimous gifts should remain known by so few." She continued, "For decades Hilary Masters has been writing some of the most elegant, intelligent, and inventive prose in American literature."

Masters has received recognition more often for his nonfiction work. The title essay for the collection *In Montaigne's Tower* (2000) was included in Phillip Lopate's *The Anchor Essay Annual: The Best of 1998*. A second essay from *In Montaigne's Tower*, "Making It Up," appears in *The Best American Essays of 1999*, edited by Edward Hoagland. Both originally appeared in the *Ohio Review* in 1997. Finally, another essay from *In Montaigne's Tower*, "Going to Cuba," was given the Monroe Spears Award as the best essay to appear in the *Sewanee Review* in 1997. Masters's short stories have also received honorable mention in *Best American Short Stories* and *The Pushcart Prize*. "The Italian Grammar," published in the Spring 1998 *Virginia Quarterly Review*, received the 1998 Balch Prize.

Son of poet Edgar Lee Masters, the author of *Spoon River Anthology* (1916), and Ellen Frances (Coyne) Masters, Hilary Thomas Masters was born on 3 February 1928 in Kansas City, Missouri. The only child of his father's second marriage, Masters spent much of his childhood (until the age of fourteen) in Kansas City at his maternal grandparents' house, while his parents lived in New York City, his father writing and his mother pursuing a master's degree in teaching from Columbia University. Masters usually spent summers with his parents in New York City, returning to Kansas City for school in the fall. He wrote about these years in his most acclaimed work, the autobiographical *Last Stands*, in which he remembers life as the son of a famous writer and the grandson of Irish immigrant Thomas Coyne, a United States Cavalry trooper in the Indian Wars.

Masters attended Davidson College from 1944 to 1946, interrupting his education to serve in the military as a correspondent in the United States Navy from 1946 to 1947. He returned stateside in 1948 and began attending Brown University, where he graduated with a B.A. in 1952. His first marriage, to Robin Owett Watt in 1954, ended with divorce. His marriage to Polly Jo McCulloch on 5 March 1955 also ended with divorce, in 1986. On 7 June 1994 Masters married Kathleen E. George, also a short-story writer and a drama professor at the University of Pittsburgh. Masters has three children: Joellen, Catherine, and John D. C.

Masters has had a varied career. From 1953 to 1956 he was a theatrical agent in New York. In 1956 he founded *The Hyde Park Record* and worked as an editor there until 1959. He has contributed short fiction and essays to *Greensboro Review, Kenyon Review, Massachusetts Review, Michigan Quarterly, Ohio Review, Prairie Schooner, Sports Illustrated, Texas Review,* and *Virginia Quarterly Review*. Besides writing, Masters is also a professional photographer. Masters has been a visiting scholar at Drake University (1975–1977), Clark University (1978), Ohio University (1979), and a Fulbright scholar in Finland (1983). In 1980 and in 1982 he was granted fellowships to Yaddo, an artists' community in Saratoga Springs, New York. Since 1983 Masters has been a professor of English and creative writing at Carnegie Mellon University. "My working experiences as a journalist, a Broadway press agent, and even some history in politics, have all found places in my writing," wrote Masters for the Carnegie Mellon English faculty website, adding, "My work sounds themes of abandonment—all kinds of abandonment, physical, spiritual and moral—while it represents men and women caught in the socio-political fabric of America."

Hammertown Tales (1986), which received mixed reviews, is Masters's first short-story collection, comprised of fourteen tales set in the fictitious New York village of Hammertown. The stories in this volume depict the characteristics of modern American regionalism. They portray life in a small American town, explore relationships, and examine the search to fill voids caused by deaths or empty relationships. Drawing the substance for his stories from everyday situations and dilemmas, Masters rarely strays from the principles of realism.

Carol Ames, in *The New York Times Book Review* (20 April 1986), praised *Hammertown Tales* as a "book of fine stories" but concluded that the collection is "not Hilary Masters' best," citing his better-known *Last Stands* as an example of his best work. The short stories share themes and stylistic qualities with *Last Stands*, invoking a reminiscent portrait of America, which perhaps inspired Ames to compare the works. In contrast to Ames's review, Stuart Wright in *The Kirkus Review* (15 December 1985) wrote that *Hammertown Tales* is "graceful, thoughtful work from an accomplished stylist, one with a fine sense of the sorrows of a disappearing America."

"The Foundation," a representative story from *Hammertown Tales*, was first published in the Winter 1979 issue of *The Ohio Review*. The story begins with a couple searching for a house foundation near some property they once owned. Trying to recapture memories, the woman is at first insistent on finding the architectural remains, while the man seems somewhat apathetic. They search through abandoned orchards for the foundation, where they wish to picnic. The tension between the two builds as they search. Finally defeated, the couple agrees to picnic by an old ruin of a wall, and as they sit, their conversation turns to an Emily Dickinson

Dust jacket for Masters's 1986 book, stories set in a fictional village in the dairy region of upstate New York

poem, relaxing the tension between them. The man begins to arrange the stones from the ruined wall into the shape of a foundation. The woman's response—and the last words of the story—as her companion arranges the rocks, confirm that the lost foundation was not what the couple needed to rekindle their memories, after all. In response to the rebuilding of the foundation, the woman says, "'Oh, don't be silly.' She flushed, but her tone was not angry. 'Come, open the wine.'" While Masters usually avoids the use of symbolism, depending more on imagery, this story treats the foundation as not only a place from the couple's past but also a symbol of the foundation of their relationship. Nonetheless, the story abides by the other principles and characteristics of realistic writing, especially the in-depth examination of everyday circumstances and characters.

The main character in "How the Indians Buried Their Dead," first published in *The Georgia Review* (Winter 1980) and included in *Hammertown Tales,* also attempts to reconnect with his past when he returns to his hometown to attend a conference after years of absence. Masters's use of imagery evokes nostalgia, per-

haps prompting George Garrett, in the introduction to *Success,* in which "How the Indians Buried Their Dead" also is collected, to note: "these stories might conceivably be called old fashioned." For example, looking down into the city from the new, modern hotel that houses the conference, the main character "can feel and smell the heat out there, like the memory of an old blanket in a summer attic." The unnamed character searches his memory for details about an old man who lived with his family and told him stories about Indians when he was young.

Curiosity compels the narrator to take a taxi to his former residence to search for clues about the old man. Things have changed. The cab driver, not wishing to enter the neighborhood, leaves him to walk the last stretch, warning, "whatever your business is, make it quick. That's my advice. Get out before it gets really dark." The man finds his childhood house and, denied entry, talks with (or rather to) the current resident through the screen door. Ultimately, the man turns back toward the modern hotel, which he sees on the city skyline "like a great rocket ship preparing to ignite its engines, preparing to pull itself up through the heavy clouds and leave all this behind. He would have to hurry." Similar to "The Foundation," "How the Indians Buried Their Dead" concludes with the protagonist accepting that the past cannot always be recovered.

Written in the first person, "Buster's Hand" relates the story of Mr. Sloan's attempt to plan a bicentennial celebration for Hammertown. The unnamed narrator, a native Hammertownian, views Mr. Sloan as an "outsider," sincerely interested in recording and preserving the history of the town but unable to fit in. To set the scene, the narrator points out that "number one, the people on this Historical Committee and especially Mr. Sloan, its chairman, don't know very much about the history of this place and, number two, there isn't an awful lot of history to know."

Filled with local color, the narration often diverts to anecdotes about Hammertown people, such as Annie Hoystradt, freezing while doing her chores, or Mrs. Sloan, who "had taken to wearing sun-bonnets in fair weather, like what women used to wear around here forty or fifty years ago." For the celebration Mr. Sloan plans to record Aunt Sally's "oral history" of the railroad and the story of Buster Ames, her husband, who was the engineer on the Poughkeepsie and Pittsfield before burning his hand off in a railroad accident. Foreshadowing the impending failure of this plan, the narrator comments, "Aunt Sally don't always remember things clear, you know. . . . She makes a lot up. It was a long time ago, anyway." When Mr. Sloan finally records Aunt Sally, rather than recounting the history of the railroad, she only rants and curses about Buster being cheated out of a pension. Mr. Sloan's effort to record the past results in bitterness for Mrs. Ames and utter failure for his project.

Similarly, "FDR Spoke Here" recollects the history of Hammertown from a first-person perspective. The narrator, a Hammertown native, again unnamed, begins:

> Some folks say they can remember young Franklin Roosevelt making that speech on the steps of Benschoten's Store when he ran for the State Senate. More likely, they heard about it from some older relative just as Florence Benschoten had heard about it from her husband, Tad–she didn't marry him and move to Hammertown until 1930–and he had heard it only described by his parents who had been there.

Despite a lack of official records indicating that Roosevelt had indeed made such a speech on the steps of the store, and the lack of actual eyewitnesses, the County Historical Society places a marker at the site of the reputed speech.

The narrator recounts the history of the spot, mentioning the Pittsfield and Poughkeepsie trains, which quit stopping at Benschoten's Store after milk was delivered by truck, and how an interstate was built around Hammertown, diverting the travelers who used to makes stops at the store. Because of the local changes, the store shuts down; the owner auctions off the supplies; and the FDR plaque turns up missing. Some young people eventually buy and renovate the store but do not succeed in selling their health food. The store is sold again, burned down, and mobile homes are moved in the lot. The original owner of the store dies, and finally the person accused of stealing the original plaque makes plans to have a marker put on the interstate saying "you are passing Hammertown, where FDR made his first speech." The bittersweet nostalgia that the current residents of the evolving Hammertown indulge in again establishes the theme of coming to terms with the past.

"The Sound of Pines" commences in a police car with two officers and a prisoner picked up for vagrancy and hitchhiking. One of the officers tries to persuade the unidentified prisoner to tell them who he is. Chatting throughout the journey about dairy land, the orange juice they stop for, and anything else, the officer finally persuades the prisoner to open up. The prisoner is going to California to plant trees in exchange for a long-term lease on the land from the state. The officer begins to warm up a little, but it is not clear whether he is being sarcastic or not until the prisoner mentions that he may have goats on his land: "'Well, that hangs it up,' the round policeman says. 'That really hangs it up. Here we are in the prime dairy land of the state, generations of the greatest Holsteins and this yo-yo talks about goats.'" The amiable break ends; the prisoner is shuffled back into the police car; and they continue the journey. The realistic conveyance of an everyday experience provides depth to the overall picture of Hammertown.

"Sam Rudder's Cottage" begins with a man taking a woman to her uncle Sam's cottage after Sam has passed away. Some hunters are interested in buying the cottage, and the unnamed niece is making up her mind what to do with it. The cottage has been locked up for about three years, and upon opening the door, the narrator and Sam's niece find stacks of magazines against the doors and all the windows locked from the inside. The niece finds a contraption on one of the windows that automatically locks when it is shut, and they surmise that Sam had done these things so he would know if there were intruders.

The niece reminisces about childhood visits to the cabin, and they leave. After they depart, the niece makes an excuse to go back and returns with a cut on her knee–indicating that she had returned, stacked the magazines up against the door again, and climbed out of the automatically locking window. The hunters later attempt to bribe the narrator to let them use the cottage without telling Sam's niece, and the narrator closes the story thus: "I tell them that, not counting the sheriff's deputies, people sometimes have a way of finding out if their property's been trespassed, and I advise them, in a friendly way, not to try it."

Because the short stories are tied together by their setting, Masters is able to provide a sweeping view of Hammertown from various angles. Masters avoids omniscient narration; he tells each story from a different, singular viewpoint, thus providing a broad perspective of Hammertown. With each story, the various levels of reality within Hammertown are added.

Success: New and Selected Short Stories (1992), Masters's second collection of short fiction, comprises sixteen tales, most of which had been published first in literary magazines, and some, including the title piece and "Grace Peck's Dog," that were republished from *Hammertown Tales.* Unlike *Hammertown Tales,* these stories do not share a commonality in plot or setting, but they all touch on similar themes and share the style inherent in most of Masters's work. Characters dealing with abandonment and/or relationships, searching for meaning and lost memories, fill the pages of this collection. Masters seems more willing to experiment in these stories, moving from the strict regionalism of Hammertown and exploring new settings, one as far away as Italy, while using different techniques, such as stream of consciousness.

The main character in "The Moving Finger" calls a former girlfriend in Chicago while on a layover at O'Hare. As in many of his other stories, Masters introduces a character trying to reconnect with his past, and like many of those stories, "The Moving Finger" ends with the character's understanding that what he is looking for cannot be found in the past. The phone call, rather than affirming his fond memories of Cindy, reminds him of her annoying compulsions and delusions. She criticizes the decisions he has made, rattles off conspiracy theories about the John F. Kennedy and Martin Luther King assassinations, and ultimately loses her temper, hanging up on him.

During his flight the character realizes that "he had been looking for some kind of fulcrum in Chicago in which to balance all this travel. He would have to look for it elsewhere, perhaps in a place so familiar that the location is temporarily out of mind." The character does not yet know what the fulcrum of his trip, or his life, is. He recognizes, however, the importance of pursuing the present and future rather than dwelling in the past. The moral, as it were, of the story is summarized

in his quotation from Omar Khayyám: "The moving finger writes, and having writ, moves on." Typically in Masters's works, the characters examine their longings and discover that what they are looking for cannot be found in the past.

Many other stories in the collection center on characters trying not to reconnect with their history, but simply to reconcile with it, sometimes feeling abandoned by deceased loved ones, at other times trying to recapture an old feeling or relationship. As Dodd put it in her *Harvard Review* article, "Hilary Masters writes, always, of place and memory, of time and change. His homeground is the rocky yet fertile soil of human connection and the soul's persistent striving toward it."

In "Ohm's Law" a widow sorts through her husband's papers. The story is told by her son, who describes the papers as "the last threads of personal history" that form a "loom over which my mother passes, back and forth, and year after year, not in anticipation of her husband's return but to unravel the thread of his complete disappearance." Masters balances the relationship between the widow and her husband (a hydroelectric engineer) with that of the widow's son, a teacher, and his lover, a student. Relationships like these– between student and teacher, older man and younger woman–fill Masters's work. One of his novels, *An American Marriage* (1969), many of his short stories, and even his autobiography deal with similar relationships. Certainly his parents' relationship, with his father nearly thirty years older than his mother, influenced Masters in his writing. In "Ohm's Law" the woman reaches closure by passing the task of sorting through the papers to her son, the narrator. The reader must decide if her son will continue her legacy. The plot of this short story, and the others, emphasizes normal daily experience, and privileges characters over plot.

"Blues for Solitaire," written in the first person with a female narrator, shifts back and forth from the narrator's memories to the present. Written in stream of consciousness, the story jumps from the narrator's father complaining about his new apartment to a phone conversation with her boyfriend and thoughts about their relationship. Masters's use of this style amplifies her struggle with her separate roles: mother, president of a credit bureau, girlfriend, and daughter. The entire story takes place within the span of a solitaire game played by her father while she is on the phone. Her father eventually scrambles the deck to get the card he needs to win, and the narrator compares her relationship with her boyfriend to a solitaire game that gets played over and over, but without the right card ever coming up. She realizes that in their relationship, "all the time, I see something that's never played out if we go by the rules."

Lurching back to Hunter on the crosstown bus, I often was tempted to get off, to double back to her. The risk of incurring my chairman's displeasure only made my such an impulse more attractive, put me in league with Shelley or Byron or one of those romantic types who were driven completely the women to control the objects of their obsession. But such domination is not in my nature But my nature does not But my temperment does not require, in the final alanysis, that sort of domination but my temperment, in the final analysis shrinks from such control and besides, Eunice's voice would restore my equilibrium. "Any socks for the wash, William?"

Anyway, that spring. "I'm sorry not to meet you today," Eva said one morning. Down the street Adlai Stevenson was demanding the the missles be removed from Cuba. "I'm going to Italy tomorrow and I have to do some things."

"Italy."

"Yes, I'm really going," she said. I imagined her eyes crinkling up, the smile: "Rome, " she specified. "I think I have a kind of job with a movie company there."

She was vague about the job her farewell was casual. After all, we had kept each other company at the Metropolitan for almost a year, but the tone in her voice sounded as if she were canceling a dentist's appointment. The tooth ache had been taken care of, and in a burst of anger which shamed me immediately, I almost asked her if Nick Jones might be accompanying her. As we know, he didn't, and as the information developed over the years, we know that Eva been embraced by far more glittering

"Isn't this your Eva?" Eunice said one Sunday morning a while back. She held out the New York Times magazine, open to an article on Rilenzo, and there were several pictures of the movie director, the largest showed him sitting looking straight into the camera, his lined face vibrant with genius, and standing behind him, her arms draped lovingly around his shoulders was Eva. "His muse and American wife who produced La Borsetta, his first triumph," the cutline below the picture read. Eva was also looking straight into the camera lens, and the two figures resembled those comfortably complacent couples found in clay on top of Etruscan tombs. She looked remarkably the same, that is not older -- her hair still dark and worn long and with bangs across her forehead above those remarkable eyes, serene now and no more uncertainty in their gaze, where a serenity had replaced that uncertain gaze which entranced us. "She must be fluent in Italian by now," Eunice observed.

Page from the revised typescript for an early draft of "The Italian Grammar," published in the Spring 1998 issue of the Virginia Quarterly Review *(Collection of Hilary Masters)*

Also first collected in *Hammertown Tales,* "Success," the title story, is narrated in first person. Similar to "Blues for Solitaire," the story jumps around in time and place within the narrator's thoughts, but the whole story takes place in a car ride with the narrator and his wife. Many of the narrator's thoughts are about his half brother, Will, who recently died. His thoughts often jump suddenly to the present, where he and his wife, Sally, are waiting for a ferry, then back to his memories. He remembers Will talking about the ferry on the way back from their father's funeral. Some of the narrator's remembrances are of their father criticizing Will: "'why, he's a runt,' Dad had said. 'He always was a runt, mentally and physically and morally. His mother spoiled him.'" His father favored the narrator because he liked the narrator's mother better than Will's mother.

In the present, Sally says to her husband, "Are you going to turn mean like that? . . . Your father was an exceptional louse." His memories return to Will, on a ferry, talking about how their dad liked this side of the river for its atmosphere and how their father kept a ferry going so he could have the barbecue served there. He remembers eating ribs with Will, who talked about another time across the river with their dad and shared how jealous he was of "Sonny" (the narrator's nickname). In the memory, the narrator returns to the other side of the river, and Will stays behind–it is the last time the narrator sees his brother, and he does not wave goodbye to him. The story concludes with Sally admonishing him, "You should have waved anyhow." The narrator is trying to reconcile his feelings regarding Will and how he is considered the successful son only because his father liked his mother better.

"Face in the Window," which takes place in Italy, departs from the regionalism of many of his stories. The main character is a professor in charge of a group of students in Italy for the summer. Overly academic, Professor Cantwell often looks over the bland faces of the students during a lecture, to see "her," a student with whom he thinks he has made a connection, Virginia Pontefore. Throughout the story, the professor fantasizes that she is different from the others, but in the end he overhears her participating in a juvenile joke and making fun of "old Cantwell." He realizes that he really is not different from any other observers of the history he is teaching them, but just another "face in the window."

Success received, for the most part, excellent reviews. In addition to Dodd's enthusiastic review, Robert Shapter said in *The Columbus Dispatch* (14 June 1992), "These stories of parents and children, broken dreams and hard-found answers are full of discoveries and delights. The values speak forcefully for themselves." He concluded that "Masters creates people and places with whom just about everyone will identify. Even the characters just offstage are deeply felt."

An exception to the positive reviews was an assertion in *Publishers Weekly* (13 January 1992) that "while Hilary Masters is truly accomplished, able to juxtapose events from the past and present gracefully, to coin arresting phrases and to manipulate symbols with enviable dexterity, none of these 16 entries seems more than an exercise in technique." More often, however, the response was positive. Constance Decker Thomson, in *The New York Times* (10 May 1992), characterized the stories as "Erudite, engaging and lovingly detailed," adding that they "feature an ambiance of quiet composure in which modest characters pursue modest longings, often across great distances. Mr. Masters excels at exploring his characters' yearnings to recover a lost home or to reconnect with a lost love."

Hilary Masters's short fiction evokes nostalgic feelings and a depth to his characters as he shares a morsel of Americana with his readers. While his autobiography and some of his essays have received broader recognition, his short fiction is exceptional, not to be circumvented in favor of his other work.

Interview:

"About the Author: Interview: Hilary Masters Author of 'Son of Spoon River,'" *Creative Nonfiction,* no. 5 <http://www.cnf.edu/thejournal/articles/issue05/05masters_ai.htm>.

James Alan McPherson

(16 September 1943 –   )

Herman Beavers
University of Pennsylvania

See also the McPherson entry in *DLB 38: Afro-American Writers After 1955: Dramatists and Prose Writers.*

BOOKS: *Hue and Cry* (Boston: Little, Brown, 1968);
Elbow Room (Boston: Little, Brown, 1977);
Crabcakes (New York: Simon & Schuster, 1998);
A Region Not Home: Reflections from Exile (New York: Simon & Schuster, 2000).

OTHER: *Railroad: Trains and Train People in American Culture,* edited by McPherson and Miller Williams (New York: Random House, 1976);
Fathering Daughters: Reflections by Men, edited by McPherson and DeWitt Henry (Boston: Beacon Press, 1998).

SELECTED PERIODICAL PUBLICATIONS–
UNCOLLECTED: "Chicago's Blackstone Rangers," *Atlantic Monthly,* 223 (May 1969): 74–84; "Chicago's Blackstone Rangers, Part II," *Atlantic Monthly,* 223 (June 1969): 92–98, 100;
"The Black Law Student: A Problem of Fidelities," *Atlantic Monthly,* 225 (April 1970): 93–100;
"Indivisible Man," *Atlantic Monthly,* 226 (December 1970): 45–60;
"On Becoming an American Writer," *Atlantic Monthly,* 242 (December 1978): 53–57;
"There Was Once a State Called Franklin," *Callaloo,* 2 (May 1979): 1–15;
"Reflections of Titus Basfield, April 1850," *Harper's,* 300 (June 2000): 99–102.

The articulated vision of James Alan McPherson needs to be understood as a product of both time and place. Though his writing has a cosmopolitan quality to it that separated him from many of his contemporaries who began writing at the same time in the 1960s, McPherson must be thought of as a Southern writer who came of age as Jim Crow segregation was being put to a slow death.

James Alan McPherson (photograph © Des Moines Register; from the dust jacket for Crabcakes, *1998)*

Born in Savannah, Georgia, on 16 September 1943, James Alan McPherson is the son of James Allen McPherson, an electrician, and his wife, Mabel (née Smalls), a housekeeper. The young McPherson grew up without the sense of fear and awe whites caused in his peers because his father dealt with white people on a daily basis. McPherson shared his father's love for comic books, but soon he traded these for the short stories of Guy de Maupassant. He attended Morris Brown College in Atlanta from 1961 to 1965 (though he spent the 1963–1964 academic year at Morgan State College in Baltimore), graduating with a B.A. in English and history. A short story of his was awarded first prize in a contest held by *Reader's Digest* among United Negro College Fund schools in 1965; later that year he was accepted into the Harvard Law School, from which he graduated in 1968. From 1968 to 1969 he also earned his Master of Fine Arts degree from the University of Iowa Writers' Workshop.

McPherson's legal training, which he undertook in the midst of the civil rights movement, has led him to adopt the lawyer's remove from what many might see as the sensationalism in human folly. Despite the fact that many writers were casting off all ties to the Western literary tradition in order to embrace the idea of being black and working in what Larry Neal and LeRoi Jones (Amiri Baraka) termed "The Black Aesthetic," McPherson fell under the influence of Ralph Ellison and adopted the older man's sense that embracing his American citizenship, despite the contradictions of the racial divide in America, would lead him closer to the core of human values he wanted to depict in his fiction.

Readers see this concentration early in McPherson's first collection of stories, *Hue and Cry* (1968), the title of which comes from a phrase in English common law. In this volume McPherson works to demonstrate that contradictions of personality, values, and fortune exist on both sides of the color line. The stories are markedly autobiographical, drawing from his boyhood in Savannah as well as his years in Cambridge, Massachusetts, where he worked as an apartment janitor while attending law school. The collection opens with "A Matter of Vocabulary," which deals with the growing pains of a thirteen-year-old boy in the South.

As the story begins, Thomas Brown is hiding in the minister's pulpit of his church when he sees several of the church deacons pocketing money collected during Sunday school. After they realize Thomas is looking at them stealing church money, they ask him why he is hiding in the pulpit. Opting not to confront them about the theft, he tells them that he was praying; but the fact that he lies weighs so heavily upon him that he refuses to return to church. Though he leaves home with his brother, Eddie, as usual on Sunday mornings, Thomas comes to enjoy spending time with the drunks waiting for the bars to open. Although he lives in the segregated South, it takes Thomas some time before he realizes that racial prejudice prevents whites from speaking to him on the street, despite the fact that he smiles and greets them warmly as his mother has taught him to do with people. Though his racial status shapes his life in a variety of ways, the most poignant effect is in the low expectations and the limited moral choices set before him. For example, when his mother confronts him about skipping church, she tells him that the world is composed only of those going to heaven and those going to hell. "Everybody on the Left is gonna fall right into the same fiery pit," she tells him, "and the ones on the Right will be raised up into glory."

What makes this story so compelling is that the reader comes to understand Thomas as a bright, obser-

vant boy whose sense of possibility is beset on all sides, from both blacks and whites, who are either threatened by his intelligence or who see him as the perfect employee. In an exchange with Milton Feinberg, the owner of the supermarket where he works after school, Thomas realizes how limited the man's view of Thomas's potential is when Feinberg tells him that there will be a place for him in the store "after you quit school." When Thomas tells him that he is not going to quit, that he intends to graduate from high school, Feinberg persists in his offer, unable to imagine anything but a life of physical labor for Thomas. Later in the story, after his brother quits his job at the same grocery store, Thomas states that he plans to keep working there. The exchange between the two brothers is punctuated by the Barefoot Lady, who comes each night to the doors of the funeral home next door to where the boys live and announces her love for the funeral director, Mr. Jones. Wondering why she does it every night, Thomas realizes that, like her, he is miserable, trapped in a life that offers little in the way of possibility.

"A Matter of Vocabulary" is not simply a story that effectively addresses issues of despair; it also confronts the deeper dilemma of how the human spirit can be crushed by a failure of imagination. Though McPherson opts not to make overt commentary about racial prejudice or the ways that the immorality of adult behavior can be justified to children, often with disastrous results, what is clear is that Thomas's greatest assets, his compassion and humility, are precisely the reasons he is under assault. In a world reduced to moral absolutes, Thomas can find no way to situate himself. Like many of McPherson's protagonists, he is an outsider looking for a place to settle; finding none, he turns inward.

The next story, "On Trains," takes up the theme of human loneliness but presents the subject through the eyes of the black porters and waiters working on a passenger train traveling west from Chicago. Again, racial tension is present, this time in the form of a Southern woman who objects to the presence of one of the black porters outside her sleeping berth during the night. Though it is the porter's job to be available to the passengers, the woman tells the conductor that she cannot sleep with a black man so close to her bed. Juxtaposed against this story is the imminent sexual liaison between John Perry, a black bartender on the train, and a Dutch female passenger. In many ways, the story suggests that "good service" on a train is based, in unspoken fashion, upon racial hierarchy. Though the porters and waiters know that their jobs depend on their ability to walk the fine line between obsequiousness or racial buffoonery and attention to duty and their knowledge of self, the story avoids being a treatise on racial injustice. It suggests that each of the characters' roles is "fixed" in immutable ways. When the old Southern woman communicates her feeling of racial superiority by failing to leave a tip, the waiters complain but understand that there are elements to the job, such as the Dutch passenger's attraction to John Perry, which reveal life to be much more complex than American race rituals might otherwise determine it to be.

Some of the best, most poignant insights in the collection are those that come from McPherson's experiences working as summer help in a railroad dining car. This experience gave rise not only to "On Trains" but also to the literary masterpiece "Solo Song: For Doc." In that story, an older waiter from a group of men who refer to themselves as "the Old School" tries to give counsel to a younger waiter and in the process ends up talking about his best friend, the now-deceased Doc Craft. The story centers on Doc's unwillingness to be forced into retirement, even after the company decides to try to catch him giving bad service. So deft is Doc's skill that it takes a last-minute change in the rule book, administered by a man named Jerry Ewald, whom the waiters all fear, to make Doc step down. Doc dies soon afterward. What makes the story so touching is its rumination upon what constitutes mastery of one's craft. Though the main characters are waiters, they could just as easily be artists.

In the nuances of the exchanges between the narrator and the young waiter, the reader finds also a rumination upon what constitutes great art and how that art can be diminished in a world lacking the imagination to correctly assess its worth. At the beginning of the story the young waiter is reading the rule book that has cost Doc his job. The young man is a figure meant to represent, at one level, the sort of mechanized, routine approach to work that the older waiter (and by extension, McPherson) opposes with passion, improvisation, and self-invention, the things that make life worthwhile. At another level, however, the younger waiter is also the artist-as-apprentice, looking, in this particular instance, in the wrong place for sources of influence and inspiration. The problem, the story suggests, is that the artist must find a way to balance a sense of craft against tradition. Hence, Doc Craft can be understood as a great man, whose purpose, in the wake of his death, is to serve a cautionary function for those who follow in his footsteps. But interestingly, McPherson's story, which operates along the lines of the classic framed tale, never allows the young man to articulate what he gleans from the older waiter's tale. Indeed, the story ends with the old waiter admonishing the young man for keeping his fingers in the pages of the "black bible" throughout the story, as if he has decided that the contents of the rule book are more important than what he

is being told. The successful juxtaposition of the oral tradition and the written word is noteworthy, not only because McPherson produces such a believable and compelling narrator but also because the first-person narration brings into the foreground exactly what all young artists have to contend with, namely the dilemma of deciding when (and from where) they should seek counsel and when they should rely on their own instincts. Though the story can be interpreted as an instance where rote learning triumphs over innovation and individuality, it can also be viewed as what Ellison has termed "antagonistic cooperation," which means that, for all the narrator's discontent, the fact that he has chosen to tell Doc's story to a younger man symbolizes his faith in the future.

Some of the other stories in *Hue and Cry* are remarkably humorous, a striking counterpoint to the fictions, plays, and poetry of the Black Arts period that either attempted to work out the contours of black racial superiority or centered on the violent overthrow of the government and physical resistance against racial oppression. McPherson's stories are characterized by their subtlety, their ability to lift the veil away from an event to reveal not only its humor but also the pathos of characters from a variety of racial, class, and national backgrounds. McPherson developed an early interest in creating characters who live on the fringe and thus live highly contingent lives. In "Gold Coast" readers see how this approach can lead to a rich existence. The narrator begins the story by observing, "That spring, when I had a great deal of potential, and no money at all, I took a job as a janitor." The story is an effective study of the nexus formed by class and race. In the 1960s, when the counterculture was seeking to simplify life by a "return to nature," becoming a janitor in spite of one's education rather than because of it was deemed a progressive move. The story argues that people require training in the practice of community and that somehow those who occupy the lower stations of life are adept in the field of interpersonal relations in ways that are threatened by upward mobility.

The most colorful of the characters is James Sullivan, the building superintendent, who takes a liking to the narrator and wants to provide guidance, whether the narrator wants it or not. He passes his three garbage cans to the narrator, failing to realize that the narrator is only passing through. The narrator, however, unlike the young waiter in "Solo Song: For Doc," understands the value of a good story. Yet, he can also walk away from the job of apartment janitor and resume his life. At the end of the story, having quit his job, he sees Sullivan on the street. "And after a few seconds of standing behind him," the narrator relates, "and knowing that he was not aware of anything at all except the two heavy

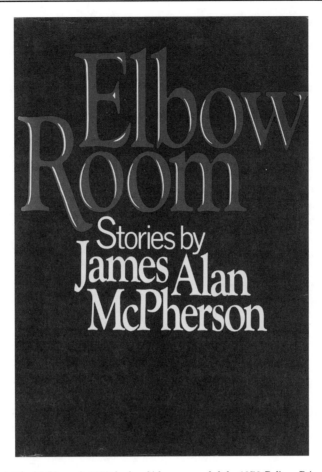

Dust jacket for McPherson's 1977 book, which was awarded the 1978 Pulitzer Prize in fiction

bags waiting to be lifted after his arms were sufficiently rested, I moved back into the stream of people which passed on the left of him. I never looked back." The ending is as much about the wages of loneliness as it is about the narrator's decision to live and not fall into a bitter remove from the rest of humanity as Sullivan has done. Though the crowd passing Sullivan might be viewed as an insensitive mass, McPherson's narrator, in making the decision to go on with his life, decides to enter it as if it were a tide carrying him out to sea. What marks this character is his self-knowledge, his ability to understand who he is, even if life is uncertain.

This narrator needs to be viewed against several other protagonists in *Hue and Cry,* many of whom are angry, listless, or simply lost. Some, like Rodney in "Private Domain," are meant to suggest the foibles that lie at the root of America's racially fixed identities. Rodney is a black man who has almost no knowledge of African American culture. The story begins with Rodney buying another black man beers in exchange for lessons on how to use black slang. The story suggests that those aspects of black culture that are deemed

intrinsic to a racialized identity are actually learned and thus of superficial value. The lasting significance of the story lies in its insistence that racial boundaries are, as W. E. B. Du Bois insisted, reminiscent of a veil, and thus they are incapable of preventing cultural practices from moving back and forth between groups until the origins of those practices are rendered uncertain.

In "All the Lonely People" and "A New Place" McPherson depicts men whose sexuality creates a sense of contingency in their own lives, as well as the lives of those men with whom they come in contact. In both instances, the stories are narrated by men whose heterosexuality is destabilized by men who either are gay, as is Alfred Bowles in "All the Lonely People," or are interpreted to be so, as is Jack in "A New Place." In fact, the narrator of "All the Lonely People" ends the story by noting, "I began to wonder about the way I am." In "A New Place" the narrator breaks ties with his roommate, Jack, and concludes that "His mind must have beat him out of the straight life." Each story presents a window on the forms of cruelty and denial that serve to buttress notions of manhood. Moreover, each story suggests that the very concept of "manhood" is a perpetually unstable enterprise that requires men to diminish women's humanity to stay safely ensconced in its parameters. "A New Place" suggests that indecision on the part of men or any instance where the individual attempts to break free of the constraints placed on him in a world of confusing signs serve to justify "man's inhumanity to man."

"An Act of Prostitution," a story that demonstrates McPherson's ability to reveal the nature of legal inequity, depicts a Monday-morning hearing conducted by Judge Bloom, who has a reputation for relishing his sentencing of wrongdoers who come before him. White attorney Jimmy Farragut is approached by a fellow lawyer who asks him to switch places on the docket so that his client will get a break. The key is Jimmy's client, Philomena Brown, a white prostitute who happens to be married to a black man and who is well known by Judge Bloom. After a courtroom disturbance, Jimmy conducts what turns into a hilarious examination of his client that leads the judge to "throw the book" at Philomena for soliciting, as the next case is called—that of an Italian youth who is being tried for his third offense, stealing a car. Though the humor is undeniable, McPherson clearly points to the hierarchy of treatment in the legal system and suggests that blacks, and anyone associated with them, are at the bottom with little recourse at their disposal.

With the success of *Hue and Cry,* McPherson moved into the spotlight as one of the most talented young American writers. Indeed, in a jacket blurb meant as a slap against members of the Black Arts Movement, Ellison wrote, "With this collection of stories, McPherson promises to move right past those talented but misguided writers of Negro American background who take being black as a privilege for being obscenely second-rate and who regard their social predicament as Negroes as exempting them from the necessity of mastering the craft and forms of fiction." McPherson formed a friendship with the older writer, leading to one of the most revealing and wide-ranging interviews with Ellison since the publication of *Invisible Man* (1952). Called "Indivisible Man," the interview features Ellison's exchanges with McPherson as well as his exchanges with young black students who, for reasons they do not understand, dislike Ellison's politics. Published in *The Atlantic Monthly* in 1970, the interview highlights McPherson's ability to make his subjects feel comfortable enough to be expansive, a talent evident in other stories McPherson did for *The Atlantic Monthly* (he became a contributing editor in 1969), including a story on the Blackstone Rangers, a prominent gang on Chicago's South Side (later the basis of one of the short stories in McPherson's second collection), and another on the black law student.

Elbow Room, his second collection of stories, appeared in 1977. The twelve stories, which include characters as morally ambivalent and misguided as those in *Hue and Cry* but with a little more human frailty, received a Pulitzer Prize in 1978, making McPherson only the second African American to receive the award and the first to receive the award in fiction. Beginning with the heartfelt remembrances of the narrator of "Why I Like Country Music" and moving through the wild antics of Billy Renfro in "The Story of a Dead Man," the desperate tale of love gone wrong in "The Story of A Scar," the political persuasiveness of "A Loaf of Bread," and the brilliant use of form in "A Sense of Story," McPherson explores the contours and nuances in various performances of American identity.

"Why I Like Country Music," the opening story, is McPherson's opportunity to revisit the ways that race straitjackets identity and also for him to put forward the notion that sometimes regional identity is as pronounced an influence as racial identity. The narrator, much to the consternation of his wife, insists upon his love of country music, despite the fact that country music is so often thought of as music that articulates a white supremacist perspective. "Hillbilly stuff is just not music," the narrator's wife warns. "It's like the New York Stock Exchange. The minute you see a sharp rise in it, you better watch out." Against what he sees as the negative assessment of country music, McPherson casts the narrator's Southern background, which is revealed to be analogous in the North to that of a refugee. This theme, the idea that contemporary circumstances have a great deal to do with American forms of mobility, with the need to break free of the constraints imposed on individuals at their respective points of origin, runs throughout the entirety of *Elbow Room.* However, McPherson wants to suggest that no matter how far people travel from their beginnings, they carry the past with them. Such is the case with the narrator of "Why I Like Country Music." He relates the story of Gweneth Lawson, his first significant love interest. Though he can lay claim to few of the details of their time together, he remembers that the highlight of the May Day celebration at his Southern elementary school in the South was square dancing with Gweneth. In the process of relating a coming-of-age tale, however, McPherson's story does much more, insisting that American culture is a matter of shared traditions that cross racial lines. The story carries further some of Ellison's most poignant observations about American culture by using square dancing, a dance form pioneered by African American slaves who were mimicking more formal English dance forms. Though square dancing is often characterized as "white," McPherson wants to propose that Americans, because they share a culture they have created jointly, are more alike than race ritual allows them to admit.

Unlike *Hue and Cry,* which is filled with closely situated delineations of character and setting, *Elbow Room* is much more attuned to acts of storymaking and storytelling, with narrators who are prone to recount how they moved from "can" to "cannot." Even in those instances where McPherson works in the third person, he is nonetheless interested in depicting the power of story, the way that storytelling shapes how people navigate the world.

For example, in "The Story of a Scar," McPherson provides a male narrator whose broken nose is the occasion for an encounter with a mature black woman whose face bears a horrible scar. In some of the most compelling writing in the volume, the narrator relates how he begins with a set of unfounded assumptions about how the woman received her scar. But the story accomplishes its intent by calling the reader's attention to the ways that storytelling requires the teller to assert and maintain authorial control of his or her story. Indeed, the inner message is that losing control of one's story is a fate worse than being scarred for life. The narrator's many intrusions, revisions, and misapprehensions of the scarred woman's story serve to remind the reader that becoming a good teller involves effective acts of listening. And the prospect of effective listening, McPherson proposes, rests on how the teller is approached. Despite warnings to the contrary, the narrator's most problematic trait is his propensity to plow ahead with the story of how the woman's face was slashed without taking care to discern the necessary details and their proper place. She compares him to her former lover, Billy Crawford, the man guilty of slashing her face in a fit of jealous rage. But the ending finds the narrator chastened to the point of realizing part of what constitutes correct listening behavior. The story ends with the simple but elegant question, "Sister, what is your name?" Concluding the story in this manner, McPherson finds a way to help readers understand that how they receive a story says as much about who they are as how they tell one.

This message, albeit in a different context, is also central to "A Sense of Story." Brilliantly rendered in the form of excerpts from a court transcript made during the criminal proceedings of a murder suspect, the story emerges through the point of view of the presiding judge. The story unfolds as the judge reads the transcript: Robert Charles has shot his boss after an argument and openly declared his guilt during an outburst in the courtroom. It falls upon the judge to determine his guilt or innocence by reading the transcript to see if the prosecution has made its case. Reading selectively, the judge determines the law is an art and that his role is that of literary critic. McPherson foregrounds the fact that the law, like literature, does not occur in a value-free environment. In fact, when one introduces the variable of race into the process, even reading the transcripts is revealed to be a highly contingent enterprise. The judge's own biases come into his reading; it does not occur to him that the boss may have done something to precipitate the violence against him.

Elbow Room culminates with the title story, which depicts a conventional narrative interrupted at several points by an editor who cannot grasp the narrator's intent. The story, which deals with the interracial marriage of Virginia Valentine and Paul Frost, functions as a racial allegory meant to suggest that redemption will come only with the kind of courage and love bound up in the birth of a child. Published in 1978, the stories gain their power from their ability to glean the sense of exhaustion that had settled in on the nation after the civil rights and Black Power movements had come to a close. Indeed, McPherson depicts African Americans who are as trapped in anomie and soullessness as racist whites.

To understand the deeper meanings of the collection, one need only turn to an essay McPherson published in 1978 after winning the Pulitzer Prize, "On Becoming an American Writer." There, McPherson insists that his purpose in writing *Elbow Room* had everything to do with trying to show the peculiarities and the possibilities of life in the United States. In many ways, he was announcing his belief that the country was still young, far away from finding a solution for its racial, class, and ethnic differences. McPherson was also clearly stating his sense that the elements for good fiction were in the interstitial, nearly accidental encounters across racial lines.

As a Southern writer, McPherson has a sense of racial tragedy equally shaped by an ability to discern vestiges of love, however ironic it might seem. As a member of the first generation of African Americans to enter the middle class via enrollment in predominantly white colleges and universities, McPherson saw *Elbow Room* as a way to chronicle the difficulty of assimilating into a new, equally rigid set of codes, as governed by rules of decorum and language as color.

This difficulty is perhaps most evident in "Widows and Orphans," in which the protagonist finds himself at a banquet honoring a former lover. He looks around the room, which is full of blacks striving for status in the city of Los Angeles, and notices their marked resemblance to Hollywood movie stars. The point is not that McPherson wishes to recapitulate the sociologist E. Franklin Frazier's criticism that the black middle class merely imitated their white counterparts, but rather that cultural references are available across racial lines and are used by blacks with the same frequency and facility as whites.

The success of *Elbow Room* left the literary community in a state of anticipation for McPherson's next book. But for twenty years there was nothing from McPherson in the genre of fiction, though he published several journalistic pieces and essays in that time. In 1981 McPherson left the faculty at the University of Virginia, where he had been living with his wife and daughter, and went to Iowa City, joining the faculty of the University of Iowa Writers' Workshop, where he quickly established himself. In the same year, he was divorced from his wife, to whom he had been married since 1973 and with whom he had a daughter, Rachel, born in 1979. The literary silence may have been generated by the fact that many critics saw in McPherson the heir apparent to the legacy of Ellison, so that the younger man felt it necessary to wait for the excitement over Ellison's expected second novel to pass. Ellison died in 1994 before the completion of the long-anticipated volume; but McPherson finally poured his talents into a new kind of writing: the personal memoir.

McPherson's flair for representing various forms of human guile is evident in his occasional and journalistic pieces. He often works impressionistically, and his best writing is often more interested in capturing nuance, the shadings of character rather than their boldest display. As a vehicle of self-representation the memoir demonstrates McPherson's ability to portray a sense of wonder and awe at human existence. This sensibility is displayed in *Crabcakes* (1998), published some twenty years after *Elbow Room*. Utilizing his powers of description and analysis, McPherson takes the reader on a journey from Iowa to Baltimore to Japan and back. In Japan he describes, first, his various failures of perception and decorum among the Japanese, only to stumble upon what the Japanese refer to as a natural way of living. Beset by the changes that come with the deaths of friends, loneliness, and shifts in political and institutional forms of kindness, McPherson's travels to the East are both a way to revisit the theme of what it means to be an American, where the frontier is thought of as that place where men can rediscover their sense of purpose, and a way to conjure up a sense of spiritual well-being. Ultimately, McPherson uses seafood–from shrimp and crawfish in Georgia, to crabcakes in Baltimore, to fugu in Japan–as metaphors for what it means to live in a community: the pleasure they elicit calls for obligation and respect in return. The conclusion of the book, with McPherson feeling a sense of *ninjo* (peace and joy), points the way to what readers can only hope

will be more tales meant to capture the eclecticism, the accidental grace, that is the American Scene.

As evidenced by the frequent performance of his stories on National Public Radio (along with a teleplay based on "Solo Song: For Doc" that was performed by Ozzie Davis and Roscoe Lee Browne in the 1980s), McPherson's short stories remain in the public consciousness. Though the expected turn for a writer of short fiction is to the novel, McPherson has distinguished himself as an essayist of deep insight and conviction as well as controlled emotional power. Following up on *Crabcakes,* in 2000 McPherson published a second collection of essays, *A Region Not Home*: *Reflections from Exile.* As with *Crabcakes,* McPherson is interested in examining the affecting community and citizenship.

In addition to "Gravitas," a piece he wrote in tribute to Ellison, "On Becoming an American Writer," and the foreword he wrote for the posthumously published collection of stories by his former student, Breece D'J Pancake, there are several essays that touch on McPherson's sense of the personal and collective costs wrought in a society where civility and judiciousness are compromised. A thread running through the collection is McPherson's depiction of his life as that of a writer in exile–from the South, from kin, from the contemporary political scene, and from the values shaping a new generation of writers. As with *Crabcakes,* McPherson grafts several other sociocultural frameworks onto the American template, only to find it lacking in the beliefs necessary to sustain an Athenian sense of purpose over the impulse to be Spartan–slow, cautious, and austere. This juxtaposition is the way for McPherson to suggest that American life, with its impulse to improvisation and flexibility, is reminiscent of "adaptable, clever" Athenian society.

In "Junior and John Doe" McPherson challenges the propensity toward racial chauvinism to be found in the racial discourse of the black community in the post-civil-rights era, where he finds "the words *they* and *them*" seem "to have become standardized ways of alluding to the relation of our inside world to the larger world outside our group." He laments that African Americans have abandoned the once-familiar moral certainty inherited from their slave ancestors in favor of a kind of moral relativism that holds results above principle. Using the word "integrated" ironically, McPherson argues that blacks, in wanting to acclimate themselves to the idea of equality, have "disrupted our historical process of making a usable identity, and many of us have settled for a simple standardization around the norms, racist and otherwise, of middle class American life."

Though McPherson's long period of silence as a fiction writer spanned twenty years, the advent of the twenty-first century finds him at work on several projects, including "Reflections of Titus Basfield, April 1850, " a short story that appeared in the 150th anniversary edition of *Harper's Magazine* (June 2000). The narrator, Basfield, describes in vivid detail the icons of the journey westward, including the Conestoga wagon, manufactured in his native state of Ohio. McPherson also includes several historical figures, ranging from George Custer to Frederick Douglass, who give credence to the transience—and instability—of the mid nineteenth century. Basfield, a graduate of Franklin College, who has "had access to the best writings of the classical world and of the Scottish Enlightenment," a "mature colored man," watches the settlers heading west on the National Road. As he notes the white slavecatchers driving coffles of recaptured slaves westward, he sees in the herders "the portrait of Achilles going into a state of aristeia—that trance-like mental state that bespeaks connections with the gods," as the herders try to make themselves seem important and superior. "My Presbyterian soul," Basfield observes, "informs me daily that evil does truly exist." McPherson ends the story with a letter from Douglass to the editor of *The London Times,* in which Douglass thanks the editor for his denouncing of Douglass's beating at the hands of a mob. What comes through, however, is Douglass's unshakeable belief in the rightness of his cause, which he (along with the editor) sees as a human one rather than a racial one.

James Alan McPherson's career as a writer of distinction continues, though he has traveled a long way from the late 1970s, when he garnered several important awards. In a March/April 2001 interview with Trent Masiki, McPherson talked about the ways that he used silence as a means of distancing himself from literary prizes and the professional jealousies that accompanied them. What comes through in his present work is the indisputable sense that he has devoted himself, both as a writer and a human being, to cultivating what he refers to in the essay "Gravitas" as "perfected friendship." This quality of human contact, which he gestures toward in *Crabcakes* during his travels in Japan, is what

McPherson historicizes in *A Region Not Home.* Writing of the concerned individuals who affirmed their connections to him during a serious illness in which he lost his memory, McPherson concludes that his exile had everything to do with "trying to learn the basic questions through reading so that, when combined with my own experiences, I could develop a national mind—a sense of how the entire culture, regional, ethnic, class, institutional functioned together, as a *whole."* As he has done throughout his career, McPherson eschews the impulse to depict life as a series of victimizations, but rather opts to create what his mentor Ellison would appreciate as an "open-ended" notion of American life.

Interview:

Trent Masiki, "James Alan McPherson: Consistently Himself," *Poets & Writers,* 29 (March/April 2001): 34–39.

References:

Herman Beavers, "I Yam What You Is and You Is What I Yam: Rhetorical Invisibility in James Alan McPherson's 'The Story of a Dead Man,'" *Callaloo,* 9 (Fall 1986): 565–577;

Beavers, *Wrestling Angels into Song: The Fictions of Ernest J. Gaines and James Alan McPherson* (Philadelphia: University of Pennsylvania Press, 1995);

Edith Blicksilver, "Interracial Relationships in Three Short Stories by James Alan McPherson," *CEA Critic,* 50 (Winter/Summer 1987–1988): 79–88;

William Domnarski, "The Voices of Misery and Despair in the Fiction of James Alan McPherson," *Arizona Quarterly,* 42 (Spring 1986): 37–44;

Mary A. Gervin, "Developing a Sense of Self: The Androgynous Ideal in McPherson's *Elbow Room,*" *CLA Journal,* 26 (December 1982): 251–255;

Jon Wallace, "The Politics of Style in Three Stories by James Alan McPherson," *Modern Fiction Studies,* 34 (Spring 1988): 17–26;

Wallace, "The Story Behind the Story in James Alan McPherson's 'Elbow Room,'" *Studies in Short Fiction,* 25 (Fall 1988): 447–452.

Vladimir Nabokov

(23 April 1899 – 2 July 1977)

Alexandra Smith
University of Canterbury, New Zealand

See also the Nabokov entries in *DLB 2: American Novelists Since World War II; DLB Yearbook: 1980; DLB Yearbook: 1991;* and *DLB Documentary Series 3.*

BOOKS: *Stikhi* (St. Petersburg: Privately printed, 1916);

Al'manakh. Dva puti, by Nabokov and Andrei Balashov (Petrograd: Privately printed, 1918);

Grozd'. Stikhi, as V. Sirin (Berlin: Gamaiun, 1923 [1922]);

Gornii put', as Vl. Sirin (Berlin: Grani, 1923);

Mashen'ka, as Vladimir Sirin (Berlin: Slovo, 1926); translated by Michael Glenny and Nabokov as *Mary,* as Nabokov (New York: McGraw-Hill, 1970; London: Weidenfeld & Nicolson, 1971);

Korol' dama valet, as Sirin (Berlin: Slovo, 1928); translated by Dmitri Nabokov and Nabokov as *King, Queen, Knave,* as Nabokov (New York: McGraw-Hill, 1968; London: Weidenfeld & Nicolson, 1968);

Zashchita Luzhina, as Sirin (Berlin: Slovo, 1930); translated by Michael Scammell and Nabokov as *The Defense,* as Nabokov (New York: Putnam, 1964; London: Weidenfeld & Nicolson, 1964);

Vozvrashchenie Chorba, as Sirin (Berlin: Slovo, 1930 [1929]);

Podvig, as Sirin (Paris: Sovremennye Zapiski, 1932); translated by Dmitri Nabokov and Nabokov as *Glory,* as Nabokov (New York: McGraw-Hill, 1971; London: Weidenfeld & Nicolson, 1972);

Kamera obskura, as Sirin (Paris: Sovremennye Zapiski, 1933); translated by Winifred Roy as *Camera Obscura,* as Vladimir Nabokoff-Sirin (London: John Long, 1935 [1936]); translated again by Nabokov as *Laughter in the Dark,* as Nabokoff (Indianapolis & New York: Bobbs-Merrill, 1938; London: Weidenfeld & Nicolson, 1961);

Otchaianie, as Sirin (Berlin: Petropolis, 1936); translated by Nabokov as *Despair,* as Nabokoff-Sirin (London: John Long, 1937); revised and retranslated

Vladimir Nabokov (photograph by Gertrude Fehr)

by Nabokov, as Nabokov (New York: Putnam, 1966; London: Weidenfeld & Nicolson, 1966);

Sogliadatai, as Sirin (Paris: Russkiia Zapiski, 1938)—comprises the title novel and twelve short stories; title novel translated by Dmitri Nabokov and Nabokov as *The Eye,* as Nabokov (New York: Phaedra, 1965; London: Weidenfeld & Nicolson, 1966);

Priglashenie na kazn', as Sirin (Paris: Dom Knigi, 1938); translated by Dmitri Nabokov and Nabokov as *Invitation to a Beheading*, as Nabokov (New York: Putnam, 1959; London: Weidenfeld & Nicolson, 1960);

The Real Life of Sebastian Knight (Norfolk, Conn.: New Directions, 1941; London: Editions Poetry, 1945);

Nikolai Gogol (Norfolk, Conn.: New Directions, 1944; London: Editions Poetry, 1947);

Bend Sinister (New York: Holt, 1947; London: Weidenfeld & Nicolson, 1960);

Nine Stories (Norfolk, Conn.: New Directions, 1947);

Conclusive Evidence: A Memoir (New York: Harper, 1951); republished as *Speak, Memory: A Memoir* (London: Gollancz, 1951); revised and enlarged as *Speak, Memory: An Autobiography Revisited* (New York: Putnam, 1967; London: Weidenfeld & Nicolson, 1967);

Dar (New York: Chekhov Publishing House, 1952); translated by Scammell and Nabokov as *The Gift* (New York: Putnam, 1963; London: Weidenfeld & Nicolson, 1963);

Stikhotvoreniia 1929–1951 (Paris: Rifma, 1952);

Lolita (Paris: Olympia Press, 1955; New York: Putnam, 1958; London: Weidenfeld & Nicolson, 1959);

Vesna v Fial'te i drugie rasskazy (New York: Chekhov Publishing House, 1956);

Pnin (Garden City, N.Y.: Doubleday, 1957; London: Heinemann, 1957);

Nabokov's Dozen: A Collection of Thirteen Stories (Garden City, N.Y.: Doubleday, 1958; London: Heinemann, 1959);

Poems (Garden City, N.Y.: Doubleday, 1959; London: Weidenfeld & Nicolson, 1961);

Pale Fire (New York: Putnam, 1962; London: Weidenfeld & Nicolson, 1962);

Notes on Prosody: From the Commentary to His Translation of Pushkin's Eugene Onegin (New York: Bollingen Foundation, 1963 [offprint]; trade edition, 1964; London: Routledge & Kegan Paul, 1965);

The Waltz Invention, translated by Dmitri Nabokov (New York: Phaedra, 1966);

Nabokov's Quartet, translated by Dmitri Nabokov (New York: Phaedra, 1966; London: Weidenfeld & Nicolson, 1967);

Nabokov's Congeries, edited by Page Stegner (New York: Viking, 1968); republished as *The Portable Nabokov* (New York: Viking, 1971);

Ada or Ardor: A Family Chronicle (New York: McGraw-Hill, 1969; London: Weidenfeld & Nicolson, 1969);

Poems and Problems (New York: McGraw-Hill, 1970 [1971]; London: Weidenfeld & Nicolson, 1972);

Transparent Things (New York: McGraw-Hill, 1972; London: Weidenfeld & Nicolson, 1973);

A Russian Beauty and Other Stories, translated by Dmitri Nabokov, Nabokov, and Simon Karlinsky (New York: McGraw-Hill, 1973; London: Weidenfeld & Nicolson, 1973);

Strong Opinions (New York: McGraw-Hill, 1973; London: Weidenfeld & Nicolson, 1974);

Lolita: A Screenplay (New York: McGraw-Hill, 1974);

Look at the Harlequins! (New York: McGraw-Hill, 1974; London: Weidenfeld & Nicolson, 1975);

Tyrants Destroyed and Other Stories, translated by Dmitri Nabokov and Nabokov (New York: McGraw-Hill, 1975; London: Weidenfeld & Nicolson, 1975);

Details of a Sunset and Other Stories, translated by Dmitri Nabokov and Nabokov (New York: McGraw-Hill, 1976; London: Weidenfeld & Nicolson, 1976);

Stikhi (Ann Arbor, Mich.: Ardis, 1979);

Lectures on Literature, edited by Fredson Bowers (New York & London: Harcourt Brace Jovanovich/ Bruccoli Clark, 1980; London: Weidenfeld & Nicolson, 1980);

Lectures on Ulysses: A Facsimile of the Manuscript (Bloomfield Hills, Mich. & Columbia, S.C.: Bruccoli Clark, 1980);

Lectures on Russian Literature, edited by Bowers (New York & London: Harcourt Brace Jovanovich/ Bruccoli Clark, 1981; London: Weidenfeld & Nicolson, 1982);

Lectures on Don Quixote, edited by Bowers (San Diego, New York & London: Harcourt Brace Jovanovich/ Bruccoli Clark, 1983; London: Weidenfeld & Nicolson, 1983);

The Man from the USSR and Other Plays, translated by Dmitri Nabokov (San Diego, New York & London: Bruccoli Clark/Harcourt Brace Jovanovich, 1984; London: Weidenfeld & Nicolson, 1985);

The Enchanter, translated by Dmitri Nabokov (New York: Putnam, 1986; London: Picador, 1987);

Carrousel; Laughter and Dreams; Painted Wood; The Russian Song (Aartswoud, The Netherlands: Spectatorpers, 1987);

The Stories of Vladimir Nabokov (New York: Knopf, 1995; London: Weidenfeld & Nicolson, 1996);

Nabokov's Butterflies: Unpublished and Uncollected Writings, edited by Brian Boyd and Robert Michael Pyle, translations by Dmitri Nabokov (Boston: Beacon Press, 2000).

TRANSLATIONS: Romain Rolland, *Nikolka persik (Colas Breugnon),* translated as Vladimir Sirin (Berlin: Slovo, 1922);

Lewis Carroll, *Ania v strane chudes,* translated as V. Sirin (Berlin: Gamiun, 1923);

Three Russian Poets: Selections from Pushkin, Lermontov, and Tyutchev (Norfolk, Conn.: New Directions, 1944 [1945]); republished as *Pushkin Lermontov Tyutchev: Poems* (London: Lindsay Drummond, 1947);

Mikhail Iur'evich Lermontov, *A Hero of Our Time,* translated by Nabokov and Dmitri Nabokov (Garden City, N.Y.: Doubleday, 1958);

The Song of Igor's Campaign: An Epic of the Twelfth Century (New York: Vintage, 1960; London: Weidenfeld & Nicolson, 1961);

Aleksandr Sergeevich Pushkin, *Eugene Onegin: A Novel in Verse,* 4 volumes (New York: Bollingen Foundation, 1964; London: Routledge & Kegan Paul, 1964); revised edition (Princeton: Princeton University Press, 1975; London: Routledge & Kegan Paul, 1976).

Russian American author Vladimir Nabokov wrote novels, short stories, poems, translations, and literary criticism. His novels firmly established him as one of the best stylists of the twentieth century. In 1955 the overwhelming success of Nabokov's novel *Lolita* enabled him to enjoy financial independence and to focus on his writing career until his death. Nabokov's lesser-known short stories, written from the early 1920s to the mid 1950s, display the same stylistic splendor and technical inventiveness as do his novels.

Chronologically, Nabokov's stories can be divided into four approximate periods: early period (1921–1928), middle period (1930–1935), high period (1936–1939), and American period (1940–1959). Nabokov's shorter fiction illuminates the evolution of his development as a prose writer, displaying his persistent search for the poetry and meaning of life. In a September 1971 interview with Stephen Jan Parker (published in 1991), Nabokov pointed out the importance of the short stories to his literary output as a whole: "In relation to the typical novel the short story represents a small Alpine, or Polar, form. It looks different, but is conspecific with the novel and is linked to it by intermediate clines." He called some of his short stories "a diminutive novel" and stressed that the process of writing them is no different than writing novels: "My short stories are produced in exactly the same way as my novels. The latter take a longer time, that's all. On the average a story of ten pages takes me a fortnight to compose, a novel of 200 pages about one year."

Nabokov stated that his fiction expresses his passionate regard for human feelings and morality. Yet, some critics have accused Nabokov of being indifferent to social and political issues of his time, comparing his stories and novels to elegantly constructed, labyrinth-like narratives and riddles. This similarity is largely because of Nabokov's curious ability to combine his passion for literature with his strong interest in chess and in crosswords. Many of Nabokov's stories share the motifs, themes, and techniques of his larger narratives, but because of their hermeneutic nature they are also accessible to general readers with no previous knowledge of his artistic persona. They function as "little tragedies," with some mythopoetic, psychological, and metaphysical overtones, as Nabokov offers comments on the paradoxes and complexity of the age of modernity to which he belonged.

Nabokov's preoccupation with the crisis of language, individuality, sexuality, and creativity manifests itself with greater vigor in his short fiction than in some of his novels. In his short stories Nabokov is not so much preoccupied with parody as in his novels, where parody can be seen as the central figure of his narrative structure. Nabokov experimented with the format of shorter fiction in order to express his subjective outlook and his poetic protest against violence, cruelty, humiliation, and vulgarity in a more striking manner than the novel would have allowed him to do.

Some stories express Nabokov's lyrical and philosophical discourses at the expense of plot structure. Thus, for example, his fragmentary stories "Solus Rex" (1940) and "Ultima Thule" (1942) were meant to be a part of Nabokov's unfinished novel "Solus Rex." Zinaida Shakhovskaia, a famous Russian émigré critic, editor, memoirist, and close friend of Nabokov, defined him as Solus Rex, a lonely literary king whose art could be fully appreciated only by fellow writers and critics.

The aristocratic spirit of Nabokov's artistic persona is best expressed in his stories, which resist conformity and ready definitions. Meanwhile, in their suggestiveness and elusiveness they often resemble the narrative style of Anton Pavlovich Chekhov and Ivan Alekseevich Bunin, while in their inventiveness and in the strange subject matter they continue the metaphysical quest of Russian Symbolist writers such as Andrei Belyi and Fedor Sologub. Nabokov's use of the pseudonym Vladimir Sirin until 1940 was not coincidental. This pseudonym reveals the author's bond with Russian Symbolist culture, with its strong orientation toward spirituality and life-creating. The name "Sirin" has associations both with a Russian mythical bird, Sirin, and with the Greek mythical sea demons called sirens, half birds and half women. Their symbol is the lyre or double flute.

As Nina Berberova (a Russian Parisian friend of Nabokov) wrote, "Nabokov is the only Russian writer (both within Russia and in emigration) who belongs to the *entire* Western world (or the world in general), not Russia alone." Nabokov presents himself in his stories as a truly cosmopolitan writer, whose work reveals the problematic nature of European identity in the twentieth century. Nabokov turned the physical displacement from his homeland into poetics of exile and estrangement, relying on his creative talent and memory to construct an immortal place of his own. As some critics believe, Nabokov created a myth about himself as an expatriate and transformed it gradually into a chain of symbols.

Vladimir Vladimirovich Nabokov was born in St. Petersburg on 23 April 1899 to Vladimir Dmitrievich Nabokov and Elena Rukavishnikov; he had two brothers and two sisters. Nabokov's father was a founder of the Constitutional Democratic Party who accepted a post in the Provisional Government in 1917. Nabokov attended the Tenishev school in St. Petersburg, and at home he had both English and French governesses. This home tuition in languages made Nabokov a fluent speaker of English, French, and Russian. In 1919 Nabokov's family moved to London, and from 1919 to 1922 Nabokov and his brother Sergei attended Cambridge University, where Vladimir Nabokov studied Romance and Slavonic languages and literatures. In 1920 the Nabokov family moved to Berlin, where Nabokov's father became the editor of the Russian newspaper *Rul'* (The Rudder). This newspaper published Nabokov's early prose works and translations of English and French poets into Russian. After graduating from Cambridge in 1922, Nabokov moved to Berlin, where he contributed to Russian periodicals and newspapers as poet, translator, prose writer, and playwright. In 1922 Nabokov's father was shot dead by right-wing monarchists in an assassination attempt on the prominent political figure Pavel Nikolaevich Miliukov. In 1923 Nabokov's mother moved to Prague, where she was offered a government pension as the widow of V. D. Nabokov. In November 1923 Nabokov met his future wife, Véra Slonim; they married in 1925. Their son, Dmitri, was born in 1934. In 1937 Nabokov and his family relocated to France, moving to the United States in 1940 because Véra Nabokov's Jewish ancestry made it unsafe for her to remain in Europe.

In 1945 Nabokov became an American citizen. By this time he was already a popular Russian writer whose work was well known in France, Germany, and the United States. From 1948 to 1958 Nabokov worked as a professor of Russian and European literature at Cornell University, where he wrote his novel *Lolita*. Four American publishers rejected this novel, but Olympia Press published it in Paris. *Lolita* was subsequently published in America in 1958. In the same year Nabokov published the superb English translation that he and his son prepared of Mikhail Iur'evich Lermontov's novel *Geroi nashego vremeni* (A Hero of Our Time,

Véra Slonim, whom Nabokov married in 1925 (courtesy of Dmitri Nabokov)

1840) as well as the collection of stories *Nabokov's Dozen*. In 1960 Nabokov and his wife settled in Switzerland, in Montreux Palace. In 1962 Nabokov's novel *Pale Fire* was published, and Stanley Kubrick's movie version of *Lolita* was released. In 1964 Nabokov published his English translation of Aleksandr Sergeevich Pushkin's novel in verse *Evgenii Onegin* (1825–1833), followed in 1967 by *Speak, Memory,* his revised autobiography. In 1973 Nabokov published another collection of stories: *A Russian Beauty and Other Stories*. His collection *Tyrants Destroyed and Other Stories* appeared in New York in 1975, followed by an additional thirteen stories–*Details of a Sunset and Other Stories*–in 1976.

Nabokov died on 2 July 1977 in Lausanne, Switzerland. He is buried in Clarens. Several of his stories, essays, and letters were published posthumously. Most of these works were prepared for publication by his son, Dmitri.

Nabokov's shorter works might be seen as preparatory sketches for his novels. As Leona Toker suggests, on some occasions they act as "channels for material that would disrupt it, or repositories for matters left over from the novel, or a development of its latent technical feats." Nabokov's stories and novels should be considered chronologically, since they share the dominant concerns (both thematic and structural) of periods of Nabokov's creative career. Thus, Julian W. Connolly attempts, though with caution, to divide Nabokov's early fiction into segments, representing stages of Nabokov's career as prose writer. According to Connolly, the first phase has a strong focus on an absent other, referring to a lost love, missing partner, or dead child. This thematic unit evokes an emotional atmosphere and mood. The next phase centers on characters' alienation from reality, through obsession with fantasies, fetishism, or loss. The third stage uses gazing as an element of narration and of constructing the protagonist's self as an other. Vladimir Alexandrov's study of Nabokov's fiction demonstrates that the human authorial consciousness adds extra depth and metaphysical dimension to Nabokov's narratives. Nabokov's later work develops more-complex structures and metafictional qualities. His irony becomes overshadowed by linguistic puzzles and the presence of a dual voice. Nabokov's stories appear simpler than his novels and thereby more accessible to general readers, although not all of them possess the same artistic qualities and refined structural techniques.

One of Nabokov's early stories, "Details of a Sunset" (first published in *Segodnia* as "Katastrofa," 1924), is permeated with melancholy. Its protagonist, Mark Standfuss, dreams about wedding his girlfriend, Klara, but his inner vision of reality is highly subjective. His obsession with Klara, the image of his dreams and happiness, leads him to profound disappointment with reality. A bus strikes Mark, fatally mauling his body, but in his mind he continues his journey to Klara, who represents his world of happiness. The story ends with the description of Mark's overwhelming pain, which prevents him from indulging his fantasy world. Nabokov highlights the importance of Mark's experience, which triggered his awakening to the world of divine beauty around him: "In bright undulations, ethereally, festively, these architectonic enchantments were receding into the heavenly distance, and Mark could not understand how he had never noticed before those galleries, those temples suspended on high." It is a story of transfiguration and transcendence that celebrates creativity beyond the physical world of the individual. Nabokov depicts his character's death in the manner of Leo Tolstoy's story *Smert' Ivana Il'icha* (The Death of Ivan Il'ich, 1886), as if Mark overcomes his isolation from the world through realization of spiritual union with the divine powers of creativity.

The Russian version of the story had the title "Katastrofa" (Catastrophe). The English version appeared in Nabokov's 1976 collection under the new title "Details of a Sunset." The renaming of the story might be explained by the fact that Nabokov's style experienced some change: by the 1970s it had become more saturated with allusions and symbols. The new title brings to the fore the striking imagery of a sunset, which epitomizes, Nabokov believed, the ability of a literary text to transgress time and space. Thus, in a letter to Professor T. G. Bergin (Cornell University), written in November 1947, Nabokov proposed a course consisting of two parts echoing each other: "Writers (Teachers, Storytellers, Enchanters) and Readers (Seekers of Knowledge, Entertainment, Magic)." In "Details of a Sunset" Nabokov presents himself both as teacher and enchanter, for the story awakens readers' appreciation of love, divinity, and beauty. It is as if Mark Standfuss is given a chance to die in a dignified manner, as a true poet who discovered the beauty of life, which transformed his vision of buildings and other objects of everyday life. Just before his death, he sees the city landscape in a new light, as divine creation: "The street was wide and gay. The colors of the sunset had invaded half of the sky. Upper stories and roofs were bathed in glorious light. Up there, Mark could discern translucent porticoes, friezes and frescoes, trellises covered with orange roses, winged statues that lifted skyward golden, unbearably blazing lyres." Enchanted by Berlin in the 1920s, one of the prominent symbols of modern metropolis, Nabokov inscribes in this story his utopian vision of modernity that could transform life. In the same vein, Nabokov's American stories describe New York of the 1940s as another powerful source of inspiration for modern writers.

In "The Potato Elf" (first published in *Russkoe ekho* as "Kartofel'nyi el'f," 1924) Nabokov brings together the same motifs of the tragedy of life, obsession, and transformation. The story records the psychological growth of Fred Dobson, a circus dwarf who performs tricks in London with a Russian magician. One day he makes love to Nora, his friend's wife. Fred deludes himself with the fantasy that Nora loves him. His obsession with his sense of emotional maturity ends when he receives a letter from Nora rejecting his love, and she leaves for America with her husband. A few months later she finds Fred, informs him that he fathered her child, and abruptly leaves him. The story ends with Fred's physical and emotional collapse: in pursuit of Nora, he overhears that her son died a few days earlier. This twist reminds Nabokov's readers of the unrealized potential of his characters. Fred believed that he matured through realization of his love for Nora. As Connolly concludes, the story "is a tale of metamorphosis and growth, and it attests to the importance of interaction with others in promoting these core transformations."

The urban setting suggests the deceptive nature of a modern metropolis. The death of the dwarf on a busy street represents a symbolic death of the Baudelairean flaneur, the modern male stroller, free of familial and communal ties. Nabokov's account of Fred's love affair forms part of a long-standing literary tradition that interprets modernity as an Oedipal revolt against the tyranny of authority, focusing on metaphors of contestation and struggle grounded in an ideal of competitive masculinity. As in the novel *Mary* (*Mashen'ka*, 1926), "The Potato Elf" draws on the love triangle; Fred falls in love with Nora and makes her pregnant while her handsome giant husband fails. The story evokes disenchantment with the equation of modernity and masculinity. Nabokov challenges the nineteenth-century preoccupation with sexuality as the truth of the self as expressed in the emerging doctrines of psychiatry and philosophy.

One interesting story of the early period, "The Return of Chorb" (first published in *Rul'* as "Vozvrashchenie Chorba," 1925), received considerable critical attention. Like other stories of this period ("Christmas," "Bakhman," "A Letter that Never Reached Russia"), it deals with the representation of loss and grief. Chorb, a Russian émigré, marries a German girl from a wealthy family. On their honeymoon in Southern France she dies in an accident (electrocuted by telegraph wire). Chorb returns to Germany to deliver the news to the Kellers, his in-laws. Unable to reach them at home, he leaves a message with the maid that his wife is ill, decides to stay overnight in the cheap hotel where he and his wife spent their wedding night, and invites a prostitute to keep him company. In the night Chorb wakes up and screams, mistaking the sleeping prostitute for his dead wife. The prostitute runs away as the Kellers appear in Chorb's room. The story epitomizes the process of alienation that Chorb experiences in his grief. He becomes obsessed with the dream of recovering the image of his dead wife, but his reemergence into the world is more shocking than his grief. In general terms this story reflects on the psychological state of Russians living in emigration after the October 1917 revolution. Nabokov views their nostalgic longing for the past as a means of escaping from reality. Nabokov's ability to produce a precisely calculated story structure, with a well-balanced mixture of plot development and mythopoetic overtones, is evident. Chorb's example illustrates the duality of life, with a blurred boundary between the physical and the invisible world of pure spirit.

Nabokov and his son translated "The Return of Chorb" into English for inclusion in *Details of a Sunset and Other Stories*. Prior to this publication, an English version of the story had been prepared by Nabokov's

Caricature of Nabokov by S. A. Tsivinskii in the 26 August 1924 issue of Segodnia *(Today), a Russian periodical that published many of his early short stories*

friend Professor Gleb Struve. In April 1975 Nabokov wrote to Struve: "I am about to publish yet another collection of stories, *Details of a Sunset,* the last raisins and petit-beurre toes from the bottom of the barrel. The volume includes 'The Return of Chorb' and 'The Passenger'—in my and Dmitri's translation. I had not looked up your versions for many years and now find them not accurate enough and too far removed from my present style in English. Please, don't be cross! Time does not move, but artistic interpretation does."

Nabokov's first novel, *Mary,* was written in 1925 in Russian and published in 1926. The novel portrays an ordinary week in the life of seven Russian émigrés in a Berlin pension. Lev Ganin, a former White Army Guard officer, discovers that his neighbor Alferov expects his wife to arrive shortly from Russia. Ganin plots to prevent the Alferovs' reunion after seeing a photograph of Alferov's wife, Mary, who was Ganin's first love; they separated during the unsettling time of the civil war in Russia. Yet, after executing his carefully planned scheme to prevent Alferov from meeting his wife at the station, Ganin decides not to escape with her; instead he goes to France on his own. In this escape into the world of new possibilities, Ganin leaves behind two heartbroken women in Berlin whom he prefers to forget, as well as a dead Symbolist poet and other Berlin acquaintances. In this novel Nabokov's antihero is born.

Nabokov's protagonists often display disenchantment with life, in the style of Pechorin, Lermontov's misfit and outsider, whose narcissistic nature alienates him from his own milieu. *Mary* provides an embryomodel of Nabokov's later fiction, presenting the author's vision of individual life as spiral. Although Ganin does not meet Mary, he undergoes a spiritual and emotional catharsis from his re-experiencing of the past. Ganin's memories of his first love signal his spiritual awakening and trigger his quest for more profound meaning in life.

Nabokov's sketch "A Guide to Berlin" (first published in *Rul'* as "Putevoditel' po Berlinu," 1925) provides illuminating background for modern drama. An introduction and five separate subchapters appear under the titles "The Pipes," "The Streetcar," "Work," "Eden," and "The Pub." Nabokov depicts alienation in a metropolis through the use of a mirror image suggesting the fragmentation of modern life into separate units and travestied images. In a satirical manner, he portrays the Berlin Zoo as a "man-made Eden on earth," which "man is able to reproduce," making fun of the hotel Eden opposite the zoo. Nabokov's dystopian vision of urban paradise on earth is further felt in his disenchantment with the streetcar, a symbol of modernity in many European narratives in the early twentieth century. Nabokov predicts "the streetcar will vanish in twenty years or so, just as the horse-drawn tram has vanished." He dismissively reveals his boredom with such a novelty: "Already I feel it has an air of antiquity, a kind of old-fashioned charm." Describing people at work randomly and dispassionately, Nabokov presents his characters as in an unusual theme park that he observes "from the crammed tram": they are all just objects of his gaze that both amuse and bore him. To complicate the structure of the sketch and to introduce his favorite device of double voice, he ends his story in a pub with a child observing the narrator talking to his companion. The narrator views himself and his companion from a distance, as part of the child's future memories. Unable to explain to his friend what he sees "down there," the narrator exclaims: "What indeed! How can I demonstrate to him that I have glimpsed somebody's future recollection?" This story brings a vision of Nabokov's own narrative as palimpsest, which the future writer—the young observer in the pub—will use to inscribe his own life into Nabokov's narrative.

Another early story, "A Nursery Tale" (first published in *Rul'* as "Skazka," 1926), links erotic overtones with the tradition of children's bedtime stories. It foreshadows Nabokov's novella *The Enchanter* (written in 1939) and his novel *Lolita*. Although the pedophilic theme is subdued in this story, it expresses the protagonist's desire for a young girl. "A Nursery Tale" portrays the erotic fantasies of a young male, Erwin, too shy to befriend women, preferring to gaze at or dream about them. The devil offers him the chance to fulfill his fantasies about a harem. The devil suggests Erwin round up as many women as he likes, as long as he finds an odd number of women within twelve hours. The devil promises to provide a villa for Erwin to stay with all his women. By midnight Erwin finds twelve and chases another to produce the odd total, but discovers that she is also number one as time runs out. Thereby the thirteen women represent his thirteen wishes that fail to materialize.

Scholars suggest Nabokov was fascinated by the difference between the numbers twelve and thirteen. His second collection of stories, *Nabokov's Dozen,* features thirteen stories, and he ensured that his next volume of short fiction in English would have thirteen entries. Before his death in 1977, Nabokov planned another collection of thirteen tales. As Priscilla Meyer explains, this obsession is linked to the difference in days between the Gregorian and Julian calendars, which increased from twelve to thirteen in the twentieth century. In numerical mysticism, thirteen is considered to be an unlucky and indivisible number, and cosmic order (represented by twelve) is restorable by removing one unit. The mystical motif of "A Nursery Tale" also has been traced to Johann Wolfgang von Goethe's *Faust* (1808, 1832) and E. T. A. Hoffmann's tales. Nabokov himself admitted in an interview that the first stories he remembered were English fairy tales.

In his lectures on the European novel at Cornell University, Nabokov told his students that any great novel is a fairy tale. By the same token, Nabokov's short stories might also be seen as fairy tales. Nabokov's narrator is often presented as a storyteller and enchanter who tries to capture his readers' imaginations. Thus, in the story "The Passenger" (first published in *Rul'* as "Passazhir," 1927) Nabokov portrays a writer who confesses to his friend that life is more inventive than any writer's imagination: "Life is more talented than we. The plots Life thinks up now and then! How can we compete with that goddess? Her works are untranslatable, indescribable." In a semihumorous vein, Nabokov alludes to his own frustration and failure to capture the sublime moments of life and to understand the psychology of modern man. The narrator of the story tells his friend about a train journey during which he encountered a crying man in his carriage, at first mistaking the man for a criminal. The writer confesses to his friend that he could have written a few stories about this man, inventing various plots, to follow the flight of his own imagination. As the narrator admits, "I would have alluded to the passionate love he had for his wife. All kinds of inventions are possible. The trouble is that we are in the dark—maybe Life had in mind something totally different, something much more subtle and deep. The trouble is that I did not learn, and shall never learn, why the passenger cried." In the story Nabokov aspires to achieve a new kind of characterization, more fluid and less stable than the fixed psychologies of nineteenth-century fiction, as exemplified in Tolstoy's novels and stories, featuring trains as symbols of modernity. In "The Passenger" Nabokov portrays himself as a modern author who observes people in order to learn various forms of modern subjectivity.

Nabokov continues the gazing theme in his novella *The Eye* (*Sogliadatai,* 1938), articulating the individual's anxiety about retaining definition of his own identity in this age of mechanical reproduction of art. Fear of others possessing the defining power worries Nabokov as creator of his own life. The plot of the story is simple: the narrator, Smurov, a young private tutor for a family with two boys, is one day punched in front of the boys by his mistress's husband. This moment of humiliation is a blow to Smurov's elevated self-consciousness: "A wretched, shivering, vulgar little man in a bowler hat stood in the center of the room, for some reason rubbing his hands. That is the glimpse I caught of myself in the mirror." Some scholars argue that the elements of suspense, which are linked to the quest for Smurov's identity, prevail in the story. Yet, the mystery of Smurov's identity remains unresolved, because Smurov's epistemological quest for his own identity leads him to dispersion and absence through aesthetic activity. Smurov's concluding remarks suggest that the key to happiness in the world is "to be nothing but a big, slightly vitreous, somewhat bloodshot, unblinking eye." The story marks Nabokov's progression from modernist to postmodernist aesthetics, with its preoccupation with the self. Bearing in mind that modernism was the art most suited to challenging political complacencies and ideological dogmas by disrupting the mimetic illusions of realist art and reflecting contradictions of modern life, Nabokov's stories of the late 1930s indicate the possibility of overcoming such contradictions through the aesthetization of life.

Nabokov in 1926 (courtesy of Dmitri Nabokov)

Two of Nabokov's novels of this period—*The Defense* (*Zashchita Luzhina,* 1930) and *Despair* (*Otchaianie,* 1936)—continue his interest in human psychology and in a world of the irrational, dreams, delusions, and obsession. *The Defense,* Nabokov's first masterpiece, portrays chess master Aleksandr Luzhin, who resembles both the famous émigré chess master Aleksandr Alekhin and Nabokov himself. Nabokov's long-standing passion for chess led some critics to believe that he had turned his fiction into metafictional play, inscribed with logical puzzles and recurrent patterns. Chessmen are familiar motifs in Nabokov's prose, secondary images in his first and late fiction. Butterflies are also prominent; apart from literature and chess, Nabokov was seriously preoccupied with lepidopterology. Butterflies often evoke memories and emotions in Nabokov's characters, bringing a sense of estrangement and of the metaphysical into the narrative.

Nabokov translated his novel *Despair* into English in 1937. Its protagonist, Hermann, is a consummate narcissist, failed as businessman but self-rediscovered as a criminal genius. He kills his double, thinking that he can thereby fake his own death. At the end of the novel

Hermann's deception is exposed, and he is captured. Nabokov's novel re-enacts the dark narratives of Pushkin and Fyodor Dostoevsky, but his protagonist is also exposed as a bad writer, perhaps an analogy with Nabokov himself. Critics have noted this work represents a striking example of Nabokov's dual-voiced narrative. Nabokov's ironic discourse was not always appreciated by his contemporaries, prompting Struve, a leading critic, to defend Nabokov's new type of description, in which he portrayed a world that was illusionary and one-dimensional behind the familiar world.

Two other novels of the 1930s–*Invitation to a Beheading* (*Priglashenie na kazn'*, first published in *Sovremennye zapiski*, 1936) and *The Gift* (*Dar*, first published in *Sovremennye zapiski*, 1937–1938)–prefigure Nabokov's politically focused narratives of the 1940s. *Invitation to a Beheading* is an anti-utopian narrative, an allegorical fantasy alluding to the totalitarian nature of Marxist and fascist utopias. The death sentence pronounced on dictator Cincinnatus C. in the novel signifies the author's symbolic rejection of tyranny and reveals his belief in the freedom in people's imagination that survives mortality. *The Gift* is Nabokov's best Russian novel. It combines Nabokov's anti-utopian sentiments with brilliant metafictional parody and with the aesthetics of the Russian nineteenth-century revolutionary writer Nikolai Gavrilovich Chernyshevsky. The protagonist of the novel, Fedor, writes a biography of Chernyshevsky, aiming to "kill" him but also to transform Chernyshevsky the man into Chernyshevsky the literary character. Russian émigré publishers deleted some passages in the novel, finding Nabokov's satire to be too dismissive of Russia's democratic and literary heritage.

"Cloud, Castle, Lake" (first published in *Russkie zapiski* as "Ozero, oblako, bashnia," 1937), a disturbing and powerful story of this period, discusses the unpleasant encounter of a young Russian émigré, Vasili Ivanovich, winner of a trip to the country, with a German group. The Germans emerge as cruel bullies who join their leader in beating up young Vasili, while he is en route to his pastoral paradise. The protagonist wishes to abandon his communal journey for his dream: an ancient black castle near a blue lake with "a large cloud reflected in its entirety." He dreams of a room with a view over the lake, "beautiful to the verge of tears." The story ends with a humane gesture from the narrator, Vasili's employer, who understands Vasili's wish to resign from his position in Berlin. The last words, "I let him go," imply the narrator's conviction that everyone should have a dream and space of his or her own. The tragic twist to the story suggests that individuality and nonconformity in 1930s Nazi Germany should not be treated as undesirable behavior or madness. Nabokov creates a striking metaphor of the collective body that represents the enormous power of mass destruction: "one collective, wobbly, many-handed being, from which one could not escape."

When "Cloud, Castle, Lake" was translated into English, Edward Weeks, editor of *The Atlantic Monthly*, welcomed it with enthusiasm. Nabokov was introduced to Weeks by Edmund Wilson. Nabokov and Weeks lunched together in 1941 in Boston. After three years of rejections from English-language publishers, Nabokov was pleasantly surprised that Weeks was eager to publish Nabokov's story in *The Atlantic Monthly*. "We are enchanted," Weeks told Nabokov; "This is genius. . . . this is what we have been looking for, we want to print it at once–give us more." *The Atlantic Monthly* published several of Nabokov's stories and poems over the next few years.

Nabokov's revolt against authoritarian regimes and tyrants is also strongly pronounced in "Tyrants Destroyed" (1938). It is the emotional monologue of an imaginary male citizen of a communist or fascist country, who realizes that to free himself from tyranny he must kill the tyrant in his mind: in other words, to liberate his consciousness he must kill his fear of tyrants. As Nabokov explains, "Hitler, Lenin, and Stalin dispute my tyrant's throne in this story–and meet again in 'Bend Sinister,' 1947, with a fifth toad. The destruction is thus complete."

Three of Nabokov's autobiographical stories– "Spring in Fialta" (first published in *Sovremennye zapiski* as "Vesna v Fial'te," 1936), "Mademoiselle O" (first published in *Mesures*, 1936) and "First Love" (first published in *The New Yorker* as "Colette," 1948)–deserve special attention for his distinctive use of memory that anticipates his later autobiographical writing. Nabokov's recollection of his Swiss governess, "Mademoiselle O," is permeated with lyrical overtones. Nabokov grew to appreciate her position in Russia as a total alien and compares her to the strange and beautiful swan featured in Charles Baudelaire's "Le Cygne" (The Swan, 1861). In "First Love" he also remembers warmly his first love, a French girl named Colette, whom he met while on a family holiday in the south of France. Subsequently the ten-year-old Nabokov met Colette for the last time in a Paris park. In this story Nabokov's poetic discourse brings together his childhood dream, intertwined with images of rainbow-colored glass, marble, and the hoop and arches of a looped fence. The poetic representation of his life as a spiral in this story resembles Henri-Louis Bergson's idea of duration and creative impulse. In Bergsonian manner, Nabokov presents a girl from the past as a desirable future unfolding its meaning to him while he relives the past in the moment of narration. Nabokov is urging readers in an age of scientific phenomena to overcome

Nabokov and his son, Dmitri, circa 1944 (courtesy of Dmitri Nabokov)

the limits of rationalism and to find intuition and memory in the knowledge of self.

"Spring in Fialta" continues the theme of the intuitive process of self-knowledge through the experience of love and loss. The protagonist, Victor, thinks to himself: "Suddenly I understood something I had been seeing without understanding." In this moment of inner truth Victor discovers Fialta, a dull and cloudy place, becoming "saturated with sunshine." The narrators of Nabokov's autobiographical stories resemble poets living aesthetically, but the message of Nabokov's stories recalls Søren Kierkegaard's statement that "every aesthetic life-view is despair."

The complex relationship between art and life is also questioned in the novel *The Real Life of Sebastian Knight* (1941), written in English and marking Nabokov's emergence as an American writer. In typical Nabokovian manner, the novel includes autobiographical overtones and allusions to chess. It depicts the narrator's search for the essence of Sebastian Knight, a half brother who died young and unrecognized as a true genius. The narrator aspires to write a biography of Sebastian Knight to disperse the myths created by his secretary's biography. The perplexing quest for Sebastian Knight leads the narrator to question his own identity and to wonder whether he himself is Sebastian Knight.

Nabokov's story "That in Aleppo Once . . ." (1943) is also partly autobiographical. The narrator, "V," a writer and collector of lichens, receives a letter from a stranger who urges "V" to write a story about his experience: the strange author of the letter believes that his wife never existed and that he deluded himself, despite the marriage certificate. The confused stranger wants "V" to use this real-life story about an illusionary wife in his writing. The narrator of the story within the story, "Aleppo," is separated from his wife while fleeing the Nazis in 1940 France. He is convinced that she disappeared not after arguing with him but because she never in fact existed. It is a psychological study of torment, jealousy, and madness.

In 1944 Nabokov wrote the story "A Forgotten Poet," which was published in 1958 in *Nabokov's Dozen*. It took him almost an entire year to write this tale of a Russian poet who supposedly drowned at the age of twenty-four in 1849, and who appears as a seventy-four-year-old man at a memorial gathering in 1899 organized by his fans to commemorate the fiftieth anniversary of his death. The poet wants to obtain the money collected by a group of poetry lovers for his monument. The surname of the poet, Perov, derives from the Russian word for "feather," which is also associated with writing, because goose feathers were used as writing tools in nineteenth-century Russia. In his speech the chairman of the gathering proclaims Perov's name to be synonymous with freedom. "To a superficial observer this freedom may seem limited to Perov's lavishness of poetical images," the speaker concludes, "But we, representatives of a more sober generation, are inclined to decipher for ourselves a deeper, more vital, more human, and more social sense in such lines of his as . . . 'then my heart goes out in its tattered cloak/to visit the poor, the blind, the foolish.'" The old man is removed from the audience by two policemen as soon as he tries to reveal his identity to the audience, admitting his need of money and protection as well as his support for the Russian monarchy. "Our empire and the throne of our father the Tsar still stand as they stood, akin to frozen thunder in their invulnerable might," the poet observes in his anniversary speech, prior to his removal from the room by police, "and the misguided youth who scribbled rebellious verse half a century ago is now a law-abiding old man respected by honest citizens."

The twist embedded in Nabokov's story has a parodic touch. Nabokov levels his criticism at the Russian myth of the national poet, constructed out of the life of Pushkin. In Russian modernism Pushkin became a cult figure associated with freedom and modernity, while in the Soviet Union he was seen as a father of socialist realism. In this story Nabokov ponders the unpredictability of literary fame, which depends on the ever-changing values and tastes of the readership. As biographer Brian Boyd points out, "A thoroughly impersonal, superbly understated re-creation of an apparently historical event in a wonderfully evoked Russia of 1899, the story is sober enough to hoodwink readers into accepting Perov as a real poet." In an ironic manner Nabokov depicts readers who refuse to accept that their favorite poet might have changed. Nabokov protests against the desire of such readers to feel free upon the poet's death to become the true authors of his texts, and against their right to mold the image of their icon as they like. In other words, Nabokov's interest in literary deception in "A Forgotten Poet" is double-edged: he differentiates between the poet and his literary masks, arguing that the poet's private life should not be seen as the main interpretative tool for his poems; and he also suggests that readers of the poet's work might be deluding themselves when they try to decipher his poems in their own way, as contemporary writing. In this story Nabokov passionately condemns the capitalist culture of mass consumption that vulgarizes the individual style and the sublime.

Nabokov's profound disillusionment with the twentieth century is revealed in his fictional twenty-first-century memoir "Time and Ebb" (first published in *The Atlantic Monthly*, 1945), narrated by a ninety-year-old

Jewish scientist of European background in New York. He suggests that all twentieth-century symbols of modernity disappeared into the unknown: "admirable monsters, great flying machines, they have gone, they have vanished like that flock of swans which passed . . . above Knights Lake in Maine" and "then nothing but a lone star remained in the sky, like an asterisk leading to an undiscoverable footnote." Nabokov wrote this story in English in 1944, in Wellesley. Boyd calls it "a little masterpiece that blends the immediate and the remote, the mundane and the eerily beautiful." The narrator lies in a hospital in the year 2024 and reflects on his childhood in America in the 1940s. The story blends science fiction with the genre of the memoir, pointing to the strangeness of life the narrator took for granted. Nabokov continues his theme of estrangement from the self and of physical displacement from the past as manifested in his early stories. For the first time in his work Nabokov uses America as the setting for a story, and in this futuristic fantasy he presents American readers with familiar landscapes in a poetic manner, adding to them a touch of magic. For example, the narrator recollects buildings, movies, planes, taxicabs, Central Park, and skyscrapers through the eyes of the enchanted boy, with warmth and sympathy:

> Upon reaching New York, travelers in space used to be as much impressed as travelers in time would have been by the old-fashioned 'skyscrapers'; this was a misnomer, since their association with the sky . . . was indescribably delicate and serene: to my childish eyes looking across the vast expanse of park land that used to grace the center of the city, they appeared remote and lilac-coloured, and strangely aquatic, mingling as they did their first cautious lights with the colors of the sunset and revealing, with a kind of dreamy candor, the pulsating insight of their semitransparent structure.

The story conveys some autobiographical overtones, hinting at Nabokov's hybrid Russian American identity. Thus the narrator states: "I suppose I am old-fashioned in my attitude toward many aspects of my life that happen to be outside my particular branch of science; and possibly the personality of the very old man I am may seem divided, like those little European towns one half of which is in France and the other in Russia." In his desire to cherish his childhood memories, the narrator of "Time and Ebb" appears to be akin to Nabokov himself, who spent many years working on his autobiographical masterpiece *Speak, Memory*.

Nabokov's story "Signs and Symbols" (first published in *The New Yorker*, 1948), praised by Boyd as "one of the greatest short stories ever written," is a complex study of maniac disorder, portraying a mad dreamer in a mental hospital. His elderly parents, a displaced Russian Jewish couple, go to the asylum to give their son his birthday present. Their son believes in a strange form of conspiracy: that everything happening around him is a secret reference to himself. A description of a thunderstorm and rain alludes to the young man's attempt at suicide. On returning home, the father suggests to his wife that they could keep their son at home, watch him at night, and call the doctor to see him twice a week. They are afraid of being responsible for his suicide. The story ends with a description of the nameless father enjoying a cup of tea and examining with pleasure "the luminous yellow, green, red little jars" of fruit preserves and jams while the telephone rings, supposedly because of someone dialing the incorrect number. The story is open-ended, but there is a hint that the phone call could be a matter of urgency, informing the parents about their son's attempt to commit suicide.

This story is a "tightly interrelating system of imagery," notes Neil Cornwell, "that reverberates beyond that story itself and back through Nabokov's earlier Russian fiction." According to Larry Andrews, "Nabokov's entire career gradually takes on the appearance of an elaborate code with an intricate symbolic meaning." William Carrol sees referential mania as "a critical disease all readers suffer from," especially readers of Nabokov's metatextual and allusive fiction, for signs and symbols play a vital role in Nabokov's worldview. Nabokov apparently worked on "Signs and Symbols" for some time. His 1944 critical study of Nikolai Vasil'evich Gogol, for example, reveals his intention to write a story of "a lunatic who constantly felt that all the parts of the landscape and movements of inanimate objects were a complex code of allusion to his own being, so the whole universe seemed to him to be conversing about him by means of signs." Arguably, Nabokov's story anticipates Jean Baudrillard's postmodernist concept of simulacra: for Baudrillard, the postmodern world is a world of simulacra, which makes people unable to differentiate between reality and simulation. In "Signs and Symbols" Nabokov expresses his critical view of any postmodern outlook that opens a way to cynicism and lack of sensitivity to the human dimension involved. As Nabokov states ironically, the referential mania sufferer "excludes real people from the conspiracy—because he considers himself to be so much more intelligent than other men." As Boyd puts it, "'Signs and Symbols' works brilliantly as poignant realism, but what makes the story such a masterpiece is the Nabokovian twist that turns the real world inside out and into an irresolvable enigma."

Nabokov discusses another example of human tragedy in an unusual psychological study, "Scenes from the Life of a Double Monster" (first published in *The Reporter*, 1958), the story of Siamese-twin brothers

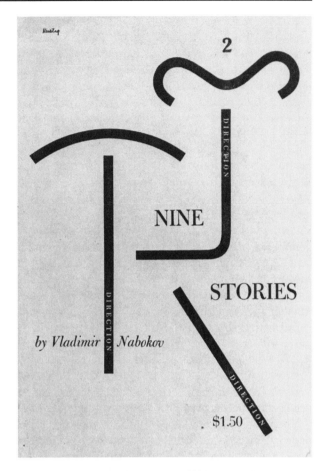

Cover for the first collection of Nabokov's stories in English, published in 1947

Floyd and Lloyd. Their life is one of total pain and misery because of their disability, which prevents them from enjoying their childhood at their grandfather's farm near Karaz, on a hill by the Black Sea. Their greedy grandfather Ahem displays the twins to visitors for money. Floyd, the narrator, "the rarest of freaks," describes in great detail their subjection to cruelty and humiliation, when various visitors expected them to perform. He comments: "They derived quite a kick from having us match wits at checkers or muzla. I suppose had we happened to be opposite-sex twins they would have made us commit incest in their presence." One day the twins were kidnapped by Uncle Novus, a showman, who never returned them to their fearful grandfather. Floyd recollects this abortive flight from their captivity twenty years later with gratitude.

On the symbolic level, Nabokov's story represents a hysterical discourse, as if the narrator needs another person through whom the whole story could be told. It is significant that Floyd speaks on behalf of both brothers. Lloyd is silent, needing Floyd to express his own suffering and his own dreams.

Nabokov's story also challenges the ethical aspects of European scientific discourse developed in the eighteenth and nineteenth centuries. St. Petersburg (Nabokov's birthplace) boasts one of the first museums in Europe that exhibited live or dead monsters, both humans and animals. Peter the Great saw the museum as a place of education, but above all one of entertainment. Nabokov's image of the double monster contains longing for the all-inclusive spirit of the Hellenistic world. Floyd dreams of encountering a stranger on a Black Sea shore who would have "experienced a thrill of ancient enchantment" and worshiped the twins as "a gentle mythological monster in a landscape of cypresses and white stones." Yet, his highly romanticized vision of himself as a gentle monster, able to evoke sympathy and "sweet tears," remains an unfulfilled fantasy. The story was written as a result of Nabokov's reading in the library at Cornell University of various nineteenth-century studies of Siamese twins. Nabokov intended to write a novel about a pair of Siamese twins, imagining a three-part tragic tale: the first part would tell about the twins' childhood in Turkey, prior to their abduction to America; the second part would tell about their marriages to two normal girls; and the third part would be a tale of unsuccessful surgery that would leave only one of them alive. The novel was never completed. Upon finishing the first part of this tale, "Scenes from the Life of a Double Monster," in October 1950, Nabokov sent it to *The New Yorker*. Although the subject was unusual and the story was vividly written, *New Yorker* editor Katharine White felt that it was missing something and rejected it. It was subsequently published in 1958.

In spring 1951 Nabokov wrote a story of two sisters. The narrator of "The Vane Sisters" (first published in the *Hudson Review*, 1958–1959) recalls his time as a teacher of French literature at a college in a small New York town. One winter day he arrives at his college to learn of Cynthia Vane's death. The narrator recounts his memories of Cynthia and her sister, Sybil, a former student who committed suicide because of a tragic love affair. Sybil's note informing the narrator of her suicidal intentions, written in bad French, was attached to one of her essays handed in to the narrator for marking; however, he discovered the note too late to help. As time passed, the narrator developed a friendship with Cynthia, a talented New York painter obsessed with spiritualism. "She was sure," Nabokov explains, "that her existence was influenced by all sort of dead friends, each of whom took turns in directing her fate." Upon receiving the news of Cynthia's death, the narrator feels unable to go to sleep, expecting some signs of Cynthia's life after death, thinking of a dream and "trying hard to unravel something Cynthia-like in it, something strange and

suggestive that must be there." The narrator experiences some mystical revelations: "I could isolate, consciously, little. Everything seemed blurred, yellow-clouded, yielding nothing tangible. Her inept acrostics, maudlin evasions. Theopathies—every recollection formed ripples of mysterious meaning. Everything seemed yellowly blurred, illusive lost." As in his earlier fiction, Nabokov mixes the surreal elements with realist description of human emotions; the depiction of otherworldly aspects of life with the philosophical discourse on the pain that is associated with the loss of human life.

"The Vane Sisters" epitomizes Nabokov's vision of art, for it deals with the death of the artist. In 1950 in one of his lectures on Franz Kafka, Nabokov explained to his students: "Beauty plus pity—that is the closest we can get to a definition of art. Where there is beauty there is pity for the simple reason that beauty must die: beauty always dies, the manner dies with the matter, the world dies with the individual." The narrator of "The Vane Sisters" tries to decipher the mysterious meaning of Cynthia's life and beauty. In his analysis of the story, Boyd points to the fact that a clue at the beginning of the story should alert readers to the acrostic message embedded in the last paragraph of the story: "Icicles by Cynthia, meter from me Sybil." As Boyd puts it, "The Vane Sisters" is one of Nabokov's best stories, for it manifests the writer's desire "to discover something that might lie beyond." It suggests, Boyd observes, "a shimmering promise behind the words: a problem set before us . . . indirect hints that our imagination can turn toward a solution." Yet, Nabokov's story does not offer any tangible definitions for the evasive meaning of the mystery of life and creativity. It might be suggested that the narrator of the story experiences some spiritual awakening that could turn him into an artist. White rejected the story for *The New Yorker*, finding it disappointing. In his letter to her, Nabokov explains the mechanism of allusive writing that can be found in "The Vane Sisters": "You may argue that reading downwards, or upwards, or diagonally is not what an editor can be expected to do; but by means of various allusions to trick-reading I have arranged matters so that the reader almost automatically slips into this discovery, especially because of the abrupt change of style." Nabokov felt frustrated with White's inability to see the "inner scheme" of his story. The situation of the two dead sisters, trying to communicate with the narrator through the symbolic language of an acrostic formed by the initial letters of the last paragraph, is rewritten in Nabokov's novel *Ada* (1969), which incorporates the theme of a ghost from the past talking to a mortal.

Nabokov working in Montreux, 1966 (courtesy of Dmitri Nabokov)

Despite their enthusiasm for the story, the staff of *The New Yorker* tried to edit the story significantly, and Nabokov had to explain the usage of such words as "spacers," "selenographers," "aclepias," and "liriodendron." Nabokov sent some materials from *Galaxy Science Fiction* magazine in support of the terms used in the story. His letter to the editors of *The New Yorker* on this subject reveals his thorough research for the story: Nabokov considered research to be a highly important component of most of his writing. Thus, he explains in an erudite and pedantic manner to the editors some of the features of the story: "The 'Indigo' Knight is the result of some of my own research; that Sir Grummore, mentioned both in Le Morte D'Arthur and in Amadis de Gaul, was a Scotsman; that L'Eau Grise is a scholarly pun; and that neither bludgeons nor blandishments will make me give up the word 'hobnailnobbing'." Some readers did not like Nabokov's story for its complexity and pretentiousness, seeing it as an unsuccessful parody of science-fiction comics. The editors of *The New Yorker* replied in a 28 February 1952 response to a reader's letter to them and defended Nabokov:

> In 'Lance' he is, of course, satirizing 'science fiction' but he is also using it as the basis of an underlying serious theme which, as we interpret it, is the constancy of human emotions in an ever-changing world. Extraordinary as an interplanetary expedition seems to us now, the emotions involved in the undertaking are no different from the emotions felt in medieval days when Lancelot, the knight, went into battle, or the emotions stirred up today when a son goes off to war. There is the same tension, the same awkward departure, the same fear of the unknown, the same anxious waiting on the part of the parents, the same courage under stress, the same sad loss of a friend, the same joyful return, the same inarticulateness in trying to communicate what one has felt and seen. No matter what changes the world goes through, our human relationships, our feelings, our reactions remain basically the same, and what seems extraordinary for us even to imagine now will be reacted to in quite an ordinary way when it comes to pass.

Nabokov was pleased with this letter, telling White that the editor "has summed up the thing in a perfectly admirable way, saying exactly what I would have liked to say (but would not have been able to do so lucidly)."

"Lance" also has some autobiographical overtones. Nabokov's first impulse for the story, as Boyd suggests, was Dmitri Nabokov's passion for mountain climbing. The story reflects the fears that Nabokov and his wife experienced regarding Dmitri's safety. In "Lance" Nabokov continues his theme of parents' love for their children and their fear of losing them, as mani-

If surreal overtones are present in most of Nabokov's short stories, science-fiction motifs become more visible in his stories written in the 1940s and 1950s. The most interesting example is "Lance," the last short story Nabokov completed, which Boyd calls "one of his best." The story was written in 1951 and published in *The New Yorker* in 1952, in spite of the fact that Nabokov felt pessimistic about the prospect of its publication after the rejection of "The Vane Sisters." Nabokov's "Lance" is an unusual hybrid of medieval chivalric romance and contemporary pulp science-fiction literature. To some extent, it is a result of Nabokov's studies in medieval French literature at Cambridge in England. Some readers found this story difficult to comprehend because of its dense structure, comprising medieval romance and parodic presentation of science-fiction tradition. White found "Lance" exciting and persuaded Harold Ross, who could not understand it, to publish it. As a result, Nabokov received $1,256 for "Lance"; as White's letter to Nabokov explains, Nabokov was paid for this story "at an unusually high word rate just on the basis of its originality."

fested in other writings such as "Signs and Symbols," "The Potato Elf," and "The Return of Chorb."

The main theme of "Lance" is courage. Lance, a brave astronaut, has a successful adventure in space and returns to earth. At some unspecified time in the future, his parents, Mr. and Mrs. Boke, see their only son off on the first manned expedition to another planet. They too display courage as they hope against hope for his return. At the end of the story Lance does return, though his friend Denny has been mysteriously killed on the expedition. Nevertheless, Lance announces his plan to go off again in November. His parents visit him in the hospital to break the news that his girlfriend, Chilla, is pregnant with his child. Lance is unemotional, obsessed with his dream to return to space. He wants to tell his parents what he and Denny saw out there, but his nurse, Mrs. Coover, prevents him from doing so. The story ends suggestively with an elevator: "Going up (glimpse of patriarch in wheelchair). Going back in November (Lancelin). Going down (the old Bokes). There are, in that elevator, two smiling women and, the object of their bright sympathy, a girl with a baby, besides the gray-haired, bent, sullen elevator man, who stands with his back to everybody." Lance, whom Nabokov characterizes as "the man of imagination and science," stands out as a new hero more developed and more courageous than heroes of antiquity or European knights of the Middle Ages. His curiosity surpasses his courage, and he seeks the infinite. Yet, the superhuman qualities developed in space turned him into a half-man and half-god. Nabokov compares Lance's transcendence of gravity to the transcendence of the grave, but Lance's dream of immortality is questioned by reference to the unknown matter Lance saw in space. Again Nabokov portrays an escapist, whose flight into the aesthetic world is not free from anxiety or humanist concerns about ethics.

Nabokov's philosophical story encapsulates the existentialist problem confronting modern man (represented in the story by Lance) and pinpointed in Kierkegaard's writings. Like Kierkegaard, Nabokov vehemently rejects Georg Wilhelm Friedrich Hegel's universalization and reduction of the individual to the stage of transcendental abstraction. The choice in itself is valuable to Nabokov the thinker, because it represents the ethical. Lance's escape into the pure aesthetic and abstraction leads to his indifference to the world around him and ends up with despair. Thus, Nabokov doubts Lance will stay sane.

Nabokov's novel *Lolita,* published in 1955 in Paris and in 1958 in America, brought him widespread popularity, but some critics believe it cost him any chance at the Nobel prize. It remains one of the most controversial novels in world literature, the story of a middle-

aged man's obsessive love with the teenage girl Lolita. Because of its pedophilic subject matter, Olympia Press, a publishing company specializing in pornography, published the novel first in Paris. Copies of the book were smuggled into America and Britain. The British government pressured France to destroy the remaining copies and to impose a ban on sales. Despite this action, Graham Greene reviewed Nabokov's book in a London *Times* article (25 December 1955), praising its stylistic splendor and including it in his list of the ten best books of 1955. Within five weeks of its 1958 publication in America it was proclaimed the most celebrated American novel. *The New York Times* listed it as one of the best-sellers of the year. Responses to Nabokov's novel were mixed. For Charles Rolo, *Lolita* was one of the funniest serious novels he had ever read: "The vision of abominable hero, who never deludes or excuses himself, brings into grotesque relief the cant, the vulgarity, and the hypocritical conventions that pervade the human comedy" (*The Atlantic Monthly,* September 1958).

In 1962 Nabokov published another novel–*Pale Fire*. It includes a 999-line poem by the late John Shade, an American poet shot dead by a madman. Supplementing this poem are a foreword, commentary, and footnotes by Charles Kinbote, a scholar who researched Shade's life and poetry. The structure of the novel is highly inventive and witty. Five years later Nabokov published his much-acclaimed autobiography *Speak, Memory*.

In 1969 Nabokov published his final major work, the novel *Ada or Ardor: A Family Chronicle*. As with *Lolita,* Nabokov's final masterpiece deals with a taboo: it is the chronicle of the incestuous love affair between Van Veen and his sister Ada. They were separated in their youth but found themselves reunited in later life, prospering together into their nineties. As some critics stated, Ada stands out as a symbol of immortalized memory. The name itself invokes two Russian words: *da* (yes) and *ad* (hell), suggesting the power of love and art to prevent destruction of some cherished memories. It is also possible to see the link between Nabokov's labyrinth of incest and George Gordon, Lord Byron's long poem *Cain* (1821), in which the name of the stepsister-wife is Adah.

Some critics note that *Ada* and *Transparent Things* (1972) could be defined as novels about last things. They reveal Nabokov the writer as gnostic seeker. According to Donald E. Morton, "*Ada* is Nabokov's fullest celebration of the powers of consciousness, and *Transparent Things* is his dramatization of the state of consciousness that lies beyond life." Morton also notes that "The privateness of these novels make them difficult for the uninitiated, but the lover of his early fiction will rejoice in them. These novels belong together in any

peace, and of nights with her, the red blaze of her hair spreading
all over the pillow, and, in the morning, again her quiet laughter,
the green dress, the coolness of her bare arms.

In the middle of a square stood a black wigwam: ~~they were~~
~~working on~~ *were being repaired* the tram tracks. He remembered how he had got today
under her short sleeve, and kissed the touching scar from her small-
pox vaccination. And now he was walking home, unsteady on his feet
from too much happiness and too much drink, swinging his slender
cane, and among the dark houses on the opposite side of the empty
street a night echo clop-clopped in time with his footfalls; but
grew silent when he turned at the corner where the same man as
always, in apron and peaked cap, stood by his grill, selling
frankfurters, crying out in a tender and sad bird-like whistle:
"Würstchen, würstchen..."

Mark felt a sort of delicious pity for the frankfurters,
the moon, the blue spark that had receded along the wire and, as
he tensed his body against a friendly fence, he was overcome with
laughter, and, bending, exhaled into a little round hole in the
boards the words "Klara, Klara, oh my darling!"

On the other side of the fence, in a gap between the buildings,
was a rectangular vacant lot. Several moving vans stood there like
enormous coffins. They were bloated from their loads. Heaven knows
what was piled inside them. Oakwood trunks, probably, and chandeliers
like iron spiders, and the heavy skeleton of a double bed. The moon

Page from the revised typescript for Vladimir and Dmitri Nabokov's translation of "Details of a Sunset,"
first published in Russian as "Katastrofa" (Catastrophe) in 1924 (courtesy of Dmitri Nabokov)

discussion of Nabokov's work, not merely because they come together in point of time, but also because they represent change in Nabokov's attitude toward his fictional material. After forty years of writing about characters bound and limited by chance, fate, and other villains, he wrote at last about freedom." Other critics comment on Nabokov's elegant use of language and composition in these novels. D. Barton Johnson, for example, considers *Ada* as "the most allusive of all Nabokov's novels."

Nabokov continued with literary activities until his death, publishing stories, poems, chess problems, and a last novel (*Look at the Harlequins!* 1974) featuring a writer living in a world of his dreams, books, and desires, ignoring his daughter's needs. All of Nabokov's novels display signs of self-reference and autobiographical overtones. Viewing all Nabokov's works together enables readers to understand his philosophy more coherently as it developed through a process of continuous discovery. On Nabokov's death, Alden Whitman wrote in *The New York Times:* (5 July 1977): "Nabokov's fiction was the refinement through memory and art of his own experience as a man who lost both his father and fatherland to violent revolution, who adopted another culture, who mastered its language as few of its own have mastered it and who never forgot his origins. . . . But as long as Western civilization survives, his reputation is safe."

The last of Nabokov's books to appear in his lifetime was the collection *Details of a Sunset and Other Stories,* published in 1976. Sunsets have a symbolic significance in Nabokov's work. Several stories in this collection were written in the 1920s but had not caught the public eye at the time. The collection evoked an enthusiastic response from reviewers. The previous collection of Nabokov's stories, *Tyrants Destroyed and Other Stories,* had been nominated for a National Book Award but failed to receive it. Some critics suggest that Nabokov's novels *The Gift* and *The Defense,* translated into English in the 1960s, overshadowed to some extent the rediscovery of his stories, which had been published previously in various European and American periodicals. Thus, in the 1940s and 1950s many of Nabokov's short stories were published by *The New Yorker.* The editors of the magazine paid handsomely for some of these stories. In 1945, for example, for his first story published by *The New Yorker*—"Double Talk"—Nabokov was paid $812.50, much more than he had ever been paid for a short story. Yet, on several occasions Nabokov had to defend his style, disliking the magazine policy of editing all submissions. In several letters to White, Nabokov insisted that the "average reader" did not read *The New Yorker,* and therefore there was no need to make Nabokov's

style more palatable to its readers: "the good reader will flit across the gaps with perfect ease."

The complexity and originality of Nabokov's style was admired by many twentieth-century prominent writers such as John Updike, Anthony Burgess, Alain Robbe-Grillet, and Greene. Yet, as J. D. O'Hara pointed out in 1977, Nabokov's position in contemporary literature was ambivalent, for he was "at once admired and forgotten." According to Boyd, intellectual fashion in the 1960s and 1970s had changed, to the effect that Nabokov's Eurocentric view of history and his antifeminist stance made him unpopular with some readers and critics. In spite of the fact that Nabokov was critical of many contemporary discourses such as Marxism, colonialism, and racism, Boyd wrote that by the 1970s "that seemed not enough to balance his unswerving allegiance to the best of western culture, the best of western freedoms." The rise of the postmodernist worldview in the United States, Europe, and Russia gives an opportunity to critics and readers alike to redefine Nabokov's role in twentieth-century literature. Some of Nabokov's short stories demonstrate his interest in subjectivity and disbelief in universal truths. Nabokov's fiction successfully illustrates several of the postmodern claims: that meaning is neither inherent in the language, nor in the world of things, for it is constructed by conventional frameworks of thought and language; that such concepts as individuality, freedom, and human subjectivity are constructs of a particular culture and time; and that literature is always metatextual and self-referential.

Longing for an ideal world and an ideal love leads to estrangement from this world—Nabokov's writings convey that message to his readers. Thereby the duality of voice in Nabokov's shorter fiction has a philosophical as well as stylistic function. Just like his novels, Nabokov's stories display concern with humanist issues. They exemplify Nabokov's important contribution to European and American tradition, to the genre of short story, and to modernism.

Letters:

The Nabokov–Wilson Letters: Correspondence Between Vladimir Nabokov and Edmund Wilson, 1940–1971, edited by Simon Karlinsky (New York: Harper & Row, 1979; London: Weidenfeld & Nicolson, 1979);
Perepiska s sestroi (Ann Arbor, Mich.: Ardis, 1985);
Vladimir Nabokov: Selected Letters, 1940–1977, edited by Dmitri Nabokov and Matthew J. Bruccoli (San Diego: Harcourt Brace Jovanovich, 1989).

Interviews:

Alfred Appel Jr., "An Interview with Vladimir Nabokov," in *Nabokov: The Man and His Work,* edited by L. S. Dembo (Madison: University of Wisconsin Press, 1967), pp. 19–44;

Stephen Jan Parker, "Vladimir Nabokov and the Short Story," in *Special Issue: V. Nabokov, Russian Literature Triquarterly,* edited by D. Barton Johnson (1991): 63–72.

Bibliographies:

Andrew Field, *Nabokov: A Bibliography* (New York: McGraw-Hill, 1973);

Samuel Schuman, *Vladimir Nabokov: A Reference Guide* (Boston: G. K. Hall, 1979);

Michael Juliar, *Vladimir Nabokov: A Descriptive Bibliography* (New York & London: Garland, 1986).

Biographies:

Andrew Field, *Nabokov: His Life in Part* (New York: Viking, 1977);

Brian Boyd, *Vladimir Nabokov: The Russian Years* (Princeton: Princeton University Press, 1990);

Boyd, *Vladimir Nabokov: The American Years* (Princeton: Princeton University Press, 1991);

Ellendea Proffer, ed., *Vladimir Nabokov: A Pictorial Biography* (Ann Arbor, Mich.: Ardis, 1991).

References:

Vladimir E. Alexandrov, *Nabokov's Underworld* (Princeton: Princeton University Press, 1991);

Alexandrov, ed., *The Garland Companion to Vladimir Nabokov* (New York: Garland, 1995);

Larry R. Andrews, "Deciphering 'Signs and Symbols,'" in *Nabokov's Fifth Arc: Nabokov and Others on His Life's Work,* edited by Julius Edwin Rivers and Charles Nicol (Austin: University of Texas Press, 1982), pp. 139–152;

Nina Berberova, *The Italics Are Mine,* translated by Philippe Radley (New York: Harcourt, Brace & World, 1969);

William Carroll, "Nabokov's Signs and Symbols," in *A Book of Things About Vladimir Nabokov,* edited by Carl R. Proffer (Ann Arbor: Ardis, 1974), pp. 203–217;

Julian W. Connolly, *Nabokov's Early Fiction: Patterns of Self and Other* (Cambridge: Cambridge University Press, 1992);

Connolly, ed., *Nabokov and His Fiction: New Perspectives* (Cambridge: Cambridge University Press, 1999);

Ned Cornwell, *Vladimir Nabokov* (Plymouth, U.K.: Northcote House / British Council, 1999);

John Burt Foster Jr., *Nabokov's Art of Memory and European Modernism* (Princeton: Princeton University Press, 1993);

Sarah Funke, *Véra's Butterflies: First Editions by Vladimir Nabokov Inscribed to His Wife* (New York: Glenn Horowitz, 1999);

D. Barton Johnson, *Worlds in Regression: Some Novels of Vladimir Nabokov* (Ann Arbor, Mich.: Ardis, 1985);

Priscilla Meyer, "The German Theme in Nabokov's Work of the 1920s," in *A Small Alpine Form: Studies in Nabokov's Short Fiction,* edited by Charles Nicol and Gennady Barabtarlo (New York: Garland, 1993), pp. 3–14;

Donald E. Morton, *Vladimir Nabokov* (New York: Ungar, 1974);

Marina Turkevich Naumann, *Blue Evenings in Berlin: Nabokov's Short Stories of the 1920s* (New York: New York University Press, 1978);

J. D. O'Hara, "Reading Nabokov," *Canto* (Spring 1977): 146–155;

Norman Page, ed., *Nabokov: The Critical Heritage* (London: Routledge & Kegan Paul, 1982);

Stephen Jan Parker, *Understanding Vladimir Nabokov* (Columbia: University of South Carolina Press, 1987);

Phyllis Roth, ed., *Critical Essays on Vladimir Nabokov* (Boston: G. K. Hall, 1984);

Stacy Schiff, *Véra (Mrs. Vladimir Nabokov): A Biography* (New York: Random House, 1999);

Zinaida Shakhovskaia, *V poiskakh Nabokova* (Paris: "La Presse Libre," 1979);

Maxim Shrayer, *The World of Nabokov's Stories* (Austin: University of Texas Press, 1999);

John O. Stark, *The Literature of Exhaustion: Borges, Nabokov, and Barth* (Durham, N.C.: Duke University Press, 1974);

Susan Elizabeth Sweeny, "The Small Furious Devil: Memory in 'Scenes from the Life of a Double Monster,'" in *A Small Alpine Form: Studies in Nabokov's Short Fiction,* edited by Charles Nicol and Gennady Barabtarlo (New York: Garland, 1993), pp. 193–216;

Leona Toker, *Nabokov: The Mystery of Literary Structure* (Ithaca, N.Y.: Cornell University Press, 1989).

Papers:

The two major repositories of Vladimir Nabokov's papers are the Library of Congress and the Vladimir Nabokov Archive in the Berg Collection of the New York Public Library.

Antonya Nelson

(6 January 1961 –   )

Sarah R. Gleeson-White
University of New South Wales

BOOKS: *The Expendables* (Athens & London: University of Georgia Press, 1990);

In the Land of Men (New York: Morrow, 1992);

Family Terrorists: A Novella and Seven Stories (New York: Houghton Mifflin, 1994; London: Picador, 1997);

Talking in Bed: A Novel (Boston: Houghton Mifflin, 1996);

Nobody's Girl (New York: Scribners, 1998);

Living To Tell (New York: Scribners, 2000).

In June 1999 an issue of *The New Yorker,* subtitled "The Future of American Fiction," listed Antonya Nelson as one of the twenty best young contemporary American writers. While Nelson has attracted critical attention within the United States with the publication of three acclaimed volumes of short stories, her name is still virtually unknown in the rest of the world. In her short fiction Nelson deals with the complexities of relationships between different generations, between men and women, women and women, best friends, lovers, and in-laws. Her stories reveal the marrow of such relationships under the rubric of "family terrorism"–games of power and manipulation, the little techniques perfected over the years to get under the skin of kinfolk and close friends. Nelson strips bare the fundamentals of human connection and its counterpart, loneliness. Her characters cover a broad spectrum of identities–academics, miners, children, animals–but are, on the whole, "good-natured foot soldiers for the common good–unambitious, undemanding, eager not to make any trouble," as Lisa Zeidner wrote in *The New York Times Book Review* (10 July 1994). By focusing on a relatively unremarkable group, Nelson is able to push the idea that the most ordinary can become–in fact, *is*–the most extraordinary. In her stories the emphasis is on the importance of the minute and the mundane in the struggle for emotional survival.

Antonya Nelson was born in Wichita, Kansas, on 6 January 1961. Her father, Francis William Nelson, was professor emeritus of English at Wichita State University, and her mother, Susan Jane (née Austin) was an

Antonya Nelson (photograph by Marion Ettlinger; from the dust jacket for Family Terrorists, *1994)*

instructor in the English department. Nelson was educated at the University of Kansas, where she received a B.A. in 1983. She married Robert L. Boswell, also a novelist and a writer of short fiction, on 28 July 1984. They have two children, Jade and Noah. Nelson completed her M.F.A. in 1986 at the University of Arizona. Since 1989 Nelson has been assistant professor in the Department of English at New Mexico State University, where she teaches creative writing. She is also a member of the faculty of the Warren Wilson College, Asheville, North Carolina, in the M.F.A. Program for Writers. She has been a visiting writer and writer in residence at several institutions, including Wichita State University (1998) and the Vermont Studio Centre, Johnson, Vermont (1999). Nelson divides her time between Las Cruces, New Mexico, and Telluride, Colorado.

Nelson's stories have appeared in various journals in the United States, including *Esquire, The New Yorker, Redbook,* and *Mademoiselle,* as well as appearing in anthologies such as *American Short Fiction* (Fall 1998). She has also written three novels: *Talking in Bed* (1996), *Nobody's Girl* (1998), and *Living To Tell* (2000). Her novels address themes that appear in her shorter fiction, including motherhood, relationships between men and women, and family dynamics. Nelson's stories have been well received by critics. Melissa Pritchard, reviewing Nelson's first collection, *The Expendables* (1990), for *The Chicago Tribune* (14 January 1990), claimed that Nelson writes with "the astute eye of a social scientist and an artist's courageous perception." Zeidner wrote that Nelson has "proved herself a master of the short story's shape. Her tales of families in transition are taut and zingy, with a tantalizing sense that we are eavesdropping on a variety of viewpoints." Nelson has won several awards, most notably the 1990 Flannery O'Connor Award for Short Fiction for *The Expendables.*

The Expendables is perhaps Nelson's strongest collection. The twelve stories are told in either the third or first person and explore themes that recur throughout Nelson's work: the rituals of marriage and death, the states of parenthood and marriage, and the process of change and growth. The concept of home is explored in "Cold Places," set in Wichita, where Nelson grew up. Hersh, a teenage girl, is a witness to her parents' marriage crisis, brought about by the appearance on their doorstep of her father's drunken mistress, Diane. Coldness saturates the story, not only metaphorically, in relationships, but also literally, in climate. Even "home" is cold, and it is in fact not a "home" as such, but a large, alienating house in which each member of the family seems to live alone. Hersh's sister, Paige, comments that "their parents' problems would have been resolved long ago if they lived in an apartment." While marital problems, particularly adultery, form the background of the story, the focus is more properly the effects of these problems on the family–particularly as experienced by young Hersh–and the way in which families are both a source of nourishment and "terrorism." Finally, her father's sexual errancy accompanies Hersh's own awakening sexuality as sexual tension mounts between herself and Diane's son, Lee.

Nelson explores similar shifts in relationships in "Listener," a Nelson Algren Award winner. The title refers not only to Julia's blind husband, Averil, to whom she regularly reads, but also to the male neighbor only ten feet "across the way" in their apartment block, with whom Julia becomes increasingly fascinated. Julia and Averil's recent move from rural Kansas to Chicago reflects their changing relationship. In the beginning Averil is seemingly dependent on Julia, who wonders "at her motives in marrying Averil. Did she really want a child instead?" With Averil's growing independence, Julia finally acknowledges her increasingly deep need of her husband.

"Listener" reflects on the short-story form itself: for Averil, short stories "end too quickly. . . . But Julia enjoys the short stories and the poems. She can read them twice in one evening if she wants. If they were powerful, she can recast their spell easily." Nelson commented in *The Writer's Chronicle* (September 1998) that she is more comfortable writing short stories than novels: "With a short story, you can interrogate at the line level . . . I think you have to give up quite a lot of control to write a novel. . . . Anything beyond 30 or 40 pages and I feel like things are leaking out the sides." The short story suits Nelson's ability to capture the minutiae of a particular emotion or impression; yet, at the same time, she indulges the novelist's ability to see a character through his or her experience by frequently revisiting her characters.

Marriage, specifically weddings, is the focus of both "Substitute" and "The Expendables." In the former, in what seems a reversal of the more clichéd flight of the groom from the altar, the would-be bride locks herself in the bathroom with a Bloody Mary on her wedding day, an occasion that provides the catalyst for the exploration of female friendship, another of Nelson's favorite themes. "The Expendables," anthologized in *American Fiction 88,* is convincingly told through the voice of an adolescent boy, Daniel, brother of the bride who is about to marry into a Mafia family. The title refers to Daniel's view of the wedding guests: "Whenever I got in a group like that, a group of sort of middle-aged people with little kids, all basically wearing the same thing, I started thinking, *This group is expendable. . . .* A group like that could vanish from the face of the earth and nobody'd notice." It is supposedly expendable people who provide the fodder for all of Nelson's stories as she seeks out the significance and resonance of the seemingly mundane and unimportant.

"Mud Season" is an exceptional and moving story in its account of Al and Lois's grieving over the recent death of their daughter Gwen, who (perhaps intentionally) rode her motorbike off a mountain road near Durango, Colorado. Nelson explores the effects of the death of a child on the parents' already-fragile marriage, a result of the husband's ongoing adultery. Lois dreams about flight, about "seeing the earth from a distance." The dream takes place in green English fields, as opposed to the Colorado mud season, that in-between season that provides a parallel with Al and Lois's similarly current liminal stage of grieving. Lois's dream of flight is a powerful motif of liberation—"the light and the freedom and the frightening unknown." The dream suggests a yearning after detachment, a freedom from the gravity of human connection, a certain numbness. Motherhood for Lois is painfully burdensome—she has been anticipating Gwen's accident "since the day she brought her first baby home from the hospital. She'd looked at the world from then on as a place full of forty-five degree angles and cliffs."

"Looking for Tower Hall" is a continuation of "Mud Season," set approximately two months later in Chicago, and is told from Gwen's brother-in-law's perspective. Gwen's parents and brother Neil visit him and his wife, Tina, in Chicago. The reader observes the further effects of the loss of a child: the father is sad and bitter, the mother is almost zombielike, numb. The suggestion is that they will be scarred for life. The story simultaneously focuses on Tina's pregnancy and the accompanying "risk" of having and loving a child: "The most dangerous thing in the world is to have a kid." "You Boys Be Good," a short, delightful story about the anxiety of awaiting the overdue return of a loved one, also explores the weight and responsibility of relationships.

Edward Allen observed in *The New York Times Book Review* (14 June 1992) that the fourteen short stories of Nelson's second collection, *In the Land of Men,* a 1992 *New York Times* Notable Book, "take place in a sort of aftermath. We come upon characters when their lives have already been fractured, displaced, uprooted." The volume includes "The Control Group," which appeared in the 1992 anthology *Prize Stories: The O. Henry Awards* and introduces the Link family, who resurface in the novella "Family Terrorists" in her third, eponymous collection (1994). "The Control Group," set in Nelson's hometown of Wichita, focuses on nine-year-old TV Mitchell, Joanne Link's foster child, whose mother has recently murdered her father, TV's grandfather. TV subsequently transfers his love from his mother to his rather stern schoolteacher, Mrs. Dugas.

Nelson has said that autobiographical sources inspired the story: her own grade-school teachers, as well as her psychologist-brother's experience with a child who was fostered out after his mother had killed her own father. Nelson wrote "The Control Group" in the third person, through the eyes of a child. On point of view, Nelson stated in a 1998 interview, "If I were to choose a small child to tell the story in the first person, I'd be putting myself under some severe limitations from the outset, and I'm not willing to do that. If it's a

child's point of view, typically I will step back and put the story in the third person so I can retain the right as a narrator to use language the child is incapable of doing."

The story from which the collection takes its title is thoroughly disturbing. "In the Land of Men" is about three brothers seeking revenge for the rape of their older sister. The boys pick up their sister from work to tell her that they have found her rapist and he is now imprisoned in the trunk of the car. It is up to her as to what action they should take: should she let her brothers deal with him, or should they hand him over to the police, who will surely let him go? In the 1998 interview Nelson said that a newspaper article inspired her story: "I was interested in taking the law into your own hands, and of a family being so motivated to find the assailant. . . . I wanted to make the issue more polarized, so I set the intentions and actions of men—the brothers—against the decision they required of the woman. As I see it the girl in the story is victimized once by the rapist and the second time by her brothers." The narrator, the boys' sister, is left in an extreme situation, and Nelson does not resolve the crisis, leaving the narrator undecided as to the course of action she will follow. The last sentence of the story is, "I'm thinking." Nelson has defended this ambiguous ending by saying that the young woman's decision is an impossible one: "To highlight that, to focus the epiphany, I had to give up the other side of the arc. I had to stop there and say, 'there is no right decision.' She's in the same situation that the reader will be in at the end of the story."

"In the Land of Men" is one of the few Nelson stories that directly confront the question of gender and the gender divide. "Human Habits" is another that addresses gender differences, although indirectly. In this story, Marta, who already has a son, Beau, marries Rory, and together they have baby David. While Marta seems bound to house and children, Rory has the option of freeing himself of these binds—an option symbolized in his maintenance of a second home in the city. Nelson has said that she empathizes with the unlikeable Rory, who entertains both a craving for familial connection as well as a seemingly opposite yearning for autonomy. In line with Nelson's continuing theme of the all-pervasiveness of family ties and obligations, the story ends with Rory unable to totally disconnect from Marta and their family. Retreating to his own home, he can still hear the sound of Marta's voice; garbage, tumbleweeds, and prickly pear have invaded his yard. "Human Habits" epitomizes the claustrophobia and the relentlessness that characterize Nelson's fictional worlds as a whole; interconnecting relationships of all kinds, while they nurture life, can also threaten to drown it.

Dust jacket for Nelson's 1992 book, stories with which she hopes to create a "little disruption in the psyche" of her reader

Nicole's loss of innocence as the world becomes tarnished with the revelation of her mother's adulterous affair and other hints of sexuality around her, including memories of her brother flashing his penis at her, and Cousin Leroy hinting that "Aunt Velvet had sex with Dog. . . . Didn't they ever wonder why she never got married? Wasn't it strange how she'd go off walking with Dog every evening for an hour? What about all those treats she brought him? And Dog went straight for crotches."

"How Much We Could See" recounts Gwen's family's annual summer holidays in Telluride (Nelson's other home), where the young female narrator, Gwen's older sister, Gwen, and their brother, Lee, befriend a local family whose son Eddie is the town bad boy. He drowns one night after a drinking binge, and Nelson describes the effects of the death on the two families. The story is about change, from childhood to adolescence, from sexual innocence to experience; it is also about the impossibility of permanence and security.

This notion of the inevitable risks of life and the inability to insulate oneself or loved ones from these risks recurs more directly in "Inertia" and "Bare Knees." In the latter, Lynnie Link–younger sister of Joanne in "The Control Group," who reappears in "Family Terrorists"–is a teenager who works at the local swimming pool as a lifeguard and finds herself unable to go to the rescue of a drowning boy. The theme of lifesaving–is it always possible?–is explored impressionistically in "Inertia," a tableau of emotion. In the background of the story is a father and his sister-in-law's concern for his daughter after her mother has committed suicide. The varying emotions of fear, anxiety, confusion, and helplessness are played out as the father tries to rescue a freezing squirrel from a rooftop. The theme is again broached in "Fair Hunt," which tells the story of Dee and James, who have moved to rural New Mexico from Houston. Dee is dying of cancer, and James does all in his power to save her, including shooting all her beloved animals so that she might return to a hygienic house after treatment, a grotesque action he comes to regret deeply.

As in her previous collection, the stories of *In the Land of Men* capture a strong sense of place. This geographic grounding often works as a contrast between the Midwest and the Southwest, the place where characters come to rebuild broken lives. In "Adobe," another story told in the first person, the female protagonist has moved from Chicago to the outskirts of Las Cruces, New Mexico. Although Allen considered "Adobe" the best story in the collection, it is slightly disappointing, mainly because of its almost paternalistic narrative stance vis-à-vis the Chicano father, Eddie, and his son, Tito, who become the focus of the female protagonist.

This type of emotional claustrophobia surfaces again in "Here On Earth," a brief and charming story of a mother reliving her past life in Chicago as she drives around the city with her daughter, Darcy. The mother makes Darcy uncomfortable with her personal reminiscences–for example, pointing out the building where she was conceived–until the end of the story describes Darcy's dream of flight, a similar dream to Lois's in "Mud Season." Flight in this story retains its sense of liberation and letting go, yet this time it is balanced, or grounded, by an acknowledgment of the simultaneous need for human contact and connection, symbolized by the young girl's need "to tell somebody."

Adolescent unease is also the subject of "Fort Despair" as well as "How Much We Could See," which once more features Gwen's family. "Fort Despair," an examination of marital love ("love came from being related to him, from habit, from knowing him so well she could predict him"), also narrates the young

While her adobe is being built, she learns to love the little boy who frequents the building site with his builder-father, and then she begins to love Eddie himself. The story ends—unconvincingly and rather cloyingly—with her falling into Eddie's arms. The building of the house is a rather obvious symbol for the rebuilding of her life and the building of her relationship with Tito and his father.

In "Goodbye, Midwest" place and relationship are again inextricably bound. Having been childhood friends in the Midwest, the female narrator and the rather wild Roxanne move to other ends of the country as their friendship falls apart. Place is a vital ingredient throughout Nelson's fiction, and a sense of place, or loss of it, becomes a metaphor for the transformation of and within relationships. The Midwest represents family and history and an accompanying claustrophobia. By contrast, the West and the Southwest represent rootlessness and a sense of freedom from family ties and shackles. There is often an accompanying tension between the urban and the rural. Connected with geographical place is an acute awareness of physical environment—climate, landscape, dwellings—that reflects an interior environment. For example, in several stories, storms and tornadoes suggest a kind of violent, yet also cathartic, form of "family terrorism."

Nelson returns to familiar themes—although place has become a lesser concern—in her third collection of stories, *Family Terrorists,* and she also picks up on some of the oddities that began to appear in *In the Land of Men,* such as the substitution of animal for human intimacy in "Fort Despair." Nelson hopes her stories will disturb readers: "That little disruption in the psyche is what I'm after. Stories ought to be a little disruptive." In "Her Secret Life" Zita is shadowed by her boyfriend's former girlfriend, Candy. Zita is simultaneously unnerved and flattered by this unusual mark of affection. When Candy finally moves to California, Zita experiences a kind of loss. Nelson handles the relationship between the two women with great delicacy as she merely hints at the possible sexual undercurrents between them.

More directly, Nelson suggests father/daughter incest in "Loaded Gun" and an illicit relationship between stepmother and stepson in "Crybaby." Even "The Written Word," told from a young boy's perspective, hints at David's odd, displaced desire for his mother, as he secretly looks at the pornographic photographs she keeps by her bedside: "a thing more powerful would overtake him, a thing so dark and sinful and inhuman he would later cry in fear for his nasty soul." David's horror at his burgeoning sexuality is the same adolescent unease in the face of an adult sexuality that Nelson describes in several other stories in *In the Land of*

Men. "The Written Word" is also concerned with David's relationship with his hated stepfather, a hatred so strong that David stages the kidnapping of his beloved baby sister in order to use the ransom money to rejoin his father in California. Although the denouement of the story is rather incredible, and the reader is left with many loose ends, "The Written Word" is nonetheless a moving story of adolescent fear and a longing for love and affirmation. Nelson also explores adolescence and sexuality in "Loaded Gun" and "Naked Ladies." In "Naked Ladies," which appeared in *The Best American Short Stories 1993,* the young female protagonist visits the house of her mother's sleazy, wealthy employer and notices on his walls a series of paintings of a naked woman. Slowly, painfully, she realizes that the model for these paintings is her mother.

The motif of innocence and experience is taken up again in "Dirty Words," included in *Prize Stories 1993: The O. Henry Awards.* This time the motif is explored through the contrast of American and European culture. Young Bette is pregnant by her older, Marxist husband, Sergio, the son of Polish immigrants. Bette feels overwhelmed by his European background and thinks that, in contrast, "her California-orange-grove life looked as naive and sunny as a sitcom. Until she'd seen him naked, Sergio had made her feel immorally young and uneducated, which was precisely what she'd come to Chicago to feel." Nelson portrays Bette's pregnancy in terms of the grotesque: "She was a large amoebic belly from which hung incidental appendages, wobbling through the world like an ugly tourist, cloddish, with a loud guffawing laugh." As with Marta in "Human Habits" from *In the Land of Men,* Bette seems weighed down by biology, by the private feminine sphere that is in strict antithesis to the public masculine sphere, Sergio's sophisticated European world of politics and the coffeehouse. While Nelson's account of Bette's pregnancy is poignant, the description of the relationship with Sergio falls back heavily on clichés and thus threatens the story as a whole.

The collection ends with its eponymous novella, "Family Terrorists," which presents the Link family—several of its members having already appeared throughout Nelson's stories—together for the first time. Zeidner wrote that Nelson finally unites the Links "so the nuclear family can explode." All the Link siblings and partners have come from around the country to bear witness to the parents' remarriage, and Lynnie's father lets her in on the burdensome secret of his affair, which ends only on the eve of his remarriage. In writing "Family Terrorists" Nelson seems to have fallen prey to the lack of control that she feels defines novel writing. Zeidner said that "Structurally, there is too much lounging and driving around, eating and drinking, cataloguing of menus and outfits . . . . By heaping up too much daily detail, not all of it absorbing, she loses some of the momentum and sharpness that make her short fiction so distinguished."

"Family Terrorists" is the culmination of the underlying theme of most of Nelson's stories: relationships, whether between kin or friends, are both nurturing and suffocating. During her drive across the country to the wedding, in the midst of a thunderstorm, Lynnie yearns for

> a car carrying a family, for a station wagon that might hold a passel of children, escorted by their bedraggled responsible father, their mother leaning over the back seat to dispense Life Savers and reassurance . . . . That was the car that would successfully ford the flood, thwart the lightning, plow some reasonably safe passage through a field full of tornadoes.

Yet, Lynnie is also aware that she is at the mercy of "family terrorism," whereby "her family always let her know the truth—that her heart was actually made of porcelain—by continuing to break it in incremental measure, one hairline crack at a time."

Antonya Nelson deserved to be included in *The New Yorker* magazine list of the twenty best young American writers today. While the content of Nelson's stories can occasionally fail to convince, her writing is sparse, piercing, and remorseless. Yet, Nelson is always empathetic, and her narrators refrain from judging the human theater in which they participate. Allen also acknowledged what he called Nelson's "unsentimental generosity toward her characters." Throughout her work is a sense of the weightiness and, at times, claustrophobia, of being alive—which means having family and friendships. Relationships such as these she seems to be saying, are what gives life its particular quality. Although her themes are similar from story to story, collection to collection, Nelson introduces such an array of characters, relationships, and circumstances—along with the force of her writing and her insight—that her stories rarely fail to move or to disturb.

Interview:

Susan McInnis, "An Interview with Antonya Nelson," *Writer's Chronicle,* 31 (September 1998): 33–37.

Josip Novakovich
(30 April 1956 –   )

David Pink
Moorhead State University

BOOKS: *Apricots from Chernobyl* (St. Paul: Graywolf Press, 1995);

Fiction Writer's Workshop (Cincinnati: Story Press, 1995);

Yolk (St. Paul: Graywolf Press, 1995);

Salvation and Other Disasters (St. Paul: Graywolf Press, 1998);

Writing Fiction Step by Step (Cincinnati: Story Press, 1998).

OTHER: *Stories in the Stepmother Tongue,* edited by Novakovich and Robert Shapard (Buffalo: White Pine Press, 2000).

Josip Novakovich has brought the soul of a Southeastern European to American short fiction. He has several times referred to himself as an expressionist, but he may also be considered a realist and, while he is uneasy with the description, a folklorist. Though he told Scott Rhoden that "the folktale style would be totally inappropriate" for him, he finds it "productive to write in village settings . . . that seems to be a folksy thing, but I use it because of its expressivity." Named by the *Utne Reader* in 1998 as one of the ten writers who is changing the face of fiction, Novakovich has been compared to Franz Kafka, Nikolai Gogol, and Isaac Babel. Because Novakovich often offers a modicum of hope along with wit, wisdom, and postmodern cynicism, some readers might be tempted to dismiss him as merely a village fabulist, but his stories reach deep to places where the heart is laid bare in all its hope and horror.

Josip Novakovich, the youngest of Josip and Ruth Navakovich's five children, was born on 30 April 1956 in Daruvar, Croatia, an ethnically mixed town of approximately twelve thousand Croatian, Serbian, Hungarian, and Czechoslovakian inhabitants. Considering the small size of Daruvar and Croatia itself, Novakovich has called his hometown "doubly provincial." Coming from a Baptist family that included woodworkers, lumberjacks, carpenters, and, in the case of his father, a wooden-shoe maker, Novakovich grew up accustomed to hard work, while observing convoluted local and state politics.

Josip Novakovich (photograph by Jeanette Novakovich; from the dust jacket for Fiction Writer's Workshop, *1995)*

In "Writing in Tongues," collected in *Apricots from Chernobyl* (1995), Novakovich explained that he encountered the English language all over Daruvar, in music, undubbed movies, sports, fashion, and cars. He came to study English in much the same way he claims to have pursued many other things in his life, as the easier of two options. When he had to choose between studying English or Russian in high school, he chose English because the class was held later in the day, which allowed him to sleep late. A relatively unmotivated student–

except when it came to reading stories–Novakovich was nearly failing English when he suffered a severely sprained ankle and had to spend time at home recuperating. He chanced on his brother Ivo's elementary English vocabulary book, which retold Greek myths. The myths stoked Novakovich's love of stories, and when his ankle healed and he returned to school, he surprised his teacher by becoming a diligent student.

Novakovich first left home in 1975 to study medicine in Novi Sad, Yugoslavia. The following year he immigrated to the United States to study psychology at Vassar College, where he earned a B.A. in 1978. He then earned a master's of divinity degree at Yale University in 1983, and attended the University of Texas at Austin to study creative writing. In 1993 he began teaching English at the University of Cincinnati, where he remained until 2001, when he was appointed an associate professor of English at Penn State university. He and his wife, Jeanette Baldwin Novakovich, have two children. He has received a Guggenheim Fellowship (1999), a 1999 American Book Award for *Salvation and Other Disasters* (1998), and a Whiting Prize for Literature (1995). He was selected a New York Public Library Writing Fellow for 2001–2002.

Much of Novakovich's fiction is about characters examining, developing, or defending their individuality, much as Novakovich has done himself. He told Rhoden, "Raised a Baptist, I was always an outsider. I'm interested in outsiders." In his world, Novakovich added, "almost everybody is an outsider. You just look for the way you are an outsider, so it's easily universal." The tension in his stories often arises from the internal and external conflicts generated by self-expression. Given the ideological conflicts that have bred war throughout the history of the Balkan region, geographical, cultural, and political landscapes often exert an overwhelming presence as well.

Novakovich's journey to writing in English was not always easy. He has noted in "Writing in Tongues" that he found himself falling into the American melting pot of a language in which "not many ingredients were allowed to melt." The considerable linguistic diversity of writers such as William Faulkner, Ernest Hemingway, and James Joyce charged Novakovich with an almost alchemical refinement of his own style. His search for his voice led Novakovich to write many narratives in which the lines between fiction and nonfiction are blurred, a situation that has become increasingly common in American and other literatures since the early 1980s.

Novakovich's first book, *Apricots from Chernobyl* (1995), is his most autobiographical, but there are elements of autobiography throughout all his writing. As he told David Pink, "I think I create various versions of myself because that's how I best know to make character–through fission method, splitting my atoms, hoping to release some energy for new stories." Many of the narratives in *Apricots from Chernobyl* were published as essays, but some were later republished as fiction. Novakovich resists such categorization, telling Pink, "in any kind of writing that matters one is at the end of one's wits, doing catch as catch can, so anything goes–memory, journals, research, imagination. The difference between the two genres lies in the description of the writing act that 'postcedes' the act; after you are done, emerging out of the chaos of writing, you can analyze: What the hell have I done?" He added that "without lawyers I doubt that we would worry about the boundaries between fiction and nonfiction so much. Hardly anybody else in the world does." Graywolf Press, the publisher of *Apricots from Chernobyl,* called the book a collection of "narratives," avoiding a designation of fiction or nonfiction. Regardless of their relationship to factuality, Novakovich's writings are remarkable in that they show little interest in what is personal to him; instead, he follows Grace Paley's advice on creative writing: "Write about what you don't know about what you know."

"Via Negativa," in *Apricots from Chernobyl,* is a good example of Novakovich's weaving autobiography and fiction into one narrative. In "Via Negativa" he ponders his father's deep religious faith. His father, a survivor of war and torture, had more than enough reasons to renounce God; yet, he believed deeply and prayed so long and hard that his knees were sometimes caked with blood. Novakovich's father loved life, worked, sang, relished the honey from his beehives, fathered five children, and when faced with his imminent death accepted it without question or complaint. Novakovich is amazed that his father could accept death so willingly and easily that his epitaph reads "Death, where is thy sting?" Years later, Novakovich questions why he does not share his father's deep and seemingly easy faith.

In contrast to his father, who appeared to have taken the direct route to belief, Novakovich searches for his faith by eliminating false paths to God. He suggests that he may have found the true path through writing fiction. The fiction writer, like a theologian, Novakovich decides, can ponder the mysteries of man and God and change his life accordingly. In this moment Novakovich undercuts much of his previous understanding of the "easy" way through which he thought his father had gained deep faith and, in so doing, pays what is perhaps a son's ultimate compliment to his father: understanding and admiring his father through his own evolutions of consciousness. "Via Negativa" shows the value of Novakovich's narrative method–mining autobiographical moments in order to treat themes that apply to many lives. Novakovich's stories often deal with everyday dramas, his touch light, leavened with genuine humor, or humorously skewed by irony.

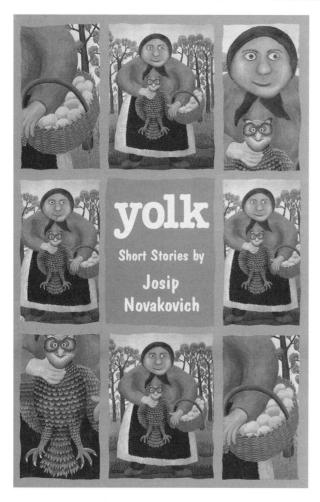

Cover for one of the 1995 collections of his writings in which Novakovich blended autobiography and fiction

In "Byeli: the Definitive Biography of a Nebraskan Tomcat" Novakovich tells the tale of one of a quartet of cats he and his wife raised while living on a farm in Nebraska. (The other cats were named Hitler, Stalin, and Churchill.) The Novakoviches let this pet tomcat inside, where, as unneutered cats are wont to do, Byeli marked his territory by spraying urine around the house. Like those who ignore a relative's or a friend's bad habits, the Novakoviches came to love Byeli despite, or because of, his cat nature. Novakovich was delighted when Byeli sprayed his tax forms—"Byeli was a stylist"—and decided to mail them that way, declaring that America should have "an organic government."

Novakovich describes Byeli and his adventures with such specificity that the creature's personality comes alive. Novakovich seems to favor writing about strong, memorable characters and does not limit his subjects to human beings. The reader feels sympathy at Byeli's death because Novakovich has depicted the cat's fierce, almost human need to assert his personality, as well as his com-

plicated mix of affection for his human masters with his occasional tyrannical and rapacious animality toward his own kind. Byeli, after all, did only what is natural for a tomcat, and in the end the Novakoviches mourn him: "It took me a long time to get used to Byeli's not existing because his ghost kept leaping everywhere for me." In his humorously stoical fashion Novakovich also notes, "No cats showed up for Byeli's funeral." Humorous as it may be, the story has deeper resonance, implying the question of how one can be a strong presence in the world without being labeled "an animal."

Strong characters also abound in *Yolk* (1995), the first of Novakovich's books whose contents have been labeled short stories. These narratives are filtered through experience and invention. In "The Burning Clog," the first story in the collection, Yozzo (Novakovich's nickname as a boy) has returned to Croatia from the United States to learn how to tell a story from Nenad, his father's longtime clog-making assistant. After having moved to America to study fiction writing, Yozzo rethinks his educational plans and returns home to learn the art of narrative fiction from the storyteller he admired as a child. Nenad quickly disillusions Yozzo by telling him that he got most of his dramatic tales of wizards, kings, and wars from the library. Moreover, he says he has run out of his stock of fictional stories.

Instead he tells Yozzo a true story about a black cat that alerted him to the arrival of German soldiers in their town during World War II. The soldiers stopped to butcher chickens belonging to villagers before marching into town to execute villagers engaged in partisan defiance of the invaders. From seeing the cat carrying a chicken head into town, Nenad deduced that the soldiers were on their way and alerted his fellow villagers. Many were saved because Nenad could "read" the story from the cat. The lesson is not lost on Yozzo, who gains from this simple tale an understanding of how story and reality are related. He realizes how the real world leads to story, which leads to salvation if the signs can only be read, and how myths and fairy tales of childhood can be replaced by stories that are even more marvelous because they are true. Such revelations become available only if one reads these stories closely and begins to understand that they are everywhere, in everyone, and in everything.

Another story in *Yolk*, "Rust" helps to delineate Novakovich's theme of transcendence, which his characters sometimes avidly resist and at other times ferociously seek. "Rust" tells the story of Marko Kovachevich, a former Communist Party member and monument sculptor who quit the party and gave up that line of sculpting because the party paid him so poorly that he took a loss on his materials. Marko turns instead to "specializing in the tombstones of deceased Party members." "Rust" captures Novakovich's themes with masterful concision. The struggle for individuality in the face of totalitarianism could not find a better, and at the same time stranger, champion or hero than Marko.

After leaving the Communist Party and its paltry commissions, Marko moonlights as an art teacher, and the narrator of the story is one of his students. For Marko, being an art teacher does not seem to matter much. He lets his students run amok while he sleeps; yet, when he does awake it is clear that he cannot escape his beliefs no matter how much the ruling class engenders ennui. Marko is not lazy; he is tired from working hard. Marko galvanizes himself and others. He quickly surveys the narrator's flaccid rendition of a tree and with a few bold, decisive strokes gives it a backbone, so that the tree seems to come alive and develop character. The narrator learns that one's philosophy, or one's artistic expression, must have backbone to make it memorable.

This epiphany comes as a shock to the narrator, who mistook Marko's art-class catnap as sloth. Journeying home years later, after having spent time studying at a Western university, the narrator seeks out Marko, who is not impressed by the narrator's studies in the "lukewarm" thought of the West, philosophies that could be sunk easily enough by hard work. He tells the stunned narrator, who has been living in a state of self-satisfied indolence, that work is part and parcel of human existence–"the whole creation travails"–and so must he. To avoid work, for Marko, is to avoid God. He says, "that's how you have to live," to avoid being destroyed by God. This statement, coming from a man the narrator has admired "most for his freedom," causes the narrator to adjust his opinion of his former teacher. He sees him now as "a slave to work." This realization leads the narrator to despair; he says, "I was more dejected than the rich young man who asked Jesus what more should he do to be saved and was told to give up all his riches to the poor." Marko, the free individualist, teaches the narrator that a totally free person who lacks a moral backbone is like the spineless, characterless tree in his painting. Disobeying state law, Marko preaches at a town-square meeting that no one should care about the ethnic distinctions that have led to so much bloodshed: "Croat . . . Serb . . . Who cares? Let me tell you. God doesn't." When he dies, having worn himself out with hard work, Marko asserts his paradoxical nonindividualist individuality by leaving instructions that his wife mark his grave with a stone he has hewn in the plainest style. Contrary to the local custom, it is totally devoid of ornamentation, as if to assert that the monument does not make the man. Contrary to the nationalistic monuments that are rusty on the outside and hollow on the inside, God expects a human being to have the backbone to stand for something.

In *Salvation and Other Disasters* (1998) Novakovich employed more traditional forms of fiction. Many of the stories have third-person or first-person narrators who are clearly not Novakovich. The first story, "Sheepskin," plays with the notion of mistaken identity and its costs. While traveling on a train, the Croatian narrator thinks that he recognizes Milos, his Serbian torturer during the Balkan Wars. The narrator decides to track Milos and look for an opportunity to exact revenge. He is surprised when Milos orders fluently in Croatian at a restaurant but convinces himself that Milos has a sinister ability to dissemble. Eventually, he shoots Milos in the back. While returning home, however, the narrator is shocked to see Milos's likeness in face after face, leading him to wonder if he murdered the wrong man. His local newspaper confirms that he has killed a fellow Croat, not Milos. The narrator begins a romantic pursuit of his victim's widow, all the while guiltily reveling in his desire to reveal himself as her husband's murderer. In the final movement of the story, he wishes that he could metamorphose into an animal, to become a fox in fields of flowers and herbs that could be made into restorative botanical teas.

"Sheepskin" displays the complexities and subtleties of Novakovich's autobiographical narratives, raising questions about the erotic nature of retaliation and how the wish for a simpler existence must be negotiated against devaluation of humanity in wartime and the acceleration of information dispersal. The pressure toward revenge, fomented by media reports of atrocities, seems to propagate a self-focus, a negation of mercy that renders life almost cartoonish in its harshness. The narrator's transmutation is impossible. He wants the reduced conscience of a fox, but, as a murderer who has also usurped his victim's place as a husband, his is not a condition any human being would see as "natural." He cannot join the guiltless, purely animal world the fox inhabits. The only other way he can find to assuage his guilt is to confess his crime to the widow, who is now his own wife, but that scenario is also untenable. In "Sheepskin" Novakovich plays with the idea that one might have the failure of existential non-being and at the same time the success of being erotically enabled through murder.

Another of Novakovich's war stories, "Crimson," revisits his theme of the complex entanglements of the Balkan conflicts. Serbian policemen with knives force Milan, a Serb peasant living in Croatia, to join the Serbian army, where his army unit is a gaggle of drinkers, smokers, and pornographic-movie watchers. (They hook up a VCR to tank batteries.) As they lob shell after shell into the Croatian city of Vukovar, Milan wonders, "what would be the point of taking a devastated city, a mound of shattered bricks?"

Cover for Novakovich's 1998 story collection, which won an American Book Award in 1999

Realizing that Milan is watching, the captain says, "after I'm done, you go ahead too, dip your little dick, and enjoy. Hahaha. You'll have a complete education today.... You'll make a soldier yet." Milan kills the captain because he thinks he recognizes the woman as his childhood sweetheart, Svyetlana. As is typical in Novakovich's war stories, it is a case of mistaken identity. The woman is Olga, not Milan's former girlfriend.

The conclusion may strike some readers as straining credulity. After Milan has saved Olga from the captain, he rapes her while she is unconscious. They meet later, in a different town, when Olga is on her way to an abortionist. He begs her not to go through with the abortion, and she agrees after he promises to take care of her. They marry, and all is fine after the baby is born until Milan sees a photograph of Olga's father and recognizes him as the man he executed. Olga ends up stabbing Milan and then saving his life by donating the blood he needs for a transfusion. The story points out the absurdity of blood conflicts in an area such as the Balkans, where interrelationships are hopelessly—or perhaps hopefully—complicated. If everyone is related in some way, then war makes even less sense than usual. Some readers, however, might see the story as plunging coincidences and complexities into absurdity.

Hyperbolic plots and straying into absurdity are dangers for an author who writes modern fables and parables. Novakovich also faces other dangers as a writer. His autobiographical writings sometimes fail to rise above sketches, as in "Bachelor Party" in *Apricots from Chernobyl*. In other cases a story that is undeniably fiction, such as "Out of the Woods" in *Salvation and Other Disasters,* does not combine autobiography and imagination as seamlessly as in a story such as "Rust."

Yet, Novakovich has written many successful stories in which memorable individuals struggle for identity in a bewildering and mysterious world. If Novakovich is a writer of the villages, it is because the world there is immediate. Characters in Novakovich's universe keep trying unsuccessfully to escape the gravitational pull of basic human needs and concerns, which appear to be a good, or at least necessary, grounding. To leave behind the mess of human and animal life for a rarefied disengagement, a philosophical or divine avatar, is to leave behind humanity and nature itself—a condition, Novakovich's fiction suggests, that is antithetical to life itself.

Milan soon has to participate more directly in the conflict when his captain orders him to shoot an old Croatian man—something he has never done before. Milan's thought that no one loves him while the man probably has many people who care about him makes him dislike the man enough that he is able to pull the trigger. Of course the captain has also threatened Milan with execution if he does not shoot the man, but this exigency seems less compelling than the lack of love in Milan's life in motivating him to carry out the murder of a civilian. Besides, the execution is easy: "it did not feel like anything as long as you concentrated on the details. He watched the crushed snail houses on the bricks, and red earthworms sliding straight, unable to coil, in the cracks between the bricks." The captain is quick to congratulate Milan, adding: "I was worried for you, that you were a sensitive, Croat-loving homosexual."

The story quickly moves to another form of violence when Milan discovers his captain raping a woman.

Interviews:

David Pink, "Josip Novakovich: Throwing Words at a Vague Shape," *A View from the Loft,* 22 (February 2000): 3–5;

Scott Rhoden, "Balkan Tales: An Interview with Josip Novakovich," *Indiana Review* (Spring 2000): 23–38.

Edward Sanders

(17 August 1939 –   )

Brooke Horvath
Kent State University

See also the Sanders entry in *DLB 16: The Beats: Literary Bohemians in Postwar America.*

BOOKS: *Poem from Jail* (San Francisco: City Lights Books, 1963);

King Lord/Queen Freak (Cleveland: Renegade Press, 1964);

The Toe Queen Poems (New York: Fuck You Press, 1964);

Peace Eye (Buffalo: Frontier Press, 1965; enlarged, 1967);

Shards of God (New York: Grove, 1970);

The Family: The Story of Charles Manson's Dune Buggy Attack Battalion (New York: Dutton, 1971; London: Hart-Davis, 1972); revised *The Family: The Manson Group and Its Aftermath* (New York: Signet-NAL, 1990);

Vote! by Sanders, Abbie Hoffman, and Jerry Rubin (New York: Warner Paperback Library, 1972);

Egyptian Hieroglyphics (Canton, N.Y.: Institute of Further Studies, 1973);

Tales of Beatnik Glory (New York: Stonehill, 1975; expanded edition, two volumes in one, New York: Citadel Underground, 1990);

20,000 A.D. (Plainfield, Vt.: North Atlantic Books, 1976);

Investigative Poetry (San Francisco: City Lights Books, 1976);

Fame & Love in New York (Berkeley: Turtle Island Foundation, 1980);

The Z-D Generation (Barrytown, N.Y.: Station Hill Press, 1981);

The Cutting Prow (Santa Barbara: Am Here Books / Immediate Editions, 1981);

Hymn to Maple Syrup and Other Poems (Woodstock, N.Y.: Poetry, Crime & Culture, 1985);

Poems for Robin (Woodstock, N.Y.: Poetry, Crime & Culture, 1987);

Thirsting for Peace in a Raging Century: Selected Poems 1961–1985 (Minneapolis: Coffee House, 1987);

Hymn to the Rebel Café (Santa Rosa: Black Sparrow, 1993);

Edward Sanders, 1995 (photograph by Mellon)

Cracks of Grace (Milwaukee: Woodland Pattern Book Center / Kenosha: Light & Dust, 1994);

Chekhov (Santa Rosa: Black Sparrow, 1995);

Der Sommer der Liebe, translated by Erwin Einzinger (St. Andra-Worder: Hannibal, 1997);

1968: A History in Verse (Santa Rosa: Black Sparrow, 1997);

America: A History in Verse, Volume I, 1900–1939 (Santa Rosa: Black Sparrow, 2000);

The Poetry and Life of Allen Ginsberg: A Narrative Poem (Woodstock, N.Y.: Overlook, 2000);

America: A History in Verse, Volume II, 1940–1961 (Santa Rosa: Black Sparrow, 2000).

PLAY PRODUCTIONS: *The Municipal Power Cantata,* by Sanders, Eli Waldron, Ilene Marder, and Martin Fleer, Woodstock, New York, Town Hall, 1978;

The Karen Silkwood Cantata, Woodstock, New York, Creative Music Studio, 1979; Annandale-on-Hudson, Bard College, 1980;

Star Peace, Oslo, International Poetry Festival, 1986;

Cassandra: A Musical Drama, Woodstock, New York, 1992, 1993.

RECORDINGS: *The Village Fugs: Ballads of Contemporary Protest, Points of View and General Dissatisfaction,* by Sanders and the Fugs (Tuli Kupferberg and Ken Weaver), Broadside Folkways, 1965; reissued as *The Fugs First Album,* ESP and Base, 1966; reissued, with additional material and booklet by Sanders, Fugs Records–Fantasy, 1994;

The Fugs, ESP and Base, 1966; reissued, with additional material and booklet by Sanders, as *The Second Fugs Album,* Fugs Records, 1993;

Tenderness Junction, by Sanders and the Fugs, Allen Ginsberg, and Gregory Corso, Reprise, 1968;

It Crawled into My Hand, Honest, by Sanders and the Fugs, Reprise, 1968;

The Belle of Avenue A, by Sanders and the Fugs, Reprise, 1969;

Golden Filth: Alive at the Fillmore East, by Sanders and the Fugs, Reprise, 1970;

Sanders' Truckstop, Reprise, 1970;

Beer Cans on the Moon, Reprise, 1972;

Refuse to Be Burnt Out, by Sanders and the Fugs, New Rose, 1985; Olufsen, 1985;

Baskets of Love, by Sanders and the Fugs, Olufsen, 1985;

No More Slavery, by Sanders and the Fugs, New Rose, 1986; Olufsen, 1986;

Star Peace, by Sanders and the Fugs, New Rose, 1987; Olufsen, 1987;

Fugs Live at Woodstock, by Sanders and the Fugs, Musik/Musik, 1989;

Songs in Ancient Greek, Olufsen, 1989;

Songs for a Portable Feast, by Sanders and the Fugs, Gazell, 1991;

Yiddish-Speaking Socialists of the Lower East Side, Hyperaction, 1991;

The Fugs Live from the Sixties, by Sanders and the Fugs, Fugs Records, 1994;

The Real Woodstock Festival, by Sanders and the Fugs, Ace, 1995;

American Bard, Olufsen, 1996.

OTHER: *Poems for Marilyn,* edited by Sanders (New York: Fuck You Press, 1962);

Bugger: An Anthology of Buttockry, edited by Sanders (New York: Fuck You Press, 1964);

Despair: Poems to Come Down By, by Sanders, Ted Berrigan, Paul Blackburn, John Keys, Al Fowler, Harry Fainlight, and Szabo (New York: Fuck You Press, 1964);

The Fugs' Song Book, edited by Sanders, Ken Weaver, and Betsy Klein (New York: Peace Eye Bookstore, 1965);

The Municipal Power Cantata, by Sanders, Eli Waldron, Ilene Marder, and Martin Fleer (Woodstock, N.Y.: Poetry, Crime & Culture, 1978);

The Party: A Chronological Perspective on a Confrontation at a Buddhist Seminary, by Sanders and his Investigative Poetry class at the Naropa Institute (Woodstock, N.Y.: Poetry, Crime & Culture, 1980);

"The Legacy of the Beats," in *Beat Culture and the New America 1950–1965,* edited by Lisa Phillips (New York: Whitney Museum of American Art / Flammarion, 1995), pp. 244–247.

SELECTED PERIODICAL PUBLICATIONS–UNCOLLECTED: "The Hairy Table," *San Francisco Earthquake,* 1 (Summer–Fall 1968): 39–44;

"Dom-Int," *Oui,* 6 (July 1977): 90–95;

"The Psychedelicatessen," *Review of Contemporary Fiction,* 19 (Spring 1999): 31–46.

Perhaps no literary/cultural movement has been as relentlessly self-documenting as the Beats, whose faces and friendships, lives and lifestyles, have been portrayed in movies and photographs, paintings and pencil sketches, memoirs, poems, and romans à clef. Yet, as the beatniks metamorphosed into hippies and the Beat Generation became the counterculture, as jazz gave way to rock, there was probably no one on the scene who observed and recorded it as affectionately, precisely, and creatively as has Edward Sanders in the thirty-two interconnected stories published as volumes one and two of *Tales of Beatnik Glory* (1975 and 1990).

Raised as "a regular American by Stevensonian Democrats," James Edward Sanders was perhaps an unlikely candidate for future Beat glory, growing up in a suburb of Kansas City, where he studied piano and drums and belonged to the DeMolays and the Society of Barbershop Quartet Singers. The son of Lyle David Sanders, a salesman and builder, and Mollie (Cravens) Sanders, Ed Sanders played football and basketball in high school, where he was president of the student council in his senior year, and bowed to his family's wishes by planning to major in engineering or physics at the University of Missouri. (He had visions of entering the space program.) In March of his senior year, however, when Sanders was seventeen, his mother died suddenly. Her passing was, he recalled in a 1990 interview, "the worst thing. I figured nothing could be worse than that. It just tore my mind apart."

That same spring, when Sanders spent a weekend at his intended alma mater, auditioning and being auditioned by fraternities, he spent a few minutes in the campus bookstore, where he discovered and purchased Allen Ginsberg's *Howl* (1956). He had already been reading the poetry of Ezra Pound and Dylan Thomas, but the impact of *Howl* was dramatic, energizing Sanders's fascination with poetry and adversarial literature. Although he prefers to downplay the autobiographical dimension of "A Book of Verse," which concludes volume one of *Tales of Beatnik Glory,* the story accurately captures this life-altering encounter with the work of Ginsberg, who became both a friend and one of Sanders's principal literary mentors:

> When he got back home, he read *Howl* and was stunned. Here was a young man whose family had prepared a map of life for him that included two avenues, either a) law school (like his uncle Milton), or b) to work in his father's dry-goods store. *Howl* ripped into his mind like the tornado that had uprooted the cherry tree in his backyard when he was a child. He began to cry. He rolled all over the floor of his bathroom crying. He walked down the stairs in the middle of the night to wake his parents and read it to them. His mother threatened to call the state police.

Sanders did enter the University of Missouri, but it was an ill-fated venture. As he explained in 1990, "I was nobody—there was no literary scene that I felt I could cooperate with, nor were there simpatico brothers and sisters with whom I could share my interest in literature, so I got out of there." Hitchhiking to New York City, Sanders found a job in a Times Square cigar store and entered New York University, still intending to study engineering but eventually majoring in classics because his mother had told him that "a gentleman always knows Greek or Latin." In Greek class during the fall of 1958, Sanders met Miriam Kittell, a writer and artist hoping to become an archaeologist. They were married three years later, on 6 October 1961, and subsequently had one daughter, Deirdre.

As Sanders worked his way toward the B.A. in Greek he earned in 1964, he became involved in the life of his times. He participated in a 1961 Walk for Peace and was arrested a few months later for obstructing the launch of Polaris submarines. The lit-

Sanders's Peace Eye bookstore in New York City, 1966

erary result was his first book, *Poem from Jail* (1963). Later he chanted the exorcism at the 1967 March on the Pentagon in protest of the war in Vietnam and helped Jerry Rubin and Abbie Hoffman found the Youth International Party (the Yippies) in 1968. Sanders was there as the turbulence of the 1960s gave way to the relative quiet of the 1970s.

In 1964, meanwhile, Sanders had opened the Peace Eye bookstore with a sign in the window identifying the proprietor as "Ed Sanders—book creep, grass cadet, fug poet, editor, squack slarfer, madman composer and poon scomp." From the back room of Peace Eye came mimeographed issues of his *Fuck You / A Magazine of the Arts* (whose contributors included Ginsberg, William S. Burroughs, Norman Mailer, and Charles Olson), and from his Fuck You Press came legendary, now-rare tomes such as *Poems for Marilyn* (1962), *The Vancouver Report* (1964) by Carol Bergé, *Roosevelt After Inauguration* (1964) by William S. Burroughs (with a cover by Allen Ginsberg), *Despair: Poems to Come Down By* (1964), *Bugger: An Anthology of Buttockry* (1964), and other pamphlets and broadsides. A summer 1965 police raid on Sanders's studio seized several underground movies made by

Sanders. In early 1966 his bookstore was raided; printed matter was seized; and Sanders was charged with possessing obscene material. The ACLU took his case, and in July 1967 a three-judge panel in New York City found Sanders innocent. The trial and the distraction of other projects caused the magazine to fold, and Peace Eye closed in early 1970.

One of the new projects distracting Sanders was the Fugs, which he started in late 1964 with Tuli Kupferberg. They soon added Ken Weaver to the group. Three Beat poets masquerading as a satiric folk-rock band, the Fugs were an underground sensation, touring and recording regularly throughout the 1960s, but their songs were sufficiently explicit sexually and controversial politically to keep them from receiving much airplay. "Amphetamine Shriek," "What Are You Doing after the Orgy," "CIA Man," and "Kill for Peace" are representative titles, although the group also set to music poems by William Blake and Algernon Charles Swinburne.

By the end of the 1960s the Fugs had disbanded. Sanders recorded a couple of solo albums and wrote a best-selling book, *The Family: The Story of Charles Manson's Dune Buggy Attack Battalion* (1971; a revised version appeared in 1990 as *The Family: The Manson Group and Its Aftermath*). In 1972 he co-authored *Vote!* with Hoffman and Rubin. By this time New York City, which had been Sanders's home throughout the 1960s, was losing its charm for him. Concerned for their safety as the Lower East Side grew more violent, the Sanderses had moved to Greenwich Village in 1970. There, Sanders's wife was mugged at knifepoint on New Year's Day of 1974. A few months later, the Sanderses moved to Woodstock, New York.

Before leaving the city, Sanders had begun *Egyptian Hieroglyphics* (1973), a book about "rebel artists in ancient Egypt" out of which, he says, grew the idea for *Tales of Beatnik Glory*. The pursuit of Manson had taken its toll on Sanders's peace of mind. Critic Thomas Meyers has argued that Sanders's fascination with Manson stemmed from his fear that Manson had taken in a dark and deadly direction ideas Sanders himself had been loudly articulating. Writing the stories in volume one of *Tales of Beatnik Glory* proved therapeutic. As Sanders explained in his introduction to *Tales of Beatnik Glory,* "I felt healed to return, in my writing, to an era which I genuinely loved and understood, and one I was sure I could limn with a wild candor featuring humor and utmost seriousness."

Despite the publication of the first volume of *Tales of Beatnik Glory,* Sanders continued to be seen primarily as a 1960s activist and former Fug. As a writer, despite a quantity of work in several forms and genres (musical cantatas, poetry manifestos, literary criticism, investigative journalism), he has remained best known as a poet and the author of *The Family*. After all, he has published eighteen volumes of poetry, including the verse biographies *Chekhov* (1995) and *The Poetry and Life of Allen Ginsberg: A Narrative Poem* (2000), as well as three book-length verse histories, *1968: A History in Verse* (1997) and the first two volumes of *America: A History in Verse* (2000). He has earned several awards and fellowships for his poetry, including the Frank O'Hara Prize (1967), a Guggenheim Fellowship (1983), and a National Endowment for the Arts Fellowship (1987). In 1988 he won an American Book Award for *Thirsting for Peace in a Raging Century: Selected Poems 1961–1985* (1987).

When asked why his fiction has been ignored, he told an interviewer for *The Review of Contemporary Fiction* (Spring 1999) that the reason was "because when I travel, I travel as a poet. I perform as a poet, and my choice of life is as a poet." Sanders also added that, before writing *Shards of God* (1970), his mock epic about the Yippies, he "had had very little experience writing prose except for term papers in college." Except for *The Family,* Sanders published little prose before *Tales of Beatnik Glory.* Most of his short fiction, published in alternative magazines, remains uncollected. For example, "The Hairy Table," which Sanders has described as "just an experiment" written backstage at a Fugs' concert in 1966, remains buried in the pages of the long-defunct magazine *San Francisco Earthquake.* Also in print are a few excerpts from "Dom-Int," a "cluster novel" (later retitled "Wounded Water"), wherein the individual stories cluster around the topic of domestic intelligence and, according to Sanders, the "means by which, at the Government's will, our lives are made to lie in total nakedness." The most readily available selection from this work appeared in the July 1977 issue of *Oui.*

Tales of Beatnik Glory is consequently the work on which Sanders's reputation as a short-story writer stands. Written during 1973 and 1974, the seventeen tales included in volume one cover events transpiring between 1958 and 1962. In a style at times reminiscent of the underground "comix" of Robert Crumb and Gilbert Shelton, *Tales of Beatnik Glory* is narrated in a voice that George Butterick, in his *DLB 16* entry on Sanders, has characterized as "one of the most celebrated idiolects of its time." As Sanders wrote in his introduction, the stories trace "the interconnected lives . . . of a group of poets, writers, painters, musicians, radicals, Freedom Riders, anti-war activists and partisans of the beat struggle in America."

Tales of Beatnik Glory opens gently and humorously with "The Mother-in-Law," a portrait of two Beats in love–she "dressed Being & Nothingness ballerina beat" and he "a filthnik"–who endure happily "years of poverty . . . roach-ridden, garbage-strewn, happy with rodents" and visits from the filthnik's initially hostile in-laws (invariably bearing gifts of groceries), who are finally won over by the birth of beatnik babies. "The Poetry Reading," which follows, continues the satirical whimsy of the book with a description of an open poetry reading at the Gaslight Café, a "goat-pen of babble," kookiness, "fingersnaps," and often pretentiously wretched verse. (Sanders includes a parody of Ginsberg's "America.")

"Total Assault Cantina," a miniature Beat version of Fyodor Dostoevsky's *Notes from the Underground* (1864), looks back on the early 1960s from the vantage point of 1973, as a once-promising novelist, now bunkered in a boarded-up basement, recalls the glory days of the once-bustling café and community center, with its press that printed "protest posters, poetry mags, draft cards, I.D., & leaflets"; its free library, free food, and use as a crashpad. He remembers how the proprietors found financial salvation when they agreed to hold a half ton of marijuana for Cousin Larry, meanwhile stealing from the dope-delivery man fifty automatic rifles intended for a right-wing paramilitary group and depositing them, amid much hilarity and mishap, in the East River.

Pathos and goofiness struggle for tonal control in "Total Assault Cantina," as well as in other stories, notably "The Cube of Potato Soaring through Vastness," about a Dadaist assault on an academic symposium on the Beats, and "Johnny the Foot," a portrait of an archetypally filthy beatnik who hits up tourists for spare change in return for a glimpse of his unwashed feet. Sanders's description of these stories, however, as works of "utmost seriousness" comes across without qualification in other tales, such as "Chessman," in which Sam Thomas–who later emerges as the central protagonist in Sanders's ensemble cast–enters the world of political activism when he attends his first protest march in support of Caryl Chessman, the so-called Red Light Bandit whose trial, conviction, and death sentence for rape made his case a cause célèbre. The description of Chessman's 1960 execution in the California gas chamber is harrowing in its details, and Sam's politicization stands as a synecdoche for the course charted by many of his generation: "It was young Sammy's first flash of solidarity. His first coordi-

nated anger-flash lined up at the barricades. Little could he guess the thrills the '60s had in store for him, in the matter of sneering and tumbling at the gray barriers."

Later in the book "The AEC Sit-In" presents the "poet"–who, along with Sam, is one of Sanders's more autobiographical characters–protesting renewed atmospheric nuclear testing and getting jailed for his trouble. "Peace Walk" details the 1962 eight-week Walk for Peace from Nashville to Washington, D.C., in which Sanders himself participated: "the danger seemed attractive, even thrillsome," Sanders's narrator recollects.

Joseph Dewey has argued persuasively that, contrary to the image of the Beats fostered by Jack Kerouac's *On the Road* (1957), the first volume of Sanders's *Tales of Beatnik Glory* presents his generation as one "in strategic retreat, negotiating for tight, protective spaces against the harsh ugliness and unbounded absurdity of the larger cultural context." Dewey notes that *Tales of Beatnik Glory* routinely locates its characters in a variety of "protective urban environments"–bookshops, converted storefronts, coffeehouses, parks, lofts, and "magic interior zones" conjured through eros and/or pharmaceuticals–that constitute safe havens "designed, sustained, and peopled against a collapsing set of larger inevitabilities." Thus, Sanders presents the basement-dwelling narrator of "Total Assault Cantina" and the vain poets safely sequestered among their own kind at the Gaslight; Louise Adams, rebel artist, converting a storefront into her "Mindscape Gallery"; John Barrett of "Vulture Egg Matzoh Brei" bopping from the Catholic Worker offices to Rienzi's Coffee House to Washington Square Park to his friend Dom's pad; and, in "Siobhan McKenna Group-Grope," seven poets reaching for nirvana via dope, recorded poetry, and group sex–or "group-grope," "bunch-punches," and "skin-clings"– in an apartment just off Avenue C.

Perhaps the stories in volume one that best make Dewey's point are "The Filmmaker" and "Raked Sand." In the first, which fictionalizes Sanders's experiences filming *Amphetamine Head*, Sam Thomas makes a 16-mm masterpiece of that name by renting "a typical two-room tub-in-the-kitchen slum apartment" and throwing a party replete with several free ounces of "the finest crushed crystals of amphetamine sulphate." A claustrophobic descent into creative frenzy, self-mutilation, apartment demolition, and "the irrationality and violence of a textbook on dictatorship" ensue before the police arrive to confront complete hallucinogenic "bombed-out chaos."

"Raked Sand" concerns the Cuban Missile Crisis of 1962. Sam and his friend Nelson await doom in

Stanley's bar until closing time, whereupon "the wet, staggering, skin-covered meat phantoms walked home." The next day Sam attempts to tell off his boss and get himself fired, but he finds that even imminent death has failed to provide the necessary chutzpah. Then he attends Louise Adams's "End-of-the-World" party. An excess of stimulation and dope (yohimbine, vodka, morning-glory seeds, and peyote) leaves a naked and sexually aroused Sam vomiting into Louise's "porcelain vortex" and staggering to the zen garden of the House of Nothingness, where he batters his dizzy head against a rock while chanting "No brain No brain No brain." Then he heads again to Stanley's and finally to his pathetic pad for a last exercise in strategic, if impotent, retreat:

> Back at the apartment, Sam rolled his final reefer. He counted his candles. There were twenty-four. He placed them in a semicircle around his couch. He crawled halfway into his sleeping bag which smelled like burnt goose feathers from an accident on a peace walk.
>
> He crossed his arms upon his chest, looking pharaonically cool. "This might be the last night. Thank God."
>
> If I die, he thought, I'm gonna continue the struggle. I ain't gonna take nothin' from nobody. He fantasized a hieroglyphic headline: BEATNIK REFUSES TO PICK GRAIN IN YARU FIELDS, OSIRIS UPSET.

Tales of Beatnik Glory is never uncritical of its subjects. Thus, although Sanders has said that one of his favorite characters is Uncle Thrills, whose chant of "imgrat" (immediate gratification of any and all desires) echoes through these stories, Sanders presents Uncle Thrills as forever busy with "the careful construction of a legend of himself as a genius." Sanders is not chary of mocking Beat pretensions to profundity and genius, nor is he hesitant to poke fun at Beat art and poetry, to glance wryly at the directions his characters take in later life (such as law school, politics, and editorial positions with large commercial presses), to expose their failures, excesses, sexism, squalor, naiveté, and the often reprehensible scams they run to turn a buck.

Johnny the Foot, for instance, may admirably flabbergast the bourgeoise as a "promulgator of revulsion" and tattooer of his penis. His obsession with joy and holiness and his defiance of unjust laws ("ahhh thou thrill of thrills!") are meant to be applauded. He is, however, presented as a comic figure. While readers are encouraged to laugh with Johnny, Sanders would have them scoff at certain

others, including artist Barton Macintyre, who manifests "just the 'correct' amount of nuttiness, drug-abuse, alcoholism, and feigned flip-out" and who whisks away to look at his work a gallery owner who has come to see Louise Adams's paintings; and Al, potato-salad provocateur at the Beat symposium, whose "salvation, he felt, was in the following: Even if I'm a punk, a poor father, a profligate, and a piss ant, if my *Verse* is there, then history will not empty out its offality upon my impish ways." Sanders invariably casts a cold eye on sellouts and poseurs, those too hungry for fame, or those self-destructively, antisocially addicted to dope.

This penchant for exaggerated send-up and satiric deflation left some reviewers of the first volume of *Tales of Beatnik Glory* uncertain as to how to interpret the meaning of the title: was the "glory" meant literally or ironically? John Yohalem, writing in the *New York Times Book Review* (9 November 1975), complained, "There is no unity of attitude or style, even within individual stories. Sanders cannot decide whether he is glorying in decadence like a shopkeeper on a spree, or striking the poses of the self-righteously liberated, or putting the whole scene down from a still more knowing standpoint." Similarly, Barry Wallenstein in *Contemporary Literature* (Autumn 1977) complained of "a tone of voice not likely to inspire genuine interest in the period" and suggested that Sanders ultimately found the Beats unworthy of "thoughtful attention" or of anything more than "flippantly casual satire."

Perhaps Yohalem's complaint is that of a modernist confronting a postmodern text, or perhaps, like Wallenstein, he is objecting to the hash-by-hookah placement of assertions such as "Everything was deity" beside a sentence that could describe an exclusive love relationship as "a pact of mono-grope relative to groin-clink." Responding to Yohalem's assessment in 1999, Sanders said, "that's missing the point. What I wanted to do was to be anthropologically exact, true to the times," which, in the period covered by the first stories, were times of "ebullience." Reiterating what he had written in the introduction to *Tales of Beat Glory,* Sanders added, "I take these stories very seriously and love those characters."

Perhaps one cause of reviewer confusion was Sanders's mixture of serious social issues with a self-indulgent pursuit of high times. In *1968: A History in Verse* (1997) Sanders wrote that he was criticized for partying in the midst of social crises, and in 1999 he articulated in no uncertain terms his defense of the high times depicted in *Tales of Beatnik Glory:* "we have to be hedonistic in a good part of our lives;

otherwise, why live? You can't be just a dreary robot slaving away. So there's that double life-track of having fun while working for a better world." Such a life plan results in a book in which neither theme nor tone can be easily categorized. Instead, the style seems to be the prose equivalent to the many-faceted reality of the period. *Tales of Beatnik Glory* exemplifies what George Butterick has described as Sanders's typical mixture of "the undeniably specific with purposeful exaggeration," of "the American idiom with ancient Egyptian hieroglyphs and Hesiodic Greek, and the sacred with the profane in a violent stew of ecstasy and purgation."

As Edward Halsey Foster has argued in *Understanding the Beats* (1992), "In one manner or another, all of the Beats pushed their work to extremes," or as Lisa Phillips explained in the essay that introduces *Beat Culture and the New America* (1995), "The search for alternative consciousness, the mystical side of the Beats, goes hand in hand with their gritty realism and rebellion. These two sides—the ecstatic and the horrific, the beatific and the beaten, define the poles of Beat experience. The extremes of mystical wonder and squalid realism, the lofty and the seedy, could be combined and expressed in the arts. . . ." The stylistic and thematic merger of seemingly mutually exclusive agendas characterizes both the voice and the subject matter of Sanders's short stories.

The poet Joel Oppenheimer was part of the scene Sanders recorded in *Tales of Beatnik Glory,* and in his review for *Liberation* magazine (Spring 1976) he observed how the book itself "becomes an action, the way things really were." Oppenheimer added that Sanders "sees what i saw then, what most of us saw—that is the wholeness, the good and bad, of this strange upsurge of reality in the middle of baghdad on the hudson. because whatever else these people, sanders' beatniks, were into, it was a reality more fine and fierce than any around them, and their concerns, for all their lunacy, should have been the world's, even if their defenses usually killed them, or burned them out." Or as Sanders told Kevin Ring in 1993, "There were many good things about the 1960s and some bad. . . . There was too much male chauvinism and we did not factor in enough . . . the impact of jealousy, envy, greed, obsession, fanaticism, lying." In these tales Sanders is as "seriously unserious" as Glenn O'Brien has suggested the Beats always were. With his "groin-clinks," "imgrat," and A-heads pulling bloody strips of skin from their lips, Sanders refuses to describe a lesser reality or to write a book less filled with manic idiocy than the years these stories document.

The initial draft of volume two of *Tales of Beatnik Glory* (1990) was completed in 1984, set aside, and then revised in 1988–1989. The new stories carry Sanders's history from 1963 through Freedom Summer of 1964. As Sanders noted in the introduction, the years between 1975 and 1990 were another "time of turbulence in my life," and volume two got sidetracked repeatedly as "other books, projects and events interceded." These projects included a series of environmental battles in upstate New York; the release of several new albums by the sporadically reuniting Fugs; the publication of five collections of poetry, the poetics manifestos *Investigative Poetry* (1976) and *The Z-D Generation* (1981), and a second novel, *Fame & Love in New York* (1980); the composition of *The Karen Silkwood Cantata* (staged in 1979) and *Star Peace* (a three-act musical drama staged in 1986 and recorded in 1987); and the release of *Songs in Ancient Greek* (1989), an album of ancient texts set to original music.

The fifteen new short stories in volume two bring back many characters from the original cast and highlight the mystical aspects and increasing drug use of the budding counterculture. Additionally, the book attempts to right the chauvinist wrongs of the Beats by offering several stories of strong women to complement the portraits of Louise Adams, dancer Claudia Pred ("Luminous Animal Theater"), and Becky Levy (an activist introduced in "Peace Walk") from volume one. As Dewey has observed, in volume two strategic withdrawal gives way to "engagement, challenge, confrontation" and to the "sweet futility" of attempting to reform "the larger culture."

"Sappho on East 7th," "Cynthia," and "A Night at the Café Perf-Po" touch most explicitly on what Sanders has termed the "spiritual hunger" of a generation John Clellon Holmes once averred was the first "in several centuries for which the act of faith has been an obsessive problem . . . ." In "Sappho on East 7th," which Sanders described as a "sho-sto-po" (a short story in verse), poet and classics graduate student John Barrett constructs a lyre with which he manages to summon the shade of the ancient Greek lyric poet Sappho, who teaches Barrett what poetry means and how to make love before taking him on a visionary journey through time. In lines that bespeak Sanders's project in *Tales of Beatnik Glory,* Sappho tells John that his muse is she "of the Retained Image," who will help him

> to sort
>   to sooth
>   to winnow
> as well as to keep
>   to save
>   to shape[.]

The main character in "Cynthia" is poet-activist Cynthia Pruitt, who after college "had been drawn to the *Catholic Worker* movement, its life of voluntary poverty, its insistence on doing good, its anti-war efforts and its direct action support of the impoverished and the weak." The story takes place the day John F. Kennedy was shot, an event that changes Cynthia's life: she finds herself morally compelled to retrieve from Sam Thomas a movie he shot of her performing fellatio. Then she races distraught into the night, where, standing "beneath the tall dark bricks" and spiked iron fence of the St. Nicholas Carpatho Russian Orthodox Greek Catholic Church at 10th and Avenue A, she receives a vision—Sappho as Catholic martyr—and as a consequence rededicates herself to helping others: "I probably prayed at that spot for at least an hour," she tells a friend eighteen years later. Cynthia's story is told retrospectively to emphasize her continuing commitment to her ideals:

> I began to feel all this joy and energy rooted in mercy. Right then, as I still knelt on St. Nicholas's steps, I remembered how Dorothy Day had quoted in her autobiography from the preamble to the International Workers of the World constitution, about a "society in which it is easier to be good."
>
> That did it. Never before had I felt such a lifting away of burdens. There was only one vow I could make—to do more—to serve—to spend years in prison against the war machine. I was willing to stay poor my whole life—I *wanted* to be poor—and, yes, chaste. . . .

Finally, in "A Night at the Café Perf-Po," another story told retrospectively, John Barrett and Sam Thomas return in 1984 to the Lower East Side and visit what was once the House of Nothingness but is now the Café Perf-Po for a performance-poetry marathon to raise money for the Live Cheap or Die Anti-Gentrification Coalition. The story is in many ways intent on sketching continuities between 1964 and 1984 (such as the antics of performance poets and those of the poets in "The Poetry Reading" from volume one) and between these years and earlier decades: Sam experiences a lengthy "past trance" in which he recalls anarchist Wolf Lesker telling how in the 1890s the House of Nothingness had housed the Anarchist Coal Collective, which had sought to help the poor through the terrible winter of 1894. Sam also recalls how Barrett had arrived late that evening in 1964, detained by his second vision of Sappho, who appeared to him this time as she had to Cynthia, "neck laden with heavy Russian crosses" and kneeling in the snow before St. Nicholas's, to deliver three cryptic words: "You'll cry too." It was a message

prophesying the fate of all rebel artists and radical activists, holy bohemian goofs and dharma bums who would presume to change the way things are.

If some of Sanders's generation connected with the spiritual through visions such as those experienced by Barrett and Cynthia, others sought the spiritual through more mundane connections—guys in shades peddling nickel bags, methamphetamine, and heroin. Although Sanders notes that LSD was appearing on the scene by 1964, the characters of these tales prefer marijuana, peyote, yohimbine bark, alcohol, and garden-variety uppers and downers, the use of which is usually treated as part of the scene or as fodder for comedy. In the introduction to the 1990 edition, however, Sanders wrote that "there were many, many lives wrecked by heroin and speed" and cautioned that "some aspects of some of the lifestyles in some of these stories can be dangerous to your health." Sanders embodies his criticism in the character of Andrew Kliver, a heroin addict. In "The Muffins of Sebek" Kliver sells some smack to a college student, who dies from an overdose; in "Farbrente Rose" Kliver's habit reprehensibly prevents him from participating in political demonstrations because he cannot risk going cold turkey if arrested; and in "Kick Grid Time for Kliver" his friends attempt to get the monkey off Kliver's back.

Several of the stories in volume two locate spiritual, ego, and emotional satisfaction in political activism. In the first story, "I Have a Dream," Sam and some other characters attend the 1963 March on Washington to hear Martin Luther King speak, to confirm Ezra Pound's fascist anti-Semitism by checking out at the Smithsonian transcripts of his Italian radio broadcasts, and to mix it up with several neonazi hecklers in the crowd. The story closes with Sam's vision of the 1960s:

> Sam Thomas was wadded up and stuffed into the paddy wagon. Before they shut the door came another startling vision. It was the hovering face of secret policeman J. Edgar Hoover, spread across the sky like a dead carp at the mouth of a sewer. Sam saw a time of crazed peril for America. There was the crackle of insane electricity in the brains of madmen, and planes swooping low over villages with fires that would not stop.

One of the most arresting stories with a political edge concerns Talbot Jenkins, a black star fullback until his knee was broken by klansman Ethrom Slage during the Freedom Rides of 1961. Set immediately after the 15 September 1963 bombing of a church that left four girls dead, "Talbot Goes to Birmingham" finds Talbot intent on killing the klansman responsible for the bombing (Ethrom again) but instead befriending Ethrom's son Johnny Ray (who figures prominently in volume three of *Tales of Beatnik Glory*) and vowing to teach him how to escape his racist upbringing. Talbot returns in "Farbrente Rose," wherein Sanders's Beats meet Rose Snyder, who, as the prose of the story evolves into poetry, recounts her life as a socialist and union organizer on the Lower East Side during the early decades of the twentieth century. Talbot appears again in "Freedom Summer," which closes the book and in which Talbot and others rush to Mississippi to rescue Sam, who has been beaten and jailed while attempting to register black voters.

True to his belief that making the world a better place should not preclude having fun, Sanders intercalates in volume two tales such as "The Schlemiel of Happening Street," in which the "dirty beatnik," his wife, and his mother-in-law make a comic guest appearance; "The Muffins of Sebek," in which Sam follows an ancient Egyptian recipe to solve his poverty-just-before-Christmas problem by manufacturing facial cream made from crocodile feces; and "Auden Buys Some Diapers," in which another impoverished beatnik scores the cash needed for diapers, spaghetti sauce, and ice-cream sundaes by forging signatures in first editions he then sells to rare-book dealers. Several stories attempt to right the wrong of Beat sexism and the marginalization and mistreatment of women through unflattering portraits of male characters and the presentation of strong female Beats. "The Wild Women of East Tenth," in which Sanders appears in the first person as the proprietor of Peace Eye and member of the Fugs, pictures three feminist free spirits from whom the author learns a lesson for the 1960s: "it was the best of times, it was the worst of times, but it was *our* times, and we owned them with our youth, our energy, our good will, our edginess. So let's party."

The lesson Sanders learned is one that Enid Baumbach, one of those wild women, is adept at teaching, and "The Van Job" recounts her fondness for recreational sex. The less-offhanded "It's Like Living with a Mongol" describes a group of protofeminists banded together to endure the difficulties of living with Beat men, who are described as "obsessive, neglectful, drug abusing, pushy, manic-depressive, overly assertive and overerotic yet indecisive and unselfconfident egomaniacs."

Reviews of the omnibus edition of *Tales of Beatnik Glory* were few but positive. *The Review of Contemporary Fiction* (Summer 1991), for instance, praised the book as a "portrait of a generation" that "has the feel of lived reality." Indeed, Sanders perhaps chose to

Dust jacket for Sanders's first volume of short stories based on his experiences among Beats and hippies during the 1960s

call these stories "tales" rather than "short stories" not only because "tales" implies a simpler, more loosely structured narrative but because "tales" has routinely been applied to short narratives whether fictional or nonfictional. Dan Barth in an the internet review for *Literary Kicks* (http://www.litkicks.com) applauded the book's humor, innovation, and ability to be both "playful and serious at the same time," and Michael Dolan, in a quirky profile of Sanders published in *New Times* (8–14 May 1991), admired not only his re-creation of "a time when it wasn't necessarily easy or safe to get and be weird in America" but also the way Sanders makes one ask, "What's so funny about peace, love, and understanding–especially in the context of riotous good times . . . ?"

Sanders, who in 1990 was projecting a third volume, now believes it will take four volumes to carry his saga through the end of the 1960s. Volume three (nine new tales) has been published in German as *Der Sommer der Liebe* (1997; The Summer of Love), but Sanders has decided not to publish an American edition until all four volumes can be brought out as a uniform set.

Volume three covers "the winter of Be-in's, the spring of the wah-wah pedal, and the Summer of Love." "Dylan's Guitar" opens the collection with the story of Johnny Ray Slage, Ethrom's son. After he receives one of Talbot's antiracist care packages that includes a guitar once owned by Bob Dylan, Johnny Ray hitchhikes to the Peace Eye bookstore and goes on to become a singing sensation: "a successful klan-to-human-being pygmalion job." "The Psychedelicatessin" offers the hippie reincarnation of the House of Nothingness (like many of the places mentioned in *Tales of Beatnik Glory,* an actual mid-1960s hang-out) and features three new strong, wild women: Vera, an actress; Lilona of the Space Shadows, a spaced-out poet often found wandering the streets; and Indian Annie, designer of hippie garb. The plot of the story turns on a raid by federal agents to confiscate Reindeer Ron's psychedelic reindeer urine, which he has ostensibly smuggled out of Siberia.

"Time, Spirit, Thrill, Dance and Music" evokes the hippie era at its zenith (spring 1967) while "The Great Tompkins Park Beatnik-to-Hippie Conversion Ceremony" treats the Death of Beat with a fingersnapping, Fug-fueled party replete with a "hashish kugel" and "a deputation of Diggers from San Francisco." "An East Village Hippie in King Arthur's Court"–a sho-sto-po also included in Sanders's *Hymn to the Rebel Café* (1993)–is a retelling of Mark Twain's *A Connecticut Yankee in King Arthur's Court* (1889), and "A Convention at Peace Eye," echoing the earlier stories of poetry readings, details the "First Annual Convention of Weird Songwriters," whose songs obsess over drugs, sex, and revolution.

Two stories fictionalize the life of James "Groovy" Hutchinson, who in Sanders's telling (as in life) spends an early October day in 1967 camped out in front of the Psychedelicatessen with his girlfriend, Lorna, (in real life, Linda Fitzpartrick) before the two are murdered in an East Side basement. Their deaths–in *Tales of Beatnik Glory* as they were at the time–are another signal of the end of the Summer of Love.

As with the earlier volumes, volume three is filled with period lore and laced with period slang: head shops and free love, the Newark riots and Vietnam, posters and magic, communes and crashpads, free stores and bad trips. Sanders once again traces the roots of the counterculture to the radicalism of Emma Goldman and others, and he continues to critique its politics. In the final story, "Beckett's Toast," Sam offers what may be Sanders's own sense at the time of the alternative futures between which America must choose: "Maybe finally a paradigm would evolve where art, economics, sharing, resistance and sustainability held hands," or "maybe the universe is always on the edge

of being devoured by an all-engulfing cancer of total evil."

In 1983 George Butterick praised Sanders's "wit, audaciousness, and high moral purpose" and his ability to "keep lively the language." Dewey ended his 1999 study by describing *Tales of Beatnik Glory* as "a vehicle for generous preservation" that continues Sanders's "determination to defy what terrifies us and what terrified the Beats: how time so quickly, so effortlessly makes relics of us all." That same year David Herd wrote that Sanders's literary career reveals an "ambitious intention . . . to contextualize the Beat way of being. What such contextualizing amounts to is an ongoing study of historical subcultures and bohemian milieus." In short, what *Tales of Beatnik Glory* offers, with "high moral purpose," is a recollection and preservation of the aspirations and the idiocies, the sincerity and the posturing, of a powerful and influential manifestation of American disaffection and disaffiliation.

Interviews:
John Wilcock, "An Interview with Ed Sanders," *Village Voice,* 17 June 1965, p. 2;

Nick Tosches, "Interview: Ed Sanders," *Fusion* (Boston), 17 October 1969, pp. 18, 26, 28, 30;

"'Sleazy Icky Yucky Mucky & Uck': An Interview with Ed Sanders," *Win,* 8 (January 1972): 6–10;

Tandy Sturgeon, "An Interview with Edward Sanders," *Contemporary Literature,* 31 (Fall 1990): 263–280;

Sean Thomas Dougherty, "Ed Sanders Interview," *Long Shot,* 13 (1992): 87–90;

Kevin Ring, "Thirsting for Peace: An Interview with Ed Sanders," *Beat Scene,* 17 (1993) <http://www.charm.net/-brooklyn/Topics/EdSandersInterview.html >;

Steve Lutrell, "Interview with Ed Sanders," 1995 <http://www.mainelink.net/~writer/café_html/fall_95/sanders1.htm l>;

Billy Bob Hargus, Interview, June 1997 <http://www.furious.com/perfect/sanders.html>;

Barry Miles, "An Interview with Ed Sanders–1 October 1968," *Review of Contemporary Fiction,* 19 (Spring 1999): 13–22;

Brooke Horvath, "Edward Sanders on His Fiction: An Interview," *Review of Contemporary Fiction,* 19 (Spring 1999): 23–30;

Wesley Joost, "Going Out in a Blaze of Leaflets," *Goblin Magazine,* 3 (n.d.) <http://www. sonic.net/~goblin/Sand.html>.

Bibliography:
Brooke Horvath, "An Edward Sanders Checklist," *Review of Contemporary Fiction,* 19 (Spring 1999): 138–143.

References:

Tom Clark, *The Great Naropa Poetry Wars* (Santa Barbara: Cadmus, 1980);

Joseph Dewey, "Helter Shelter: Strategic Interment in *Tales of Beatnik Glory*," *Review of Contemporary Fiction,* 19 (Spring 1999): 101–111;

Michael Dolan, "The Mod Couple," *New Times,* 8–14 May 1991, pp. 14–16, 18–19, 21;

Edward Dorn, *Views,* edited by Donald Allen (San Francisco: Four Seasons Foundation, 1980), pp. 79–82;

Kerry Driscoll, "'A Droll Stroll along Green Grab Creek,'" *Credences,* new series 1 (Fall-Winter 1981–1982): 181–184;

John Gruen, *The New Bohemia: The Combine Generation* (New York: Shorecrest, 1966);

Stephanie Harrington, "Ed Sanders: Rolling Stoned with Joyous 'Pornographer,'" *Village Voice,* 27 January 1966, pp. 1, 27;

David Herd, "'After All, What Else Is There to Say?' Ed Sanders and the Beat Aesthetic," *Review of Contemporary Fiction,* 19 (Spring 1999): 122–137;

Brooke Horvath, ed., Edward Sanders number, *Review of Contemporary Fiction,* 19 (Spring 1999);

David Jackson, "Tales of Ed Sanders: The Superbeat Moves On," *Village Voice,* 22–28 July 1981, pp. 32–33;

Allan Katzman, "Poet Arrested for Obscenity," *East Village Other,* 1–14 February 1966, pp. 1, 6;

Thomas Myers, "Rerunning the Creepy-Crawl: Ed Sanders and Charles Manson," *Review of Contemporary Fiction,* 19 (Spring 1999): 81–90;

Abe Peck, *Uncovering the Sixties: The Life and Times of the Underground Press* (New York: Pantheon, 1985);

Nick Tosches, "Stalking Manson–The Sanders Sage," *Fusion* (Boston), 24 December 1971, pp. 14–16;

Barry Wallenstein, "The Beats," *Contemporary Literature,* 18 (Autumn 1977): 542–551.

Papers:

Some of Edward Sanders's papers from the 1960s and early 1970s are in the library at the University of Connecticut, Storrs.

Melanie Rae Thon

(23 August 1957 –   )

Kelli Wondra

BOOKS: *Meteors in August* (New York: Random House, 1990);

Girls in the Grass (New York: Random House, 1991);

Iona Moon (New York: Poseidon, 1993; London: Penguin, 1993);

First, Body (Boston: Houghton Mifflin, 1997);

Sweet Hearts (Boston: Houghton Mifflin, 2000).

Melanie Rae Thon has established a reputation for writing tough and lyrical portraits of those who live on the fringes of American society. *Girls in the Grass* (1991) and *First, Body* (1997), her two volumes of short stories, have been praised by reviewers for their powerful lyric visions, compelling characters, and blues-styled rhythms. Working in both first- and third-person voices, Thon creates such vivid portraits of her characters that, as Geri Gourley wrote in *The Bergen Record* (16 February 1997), "You feel their torment in the urgent pace of her narratives." Rand Richards Cooper wrote in *The New York Times* (16 February 1997) that Thon's range of marginal and miserable voices makes her "more American" than many of her writing peers.

Thon's short stories share many of the thematic and stylistic elements that appear in her novels *Meteors in August* (1990) and *Iona Moon* (1993). Of these shared elements, the strongest is the reliance on lyric voices that move freely between past and present. Pointing to frequent shifts in time throughout the stories in *First, Body,* Cooper defined Thon's style as impressionistic. Additionally, the short stories and novels often cover the same geographic territory.

Meteors in August, which takes place in Willis, Montana, was described by reviewer Carolyn See in *The Los Angeles Times* (17 September 1990) as a universe that is "lovely and brutal." Karen Rile, writing for *The San Francisco Chronicle* (15 August 1993), characterized the geography of *Iona Moon,* which is set in White Falls, Idaho, as "a comfortless landscape crawling with predators, sexual and otherwise." Both descriptions could easily summarize many of the settings that appear in Thon's short fiction. The protagonists in Thon's nov-

Melanie Rae Thon (photograph © Bruce Hillard; from the dust jacket for Girls in the Grass, *1991)*

els—Lizzie of *Meteors in August* and Iona of *Iona Moon*—suffer a sexually related crisis and then must come to terms with its personal, social, and philosophical consequences. In *Girls in the Grass* and *First, Body,* Thon's characters face coming of age, sexual abuse, racial intolerance, privation, and the search for salvation. While some reviewers have labeled her work as grim and edgy, others have interpreted her dark tone as a kind of testimony to the resilience of the human spirit, even in the most extreme circumstances of life.

The youngest of four children, Melanie Rae Thon was born in Kalispell, Montana, on 23 August 1957 to Lois Ann (née Lockwood), a homemaker, and Raymond Albert Thon, an architect. In an unpublished interview (11 May 2000) Thon spoke briefly about her family's history: "My father's ancestors were among the first white settlers in Montana. Our long frontier history—and the extremity of life and landscape in Montana—has had a huge impact on my life—both consciously and unconsciously." Speaking to Caryl Phillips in an interview published in *Bomb Magazine* (Summer 1993), Thon also affirmed that she will "always return to that landscape. No matter how long I live somewhere else, those images are imbedded in ways I can't escape." From the time she was a young girl, Thon knew that she wanted to write, calling herself a writer before she even entered college. Thon earned her B.A. in English from the University of Michigan, Ann Arbor, in 1980 and then completed an M.A. in creative writing at Boston University in 1982. Thon has said that although she did not publish any of her work done in graduate school, "I don't consider that time a waste. I was building many skills: most importantly, I was learning the tolerance for revision, which I really didn't have before that." Since finishing graduate school she has taught at Wheelock College, Emerson College, the University of Massachusetts at Boston, Ohio State University (where she was named Graduate Professor of the Year in 1998), Harvard University Extension School, Syracuse University, and the University of Utah, Salt Lake City. Thon views teaching and its reciprocal influence on her own work with enthusiasm: "I'm certainly in the group of writers who love to teach. Being rigorous in the way that I look at other people's work, being forced to understand how ideas and language converge makes me capable of doing more in my own work." Before appearing in these two collections, many of her short stories were published in literary magazines such as *Antaeus, Ontario Review, Granta,* and *Ploughshares.*

The stories included in *Girls in the Grass* can be grouped into two categories: coming-of-age stories in which young girls and boys are working out their growing awareness of sex and sexuality as it relates to the moral structure of the world around them, and the confessional stories of older characters reflecting on moments of failure.

"Girls in the Grass," the first story in the collection, is set in Montana and presents an energetic and charming first-person account of three young girls, Meg, Lyla, and the unnamed narrator, during the summer before they enter high school. Using the game of Truth or Dare as a framing device for the action, Thon weaves together the events of that summer. The girls rely on the game as a way to explore their flourishing sense of sexuality. With each dare the girls use each other to practice kissing and petting. Thon subtly suggests that the narrator is a budding lesbian who is aware of her own sexual prowess. Early in the story the narrator boasts, "Sometimes I get carried away and they say not so far, close your lips, don't use your tongue like that, it tickles. They babble on and on and I let them because I know that when they've had their say, they'll both take turns kissing me again." When Meg announces that her family is moving to California, the others must deal with the rupture of their intimate circle. In the final game of Truth or Dare, the narrator dares Lyla to kiss her, but Lyla admonishes, "we're getting too old for these games. Know what I mean?" Much of the charm of the story is connected to the three quirky, innocent female characters. With this story Thon creates a snapshot of a time in the narrator's life when the inklings of sex are part of adolescent play and its consequences are not to be feared yet.

"Iona Moon" and "Snake River" are linked together by the characters Iona Moon, Jay Tyler, and Willy Hamilton, who also appear as central characters in Thon's novel *Iona Moon.* Both short stories function as entry points into the world of White Falls, Idaho. "Iona Moon" is told primarily from Willy and Iona's points of view, while "Snake River" centers on the character of Jay Tyler. Sex becomes a defining act for each of the characters. Although Iona's introduction to sex is brutal, it becomes empowering. For Willy, sex is an ideal, a marker that allows him to classify and categorize girls and to separate the "good" ones from the "bad." He prefers "Girls who could pull you right to the edge and still always, always say no." For Jay, who impregnates his young Catholic girlfriend and then must tolerate her family's hatred of him, sex becomes an aversion. In the interview in *Bomb* magazine, Thon explained Iona's sexuality:

> She's desirable because she's passionate. She's not afraid of her own body. She's not afraid of her own sexuality. . . . It gives her a great deal of power over the boys who are attracted to her. . . . I think that's why she's discardable. If she becomes too threatening they can revert to their moralistic sensibilities; they can think of her as dirty—physically and spiritually.

Examined in isolation as short stories, "Iona Moon" and "Snake River" can seem to be overwhelmingly dark; yet, in the context of the novel, each episode carefully plots a course toward the conclusion, which, as T. M. McNally asserted in his review of *Iona Moon* in *The Washington Post* (25 July 1993) is "not about hardship and grief, but

Dust jacket for Thon's 1991 book, in which the title story depicts three young adolescents exploring their sexuality

about our interconnected need, and ability, to survive what life brings us."

In "Iona Moon" and "Repentance," the young protagonists, Iona and Margaret, learn that giving in to one's sexual desires often leads them to ignore the needs of others—with serious consequences. Iona allows her desire to seduce Willy to distract her from running an errand for her dying mother. In this instance the issue of sexuality also is complicated by the fact that in her childhood, Iona had been molested by her older brother, Leon. While readers can admire Iona's sexual empowerment and her pragmatic approach to sex, they must also understand that her strength comes at a cost.

In "Repentance" Margaret, engrossed in the physical sensations aroused by playing surgery with her friend Delana, ignores the calls of her grandmother, who has suffered a serious fall and eventually dies. Wishing to avoid punishment, Margaret lies about the circumstances surrounding the accident. In one moment Margaret tells her grandmother that she did not hear her cries for help

because she was sleeping, but then, in a delicate moment of subtext, immediately confesses to herself that "This is my worst lie, because it matters." Margaret's guilt permeates the narrative from that point forward. In the final moments of the story she is seen lying in her bed, tense and taut. Outside of her door she hears her mother pacing through the house. Knowing that her mother feels at fault for having been out of the house when the grandmother's accident happened, Margaret longs to confess the lies so that she might relieve some of her mother's own guilt and grief. She does not.

Shifts in point of view and multiple themes make "Punishment" the most complex story in *Girls in the Grass*. Thon explores racial oppression and sexual abuse among characters residing on a plantation in antebellum Louisville, Georgia. The narration is split between Selina, a ninety-year-old white woman, and Lize, the ghost of her household slave. Lize, who had just given birth, was pulled from her own family in order to nurse Selina's infant brother. While serving in the household, Lize was raped by Selina's father. Lize also learned that during the absence from her own family, her infant son starved to death. In retaliation Lize smothered the white infant while nursing him and was hanged for her actions. Lize, speaking from across the years, delivers ponderous descriptions of her ancestors' enslavement, of her husband's disfigurement at the hands of a brutal overseer, and of her child's starvation. Thon sustains dramatic tension by pulling the reader deep within the physical reality of Lize's life as a slave and by juxtaposing her physical anguish and resulting fury with that of Selina's increasing guilt and fear. Selina's feelings of guilt are compounded by her belief that Lize can see into her dreams, and she is especially fearful that Lize knows of her erotic dreams about Lize's husband, Abe. Selina is further tortured by the sexual threat that her father poses to her. The metaphoric implications of desire, incest, and rape culminating in genocide are harshly drawn when Lize accuses Selina: "Whitewoman, you all look the same to me. You all kill us with desire." After the Civil War, Selina fled to Chicago, hoping that with the death of her father and the passing of time, her guilt would abate. It has not, and the specter of Lize consumes her life.

Thon also uses alternating points of view in "The Spanish Boy" to develop its dramatic tension and to provide commentary on its theme. Through a series of contrasting lyric and dramatic episodes, Pauline and Nick reveal to the reader their drastically different perceptions of their marriage. The turning point in the story happens after an episode of lovemaking, which provokes markedly different interpretations from both narrators. Sex, in this story, is used as a sort of litmus test. Pauline, sensing that her husband does not love and respect her, uses the physical act as a way to prove her husband's ignorance and egoism. The session culminates in her decision to leave the marriage. Nick, ignorant of Pauline's intentions, is at first frightened by the vulgarity of the sex but gives in to the intoxicating sense of power that he feels when he brutalizes her. When he wakes, he notes Pauline's absence but feels that the sexual episode of the night before had made him "strong enough to comfort her." The last image of Nick reveals him lying in bed, aware that Pauline is not present, simply wondering "how long she'd been gone and why." The story closes with Pauline alone in the kitchen, contemplating her need to make Nick humiliate and dominate her, but knowing too that she will leave him.

In contrast to the sexual awakenings that take place in "Girls in the Grass" and "Repentance" and the sexual brutality of the other stories, Thon charts the spiritual awakenings of two young boys, Ben in "The Sacrifice" and Cal in "Chances of Survival" (along with its companion story, "Lizards"), who must each come to terms with the real meaning of their mothers' pregnancies. Both stories capture the wonder and youthful confusion of contemplating the divine. "The Sacrifice" revolves around Ben, a young African American boy, and his family, who have left Georgia for Detroit. Ben's primary conflict arises during a series of revivalist church services he attends with his pregnant mother, and during which he eventually rejects "this white Jesus who cared so little for the shriveled soul of one small Black boy in Detroit." Lyric passages capture the energy and intensity of these services. During one hot July evening in church, surrounded by ecstatic voices and people in the throes of divine ecstasy, Ben is overcome by apocalyptic visions of his own spiritual death and the destruction of the church. Succumbing to the power of his vision, Ben collapses, and the churchgoers mistake it as a sign that he was saved with "so much force" that it left him "too limp to stand." The story concludes rather ambivalently with the introduction of a shadowy figure, a variation of the wounded, white Jesus, who follows Ben and his father through the woods while they are hunting.

Lacking the overt lyric power of "The Sacrifice," "Chances of Survival" and "Lizards" both focus on a young boy named Cal, whose family has just moved from Idaho to Arizona. Learning that his mother is unexpectedly pregnant, Cal tries to accept that the new baby will change his family life even more. Heavily influenced by sermons he hears in church, Cal attempts to reason out God's purpose for him in life. Afraid that he will forget God, he takes to wearing a heavy, maroon robe. The discomfort of wearing the robe, or as Cal says, its "bristly warmth," reminds him that "God was watching. . . . The robe protected him, saved him from his own forgetfulness." Cal develops a crush on his teacher, Miss Faye, whose instruction in math gives him the confidence to proclaim "He was the Lord of the Numbers." Miss Faye, whom Cal also frequently fantasizes about, provides a con-

trasting female presence to his mother, who he imagines as a "rare white whale." The encouragement and happiness that he finds in his vivid fantasy life with Miss Faye is destroyed when she suddenly disappears. When Cal learns that she was stalked and disfigured by a brutal drifter, the fear his discovery inspires drives him back to his robe. The lizards are symbolically part of Cal's atonement for having violated his mother's command not to bring them into the house–he had hidden them in a box under his bed. After she suffers a violent nightmare in which she believes the lizards are crawling all over her, Cal releases them outdoors.

The remaining stories in *Girls in the Grass* present adults ruminating over past mistakes that continue to haunt them. Ted Brandon, the protagonist in "Small Crimes," is a creative-writing teacher, a has-been poet, and an alcoholic who seduces a series of college girls. Playing off his former acclaim as a writer, he uses his power as a teacher to play on the fears and desires of the young women in his writing classes. Thon's focus on the "ritual" of the seduction allows the reader to see the extent to which Brandon has developed his art, which includes all manner of details down to the timing of his entrance at a café around the corner from his apartment. At first it seems that the seduction and the sex make Brandon the criminal, but as he unfolds his own chain of tragedies–part of the seduction is designed to get sympathy from the women, thus enhancing his chances of getting them into bed–the reader sees that his real crime is the rejection of his daughter. Ted Brandon is not looking for a fling, but rather a captive audience who will hear his confession and even act as a surrogate daughter, hopefully forgiving him. Brandon is strongly self-conscious, and when he remarks that "Confessions are not made for the ones who hear them," it becomes clear that he is not seeking forgiveness from his students, but from himself. Indeed, many of the characters in this collection seek catharsis, and by revealing that which is secret and sinful, they hope to atone for their wrongs and go on with their lives.

In "Sisters," the final story of the collection, the unnamed first-person narrator claims, "People still think my sister killed a man." Under the shadow of her wild and willful sister, Grace, the narrator tries over the years to play peacemaker when her father and then her mother both push Grace out of the family. The sisters' relationship is laced with no ordinary sibling rivalry: Grace is a flawed female warrior who lashes out at her family by turning to alcohol and self-destructive behavior. Each time Grace reappears in her sister's life, she undermines the security that her sister has worked hard to achieve; each time Grace vanishes, she steals a modest amount of money and robs the narrator of her esteem. Equally remarkable to the episodes of self-doubt is the narrator's insistence on not naming herself. In a moment of fantasized revenge, she wishes that she could find the baby that Grace gave up for adoption: "I will say I am her mother. I will live with Grace's name and take this child away, north, to Alaska, where Grace, who hates the cold, will never find us." Even in private fantasy, the narrator effaces her own identity.

Response to *Girls in the Grass* was mostly positive. Beverly Langer of *The San Francisco Chronicle* (7 July 1991) singled out Thon's ability to create characters that one "is tempted to fall in love with . . . and to join them in that quest for a state of grace." In addition to the characters, Constance Decker Thompson, a reviewer for *The New York Times* (14 July 1991) added that the "taut, magic current" of Thon's prose and its "exhilarating rhythmic punch" were the elements that kept the reader engaged. Some critics, however, such as Carolyn See of *The Los Angeles Times* (8 July 1991) claimed that "The pieces are uneven, written in very different styles. Some of them seem literary to a fault." In general, however, most critics were not bothered by Thon's narrative style.

First, Body, Thon's second collection, came out in 1997. As the title alludes, all the characters in this collection are intensely aware of their physical conditions, most of which are extreme. If the characters are not physically afflicted, then their psyches afflict their bodies. In these stories characters exhibit an enhanced awareness of their own physical and mental pain so vivid that it becomes a part of the reader's sensory landscape. In one of the more visceral responses to *First, Body,* Betsy Willeford wrote in *The Palm Beach Post* (2 March 1997) that "Thon crawls into a character as if it were the carcass of an animal," and added that her stories "are a series of self-consuming illuminations, small fires in the rain." Reviewers also responded to the intensity of *First, Body* with admiration and alarm. Geri Gourley classified the cumulative effect of the intensity of these narratives as a sort of "emotional claustrophobia." In this collection Thon relies primarily on the first-person voice to establish character. Christopher Tilghman, writing for *Ploughshares* (Spring 1997), proposed that *First, Body* is a distinct departure from Thon's earlier works and that her powerful vision is "driving her far away from the conventional structures of her earlier stories and novels."

"First, Body," the lead story in the collection, focuses on Sid Elliot, a compassionate but misunderstood Vietnam vet who works as an orderly in a Seattle hospital. Having survived the horrors and misery of Vietnam, Sid cannot escape one particular vision of the war: his discovery of the body of a young girl, a guerilla fighter, who had been killed by Sid's unit. Although Sid is acutely aware that "She's the one who strung the wire, the one who made a booby trap with your grenade," in death "she's not anyone's enemy—she's just a dead girl in the grass, and you leave her there by the river." No longer able to objectify her or others, Sid allows his compassion and empathy to influence how he conducts himself in everyday life, which becomes his downfall.

Early in the story, Sid falls in love with Roxanne, a drug addict and alcoholic whom he meets in the park. She moves in with him, and his own recently acquired sobriety influences her to stop drinking. They share a brief period of happiness that ends after Roxanne resumes drinking and disappears. At work, Sid's desire to render assistance to a young girl in the throes of withdrawal places him in danger when she bites him in the ensuing scuffle. For this "inappropriate interference with a patient" he is reassigned to the morgue. In the morgue his desire to show Gloria Luby, a 326-pound dead woman, "some trace of respect," once again places him in physical jeopardy as he succeeds in seriously injuring himself in the attempt to carry her to the morgue table. His empathy for others is so strong that even in her absence, Sid worries for Roxanne and believes that he sees her in patients who pass through the morgue. In Gloria Luby, Sid sees what her doctors did not: a woman, complete with failures, who still deserved a little dignity. While Sid recovers from knee surgery, he experiences Demerol-induced hallucinations of Roxanne and Gloria Luby: in these visions Roxanne pushes him further away while Gloria thanks him by silently lying down next to him as he sleeps. Trying to guard himself against bitterness, Sid "tries to be tender. He prays to be strong."

"Father, Lover, Deadman, Dreamer" is the lyrical account of Ada, a young woman from rural Montana who realizes the legacy of alcohol and guilt after she kills a man in a hit-and-run accident. "I was a natural liar, like my mother," says Ada in the opening line. Wishing desperately that she could go back to that moment in time and ease her victim's suffering, along with her own, Ada reexamines how her mother's addictions and her father's blindness allowed her to tell a lie "that came so easily." She indulges in complex fantasies in which the man she hit, Vincent Blew, is no longer just a body on the road. In these fantasies he speaks to her. Unable to accept the uncomfortable silence that develops when she is sure that her father realizes that she hit and killed a man, Ada runs away. Obsessed by the idea that she has become her mother, she engages in a series of one-night stands and haunts the local bar her mother often visited. Some of her evenings are spent parked outside of her dying father's house, watching him and wishing that she could ease his pain and hers by changing the past.

The legacy of racial intolerance is a theme that frequently appears in Thon's fiction. In her novels Thon has chosen to examine tensions that arise between the Native American and white cultures who inhabit Idaho and Montana. In her short stories tension between African American and white characters is a frequent point of exploration. In her small-town settings, where resources are scarce and personal stakes often high, Thon finds that a "pervasive aspect of that culture is violence." Speaking to Phillips on the issue of cultural appropriation, Thon said, "I believe it's important for people to transcend who they are as individuals. That's one reason we write, to get outside of ourselves, to try to understand something beyond our particular experience."

In contrast to "Punishment" from *Girls in the Grass*, "Little White Sister" presents readers with an older, African American man who is haunted by the guilt he experiences after he refuses to help a young white woman, a drug addict, who pounds on his door. Jimmy spends most of his story detailing how his relationship with a white woman who became his partner in drug abuse and crime led to a nine-year prison sentence for armed robbery. Where "Punishment" explored oppression and rage, "Little White Sister" offers a more pitiful reality when Jimmy says "I drink port because it's sweet, gin because it's bitter, back to back, one kills the taste of the other. . . . Three days now since we found her and I see her whole life, like she's my sister and I grew up with her." Of this character Thon has said, "He's trying to understand her life, as I'm trying to understand his. So, this man and I were engaged in the same process."

Dora, the narrator of "Necessary Angels," relives the passion and fear she experienced as a teenager when she had an affair with a young, African American man named Lewis. Both are trapped in a world where they know "They will be caught. It is necessary." During one tryst in Lewis's car, they are attacked by a gang of white kids. After discovering she is pregnant with Lewis's baby, Dora undergoes an abortion. They sever their relationship. As she grows older, Dora learns that Lewis has become an emergency medical technician, and she finds herself working as a lab technician. They have become the "necessary angels" of the story, helping others, perhaps out of the desire to transcend their own pain.

In "Nobody's Daughters" Nadine narrates her own story in three installments: "In These Woods," "Xmas, Jamaica Plain," and "Home." Driven away from home by her mother's new husband and his sons, Nadine hitchhikes, steals, and turns tricks in order to survive. Haunted by memories of her sister, Clare, who died of AIDS, Nadine allows Clare to function as her spirit guide, helping her out of scrapes with strangers on the road. While the tone of "Nobody's Daughter" is predominantly dark, Nadine finds some fleeting joy in "Xmas, Jamaica Plain" as she addresses the woman whose house she broke into and ransacked during Christmas vacation. In this section Nadine enjoys the company of Emile, a teenage male prostitute. Seeking shelter from the brutal cold of the streets, they break into a house located on the edge of a Boston suburb, where they eat, sleep, and play to their hearts' content. Broken by his life on the street, Emile decides to end his life by overdosing on the woman's sleeping pills.

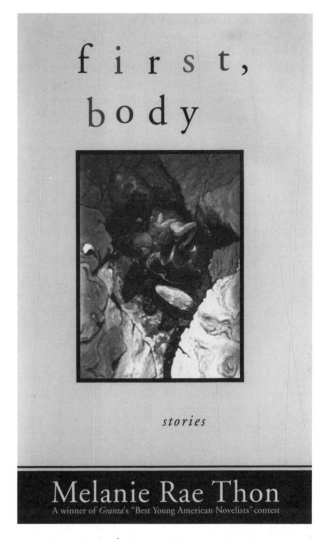

Dust jacket for Thon's 1997 book, stories about characters in extreme mental or physical conditions

Nadine, urged on by Clare, flees the scene. Nadine's need to speak to the woman, who will come home to find Emile dead on her bathroom floor, is fueled by her first disagreement with Clare. After a night of walking away from the house, she sees a car sitting on the street with its engine running and its driver standing on a porch. Seeing a baby in the backseat, however, Nadine decides not to steal the car. In a rare moment of redemption, she is proud that she "let one thing go." At the end of the section she says, "I forgive myself for everything else." "Home" is the abysmal final installment of Nadine's story, in which she contacts her mother to inform her of Clare's death. Nadine cannot forgive their mother for allowing them to run away, and she allows Clare to guide her once more onto the road, seeking a place where she can be "whole" again.

"Bodies of Water" features Elena, Thon's only upper-class character. Emotionally she is as disenfranchised and disenchanted as the other people in the collection. Two days after having been mugged on a Seattle street, Elena makes her way home in a violent rainstorm to find that the young boy who had stolen her purse has now broken into her house. While the storm rages outside, Elena is trapped inside her home with a young predator who inspires in her the same fear and remorse she felt years earlier after being raped by a group of young men in her father's orchard. Although Elena is surrounded by the hallmarks of comfort and security, her narrative takes on the same broken and fragmentary style of the other less fortunate characters in this collection. As Elena becomes more keenly aware of the danger that she is in, the young boy's physical presence dominates the house and his voice encroaches on the narrative. Once the boy leaves, Elena comes out from her hiding place in the attic. Realizing that "no one will understand" what has happened to her, Elena decides merely to "erase" his presence from the house. Thon closes the story with the strongest symbolic image in the collection: nature personified in the voice of the rain. Stepping outside of material reality, the rain reassures Elena as it says to her: "I have a body like yours and like your mother's. I have a body like your daughter's. I have a body. It's the boy's, and it's your sister's. They've stepped between the raindrops. They flow away. They're mostly water."

In "The Snow Thief," the briefest story in the collection, the narrator, Marie, chronicles her awakening sense of self after the death of her parents. At the beginning of the story, Marie's father has just died from a stroke. In the aftermath of his death, the mother begins to suffer the same fate, slowly dying from a series of strokes. Marie watches as her mother progressively forgets everything from her own body to her children. "The Snow Thief" goes beyond Marie's minute-to-minute lyric reflections and is densely infused with hunt-related metaphors. In her mind's eye Marie sees her father hunting her mother, with each shot taking her "piece by piece." As in "Iona Moon," the theme of incest is woven into the protagonist's life. Memory and consciousness form the other thematic exploration in the story. Having engaged in a sexual act with her brother, Marie relates her disappointment that he will not acknowledge their sexual liaison, and she bears the burden of it alone. "First love gone to this," she muses; "If I said, 'Remember?,' Wayne would say I'd had a dream." Memory is connected to sin and punishment, and Marie believes that "This is how God gets revenge: he leaves one to remember and one to forget." After the death of her mother, Marie goes back to the woods, where she has a vision of her parents moving quickly away from her. Trying to shut out the bitter cold, Marie says, "I forget my body." "The Snow Thief" concludes with a moment of ambiguity by leaving Marie suspended in a moment of keen awareness, knowing that she can choose between life and death, between brooding over the past and moving into the future–but doing neither.

Thon's short fiction has been greeted by mixed critical response. In his review of *First, Body* Tilghman praised Thon's moral agenda and the compassion with which she creates her characters. For Willeford, the reader's reward lies in Thon's "poetic prose, honest emotion, and richly rendered lives." The intensity with which Thon is able to evoke time, place, and character, and the resulting lack of aesthetic distance in her novels and stories, is a criticism frequently leveled against her. Carolyn See challenged Thon's insistence on focusing solely on suffering characters and pointed out that while there is truth in their experiences, "There are other truths as well." Claire Messud, reviewer for *The Times Literary Supplement* (23 July 1993), praised "Thon's integrity and beautiful turns of phrase" but longed to escape from the oppressive world of *Iona Moon*. Messud's deeper objection, however, was to the source from which Thon drew her characters, and Messud also advocated "a five year moratorium" on:

> sexy girls with hearts of gold from the wrong side of the tracks; on soothsaying women and limbless or mutilated men of all ages and ethnic origins; on incest and child sexual abuse; on alcoholic and/or tranquilized housewives in upper-middle-class families; on high school heroes who don't make good; on funeral-parlour employees; and, above all, on small towns like White Falls, Idaho.

More balanced reviews, such as that by Cooper, accept that Thon's work often veers away from realism and suggests that the lack of aesthetic distance in *First, Body* is an act of "solidarity" on Thon's behalf and reminds readers that if the characters in her stories do not "get any respite, why should we?"

In 1996 Thon was named by *Granta* as one of the Best Young American Novelists. In 1997 she was the recipient of a Whiting Writers Award. Her innovative work has also earned her fellowships from the Massachusetts Artists Foundation (1988), the National Endowment for the Arts (1992), the New York Foundation for the Arts (1996), and the Ohio Arts Council (2000). Hailed by Phillips as "a serious and powerful voice in contemporary American fiction," Thon has made contributions to the field of short fiction that place her firmly alongside writers such as Sherman Alexie and Edwidge Danticat. While Thon does not enjoy the commercial recognition that others do, she has earned the critical admiration of fellow writers, including Cooper, Tilghman, and Joyce Carol Oates.

Interview:

Caryl Phillips, "Interview with Melanie Rae Thon," *Bomb,* 44 (Summer 1993): 241–250.

Christopher Tilghman

(circa 1948 –   )

Kelli Wondra

BOOKS: *In a Father's Place* (New York: Farrar, Straus & Giroux, 1990; London: Sinclair-Stevenson, 1990);

Mason's Retreat (New York: Random House, 1996; London: Chatto & Windus, 1996);

The Way People Run (New York: Random House, 1999; London: Chatto & Windus, 1999).

Christopher Tilghman's collections of short stories, *In a Father's Place* (1990) and *The Way People Run* (1999), have been praised for mature character voices, detailed settings, and precisely crafted plots that guide his characters toward life-affirming epiphanies. Family history and geographic location provide the common ground for many of his stories. Insisting on "event and consequence and people" as the essential elements of storytelling, Tilghman has written stories that have led reviewers to compare him to Flannery O'Connor, William Faulkner, John Cheever, Ernest Hemingway, and Anton Chekhov.

Even as a child Tilghman was interested in writing, an interest fostered perhaps by his father, who was an executive at Houghton Mifflin. Born in Boston, Christopher Tilghman attended St. Paul's preparatory school and spent summers at a farm in Maryland that his family had owned since the seventeenth century. Tilghman dabbled in writing throughout his school years; yet, when he entered Yale University, he chose to study French literature. While at Yale, he dedicated much of his time to music, playing bass in a jazz band and toying with the idea of becoming a professional saxophonist. He considered staying at Yale for a fifth year in order to get a bachelor's degree in music. When he was drafted into the U.S. Army in 1968, though, his plans changed. He decided instead to enter the U.S. Navy officer program, serving three years during the Vietnam War. Speaking to Don Lee for an article published in *Ploughshares* (Winter 1992–1993), Tilghman described the night on shipboard in the North Atlantic when he decided to become a writer: "It was one of those defining moments. . . . I was on watch, and it was

Christopher Tilghman (photograph by Richard Howard; from the dust jacket for The Way People Run, *1999)*

cold as hell, and I was miserable. I'd been doing a lot of writing then, mostly journal entries, and I suddenly knew what I really wanted to do was write fiction."

After his service in the navy ended, Tilghman and his first wife lived in New Hampshire, where he spent two years working on a novel that was never published. As he told Lee, Tilghman became a self-professed hippie: "I had the long hair, the full beard—the full catastrophe." Eschewing the conveniences of society, he strove to be completely self-reliant and to that end learned skills as varied as cabinetry, carpentry, sawmilling, auto mechanics, and butchery. Over a period of ten years these life experiences helped Tilghman develop the diverse stock of characters who populate the equally diverse settings of his stories. Tilghman, who has taught creative writing at Emerson College and at the University of Virginia, has earned several awards for his writing, including a Guggenheim Fellowship, a Whiting Writer's Award, and an Ingram Merrill Foundation Award. Tilghman and his second wife, Caroline Preston, have three sons.

When *In a Father's Place* was published in 1990, reviewers praised Tilghman for his narrative craftsmanship as well as for the sensitivity of his focus on family. John Casey, whose review appeared in *The New York Times Book Review* (6 May 1990), commended Tilghman's handling of tone and plot and said that "each story becomes increasingly charged with feeling and yet increasingly clarified; quick reflective realizations guide the narrative." Writing for *The New York Times* (3 April 1990), Michiko Kakutani noted Tilghman's "remarkable gift in these stories for delineating the complexities of familial love." Family, loyalty, and salvation are the thematic moorings that anchor these stories in place. Relying almost exclusively on the third-person narration, Tilghman depicts characters who confront intense episodes of family pain and anguish and strive toward reconciliation or grace. Reviewers have also explored the complex interplay among geography, mood, and character. The connection is not accidental. Describing his creative process in an interview with Bonnie Lyons and Bill Oliver, published in 1995, Tilghman explained: "Almost always I start with a visual image. Sometimes it's just a photograph, sometimes it's just something in my head. And that visual image has a great deal to do with the place and landscape. . . . My stories are rooted in place." For Tilghman place is more than a series of poetic descriptions; it is also a repository for history. He said, "You can't think about a place and not think about its history. Each parcel of land contains everything that has happened there. You talk about evoking place, it has got to be sensual, but also cultural, geographical, historical." In six of the seven stories collected in *In a Father's Place* geographical setting provides, to various degrees, mitigating factors that enhance the central conflict.

Set on the Eastern Shore of Maryland, "On the Rivershore," the first story in the collection, centers on twelve-year-old Cecil Mayberry, who, after seeing his father brutally murder a local waterman, Tommie Todman, must decide to whom to report the crime. Within the span of twenty-six pages Tilghman creates a miniature historical novel, documenting through the eyes of his young protagonist the intense rivalry between farmers and watermen. Tilghman's geographical descriptions are vividly authentic, creating what reviewer Ann Hulbert of *The New Republic* (4 June 1990) called a

"physical and psychological challenge." The opening image of "On the Rivershore" features Cecil on a sandy beach along the Chester River, which functions as a "narrow divider" between the watermen and the farmers. From this vantage point, stranded between the two worlds, Cecil witnesses his father's act of transgression. Even at the age of twelve he has an understanding of the troubled relationship between the two groups. Sensing the danger his father could be in should the watermen discover what has happened, Cecil flees to the estate of his father's employer, Mr. McHugh, and begs him to protect his father. A brusque, compassionate patriarchal figure who is spiritually strong but physically weak, McHugh gathers his resources in an effort to protect Cecil's father but reminds the young boy, "What we're doing here is wrong by every standard but one. You'd better remember that all your life if that's what it takes." As McHugh and his farmhands—including Cecil and his father, Larry—are about to dump Tommie's corpse in the river, they are confronted by a group of watermen. Alternating rapidly between sections of tautly drawn dialogue and lyric passages, Tilghman details the fierce territorial nature of the two groups in full detail as the watermen threaten to turn over the farmers to the local authorities. As the men argue the value of Tommie Todman's life and whether Larry Mayberry should be taken to the authorities, one of the farmers urges the others to remember that "the boy is the issue. Not us." Eventually, the men agree to dump the corpse in the bay. Tilghman brings the story full circle thirty years later as Cecil and his children, who have returned for a funeral, are walking on the beach and Cecil ponders the changes that have occurred in the years since Tommie Todman's murder.

The Maryland coast also provides the setting for the title story, "In a Father's Place," which takes place on an estate that has been in Dan's family since the seventeenth century. This time, however, the characters are well-to-do and well educated. In the opening scene Dan, having just awoken from a sleep induced by the "lapping rhythm of a muggy Chesapeake evening," greets his son, Nick, and his contentious girlfriend, Patty, who have arrived from New York City. Even before Dan notices that Patty is preoccupied with taking a silent inventory of the antique furnishings, he briefly considers that "maybe no new lover ever walked into fair ground in this house." From the outset it is clear that Patty is the antagonist even before she reveals that she is a deconstructionist and that Nick's new novel is an attempt to deconstruct the family. Tilghman contrasts protagonist and antagonist. Dan is a patriarch, comfortable with the trappings of tradition, a Chesapeake Bay native who recognizes that embracing the land and the water is in itself a form of salvation. Patty, on the other hand, is uncomfortable in the house and ambivalent toward the things that represent the family's posterity. She spends her time reading a book by Deconstructionist Jacques Derrida on the screened porch, never venturing onto the estate to examine the family in a larger context or out to the bay to understand its elemental impact on the family. The tension between Patty and the rest of the family (which includes Dan's daughter, Rachel) escalates.

While Nick is sailing the bay with Rachel, Dan and Patty have their final confrontation. Tired of Patty's condescension and enmity, Dan evicts her from the house. Wondering how Nick will react to his action, Dan thinks back to an episode in his own life when a former lover had made him miserable:

> This was the soul of the Chesapeake country. . . . The water was there, in the end, with Sheila, because he had triumphed over her, had fought battles for months in telephone calls that lasted for hours and evenings drowned her in liquor, until one morning he had awakened and listened to the songs from the water and realized that he was free.

As the story closes, Dan's final thoughts are a peaceful, exalted reverie on the land, his life, and his family.

"Norfolk, 1969" and "A Gracious Rain" focus more intimately than the other stories in the collection on transactions between husbands and wives as their relationships evolve and they discover that love and commitment do not always guarantee survival. In "Norfolk, 1969" Charlie and Julie find the bond between them weakening while he is away at sea serving in the navy during the Vietnam War and she is making a life for herself in Norfolk. As in many of the stories of this collection, setting is linked to dramatic changes in character. The most dramatic change for Charlie occurs while he is at sea. Far from land and from the growing antiwar protest, he becomes aware of the powerful allure of the ocean, where deep in the "shimmering sea piled on gray days with black waves" he discovers his "elemental soul." On his return home Charlie finds the philosophical and spiritual distance between himself and his wife has grown considerably. They both recognize the breach in their relationship, which is shown most starkly when Julie "saw him struggling to be liked and to like, and she tried to help. But as much as she tried, she never quite overcame a conviction in his heart that she agreed with her friends, that in these temples of the sixties, her husband, Charlie, was unwashed." Knowing that the marriage is in jeopardy, Charlie resolves to bridge the distance between them, but his resolution is not enough to stop the rift, which deepens when they both participate in an antiwar demonstration and Julie takes her protest further

than Charlie dares. The passage of time eases Charlie's pain. The story closes some twenty years later, as Charlie speculates on the literal and symbolic ties to the sea that anchor him to Norfolk in 1969.

Set in Cookestown, Maryland, "A Gracious Rain" veers slightly into the realm of magical realism, when a man's devotion to his family is proven after he dies. Stanley, a machinist whose nickname is "Preacher," is preoccupied by the notion that "life had a reason and a reward, that life was a blessing." From the opening image of Stanley sitting on his front porch and surveying the houses of Cookestown in the setting sun, to the "frying pork and fresh dinner rolls" and the "sharp yips of children playing," the story is saturated with sensory detail that celebrates the corporeal as well as the spiritual. Through Stanley, Tilghman expresses his own quest. As he told Lyons and Oliver, "I'm looking to glorify my life and my children and the time I get to spend with them and everything I love." In direct contrast to Stanley's state of grace is the doubt and insecurity of the Reverend James Broadhurst, who seems to dwell on the possibility that God might forsake his people in their most vulnerable moments. The key to understanding Broadhurst's "brooding," as Stanley calls it, is to realize that as a single man, Broadhurst lives alone in his isolated parsonage, and his loneliness feeds his sense of isolation. Stanley and his wife, Beth, share a connection so deep that she senses Stanley's death in the moment just before Officer Stapleton and Reverend Broadhurst arrive to deliver the news. After this element of magical realism, the story works its way through the hours immediately after Stanley's death. Stanley does not reenter the story until near the end, after an extended conversation between Broadhurst and Beth, during which the reader learns that the minister harbors romantic feelings for her. Having witnessed their conversation, Stanley provides a sweet but ironic commentary on the things that he remembers about his life with Beth. Finally Stanley, back in his place on the front porch, reveals to the reader that "Life, in other words, went on." The story concludes as he basks in the comfort of this discovery and settles into his old chair to observe the neighborhood "under a gracious rain falling lightly on the resting land."

"Hole in the Day" begins after Lonnie, pregnant with her fifth child, has abandoned her husband, Grant, and their four young children, leaving their South Dakota farm. Although the message of this story is ultimately life affirming, it is darker in tone than the other stories in the collection because its central characters become imprisoned by their physical intimacy and by Lonnie's fertility. Acutely sensitive to their biological states and to each other, their heightened awareness allows Lonnie to "feel the suckling at her breast"—even

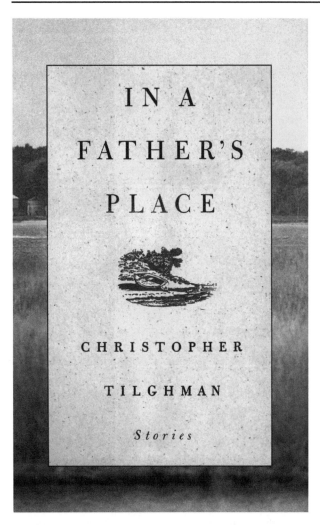

Dust jacket for Tilghman's first book (1990), stories that novelist John Casey described as "increasingly charged with feeling and yet increasingly clarified"

when she is just a few weeks pregnant—and allows Grant to track Lonnie merely by intuiting her presence. The landscape is a mythopoetic map that helps Grant track his wife. In the description that opens the story Grant is "listening to the sound of the grass." As he continues to obsess about Lonnie, "The grass tells him to forget her, *Forget Lonnie the whore.*" Driven by the urge to protect his family, Grant frantically searches the towns scattered along the lonely highways of South Dakota and Montana. The family is eventually reunited, as the tone of the story vacillates between despair and joy; its extremes reflect the pioneer spirit that is required to survive under harsh conditions.

Set on an isolated Montana ranch, "Loose Reins" depicts Hal's struggle to accept his mother's marriage to Roy, a former ranch hand. Haunted by old jealousies and insecurities, Hal attempts throughout the story to overcome his bitterness toward his deceased father, who

was a harsh and silent stranger, and to reconcile his feelings toward Roy, whom he finds equally enigmatic. Tilghman's rich and complex portraits of Roy and Jean provide a warm balance to Hal's often cold and childish actions. Jean, a transplanted Easterner who has assimilated fully into frontier culture, is a strong and sympathetic woman, while Roy, a recovered alcoholic, provides an unexpectedly compelling surrogate father to Hal. Most of the narrative is given over to Hal's selfish ruminations. In the conclusion Hal has a flash of insight as, watching from a distance, he catches a glimpse of Roy kissing Jean and realizes that "he didn't know, had never known, the last name of the man who was now his mother's husband." In this single, small epiphany Hal begins to ponder the possibility of forgiving his parents and himself.

"Mary in the Mountains" departs from the linear plot structure of the other six stories. By juxtaposing past with present in a series of fragments from a letter and episodes told in third-person narration, Tilghman presents Mary's account of her doomed marriage to Will. The letter, which includes allegorical images and acerbic descriptions of Mary's current life, seems especially eloquent after the reader learns in one of the third-person passages that Mary "stuttered, often on Ts and Ws." Reflecting on the news that Will has just become a father—something he was unable to do with Mary, who suffered a series of miscarriages—Mary does not immediately forgive Will for his extramarital affair or for the humiliating way he treated her. Yet, she does cherish her memories of their marriage and believes that without them her life would be less full. "I've never lost anyone," she writes, "that is what will save me. The memories are my grace, and all of you, as you can hear me say, are w-w-welcome in my heart."

In a Father's Place received wide critical acclaim. In her review for *The New Republic* (4 June 1990), Ann Hulbert lauded Tilghman's ability to give each of the stories a "serene pace, the calm born not of detachment but of devoted interest in small details, which open into larger spaces." Thomas D'Evelyn, whose review appeared in *The Christian Science Monitor* (15 June 1990), acknowledged Tilghman's eloquence, intelligence, and craft and noted that "these stories reek experience." When reviewers mentioned stylistic weaknesses, they tended to focus on three stories in particular: "A Gracious Rain," "Mary in the Mountains," and "In a Father's Place." Richard Eder, writing for *The Los Angeles Times* (29 April 1990), felt that "A Gracious Rain" was a "contrived *Our Town*–like sketch." In *The New York Times* (3 April 1990), Michiko Kakutani noted that the "self-conscious, structural conceits" that are a part of "Mary in the Mountains" and "A Gracious Rain" made them less effective than the other stories in the collection. Reviewing the collection for *The New York Review of Books* (16 August 1990), Robert Towers noted that with Patty's character development in "In a Father's Place" "Tilghman seems ill at ease in presenting the intellectual credentials of this fierce young woman and the deepening conflict between her and Dan." In his review for *The New York Times Book Review* (6 May 1990) John Casey also pointed out that the relationship between Dan and Patty was somewhat predictable, in part because Patty is "a stage villain." Relatively speaking, these flaws are minor, and Hulbert's closing remark accurately represents the general response to Tilghman's collection: "In the ample vision of Tilghman's stories, small metamorphoses always matter."

The contents of Tilghman's second collection of short stories, *The Way People Run* (1999) aptly attest to Tilghman's ability to synthesize complex characterization and concise plot structure. The element of "mundane realism" that Hulbert commended in *In a Father's Place* is the stylistic element that unifies the stories in *The Way People Run*. Relying solely on third-person narration, Tilghman created six strikingly vivid portraits that, in the words of Matthew Gilbert of *The Boston Globe* (23 May 1999), detail "a sensual, organic, and spiritual place in which men are interconnected with the family members from whom they run, and the American landscapes through which they run." Where geography and history were influential narrative elements of the stories in the first collection, the stories of the second collection rely more heavily on the lyric mode. This time Tilghman seems more concerned with mapping the emotional geography of his characters' crises rather than evoking the grandeur of the places they occupy. While images of water and land are still powerful, they have more poetic resonance and less immediate impact on plot or character development.

"Room for Mistakes" is a continuation of "Loose Reins," beginning just after the death of Hal's mother, Jean. During the seven years that have elapsed between the two stories, Hal has "been trying to make amends." In the harshest part of winter he and his wife, Marcie, make the drive from Massachusetts to Montana. Already poised on the brink of a midlife crisis, Hal is distraught to learn that in the months that led up to her death, Jean had concealed from him the gravity of her condition. Old insecurities and wounds are reopened at the reading of Jean's will when Hal learns that she has left the ranch to Roy. In a painful scene with Roy, Hal finds it impossible to hide the agony of his rejection, and stripped of his adult defenses in this moment of vulnerability, he cries out to Roy to tell him what to do. Roy, aware of the pain inflicted on Hal by both parents, offers him the ultimate mercy: to move back home and, in seeming defiance of Jean's last wishes, to work the

ranch alongside Roy. Hal's discovery of such unexpected grace is bolstered when Roy remarks, "It's a good life. There's room for mistakes. I'm here to testify to that. There's mercies all through it."

"Room for Mistakes" ends on this decidedly optimistic note, and, with the exception of the title story and "A Suitable Goodbye," that same optimism permeates *The Way People Run*. Perhaps most optimistic of all the stories is "The Late Night News," in which Martin Grey, an inebriated, fifty-something loner holed up in his decaying family estate on the Chesapeake Bay, finds himself in a one-on-one confrontation with a young man who breaks into the house. Unbalanced by an evening of solitary drinking, Martin is unprepared for his youthful adversary. The wryly ironic story rises to near farce when Martin gives away his presence to the would-be burglar by accidentally throwing his tumbler into the fireplace. Then he realizes that the "weapon" he has grabbed from the hearth is a fireplace shovel: "God, he thought, even as he began to advance into the kitchen and toward the swinging door into the main hall, what a caricature! Trying to scare housebreakers away with a highball glass and a fire tool." A tense standoff between Martin and the young interloper is interrupted by Martin's wild strands of thoughts, which range from bitter self-condemnation to college memories and odd bits of family trivia. In a moment of violence between the two at the end of the story, Martin receives a well-deserved blow from the young man. As the attacker flees, Martin realizes that it was neither race nor age that prompted the attack but rather his own foolish behavior. Instead of seeing the young man as a criminal, he sees him as a "visitation" or a "messenger from the dark," which prompts him to reexamine the role of alcohol in his life.

"Something Important" and "Things Left Undone" present two men who work to maintain their equilibrium in the face of family crisis. Peter in "Something Important" must confront his wife's desire for a divorce, a fact he learns from his brother, Mitch. In "Things Left Undone" Denny and Susan nearly destroy their marriage in the aftermath of their infant son's death. The day-to-day battles that Peter faces in rebuilding his relationship with his brother and that Denny and Susan face in accepting their son's death are the rocky terrain of rejection and loss that Tilghman's characters must traverse as they try to remap and redefine what it means to be a family.

"A Suitable Good-bye" and "The Way People Run" contemplate what happens when characters willingly withdraw from the security of their families. Lee in "A Suitable Good-bye" and Barry in "The Way People Run" endlessly search for some sense of freedom and identity. Invited to join his mother on her pilgrimage to Hattiesburg, Mississippi, to find her father's grave, Lee, a freelance consultant in New York, hopes this adventure will distract him from his pressing economic woes in Manhattan. Instead he finds himself constantly questioning his existence and looking for a solution, "as if there were a calculus that could help him understand his life." Instead of seeing through his mother's search, Lee returns to Manhattan to take a job. He has failed to recognize, as his mother points out, the obvious parallel that exists between her father (who committed suicide and who seems forever lost) and himself (who has allowed his career to place him in self-imposed exile). If Lee has an epiphany, it is only the realization that he is "the same old Lee, looking for an exit." This thought, however, is undercut by the sardonic remarks of a fellow plane passenger, and the reader is left to speculate whether or not Lee will make a change in his life.

Barry, the central character of "The Way People Run," is a Wall Street financier wandering the country in a desperate search for a job and a sense of purpose. Visiting his grandfather's abandoned farm, he finds an impressive junkyard of automobiles, which he reveres as a kind of monument. At first it inspires in him a sense of hope, and he decides "there are invitations on the tip of every blade of grass," but his euphoria is replaced with doubt and he resumes his wandering. Lee and Barry are antiheroes searching for contentment outside of their familial bonds. What they find in their travels, however, is that the American landscape offers them no solace, and without the bonds of love and security provided by family, they continue to wander aimlessly.

Critical response to Tilghman's second collection was enthusiastic. Writing for *Salon.com* (20 May 1999), Gary Krist summed up the appeal of the stories by asserting:

> Christopher Tilghman is hopelessly out of step with the times. I mean that as a compliment. In a publishing environment that seems fixated on attention-getting ploys and high-concept, Tilghman persists in writing the kind of fiction we're all supposedly too busy to read—unhurried, carefully observed, 100 percent gimmick-free stories steeped in an old-fashioned brew of local tradition, family history and natural landscape.

In his review for *The Boston Globe* (23 May 1999) Matthew Gilbert praised Tilghman's use of language as "deliberate and straightforward." Still other critics, such as Wendi Kaufman in *The Washington Post* (16 May 1999), praised *The Way People Run* and its "close and

steady look not at what people run from but rather what they run toward: home, a place that lies at the intersection of past and future, the elusive promise of the even-keeled domestic space waiting beyond the next curve in the road." Rand Richards Cooper of *The New York Times* (4 July 1999) also found Tilghman's characters compelling: "His people drift there on ambition alone; when that fails them, they set forth on bemused pilgrimages to country places connected, however tenuously, with an ancestral idea of home." Cooper also found Tilghman's tone to be the root of the weakness of the stories, however, saying that his lyricism often seemed "little more than a reflex." He added, "Retrospection blurs into melancholy, creating characters with an attenuated capacity for living in the present. You feel like shaking them." Similarly, while Krist was delighted with Tilghman's exploration of the road to wisdom, he conceded that the stories were flawed by "their tendency toward earnestness. . . . There are times when I would welcome a drop or two of irony in the narrative, no matter how tragic the story being told."

Family and its companion element, tradition, are the two constants in Tilghman's fiction, whether it be in the neatly written short stories of *In a Father's Place* and *The Way People Run* or his novel, *Mason's Retreat* (1996). In Tilghman's universe, to be connected to one's family and to celebrate tradition is akin to occupying Eden; to be adrift from one's family is hell. Tilghman's rejection of postmodernist techniques and sensational themes has earned him a distinct place in the contemporary writers' market. As Gail Caldwell remarked in her review of *Mason's Retreat* for *The Boston Globe* (7 April 1996), "It's a bit of a dare to write a novel this old-fashioned in today's climes, for Tilghman proposes neither to re-arrange the form nor to avoid the timeless sentiments of love and betrayal, family ghosts and blood connections. Instead he has elected to give us a story written for the pure sake of story. . . ."

Tilghman's three books have earned him solid critical acclaim, and as David Weigand wrote in *The San Francisco Chronicle* (27 June 1999), *The Way People Run* is "continuing proof of Tilghman's careful skills to keep us reading and waiting, no matter how long, for his next project."

References:

Don Lee, "About Christopher Tilghman: A Profile," *Ploughshares*, 18 (Winter 1992–1993): 228–231;

Bonnie Lyons and Bill Oliver, "Places and Visions: An Interview with Christopher Tilghman," *Literary Review*, 38 (Winter 1995): 244–255.

Douglas Woolf

(2 March 1922 – 18 January 1992)

Richard L. Blevins
University of Pittsburgh at Greensburg

BOOKS: *The Hypocritic Days* (Majorca, Spain: Divers Press, 1955);

Fade Out (New York: Grove, 1959; London: Weidenfeld & Nicolson, 1968);

Wall to Wall: A Novel (New York: Grove, 1962);

Signs of a Migrant Worrier (Eugene, Ore.: Coyote's Journal, 1965);

Ya! John-Juan: Two Novels (New York: Harper & Row, 1971);

Spring of the Lamb: A Tale, with *Broken Field Runner: A Douglas Woolf Notebook,* by Paul Metcalf (Kendal, U.K.: Jargon Society, 1972);

On Us (Santa Rosa, Cal.: Black Sparrow Press, 1977);

HAD: A Tale (Eugene, Ore.: Wolf Run Books, 1977);

Future Preconditional: A Collection (Toronto: Coach House Press, 1978);

The Timing Chain: A Novel (Bolinas, Cal.: Tombouctou, 1985);

Loving Ladies: To Maine and Back & Beyond: Concerning Mainly One of My Daughters, One of My Wives, and One of My Mothers (Minneapolis: Zelot Press, 1986);

Hypocritic Days & Other Tales, edited by Sandra Braman (Santa Rosa, Cal.: Black Sparrow Press, 1993).

OTHER: "Work in Flight Grounded," in *The Moderns: An Anthology of New Writing in America,* edited by LeRoi Jones (New York: Corinth Books, 1963), pp. 80–94;

"Prosit," in *New American Story,* edited by Donald Allen and Robert Creeley (New York: Grove, 1965), pp. 277–278;

Larry Eigner, *Country Harbor Quiet Act Around,* edited by Barrett Watten, introduction by Woolf (Kensington, Cal.: This Press, 1978);

Vital Statistics [Eugene, Oregon], nos. 1–3 (1978–1980), edited by Woolf and Sandra Braman.

SELECTED PERIODICAL PUBLICATIONS– UNCOLLECTED: "Radioactive Generation," *Inland,* 1 (Autumn 1960): 33–34;

Douglas Woolf (photograph from the cover of Wall to Wall, *1962)*

"Who's Afraid of Leonard Woolf?" *Evergreen Review,* 31 (October–November 1963): 111–114;

"In Walks Everyone," *Wild Dog,* 5 (January 1964): 16–17;

"To Who Is Concerned," *TriQuarterly,* 19 (Fall 1970): 135;

"Unpublished Letter to *The Times,*" *Earth Ship,* 3 (February–April 1971): 1;

"Title O," *Periodics,* 2 (Fall 1977): 13–19.

Douglas Woolf's reputation as a young writer was launched with the publications by Grove Press of two novels, *Fade Out* (1959) and *Wall to Wall* (1962), but his readership may best remember him for his contributions of short fiction to many of the notable small presses of his era, including Origin, The Divers Press, Black Sparrow, Coyote's Journal, The Jargon Society, Coach House Press, Tombouctou, and his own imprint (with Sandra Braman, his second wife), Wolf Run Books. *Fade Out* became a best-seller—but only in its 1968 Polish translation—and *Wall to Wall* was a runner-up in 1961 for the $10,000 *Formentor* international prize in the novel. In 1971 Harper and Row brought out a double-novel edition of *Ya! John-Juan* that was quickly remaindered; Woolf bought the leftover stock and sold the book himself on his restless transcontinental treks. Woolf emerged as an influential short-fiction writer in 1965, with the publication of his first collection of stories, *Signs of a Migrant Worrier,* and with his inclusion in the Donald Allen-Robert Creeley anthology *New American Story*. He was recognized as one of the leading practitioners in prose of the "composition by field" method being advanced by the Black Mountain school of writers, which was largely dominated by poets including Creeley, Charles Olson, and Robert Duncan. His next collection of short stories, *Future Preconditional* (1978), was an American Book Award winner.

Among his contemporaries, who included fiction writers Fielding Dawson, Michael Rumaker, William Eastlake, and Paul Metcalf, as well as poets Creeley, Edward Dorn, Jonathan Williams, George Bowering, and Larry Eigner, Woolf was a literary maverick who achieved a highly personal prose style by melding the presentation of an "artless" and naively comedic surface, apparently unencumbered with the self-conscious making of fiction, with a bleak, satiric purpose. Creeley noted in publicity material for a 1984 Dalkey Archive Press edition of *Wall to Wall* that "Douglas Woolf has a tone, always, of wry, persistently awake questioning, of a superficially bland but harshly abrasive content." Woolf is the author of particular personal accounts of American life in the second half of the twentieth century, as told by and about the culturally disenfranchised and otherwise forgotten dropouts from the middle class. Except for "The Kind of Life We've Planned" (1954), about an arrogant golfer who, after he rejects his pregnant girlfriend, is clubbed to death on a golf course by two resentful "duffers" unaware that they represent revenge—a story he wrote following what he estimated to be the *New Yorker* model—he was usually careful in his fiction to hide social critique behind kinder masks of absurdity and dark comedy. Woolf ranks, with Americans Edgar Allan Poe and William S. Burroughs and French authors Louis-Ferdinand Celine and Antonin Artaud, among the great authors of paranoia.

Douglas Gordon Woolf Jr. was born in New York City on 2 March 1922 to Douglas and Dorothy Woolf, who subsequently divorced and both remarried during the author's childhood. He grew up in the suburbs of Connecticut, near the Mark Twain Library, in a world of affluence and privilege. His father sold Persian rugs and edited a journal on textiles. His architect stepmother was the granddaughter of Thomas Edison. Woolf's nearly lifelong wanderlust and his habit of associating travel and literature date back at least to his trip to Florida with his stepfather Keeffe's father, who was an itinerant journalist and Irish storyteller. However, the teenaged Woolf was profoundly affected by his parents' breakup, divorce, and remarriages; his feeling of being tossed back and forth between two families, the Woolfs and the Keeffes, is evident in stories such as "The Pilgrimage" and "You Can't Get Another One."

Woolf first escaped his family by attending Harvard, where he was friends with Norman Mailer and John F. Kennedy, from 1939 to 1942. Afterward, his service in World War II, first as an ambulance driver in North Africa and then as a navigator in the U.S. Army Air Force, provided him with one of the themes of his early stories: the world-weary veteran's moment of return to civilian life. Woolf himself chose not to resume the comfortable life of an American bourgeoisie. He worked as a screenwriter in Hollywood long enough to marry Yvonne Elyce Stone, a local girl from a wealthy family, whose mother ran a successful dance studio. He also flirted with an academic life, earning an A.B. at the University of New Mexico, Albuquerque, in 1950 and working toward his masters' degree at the University of Arizona, Tucson, in 1954; but his manuscript for *The Hypocritic Days* (1955) was not accepted for his thesis. Instead, *The Hypocritic Days* was published as Woolf's first book by Creeley's Divers Press in Majorca, Spain.

His formative relationship with Creeley is indicative of Woolf's sense of isolation in his own community of writers: Creeley also had left Harvard for the American Field Service, but the book project was carried off, without a personal meeting, via international air mail. (Woolf also felt that his long correspondence with Eigner was most important to him, but they never met in person either.) After the war, Woolf seemed to be drawn to the deserts and wastelands of the American Far West, perhaps because of the persistent memory of his life-altering experiences in the deserts of North Africa. Ignoring offers from his family for financial support for his writing, he launched himself on what might be called, after the title for his first published collection of stories, a life as "a migrant worrier," content to work

THE LOVE LETTER

The Scene is your neighborhood branch of the Post Office Department.
A facade dividing the public from the working area is far downstage,
giving a closed-in feeling, and allowing little room in front for
any except crosswise action. The clerks ~~workers~~ behind the facade seem
to have all the room and light. On the right are post office boxes,
rather outsized, remindful also of a honeycomb, catacombs, or a
punchboard, depending on who you are and where standing. You are
waiting in one of several lines, ~~behind those on stage with their~~
~~backs to you,~~ waiting to approach your own post office box perhaps,
or one of the three service windows visible from where you stand.
(All seats are tied back with brown cord. No one will be seated
until after the play unless in a wheelchair.) While you wait, you
watch luckier people in front squeeze forward, or dart in from
right, go to their boxes or, those with packages to send or receive,
to the Stamps-Sales & Service window, the first and largest of the
three windows, just left of center stage. Few go on to the other
two windows, the Money Order-Real Estate window, or the Council
window at far left stage, although clerks ~~workers~~ stand behind each of these
windows too. Offstage right a heavy swinging door creaks and whooshes
each time a client enters or departs. You feel drafts, and restlessness. You have time to notice the people in front of you, that they
are well-dressed, the men wear felt hats, overcoats, scarves, carry

Page from the revised typescript for a story collected in Woolf's 1965 book, Signs of a Migrant Worrier
(Douglas Woolf Papers, University of Delaware Library)

odd dead-end jobs before writing his next book in a few months of deliberate isolation. Some details of his itinerant jobs became part of his fiction. He was a migrant farm worker on several occasions. He filled cigarette machines ("Quadrangle"), and he sold ice cream from a musical truck ("The Ice Cream Man"); he spent summers in a fire tower in the New Mexico wilderness ("Slayer of the Alien Gods"), and he washed windows at a Miami luxury hotel ("The Third Doorman"); he returned automobiles cross-country for rental agencies (the unpublished "Woolf's Guide to New York"), and he conducted door-to-door interviews for directories ("Market Research"). More than once, he sold his own blood for cash ("Bank Day"). In an unpublished biography, Braman recalls that when Woolf and Yvonne "had enough money, they would take to the woods or desert altogether with children Gale and Lorraine, living under blankets spread over tree branches, in abandoned ghost towns, in shacks, in the car, while Doug wrote." Woolf and his first wife divorced, and he married Braman in 1973. Braman has left a record of a three-year perpetual "reading tour" in the 1970s, a time of hawking his books on the streets, in her collection *A True Story* (1985).

Woolf's habit was to compose a whole text over a few months' time, writing on the run and in fits and starts. He worked out *The Hypocritic Days,* by his own account (in an author's statement for *New American Story,* 1965), "in a lookout tower on Cibola National Forest . . . in three sleepless months sitting on a ruptured disc." *Fade Out* was mostly written while living in an Arizona ghost town. *Wall to Wall* was composed rapidly in an Arizona copper town. A late novel, *The Timing Chain* (1985), "was begun in a summer cabin in northern Minnesota in the winter of '83, finished in northern Arizona in the spring–summer '83," his note informs the reader. "Research" on the unpublished "Woolf's Guide to New York," the novelist explains, "was begun in Manhattan in the Spring of '22"–the time of his birth, of course– "and finally collected in the mountains of Eastern Oregon summer '79, and Portland, Ore., winter '79–'80."

In terms of length, *Ya! John-Juan* and *The Timing Chain* make short novels or novellas (a term Woolf never seems to have used to characterize his books). But *The Hypocritic Days,* published as his first novel and divided into five chapters, was collected as a seventy-page story in *Hypocritic Days & Other Tales* (1993). His contribution to the anthology *New American Story* was a chapter from *Wall to Wall.* A novel, he once cryptically remarked on the dust jacket of *Wall to Wall,* "must be more nearly poetry than reportage." (His poem sequence, "God's Teagarden," composed while listening to jazz and titled after Jack Teagarden, has remained unpublished.) Woolf only twice published his stories in

book form: *Signs of a Migrant Worrier,* in a short-run small-press edition, and *Future Preconditional.* Braman, for her edition of *Hypocritic Days & Other Tales,* chooses to reprint the short novels *Spring of the Lamb, The Timing Chain,* and *HAD* (1977), following Woolf's editorial precedent of collecting *HAD* in *Future Preconditional.*

Woolf waited until 1965, after he had written for more than two decades and published three novels, before he collected seven short stories for *Signs of a Migrant Worrier.* Taking on the identity of a migrant worker who writes fiction on the run, he informs his reader in a foreword that this book is "a collection of worries." This concept of form further suggests that the storyteller considers his fictions to be open and ongoing, rather than closed and static. Woolf's great theme– the alienation of the individual in the postmodern New World–is examined, but not resolved, in four distinct types of narratives. Some are stories of the causes of alienation, namely the discontinuities of family history and the effects of postwar stress. Perhaps the purest Woolf stories are fictive case studies, often told by a Poe-like unreliable narrator who speaks from the paranoid condition. Such stories examine the state of mind of the protagonist who, excluded from one world, makes his own reality. Other stories take society to task for marginalizing its individuals into an existential abyss. A few Woolf stories experiment with ways of escaping from the wasteland of contemporary civilization by reestablishing the naive, animalistic aspects of human nature or, in the case of Native Americans, by an attempt to make new the primitive, ancestral cosmology.

"Off the Runway," the initial story in *Signs of a Migrant Worrier,* establishes Woolf's fundamental background of paranoia, as well as an autobiographical rationale for reading the subsequent stories. In this story the causes for the alienation of the male protagonist are his submission to family history and the aftershocks of his war experiences. Woolf introduces his reader to the Childs, mother and adult son, as they ride in a cab through Boston, bound for the airport. The son's chances for escaping his alienated condition by leaving Back Bay for Seattle are minimalized by the mother. She persists in calling him "Child"; she treats him like her child, even though he had flown in the war and their upcoming flight is her first; he is not leaving her but traveling with her; even the brand-name candy she forces on him, Chiclets, makes a humiliating pun on her relationship with her son. She mothers him, insisting he wear a hat she has bought for him for the trip. Child's awkwardness in handling this absurd fedora provides comic moments through the story, and his losing, recovering, and juggling of the hat becomes a metaphor for his own condition after the war, where he first suffered the sense of losing himself.

Woolf launches his characters on a dark, fated journey over a bright, calm sea of comedy. Dialogue in this story of strained relationships is persistently humorous; characters often exclaim "Wonderful!" in spite of the air turbulence. The pilot (John Stevens), copilot (John Whitman), and stewardess (Joan Johns) are all Johns. When the plane is forced to make an unscheduled landing in Nebraska, the passengers drink in a generalized hilarity. Aloft again, with the mother stimulated by her window seat and Child "dreaming of coming to life," it is determined that the plane cannot land because of a power failure.

Three stories in *Signs of a Migrant Worrier,* "Fair-Weather-Wise," "Bank Day," and "The Flyman," are case studies in the workings of the American mind rendered paranoid. This trilogy represents some of Woolf's strongest story writing. "Fair-Weather-Wise" is a tale wholly given over to the perspective of the character Howard's paranoid knowledge of Eisenhower-era America. Written in 1960, Woolf's story features what Howard alternately calls "blowbirds" or "blowboys" or "blowfish"–hermetic terms for the birds that spoil the peace and tranquility of Howard's neighborhood. Howard has declared every Saturday night to be "a time of keen joy," time for the family to listen to the radio together. The detail of Howard's placing the radio in the oven and turning the volume up loud to approximate stereo betrays his irrational state of mind to the reader in a way his readers came to expect from a Woolf text. Details from the schizophrenic knowledge of his protagonists are often bizarrely comedic, as with Lou Well's painstakingly exacting recipe for "TV cooking" in *The Timing Chain,* meaning how to heat one's TV dinner on top of the television. The fair weather of the story title, which is given mostly to a walk by father and daughter until dark and the time for the radio with the mother, is antithetical to the foggy weather Howard has had to endure in the middle-class residential neighborhood.

"Bank Day" is a case study that opens with a dream about a gift of a small sum of money received by the protagonist, but "not for anything he had done." John, although unemployed, wakes his pregnant wife with a joyful "Bank day today," suggesting, as it turns out, a payday that no character in the story can count on. Woolf suggests that the day is somehow significant in an American way: the date is shared by Gene Autry's birthday and the Battle of the Alamo. The significant difference between Autry, a popular Hollywood cowboy celebrity, and the historical place where real Western heroes fought and died, goes unnoted by the characters, who live their lives in postmodern ennui.

John, an "unused cook" who had spent half his life in the army, eats cat food (as Woolf sometimes had to). He carries an undefined piece of wood out of the house that morning, and it becomes his meager addition to the barrel fire that warms a line of out-of-work men. Only at this point in the story do Woolf's puns become clear. John is banking the coals of the fire to warm himself before selling his own blood to a blood bank. At the end of the story, as he is giving blood, John thinks: "Yet he did not allow himself to brood long on tomorrow's uncertainties, but centered all his failing attention on the warm, snug feeling of the man who knows that for today at least he still has it made." Success, in a paranoid condition, is defined in terms of moments at peace with one's self.

"The Flyman" opens with a sentence describing a moving van into which had been "shoved . . . the last slippery convenience," a phrase that conveys Woolf's attitude toward the slippery vagaries of so-called consumer society and its objects of value more than it accurately depicts the difficulty of gripping a large appliance. George Nader is relocating to St. Paul because of his wife's job; to Woolf, the Naders' empty house is a "seeming inconvenience." George is unmoved by the dislocation of the household objects from his childless and waning marriage–indeed, he is relieved to be away from his wife's clocks and mirrors and guests for a time. His possessions are flyswatters; a turtle bowl (his pet turtle was his first "fly trap"); an "ingenious, tactically flawless" system of flypaper he has situated through the house, which mostly catches and infuriates his wife; and a garage shop occupied by his inventions, the "gyrotraps" for flies. Woolf creates a character whose acts are obsessive events, not actions in the world. George remains unchanged even in the middle of relocating his home. He cannot leave his true self behind.

Often Woolf practices fiction as a form of paranoid delusion. The obsessive-compulsive George in "The Flyman" only thinks himself to be an inventor; John, happily readying himself to sell his blood in "Bank Day," only deludes himself into thinking he is content. Woolf's protagonists alternate between sympathy for all living things and a paranoid fear of the encroachment of others. Even in stories that are sympathetic to the protagonist's condition, Woolf's reader is always privy to the character's obsessive creation of a world apart from the common life. "The Flyman" further reveals something of Woolf's notion of the creative mind. In Woolf, there is no special claim for genius, only the unhealthy mind enacting its unmediated eccentricity. Fiction offers no insight, then, into personality through the manipulation of characters. Dorn remarked in his introduction to *Hypocritic Days & Other Tales* that

Cover for Woolf's 1978 book, in which some of the stories suggest ways of escaping alienation, the theme of much of his fiction

Woolf, in his writing, is "impartial as an ethnologist among savages." Perhaps even beyond impartiality, in a story such as "The Flyman," Woolf is careful not to affect the native culture with his civilized presence.

The three remaining stories in *Signs of a Migrant Worrier* are more-overt critiques of how society and its holding patterns of normal behavior alienate the individual. "Stand Still" opens on yet another Woolfean morning, the day after Stuart Toll and his wife celebrated his resolve to give up smoking during the relief of his midyear break from teaching high school. He had resolved the night before to spend this whole day in his room thinking about ways to escape his middle-class family life in an Arizona housing project. Stuart envies the garbage men, "who by their chosen profession had their own view." But, when he alone observes the act of one worker appearing to make love to a life-sized female doll atop his garbage truck, he becomes an uneasy storyteller. His neighbors and even his wife ask

him no questions when he tells them what he has seen. His life is at a standstill; he makes himself immobile at the end of the story, conversation or conclusion unpursued.

In "Cougher" John Forbes is a man in a waiting room who suffers a coughing fit and tries to control it before his Kafka-like interview with a forbidding bureaucrat known only as "the writer at desk 3." When the writer challenges Forbes concerning gaps in his employment record, Forbes explains that he was "retenu," just traveling for months at a time, in 1951–1952 and 1953–1954 (following Woolf's own journey as a migrant worker). When the employer declares "You're finished, John," Forbes becomes another kind of writer, asking for "a pencil . . . a graphite stick" in the now-dark office.

"The Love Letter" opens with "stage directions" that set the story in another public office, this time in a post-office branch. Woolf allows the "audience" to see the workers and the customers on both sides of the clerks' partition, fashioning a paradigm for Woolf's attention to the everyday barriers that separate workers and others. Further, Woolf invites the reader of the story to get in line behind a window and thus become an actor participating in the play. The calendar says it is 31 December as Arnold A. Prebble comes into the post office to renew his lease on his mailbox. As in "Cougher," the resulting interview with a bureaucrat places the man in trouble. Another of Woolf's crimeless victims, Arnold is charged with "confusing" the post office because he has received a love letter and postcards promising love letters to follow. He spends his time hoping for love letters that never come; his desire is his crime. Woolf's theme seems to be on the theatrical nature of the epistolary novel, which renders its characters both intimates and observers. His social commentary is on the societal obstructions in the way of what Warren Tallman in *New American Story* identified in Woolf's stories as "the need to give and receive love and friendship."

The stories published thirteen years later, in Woolf's second collection, *Future Preconditional*, investigate the nature and causes of modern alienation along similar lines, while adding the new category of stories about nonparanoid ways of escaping alienation by identifying with family and cultural heritage. "Note for an Autobituary," written in 1961, is a short (mostly one extended paragraph) but detailed memoir of Woolf's experience as an ambulance driver in North Africa two decades earlier. The story is dominated by the African sun and a single moral dilemma. The narrator volunteers to drive a corpse back from a firing-squad execution. The dilemma does not involve the dead man's guilt—he was guilty—but rather the narrator's horrible realization that "no man could know that much, in the face of such knowledge he [the condemned man] would have to give up knowing anything." Before the Sudanese firing squad, the condemned man is heard by the narrator to chant "Pas les noirs" ("Not the blacks"), ending the story with an ambiguous racist/existential utterance.

"The Ice Cream Man" is told by a superanalytical narrator, Bobby Knight's father, whose problem child has been recently released into his custody. Knight claims the ice-cream vendor was "the only person who in fact ever tried to save us." Woolf's narrator displays a disturbing love of reassessing situations and developments surrounding the ice-cream-truck driver and describes him at length as a kind of migrant philosopher who dispensed love and pleasure to the boy.

In "The Contest" Gerald Blake "was not a familiar type" of middle-class, middle-aged male during the Grey Flannel Era, because "he had not been tranquilized yet. He was in love, rapt, with his wife's body" after fifteen years of marriage. He decides, however, to make public his private hobby—photographing his wife—by sending a sexually intimate picture to a photography magazine. The photo is published, and the resulting scandal quickly ends their happy lives. This tale is a cautionary one, and Woolf eschews narrative development for the moral statement; this time, the story writer—and not his protagonist—seems paranoid about society.

The story "Slayer of the Alien Gods" presents one way of escaping the meaninglessness of modern life. A Navajo Indian Service worker, George, is an army veteran who, like a formulaic hero in a Western novel, does all things well—even the way he trots, which becomes a motif in the tale. The thumping of his own heart, which furnishes the countering motif through the story, is the one thing he cannot control. George tends to translate the people and events of his life into figures and legends of the tribal cosmology. When he and his wife disagree, he calls her Estsanatlehi, Changing Woman. When he is called to help fight a forest fire, he takes Jimmie, another Native American, with him. Jimmie dreams of discovering uranium with his Geiger counter; George thinks in terms of Navajo myths that explain the origins and nature of uranium as the entrails of Yeitso, the first of the alien gods. Yeitso was slain by the two war-god brothers (Jimmie, like George, is a veteran), the children of Changing Woman (George's wife, Nancy), and the Sun (the wild fire that "burns everybody, like the sun"). George recalls the myth for Jimmie's benefit as they arrive at Hosta Butte, the scene of the fire; Jimmie claims that the fire is Yeitso, that George is the slayer of the alien gods, and that he is the child of the water. George continues retelling the legend, not even interrupted now by the two-way radio, climaxing with the slayer of the alien gods cutting lines across the valley—as George and Jimmie march out to the fire line, in military step, with their shovels—so Yeitso would not live again.

Collected in *Hypocritic Days & Other Tales,* "Just the Three of Us," written when Woolf was twenty-two years old, and "Company" (1947) are early tales of the causes of alienation. "Just the Three of Us" is set determinedly in what Woolf saw in 1944 as the domestic scene in suburban New York. The father, who cannot "think of a venomous snake of five letters ending in t," and his wife, who must mix salad dressing herself because she gave the help the night off, are ensconced in the brand-name products (Kem-Tone, Brillo) as well as the clichéd language ("too much work for one person . . . home sweet home . . . it's been a long time") of the middle class. The parents are expecting the arrival of their son, John Hawkins, who makes the third member in Woolf's title. Their boy returns from the war on furlough, although the reader learns only late in the story that he has been in Alaska, not at the front. John arrives drunk, carrying a whiskey bottle and a suitcase, and promptly falls asleep. The mother is proud of his service ribbons but hides him from the neighbors; the father reacts by placing three ice cubes in drinking glasses so he and his wife can share the rest of John's bottle of Carstairs.

"Company" opens with Arthur Haley, recently mustered out of the U.S. Army Air Force as a lieutenant, standing at the front door of the Potters, an Oklahoma family with whom he had lived during flight training. Haley has quit a series of odd jobs in New York and is making his way to the West Coast, while the Potter family seems to enjoy, in contrast, small-town stability. Only late in the story, and through understated conversation, does it become clear that Haley had impregnated the Potters' daughter, Marcia—and the baby is now two years old. Finding out his child is a girl, Haley abruptly leaves. The small-town stability seems only a surface now, and Haley wants nothing of the regular civilian life.

Two stories featuring Milton Weatherwax, "Mr. Weatherwax and Psyche" (originally collected in *Future Preconditional*) and "Mr. Weatherwax Takes the Cure" (in the Braman edition), both written in 1950, are fantasies concerning commercial advertising images of the American woman. "Mr. Weatherwax and Psyche" opens with a statement of the Weatherwax dilemma: "When a man reaches fifty without having once been unfaithful to his wife, and in a deeper sense to his mother too, he begins to look closely at the paintings of nudes . . . and at the portrait of Psyche on the White Rock carbonated water bottle." His wife prefers him drunk so she can handle him at night—he has been breaking things about the house lately. When he goes outside to put the car in the garage for the night, he has a vision of a kissable Psyche inside the car, waiting for him. The story ends with Weatherwax and his wife inside the house, hearing the crash of the car into the garage. He figures Psyche is a bad driver; his wife asks if he had remembered to put on the hand brake. In "Weatherwax Takes the Cure" his wife asks Weatherwax to give her a home permanent and set her hair "in curlers, not snakes" like a Medusa. In spite of her instructions, Weatherwax manages to confuse the neutralizer bottle for a bottle of booze. This time, the Toni Twins appear surrealistically before his intoxicated eyes. When he reaches to touch a twin, he gropes his wife—she is "the cure" that sobers him.

"The Cure" is also the title of a Woolf story, collected in the posthumous edition, in which he criticizes the intrusions of society in the name of normality. Dave Hobart returns from a two-week alcohol detoxification session at Restview. His wife had spent the two weeks on vacation at her sister's. Hobart is passive and defeated, until they discover their pet cat is dead, having been locked in the guestroom during the interim. Hobart becomes bitter, thinking that the cat represents what his wife has done to him.

"Juncos and Jokers Wild" is undisguised autobiography from the period of Woolf's first marriage; the unnamed narrator is clearly Woolf himself, and the daughters bear Woolf's daughters' names. The piece teaches escape from alienation by identifying with animal life even while remaining a defenseless slave to obsessions. Like George in "The Flyman," the narrator claims he does not share his two daughters' sense of dislocation after their move from the Southwest to northern Idaho: instead, he finds it "odd and exciting, as though in a bird heaven the juncos chose to be mice." Out of the desert and into the forest around Wallace, Idaho, he discovers "little birds living down on the ground, what to think of that?" What he thinks is that he has located a bower of "perfect isolation" outside of Wallace—a best-loved place for Woolf, whose ashes were scattered beside the cabin he writes about—that "can never last," because the novel he is writing there will be finished, and his children will grow up and away. He talks about his progress on a manuscript in

terms of the developments inside a birds' nest. The morning after Woolf beats a snake to death in order to save the life of a baby bird, his younger daughter, Lorraine, gathers the feathers from the site of the struggle. The feathers are the start of her first collection, which grows "overnight" supplemented by friends and family. Contrary to the uncurbed behavior of Woolf's collector in "The Flyman," however, Lorraine decides one day to let her feather collection go in a strong wind. The next summer, his other daughter, Gale, first tries collecting, and her postcard collection grows out of control before long. The story ends with Woolf unable to advise his daughters but delivering nonetheless a commentary on lifestyle: "Don't collect, Don't ask, Go it alone, Travel light, Help less?"

A decade after writing "Juncos and Jokers Wild," Woolf produced the novellas *Spring of the Lamb,* an imaginative record of the perceptions of a lamb starting soon after birth, and *HAD,* narrated by a bird. (Woolf talked about completing his trilogy with a third novella that was to be told from the point of view of a potato.) Woolf's ill health curbed his wandering by the mid 1980s, though he continued to move from college town to college town, following Braman on her academic career, even after their divorce. He died in Urbana, Illinois, on 18 January 1992.

At his death, Douglas Woolf was celebrated as a gifted writer. On 31 May 1992, at St. Marks Church-in-the-Bowery in New York City, Woolf was memorialized by writers including Michael Andre, Norman Mailer, Alice Notley, Martha King, Hubert Selby Jr., Gilbert Sorrentino, Lewis Warsh, Rumaker, Williams, Metcalf, Dawson, Eigner, and Creeley, who organized the service. Woolf awaits his biographer and the first book-length critical study of five decades of uncompromisingly original American fiction.

Reference:

Review of Contemporary Fiction, special Woolf issue, edited by John O'Brien, 2 (Spring 1982).

Papers:

Douglas Woolf's literary papers and correspondence are housed at the University of Delaware. Among other important collections are the Donald Allen Collection at the University of California at San Diego and the Larry Eigner Papers at Stanford University.

Books for Further Reading

Allen, Frederick Lewis. *The Big Change: America Transforms Itself, 1900–1950.* New York: Harper, 1952.

Allen, Walter. *The Short Story in English.* Oxford: Clarendon Press / New York: Oxford University Press, 1981.

Aycock, Wendell M., ed. *The Teller and the Tale: Aspects of the Short Story.* Lubbock: Texas Tech University Press, 1982.

Barthes, Roland. *S/Z,* translated by Richard Miller. New York: Hill & Wang, 1974.

Bates, H. E. *The Modern Short Story: A Critical Survey.* Boston: The Writer, 1972.

Bayley, John. *The Short Story: Henry James to Elizabeth Bowen.* New York: St. Martin's Press, 1988.

Beachcroft, T. O. *The Modest Art: A Survey of the Short Story in English.* London & New York: Oxford University Press, 1968.

Boland, John. *Short Story Technique.* Crowborough, U.K.: Forest House Books, 1973.

Bonheim, Helmut. *The Narrative Modes: Techniques of the Short Story.* Cambridge: D. S. Brewer, 1982.

Bruck, Peter, ed. *The Black American Short Story in the 20th Century: A Collection of Critical Essays.* Amsterdam: Grüner, 1977.

Chatman, Seymour. *Story and Discourse: Narrative Structure in Fiction and Film.* Ithaca, N.Y.: Cornell University Press, 1978.

Current-García, Eugene, and Walton R. Patrick, eds. *What Is the Short Story?* Glenview, Ill.: Scott, Foresman, 1974.

Dijk, Teun A. van. *Macrostructures: An Interdisciplinary Study of Global Structures in Discourse, Interaction, and Cognition.* Hillsdale, N.J.: L. Erlbaum Associates, 1980.

Eikhenbaum, B. M. *O. Henry and the Theory of the Short Story,* translated by I. R. Titunik. Ann Arbor: University of Michigan Department of Slavic Languages and Literatures, 1968.

Friedman, Norman. *Form and Meaning in Fiction.* Athens: University of Georgia Press, 1975.

Gerlach, John. *Toward the End: Closure and Structure in the American Short Story.* University: University of Alabama Press, 1985.

Hanson, Clare. *Short Stories and Short Fictions, 1880–1980.* New York: St. Martin's Press, 1985.

Hendin, Josephine. *Vulnerable People: A View of American Fiction Since 1945.* New York & London: Oxford University Press, 1978.

Hooper, Brad. *Short-Story Writers and Their Work: A Guide to the Best.* Chicago: American Library Association, 1988.

Ingram, Forrest L. *Representative Short-Story Cycles of the Twentieth Century: Studies in a Literary Genre.* The Hague: Mouton, 1971.

Jameson, Frederic. *The Prison-House of Language: A Critical Account of Structuralism and Russian Formalism.* Princeton: Princeton University Press, 1972.

Kenner, Hugh. *A Homemade World: The American Modernist Writers.* New York: Knopf, 1974.

Klinkowitz, Jerome. *The Practice of Fiction in America: Writers from Hawthorne to the Present.* Ames: Iowa State University Press, 1980.

Klinkowitz. *The Self-Apparent Word: Fiction as Language/Language as Fiction.* Carbondale: Southern Illinois University Press, 1984.

Klinkowitz. *Structuring the Void: The Struggle for Subject in Contemporary American Fiction.* Durham: Duke University Press, 1992.

Leitch, Thomas M. *What Stories Are: Narrative Theory and Interpretation.* University Park: Pennsylvania State University Press, 1986.

Levin, Gerald, ed. *The Short Story: An Inductive Approach.* New York: Harcourt, Brace & World, 1967.

Lohafer, Susan. *Coming to Terms with the Short Story.* Baton Rouge: Louisiana State University Press, 1983.

Lohafer and Jo Ellyn Clarey, eds. *Short Story Theory at a Crossroads.* Baton Rouge: Louisiana State University Press, 1989.

Magill, Frank N., ed. *Critical Survey of Short Fiction,* 7 volumes. Pasadena: Salem, 1993.

Mann, Susan Garland. *The Short-Story Cycle: A Genre Companion and Reference Guide.* New York: Greenwood Press, 1989.

May, Charles E. *The Short Story: The Reality of Artifice.* New York: Twayne, 1995.

May, ed. *Fiction's Many Worlds.* Lexington, Mass.: D. C. Heath, 1993.

May, ed. *The New Short Story Theories.* Athens: Ohio University Press, 1994.

May, ed. *Short Story Theories.* Athens: Ohio University Press, 1976.

O'Connor, Frank. *The Lonely Voice: A Study of the Short Story.* Cleveland: World, 1963.

O'Faolain, Sean. *The Short Story.* New York: Devin-Adair, 1951.

Peden, William. *The American Short Story: Continuity and Change, 1940–1975.* Boston: Houghton Mifflin, 1975.

Prince, Gerald. *A Grammar of Stories: An Introduction.* The Hague: Mouton, 1973.

Prince. *Narratology: The Form and Functioning of Narrative.* New York: Mouton, 1982.

Reid, Ian. *The Short Story.* New York: Routledge, 1991.

Rohrberger, Mary. *Hawthorne and the Modern Short Story: A Study in Genre.* The Hague: Mouton, 1966.

Rohrberger. *Story to Anti-Story.* Boston: Houghton Mifflin, 1979.

Ross, Danforth. *The American Short Story*. Minneapolis: University of Minnesota Press, 1961.

Scholes, Robert. *Structuralism in Literature: An Introduction*. New Haven: Yale University Press, 1974.

Shaw, Valerie. *The Short Story: A Critical Introduction*. New York & London: Longman, 1983.

Stephens, Michael. *The Dramaturgy of Style: Voice in Short Fiction*. Carbondale: Southern Illinois University Press, 1986.

Stummer, Peter O., ed. *The Story Must Be Told: Short Narrative Prose in the New English Literatures*. Würzburg: Königshausen & Neumann, 1986.

Summers, Hollis, ed. *Discussions of the Short Story*. Boston: D. C. Heath, 1963.

Todorov, Tzvetan. *The Poetics of Prose*, translated by Richard Howard. Ithaca, N.Y.: Cornell University Press, 1977.

Voss, Arthur. *The American Short Story: A Critical Survey*. Norman: University of Oklahoma Press, 1973.

Walker, Warren S. *Twentieth-Century Short-Story Explication, New Series*. Hamden, Conn.: Shoe String Press, 1993.

Weaver, Gordon, ed. *The American Short Story, 1945–1980: A Critical History*. Boston: Twayne, 1983.

Weixlmann, Joe. *American Short-Fiction Criticism and Scholarship, 1959–1977: A Checklist*. Chicago: Swallow Press, 1982.

West, Ray. *The Short Story in America, 1900–1950*. Chicago: Regnery, 1952.

Williams, William Carlos. *A Beginning on the Short Story: Notes*. Yonkers, N.Y.: Alicat Bookshop Press, 1950.

Contributors

Ned Balbo . . . . *Loyola College, Maryland*

Herman Beavers . . . .*University of Pennsylvania*

Richard L. Blevins . . . . *University of Pittsburgh at Greensburg*

Jay Boyer. . . . .*Arizona State University*

John Breitmeyer . . . . *University of South Carolina*

Maureen P. Carroll . . . . *University of Hartford*

Cynthia A. Davidson. . . . .*State University of New York at Stony Brook*

Carol Frost . . . .*Hartwick College*

Paula E. Geyh . . . . *Southern Illinois University, Carbondale*

Sarah R. Gleeson-White . . . . *University of New South Wales*

Geoffrey H. Goodwin . . . .*Naropa University*

John C. Hawley. . . . . *Santa Clara University*

Leslie Haynsworth . . . . *Columbia College*

Dennis Held . . . .*Lewis-Clark State College*

Denis Hennessy. . . . . *State University of New York at Oneonta*

Brooke Horvath . . . . *Kent State University*

John Hughes . . . . *Valencia Community College*

Sigrid Kelsey . . . . *Louisiana State University*

Mary Beth Long . . . . *University of Massachusetts*

J. V. Long . . . . *Portland State University*

Joseph McNicholas . . . . *State University of New York at Oneonta*

Patrick Meanor . . . . *State University of New York at Oneonta*

Robert Miltner. . . . . *Kent State University, Stark Campus*

David Pink . . . .*Minnesota State University Moorhead*

Ann V. Simon . . . .*University of California at Berkeley*

Alexandra Smith . . . . *University of Canterbury, New Zealand*

William L. Stull. . . . . *University of Hartford*

Norma Tilden . . . . *Georgetown University*

Brad Vice . . . .*Arkansas Tech University*

Brandy Brown Walker . . . . *Georgia Institute of Technology*

Robin A. Werner. . . . . *Tulane University*

Kathryn West . . . .*Bellarmine University*

Kelli Wondra. . . . . *New York City*

Joseph J. Wydeven . . . . *Bellevue University*

Cumulative Index

Dictionary of Literary Biography, Volumes 1-244
Dictionary of Literary Biography Yearbook, 1980-2000
Dictionary of Literary Biography Documentary Series, Volumes 1-19
Concise Dictionary of American Literary Biography, Volumes 1-7
Concise Dictionary of British Literary Biography, Volumes 1-8
Concise Dictionary of World Literary Biography, Volumes 1-4

Cumulative Index

DLB before number: *Dictionary of Literary Biography,* Volumes 1-244
Y before number: *Dictionary of Literary Biography Yearbook,* 1980-2000
DS before number: *Dictionary of Literary Biography Documentary Series,* Volumes 1-19
CDALB before number: *Concise Dictionary of American Literary Biography,* Volumes 1-7
CDBLB before number: *Concise Dictionary of British Literary Biography,* Volumes 1-8
CDWLB before number: *Concise Dictionary of World Literary Biography,* Volumes 1-4

C

H

O

Q

R

Cumulative Index